A Forest of Voices

A Forest of Voices *Second Edition*

Conversations in Ecology

CHRIS ANDERSON
Oregon State University

LEX RUNCIMAN
Linfield College

Mayfield Publishing Company
Mountain View, California
London • Toronto

Library of Congress Cataloging-in-Publication Data
Anderson, Chris
    A forest of voices : conversations in ecology / Chris Anderson,
Lex Runciman. — 2nd ed.
      p.   cm.
    Includes bibliographical references and index.
    ISBN 0-7674-1147-1
    1. English language—Rhetoric.   2. Environmental protection
Problems, exercises, etc.   3. Readers—Environmental protection.
4. Nature Problems, exercises, etc.   5. College readers.
6. Readers—Nature.   7. Report writing.   I. Runciman, Lex.
II. Title.
PE1408.A577   2000
808'.0427—dc21   99-39787
                                                  CIP

Manufactured in the United States of America
10   9   8   7   6   5   4   3

Mayfield Publishing Company
1280 Villa Street
Mountain View, California 94041

Sponsoring editor, Reneé Deljon; production editor, Carla White Kirschenbaum; manuscript editor, Robin Kelly; design manager and cover designer, Glenda King; text design, Linda M. Robertson; manufacturing manager, Randy Hurst. The text was set in 11/12 Bembo by Thompson Type and printed on 45# Chromaton Matte by Banta Book Group.

Cover image: Christopher Brown, *The Birder's Log,* 1993. Pastel on paper. Photograph © 1995 M. Lee Fatherree. Courtesy of Palo Alto Art Center, Palo Alto, California.

To the Instructor

Environmental questions are like a forest: complicated, interrelated, mutually dependent. Things are rarely what they seem, as all your students' college courses finally demonstrate, whatever their subject. There's always more than meets the eye. Whether in organic chemistry or the early romantic poets, the point is that there are no easy answers, that claims should never be made without adequate support.

The reading and writing assignments in this book introduce students to a forest of voices and ideas on topics relevant to environmental and ecological issues, and they invite students to read and reread, think and think again. Though it's a third shorter than the first edition, this second edition contains twenty-nine new selections and offers better gender-balance and greater ethnic, cultural, and geographic diversity. The collection offers pieces that challenge other pieces, pieces that shrug their shoulders, and pieces that shout for joy. Our most acclaimed environmental writers are here, as are lesser-known writers. The conversation ranges from grizzlies to butterflies, from the mountains to the ocean floor, and all of the academic disciplines are represented, from the sciences to the humanities.

The book begins with a much condensed version of Part I: Writing to Read. This section offers the same strategies for managing the processes of reading and writing as those in the first edition, all concisely presented and now without separate exercises. The reading selections that follow in Part II: Reading to Write are grouped into six new chapters, each divided into two equal subsections: Chapter 2, Rooms and Homes, Country and City, asks students to think about the world around them growing up and right now, whether rural or urban; Chapter 3, Where Wilderness Begins, invites students to step outside of that familiar world and start exploring; Chapter 4, Animal Lives, uses the topic of animals wild and tame to probe further into the environmental debate; Chapter 5, Limits: Challenges and Progress, sketches a history of environmental decline and our various efforts to reverse this decline; Chapter 6, Evolving Ethics, explores the ethical questions such as what is the value of land? Who has the right to determine its use? Which animals do we protect? What are hunters' ethics?; and Chapter 7, Practicing Knowledge, challenges students to think about what can actually be done to improve and sustain our various environments.

The general movement, then, is as it was in the first edition, from familiar to unfamiliar, contemplation to action. Questions and topics at the end of individual selections try to complicate students' understanding and lead them to their own questions and writing.

Our goals in all this are ethical as well as intellectual, though our approach to ethics is through the use of language. In our view that's the real stumbling block in the environmental debate. What undermines us are the slogans, the easy oppositions. We can't seem to talk about the issues without squaring off into silly, debilitating distinctions like spotted owls versus loggers, environmentalists versus developers, as if an issue so rooted and layered could ever be reduced to dualities and bumperstickers.

What we need is the humane and reasoned thinking of our best writers, voices old and new. What we need, further, is both humility and finesse, and the purpose of *A Forest of Voices* is to help toward this end. Finally, the goal of the book is to encourage a genuine conversation among students, their friends, their families, their communities, and their elected officials. The goal ultimately is to encourage conversations (silent, spoken, written, acted) about what really matters and what's really true, a conversation as rich and deep as the forest itself.

ACKNOWLEDGMENTS

Our thanks to Renée Deljon of Mayfield Publishing, who asked us to do this second edition and who guided it quickly and deftly along, with all solicitousness, bringing the book back when we thought it long gone. Our thanks to the readers who helped us shape the second edition: Roy K. Bird, University of Alaska, Fairbanks; Carl Herndl, New Mexico State University; Sandy Jordan, University of Houston; Daniel J. Philippon, University of Minnesota, Twin Cities; Randall Roorda, University of Missouri, Kansas City; Scott Slovic, University of Nevada, Reno. And once again our thanks to the reviewers who helped us with the first edition: Charles Schuster, Johanna W. Atwood, Alys Chulhane, Karen Dick, Lydia Equitz, Kerry Hansen, Roberta Harvey, Matt Matcuk, and Donna Strickland. Our thanks to all those at Mayfield Publishing who helped in the development and production of the book: Rick Roehrick, Developmental Editor; Carla White Kirschenbaum, Senior Production Editor; Glenda King, Design Manager; and Marty Granahan, Permissions Editor.

Our thanks as always to our families, the one in Corvallis and the one in McMinnville. And our thanks to each other. Of all the many reasons to write a book, friendship is one of the best.

To the Student

Environmental questions are like a forest: complicated, interrelated, mutually dependent. Things are rarely what they seem, as all your college courses finally demonstrate, whatever their subject. There's always more than meets the eye. Whether in organic chemistry or the early romantic poets, the point is that there are no easy answers, that claims should never be made without adequate support.

The reading and writing assignments in this book introduce you to a forest of voices and ideas on topics relevant to environmental and ecological issues, and invite you to read and reread, think and think again. The collection may surprise you. Its readings are ethnically, culturally, and geographically diverse, offering pieces by women and people of color, pieces that challenge other pieces, pieces that shrug their shoulders, and pieces that shout for joy. Our most acclaimed environmental writers are here, as well as those writers who are lesser known. The conversation ranges from grizzlies to butterflies, from the mountains to the ocean floor, and all the academic disciplines are represented, from the sciences to the humanities.

The book begins with Part I: Writing to Read, which offers numerous strategies for managing the processes of reading and writing, all concisely presented. The reading selections that follow in Part II: Reading to Write are grouped into six chapters, each divided into two equal subsections: Chapter 2, Rooms and Homes, Country and City, asks you to think about the world around you growing up and right now, whether rural or urban; Chapter 3, Where Wilderness Begins, invites you to step outside and start exploring; Chapter 4, Animal Lives, uses the topic of animals wild and tame to probe further into the environmental debate; Chapter 5, Limits: Challenges and Progress, sketches a history of environmental decline and our various efforts to reverse this decline; Chapter 6, Evolving Ethics, explores the ethical questions such as what is the value of land? Who has the right to determine its use? Which animals do we protect? What are hunters' ethics?; and Chapter 7, Practicing Knowledge, challenges you to think about what can actually be done.

The general movement, then, is from familiar to strange, contemplation to action. Questions and topics at the end of individual selections try to complicate your understanding and lead you to your own questions and your own writing.

Our goals in all this are ethical as well as intellectual, though our approach to ethics is through the use of language. In our view that's the real stumbling block in the environmental debate—what undermines us are the slogans, the easy oppositions. We can't seem to talk about the issues without squaring off into silly, debilitating distinctions like spotted owls versus loggers, environmentalists versus developers, as if an issue so rooted and layered could ever be reduced to dualities and bumperstickers.

What we need is the humane and reasoned thinking of our best writers. What we need is both humility and finesse, and the purpose of *A Forest of Voices* is to help toward this end. Finally, the goal of the book is to encourage a genuine conversation among you and your peers, you and your friends, you and your family, you and your community, you and your elected officials. The goal ultimately is to encourage a conversation about what really matters and what's really true, a conversation as rich and deep as the forest itself.

Contents

Part I
Writing to Read

1

Joining the Conversation

Keeping a Reading Journal

The kind of reading you have to do in college is usually complex and demanding, and even the best students don't understand everything the first time through. College reading asks you to think—and think again; read—and revise your readings; understand—and understand more completely.

ACADEMIC READING: SOME INITIAL ADVICE

1. Read in a setting that lets you think. Reading, like every other act, depends in many ways on its environment. Whatever environment you choose, arrange your week so that you have good reading time there.

2. Set aside enough time to read. Reading slowly isn't a problem if you set aside enough time—and even fast readers need time to reread difficult pieces. If your schedule is too full for large blocks of reading time, plan on several shorter blocks of time.

3. Don't panic, and don't give up. By its nature, academic reading often deals with topics you don't know very much about; the topics often are complicated, with many levels of meaning. So expect some struggle and work when you read college texts. There's nothing wrong or lacking in you. No one else is having an easier time of it.

MAKING JOURNAL ENTRIES

As you read the selections in this book, keep paper and pencil handy so that you can use informal writing—writing you do quickly for yourself—as a way to make your reading process more conscious and more rewarding. Journal entries have several advantages: They're on paper (so you don't have to rely entirely on memory), they're relatively compact (you don't have to thumb through a book reading marginal notes), and they make rethinking easier (rereading a journal entry, you invariably find yourself agreeing or disagreeing with what you thought earlier).

Here is an example.

March 4th. "Dogs, and the Tug of Life" is a strange essay. Odd. It's hard to follow. Keeps jumping around. I'm not clear what Hoagland's main point is—that having a dog is good or bad? That dogs are really wild after all? The idea that pets reflect their masters, maybe? (No, more than that.) I keep thinking of my dog, Max. Part border collie and part who knows what. He's just a silly, friendly dog and I love coming home to him, taking him for a walk. I don't think much about him at all. I don't *think* when I'm with him. That's the point, just to let go, to come home from college and just be with my dog, have him lick my face, be happy to see me. And so I resist Hoagland making such a big deal out of pets, reading things into what's simple and natural. (Although maybe *that's* the point, his point: all this is deeper than it seems.)

THE PROCESS OF READING: PREREADING

Before you actually begin reading the first word of the first sentence, preread. Prereading means scanning the assignments with the following questions in mind, jotting down your answers briefly, and then using those answers to help you plan and to give your reading a preliminary context.

What is this reading's genre? poetry? fiction? nonfiction prose? If nonfiction prose, what kind? an autobiographical account? a discussion of an issue? an argument in favor of something? part of a textbook?

Is it contemporary or older?

Is it long or short? in pieces or one whole?

Do you know anything about the author (what do the headnotes tell you, for example)?

Can you tell what audience this writer wants to talk to?

Can you tell why this writer wants to talk to these readers?

What do you already know about this subject?

FIRST READING

Begin reading by using your common sense and trusting your initial, intuitive responses. Some of what you'll read will be clear right from the start; other parts will seem fuzzy or only partly clear or (sometimes) entirely unclear. As you read, keep track of what you understand and what you don't.

Open your journal so that you have two blank pages facing each other, or draw a line down the center of a single page. On the left side, jot down quickly what you understand or what you can relate to. Write a phrase or key word along with the page number. On the right side, jot down questions or things you don't understand or can't relate to. Do this as you actually read (read with a pencil or pen in your hand).

After your first reading of one of the selections in this book, use one of the following suggestions to write a journal entry.

1. Tell the story of your reading, in chronological order from start to finish. (For example: "When I first started, I was confused. I couldn't understand what the author was saying because I didn't understand some of the words. But then, about the second page, the passage about environmental impact statements really jumped out at me and made sense, and from then on I was right with the author. Suddenly the subtitles were very clear and logical, and I was able to read right to the end, agreeing all the way.")
2. Explain anything in the reading that surprised you, that you didn't expect.
3. Which passages stood out (either in good ways or in problematic ones), and why?
4. Talk about how this reading helps you understand something in your own life.
5. Talk about how this reading complicates or confuses something you've taken for granted or not thought about much before now.

ANNOTATING

While reading, you can also annotate—or make brief notes about—the text. Your notes may explain or clarify or may offer comment. Think of annotating the text itself as abbreviated journal writing and of the journal as an elaboration of your reactions. Some of the same thought processes are involved in annotating as in journal writing.

What good annotating encourages is what the journal encourages: active, involved reading. Here are some ideas on what to mark and how to comment.

Mark any passage that interests, compels, excites, confuses you—anything that seems important. Draw a line, bracket, star, or circle. In the margins, write a short phrase or question that summarizes the point.

Record enthusiasms: "Yes." "I agree with this." "Of course."

Record resistances and questions: "What?" "Give me a break." "I'm not following this."

Mark statements that summarize the theme of the piece, and mark the topic sentences in important paragraphs. Mark anything that summarizes main ideas.

Notice patterns and evolving themes. At the top of a page, write your reactions: "Rejection of romanticism." "Statistics used to overwhelm us." "Notice all the images of passageways."

Outline the selection. Put numbers and letters in the margins indicating the main sections.

Write subtitles for major sections.

Write questions to ask in class.

After annotating a selection in this book for the first time, exchange and discuss your notes with one or two of your classmates. What did you mark in common? What do your annotations reveal about the way you think? about the nature of the piece?

REREADING

The next step is rereading, going back through the text and trying to understand both what it's saying and how you're responding to it. This is the stage when you start dealing with complexities, so you have to be patient with yourself and the writer. Here are some suggestions.

- Reflect. Where did you get bogged down or have difficulty, and why? What in the form or content of the piece made the reading hard for you? If the reading was easy and fun, what made it easy and fun—the author's language, your prior knowledge of the subject? To put this another way, what kind of reader does the author suppose you are? What does the author assume you know? What does the author expect you to be able to do? How could you become that reader?

- Translate. Take any passage that isn't clear and try to put it into your own words. Make it as simple and direct and clear as you can. Be slangy. Find a commonsense, everyday, contemporary example of the idea or form.

- Interpret. Do the examples support the writer's claims, or is there some slippage or disjunction? Is this a well-written, honest piece, even though you just can't buy it? Does this piece overturn or call into question any of your own beliefs? Does the writing ring true in your own experience? How does it compare with other pieces you've read?

- Organize. Review the notes you took as you read. Try to find connections among key points. Are some points subordinate to one greater point? Are there, say, three major points to which everything else is secondary? Do your comments line up as a series of oppositions, paradoxes, or contradictions? Try sketching, doodling, looping, outlining.

Use any of the following suggestions to make an extended journal entry (more than half a page) based on your rereading.

1. Outline a possible research project based on a topic you read about in the reading selection. What else would you like to know? Why would it be helpful to know these things?

2. Teach the reading selection to someone in the class who hasn't been able to read it. What can you say that will give the person a basic grasp of the selection?

3. Think imaginatively and metaphorically: think of this reading selection as medicine—for example, a cure for something. What's the disease, and why does this reading cure it? Or what kind of weather is the reading like? What would the reading look like if it were a landscape? What kind of music is the reading like, or what kind of clothes? Who would play the author or main character in the movie, and what kind of movie would it be?

FREEWRITING

The technique of freewriting can be a very useful way of responding to something you have just read. To freewrite, simply start writing and don't stop for about five or ten minutes, or until you've run out of steam. Write nonstop, at a comfortable pace, not letting your pen leave the page. Record everything that's in your head at the moment. If you don't know what to say, write "I don't know what to say" until you think of something, or repeat the last word of the last sentence until you find your way. Don't worry about making errors in grammar, punctuation, or spelling or even about saying something stupid or off the point. Just keep writing. Don't let your pen leave the page or your fingers the keyboard. Concentrate on what you're thinking, as if the words were transparent, not there at all.

Try to stay on the point, focused on the reading. But if you find yourself wandering into new territory, don't pull back too soon. You may be exploring something unusual and important.

FURTHER ADVICE AND PERSPECTIVES

Like the writing process, reading always involves some kind of revision, re-seeing. Reading once is not enough. Here are some further ideas to keep in mind.

- Be generous and open-minded. It's hard to understand any reading when you've made up your mind in advance. Reading involves, after all, a kind of careful listening; it requires paying attention. So try not to dismiss any author offhandedly, even when you disagree. Give the author the benefit of the doubt, the way you do when you meet someone in person; show some courtesy.

- Keep in mind that meaning is never absolute. A text isn't cast in concrete, its meaning fixed once and for all. Meaning is what you make for yourself as you read a text. You bring to the reading your values, beliefs, and experience, and these qualities condition what it's possible for you to understand in that text.

- Consider the rhetorical context. A piece of writing comes from somewhere and is directed to a particular audience. That is its rhetorical context. The author wrote it for a reason.

    In the same way, it's important to know the *aim* of a piece of expository writing. Is it intended *to inform, to argue a position,* or *to reflect and explore*? These are the three main purposes a piece of writing can serve.

    In other words, not only do the readings in this book all concern the theme of the environment, they also all *have* an environment. And that environment is as important to understand as the reading itself.

- Look for what *isn't* said. A literary text like a poem or short story *shows* rather than *tells.* It gives scenes, metaphors, and images that usually stand on their own without explicit commentary from the writer. Rarely does a poet or fiction writer step forward and say, "And the moral of this story is. . . ." Literature doesn't want to tell you something; it wants to make an experience for you.

    An expository or explanatory reading is more explicit than literature. There's usually a very clear thesis statement right at the beginning, and the author tries to take us step by step through the details and information. But even in expository prose some of the most important things are not said explicitly. Often the writer will assume we know historical facts or the methods of a discipline. The writer may be continuing a discussion that's been going on for years and may assume we are aware of the background. Often there will be some key assumption that isn't stated directly, something the writer is taking for granted.

- Think about likenesses and differences. One key way to read is to look for how the ideas and feelings embodied in the reading are like your own, familiar, in keeping with who you already are, relevant to your situation, contemporary. Try to imaginatively close the gaps between yourself and your reading. Imagine living in the world of the author who wrote what you're reading. Once you've worked hard to understand the author in these ways, step back again and think about how different that author is from you and how different that author's life and world appear to you.

- Rely on the instructor and your classmates. Students often worry when they can't figure out a reading all by themselves. Just as a now–outdated assumption suggested that writers worked all alone by lamplight in some lonely garret, students often seem to assume that readers are supposed to understand things on their own; and if they can't, there's something wrong with them. But reading, like writing, is a collaborative act. It depends on community and discussion. Of course, teachers have insights and information you need in order to understand some of the reading you do. They're apt to be more experienced with the content and ideas of college coursework. Your responsibility is to do the best you can in advance, to learn from your instructor, and to read again, bringing all you've learned into the class.

  Your classmates are also part of the process. Each person in a class sees something the rest haven't; and together these insights make up a larger, fuller, richer understanding of the subject. Take advantage of any opportunities for classroom discussion. Ask that nagging question you've written in one of your journal entries. Respond to what others say. Write down what others say. Whenever your class offers opportunities for discussion, take that dialogue you've developed with the text and use it to help others and to ask for help.

WRITING AND READING

Implicit in everything we recommend in this book is the belief that writing is the best way to read. To understand a difficult reading selection, you need to write about it, briefly and informally at first and later at length and with revision. Through writing you enter into a reading. Consider the following questions and ideas as you write about what you read.

Recall your prereading of this selection, and look back over any earlier journal entries. How have those earlier understandings changed? Did what you guess at the start prove accurate? What did you understand accurately from the first? What did you misunderstand at first but now understand?

If you were going to write two questions to focus class discussion, what would they be? (Make sure that both of your questions include a specific reference to a particular section or part of the reading itself.)

What do you like in this reading? What do you find praiseworthy?

What do you dislike in this reading, and where does your dislike come from? Do you dislike it because you disagree with it? because it doesn't persuade you?

What biases, experiences, and beliefs do you bring to the reading, and how do they influence your understanding, whether or not you like the reading?

What argument (either direct or indirect) does this selection make? What does the author want readers to understand or think or do?

Think of what you've read as answering a significant question that was on the writer's mind. What was this question? How would you begin to answer it?

Write a letter to the author or to one of the characters. Tell that person what you think about what you've read. Or become one of the characters or the author and write back, or write something from that person's point of view.

Write more about the relationship between the reading and your experience. Write from both directions: How does the reading help you understand your life, and how does your life help you understand the reading? How do the reading and your life influence each other, pull against each other, warp or change each other, slide into each other—clash, merge, split?

After doing a number of entries over several weeks, review what you've written and try to summarize and analyze it. Describe your intellectual landscape. Narrate your intellectual journey. Categorize the entries. What have you learned?

As you review numerous entries about different works, do you see any entries that seem connected to each other? Looking back now, do you see a pattern? a series of oppositions? paradoxes? questions?

Summarize, explain, extend, illustrate, apply, react to what you think are the most important and interesting ideas from class lectures and discussions.

Write a memo to your instructor asking questions about a lecture or offering comments you didn't have a chance to make in class.

Write an open memo to the class offering comments and reactions about a class discussion.

Writing Essays

THE ESSAY AS A REVISED JOURNAL ENTRY

An essay is in many ways like a journal entry.

It's informal in style, free of fancy words and unnecessary jargon.

It's personal, drawing on the writer's own experience, admitting biases and enthusiasms.

It doesn't have to come to definitive answers or demonstrate a thesis beyond any doubt; it can ask questions and try out different possibilities.

It doesn't have to follow a specific format like the traditional five-paragraph theme; it can be organized organically, naturally.

An essay is different from a journal entry in the following ways.

It's proofread: grammar, spelling, and punctuation count.

It's precise; there are no wasted words.

It's the product of thinking, rethinking, and reconsidering. If a journal entry means "let's think about this," then an essay means "let's think about this, think about it again, raise new questions about it, look at it from another perspective, and then see if we can say what we think is true."

It's detailed and grounded in evidence. Although you don't have to come to a definite conclusion, you do need to show where your responses come from in the reading.

It's organized. It doesn't have to follow a prescribed format, but it must have a coherent shape and clear transitions.

A journal entry records first thoughts. An essay, on the other hand, records second and third and fourth thoughts. In a journal you don't have to worry about the shape of the sentences and paragraphs. Essay writing uses the same kind of thinking as journal writing but requires the clearest sentences and most organized paragraphs you can write. A journal is private, written primarily to prompt and record your thinking as it happens; an essay is public, a piece of writing for a reader who needs to have assumptions explained and detail presented.

THE NATURAL STYLE

When students move from journals to essays, they're often tempted to get wordy and abstract and indirect, giving up the gains of journal writing. Essays give writers permission to be informal and direct, writing with the same honesty they bring to journals. The premise of essay writing is that direct sentences are not only acceptable but also better—more precise, more insightful, more powerful stylistically. When you revise a journal entry, you often need to reword phrases for greater clarity or include clearer transitions; but the key is not to lose your natural rhythms in the process.

PATTERNS FOR ESSAY STRUCTURE

If you think of an essay as writing that grows directly out of your own thinking, then its structure can follow the natural movement of your mind as you explore and work through an important idea. On the other hand, formulas are good as long as there are lots of them, and as long as you don't force yourself to follow any particular one to the letter.

The list that follows describes ten patterns that will help you understand how to structure an essay. Use these patterns as strategies to help your essay writing. All are simplified patterns that can be varied and adapted in many ways. The tenth pattern, called TRIAC, is described in the subsection that follows this one.

1. Spot of time/mind-movie

   Spot of time: First, describe as directly and in as much detail as you can some significant moment from your recent experience, some moment that stands out from the rest, when you felt greater joy or had deeper insight into something.

   Mind-movie: In the second half of the essay, think aloud about what the experience might mean. *Read* the experience. Tell the story of your thinking and feeling about the experience, in chronological order, including how you feel and think about it now that it's passed. Use ideas and short quotations from your reading of other essays, stories, or articles.

2. Passage/mind-movie

   Passage: First, take a significant passage from the reading, some passage that stands out from the rest (just as the spot of time stands out in your experiences). Describe the passage as clearly and directly as you can, putting it into your own words.

   Mind-movie: Next, tell the story of your thinking about the passage, in chronological order: what you thought first, then second, then third, along with any confusions and questions. Conclude by explaining where you are right now. Use relevant ideas and terms from lectures and class discussions, other readings in the book, and other classes.

3. Mind-movie

   Simply tell the story of your thinking about the reading or a question from the reading. You can explain what you first thought, then what you thought next, and so on, from the beginning of the process. Or you can zero in on what you're thinking at this moment—videotaping everything that's going on in your head, all the levels and layers, right now.

4. Ideas before/ideas after

   Ideas before: Begin by describing everything you thought about a particular issue or subject before you did the reading. Describe what you thought about the reading selection before class discussion and lectures took place.

   Ideas after: Next, discuss how the reading has confirmed your ideas, reinforced and strengthened them; or how it has changed your mind, overturned what you thought; or how your ideas have been complicated at least. Describe what you think about the reading selection now, in light of what you learned in class.

5. Confusion to clarity

   Confusion: Start by identifying and describing why you were confused in the beginning, what the problem was.

Clarity: Then discuss what you understand now and how you came to understand it, as well as whatever problems remain.

6. Response/sources

   Response: Explain a reaction you had to one of the readings: confusion, anger, frustration, agreement, excitement.

   Sources: Then try to figure out the sources of this response. What features of the style and structure of the piece caused you to feel this way? What convictions or experiences did you bring to the reading, and how have they helped to prompt your response?

7. Oppositions, paradoxes, contradictions

   List and explain the ideas in the reading that seem to be at odds with each other or in some tension—on the one hand, this; on the other hand, that. An entire essay can be focused on only one such tension. Or an essay can express a confusion, the way things seem to you right now. Or you can write to express a conviction, what you're sure is at the heart of the reading, some underlying problem or paradox the reading confronts.

8. Reading/experience

   Reading: Take an important passage or idea and explain it clearly in your own words.

   Experience: Take an experience from your life, describe it in detail, and then explain how that experience illustrates the idea in the reading, how it is an example of it. Or show how your experience complicates, challenges, or questions the issue in the reading.

9. The selection is like me/unlike me

   The selection is like me: Begin by discussing how your experience is similar to the author's, how you can relate to it, and how you agree with it.

   The selection is unlike me: Then move to contrast, to show how the author's experience is different from yours, at odds with it, its values separate and its history remote.

THE FINAL PATTERN: TRIAC

Notice that most of the patterns we've suggested move in some way from the general to the particular or from the particular to the general. That's the key to any structure. A claim gets made or an idea is stated; then the writer naturally moves to defending the claim, explaining the idea, filling in the details. All writing is an ebb and flow between the general and the particular, the claim and the support.

Supporting details often are missing from journal entries. Writing quickly, without revising, allows you to be free to generalize. Revising the journal entry means taking that good, quick idea and showing where it came from, what details give rise to it, what particulars support it.

Sometimes it's just the opposite. Your journal entry may record details and observations but may not explain the significance of those facts. Revising the entry for an essay involves pulling the particulars together under some unifying concept.

Here's a slightly more systematic way to understand and organize this movement. It's a structure that can be used within paragraphs and across numerous paragraphs in whole essays. In this pattern each letter stands for a part of the essay.

> *T = theme, topic, thesis:* State what the essay is about, the topic the essay addresses, or what you will argue or claim. This opening may run only a sentence or so; rarely will it be longer than a paragraph.

> *R = restatement, restriction, refinement:* Rephrase the theme or thesis in sharper, slightly more particular ways. This restatement is often preceded with transitions like *that is, in other words,* or *what I mean is.* Again, this restatement may run only a sentence or a few sentences.

> *I = illustration, example:* Support your ideas. Give examples. Illustrate. Sentences that do this are often preceded with the transitional phrases *for instance* or *for example.* These discussions form the heart of an essay or paragraph; they give the details that make the writing convincing and interesting.

> *A = analysis:* Analysis means telling readers how to understand the examples or illustrations. It means making logical, commonsense inferences between causes and effects, intentions and actions. Words like *since, therefore, because, however,* and *nevertheless* all work to signal your logic.

> *C = conclusion, closure:* Anytime you're ready to draw together several threads of your logic, you're making a conclusion. Such sentences or paragraphs are often preceded with *in conclusion* or *thus,* though these transitions aren't always necessary and can sound a little clunky. Conclusions can appear in the middle of an essay and more than once.

On the paragraph level TRIAC is a particularly good way of organizing a discussion of quotations or paraphrases from the reading. In essence, TRIAC gives you a recipe.

> T = your claim about a passage
> R = a refined statement of that claim
> I = the passage itself, quoted or paraphrased

A = analysis of how the passage illustrates your claim

C = statement you now have clearly shown to be true

It's a structure that can vary, too. For example, the steps can go in different orders, such as IATC.

I = intriguing illustration or example to begin

A = analysis of this illustration, how it works, why it works this way

T = your sense of the theme of the passage, your real topic

C = your concluding discussion of what now seems true to you and should seem true to your readers

Or you could use TITITIAC—three pairs of thesis/illustrations followed by analysis of how these three add up and a concluding discussion of what now seems accurate or true. TRIAC, in other words, is a structure that can work in lots of different sequences and combinations.

QUOTING AND PARAPHRASING

Using quotations helps you be specific; quotations help you (and your readers) see where an idea came from or what parts of a reading provoked your response. Let's say that you've been struck by a highly quotable passage in Wendell Berry's "Getting Along with Nature" and want to use it in an essay. You have several options.

- You can quote the whole passage. Quoting the whole passage tells readers that they really need to read it all in the exact words of the author. To quote an entire passage, use a lead-in phrase and then indent the passage as a block.

  As Wendell Berry puts it in "Getting Along with Nature":
  > We go to wilderness places to be restored, to be instructed in the natural economies of fertility and healing, to admire what we cannot make. Sometimes, as we find to our surprise, we go to be chastened or corrected. And we go in order to return with renewed knowledge by which to judge the health of our human economy and our dwelling places.

  Wilderness, in other words, teaches us and heals us in ways that nothing else can.

  Whenever you want to quote a passage longer than three or four lines, you need to block it like this. Notice that in a block quotation you don't use quotation marks before and after the passage.

- You can use a shorter part of the passage. To use just part of a passage, use a lead-in phrase, and then quote the lines. But this time there's no need to indent the passage as a block. Work the lines into the paragraph and use quotation marks.

As Wendell Berry puts it in "Getting Along with Nature," "We go to wilderness places to be restored, to be instructed in the natural economies of fertility and healing, to admire what we cannot make." Wilderness, in other words, teaches us and heals us in ways that nothing else can.

- You can work smaller phrases into your own sentences. Instead of quoting all or part of the passage in whole sentences, take some piece of the author's sentence and blend it into your own language.

  Sometimes, we go to wilderness areas, as Wendell Berry says, "to be chastened or corrected." This is often a surprise. We don't expect to be shown the errors of our ways, but we are; and we return to civilization a little sheepish, aware of our mistakes.

  In general, try not to quote more than you really need to. Sometimes, a long passage is so good that you've got to use all of it, but you should do extensive quoting only now and then. Even in a long term paper you shouldn't have more than one or two long quotations.
  Here are further tips for all three kinds of quoting.

  Notice that commas and periods always go inside quotation marks.
  Notice that in all three examples the quotation is followed by some explanation in the student's own words. It's not enough just to quote the piece. You've got to explain it a little, both because important quotations are usually not self-explanatory and because part of your job is to show that you've actually understood what you're quoting. You're showing that the quotation actually fits the claim you're making about it, that it belongs in the paragraph.
  Lead-in and transitional phrases are always necessary: *As Berry says, According to Berry, As Berry puts it, In Berry's words, Berry says, Berry exclaims, Berry insists, Berry argues.* These phrases can go at the beginning, in the middle, or at the end of a quotation. Varying the sequence can help the sentences flow more smoothly.

  As Berry insists, "whether we go to those places or not, we need to know that they exist."

  Berry argues that "whether we go to those places or not, we need to know that they exist."

  "Whether we go to those places or not," Berry insists, "we need to know that they exist."

- Finally, you can paraphrase the quotation. That is, you can put the idea into your own words, acknowledging in some way that it isn't your own. This is what the follow-up sentences—"Wilderness, in other words, teaches us and heals us in ways that nothing else can"—are doing in the earlier examples. The transition *in other words* is the obvious indication of the paraphrase.

One way to imagine the sequence when you're quoting is like this:

thesis
lead-in phrase
long or short quotation or a brief quotation worked into your own
    sentences
follow-up paraphrase

But it's also good to leave out the quotations and simply give the sense of the author's meaning yourself. You show that you've absorbed the meaning and can give it back in your own way.

> Berry's point in "Getting Along with Nature" is that we all need wilderness areas. We need to get away from the unnatural "economies" that surround us everywhere in the city and encounter the "natural economies" of wilderness, because these natural economies teach us things. They teach us what we're doing wrong. They teach us by contrast—and in the process "chasten" and "correct" us.

Here is a shorter version.

> Berry's point is that wilderness teaches us what we're doing wrong and shows us an alternative "economy," something different from the world of malls and tract houses, something we can "admire."

Notice that in paraphrase it's good to quote a word now and then. But the student is controlling the sentence rhythms, directing the sequence, and emphasizing what he or she thinks should be emphasized.

HOW THE ESSAY HELPS YOU WITH TERM PAPERS

Writing essays is good training for writing term papers (as well as something worthwhile to do in itself). The permissions of the essay form give you a chance to learn what's basic to all good writing.

Writing clearly and straightforwardly: Using *I* and writing in your own voice prepares you for writing the direct, precise sentences that good term papers require.
Grounding claims: Testing ideas in your own experience prepares you for grounding claims in the kinds of evidence found through research.
Getting beyond the easy generalization: Exploring meaning in your own reading experience, not settling for the easy answers, prepares you for the complexities of a longer project.

You usually don't use *I* in a term paper, of course, and you usually don't write directly about your own experience. There are further adjustments to be made, more distancing to do, as you move from the essay to the longer paper. But the essay, like the journal, is a way of learning what's fundamental to academic thinking. It's a way of learning to read past the obvious, to get to the rich particulars. You can structure an essay with the following basic pattern to reach directly for the truth in a straightforward manner.

Everyone says _____.
But in my own experience I have found _____.

Writing Summaries

In this chapter we move from the informal, open-ended writing of journals and short essays to the stricter, objective form of the summary. The task here is not to show *your* thinking but to report the thinking of someone else—to show that you've understood what someone else has to say. A summary focuses on the text itself, not on reactions to the text.

READING TO WRITE A SUMMARY

Knowing that you'll be writing a summary, you should pay special attention to figuring out the mental moves that piece of writing makes. Here are some questions to be aware of as you read a piece you plan to summarize.

- What do the title and first page or so of the reading identify as this writer's main interest? If you can find a sentence that directly tells you, copy it down. If not, finish this sentence after you've read the first page: "So far, it looks like the writer in this piece aims to . . ." Then add another sentence of your own that adds further explanation.

- Has the writer of this piece used subheadings or other divisions (for instance, asterisks or extra white space) to show shifts in content? If so, pay attention to them. Try to explain the reasons that the piece shifts where it does.

- Realizing that virtually all writing is made up of examples (stories, images, illustrations) and larger assertions, see whether you can identify which is which. Which examples or illustrations are longest? On what does this writer spend the most words?

- Use the TRIAC scheme to identify the major pieces in the selection as a whole: Which paragraphs or parts of paragraphs fill the T slot, which the A slot, and so on? Use TRIAC to look within paragraphs as well: Which sentences fill the T slot in a given paragraph, which the A slot?

- Does this piece tell a story? Does it move in a chronological order (first this happened, then this, then this)? Or does it move from major topic to major topic? If it moves in chronological order to tell a story, what is the story? What is the story about? If it moves from major topic to major topic, what are these topics?

Using these questions while reading Melissa Greene's "No Rms, Jungle Vu," you might make notes in your journal similar to the following sample journal entry.

Title, first page: This title's a little strange. It looks like something from a classified ad, maybe an advertisement for an apartment or something. Except where would you have an apartment that has no rooms and gives a view of the jungle? Once I begin reading, things get clearer: it's a zoo—the design of a zoo—that she's talking about. And once that's clear, the title makes sense.

Subheadings, other divisions: No subheadings, though I see that the piece does divide into sections separated by three dots. Just looking quickly, I see a first section that's sort of long, a second one that's much shorter, a third long one with a subdivision in it (white space), then a quite short ending section.

Examples, assertions: Just looking at how the first section starts, it opens with assertions—Jon Coe telling us something he believes: how zoo design should work—it should "make the hair stand up on the back of your neck." Then the section goes on with what looks like a careful discussion of the Woodland Park gorilla exhibit as a major example, how it's a model for other places. And this section also tells us what it's like to actually go to this exhibit, where we'd stand and what we'd see and how it's all been arranged to keep the gorillas where they're in easy view. The heated boulders is a nifty idea. This organization seems pretty straightforward: assertion, then example.

The second section looks like it's establishing the recent history of zoo design—how this kind of design started. It's telling that story.

Chronology, major topics: This piece starts by establishing its major focus: the revolution in zoo design. The second section tells the story of its immediate origin. The third section really has two topics—the changes in science and the loss of wilderness. Both have driven this new kind of design. Section three does a lot of comparing/contrasting (zoos now versus older ones) to show the changes, and it uses explanations and quotations to talk about the loss of wilderness and what that means for zoos and their goals. The last section seems to be a short example, a story really. Except for the last section, the overall organization relies on opening assertions followed by examples and explanations.

WRITING THE SUMMARY

Usually, a summary performs three main functions: It describes *what the writing does,* it discusses *how the writing does it,* and it explains *why the author has written the piece.* A summary will also include any important information about the author and any crucial information about the context in which the piece was written. If the summary must be very short (say five hundred words), then these major discussion points may require only a paragraph each. And the summary might open by discussing all of them. So, for example, a summary of "No Rms, Jungle Vu" by Melissa Greene might begin in this way.

> When we go to zoos, we might not think of them as places that have actually been designed. Melissa Greene's "No Rms, Jungle Vu" shows us otherwise. Her factual essay takes us into the world of zoo design, introduces readers to some of the major designers, and explains how dramatically zoos have changed since 1970.

An opening like this gives us a good bit of information: We know who wrote the piece, we know its primary focus, we know its title, we know that it's an essay (not a poem or short story), and we know its basic aims. Later sentences and paragraphs would identify Greene's major assertions and major examples. Remember that, as a general rule, the most important points will be those that are discussed the longest. In general, then, look for the longest explanations or the longest stories: They usually focus on the most important and most complicated main points.

USING QUOTATIONS IN SUMMARIES

Summaries are hard to write partly because they must take complicated or well-detailed information and present it briefly. The great temptation here is to generalize, to make your summary too vague, so that it doesn't really communicate a clear sense of the piece you're summarizing. Using brief quotations can remedy this problem and give your readers a clearer sense of the original.

Why use brief quotations (at most, usually no more than a sentence or so for any one purpose) rather than long ones? Remember that to be really effective and truly save readers time, a summary has to be short, concise. Thus it should use quotations to help flesh out only the most important aspects of the original piece you're summarizing. Sometimes you may decide to quote a sentence or a part of one, as in this example.

> Greene features the Woodland Park gorilla exhibit in Seattle as "an international standard for the replication of wilderness in a zoo exhibit."

Sometimes you may decide to quote parts of two or more sentences within a statement of your own.

Greene explains that in the past zoos were often designed by local architects who "did the suburban hospital," whereas today zoo architecture is a specialty aimed at creating "astoundingly realistic habitats for the animals."

EVALUATING AND REVISING SUMMARY DRAFTS

Good summaries spend their words carefully, and they work to accurately reflect the intentions and major features of the original. Thus minor points of the original are left out of the summary or are mentioned only briefly; major points and major illustrations or explanations receive most of the attention and most of the summary's words. In addition, a good summary flows easily, with its logic and progression consistently clear to readers. With these traits in mind we can make a checklist that should help you evaluate and revise your own draft.

Read the draft as though you have no knowledge of the original reading. On the basis of the summary draft only, list the main points (the main logic, the major explanations or illustrations) in the reading.

Does your summary quote from the original, and do the quotations support the original author's most important points? Which other points (if any) should also be supported with quotations from the original? Should any quotations now in the draft be cut or shortened?

Which sentences or paragraphs in your summary draft seem confusingly worded or likely to be misunderstood?

Which parts of the draft will benefit most from revision?

How do the main points in your summary draft compare with the points you first made in journal entries? Does your draft accurately reflect the original reading? Does it leave out or pay too little attention to something important? Where does it spend too much time (and too many words), and where does it spend too few?

Writing Arguments

A good argumentative paper convinces readers of several things. It convinces them that:

You investigated an issue thoroughly.
You understood it because you present credible evidence.

You made clear decisions about how to weigh and value that
evidence.
You presented your findings in accessible, rational ways.
Your position is at least as well considered as their own.

A good argument speaks to an audience of people just like you, people of
goodwill and intelligence who may not agree with you or who may not
understand your position. In writing arguments, your purpose is not to
seize ground but to find common ground.

USING JOURNAL ENTRIES TO HELP
YOU DECIDE YOUR POSITION

You will rarely be asked to write an argument on an issue that's
simple or self-evident. Simple or obvious issues (should you stop at a red
light, for instance) aren't really debatable; there is no genuine basis for
argument or disagreement. Issues worth arguing about are arguable because
they're complicated and because thoughtful, honest people can disagree
about them. Here are some useful suggestions to keep in mind as you
begin the process of writing an argument.

- Start by identifying the main issue. What is the question or set of questions that forms the center of the discussion? To find the questions, look
for (or listen for) the statements that discuss some action or outcome.
Such statements will either agree with this action/outcome or disagree
with it. In John Muir's piece "Hetch Hetchy Valley," for example, the
immediate question can be seen in this sentence: "Sad to say, this most
precious and sublime feature of the Yosemite National Park, one of the
greatest of all our natural resources for the uplifting joy and peace and
health of the people, is in danger of being dammed and made into a
reservoir to help supply San Francisco with water and light. . . ." The
possible action here is the damming of a river, and the possible outcomes
are two: (1) a valley flooded and made into a reservoir and (2) additional
water and electricity made available for San Francisco. And even this one
sentence clearly indicates that Muir disagrees with the proposed action
and possible outcomes: Thinking about it is "sad to say."

- Think about audience and purpose. Who cares about this issue, and
why? If the situation isn't clear in your mind, try to dramatize it as
concretely as you can: Someone is standing up in front of some particular
group at a particular time saying these things. Visualize the group.

- State the issue in a question (or a series of questions). Returning to the
John Muir piece, you might ask questions such as the following. Should
the Tuolumne River be dammed and the Hetch Hetchy Valley be
flooded? What would be gained by doing this? What would be lost by
doing this? Who or what would benefit by the damming? Who or what
would be sacrificed? Do the benefits outweigh the sacrifices? why or
why not?

- Identify your own preliminary judgment. If you had to pick a side or choose a position right now, what choice would you make? What reasons do you have now?

- Consult those who have already taken a side. This consultation may take the form of discussion (in class or out). Or it may take the form of reading from other sources (we'll say more about research later).

- Do a two-column, quick review of what you know with regard to your issue. Put all of the arguments for one side in one column, and put the rebuttals or counterarguments in the other column. Use key words or phrases, not full sentences, and try to put all of the major information you have on a single sheet of paper.

- Revise and refine your own judgment. At some point you must make a decision about what you believe is true and why you believe it. Are you ready to do that now? If not, what nagging questions do you need to answer?

- Look for areas of agreement. Despite different values or conclusions, what would all concerned parties agree with or affirm? Finding some common ground can often be the key to encouraging your readers to listen to what you have to say.

RETHINKING ASSUMPTIONS

One of the challenges in arguing is getting outside our own natural, instinctive assumptions. All of us feel and think certain things automatically, intuitively, because of who we are and where we come from. Although these assumptions may be right and good, they need to be extracted and examined. Here is a series of strategies and questions, borrowed from writing teacher Douglas Hunt, that can help you examine your assumptions.

1. Identify a position that seems obvious or natural to you, something you believe now without even thinking about it.
2. Write down the elements in your experience that make this idea or position seem natural to you.
3. Make a list of any reasons you can think of to question this idea. Why would others question it? Come to think of it, why should *you* question it?
4. Make a list of all the reasons you can think of to believe in this position after all. What were you thinking or feeling underneath?
5. Explain why this isn't a black-and-white issue, why it isn't clearly one way or the other but is complex (and so worth arguing about).
6. Explain the consequences of persuading your readers to accept the position: What would happen if everyone agreed with you? disagreed?

USING TRIAC TO STRUCTURE AN ARGUMENT

Earlier in this section we discussed TRIAC as one pattern to use in writing an essay. This pattern can be particularly useful with argument.

T = Topic (or Issue) and Thesis: State the topic, the issue or controversy that you want your readers to look at. In an argument, this opening should give a wide view, mentioning the two or three major positions people have taken on the issue. The tone here is that of an objective reporter surveying the range of responses to the controversy. For example, after reading Wendell Berry's "Out of Your Car, Off Your Horse," you might decide that the topic is, Price and convenience are two factors that affect the choices we make in food buying.

R = Restatement, Restriction, Refinement: Return to the position that you advocate, rephrasing the overall question and restricting it in sharper, more particular ways. Returning to the Wendell Berry example, you don't just want to look at price or convenience; you also want to encourage readers to tie their food buying to ecological thinking. The tone here shifts, becoming less neutral and surer of its own truth. This is when you tell readers what you think. This section establishes the foundation on which your argument will build, and it normally includes a list of the major reasons that the next sections of your paper will discuss at some length.

I = Illustrations, Examples: By illustrations or examples we mean your reasons, your facts, data, or testimony from authorities—whatever it is that you have learned (either from your own experience or your research) that has helped you take your position. This section is your teaching section. It's where you introduce readers to the new information that has significantly affected your own view and that, presumably, will educate your readers, too.

A = Analysis: Once readers feel more fully educated about the issue, they need to see how these new understandings add up. That's what your analysis section does: It tells readers how the various pieces interrelate. In a way, you are assembling a puzzle, putting together various understandings until they form a complete picture.

C = Conclusion: Analysis inevitably leads to conclusion. In an argument, each piece of evidence and each reason you have should lead to its own conclusion. Thus if you have three main reasons, you should have three conclusions, each of which asserts some truth. These three conclusions should also add up to some greater truth.

REVISING THE DRAFT OF YOUR ARGUMENT

Once you have a more or less complete draft, get responses to it from other readers such as fellow students or writing center staff. Other readers will be able to see inconsistencies or holes in your argument. If you cannot involve other readers, you may still be able to pretend that you're reading for the first time. Either way, here are some directions to organize a writing group discussion or to help you see your draft as others do.

> Find the part of the draft that most clearly states the overall issue. Is it as clear as it should be? Does it appear at the right place in the draft?
>
> Find the part of the draft that most clearly states the specific argument the paper will work to illustrate and make clear. Is it as clear as it should be? How could it be misinterpreted? Is it placed where it should be?
>
> List the major reasons, evidence, or examples the argument gives.
>
> Evaluate each of the reasons or examples. Is each discussed clearly? What questions come up as you read this part of the discussion?
>
> Ask yourself where readers could misread or misinterpret what the draft says now. Make a list of these problem areas.
>
> Pay attention to how the argument ends. Does it close with a strongly stated set of conclusions (because W, X, and Y are true and because Z is related, then Z is true)? Does the concluding position fit with the writing and thinking that precedes it? If not, what seems to be wrong?

You can also try filling out a chart of the argument, similar to the one that follows. In the process of filling it out, you should get a clearer view of your own draft. Use just key words and phrases, and try to summarize each of the sections.

Opening identification of issue + range of responses

_____

_____

_____

Refocusing of issue, author's position, list of major reasons

_____

_____

_____

Discussion of reasons and evidence + preliminary conclusions

_____

_____

_____

Ending interpretations, analyses, conclusions

_____

_____

_____

ARGUING TO PERSUADE OTHERS

Argument is more than a form of inquiry, of course. Often the task is not to figure out what you think but to persuade someone else that what you think is valid and right, or at least worth taking seriously. An argument focuses on readers, not on your own thinking. Your goal is to change minds, to move people to action. Everything we've said earlier in this chapter will help you do this. But writing to convince readers whom you know oppose you presents some additional challenges. To reach these readers, you also need to understand their values and their reasons, which means looking carefully at divergent viewpoints. Here are three things to look at closely.

1. Look at how the other person frames the controversy. Consider, for example, the question of mass transit versus individual commuters driving their own cars. People who advocate mass transit would probably frame the question in terms of air pollution (mass transit reduces it), ease (someone else drives, no parking hassles), and perhaps expense (no parking fees, less upkeep on a car, maybe even one less car). On the other hand, those who individually commute might frame the question first and foremost in terms of freedom and convenience (cars aren't bound by transit schedules or limited to transit routes). Clearly the two sides view the question in quite different terms.

If you were to write an argument that focuses on this question, you'd need to make sure that part of your paper showed your understanding of your readers' different perspectives. Your argument certainly wouldn't need to agree with those perspectives, but you would want to show that you've considered your readers' viewpoints and can effectively build on that understanding to offer a better, more persuasive alternative.

2. As you look at your readers' different views, also pay attention to what they present as evidence or proof. Try to summarize this evidence briefly in your own words as a way to test whether you really understand what you're hearing. This summary will help you as you construct your own argument, because as someone who wants to change readers' minds, you will need to counter this evidence with better evidence of your own. For example, if an argument presents a first-person story as its proof (for example, the story of how an individual commute in one's own car gives a person flexibility), then you might want to try telling a story (a different story) that illustrates your way of seeing this issue.

3. See if you can identify any values or truths that you and your readers share. For example, virtually all commuters will value less tension in their lives, minimum expense, dependability of schedule, and the like. Identifying such common ground can be an important step toward understanding your opposition, and it can lead to the development of counter-arguments or compromise positions.

THE REASONABLE VOICE

In writing an argument, your first goal is to make sure that the argument is actually read by those you want to reach; an unread argument—however brilliantly constructed—always fails. So you want to be careful not to call your readers (or their views) foolish, misguided, inadequate, or uninformed. Thus instead of saying something like "these sadly incomplete views fail to fully understand X," you could work to raise more questions about X: "Let's look at X more closely. Does X really mean . . . ?" Also, try to avoid any specific words that may trigger a negative reaction from your readers. For example, people who prefer to drive their own cars to work probably will flare up at the identification of their cars as "gas-guzzlers."

Gathering and Using Information

For excellence, the presence of others is always required.

—HANNAH ARENDT

Research isn't just something a college writing assignment forces you into. You gather and use information from the moment you get up in the morning. For example, you might listen to a traffic report to find out what your commute will be like, or you might check an outdoor thermometer to find out if it's warm enough for a bicycle ride. Research, or gathering information, helps us make wise decisions.

The readings in this book depend on research that is not dissimilar from the research you do every day. The selections fall into roughly three categories: literary readings (poems and short stories), personal essays drawing mostly from personal experience (Joan Didion's "On Going Home," for instance), and essays that depend heavily on information from other experts and sources (Samuel W. Matthews's "Under the Sun," for example). Some involve looking out the window at the sky, in other words; others involve checking the newspaper; many involve both.

SOME TIPS FOR COMING UP WITH TOPICS (AND KEEPING THEM MANAGEABLE)

The hard part in doing research for papers, of course, is finding a good topic you really care about—and then keeping the topic focused to a narrow, manageable scale. Here are some practical tips.

- Think in terms of questions that interest you. When you shop for a stereo or a car, you're interested in answering a question: Which stereo should I buy, or which car should I buy? And to answer broad questions like these, you naturally start asking smaller, more specific ones. How much do stereos cost? What features do they have? Suppose something breaks—is there a warranty? Do I know anyone who already has this model? If so, would this person buy the same stereo again? Thinking in terms of such questions can help you see how focused your topic really is. If your research interest is too broad, you'll find yourself writing a book instead of an essay.

- Do your thinking in writing. Don't just let your thoughts about research swirl around in your brain, ungrounded. Get them on the page in a reading or research journal.

- Think about what's most important in your own life right now. Think about some important personal experience, and then move outward to larger issues. Let's say that in the past few months you've become bothered by the noise in the dorm or apartment where you live. The stereos are always booming. Laughter is always coming through the walls. You probably have enough energy built up on this issue to begin asking the broader questions that only research can answer.

    Is your experience representative? For example, are many people bothered by noise? Have there been other complaints locally? Have other communities struggled with noise problems?

    Is your experience part of larger trends or larger issues? What effects does noise have on the nervous system, mood, or behavior, for instance? Are these effects representative of the overall impact the environment has on the way we think and feel?

    Do experts agree with you, and do they have ideas that relate to your experience? For example, what do scientists think about the effects of noise? What do moralists think about the rights and responsibilities of people living in groups?

- Form opinions early and often. Play your hunches. Begin your research with a possible thesis or two. People usually have an intuition about what they'll find when they begin doing research. They might have a deep bias or a preformed notion that's gotten them a little interested in pursuing the topic further. It's good to use this kernel of an opinion as an organizing point, a direction finder. It's not that you're going into the research with your mind made up completely, looking to bend information to preconceived notions. You'll change your mind several times before you're done, a new thesis replacing the old. But if you start the process with a clear argument or hypothesis, it gives you some perspective for handling the great amount of information you're sure to find.

- Figure out whether you're reporting or arguing. One reason for doing research is to find statistics, scientific studies, and expert opinion to support an argument. You can also simply report research, seeking to inform rather than persuade. Having that purpose in mind as you walk through the library doors can help guide you, too.

- Think small from the beginning. It will be obvious as soon as you start searching the data banks and indexes that a topic like "ecology" won't get you anywhere. You'll get lost in a forest of sources. And a term paper on a subject like ecology would either be a superficial and useless ten pages or a thousand-page monster. So think small from the beginning.

- Think locally. In any community there are always examples of national events issues expressed in local terms. Focus on the local scale. If you're concerned about child abuse, for example, begin by checking the local papers and seeing how that issue is played out in your community.

- Think of a real audience. Teachers aren't the only audience for research papers. In the world outside the classroom all kinds of people want all kinds of information. Try to translate your possible research project out of the classroom (even if that's the only place the paper will go). Ask yourself, Who do I know who would need to know this?

USING DATABASES TO DO RESEARCH

Most on-line library catalogues list books but not articles from periodicals. The different CD-ROM (computer disk, read-only memory) indexes list primarily articles from journals and magazines, although sometimes chapters or parts of books are also included. These two sets of databases are sometimes in different places (on different computers), and they often require slightly different procedures.

All databases are typically organized in three ways: by author, by title of a work, and by subject. If you know you want to find work by a particular author, either a book or an article, you shouldn't have much trouble, especially if you know the author's full name. But most of the time, you're looking not for a particular author but rather for answers to some particular questions. And this means searching according to subject.

All on-line library catalogues (the ones for books) can be accessed by subject. To search by subject, you need to identify the words that the particular index program will recognize in order to retrieve the information you want. Some words are so broad (and so frequently used in the titles of articles) that the search yields more information than you want. Suppose you sit down at a computer terminal in your library, access an index, and type in the word *environment*. Chances are that the screen will then present you with many more articles and citations than you know what to do with. Similarly, typing *Cherokee* and nothing else (called a single-level search) may give you a list of articles dealing with an automobile that has the brand name Cherokee. Index programs typically let you type more than one search word; so after you type *ecology*, you could type *acid rain* and *New England* (a three-level search). In general, searching in this narrow, more focused way will give you a shorter, more specific list of articles.

Remember that databases typically give you only publication information: an article's title, its author(s), publisher, volume number or month and year of publication, and page numbers. Some indexes will also give you a very brief summary. The point to remember here is that locating promising articles in a database is not the same as actually being able to read and use these articles. Does your library have these publications, or can you get a copy of this article through interlibrary loan (and get it early enough to use it)?

A WARNING ABOUT INTERNET RESEARCH

If you have ready access to the Internet (via your own computer or one in a library or computer lab at school), then you may well see Internet searching as the easiest way to locate the information you need. Unfortunately, not all information on the Internet is reliable; some of it is, and some of it is pure garbage.

Think of it this way: The Internet is merely a very large bulletin board. Anyone who knows how to construct a Web page can post on this "bulletin board." And the Web page of a prankster can look every bit as professional as the Web page constructed by a PhD in the field. You need to evaluate Web pages before you accept what they offer. Here are some tips.

- Pay attention to the Web address: sites that end in .edu are associated with educational institutions, sites ending in .com are associated with for-profit businesses or organizations, and sites ending in .org are associated with nonprofit (often advocacy) groups. In general, educators pursue truth, businesses pursue profit, and advocacy groups pursue their stated goals. These various pursuits often need to be considered as you decide whether the information you're finding is accurate and complete.

- Look for a clear statement of site authorship; be wary of a site that seems to lack an author. If you can find out more about that author, do so.

- Look for links to other authoritative sites, and check them to see if they work and are current. Be wary of sites that don't have links or that include links to irrelevant sites.

- Be wary of Web-published information that you cannot verify with other media (printed magazines, academic journals, or books, for example). In fact, be wary of any information that seems absolutely unique, uncorroborated, or unsupported elsewhere.

- When you're not sure of the information you get from the Web, ask experts for help. Ask your reference librarian or your course instructor for their evaluations.

When it comes to any research—and especially Internet research—accuracy matters, because it affects your credibility and your impact as a writer. The responsibility to report accurate information rests squarely with you.

HANDLING WHAT YOU FIND

It's not hard to find information. More often, the problem is the opposite: You've got more information than you know what to do with, and it all looks equally important at first, deserving of your attention. Here's some advice for handling the panic you may feel as the sources start piling up.

- Go back to your original reasons for doing this research. What are you looking for anyhow? What are you trying to find out? Remembering why you're researching should help you see what's important and what's not.

- Read your material just closely enough to get an overview. "Freeread" and plan on rereading later. Get a feel for what seems important, and set those sources aside. Reject sources that don't seem useful. Get a sense of the lay of the land, the topography. Look for repetitions in different sources, the ideas and questions that keep coming up. Look for contradictions.

- Find a central book or article in the subject and move out from there. Often a particular source will seem the most authoritative. It's the one everyone else refers to, or it's the one that you understood and liked the best, trusted the most. Usually it's a book-length study, and usually (though not always) it's fairly recent. Use that book to organize your other research. Read it carefully. Use its endnotes and bibliography to find further research.

- Keep a research log. A research log is a very practical tool, partly because it records everything you actually *did* on any given day: not just the title of the book or article you found but also where in your particular library you found it; whether the book was missing from the shelves and how long it will take to get it; and so on. Buy a separate little notebook and write down everything, especially call numbers, authors, and titles.

- Read only as carefully as you need to. There are three kinds of sources, three piles to put things in: (1) the central source or sources, the ones you read line by line; (2) the useless sources, the ones you can put aside; (3) the sources that might be good or have some useful information but don't demand close reading. Skim the third group; read them quickly. Jump through the subtitles until you get to what you want. Read quickly until something in the piece catches your eye.

- Remember how little material you can actually use. Earlier in this chapter we suggested that it's good to avoid using block quotations more than once or twice, even in a long paper. In fact, the hardest part about writing a research paper is leaving things out: It was so hard to find the material in the first place, it's a shame not to include it. But you've got to be ruthless. Look for three or four long quotations at the most. Make a list of a half-dozen to a dozen phrases and short passages you want to include, too. Leave everything else aside.

- Summarize and paraphrase as much as you can. These are skills we've talked about before, and they're essential now. The majority of the information you've found won't appear in the form of direct quotations in your own paper. It will appear in your own words (with sources cited).

- Find the quotable quotations. Look for the passage or sentence that stood out most to you as you read—the one that best explained or summarized the piece, that was the most beautiful or interesting. Find the passage that summarizes the idea of the selection. This passage often appears at the beginning or at the end, though it can appear elsewhere. Keep TRIAC in mind; often the most quotable statements are the T and R and C statements.

- Work from the books and articles themselves. On short projects that don't need too many sources, it's useful sometimes simply to pile up the books and journals on your desk, with slips of paper to mark the passages you want to use.

- Make copies. Copying makes elaborate note taking unnecessary most of the time, particularly for short to medium-length projects. Simply copy the half-dozen major sources or parts of sources; then annotate the copy, marking the passages you want to quote. It's useful sometimes to put numbers in the margins to keep track of things, though you may be able to keep all of this organization in your head if there aren't too many sources. *Copy whatever other pages you'll need in order to document the source: its title, author, magazine or journal name, volume and/or issue, and page numbers.*

- Try using index cards. The advantage of index cards is that they allow you to establish categories, and for long, complex projects that's sometimes the only way to make sense of all the information. Typically you use one index card for each source.

    Remember to record all of the publication information you'll need later: author, title, library call number or location (in case you need to find this source again), publisher, publication date, volume number (for magazines or journals), and page numbers. In the heat of your search this record keeping may seem tedious or unnecessary, but doing it accurately (rather than sloppily or not at all) will save your sanity later.

    Next, indicate in your own words how or why you might use this source. Using index cards pushes you to summarize, and they make it easier for you to find order in your information (by ordering and reordering the cards themselves).

• Stop now and then to write. During the research phase you may at times feel overwhelmed, tired, or frustrated. So stop and write for a few minutes. Freewrite. Make a list. There will also be moments when you feel that things are coming together, that you've found your theme. There will be moments (believe it or not) when you feel elated. Again, stop and write. Periodically in the process, write out progress reports, interim stories of your thinking.

A particularly good journal topic at this point is the notion of surprise. You started with a thesis but maybe it's changed now. How? What material wasn't there that you expected to find? How has your research challenged, complicated, undermined your assumptions?

There's probably a new thesis here, a good focus for a paper. Write it down: "Like everyone else, I used to think _____. But research shows, in fact, that _____." Let this statement be your guide for the remainder of your work in the library.

DOCUMENTING SOURCES

The specific ways that writers cite their sources in the paper itself vary among academic disciplines. In the humanities (literature, music, art, and so on) most writers follow the guidelines of the Modern Language Association (MLA). The social sciences and many natural sciences follow the guidelines of the American Psychological Association (APA). And there are many other such guidelines. We can't tell you which set of guidelines is right for you, especially since much of the material in this book could easily be classified as literature and as natural science. We can tell you, though, that the old system of numbered footnotes has been almost entirely replaced by a system that uses parentheses to indicate source information; both the current MLA and APA systems use parenthetical citations in the text itself. And both systems rely on a page at the end of the paper that lists all of the sources cited.

Chapter 1 Essay Topics

1. Sketch a profile of yourself as a reader. Write a reading autobiography. Here are some questions to help you start brainstorming details. (Don't feel that you have to take up each one in order. Simply start writing as soon as you've gotten enough ideas and images.)

Did you read a lot or a little growing up? Did your parents read and, if so, what did they read? Did you have books in your house? Have your tastes and interests changed? how? Do you remember one treasured book from your growing up? Do you read for pleasure now? What is your favorite book, and why? What is the last book you read, why did you read it, and what was the experience of reading it? If you don't read for pleasure, what do you do instead, and what are the benefits of doing those things? the disadvantages? What role does television play in your reading life? Have you always intended to do more reading but for some reason haven't gotten to it? Why haven't you gotten to it? What do you feel the moment you get a reading assignment in one of your classes this term? dread? anticipation? What's the difference between the reading you enjoy (if you enjoy reading) and the reading you're assigned? Do you know people who read a lot? What kind of people are they? Would you like to be more like these people? What do you enjoy doing most, and how does this activity compare with the act of reading? Is it at odds with reading or in keeping with it?

After you've filled in your portrait with details, conclude by reflecting on the implications. How do you think your experiences with reading and your attitudes about reading will influence your approach to this book? to college in general? In your own life, what's the relationship between reading and writing?

2. Write an essay reflecting on how you "read" other things in your life besides books and articles—*reading* in the sense of interpreting a person, thing, or experience, decoding the details on the surface, seeing past the surface to what's underneath.

For example, a person good at auto mechanics can read an engine, figuring out the problem with the fuel filter or the wheel bearings by interpreting the external signs—the sounds, the smells, the appearance of things. A forester can read a forest, determining the best approach to logging or reforestation by the lay of the land, the health and distribution of trees, the density of wildlife, and so on. A cook can read a cake or sauce, deciding when to add ingredients or turn off the heat.

In our day-to-day experiences we're reading all the time: making inferences about people on the basis of their body language, their clothing, what they say and how they say it, and what they don't say. Reading is what we have to do whenever the answer or the reality of something isn't immediately obvious.

Write an essay describing something you know how to read, and compare this experience to the reading of books and articles. How are these acts of interpretation different and the same? What can one tell you about the other? How did you learn to become expert in this other kind of reading? What have you gained from it?

3. Write about a time when reading really worked for you—a time when you were very moved by a book or story or poem or essay or a time when you learned something important from a reading.

What was the content of the reading? What was its style? Why did you do the reading? Was it assigned, or did you choose it yourself? Where did you read it, and how long did it take? Did you write about it or take notes on it? Describe how you felt during and after the reading—sad, elated, happy, confused. What was it that caused these feelings? If you got information from a piece, what information did you get, why did you want it, and how did the text deliver it? What did you do to make the reading successful? How were you prepared? How did you act?

Finally, compare this positive experience to a negative one—to a time when reading was hard or frustrating. What's the difference? What can you do to change things? What things can't you change, and how can you manage those things?

4. *"Screenings" or "Best Pieces."*
This is a preliminary form, a step toward an essay. Simply go through your journal and screen out what you think are your best entries or the best parts of entries. Clean these up (proofreading and correcting any grammatical mistakes); then type them, leaving blank space between the entries. You don't need to add any text or arrange the pieces in any particular order.

5. *Collages.*
This is another preliminary form, a step up from a screening. Go through the same process of screening out the best pieces, proofreading, and typing; but this time, try to arrange the pieces in some kind of order. Use blank spaces as transitions; there's no need to add transitions or do any other blending. But try to see whether there's a pattern among the pieces: imagistic, associative, alternating (long/short, personal/analytical), thematic. Think of the pieces as a puzzle you've made up yourself; then try to assemble the pieces. It's helpful even to cut out these pieces (literally, with scissors) and spread them on a table so you can see them better. Be intuitive. Be playful. Think of this task as an arts and crafts project.

As a final stage, after completing the collage, you may want to experiment with blending the pieces into a single, coherent essay. Is it possible to put some pieces together without elaborate transition—pieces that seemed unrelated at first but that now might blend? What transitions are necessary? Do you need to write a few extra pieces?

6. Write an essay reflecting on the essay. Here are some questions to get you thinking. When you hear the word *essay,* what associations immediately come to mind? what images? From past experience, come up with a list of rules and requirements for good essay writing, and then compare this list with the suggestions in this chapter. Read several of the essayists in this book, such as Joan Didion, Lewis Thomas, Wendell Berry, and Barry Lopez. Do these writers break any of the rules you learned before now? Do they surprise you? What new rules or new standards do they introduce? What values seem implicit in the way the essay was taught to you in school, and what values are implicit in the way we're talking about the essay in this chapter (assuming they are different)?

7. Write an essay reflecting on your style of thinking. Maybe you've taken a test establishing your psychological profile or have read educational theorists talking about learning styles. Using any of that terminology or simply your own language, try to describe how you think you think. If

you've been keeping a journal, reread it as "data" for this study. Step back and see whether you can identify patterns in the way you've written, questions you've especially liked to answer, moves you typically make as a reader and a writer. Maybe you like going from the general to the particular, or maybe you find it hard to come up with particulars. Maybe you find yourself typically resisting something at first and then opening up to it, or vice versa. Maybe you're very personal as a thinker, or very abstract. Maybe you like to jump from point to point, or maybe you stick to the same idea for pages. If you haven't kept a journal, simply reflect on what happens as you do a reading for school, write a paper, or learn a new job—what you do when you think.

Try to come to some conclusions. Given the way you think, what kind of career are you best suited for? Are there things about your style that you'd just as soon change? How and why? Do the essay patterns proposed in this chapter help you in your thinking, clarify or modify it in any way? Can you come up with usable patterns that correspond to your own style of thought?

Part II
Reading to Write

2

Rooms and Homes,
Country and City

Almost uniquely among species, human beings can live at polar research stations and in equatorial jungles. We can even re-create the conditions we need to live outside the earth's atmospheric envelope. We modify whatever we find to create conditions favorable to us: we make cities, towns, shopping malls, freeways, fences, yards. We paint walls, hang photographs or posters or other art, lay carpets, and post refrigerator magnets—all in an effort to make ourselves at home.

The readings in this chapter examine the places that people have made and places that have made us. To some extent, we know who we are by knowing our places, our homes.

MY NEIGHBORHOOD

THEME FOR ENGLISH B

Langston Hughes

Poet Langston Hughes was a prominent figure in the Harlem Renaissance, a literary and artistic movement centered in the New York City region of Harlem during the 1920s. Hughes wrote sixteen books of poetry, two novels, and numerous plays and short stories invoking both lyricism and realism in the life of African Americans. In this frequently anthologized poem, he describes the thoughts of a young black student in a composition course.

The instructor said,

> *Go home and write*
> *a page tonight.*
> *And let that page come out of you—*
> *Then, it will be true.*   5

I wonder if it's that simple?
I am twenty-two, colored, born in Winston-Salem.
I went to school there, then Durham, then here
to this college on the hill above Harlem.
I am the only colored student in my class.   10
The steps from the hill lead down into Harlem,
through a park, then I cross St. Nicholas,
Eighth Avenue, Seventh, and I come to the Y,
the Harlem Branch Y, where I take the elevator
up to my room, sit down, and write this page: 15

It's not easy to know what is true for you or me
at twenty-two, my age. But I guess I'm what
I feel and see and hear, Harlem, I hear you:
hear you, hear me—we two—you, me, talk on this page.
(I hear New York, too.) Me—who?   20

Well, I like to eat, sleep, drink, and be in love.
I like to work, read, learn, and understand life.
I like a pipe for a Christmas present,
or records—Bessie, bop, or Bach.
I guess being colored doesn't make me *not* like   25
the same things other folks like who are other races.
So will my page be colored that I write?

Being me, it will not be white.
But it will be

a part of you, instructor.
You are white—   30
yet a part of me, as I am a part of you.
That's American.
Sometimes perhaps you don't want to be a part of me.
Nor do I often want to be a part of you.
But we are, that's true!   35
As I learn from you,
I guess you learn from me—
although you're older—and white—
and somewhat more free.
                                                                                         40
This is my page for English B.

                                                                                    1959

Reading and Responding

1. The opening lines of this poem quote an instructor who gives an assignment: "Go home and write / a page tonight. / And let that page come out of you— / Then, it will be true." The instructor's assignment includes an interesting definition of truth. Why would something be true if it came "out of you"? What would make that writing "true"? Freewrite about this notion of truth. Could something that came out of you in this way ever be false?

2. Does the poem sound true to you? What makes it sound that way? How can you sound true when you write academic papers? Take about fifteen minutes to write your responses to these questions.

Working Together

1. Write a group poem, based on lines 7–15 of Hughes's poem, that describes everyone in your group. Write the nine lines for each individual group member, replacing the words that are specific to Hughes with words that describe that person's life. Begin with "I am . . ." and finish it in whatever way is appropriate to that person. Imitate the poem's overall format and style. When you compile your group poem, you might end up with forty-five lines for a five-person group.

2. As a group, decide on a list of five words or phrases that describe the poem "Theme for English B." For each word or phrase, identify a part of the poem that particularly expresses that quality. Write two sentences that explain what you mean by that word or phrase. In a five-person group, each person should be ready to report a different word or phrase, read the part of the poem that supports it, and then explain the group's reasoning.

3. As a group, look for similarities and differences between the sort of truth that forms the topic of "Theme for English B" and the sort of

truth that you're usually asked to write about in academic courses. Try to identify three major similarities and three major differences. Decide as a group which kind of writing is easier—the sort of writing the poem suggests, or the sort of writing you usually do in other courses. Be ready to talk about your reasoning.

Rethinking and Rewriting

1. Write your own "Theme for English B." Imitate the format (the line breaks and the sort of content) if you want. Change the content in any way that truthfully reflects you and your own life. Give the poem an appropriate title that reflects the name of your English course. Once you've finished, write a prose paragraph (at least five sentences) that discusses what it was like to write your poem.

2. Write a version of "Theme for English B" that reflects another person's experience. Follow the general cues that Hughes's poem gives you in terms of content, but write about the person you selected, either from that person's viewpoint or using third-person voice. Talk with the person beforehand. Once you've finished, write a paragraph (at least five sentences) about researching and writing this poem.

3. Write a three-page prose self-introduction that begins to give readers a sense of your home. Aim for the sort of truth that the poem gives. Include at least two quotes from "Theme for English B" as a way of making connections between what Hughes says and what you want to say.

COMING AROUND THE BEND
Thoughts on Cultivating the Unexpected

Sarah Rabkin

A lecturer in the Writing Program at the University of California in Santa Cruz, Sarah Rabkin specializes in science and environmental writing, journalism, and the personal essay. In this essay, Rabkin suggests that we can learn a great deal by observing our own neighborhoods. This essay appeared in the environmental quarterly Isle *(spring 1997).*

When I was in my teens, I came upon John Muir's description of his first glimpse across California's Central Valley, from the grassy crest of the Coast Range to the granite peaks of the Sierra Nevada. Standing at the summit of Pacheco Pass in April, Muir looked over a sea of wildflowers that stretched to the north and south farther than he could see. Nearly a hundred miles ahead to the east, the Sierra rose from a belt of pink and yellow foothills into purple mountains capped with a pearl-gray frosting of snow: "a wall of light ineffably fine," he wrote, "and as beautiful as a rainbow."

Reading Muir's passage, I thought about riding inland from Berkeley toward the mountains in my family's car. We would wind gently up the coastal slopes until, coming around a bend in the highway, we reached a vantage point similar to Muir's. Peering eastward through yellow-gray smog, I beheld the great valley below, plowed and platted, the Sierra a dirty mirage in the distance. My spirits always sank at that sight. Only about a century had passed between Muir's viewing and mine, and the contrast attested to rapid and violent changes in the California landscape.

Years later, I taught a group of ten-year-old girls in an after-school workshop on nature notebooks. On the first day, as we sat introducing ourselves, I asked them to think out loud about nature. What exactly does the word mean? What is natural and what is not? After the girls had talked for a while, I asked them whether they considered humans a part of nature. "We used to be," said one, "but we domesticated ourselves."

We, wielders of combines and chain saws, bulldozers and backhoes, have indeed domesticated ourselves and our surroundings—and now we are asking, with increasing urgency, what we have lost in the process. Among the spiritual satisfactions that we forfeit when we tame the landscape is that of coming around a bend, as John Muir did when he topped Pacheco Pass for the first time, and discovering something wide open and wild. Muir tried to keep his contemporaries from closing in on the last of the untrampled places. Today, we in the West struggle to hold back development from a few remaining parks and wilderness areas, what Wallace Stegner called the geography of hope, in order to preserve not only the land but also the pioneer's sense of limitless possibility within ourselves.

Towns and cities cannot substitute for wilderness, and yet they, too,   5
can offer moments of private pioneering, of coming-around-the-bend.
One morning I found myself in an unfamiliar Santa Cruz neighborhood
within a mile of my home, on a side street where I had never walked
before. I could hear the traffic a few blocks away at the grocery store where
I shop every weekend, but I couldn't picture my position in relation to
other streets, and suddenly I had no idea what lay around the corner ahead
of me. In a small way, I was lost.

With the momentary disorientation came unanticipated pleasure. I
had no mental map for this place—no internal map of what to expect as I
gazed down the winding street. I became elated, charged with a sense of
adventure. If I did not know what waited around the bend, it seemed,
then anything might appear there, including a spectacular flower garden, a
funky Victorian cottage, the season's best blooming eucalyptus, or a stranger
who would turn out to become a friend. I found myself savoring the moment and reluctant to return to familiar ground.

This brief encounter with the unpredictable reminded me of being
on the trail and the road, and it illuminated one reason why I love to travel.
Visiting a place for the first time, whether a mountain river or a roaring
city, makes almost everything worth examining, because very little is dis-
missably familiar. Unable to slip the scene into a comfortable context of
memory, the mind refuses to shut out any possibility, and the senses open
up to every stimulus. The world is new.

As I wandered my small stretch of personal frontier in Santa Cruz
that morning, I wondered what it would take to cultivate the traveler's
openness as a perpetual state of mind, even amid the dailiness of home.
Optimistic artists and dreamers do seem able to retain this ability to see
their surroundings as if for the first time, while the more demoralized
among us have lost faith in the idea that something unexpected, rejuvenat-
ing, and good could lie just around the corner. Most of us find our outlook
swinging gently between those extremes, but the environments where we
live and work—the shapes, smells, textures, and colors of the spaces we
encounter every day—can affect the pendulum's tendency profoundly.

Although we have lost the literal frontier, we have not shed our need
for the inviting unknown place that lies ahead and beyond. Most of us live
in cities, so preserving wilderness areas and establishing national parks,
though essential, is not enough. We need to create inviting spaces close to
home that offer a sense of mystery and promise, and that elevate rather
than diminish our spirits. Public gardens, parks, and pathways, restored
riverfronts, pedestrian malls, museums, cathedrals—all kinds of city places
have that power. I remember touring a large Massachusetts Institute of
Technology dormitory whose curving hallways produced a sense of intimacy in the alcoves outside rooms and an exhilarating curiosity about what
and whom one would encounter around the next bend.

Perhaps the most magical urban spaces of all, at least to me, are   10
bookstores and libraries. If I were an architect or planner, I think I would

pay close attention to the places where books are bought and borrowed. Buildings that house books unite two kinds of architecture, literal and literary, and I suspect they can teach us a lot about how to create environments full of hope and goodwill.

When it comes to design and furnishing, the best book places have their signature touches: the parquet floor, the vaulted ceiling, the loft hung with photographs of visiting writers from over the years, the rocking horse in the corner. But interwoven with the physical arrangement of space is a more complex design—one that changes with the inventory and varies with each visitor, composed of the invisible lines of ideas that interconnect books and browsers. In the best, one-of-a-kind bookshops, as in the most enticing outdoor landscapes, mystery and possibility are written into every nook and corner.

One of my favorite local bookstores sells a sweatshirt emblazoned with a line from Vincent van Gogh: "I think that I still have it in my heart someday to paint a bookshop with the front yellow and pink in the evening . . . like a light in the midst of darkness." I don't know whether van Gogh ever painted his bookshop, but if he did, it would have been a Bookshop Santa Cruz or an Elliott Bay Book Company, not a franchised, sterilized, predictable space where the beep of the electronic cash register is louder than the thoughts of the browsers.

As a society, we can create the kind of surroundings that encourage joyful creativity in each of us—or the kind that drive us to depression. Someone who grows up in a bleak neighborhood accustomed to fearing danger around the corner has slim chances, I think, of learning to trust in the world's miracles. Those who plan neighborhoods and commercial streets, who build fences, developments, and dams, who design buildings and parks, do not determine everything about our surroundings, but they do have tremendous power to influence attitudes by shaping our physical world.

Domesticating ourselves does not have to be a deadly process. We can plant splashes of unexpected color and scent in our cities and build hundred-mile trails around and out of them. We can restore urban waterways, fund art on the streets, make resting alcoves and miniparks along crowded boulevards, create tree buffers to temper the noise and danger of traffic alongside pedestrian walkways, and push for bike paths and public transportation and cleaner air. And we can support independent booksellers and local libraries. Whether it is from Muir's luminous wall of mountains or van Gogh's illuminated bookshop window, we need the light of hope, discovery, and possibility to shine on the places where we spend our lives.

Reading and Responding

1. Reread Rabkin's essay with a piece of paper (or notebook) in front of you. As you finish the second paragraph (about what Rabkin remembered

about "riding inland from Berkeley toward the mountains in my family's car"), pause and write a paragraph about something you remember seeing from a car window, bus window, or train window—some view that gave you a sense of distance. Write about what you saw. Then explain how you felt seeing it.

2. Freewrite about the first time you walked somewhere and, as Rabkin puts it, had "no idea what lay around the corner" ahead of you. Where was this? How old were you? What feelings did you have as you experienced this new place on foot?

3. As you think about the city, suburb, town, or other landscape you know well, what place do you like to visit occasionally that offers what Rabkin terms a "sense of mystery and promise"? Write about going to this place and what it gives you.

Working Together

1. Take a group walk—on campus, say from the bookstore to the soccer field—following a route that at a normal pace would take about ten minutes; plan on at least a half an hour for your walk, though. Take a notebook with you, and walk this route paying uncommon attention, stopping to write briefly about whatever surprises you or catches your attention. Anyone in the group may ask to stop for a while by simply saying "notebook" as a way of indicating a pause in order to note something. Every time someone calls for a pause, write something down about what you see. Decide in advance who will say "notebook" first, who will say it second, and so on. Everyone should have a turn. If you finish the walk before each member of the group has called for a pause, walk the same route again until each group member has had a turn.

2. Based on the activity in item 1, work as a group to write a description of this part of the campus as seen by your group. What did you notice that you might otherwise have missed or given only very brief attention? What have you learned about your campus from this more focused kind of looking?

3. Talk in your group about a place on campus that seems to draw people to it because of its location or design, not because they need to do business there. What is it about the design that makes this place attractive? What decisions were made to either create this place or keep it as it is?

Rethinking and Rewriting

1. Write a letter of at least two pages to someone urging him or her to visit a constructed place (that is, a place developed and built by human effort, not by nature) that you value and visit often, or would if you could. In the letter, explain what the person would find in this place;

explain what to look for, or where to go exactly, to experience the place as you would. Your letter should make the person want to go to this place, and it should deliver a taste of the site so your reader knows something new even if he or she never actually visits the place you described.

2. Write an essay that re-creates a journey—a walk, a train or bus ride, and so on—through a cityscape or urban area you're just learning. Let the essay follow your actions chronologically (from beginning to end), by location (from start to finish), and through your consciousness (your senses, your surprises, worries, elations, your curiosity, your judgment). Be a tour guide and take your readers on this journey.

THE SILENT NEIGHBORHOOD

Annie Dillard

> *Annie Dillard won the Pulitzer Prize at age twenty-nine for her first book,* Pilgrim at Tinker's Creek *(1974). Since then she has been one of our most influential writers. Her subsequent books include* Teaching a Stone to Talk, The Writing Life, *and, most recently,* For the Time Being *(1999). The following evocation of early childhood is from the opening of her autobiography,* An American Childhood.

The story starts back in 1950, when I was five.

Oh, the great humming silence of the empty neighborhoods in those days, the neighborhoods abandoned everywhere across continental America—the city residential areas, the new "suburbs," the towns and villages on the peopled highways, the cities, towns, and villages on the rivers, the shores, in the Rocky and Appalachian mountains, the piedmont, the dells, the bayous, the hills, the Great Basin, the Great Valley, the Great Plains— oh, the silence!

For every morning the neighborhoods emptied, and all vital activity, it seemed, set forth for parts unknown.

The men left in a rush: they flung on coats, they slid kisses at everybody's cheeks, they slammed house doors, they slammed car doors; they ground their cars' starters till the motors caught with a jump.

And the Catholic schoolchildren left in a rush; I saw them from our dining-room windows. They burst into the street buttoning their jackets; they threw dry catalpa pods at the stop sign and at each other. They hugged their brown-and-tan workbooks to them, clumped and parted, and proceeded toward St. Bede's church school almost by accident. 5

The men in their oval, empty cars drove slowly among the schoolchildren. The boys banged the cars' fenders with their hands, with their jackets' elbows, or their books. The men in cars inched among the children; they edged around corners and vanished from sight. The waving knots of children zigzagged and hollered up the street and vanished from sight. And inside all the forgotten houses in all the abandoned neighborhoods, the day of silence and waiting had begun.

The war was over. People wanted to settle down, apparently, and calmly blow their way out of years of rationing. They wanted to bake sugary cakes, burn gas, go to church together, get rich, and make babies.

I had been born at the end of April 1945, on the day Hitler died; Roosevelt had died eighteen days before. My father had been 4-F in the war, because of a collapsing lung—despite his repeated and chagrined efforts to enlist. Now—five years after V-J Day—he still went out one night a week as a volunteer to the Civil Air Patrol; he searched the Pittsburgh skies for new enemy bombers. By day he worked downtown for American Standard.

Every woman stayed alone in her house in those days, like a coin in a safe. Amy and I lived alone with our mother most of the day. Amy was three years younger than I. Mother and Amy and I went our separate ways in peace.

The men had driven away and the schoolchildren had paraded out of sight. Now a self-conscious and stricken silence overtook the neighborhood, overtook our white corner house and myself inside. "Am I living?" In the kitchen I watched the unselfconscious trees through the screen door, until the trees' autumn branches like fins waved away the silence. I forgot myself, and sank into dim and watery oblivion.

A car passed. Its rush and whine jolted me from my blankness. The sound faded again and I faded again down into my hushed brain until the icebox motor kicked on and prodded me awake. "You are living," the icebox motor said. "It is morning, morning, here in the kitchen, and you are in it," the icebox motor said, or the dripping faucet said, or any of the hundred other noisy things that only children can't stop hearing. Cars started, leaves rubbed, trucks' brakes whistled, sparrows peeped. Whenever it rained, the rain spattered, dripped, and ran, for the entire length of the shower, for the entire length of days-long rains, until we children were almost insane from hearing it rain because we couldn't stop hearing it rain. "Rinso white!" cried the man on the radio. "Rinso blue." The silence, like all silences, was made poignant and distinct by its sounds.

What a marvel it was that the day so often introduced itself with a firm footfall nearby. What a marvel it was that so many times a day the world, like a church bell, reminded me to recall and contemplate the durable fact that I was here, and had awakened once more to find myself set down in a going world.

In the living room the mail slot clicked open and envelopes clattered down. In the back room, where our maid, Margaret Butler, was ironing, the steam iron thumped the muffled ironing board and hissed. The walls squeaked, the pipes knocked, the screen door trembled, the furnace banged, and the radiators clanged. This was the fall the loud trucks went by. I sat mindless and eternal on the kitchen floor, stony of head and solemn, playing with my fingers. Time streamed in full flood beside me on the kitchen floor; time roared raging beside me down its swollen banks; and when I woke I was so startled I fell in.

Who could ever tire of this heart-stopping transition, of this breakthrough shift between seeing and knowing you see, between being and knowing you be? It drives you to a life of concentration, it does, a life in which effort draws you down so very deep that when you surface you twist up exhilarated with a yelp and a gasp.

Who could ever tire of this radiant transition, this surfacing to awareness and this deliberate plunging to oblivion—the theater curtain rising and falling? Who could tire of it when the sum of those moments at the edge—the conscious life we so dread losing—is all we have, the gift at the moment of opening it? *15*

Six xylophone notes chimed evenly from the radio in the back room where Margaret was ironing, and then seven xylophone notes chimed. With carefully controlled emotion, a radio woman sang:

What will the weather be?
Tell us, Mister Weather Man.

Mother picked up Amy, who was afraid of the trucks. She called the painters on the phone; it was time to paint the outside trim again. She ordered groceries on the phone. Larry, from Lloyd's Market, delivered. He joked with us in the kitchen while Mother unpacked the groceries' cardboard box.

I wandered outside. It was afternoon. No cars passed on the empty streets; no people passed on the empty sidewalks. The brick houses, the frame and stucco houses, white and red behind their high hedges, were still. A small woman appeared at the far, high end of the street, in silhouette against the sky; she pushed a black baby carriage tall and chromed as a hearse. The leaves in the Lombardy poplars were turning brown.

"Lie on your back," my mother said. She was kind, imaginative. She had joined me in one of the side yards. "Look at the clouds and figure out what they look like. A hat? I see a camel."

Must I? Could this be anybody's idea of something worth doing? *20*

I was hoping the war would break out again, here. I was hoping the streets would fill and I could shoot my cap gun at people instead of at mere sparrows. My project was to ride my swing all around, over the top. I bounced a ball against the house; I fired gravel bits from an illegal slingshot Mother gave me. Sometimes I looked at the back of my hand and tried to memorize it. Sometimes I dreamed of a coal furnace, a blue lake, a redheaded woodpecker who turned into a screeching hag. Sometimes I sang uselessly in the yard, "Blithar, blithar, blithar, blithar."

It rained and it cleared and I sent Popsicle sticks and twigs down the gritty rivulet below the curb. Soon the separated neighborhood trees lost their leaves, one by one. On Saturday afternoons I watched the men rake leaves into low heaps at the curb. They tried to ignite the heaps with matches. At length my father went into the house and returned with a yellow can of lighter fluid. The daylight ended early, before all the men had burned all their leaves.

It snowed and it cleared and I kicked and pounded the snow. I roamed the darkening snowy neighborhood, oblivious. I bit and crumbled on my tongue the sweet, metallic worms of ice that had formed in rows on my mittens. I took a mitten off to fetch some wool strands from my mouth. Deeper the blue shadows grew on the sidewalk snow, and longer; the blue shadows joined and spread upward from the streets like rising water. I walked wordless and unseeing, dumb and sunk in my skull, until— what was that?

The streetlights had come on—yellow, bing—and the new light woke me like noise. I surfaced once again and saw: it was winter now, winter again. The air had grown blue dark; the skies were shrinking; the streetlights had come on; and I was here outside in the dimming day's snow, alive.

Reading and Responding

1. Imagine that you're five years old and at home, wherever home was. It's morning. Do a one-page freewrite—not letting your pen leave the page, not worrying about grammar and punctuation, just recording your thoughts and feelings as they come to you—describing what you see and feel in your mind.
2. Freewrite about some early memory that you connect with home. Write quickly and don't worry about errors; just write what you remember and speculate about what you don't remember.

Working Together

1. Make a list of the many details Annie Dillard uses in this essay, the concrete sensations she describes, the sights, sounds, and smells. List the nouns, verbs, and adjectives. Combine your list with those of classmates. As a group, come to a conclusion about how all of those details add up: What's their effect on you as a reader?
2. Dillard describes a time when she was glad to be alive, full of energy and awareness and attention. Try to remember how you felt when you were five. Did you feel the same as Dillard? Compare that five-year-old feeling with the feeling you had just this morning, on the way to class, for example. As a group, come up with a list of five phrases that describe how you felt when you were young and another list of five phrases describing how you felt this morning. As you look at these two lists, how do you account for the differences?

Rethinking and Rewriting

1. Return to your earlier freewrite, and make a list of new details—new sights and sounds and smells—that you can add to it.
2. Revise and extend your earlier freewrite into a short essay that recalls what home was for you when you were five years old. Add the list of details and as many more as you can think of. Your task in this essay is

to re-create the experience of being where you were all those years ago. Like Dillard, re-create a single day in that life. As you polish this essay, try to make your sentences as direct and straightforward, as strong and clear, as Dillard's. Optional: Make this the first part of a two-part essay comparing home when you were five and home for you now, the way you felt then and the way you feel right now.

MY NEIGHBORHOOD

Ishmael Reed

African American novelist, playwright, and essayist Ishmael Reed teaches at the University of California, Berkeley. His work includes the novel Reckless Eyeballing *(1986) and the essay collection* Writing Is Fightin' *(1988). He is also the editor of the recently published* Multi America: Essays on Cultural Wars and Cultural Peace *(1998), a collection of essays by writers of color. In the following essay, first published in* California *magazine, Reed praises the Oakland, California, neighborhood where he lives.*

My stepfather is an evolutionist. He worked for many years at the Chevrolet division of General Motors in Buffalo, a working-class auto and steel town in upstate New York, and was able to rise from relative poverty to the middle class. He believes that each succeeding generation of Afro-Americans will have it better than its predecessor. In 1979 I moved into the kind of neighborhood that he and my mother spent about a third of their lives trying to escape. According to the evolutionist integrationist ethic, this was surely a step backward, since "success" was seen as being able to live in a neighborhood in which you were the only black and joined your neighbors in trying to keep out "them."

My neighborhood, bordered by Genoa, Market Street, and 48th and 55th streets in North Oakland, is what the media refer to as a "predominantly black neighborhood." It's the kind of neighborhood I grew up in before leaving for New York City in 1962. My last New York residence was an apartment in a brownstone, next door to the building in which poet W. H. Auden lived. There were trees in the backyard, and I thought it was a swell neighborhood until I read in Robert Craft's biography of [the composer] Stravinsky that "when Stravinsky sent his chauffeur to pick up his friend Auden, the chauffeur would ask, 'Are you sure Mr. Auden lives in this neighborhood?'" By 1968 my wife and I were able to live six months of the year in New York and the other six in California. This came to an end when one of the people I sublet the apartment to abandoned it. He had fled to England to pursue a romance. He didn't pay the rent, and so we were evicted long distance.

My first residence in California was an apartment on Santa Ynez Street, near Echo Park Lake in Los Angeles, where I lived for about six months in 1967. I was working on my second novel, and Carla Blank, my wife, a dancer, was teaching physical education at one of Eddie Rickenbacker's camps, located on an old movie set in the San Bernardino Mountains. Carla's employers were always offering me a cabin where they promised I could write without interruption. I never took them up on the offer, but for years I've wondered about what kind of reception I would have received had they discovered that I am black.

During my breaks from writing I would walk through the shopping areas near Santa Ynez, strolling by vending machines holding newspapers whose headlines screamed about riots in Detroit. On some weekends we'd visit novelist Robert Gover (*The One Hundred Dollar Misunderstanding*) and his friends in Malibu. I remember one of Gover's friends, a scriptwriter for the *Donna Reed Show*, looking me in the eye and telling me that if he were black he'd be "on a Detroit rooftop, sniping at cops," as he reclined, glass of scotch in hand, in a comfortable chair whose position gave him a good view of the rolling Pacific.

My Santa Ynez neighbors were whites from Alabama and Mississippi, 5 and we got along fine. Most of them were elderly, left behind by white flight to the suburbs, and on weekends the street would be lined with cars belonging to relatives who were visiting. While living here I observed a uniquely Californian phenomenon. Retired men would leave their houses in the morning, enter their cars, and remain there for a good part of the day, snoozing, reading newspapers, or listening to the radio.

I didn't experience a single racial incident during my stay in this Los Angeles neighborhood of ex-southerners. Once, however, I had a strange encounter with the police. I was walking through a black working-class neighborhood on my way to the downtown Los Angeles library. Some cops drove up and rushed me. A crowd gathered. The cops snatched my briefcase and removed its contents—books and notebooks having to do with my research of voodoo. The crowd laughed when the cops said they thought I was carrying a purse.

In 1968 my wife and I moved to Berkeley, where we lived in one Bauhaus box after another until about 1971, when I received a three-book contract from Doubleday. Then we moved into the Berkeley Hills, where we lived in the downstairs apartment of a very grand-looking house on Bret Harte Way. There was a Zen garden with streams, waterfalls, and bridges outside, along with many varieties of flowers and plants. I didn't drive, and Carla was away at Mills College each day, earning a master's degree in dance. I stayed holed up in that apartment for two years, during which time I completed my third novel, *Mumbo Jumbo*.

During this period I became exposed to some of the racism I hadn't detected on Santa Ynez or in the Berkeley flats. As a black male working at home, I was regarded with suspicion. Neighbors would come over and warn me about a heroin salesman they said was burglarizing the neighborhood, all the while looking over my shoulder in an attempt to pry into what I was up to. Once, while I was eating breakfast, a policeman entered through the garden door, gun drawn. "What on earth is the problem, officer?" I asked. He said they got word that a homicide had been committed in my apartment, which I recognized as an old police tactic used to gain entry into somebody's house. Walking through the Berkeley Hills on Sundays, I was greeted by unfriendly stares and growling, snarling dogs. I remember one pest who always poked her head out of her window whenever I'd walk down Bret Harte Way. She was always hassling me about parking my car in front of her house. She resembled Miss Piggy. I came to think of this section of Berkeley as "Whitetown."

Around 1974 the landlord raised the rent on the house in the hills, and we found ourselves again in the Berkeley flats. We spent a couple of peaceful years on Edith Street, and then moved to Jayne Street, where we encountered another next-door family of nosy, middle-class progressives. I understand that much time at North Berkeley white neighborhood association meetings is taken up with discussion of and fascination with blacks who move through the neighborhoods, with special concern given those who tarry, or who wear dreadlocks. Since before the Civil War, vagrancy laws have been used as political weapons against blacks. Appropriately, there has been talk of making Havana—where I understand a woman can get turned in by her neighbors for having too many boyfriends over—Berkeley's sister city.

In 1976 our landlady announced that she was going to reoccupy the Jayne Street house. I facetiously told a friend that I wanted to move to the most right-wing neighborhood he could think of. He mentioned El Cerrito. There, he said, your next-door neighbor might even be a cop. We moved to El Cerrito. Instead of the patronizing nosiness blacks complain about in Berkeley, I found the opposite on Terrace Drive in El Cerrito. The people were cold, impersonal, remote. But the neighborhood was quiet, serene even—the view was Olympian, and our rented house was secluded by eucalyptus trees. The annoyances were minor. Occasionally a car would careen down Terrace Drive full of white teenagers, and one or two would shout, "Hey, nigger!" Sometimes as I walked down The Arlington toward Kensington Market, the curious would stare at me from their cars, and women I encountered would give me nervous, frightened looks. Once, as I was walking to the market to buy magazines, a white child was sitting directly in my path. We were the only two people on the street. Two or three cars actually stopped, and their drivers observed the scene through their rearview mirrors until they were assured I wasn't going to abduct the child.

At night the Kensington Market area was lit with a yellow light, especially eerie during a fog. I always thought that this section of Kensington would be a swell place to make a horror movie—the residents would make great extras—but whatever discomfort I felt about traveling through this area at 2 a.m. was mixed with the relief that I had just navigated safely through Albany, where the police seemed always to be lurking in the shadows, prepared to ensnare blacks, hippies, and others they didn't deem suitable for such a neighborhood.

In 1979 our landlord, a decent enough fellow in comparison to some of the others we had had (who made you understand why the communists shoot the landlords first when they take over a country), announced he was going to sell the house on Terrace Drive. This was the third rented house to be sold out from under us. The asking price was way beyond our means, and so we started to search for another home, only to find that the

10

ones within our price range were located in North Oakland, in a "predominantly black neighborhood." We finally found a huge Queen Anne Victorian, which seemed to be about a month away from the wrecker's ball if the termites and the precarious foundation didn't do it in first, but I decided that I had to have it. The oldest house on the block, it was built in 1906, the year the big earthquake hit Northern California, but left Oakland unscathed because, according to Bret Harte, "there are some things even the earth can't swallow." If I was apprehensive about moving into this neighborhood—on television all black neighborhoods resemble the commotion of the station house on *Hill Street Blues*—I was later to learn that our neighbors were just as apprehensive about us. Were we hippies? Did I have a job? Were we going to pay as much attention to maintaining our property as they did to theirs? Neglected, the dilapidated monstrosity I'd got myself into would blight the entire block.

While I was going to college I worked as an orderly in a psychiatric hospital, and I remember a case in which a man was signed into the institution, after complaints from his neighbors that he mowed the lawn at four in the morning. My neighbors aren't that finicky, but they keep very busy pruning, gardening, and mowing their lawns. Novelist Toni Cade Bambara wrote of the spirit women in Atlanta who plant by moonlight and use conjure to reap gorgeous vegetables and flowers. A woman on this block grows roses the size of cantaloupes.

On New Year's Eve, famed landscape architect John Roberts accompanied me on my nightly walk, which takes me from 53rd Street to Aileen, Shattuck, and back to 53rd Street. He was able to identify plants and trees that had been imported from Asia, Africa, the Middle East, and Australia. On Aileen Street he discovered a banana tree! And Arthur Monroe, a painter and art historian, traces the "Tabby" garden design—in which seashells and plates are mixed with lime, sand, and water to form decorative borders, found in this Oakland neighborhood, and others—to the influence of Islamic slaves brought to the Gulf Coast.

I won over my neighbors, I think, after I triumphed over a dozen [15] generations of pigeons that had been roosting in the crevices of this house for many years. It was a long and angry war, and my five year old constantly complained to her mother about Daddy's bad words about the birds. I used everything I could get my hands on, including chicken wire and mothballs, and I would have tried the clay owls if the only manufacturer hadn't gone out of business. I also learned never to underestimate the intelligence of pigeons; just when you think you've got them whipped, you'll notice that they've regrouped on some strategic rooftop to prepare for another invasion. When the house was free of pigeons and their droppings, which had spread to the adjoining properties, the lady next door said, "Thank you."

Every New Year's Day since then our neighbors have invited us to join them and their fellow Louisianans for the traditional Afro-American good luck meal called Hoppin' John. This year the menu included blackeyed peas, ham, corn bread, potato salad, chitterlings, greens, fried chicken, yams, head cheese, macaroni, rolls, sweet potato pie, and fruitcake. I got up that morning weighing 214 pounds and came home from the party weighing 220.

We've lived on 53rd Street for three years now. Carla's dance and theater school, which she operates with her partner, Jody Roberts—Roberts and Blank Dance/Drama—is already five years old. I am working on my seventh novel and a television production of my play *Mother Hubbard*. The house has yet to be restored to its 1906 glory, but we're working on it.

I've grown accustomed to the common sights here—teenagers moving through the neighborhood carrying radios blasting music by Grandmaster Flash and Prince, men hovering over cars with tools and rags in hand, decked-out female church delegations visiting the sick. Unemployment up, one sees more men drinking from sacks as they walk through Market Street or gather in Helen McGregor Plaza, on Shattuck and 52nd Street, near a bench where mothers sit with their children, waiting for buses. It may be because the bus stop is across the street from Children's Hospital (exhibiting a brand-new antihuman, postmodern wing), but there seem to be a lot of sick black children these days. The criminal courts and emergency rooms of Oakland hospitals, both medical and psychiatric, are also filled with blacks.

White men go from door to door trying to unload spoiled meat. Incredibly sleazy white contractors and hustlers try to entangle people into shady deals that sometimes lead to the loss of a home. Everybody knows of someone, usually a widow, who has been gypped into paying thousands of dollars more than the standard cost for, say, adding a room to a house. It sure ain't El Cerrito. In El Cerrito the representatives from the utilities were very courteous. If they realize they're speaking to someone in a black neighborhood, however, they become curt and sarcastic. I was trying to arrange for the gas company to come out to fix a stove when the woman from Pacific Gas and Electric gave me some snide lip. I told her, "Lady, if you think what you're going through is an inconvenience, you can imagine my inconvenience paying the bills every month." Even she had to laugh.

The clerks in the stores are also curt, regarding blacks the way the media regard them, as criminal suspects. Over in El Cerrito the cops were professional, respectful—in Oakland they swagger about like candidates for a rodeo. In El Cerrito and the Berkeley Hills you could take your time paying some bills, but in this black neighborhood if you miss paying a bill by one day, "reminders" printed in glaring and violent typefaces are sent to you, or you're threatened with discontinuance of this or that service. Los Angeles police victim Eulia Love, who was shot in the aftermath of an argument over an overdue gas bill, would still be alive if she had lived in El Cerrito or the Berkeley Hills.

I went to a bank a few weeks ago that advertised easy loans on television, only to be told that I would have to wait six months after opening an account to be eligible for a loan. I went home and called the

20

same bank, this time putting on my Clark Kent voice, and was informed that I could come in and get the loan the same day. Other credit unions and banks, too, have different lending practices for black and white neighborhoods, but when I try to tell white intellectuals that blacks are prevented from developing industries because the banks find it easier to lend money to communist countries than to American citizens, they call me paranoid. Sometimes when I know I am going to be inconvenienced by merchants or creditors because of my 53rd Street address, I give the address of my Berkeley studio instead. Others are not so fortunate.

Despite the inconveniences and antagonism from the outside world one has to endure for having a 53rd Street address, life in this neighborhood is more pleasant than grim. Casually dressed, well-groomed elderly men gather at the intersections to look after the small children as they walk to and from school, or just to keep an eye on the neighborhood. My next-door neighbor keeps me in stitches with his informed commentary on any number of political comedies emanating from Washington and Sacramento. Once we were discussing pesticides and the man who was repairing his porch told us that he had a great garden and didn't have to pay all that much attention to it. As for pesticides, he said, the bugs have to eat, too.

There are people on this block who still know the subsistence skills many Americans have forgotten. They can hunt and fish (and if you don't fish, there is a man who covers the neighborhood selling fresh fish and yelling, "Fishman," recalling a period of ancient American commerce when you didn't have to pay the middleman). They are also loyal Americans—they vote, they pay taxes—but you don't find the extreme patriots here that you find in white neighborhoods. Although Christmas, Thanksgiving, New Year's, and Easter are celebrated with all get-out, I've never seen a flag flying on Memorial Day, or on any holiday that calls for the showing of the flag. Blacks express their loyalty in concrete ways. For example, you rarely see a foreign car in this neighborhood. And this 53rd Street neighborhood, as well as black neighborhoods like it from coast to coast, will supply the male children who will bear the brunt of future jungle wars, just as they did in Vietnam.

We do our shopping on a strip called Temescal, which stretches from 46th to 51st streets. Temescal, according to Oakland librarian William Sturm, is an Aztec word for "hothouse," or "bathhouse." The word was borrowed from the Mexicans by the Spanish to describe similar hothouses, early saunas, built by the California Indians in what is now North Oakland. Some say the hothouses were used to sweat out demons; others claim the Indians used them for medicinal purposes. Most agree that after a period of time in the steam, the Indians would rush en masse into the streams that flowed through the area. One still runs underneath my backyard—I have to mow the grass there almost every other day.

Within these five blocks are the famous Italian restaurant Bertola's, *25*
"Since 1932"; Siam restaurant; La Belle Creole, a French-Caribbean res-

taurant; Asmara, an Ethiopian restaurant; and Ben's Hof Brau, where white and black senior citizens, dressed in the elegance of a former time, congregate to talk or to have an inexpensive though quality breakfast provided by Ben's hardworking and courteous staff.

The Hof Brau shares its space with Vern's market, where you can shop to the music of DeBarge. To the front of Vern's is the Temescal Delicatessen, where a young Korean man makes the best po'boy sandwiches north of Louisiana, and near the side entrance is Ed Fraga's Automotive. The owner is always advising his customers to avoid stress, and he says goodbye with a "God bless you." The rest of the strip is taken up by the Temescal Pharmacy, which has a resident health advisor and a small library of health literature; the Aikido Institute; an African bookstore; and the internationally known Genova deli, to which people from the surrounding cities travel to shop. The strip also includes the Clausen House thrift shop, which sells used clothes and furniture. Here you can buy novels by J. D. Salinger and John O'Hara for ten cents each.

Space that was recently occupied by the Buon Gusto Bakery is now for rent. Before the bakery left, an Italian lady who worked there introduced me to a crunchy, cookie-like treat called "bones," which she said went well with Italian wine. The Buon Gusto had been a landmark since the 1940s, when, according to a guest at the New Year's Day Hoppin' John supper, North Oakland was populated by Italians and Portuguese. In those days a five-room house could be rented for $45 a month, she said.

The neighborhood is still in transition. The East Bay Negro Historical Society, which was located around the corner on Grove Street, included in its collection letters written by nineteenth-century macho man Jack London to his black nurse. They were signed, "Your little white pickaninny." It's been replaced by the New Israelite Delight restaurant, part of the Israelite Church, which also operates a day care center. The restaurant offers homemade Louisiana gumbo and a breakfast that includes grits.

Unlike the other California neighborhoods I've lived in, I know most of the people on this block by name. They are friendly and cooperative, always offering to watch your house while you're away. The day after one of the few whites who lives on the block—a brilliant muckraking journalist and former student of mine—was robbed, neighbors gathered in front of his house to offer assistance.

In El Cerrito my neighbor was indeed a cop. He used pomade on his curly hair, sported a mustache, and there was a grayish tint in his brown eyes. He was a handsome man, with a smile like a movie star's. His was the only house on the block I entered during my three-year stay in that neighborhood, and that was one afternoon when we shared some brandy. I wanted to get to know him better. I didn't know he was dead until I saw people in black gathered on his doorstep.

I can't imagine that happening on 53rd Street. In a time when dour thinkers view alienation and insensitivity toward the plight of others as characteristics of the modern condition, I think I'm lucky to live in a neighborhood where people look out for one another.

A human neighborhood.

Reading and Responding

1. Have you ever moved to a new home? If so, freewrite about that experience. What was it like to move?
2. As you read about the reactions that various neighbors and others have to Ishmael Reed's presence, what's your reaction? Talk about the parts of this essay that provoke the strongest reaction from you.

Working Together

1. Talk about the various groups that you belong to and about the ways that other people judge you simply because you're a member of that group. Identify three examples that you can present to the class.
2. Pretend that you are Ishmael Reed. What do you say to your father about the neighborhood you live in now (at the end of the essay)? Does living where you live now mean "success"?

Rethinking and Rewriting

1. Write an essay that begins by discussing the very best place you've ever lived and then goes on to describe your ideal neighborhood. What are its features, and who are your neighbors? What would you take from that very best place, and what would you add to it to make this ideal neighborhood?
2. Write an essay that discusses an occasion when you've been uncomfortable in some part of a city. Make sure the essay explains where you were, how you got there, and why you were uncomfortable. Then talk about some occasion when you had a great time in a city (again, make sure it's clear where you were and what were the conditions that contributed to how you felt). End by looking at these two experiences. What made for the comfort; what made for the discomfort?

O ROTTEN GOTHAM

Tom Wolfe

As a journalist writing features in the sixties, Tom Wolfe developed the approach to nonfiction that he later called "New Journalism," a style of writing that applies the techniques of fiction to the telling of "true" stories. Wolfe's study of the counterculture, The Electric Kool-Aid Acid Test *(1968) and his later portrayal of the first astronauts,* The Right Stuff *(1979), established him as one of our most important writers of literary journalism. Wolfe also has written two novels, including the recent* A Man in Full *(1998). In the following study of the effects of overcrowding in New York, Wolfe demonstrates the intensity that made him famous.*

I just spent two days with Edward T. Hall, an anthropologist, watching thousands of my fellow New Yorkers short-circuiting themselves into hot little twitching death balls with jolts of their own adrenalin. Dr. Hall says it is overcrowding that does it. Overcrowding gets the adrenalin going, and the adrenalin gets them hyped up. And here they are, hyped up, turning bilious, nephritic, queer, autistic, sadistic, barren, batty, sloppy, hot-in-the-pants, chancred-on-the-flankers, leering, puling, numb—the usual in New York, in other words, and God knows what else. Dr. Hall has the theory that overcrowding has already thrown New York into a state of behavioral sink. Behavioral sink is a term from ethology, which is the study of how animals relate to their environment. Among animals, the sink winds up with a "population collapse" or "massive die-off." O rotten Gotham.

It got to be easy to look at New Yorkers as animals, especially looking down from some place like a balcony at Grand Central at the rush hour Friday afternoon. The floor was filled with the poor white humans, running around, dodging, blinking their eyes, making a sound like a pen full of starlings or rats or something.

"Listen to them skid," says Dr. Hall.

He was right. The poor old etiolate animals were out there skidding on their rubber soles. You could hear it once he pointed it out. They stop short to keep from hitting somebody or because they are disoriented and they suddenly stop and look around, and they skid on their rubber-sole shoes, and a screech goes up. They pour out onto the floor down the escalators from the Pan-Am Building, from 42nd Street, from Lexington Avenue, up out of subways, down into subways, railroad trains, up into helicopters—

"You can also hear the helicopters all the way down here," says Dr. Hall. The sound of the helicopters using the roof of the Pan-Am Building nearly fifty stories up beats right through. "If it weren't for this ceiling"—he is referring to the very high ceiling in Grand Central—"this place would be unbearable with this kind of crowding. And yet they'll probably never 'waste' space like this again."

They screech! And the adrenal glands in all those poor white animals enlarge, micrometer by micrometer, to the size of cantaloupes. Dr. Hall pulls a Minox camera out of a holster he has on his belt and starts shooting away at the human scurry. The Sink!

Dr. Hall has the Minox up to his eye—he is a slender man, calm, 52 years old, young-looking, an anthropologist who has worked with Navajos, Hopis, Spanish-Americans, Negroes, Trukese. He was the most important anthropologist in the government during the crucial years of the foreign aid program, the 1950's. He directed both the Point Four training program and the Human Relations Area Files. He wrote *The Silent Language* and *The Hidden Dimension,* two books that are picking up the kind of "underground" following his friend Marshall McLuhan started picking up about five years ago. He teaches at the Illinois Institute of Technology, lives with his wife, Mildred, in a high-ceilinged town house on one of the last great residential streets in downtown Chicago, Astor Street; has a grown son and daughter, loves good food, good wine, the relaxed, civilized life—but comes to New York with a Minox at his eye to record—perfect!—The Sink.

We really got down in there by walking down into the Lexington Avenue line subway stop under Grand Central. We inhaled those nice big fluffy fumes of human sweat, urine, effluvia, and sebaceous secretions. One old female human was already stroked out on the upper level, on a stretcher, with two policemen standing by. The other humans barely looked at her. They rushed into line. They bellied each other, haunch to paunch, down the stairs. Human heads shone through the gratings. The species North European tried to create bubbles of space around themselves, about a foot and a half in diameter

"See, he's reacting against the line," says Dr. Hall.

—but the species Mediterranean presses on in. The hell with bubbles   *10* of space. The species North European resents that, this male human behind him presses forward toward the booth . . . *breathing* on him, he's disgusted, he pulls out of the line entirely, the species Mediterranean resents him for resenting it, and neither of them realizes what the hell they are getting irritable about exactly. And in all of them the old adrenals grow another micrometer.

Dr. Hall whips out the Minox. Too perfect! The bottom of The Sink.

It is the sheer overcrowding, such as occurs in the business sections of Manhattan five days a week and in Harlem, Bedford-Stuyvesant, southeast Bronx every day—sheer overcrowding is converting New Yorkers into animals in a sink pen. Dr. Hall's argument runs as follows: all animals, including birds, seem to have a built-in, inherited requirement to have a certain amount of territory, space, to lead their lives in. Even if they have all the food they need, and there are no predatory animals threatening them, they cannot tolerate crowding beyond a certain point. No more than two hundred wild Norway rats can survive on a quarter acre of ground, for example, even when they are given all the food they can eat. They just die off.

But why? To find out, ethologists have run experiments on all sorts of animals, from stickleback crabs to Sika deer. In one major experiment, an ethologist named John Calhoun put some domesticated white Norway rats in a pen with four sections to it, connected by ramps. Calhoun knew from previous experiments that the rats tend to split up into groups of ten to twelve and that the pen, therefore, would hold forty to forty-eight rats comfortably, assuming they formed four equal groups. He allowed them to reproduce until there were eighty rats, balanced between male and female, but did not let it get any more crowded. He kept them supplied with plenty of food, water, and nesting materials. In other words, all their more obvious needs were taken care of. A less obvious need—space—was not. To the human eye, the pen did not even look especially crowded. But to the rats, it was crowded beyond endurance.

The entire colony was soon plunged into a profound behavioral sink. "The sink," said Calhoun, "is the outcome of any behavioral process that collects animals together in unusually great numbers. The unhealthy connotations of the term are not accidental: a behavioral sink does act to aggravate all forms of pathology that can be found within a group."

For a start, long before the rat population reached eighty, a status hierarchy had developed in the pen. Two dominant male rats took over the two end sections, acquired harems of eight to ten females each, and forced the rest of the rats into the two middle pens. All the overcrowding took place in the middle pens. That was where the "sink" hit. The aristocrat rats at the ends grew bigger, sleeker, healthier, and more secure the whole time.

In The Sink, meanwhile, nest building, courting, sex behavior, reproduction, social organization, health—all of it went to pieces. Normally, Norway rats have a mating ritual in which the male chases the female, the female ducks down into a burrow and sticks her head up to watch the male. He performs a little dance outside the burrow, then she comes out, and he mounts her, usually for a few seconds. When The Sink set in, however, no more than three males—the dominant males in the middle sections—kept up the old customs. The rest tried everything from satyrism to homosexuality or else gave up on sex altogether. Some of the subordinate males spent all their time chasing females. Three or four might chase one female at the same time, and instead of stopping at the burrow entrance for the ritual, they would charge right in. Once mounted, they would hold on for minutes instead of the usual seconds.

Homosexuality rose sharply. So did bisexuality. Some males would mount anything—males, females, babies, senescent rats, anything. Still other males dropped sexual activity altogether, wouldn't fight and, in fact, would hardly move except when the other rats slept. Occasionally a female from the aristocrat rats' harems would come over the ramps and into the middle sections to sample life in The Sink. When she had had enough, she would run back up the ramp. Sink males would give chase up to the top of the ramp, which is to say, to the very edge of the aristocratic preserve. But one glance from one of the king rats would stop them cold and they would return to The Sink.

The slumming females from the harems had their adventures and then returned to a placid, healthy life. Females in The Sink, however were ravaged, physically and psychologically. Pregnant rats had trouble continuing pregnancy. The rate of miscarriages increased significantly, and females started dying from tumors and other disorders of the mammary glands, sex organs, uterus, ovaries, and Fallopian tubes. Typically, their kidneys, livers, and adrenals were also enlarged or diseased or showed other signs associated with stress.

Child-rearing became totally disorganized. The females lost the interest or the stamina to build nests and did not keep them up if they did build them. In the general filth and confusion, they would not put themselves out to save offspring they were momentarily separated from. Frantic, even sadistic competition among the males was going on all around them and rendering their lives chaotic. The males began unprovoked and senseless assaults upon one another, often in the form of tail-biting. Ordinarily, rats will suppress this kind of behavior when it crops up. In The Sink, male rats gave up all policing and just looked out for themselves. The "pecking order" among males in The Sink was never stable. Normally, male rats set up a three-class structure. Under the pressure of overcrowding, however, they broke up into all sorts of unstable subclasses, cliques, packs—and constantly pushed, probed, explored, tested one another's power. Anyone was fair game, except for the aristocrats in the end pens.

Calhoun kept the population down to eighty, so that the next stage, "population collapse" or "massive die-off," did not occur. But the autopsies showed that the pattern—as in the diseases among the female rats—was already there.

The classic study of die-off was John J. Christian's study of Sika deer on James Island in the Chesapeake Bay, west of Cambridge, Maryland. Four or five of the deer had been released on the island, which was 280 acres and uninhabited, in 1916. By 1955 they had bred freely into a herd of 280 to 300. The population density was only about one deer per acre at this point, but Christian knew that this was already too high for the Sikas' inborn space requirements, and something would give before long. For two years the number of deer remained 280 to 300. But suddenly, in 1958, over half the deer died; 161 carcasses were recovered. In 1959 more deer died and the population steadied at about 80.

In two years, two-thirds of the herd had died. Why? It was not starvation. In fact, all the deer collected were in excellent condition, with well-developed muscles, shining coats, and fat deposits between the muscles. In practically all the deer, however, the adrenal glands had enlarged

20

by 50 percent. Christian concluded that the die-off was due to "shock following severe metabolic disturbance, probably as a result of prolonged adrenocortical hyperactivity. . . . There was no evidence of infection, starvation, or other obvious cause to explain the mass mortality." In other words, the constant stress of overpopulation, plus the normal stress of the cold of the winter, had kept the adrenalin flowing so constantly in the deer that their systems were depleted of blood sugar and they died of shock.

Well, the white humans are still skidding and darting across the floor of Grand Central. Dr. Hall listens a moment longer to the skidding and the darting noises, and then says, "You know, I've been on commuter trains here after everyone has been through one of these rushes and I'll tell you, there is enough acid flowing in the stomachs in every car to dissolve the rails underneath."

Just a little invisible acid bath for the linings to round off the day. The ulcers the acids cause, of course, are the one disease people have already been taught to associate with the stress of city life. But overcrowding, as Dr. Hall sees it, raises a lot more hell with the body than just ulcers. In everyday life in New York—just the usual, getting to work, working in massively congested areas like 42nd Street between Fifth Avenue and Lexington, especially now that the Pan-Am Building is set in there, working in cubicles such as those in the editorial offices at Time-Life, Inc., which Dr. Hall cites as typical of New York's poor handling of space, working in cubicles with low ceilings and, often, no access to a window, while construction crews all over Manhattan drive everybody up the Masonite wall with air-pressure generators with noises up to the boil-a-brain decibel levels, then rushing to get home, piling into subways and trains, fighting for time and for space, the usual day in New York—the whole now-normal thing keeps shooting jolts of adrenalin into the body, breaking down the body's defenses and winding up with the work-a-daddy human animal stroked out at the breakfast table with his head apoplexed like a cauliflower out of his $6.95 semispread Pima-cotton shirt, and nosed over into a plate of No-Kloresto egg substitute, signing off with the black thrombosis, cancer, kidney, liver, or stomach failure, and the adrenals ooze to a halt, the size of eggplants in July.

One of the people whose work Dr. Hall is interested in on this score 25 is Rene Dubos at the Rockefeller Institute. Dubos's work indicates that specific organisms, such as the tuberculosis bacillus or a pneumonia virus, can seldom be considered "the cause" of a disease. The germ or virus, apparently, has to work in combination with other things that have already broken the body down in some way—such as the old adrenal hyperactivity. Dr. Hall would like to see some autopsy studies made to record the size of adrenal glands in New York, especially of people crowded into slums and people who go through the full rush-hour-work-rush-hour cycle every day. He is afraid that until there is some clinical, statistical data on how overcrowding actually ravages the human body, no one will be willing to do anything about it. Even in so obvious a thing as air pollution, the pattern is familiar. Until people can actually see the smoke or smell the sulphur or feel the sting in their eyes, politicians will not get excited about it, even though it is well known that many of the lethal substances polluting the air are invisible and odorless. For one thing, most politicians are like the aristocrat rats. They are insulated from The Sink by practically sultanic buffers—limousines, chauffeurs, secretaries, aides-de-camp, doormen, shuttered houses, high-floor apartments. They almost never ride subways, fight rush hours, much less live in the slums or work in the Pan-Am Building.

We took a cab from Grand Central to go up to Harlem, and by 48th Street we were already socked into one of those great, total traffic jams on First Avenue on Friday afternoon. Dr. Hall motions for me to survey the scene, and there they all are, humans, male and female, behind the glass of their automobile windows, soundlessly going through the torture of their own adrenalin jolts. This male over here contracts his jaw muscles so hard that they bunch up into a great cheese Danish pattern. He twists his lips, he bleeds from the eyeballs, he shouts . . . soundlessly behind glass . . . the fat corrugates on the back of his neck, his whole body shakes as he pounds the heel of his hand into the steering wheel. The female human in the car ahead of him whips her head around, she bares her teeth, she screams . . . soundlessly behind glass . . . she throws her hands up in the air, Whaddya expect me—Yah, yuh stupid—and they all sit there, trapped in their own congestion, bleeding hate all over each other, shorting out the ganglia and— goddam it—

Dr. Hall sits back and watches it all. This is it! The Sink! And where is everybody's wandering boy?

Dr. Hall says, "We need a study in which drivers who go through these rush hours every day would wear GSR bands."

GSR?

"Galvanic skin response. It measures the electric potential of the skin,   *30* which is a function of sweating. If a person gets highly nervous, his palms begin to sweat. It is an index of tension. There are some other fairly simple devices that would record respiration and pulse. I think everybody who goes through this kind of experience all the time should take his own pulse—not literally—but just be aware of what's happening to him. You can usually tell when stress is beginning to get you physically."

In testing people crowded into New York's slums, Dr. Hall would like to take it one step further—gather information on the plasma hydrocortisone level in the blood or the corticosteroids in the urine. Both have been demonstrated to be reliable indicators of stress, and testing procedures are simple.

The slums—we finally made it up to East Harlem. We drove into 101st Street, and there was a new, avant-garde little church building, the Church of the Epiphany, which Dr. Hall liked—and, next to it, a pile of rubble where a row of buildings had been torn down, and from the back windows of the tenements beyond several people were busy "airmailing," throwing garbage out the window, into the rubble, beer cans, red shreds, the No-Money-Down Eames roller stand for a TV set, all flying through the air onto the scaggy sump. We drove around some more in Harlem, and a sequence was repeated, trash, buildings falling down, buildings torn down, rubble, scaggy sumps or, suddenly, a cluster of high-rise apartment projects, with fences around the grass.

"You know what this city looks like?" Dr. Hall said. "It looks bombed out. I used to live at Broadway and 124th Street back in 1946 when I was studying at Columbia. I can't tell you how much Harlem has changed in twenty years. It looks bombed out. It's broken down. People who live in New York get used to it and don't realize how filthy the city has become. The whole thing is typical of a behavioral sink. So is something like the Kitty Genovese case—a girl raped and murdered in the courtyard of an apartment complex and forty or fifty people look on from their apartments and nobody even calls the police. That kind of apathy and anomie is typical of the general psychological deterioration of The Sink."

He looked at the high-rise housing projects and found them mainly testimony to how little planners know about humans' basic animal requirements for space.

"Even on the simplest terms," he said, "it is pointless to build one of ³⁵ these blocks much over five stories high. Suppose a family lives on the fifteenth floor. The mother will be completely cut off from her children if they are playing down below, because the elevators are constantly broken in these projects, and it often takes half an hour, literally half an hour, to get the elevator if it is running. That's very common. A mother in that situation is just as much a victim of overcrowding as if she were back in the tenement block. Some Negro leaders have a bitter joke about how the white man is solving the slum problem by stacking Negroes up vertically, and there is a lot to that."

For one thing, says Dr. Hall, planners have no idea of the different space requirements of people from different cultures, such as Negroes and Puerto Ricans. They are all treated as if they were minute, compact middle-class whites. As with the Sika deer, who are overcrowded at one per acre, overcrowding is a relative thing for the human animal, as well. Each species has its own feeling for space. The feeling may be "subjective," but it is quite real.

Dr. Hall's theories on space and territory are based on the same information, gathered by biologists, ethologists, and anthropologists, chiefly, as Robert Ardrey's. Ardrey has written two well-publicized books, *African Genesis* and *The Territorial Imperative*. *Life* magazine ran big excerpts from *The Territorial Imperative,* all about how the drive to acquire territory and property and add to it and achieve status is built into all animals, including man, over thousands of centuries of genetic history, etc., and is a more powerful drive than sex. *Life*'s big display prompted Marshall McLuhan to crack, "They see this as a great historic justification for free enterprise and Republicanism. If the birds do it and the stickle-back crabs do it, then it's right for man." To people like Hall and McLuhan, and Ardrey, for that matter, the right or wrong of it is irrelevant. The only thing they find inexcusable is the kind of thinking, by influential people, that isn't even aware of all this. Such as the thinking of most city planners.

"The planners always show you a bird's-eye view of what they are doing," he said. "You've seen those scale models. Everyone stands around the table and looks down and says that's great. It never occurs to anyone that they are taking a bird's-eye view. In the end, these projects do turn out fine, when viewed from an airplane."

As an anthropologist, Dr. Hall has to shake his head every time he hears planners talking about fully integrated housing projects for the year 1980 or 1990, as if by then all cultural groups will have the same feeling for space and will live placidly side by side, happy as the happy burghers who plan all the good clean bird's-eye views. According to his findings, the very fact that every cultural group does have its own peculiar, unspoken feeling for space is what is responsible for much of the uneasiness one group feels around the other.

It is like the North European and the Mediterranean in the subway   40
line. The North European, without ever realizing it, tries to keep a bubble of space around himself, and the moment a stranger invades that sphere, he feels threatened. Mediterranean peoples tend to come from cultures where everyone is much more involved physically, publicly, with one another on a day-to-day basis and feels no uneasiness about mixing it up in public, but may have very different ideas about space inside the home. Even Negroes brought up in America have a different vocabulary of space and gesture from the North European Americans who, historically, have been their models, according to Dr. Hall. The failure of Negroes and whites to communicate well often boils down to things like this: some white will be interviewing a Negro for a job; the Negro's culture has taught him to show somebody you are interested by looking right at him and listening intently to what he has to say. But the species North European requires something more. He expects his listener to nod from time to time, as if to say, "Yes, keep going." If he doesn't get this nodding, he feels anxious, for fear the listener doesn't agree with him or has switched off. The Negro may learn that the white expects this sort of thing, but he isn't used to the precise kind of nodding that is customary, and so he may start overresponding, nodding like mad, and at this point the North European is liable to think he has some kind of stupid Uncle Tom on his hands, and the guy still doesn't get the job.

The whole handling of space in New York is so chaotic, says Dr. Hall, that even middle-class housing now seems to be based on the bird's-eye models for slum projects. He took a look at the big Park West Village development, set up originally to provide housing in Manhattan for families in the middle-income range, and found its handling of space very much like a slum project with slightly larger balconies. He felt the time has come to start subsidizing the middle class in New York on its own terms—namely, the kind of truly "human" spaces that still remain in brownstones.

"I think New York City should seriously consider a program of encouraging the middle-class development of an area like Chelsea, which is already starting to come up. People are beginning to renovate houses there on their own, and I think if the city would subsidize that sort of thing with tax reliefs and so forth, you would be amazed at what would result. What New York needs is a string of minor successes in the housing field, just to show everyone that it can be done, and I think the middle class can still do that for you. The alternative is to keep on doing what you're doing now, trying to lift a very large lower class up by main force almost and finding it a very slow and discouraging process.

"But before deciding how to redesign space in New York," he said, "people must first simply realize how severe the problem already is. And the handwriting is already on the wall."

"A study published in 1962," he said, "surveyed a representative sample of people living in New York slums and found only 18 percent of them free from emotional symptoms. Thirty-eight percent were in need of psychiatric help, and 23 percent were seriously disturbed or incapacitated. Now, this study was published in 1962, which means the work probably went on from 1955 to 1960. There is no telling how bad it is now. In a behavioral sink, crises can develop rapidly."

Dr. Hall would like to see a large-scale study similar to that undertaken by two sociopsychologists, Chombart de Lauwe and his wife, in a French working-class town. They found a direct relationship between crowding and general breakdown. In families where people were crowded into the apartment so that there was less than 86 to 108 square feet per person, social and physical disorders doubled. That would mean that for four people the smallest floor space they could tolerate would be an apartment, say, 12 by 30 feet.

What would one find in Harlem? "It is fairly obvious," Dr. Hall wrote in *The Hidden Dimension,* "that the American Negroes and people of Spanish culture who are flocking to our cities are being very seriously stressed. Not only are they in a setting that does not fit them, but they have passed the limits of their own tolerance of stress. The United States is faced with the fact that two of its creative and sensitive peoples are in the process of being destroyed and like Samson could bring down the structure that houses us all."

Dr. Hall goes out to the airport, to go back to Chicago, and I am coming back in a cab, along the East River Drive. It is four in the afternoon, but already the damned drive is clogging up. There is a 1959 Oldsmobile just to the right of me. There are about eight people in there, a lot of popeyed silhouettes against a leopard-skin dashboard, leopard-skin seats—and the driver is classic. He has a mustache, sideburns down to his jaw socket, and a tattoo on his forearm with a Rossetti painting of Jane Burden Morris with her hair long. All right; it is even touching, like a postcard photo of the main drag in San Pedro, California. But suddenly Sideburns guns it and cuts in front of my cab so that my driver has to hit the brakes, and then hardly 100 feet ahead Sideburns hits a wall of traffic himself and has to hit his brakes, and then it happens. A stuffed white Angora animal, a dog, no, it's a Pekingese cat, is mounted in his rear window—as soon as he hits the brakes its *eyes* light up, Nighttown pink. To keep from ramming him, my driver has to hit the brakes again, too, and so here I am, out in an insane, jammed-up expressway at four in the afternoon, shuddering to a stop while a stuffed Pekingese grows bigger and bigger and brighter in the eyeballs directly in front of me. Jolt! Nighttown pink! Hey— that's me the adrenalin is hitting, *I* am this white human sitting in a projectile heading amid a mass of clotted humans toward white Angora stuffed god-dam leopard-dash Pekingese freaking cat—kill that damned Angora—Jolt!— got me—another micrometer on the old adrenals—

Reading and Responding

1. Explain anything in the language or ideas of this essay that surprised you.
2. Mark a passage you especially liked or a passage that confused you, and explain why you had the reaction you did.
3. Freewrite about a city you know. Does the term *behavioral sink* apply? Talk about why it does and/or why it doesn't.

Working Together

1. Make a list of all the *do's* and *don't's* you've been taught for writing term papers or research papers, particularly for the style and form of those papers. Make a list of all the ways Tom Wolfe fulfills those requirements and all the ways he violates those rules.
2. Discuss why you think Wolfe would want to stretch and intensify the conventional forms of writing the way he does. How do you think he wants readers to respond? How did you respond?
3. Discuss whether you want to live in a big city. Make a list of advantages and disadvantages as seen by the members of your group.
4. List at least five significant things about New York City that you think Wolfe has neglected to mention. As a group, write a paragraph that comments on Wolfe's views.

Rethinking and Rewriting

1. Both Dillard in "The Silent Neighborhood" and Wolfe in "O Rotten Gotham" talk about the ways that environment affects behavior. Explain,

first, how the empty suburb affects how Dillard felt as a girl and, second, how overcrowding in New York influences behavior according to Wolfe.

2. Go to the library and look up the works of Edward T. Hall. Write a paper that compares Hall's language and form with Wolfe's; argue for the style or approach you like best.

3. Take any textbook or academic article you're reading for another course, and write about those ideas, adopting Wolfe's writing style. Juice up your term paper. Write a hyper–term paper.

EXILE: EL PASO, TEXAS

Benjamin Saenz

> *Benjamin Saenz is assistant professor of English and a member of the Chicano Studies Research Program at the University of Texas, El Paso. He writes poetry, novels, and children's books. Saenz recently wrote* A Gift *from* Papá Diego *(1998). The following essay describes the border not just between Mexico and the United States but between the urban and the wild, culture and landscape.*

That morning—when the day was new, when the sun slowly touched the sky, almost afraid to break it—that morning I looked out my window and stared at the Juárez Mountains. Mexican purples—burning. I had always thought of them as sacraments of belonging. That was the first time it happened. It had happened to others, but it had never happened to me. And when it happened, it started a fire, a fire that will burn for a long time.

As I walked to school, I remember thinking what a perfect place Sunset Heights was; turn of the century houses intact; remodeled houses painted pink and turquoise; old homes tastefully gentrified by the aspiring young; the rundown Sunset Grocery store decorated with the protest art of graffiti on one end and a plastic-signed "Circle K" on the other.

This was the edge of the piece of paper that was America, the border that bordered the University—its buildings, its libraries; the border that bordered the freeway—its cars coming and going, coming and going endlessly; the border that bordered downtown—its banks and businesses and bars; the border that bordered the border between two countries.

The unemployed poor from Juárez knocking on doors and asking for jobs—or money—or food. Small parks filled with people whose English did not exist. The upwardly mobile living next to families whose only concern was getting enough money to pay next month's rent. Some had lived here for generations, would continue living here into the next century; others would live here a few days. All this color, all this color, all this color beneath the shadow of the Juárez Mountains. Sunset Heights: a perfect place with a perfect name, and a perfect view of the river.

After class, I went by my office and drank a cup of coffee, sat and read, and did some writing. It was a quiet day on campus, nothing but me and my work—the kind of day the mind needs to catch up with itself, the kind of uneventful day so necessary for living. I started walking home at about three o'clock, after I had put my things together in my torn backpack. I made a mental note to sew the damn thing. *One day everything's gonna come tumbling out—better sew it.* I'd made that mental note before.

Walking down Prospect, I thought maybe I'd go for a jog. I hoped the spring would not bring too much wind this year. The wind, common desert rain; the wind blew too hard and harsh sometimes; the wind unsettled the desert—upset things, ruined the calmness of the spring. My mind wandered, searched the black asphalt littered with torn papers; the chained dogs in the yards who couldn't hurt me; the even bricks of all the houses I passed. I belonged here, yes. I belonged. Thoughts entered like children running through a park. This year, maybe the winds would not come.

I didn't notice the green car drive up and stop right next to me as I walked. The border patrol interrupted my daydreaming: "Where are you from?"

I didn't answer. I wasn't sure who the agent, a woman, was addressing. She repeated the question in Spanish, "*¿De dónde eres?*"

Without thinking, I almost answered her question—in Spanish. A reflex. I caught myself in midsentence and stuttered in a nonlanguage.

"*¿Dónde naciste?*" she asked again.

By then my mind had cleared, and quietly I said: "I'm a U.S. citizen."

"Were you born in the United States?"

She was browner than I was. I might have asked her the same question. I looked at her for awhile—searching for something I recognized.

"Yes," I answered.

"Where in the United States were you born?"

"In New Mexico."

"Where in New Mexico?"

"Las Cruces."

"What do you do?"

"I'm a student."

"And are you employed?"

"Sort of."

"Sort of?" She didn't like my answer. Her tone bordered on anger. I looked at her expression and decided it wasn't hurting anyone to answer her questions. It was all very innocent, just a game we were playing.

"I work at the University as a teaching assistant."

She didn't respond. She looked at me as if I were a blank. Her eyes were filling in the empty spaces as she looked at my face. I looked at her for a second and decided she was finished with me. I started walking away. "Are you sure you were born in Las Cruces?" she asked again.

I turned around and smiled, "Yes, I'm sure." She didn't smile back. She and the driver sat there for awhile and watched me as I continued walking. They drove past me slowly and then proceeded down the street.

I didn't much care for the color of their cars.

"Sons of bitches," I whispered, "pretty soon I'll have to carry a passport in my own neighborhood." I said it to be flippant; something in me rebelled against people dressed in uniforms. I wasn't angry—not then, not at first, not really angry. In less than ten minutes I was back in my apartment playing the scene again and again in my mind. It was like a video I played over and over—memorizing the images. Something was wrong. I was embarrassed, ashamed because I'd been so damned compliant like a piece of tin foil in the uniformed woman's hand. Just like a child in the principal's office, in trouble for speaking Spanish. "I should have told that witch exactly what I thought of her and her green car and her green uniform."

I lit a cigarette and told myself I was overreacting. "Breathe in—   *30* breathe out—breathe in—breathe out—no big deal—you live on a border. These things happen—just one of those things. Just a game . . ." I changed into my jogging clothes and went for a run. At the top of the hill on Sunbowl Drive, I stopped to stare at the Juárez Mountains. I felt the sweat run down my face. I kept running until I could no longer hear *Are you sure you were born in Las Cruces?* ringing in my ears.

School let out in early May. I spent the last two weeks of that month relaxing and working on some paintings. In June I got back to working on my stories. I had a working title, which I hated, but I hated it less than the actual stories I was writing. It would come to nothing; I knew it would come to nothing.

From my window I could see the freeway. It was then I realized that not a day went by when I didn't see someone running across the freeway or walking down the street looking out for someone. They were people who looked not so different from me—except that they lived their lives looking over their shoulders.

One Thursday, I saw the border patrol throw some men into their van—throw them—as if they were born to be thrown like baseballs, like rings in a carnival ringtoss, easy inanimate objects, dead bucks after a deer hunt. The illegals didn't even put up a fight. They were aliens, from some-where else, somewhere foreign, and it did not matter that the "somewhere else" was as close as an eyelash to an eye. What mattered was that someone had once drawn a line, and once drawn, that line became indelible and hard and could not be crossed.

The men hung their heads so low that they almost scraped the littered asphalt. Whatever they felt, they did not show; whatever burned did not burn for an audience. I sat at my typewriter and tried to pretend I saw nothing. *What do you think happens when you peer out windows? Buy curtains.*

I didn't write the rest of the day. I kept seeing the border patrol   *35* woman against a blue sky turning green. I thought of rearranging my desk so I wouldn't be next to the window, but I thought of the mountains. No, I would keep my desk near the window, but I would look only at the mountains.

Two weeks later, I went for a walk. The stories weren't going well that day; my writing was getting worse instead of better; my characters were getting on my nerves—I didn't like them—no one else would like them either. They did not burn with anything. I hadn't showered, hadn't shaved, hadn't combed my hair. I threw some water on my face and walked out the door. It was summer; it was hot; it was afternoon, the time of day when everything felt as if it were on fire. The worst time of the day to take a walk. I wiped the sweat from my eyelids; it instantly reappeared. I wiped it off again, but the sweat came pouring out—a leak in the dam. Let it leak. I laughed. A hundred degrees in the middle of a desert afternoon. Laughter poured out of me as fast as my sweat. I turned the corner and headed back home. I saw the green van. It was parked right ahead of me.

A man about my height got out of the van and approached me. Another man, taller, followed him. *"¿Tienes tus papeles?"* he asked. His gringo accent was as thick as the sweat on my skin.

"I can speak English," I said. I started to add: *I can probably speak it better than you,* but I stopped myself. No need to be aggressive, no need to get any hotter.

"Do you live in this neighborhood?"

"Yes."   40

"Where?"

"Down the street."

"Where down the street?"

"Are you planning on making a social visit?"

He gave me a hard look—cold and blue—then looked at his partner.   45
He didn't like me. I didn't care. I liked that he hated me. It made it easier.

I watched them drive away and felt as hot as the air, felt as hot as the heat that was burning away the blue in the sky.

There were other times when I felt watched. Sometimes, when I jogged, the green vans would slow down, eye me. I felt like prey, like a rabbit who smelled the hunter. I pretended not to notice them. I stopped pretending. I started noting their presence in our neighborhood more and more. I started growing suspicious of my own observations. Of course, they weren't everywhere. But they *were* everywhere. I had just been oblivious to their presence, had been oblivious because they had nothing to do with me; their presence had something to do with someone else. I was not a part of this. I wanted no part of it. The green cars and the green vans clashed with the purples of the Juárez Mountains. Nothing looked the same. I never talked about their presence to other people. Sometimes the topic of the *Migra* would come up in conversations. I felt the burning; I felt the anger, would control it. I casually referred to them as the Gestapo, the traces of rage carefully hidden from the expression on my face—and everyone would laugh. I hated them.

When school started in the fall, I was stopped again. Again I had been walking home from the University. I heard the familiar question: "Where are you from?"

"Leave me alone."

"Are you a citizen of the United States?"   50

"Yes."

"Can you prove it?"

"No. No, I can't."

He looked at my clothes: jeans, tennis shoes, and a casual California shirt. He noticed my backpack full of books.

"You a student?"   55

I nodded and stared at him.

"There isn't any need to be unfriendly—"

"I'd like you to leave me alone."

"Just doing my job," he laughed. I didn't smile back. *Terrorists. Nazis did their jobs. Death squads in El Salvador and Guatemala did their jobs, too.* An unfair analogy. An unfair analogy? Yes, unfair. I thought it; I felt it; it was no longer my job to excuse—someone else would have to do that, someone else. The Juárez Mountains did not seem purple that fall. They no longer burned with color.

60

In early January I went with Michael to Juárez. Michael was from New York, and he had come to work in a home for the homeless in South El Paso. We weren't in Juárez very long—just looking around and getting gas. Gas was cheap in Juárez. On the way back, the customs officer asked us to declare our citizenship. "U.S. citizen," I said. "U.S. citizen," Michael followed. The customs officer lowered his head and poked it in the car. "What are you bringing over?"

"Nothing."

He looked at me. "Where in the United States were you born?"

"In Las Cruces, New Mexico."

He looked at me a while longer. "Go ahead," he signaled.

I noticed that he didn't ask Michael where he was from. But Michael   65
had blue eyes; Michael had white skin. Michael didn't have to tell the man in the uniform where he was from.

That winter, Sunset Heights seemed deserted to me. The streets were empty like the river. One morning, I was driving down Upson Street toward the University, the wind shaking the limbs of the bare trees. Nothing to shield them—unprotected by green leaves. The sun burned a dull yellow. In front of me, I noticed two border patrol officers chasing someone, though that someone was not visible. One of them put his hand out, signaling me to slow down as they ran across the street in front of my car. They were running with their billy clubs in hand. The wind blew at their backs as if to urge them on, as if to carry them.

In late January, Michael and I went to Juárez again. A friend of his was in town, and he wanted to see Juárez. We walked across the bridge across the river, across the line into another country. It was easy. No one there to stop us. We walked the streets of Juárez, streets that had seen better years, that were tired now from the tired feet that walked them. Michael's friend wanted to know how it was that there were so many beggars. "Were there always so many? Has it always been this way?" He didn't know how it had always been. We sat in the Cathedral and in an old chapel next to it and watched people rubbing the feet of statues; when I touched a statue, it was warmer than my own hand. We walked in the marketplace and inhaled the smells. Grocery stores in the country I knew did not have such smells. On the way back we stopped in a small bar and had a beer. The beer was cold and cheap. Walking back over the bridge, we stopped at the top and looked out at the city of El Paso. "It actually looks pretty from here, doesn't it?" I said. Michael nodded. It did look pretty. We looked off to the side—down the river—and for a long time watched the people trying to get across. Michael's friend said it was like watching *The CBS Evening News.*

As we reached the customs building, we noticed that a border patrol van pulled up behind the building where the other green cars were parked. The officers jumped out of the van and threw a handcuffed man against one of the parked cars. It looked like they were going to beat him. Two more border patrol officers pulled up in a car and jumped out to join them. One of the officers noticed we were watching. They straightened the man out and walked him inside—like gentlemen. They would have beat him. They would have beat him. But we were watching.

My fingers wanted to reach through the wire fence, not to touch it, not to feel it, but to break it down, to melt it down with what I did not understand. The burning was not there to be understood. Something was burning, the side of me that knew I was treated different, would always be treated different because I was born on a particular side of a fence, a fence that separated me from others, that separated me from the past, that separated me from the country of my genesis and glued me to the country I did not love because it demanded something of me I could not give. Something was burning now, and if I could have grasped the source of that rage and held it in my fist, I would have melted that fence. Someone built that fence; someone could tear it down. Maybe I could tear it down; maybe I was the one. Maybe then I would no longer be separated.

The first day in February, I was walking to a downtown Chevron station to pick up my car. On the corner of Prospect and Upson, a green car was parked—just sitting there. A part of my landscape. I was walking on the opposite side of the street. For some reason, I knew they were going to stop me. My heart clenched like a fist; the muscles in my back knotted up. *Maybe they'll leave me alone. I should have taken a shower this morning. I should have worn a nicer sweater. I should have put on a pair of socks, worn a nicer pair of shoes. I should have cut my hair; I should have shaved . . .*

The driver rolled down his window. I saw him from the corner of my eye. He called me over to him—*whistled me over*—much like he'd call a dog. I kept walking. He whistled me over again. *Here, boy.* I stopped for a second. Only a second. I kept walking. The border patrol officer and a policeman rushed out of the car and ran toward me. I was sure they were going to tackle me, drag me to the ground, handcuff me. They stopped in front of me.

"Can I see your driver's license?" the policeman asked.

"Since when do you need a driver's license to walk down the street?" Our eyes met. "Did I do something against the law?"

The policeman was annoyed. He wanted me to be passive, to say: "Yes, sir." He wanted me to approve of his job.

"Don't you know what we do?"   75

"Yes, I know what you do."

"Don't give me a hard time. I don't want trouble. I just want to see some identification."

I looked at him—looked, and saw what would not go away: neither him, nor his car, nor his job, nor what I knew, nor what I felt. He stared back. He hated me as much as I hated him. He saw the bulge of my cigarettes under my sweater and crumpled them.

I backed away from his touch. "I smoke. It's not good for me, but it's not against the law. Not yet, anyway. Don't touch me. I don't like that. Read me my rights, throw me in the can, or leave me alone." I smiled.

"No one's charging you with anything."   80

My eyes followed them as they walked back to their car. Now it was war, and *I had won this battle.* Had I won this battle? Had I won?

This spring morning, I sit at my desk, wait for the coffee to brew, and look out my window. This day, like every day, I look out my window. Across the street, a border patrol van stops and an officer gets out. So close I could touch him. On the freeway—this side of the river—a man is running. I put on my glasses. I am afraid he will be run over by the cars. I cheer for him. *Be careful. Don't get run over.* So close to the other side he can touch it. The border patrol officer gets out his walkie-talkie and runs toward the man who has disappeared from my view. I go and get my cup of coffee. I take a drink—slowly, it mixes with yesterday's tastes in my mouth. The officer in the green uniform comes back into view. He has the man with him. He puts him in the van. I can't see the color in their eyes. I see only the green. They drive away. There is no trace that says they've been there. The mountains watch the scene and say nothing. The mountains, ablaze in the spring light, have been watching—and guarding— and keeping silent longer than I have been alive. They will continue their vigil long after I am dead.

The green vans. They are taking someone away. They are taking. Green vans. This is my home, I tell myself. But I am not sure if I want this to be my home anymore. The thought crosses my mind to walk out of my apartment without my wallet. The thought crosses my mind that maybe the *Migra* will stop me again. I will let them arrest me. I will let them warehouse me. I will let them push me in front of a judge who will look at me like he has looked at the millions before me. I will be sent back to

Mexico. I will let them treat me like I am illegal. But the thoughts pass. I am not brave enough to let them do that to me.

Today, the spring winds blow outside my window. The reflections in the pane, graffiti burning questions into the glass: *Sure you were born . . . Identification . . . Do you live? . . .* The winds will unsettle the desert— cover Sunset Heights with green dust. The vans will stay in my mind forever. I cannot banish them. I cannot banish their questions: *Where are you from?* I no longer know.

This is a true story.

Reading and Responding

1. As you reread this piece, look for two kinds of information: (a) simple facts about the narrator (such as age and occupation), and (b) instances in which the narrator expresses strong emotion or opinion. List the facts as you find them, and mark in the margins those places that seem to show strong emotion or opinion. Try to identify the factors or causes that provoke this emotion.
2. Have you ever traveled in a border area—either literally (as in the border between countries) or metaphorically (as in the border between cultures or groups of people)? Or have you ever felt yourself in one group and somehow distanced or divided from some other group? In a paragraph or so, describe how borders affected the people there.

Working Together

1. Compare notes about the instances in which the narrator shows strong emotion. What values or attitudes or assumptions underpin or provide the foundation for these emotions? What does this narrator believe in or want to believe in?
2. Consider the concept of home. What forces in this narrator's life complicate this notion of home? Which of these forces are public and general, and which are private and personal? Is it reasonable to even try to separate the public and the private in a piece like this one?
3. What is the argument for having distinct and clear borders? What makes it a complicated argument? As a group, make a list of reasons.
4. What is the argument for fluid borders with much mixing and inter-change? Why is this a complicated argument? As a group, make a list of reasons.
5. To what extent does "Exile: El Paso, Texas" provoke your sympathy, and to what extent does it provoke your disagreement? As a group, construct a paragraph that reflects the viewpoints of all group members.

Rethinking and Rewriting

1. Write an essay that tells the story of a few weeks of your own life, setting it in relationship to the few weeks of the narrator's life in "Exile: El Paso, Texas." Use the concepts of exile and home to compare your experience with Saenz's experience. Assume that your readers are familiar with "Exile: El Paso, Texas." Refer to the essay whenever you need to, without summarizing it. Instead, let readers understand your own experience as it compares to "Exile: El Paso, Texas."

2. Research the border between Mexico and the United States. What do people (national politicians, local politicians, business people, workers, residents) say about this border? Record their positions and tell why people disagree. Explain the complications and contradictions of the issue as clearly as your research allows. Avoid arguing your own position.

3. Write an essay that begins by advancing the argument in favor of strict borders between Mexico and the United States. Explain why border police and careful enforcement are necessary. Then end your essay by critiquing that argument. Do you agree or disagree with the argument? Do you agree with part of it? Explain your reasoning.

ENCLOSED. ENCYCLOPEDIC. ENDURED. ONE WEEK AT THE MALL OF AMERICA

David Guterson

Novelist David Guterson is a frequent contributor to Harper's *magazine. His first novel,* Snow Falling on Cedars, *won the 1995 PEN/Faulkner award. A second novel,* East of the Mountains, *was published in 1999. In the following piece, Guterson combines factual research with his own emotional responses to describe Minneapolis's Mall of America.*

Last April, on a visit to the new Mall of America near Minneapolis, I carried with me the public-relations press kit provided for the benefit of reporters. It included an assortment of "fun facts" about the mall: 140,000 hot dogs sold each week, 10,000 permanent jobs, 44 escalators and 17 elevators, 12,750 parking places, 13,300 short tons of steel, $1 million in cash disbursed weekly from 8 automatic-teller machines. Opened in the summer of 1992, the mall was built on the 78-acre site of the former Metropolitan Stadium, a five-minute drive from the Minneapolis–St. Paul International Airport. With 4.2 million square feet of floor space—including twenty-two times the retail footage of the average American shopping center—the Mall of America was "the largest fully enclosed combination retail and family entertainment complex in the United States."

Eleven thousand articles, the press kit warned me, had already been written on the mall. Four hundred trees had been planted in its gardens, $625 million had been spent to build it, 350 stores had been leased. Three thousand bus tours were anticipated each year along with a half-million Canadian visitors and 200,000 Japanese tourists. Sales were projected at $650 million for 1993 and at $1 billion for 1996. Donny and Marie Osmond had visited the mall, as had Janet Jackson and Sally Jesse Raphael, Arnold Schwarzenegger, and the 1994 Winter Olympic Committee. The mall was five times larger than Red Square and twenty times larger than St. Peter's Basilica; it incorporated 2.3 miles of hallways and almost twice as much steel as the Eiffel Tower. It was also home to the nation's largest indoor theme park, a place called Knott's Camp Snoopy.

On the night I arrived, a Saturday, the mall was spotlit dramatically in the manner of a Las Vegas casino. It resembled, from the outside, a castle or fort, the Emerald City or Never-Never Land, impossibly large and vaguely unreal, an unbroken, windowless multi-storied edifice the size of an airport terminal. Surrounded by parking lots and new freeway ramps, monolithic and imposing in the manner of a walled city, it loomed brightly against the Minnesota night sky with the disturbing magnetism of a mirage.

I knew already that the Mall of America had been imagined by its creators not merely as a marketplace but as a national tourist attraction, an immense zone of entertainments. Such a conceit raised provocative questions, for our architecture testifies to our view of ourselves and to the condition of our souls. Large buildings stand as markers in the lives of nations and in the stream of a people's history. Thus I could only ask myself: Here was a new structure that had cost more than half a billion dollars to erect—what might it tell us about ourselves? If the Mall of America was part of America, what was that going to mean?

I passed through one of the mall's enormous entranceways and took   5
myself inside. Although from a distance the Mall of America had appeared menacing—exuding the ambience of a monstrous hallucination—within it turned out to be simply a shopping mall, certainly more vast than other malls but in tone and aspect, design and feel, not readily distinguishable from them. Its nuances were instantly familiar as the generic features of the American shopping mall at the tail end of the twentieth century: polished stone, polished tile, shiny chrome and brass, terrazzo floors, gazebos. From third-floor vistas, across vaulted spaces, the Mall of America felt endlessly textured—glass-enclosed elevators, neon-tube lighting, bridges, balconies, gas lamps, vaulted skylights—and densely crowded with hordes of people circumambulating in an endless promenade. Yet despite the mall's expansiveness, it elicited claustrophobia, sensory deprivation, and an unnerving disorientation. Everywhere I went I spied other pilgrims who had found, like me, that the straight way was lost and that the YOU ARE HERE landmarks on the map kiosks referred to nothing in particular.

Getting lost, feeling lost, being lost—these states of mind are intentional features of the mall's psychological terrain. There are, one notices, no clocks or windows, nothing to distract the shopper's psyche from the alternate reality the mall conjures. Here we are free to wander endlessly and to furtively watch our fellow wanderers, thousands upon thousands of milling strangers who have come with the intent of losing themselves in the mall's grand, stimulating design. For a few hours we share some common ground—a fantasy of infinite commodities and comforts—and then we drift apart forever. The mall exploits our acquisitive instincts without honoring our communal requirements, our eternal desire for discourse and intimacy, needs that until the twentieth century were traditionally met in our marketplaces but that are not met at all in giant shopping malls.

On this evening a few thousand young people had descended on the mall in pursuit of alcohol and entertainment. They had come to Gators, Hooters, and Knuckleheads, Puzzles, Fat Tuesday, and Ltl Ditty's. At Players, a sports bar, the woman beside me introduced herself as· "the pregnant wife of an Iowa pig farmer" and explained that she had driven five hours with friends to "do the mall party scene together." She left and was replaced by Kathleen from Minnetonka, who claimed to have "a real shopping thing—I can't go a week without buying new clothes. I'm not fulfilled until I buy something."

Later a woman named Laura arrived, with whom Kathleen was acquainted. "I *am* the mall," she announced ecstatically upon discovering I was a reporter. "I'd move in here if I could bring my dog," she added. "This place is heaven, it's a *mecca.*"

"We egg each other on," explained Kathleen, calmly puffing on a cigarette. "It's like, sort of, an addiction."

"You want the truth?" Laura asked. "I'm constantly suffering from megamall withdrawal. I come here all the time."

Kathleen: "It's a sickness. It's like cocaine or something; it's a drug."

Laura: "Kathleen's got this thing about buying, but I just need to *be* here. If I buy something it's an added bonus."

Kathleen: "She buys stuff all the time; don't listen."

Laura: "Seriously, I feel sorry for other malls. They're so small and *boring.*"

Kathleen seemed to think about this: "Richdale Mall," she blurted finally. She rolled her eyes and gestured with her cigarette. "Oh, my God, Laura. Why did we even *go* there?"

There is, of course, nothing naturally abhorrent in the human impulse to dwell in marketplaces or the urge to buy, sell, and trade. Rural Americans traditionally looked forward to the excitement and sensuality of market day; Native Americans traveled long distances to barter and trade at sprawling, festive encampments. In Persian bazaars and in the ancient Greek agoras the very soul of the community was preserved and could be seen, felt, heard, and smelled as it might be nowhere else. All over the planet the humblest of people have always gone to market with hope in their hearts and in expectation of something beyond mere goods—seeking a place where humanity is temporarily in ascendance, a palette for the senses, one another.

But the illicit possibilities of the marketplace also have long been acknowledged. The Persian bazaar was closed at sundown; the Greek agora was off-limits to those who had been charged with certain crimes. One myth of the Old West we still carry with us is that market day presupposes danger; the faithful were advised to make purchases quickly and repair without delay to the farm, lest their attraction to the pleasures of the marketplace erode their purity of spirit.

In our collective discourse the shopping mall appears with the tract house, the freeway, and the backyard barbecue as a product of the American postwar years, a testament to contemporary necessities and desires and an invention not only peculiarly American but peculiarly of our own era too. Yet the mall's varied and far-flung predecessors—the covered bazaars of the Middle East, the stately arcades of Victorian England, Italy's vaulted and skylit gallerias, Asia's monsoon-protected urban markets—all suggest that the rituals of indoor shopping, although in their nuances not often like our own, are nevertheless broadly known. The late twentieth-century American contribution has been to transform the enclosed bazaar into an economic institution that is vastly profitable yet socially enervated, one that redefines in fundamental ways the human relationship to the marketplace. At the Mall of America—an extreme example—we discover ourselves thoroughly lost among strangers in a marketplace intentionally designed to serve no community needs.

In the strict sense the Mall of America is not a marketplace at all—the soul of a community expressed as a *place*—but rather a tourist attraction. Its promoters have peddled it to the world at large as something more profound than a local marketplace and as a destination with deep implications. "I believe we can make Mall of America stand for all of America," asserted the mall's general manager, John Wheeler, in a promotional video entitled *There's a Place for Fun in Your Life*. "I believe there's a shopper in all of us," added the director of marketing, Maureen Hooley. The mall has memorialized its opening-day proceedings by producing a celebratory videotape: Ray Charles singing "America the Beautiful," a laser show followed by fireworks, "The Star-Spangled Banner" and "The Stars and Stripes Forever," the Gatlin Brothers, and Peter Graves. "Mall of America . . . ," its narrator intoned. "The name alone conjures up images of greatness, of a retail complex so magnificent it could only happen in America."

Indeed, on the day the mall opened, Miss America visited. The mall's   20
logo—a red, white, and blue star bisected by a red, white, and blue ribbon—decorated everything from the mall itself to coffee mugs and the flanks of buses. The idea, director of tourism Colleen Hayes told me, was to position America's largest mall as an institution on the scale of Disneyland or the Grand Canyon, a place simultaneously iconic and totemic, a revered symbol of the United States and a mecca to which the faithful would flock in pursuit of all things purchasable.

On Sunday I wandered the hallways of the pleasure dome with the sensation that I had entered an M. C. Escher drawing—there was no such thing as up or down, and the escalators all ran backward. A 1993 Ford Probe GT was displayed as if popping out of a giant packing box; a full-size home, complete with artificial lawn, had been built in the mall's rotunda. At the Michael Ricker Pewter Gallery I came across a miniature tableau of a pewter dog peeing on a pewter man's leg; at Hologram Land I pondered 3-D hallucinations of the Medusa and Marilyn Monroe. I passed a kiosk called The Sportsman's Wife; I stood beside a life-size statue of the Hamm's Bear, carved out of pine and available for $1,395 at a store called Minnesot-ah! At Pueblo Spirit I examined a "dream catcher"—a small hoop made from deer sinew and willow twigs and designed to be hung over its owner's bed as a tactic for filtering bad dreams. For a while I sat in front of Glamour Shots and watched while women were groomed and brushed for photo sessions yielding high-fashion self-portraits at $34.95 each. There was no stopping, no slowing down. I passed Mug Me, Queen for a Day, and Barnyard Buddies, and stood in the Brookstone store examining a catalogue: a gopher "eliminator" for $40 (it's a vibrating, anodized-aluminum stake), a "no-stoop" shoehorn for $10, a nose-hair trimmer for $18. At the arcade inside Knott's Camp Snoopy I watched while teenagers played Guardians of the 'Hood, Total Carnage, Final Fight, and Varth Operation Thunderstorm; a small crowd of them had gathered around a lean, cool character who stood calmly shooting video cowpokes in a game called Mad Dog McCree. Left thumb on his silver belt buckle, biceps pulsing, he banged away without remorse while dozens of his enemies crumpled and died in alleyways and dusty streets.

At Amazing Pictures a teenage boy had his photograph taken as a bodybuilder—his face smoothly grafted onto a rippling body—then proceeded to purchase this pleasing image on a poster, a sweatshirt, and a coffee mug. At Painted Tipi there was wild rice for sale, hand-harvested from Leech Lake, Minnesota. At Animalia I came across a polyresin figurine of a turtle retailing for $3,200. At Bloomingdale's I pondered a denim shirt with its sleeves ripped away, the sort of thing available at used-clothing stores (the "grunge look," a Bloomingdale's employee explained), on sale for $125. Finally, at a gift shop in Knott's Camp Snoopy, I came across a game called Electronic Mall Madness, put out by Milton Bradley. On the box, three twelve-year-old girls with good features happily vied to beat one another to the game-board mall's best sales.

At last I achieved an enforced self-arrest, anchoring myself against a bench while the mall tilted on its axis. Two pubescent girls in retainers and braces sat beside me sipping coffees topped with whipped cream and chocolate sprinkles, their shopping bags gathered tightly around their legs, their eyes fixed on the passing crowds. They came, they said, from Shakopee— "It's nowhere," one of them explained. The megamall, she added, was "a buzz at first, but now it seems pretty normal. 'Cept my parents are like Twenty Questions every time I want to come here. 'Specially since the shooting."

On a Sunday night, she elaborated, three people had been wounded when shots were fired in a dispute over a San Jose Sharks jacket. "In the *mall*," her friend reminded me. "Right here at megamall. A shooting."

"It's like nowhere's safe," the first added.   25

They sipped their coffees and explicated for me the plot of a film they saw as relevant, a horror movie called *Dawn of the Dead,* which they had each viewed a half-dozen times. In the film, they explained, apocalypse had come, and the survivors had repaired to a shopping mall as the most likely place to make their last stand in a poisoned, impossible world. And this would have been perfectly all right, they insisted, except that the place had also attracted hordes of the infamous living dead—sentient corpses who had not relinquished their attraction to indoor shopping.

I moved on and contemplated a computerized cash register in the infant's section of the Nordstrom store: "The Answer Is Yes!!!" its monitor reminded clerks. "Customer Service Is Our Number One Priority!" Then back at Bloomingdale's I contemplated a bank of televisions playing incessantly an advertisement for Egoïste, a men's cologne from Chanel. In the ad a woman on a wrought-iron balcony tossed her black hair about and screamed long and passionately; then there were many women screaming passionately, too, and throwing balcony shutters open and closed, and this was all followed by a bottle of the cologne displayed where I could get a good look at it. The brief, strange drama repeated itself until I could no longer stand it.

America's first fully enclosed shopping center—Southdale Center, in Edina, Minnesota—is a ten-minute drive from the Mall of America and thirty-six years its senior. (It is no coincidence that the Twin Cities area is such a prominent player in mall history: Minnesota is subject to the sort of severe weather that makes climate-controlled shopping seductive.) Opened in 1956, Southdale spawned an era of fervid mall construction and generated a vast new industry. Shopping centers proliferated so rapidly that by the end of 1992, says the National Research Bureau, there were nearly 39,000 of them operating everywhere across the country. But while malls recorded a much-ballyhooed success in the America of the 1970s and early 1980s, they gradually became less profitable to run as the exhausted and overwhelmed American worker inevitably lost interest in leisure shopping. Pressed for time and short on money, shoppers turned to factory outlet centers, catalogue purchasing, and "category killers" (specialty stores such as Home Depot and Price Club) at the expense of shopping malls. The industry, unnerved, re-invented itself, relying on smaller and more convenient local centers—especially the familiar neighborhood strip mall—and building far fewer large regional malls in an effort to stay afloat through troubled times. With the advent of cable television's Home Shopping Network and the proliferation of specialty catalogue retailers (whose access to computerized market research has made them, in the Nineties, powerful competitors), the mall industry reeled yet further. According to the International Council of Shopping Centers, new mall construction in 1992 was a third of what it had been in 1989, and the value of mall-construction contracts dropped 60 percent in the same three-year period.

Anticipating a future in which millions of Americans will prefer to shop in the security of their living rooms—conveniently accessing online retail companies as a form of quiet evening entertainment—the mall industry, after less than forty years, experienced a full-blown mid-life crisis. It was necessary for the industry to re-invent itself once more, this time with greater attentiveness to the qualities that would allow it to endure relentless change. Anxiety-ridden and sapped of vitality, mall builders fell back on an ancient truth, one capable of sustaining them through troubled seasons: they discovered what humanity had always understood, that shopping and frivolity go hand in hand and are inherently symbiotic. *If you build it fun, they will come.*

The new bread-and-circuses approach to mall building was first ventured in 1985 by the four Ghermezian brothers—Raphael, Nader, Bahman, and Eskandar—builders of Canada's $750 million West Edmonton   30

Mall, which included a water slide, an artificial lake, a miniature-golf course, a hockey rink, and forty-seven rides in an amusement park known as Fantasyland. The complex quickly generated sales revenues at twice the rate per square foot of retail space that could be squeezed from a conventional outlet mall, mostly by developing its own shopping synergy: people came for a variety of reasons and to do a variety of things. West Edmonton's carnival atmosphere, it gradually emerged, lubricated pocketbooks and inspired the sort of impulse buying on which malls everywhere thrive. To put the matter another way, it was time for a shopping-and-pleasure palace to be attempted in the United States.

After selling the Mall of America concept to Minnesotans in 1985, the Ghermezians joined forces with their American counterparts—Mel and Herb Simon of Indianapolis, owners of the NBA's Indiana Pacers and the nation's second-largest developers of shopping malls. The idea, in the beginning, was to outdo West Edmonton by building a mall far larger and more expensive—something visionary, a wonder of the world—and to include such attractions as fashionable hotels, an elaborate tour de force aquarium, and a monorail to the Minneapolis–St. Paul airport. Eventually the project was downscaled substantially: a million square feet of floor space was eliminated, the construction budget was cut, and the aquarium and hotels were never built (reserved, said marketing director Maureen Hooley, for "phase two" of the mall's development). Japan's Mitsubishi Bank, Mitsui Trust, and Chuo Trust together put up a reported $400 million to finance the cost of construction, and Teachers Insurance and Annuity Association (the majority owner of the Mall of America) came through with another $225 million. At a total bill of $625 million, the mall was ultimately a less ambitious project than its forebear up north on the Canadian plains, and neither as large nor as gaudy. Reflecting the economy's downturn, the parent companies of three of the mall's anchor tenants—Sears, Macy's, and Bloomingdale's—were battling serious financial trouble and needed substantial transfusions from mall developers to have their stores ready by opening day.

The mall expects to spend millions on marketing itself during its initial year of operation and has lined up the usual corporate sponsors— Ford, Pepsi, US West—in an effort to build powerful alliances. Its public-relations representatives travel to towns such as Rapid City, South Dakota, and Sioux City, Iowa, in order to drum up interest within the Farm Belt. Northwest Airlines, another corporate sponsor, offers package deals from London and Tokyo and fare adjustments for those willing to come from Bismarck, North Dakota; Cedar Rapids, Iowa; and Kalamazoo or Grand Rapids, Michigan. Calling itself a "premier tourism destination," the mall draws from a primary tourist market that incorporates the eleven Midwest states (and two Canadian provinces) lying within a day's drive of its parking lots. It also estimates that in its first six months of operation, 5.3 million out of 16 million visitors came from beyond the Twin Cities metropolitan area.

The mall has forecast a much-doubted figure of 46 million annual visits by 1996—four times the number of annual visits to Disneyland, for example, and twelve times the visits to the Grand Canyon. The number, Maureen Hooley explained, seems far less absurd when one takes into account that mall pilgrims make far more repeat visits—as many as eighty in a single year—than visitors to theme parks such as Disneyland. Relentless advertising and shrewd promotion, abetted by the work of journalists like myself, assure the mall that visitors will come in droves—at least for the time being. The national media have comported themselves as if the new mall were a place of light and promise, full of hope and possibility. Meanwhile the Twin Cities' media have been shameless: on opening night Minneapolis's WCCO-TV aired a one-hour mall special, hosted by local news anchors Don Shelby and Colleen Needles, and the *St. Paul Pioneer Press* (which was named an "official" sponsor of the opening) dedicated both a phone line and a weekly column to answering esoteric mall questions. Not to be outdone, the *Minneapolis Star Tribune* developed a special graphic to draw readers to mall stories and printed a vast Sunday supplement before opening day under the heading A WHOLE NEW MALLGAME. By the following Wednesday all perspective was in eclipse: the local press reported that at 9:05 a.m., the mall's Victoria's Secret outlet had recorded its first sale, a pair of blue/green silk men's boxer shorts; that mall developers Mel and Herb Simon ate black-bean soup for lunch at 12:30 p.m.; that Kimberly Levis, four years old, constructed a rectangular column nineteen bricks high at the mall's Lego Imagination Center; and that mall officials had retained a plumber on standby in case difficulties arose with the mall's toilets.

From all of this coverage—and from the words you now read—the mall gains status as a phenomenon worthy of our time and consideration: place as celebrity. The media encourage us to visit our megamall in the obligatory fashion we flock to *Jurassic Park*—because it is there, all glitter and glow, a piece of the terrain, a season's diversion, an assumption on the cultural landscape. All of us will want to be in on the conversation and, despite ourselves, we will go.

Lost in the fun house I shopped till I dropped, but the scale of the mall eventually overwhelmed me and I was unable to make a purchase. Finally I met Chuck Brand on a bench in Knott's Camp Snoopy; he was seventy-two and, in his personal assessment of it, had lost at least 25 percent of his mind. "It's fun being a doozy," he confessed to me. "The security cops got me figured and keep their distance. I don't get hassled for hanging out, not shopping. Because the deal is, when you're seventy-two, man, you're just about all done shopping."

After forty-seven years of selling houses in Minneapolis, Chuck comes to the mall every day. He carries a business card with his picture on it, his company name and phone number deleted and replaced by his pager code. His wife drops him at the mall at 10:00 a.m. each morning and picks

35

him up again at six; in between he sits and watches. "I can't sit home and do nothing," he insisted. When I stood to go he assured me he understood: I was young and had things I had to do. "Listen," he added, "thanks for talking to me, man. I've been sitting in this mall for four months now and nobody ever said nothing."

The next day I descended into the mall's enormous basement, where its business offices are located. "I'm sorry to have to bring this up," my prearranged mall guide, Michelle Biesiada, greeted me. "But you were seen talking to one of our housekeepers—one of the people who empty the garbage?—and really, you aren't supposed to do that."

Later we sat in the mall's security center, a subterranean computerized command post where two uniformed officers manned a bank of television screens. The Mall of America, it emerged, employed 109 surveillance cameras to monitor the various activities of its guests, and had plans to add yet more. There were cameras in the food courts and parking lots, in the hallways and in Knott's Camp Snoopy. From where we sat, it was possible to monitor thirty-six locations simultaneously; it was also possible, with the use of a zoom feature, to narrow in on an object as small as a hand, a license plate, or a wallet.

While we sat in the darkness of the security room, enjoying the voyeuristic pleasures it allowed (I, for one, felt a giddy sense of power), a security guard noted something of interest occurring in one of the parking lots. The guard engaged a camera's zoom feature, and soon we were given to understand that a couple of bored shoppers were enjoying themselves by fornicating in the front seat of a parked car. An officer was dispatched to knock on their door and discreetly suggest that they move themselves along; the Mall of America was no place for this. "If they want to have sex they'll have to go elsewhere," a security officer told me. "We don't have anything against sex, per se, but we don't want it happening in our parking lots."

I left soon afterward for a tour of the mall's basement, a place of perpetual concrete corridors and home to a much-touted recyclery. Declaring itself "the most environmentally conscious shopping center in the industry," the Mall of America claims to recycle up to 80 percent of its considerable refuse and points to its "state-of-the-art" recycling system as a symbol of its dedication to Mother Earth. Yet Rick Doering of Browning-Ferris Industries—the company contracted to manage the mall's 700 tons of monthly garbage—described the on-site facility as primarily a public-relations gambit that actually recycles only a third of the mall's tenant waste and little of what is discarded by its thousands of visitors; furthermore, he admitted, the venture is unprofitable to Browning-Ferris, which would find it far cheaper to recycle the mall's refuse somewhere other than in its basement.

A third-floor "RecycleNOW Center," located next to Macy's and featuring educational exhibits, is designed to enhance the mall's self-styled image as a national recycling leader. Yet while the mall's developers gave

40

Macy's $35 million to cover most of its "build-out" expenses (the cost of transforming the mall's basic structure into finished, customer-ready floor space), Browning-Ferris got nothing in build-out costs and operates the center at a total loss, paying rent equivalent to that paid by the mall's retailers. As a result, the company has had to look for ways to keep its costs to a minimum, and the mall's garbage is now sorted by developmentally disabled adults working a conveyor belt in the basement. Doering and I stood watching them as they picked at a stream of paper and plastic bottles; when I asked about their pay, he flinched and grimaced, then deflected me toward another supervisor, who said that wages were based on daily productivity. Did this mean that they made less than minimum wage? I inquired. The answer was yes.

Upstairs once again, I hoped for relief from the basement's oppressive, concrete gloom, but the mall felt densely crowded and with panicked urgency I made an effort to leave. I ended up instead at Knott's Camp Snoopy—the seven-acre theme park at the center of the complex—a place intended to alleviate claustrophobia by "bringing the outdoors indoors." Its interior landscape, the press kit claims, "was inspired by Minnesota's natural habitat—forests, meadows, river banks, and marshes . . ." And "everything you see, feel, smell and hear adds to the illusion that it's summertime, seventy degrees and you're outside enjoying the awesome splendor of the Minnesota woods."

Creators of this illusion had much to contend with, including sixteen carnival-style midway rides, such as the Pepsi Ripsaw, the Screaming Yellow Eagle, Paul Bunyan's Log Chute by Brawny, Tumbler, Truckin', and Huff 'n' Puff; fifteen places for visitors to eat, such as Funnel Cakes, Stick Dogs and Campfire Burgers, Taters, Pizza Oven, and Wilderness Barbecue; seven shops with names like Snoopy's Boutique, Joe Cool's Hot Shop, and Camp Snoopy Toys; and such assorted attractions as Pan for Gold, Hunter's Paradise Shooting Gallery, the Snoopy Fountain, and the video arcade that includes the game Mad Dog McCree.

As if all this were not enough to cast a serious pall over the Minnesota woods illusion, the theme park's designers had to contend with the fact that they could use few plants native to Minnesota. At a constant temperature of seventy degrees, the mall lends itself almost exclusively to tropical varieties—orange jasmine, black olive, oleander, hibiscus—and not at all to the conifers of Minnesota, which require a cold dormancy period. Deferring ineluctably to this troubling reality, Knott's Camp Snoopy brought in 526 tons of plants—tropical rhododendrons, willow figs, buddhist pines, azaleas—from such places as Florida, Georgia, and Mississippi.

Anne Pryor, a Camp Snoopy marketing representative, explained to 45
me that these plants were cared for via something called "integrated pest management," which meant the use of predators such as ladybugs instead of pesticides. Yet every member of the landscape staff I spoke to described a campaign of late-night pesticide spraying as a means of controlling the theme park's enemies—mealybugs, aphids, and spider mites. Two said they

had argued for integrated pest management as a more environmentally sound method of controlling insects but that to date it had not been tried.

Even granting that Camp Snoopy is what it claims to be—an authentic version of Minnesota's north woods tended by environmentally correct means—the question remains whether it makes sense to place a forest in the middle of the country's largest shopping complex. Isn't it true that if people want woods, they are better off not going to a mall?

On Valentine's Day last February—cashing in on the promotional scheme of a local radio station—ninety-two couples were married en masse in a ceremony at the Mall of America. They rode the roller coaster and the Screaming Yellow Eagle and were photographed beside a frolicking Snoopy, who wore an immaculate tuxedo. "As we stand here together at the Mall of America," presiding district judge Richard Spicer declared, "we are reminded that there is a place for fun in your life and you have found it in each other." Six months earlier, the Reverend Leith Anderson of the Wooddale Church in Eden Prairie conducted services in the mall's rotunda. Six thousand people had congregated by 10:00 a.m., and Reverend Anderson delivered a sermon entitled "The Unknown God of the Mall." Characterizing the mall as a "direct descendant" of the ancient Greek agoras, the reverend pointed out that, like the Greeks before us, we Americans have many gods. Afterward, of course, the flock went shopping, much to the chagrin of Reverend Delton Krueger, president of the Mall Area Religious Council, who told the *Minneapolis Star Tribune* that as a site for church services, the mall may trivialize religion. "A good many people in the churches," said Krueger, "feel a lot of the trouble in the world is because of materialism."

But a good many people in the mall business today apparently think the trouble lies elsewhere. They are moving forward aggressively on the premise that the dawning era of electronic shopping does not preclude the building of shopping-and-pleasure palaces all around the globe. Japanese developers, in a joint venture with the Ghermezians known as International Malls Incorporated, are planning a $400 million Mall of Japan, with an ice rink, a water park, a fantasy-theme hotel, three breweries, waterfalls, and a sports center. We might shortly predict, too, a Mall of Europe, a Mall of New England, a Mall of California, and perhaps even a Mall of the World. The concept of shopping in a frivolous atmosphere, concocted to loosen consumers' wallets, is poised to proliferate globally. We will soon see monster malls everywhere, rooted in the soil of every nation and offering a preposterous, impossible variety of commodities and entertainments.

The new malls will be planets unto themselves, closed off from this world in the manner of space stations or of science fiction's underground cities. Like the Mall of America and West Edmonton Mall—prototypes for a new generation of shopping centers—they will project a separate and distinct reality in which an "outdoor café" is not outdoors, a "bubbling brook" is a concrete watercourse, and a "serpentine street" is a hallway. Safe, surreal, and outside of time and space, they will offer the mind a potent dreamscape from which there is no present waking. This carefully controlled fantasy—now operable in Minnesota—is so powerful as to inspire psychological addiction or to elicit in visitors a catatonic obsession with the mall's various hallucinations. The new malls will be theatrical, high-tech illusions capable of attracting enormous crowds from distant points and foreign ports. Their psychology has not yet been tried pervasively on the scale of the Mall of America, nor has it been perfected. But in time our marketplaces, all over the world, will be in essential ways interchangeable, so thoroughly divorced from the communities in which they sit that they will appear to rest like permanently docked spaceships against the landscape, windowless and turned in upon their own affairs. The affluent will travel as tourists to each, visiting the holy sites and taking photographs in the catacombs of far-flung temples.

Just as Victorian England is acutely revealed beneath the grandiose *50* domes of its overwrought train stations, so is contemporary America well understood from the upper vistas of its shopping malls, places without either windows or clocks where the temperature is forever seventy degrees. It is facile to believe, from this vantage point, that the endless circumambulations of tens of thousands of strangers—all loaded down with the detritus of commerce—resemble anything akin to community. The shopping mall is not, as the architecture critic Witold Rybczynski has concluded, "poised to become a real urban place" with "a variety of commercial and noncommercial functions." On the contrary, it is poised to multiply around the world as an institution offering only a desolate substitute for the rich, communal lifeblood of the traditional marketplace, which will not survive its onslaught.

Standing on the Mall of America's roof, where I had ventured to inspect its massive ventilation units, I finally achieved a full sense of its vastness, of how it overwhelmed the surrounding terrain—the last sheep farm in sight, the Mississippi River incidental in the distance. Then I peered through the skylights down into Camp Snoopy, where throngs of my fellow citizens caroused happily in the vast entrails of the beast.

Reading and Responding

1. Guterson starts this piece by giving you quite a number of facts. What's your response to these facts? In a paragraph or so, talk about the effects they have on you.
2. Once Guterson gets inside the mall, he both observes (tells you what he sees, hears, and so on) and judges (tells you what he thinks of what he sees, hears, and so on). As you read, make a list of these observations; and next to it, make a list of his judgments.

Working Together

1. Look closely at how Guterson ends this piece. Paying special attention to this ending, try to summarize his main points in a paragraph.
2. As a group, talk about how reading Guterson's piece has made you think about malls in new ways. Phrased another way, how has reading this essay changed the way you look at malls? What aspects of Guterson's view are new to you?

Rethinking and Rewriting

1. Go to a mall and take your notebook with you. As you walk in and walk around, assume that the mall is a town. What's in this town? What's not in this town? Who lives in this town? What kind of people do you not see in this town? Is it pleasant to be in this town? What can you do here, and what can you not do here? Finally, draw on your notes and experience and write an essay that presents your answers to these questions and ends by discussing the advantages and the disadvantages of this town.
2. Does David Guterson's writing seem objective and neutral, or does it seem as though Guterson wants to convince you of something? In an essay, describe at least one section in which the writing seems objective and another in which the writer apparently wants to convince readers of something. End your essay by arguing either that Guterson is, in fact, a neutral observer or that he writes to persuade.

THE PROBLEM OF PLACE IN AMERICA

Ray Oldenburg

Ray Oldenburg, a sociologist, teaches at the University of West Florida in Pensacola. The following is an excerpt from his book about the concept of place in America, The Great Good Place: Cafés, Coffee Shops, Community Centers, Beauty Parlors, General Stores, Bars, Hangouts and How They Get You Through the Day *(1989).*

A number of recent American writings indicate that the nostalgia for the small town need not be construed as directed toward the town itself: it is rather a "quest for community" (as Robert Nisbet puts it)—a nostalgia for a compassable and integral living unit. The critical question is not whether the small town can be rehabilitated in the image of its earlier strength and growth—for clearly it cannot—but whether American life will be able to evolve any other integral community to replace it. This is what I call the problem of place in America, and unless it is somehow resolved, American life will become more jangled and fragmented than it is, and American personality will continue to be unquiet and unfulfilled.

MAX LERNER, *America as a Civilization,* 1957

The ensuing years have confirmed Lerner's diagnosis. The problem of place in America has not been resolved and life *has* become more jangled and fragmented. No new form of integral community has been found; the small town has yet to greet its replacement. And Americans are not a contented people.

What may have seemed like the new form of community—the automobile suburb—multiplied rapidly after World War II. Thirteen million plus returning veterans qualified for single-family dwellings requiring no down payments in the new developments. In building and equipping these millions of new private domains, American industry found a major alternative to military production and companionate marriages appeared to have found ideal nesting places. But we did not live happily ever after.

Life in the subdivision may have satisfied the combat veteran's longing for a safe, orderly, and quiet haven, but it rarely offered the sense of place and belonging that had rooted his parents and grandparents. Houses alone do not a community make, and the typical subdivision proved hostile to the emergence of any structure or space utilization beyond the uniform houses and streets that characterized it.

Like all-residential city blocks, observed one student of the American condition, the suburb is "merely a base from which the individual reaches out to the scattered components of social existence."[1] Though proclaimed as offering the best of both rural and urban life, the automobile suburb had the effect of fragmenting the individual's world. As one observer wrote: "A man works in one place, sleeps in another, shops somewhere else, finds pleasure or companionship where he can, and cares about none of these places."

The typical suburban home is easy to leave behind as its occupants move to another. What people cherish most in them can be taken along in the move. There are no sad farewells at the local taverns or the corner store because there are no local taverns or corner stores. Indeed, there is often more encouragement to leave a given subdivision than to stay in it, for neither the homes nor the neighborhoods are equipped to see families or individuals through the cycle of life. Each is designed for families of particular sizes, incomes, and ages. There is little sense of place and even less opportunity to put down roots.

Transplanted Europeans are acutely aware of the lack of a community life in our residential areas. We recently talked with an outgoing lady who had lived in many countries and was used to adapting to local ways. The problem of place in America had become her problem as well:

> After four years here, I still feel more of a foreigner than in any other place in the world I have been. People here are proud to live in a "good" area, but to us these so-called desirable areas are like prisons. There is no contact between the various households, we rarely see the neighbors and certainly do not know any of them. In Luxembourg, however, we would frequently stroll down to one of the local cafés in the evening, and there pass a very congenial few hours in the company of the local fireman, dentist, bank employee or whoever happened to be there at the time. There is no pleasure to be had in driving to a sleazy, dark bar where one keeps strictly to one's self and becomes fearful if approached by some drunk.

Sounding the same note, Kenneth Harris has commented on one of the things British people miss most in the United States. It is some reasonable approximation of the village inn or local pub; our neighborhoods do not have it. Harris comments: "The American does not walk around to the local two or three times a week with his wife or with his son, to have his pint, chat with the neighbors, and then walk home. He does not take out the dog last thing every night, and break his journey with a quick one at the Crown."[2]

The contrast in cultures is keenly felt by those who enjoy a dual residence in Europe and America. Victor Gruen and his wife have a large place in Los Angeles and a small one in Vienna. He finds that: "In Los Angeles we are hesitant to leave our sheltered home in order to visit friends or to participate in cultural or entertainment events because every such outing involves a major investment of time and nervous strain in driving long distances."[3] But, he says, the European experience is much different:

5

"In Vienna, we are persuaded to go out often because we are within easy walking distance of two concert halls, the opera, a number of theatres, and a variety of restaurants, cafés, and shops. Seeing old friends does not have to be a prearranged affair as in Los Angeles, and more often than not, one bumps into them on the street or in a café." The Gruens have a hundred times more residential space in America but give the impression that they don't enjoy it half as much as their little corner of Vienna.

But one needn't call upon foreign visitors to point up the shortcomings of the suburban experiment. As a setting for marriage and family life, it has given those institutions a bad name. By the 1960s, a picture had emerged of the suburban housewife as "bored, isolated, and preoccupied with material things."[4] The suburban wife without a car to escape in epitomized the experience of being alone in America.[5] Those who could afford it compensated for the loneliness, isolation, and lack of community with the "frantic scheduling syndrome" as described by a counselor in the northeastern region of the United States:

> The loneliness I'm most familiar with in my job is that of wives and mothers of small children who are dumped in the suburbs and whose husbands are commuters . . . I see a lot of generalized loneliness, but I think that in well-to-do communities they cover it up with a wealth of frantic activity. That's the reason tennis has gotten so big. They all go out and play tennis.[6]

A majority of the former stay-at-home wives are now in the labor force. As both father and mother gain some semblance of a community life via their daily escapes from the subdivision, children are even more cut off from ties with adults. Home offers less and the neighborhood offers nothing for the typical suburban adolescent. The situation in the early seventies as described by Richard Sennett is worsening:

> In the past ten years, many middle-class children have tried to break out of the communities, the schools and the homes that their parents have spent so much of their own lives creating. If any one feeling can be said to run through the diverse groups and life-styles of the youth movements, it is a feeling that these middle-class communities of the parents were like pens, like cages keeping the youth from being free and alive. The source of the feeling lies in the perception that while these middle-class environments are secure and orderly regimes, people suffocate there for lack of the new, the unexpected, the diverse in their lives.[7]

The adolescent houseguest, I would suggest, is probably the best and quickest test of the vitality of a neighborhood; the visiting teenager in the subdivision soon acts like an animal in a cage. He or she paces, looks unhappy and uncomfortable, and by the second day is putting heavy pressure on the parents to leave. There is no place to which they can escape and join their own kind. There is nothing for them to do on their own.

There is nothing in the surroundings but the houses of strangers and no-body on the streets. Adults make a more successful adjustment, largely because they demand less. But few at any age find vitality in the housing developments. David Riesman, an esteemed elder statesman among social scientists, once attempted to describe the import of suburbia upon most of those who live there. "There would seem," he wrote, "to be an aimless-ness, a pervasive low-keyed unpleasure."[8] The word he seemed averse to using is *boring.* A teenager would not have had to struggle for the right phrasing.

Their failure to solve the problem of place in America and to provide a community life for their inhabitants has not effectively discouraged the growth of the postwar suburbs. To the contrary, there have emerged new generations of suburban development in which there is even less life out-side the houses than before. Why does failure succeed? Dolores Hayden supplies part of the answer when she observes that Americans have substi-tuted the vision of the ideal home for that of the ideal city.[9] The purchase of the even larger home on the even larger lot in the even more lifeless neighborhood is not so much a matter of joining community as retreating from it. Encouraged by a continuing decline in the civilities and amenities of the public or shared environment, people invest more hopes in their private acreage. They proceed as though a house can substitute for a com-munity if only it is spacious enough, entertaining enough, comfortable enough, splendid enough—and suitably isolated from that common horde that politicians still refer to as our "fellow Americans."

Observers disagree about the reasons for the growing estrangement between the family and the city in American society.[10] Richard Sennett, whose research spans several generations, argues that as soon as an Ameri-can family became middle class and could afford to do something about its fear of the outside world and its confusions, it drew in upon itself, and "in America, unlike France or Germany, the urban middle-class shunned pub-lic forms of social life like cafés and banquet halls."[11] Philippe Ariès, who also knows his history, counters with the argument that modern urban development has killed the essential relationships that once made a city and, as a consequence, "the role of the family overexpanded like a hyper-trophied cell" trying to take up the slack.[12]

In some countries, television broadcasting is suspended one night a week so that people will not abandon the habit of getting out of their homes and maintaining contact with one another. This tactic would prob-ably not work in America. Sennett would argue that the middle-class family, given its assessment of the public domain, would stay at home anyway. Ariès would argue that most would stay home for want of places to get together with their friends and neighbors. As Richard Goodwin declared, "there is virtually no place where neighbors can anticipate un-planned meetings—no pub or corner store or park."[13] The bright spot in this dispute is that the same set of remedies would cure both the family and the city of major ills.

Meantime, new generations are encouraged to shun a community life   15
in favor of a highly privatized one and to set personal aggrandizement
above public good. The attitudes may be learned from parents but they are
also learned in each generation's experiences. The modest housing developments, those *un*exclusive suburbs from which middle-class people graduate as they grow older and more affluent, teach their residents that future
hopes for a good life are pretty much confined to one's house and yard.
Community life amid tract housing is a disappointing experience. The
space within the development has been equipped and staged for isolated
family living and little else. The processes by which potential friends might
find one another and by which friendships not suited to the home might
be nurtured outside it are severely thwarted by the limited features and
facilities of the modern suburb.

The housing development's lack of informal social centers or informal public gathering places puts people too much at the mercy of their
closest neighbors. The small town taught us that people's best friends and
favorite companions rarely lived right next door to one another. Why
should it be any different in the automobile suburbs? What are the odds,
given that a hundred households are within easy walking distance, that one
is most likely to hit it off with the people next door? Small! Yet, the closest
neighbors are the ones with whom friendships are most likely to be attempted, for how does one even find out enough about someone a block
and a half away to justify an introduction?

What opportunity is there for two men who both enjoy shooting,
fishing, or flying to get together and gab if their families are not compatible? Where do people entertain and enjoy one another if, for whatever
reason, they are not comfortable in one another's homes? Where do people
have a chance to get to know one another casually and without commitment before deciding whether to involve other family members in their
relationship? Tract housing offers no such places.

Getting together with neighbors in the development entails considerable hosting efforts, and it depends upon continuing good relationships
between households and their members. In the usual course of things,
these relationships are easily strained or ruptured. Having been lately
formed and built on little, they are not easy to mend. Worse, some of the
few good friends will move and are not easily replaced. In time, the over-
tures toward friendship, neighborliness, and a semblance of community
hardly seem worth the effort.

In the Absence of an Informal Public Life

We have noted Sennett's observation that middle-class Americans are
not like their French or German counterparts. Americans do not make
daily visits to sidewalk cafés or banquet halls. We do not have that third
realm of satisfaction and social cohesion beyond the portals of home and
work that for others is an essential element of the good life. Our comings

and goings are more restricted to the home and work settings, and those two spheres have become preemptive. Multitudes shuttle back and forth between the "womb" and the "rat race" in a constricted pattern of daily life that easily generates the familiar desire to "get away from it all."

A two-stop model of daily routine is becoming fixed in our habits as   20
the urban environment affords less opportunity for public relaxation. Our most familiar gathering centers are disappearing rapidly. The proportion of beer and spirits consumed in public places has declined from about 90 percent of the total in the late 1940s to about 30 percent today.[14] There's been a similar decline in the number of neighborhood taverns in which those beverages are sold. For those who avoid alcoholic refreshments and prefer the drugstore soda fountain across the street, the situation has gotten even worse. By the 1960s, it was clear that the soda fountain and the lunch counter no longer had a place in "the balanced drug store."[15] "In this day of heavy unionization and rising minimum wages for unskilled help, the traditional soda fountain should be thrown out," advised an expert on drugstore management. And so it has been. The new kinds of places emphasize fast service, not slow and easy relaxation.

In the absence of an informal public life, people's expectations toward work and family life have escalated beyond the capacity of those institutions to meet them. Domestic and work relationships are pressed to supply all that is wanting and much that is missing in the constricted life-styles of those without community. The resulting strain on work and family institutions is glaringly evident. In the measure of its disorganization and deterioration, the middle-class family of today resembles the low-income family of the 1960s.[16] The United States now leads the world in the rate of divorce among its population. Fatherless children comprise the fastest-growing segment of the infant population. The strains that have eroded the traditional family configuration have given rise to alternate life-styles, and though their appearance suggests the luxury of choice, none are as satisfactory as was the traditional family when embedded in a supporting community.

It is estimated that American industry loses from $50 billion to $75 billion annually due to absenteeism, company-paid medical expenses, and lost productivity.[17] Stress in the lives of the workers is a major cause of these industrial losses. Two-thirds of the visits to family physicians in the United States are prompted by stress-related problems.[18] "Our mode of life," says one medical practitioner, "is emerging as today's principal cause of illness."[19] Writes Claudia Wallis, "It is a sorry sign of the times that the three best-selling drugs in the country are an ulcer medication (Tagamet), a hypertension drug (Inderal), and a tranquilizer (Valium)."[20]

In the absence of an informal public life, Americans are denied those means of relieving stress that serve other cultures so effectively. We seem not to realize that the means of relieving stress can just as easily be built into an urban environment as those features which produce stress. To our considerable misfortune, the pleasures of the city have been largely reduced to consumerism. We don't much enjoy our cities because they're not very enjoyable. The mode of urban life that has become our principal cause of illness resembles a pressure cooker without its essential safety valve. Our urban environment is like an engine that runs hot because it was designed without a cooling system.

Unfortunately, opinion leans toward the view that the causes of stress are social but the cures are individual. It is widely assumed that high levels of stress are an unavoidable condition of modern life, that these are built into the social system, and that one must get outside the system in order to gain relief. Even our efforts at entertaining and being entertained tend toward the competitive and stressful. We come dangerously close to the notion that one "gets sick" in the world beyond one's domicile and one "gets well" by retreating from it. Thus, while Germans relax amid the rousing company of the *bier garten* or the French recuperate in their animated little bistros, Americans turn to massaging, meditating, jogging, hot-tubbing, or escape fiction. While others take full advantage of their freedom to associate, we glorify our freedom *not* to associate.

In the absence of an informal public life, living becomes more expensive. Where the means and facilities for relaxation and leisure are not publicly shared, they become the objects of private ownership and consumption. In the United States, about two-thirds of the GNP is based on personal consumption expenditures. That category, observes Goodwin, contains "the alienated substance of mankind."[21] Some four *trillion* dollars spent for individual aggrandizement represents a powerful divisive force indeed. In our society, insists one expert on the subject, leisure has been perverted into consumption.[22] An aggressive, driving force behind this perversion is advertising, which conditions "our drive to consume and to own whatever industry produces."[23]

Paragons of self-righteousness, advertisers promulgate the notion that society would languish in a state of inertia but for their efforts. "Nothing happens until somebody sells something," they love to say. That may be true enough within a strictly commercial world (and for them, what else is there?) but the development of an informal public life depends upon people finding and enjoying one another outside the cash nexus. Advertising, in its ideology and effects, is the enemy of an informal public life. It breeds alienation. It convinces people that the good life can be individually purchased. In the place of the shared camaraderie of people who see themselves as equals, the ideology of advertising substitutes competitive acquisition. It is the difference between loving people for what they are and envying them for what they own. It is no coincidence that cultures with a highly developed informal public life have a disdain for advertising.[24]

The tremendous advantage enjoyed by societies with a well-developed informal public life is that, within them, poverty carries few burdens other than that of having to live a rather Spartan existence. But there is no stigma and little deprivation of experience. There is an engaging and sustaining public life to supplement and complement home and work routines. For those on tight budgets who live in some degree of austerity, it compensates for the lack of things owned privately. For the affluent, it offers much that money can't buy.

The American middle-class life-style is an exceedingly expensive one—especially when measured against the satisfaction it yields. The paucity of collective rituals and unplanned social gatherings puts a formidable burden upon the individual to overcome the social isolation that threatens. Where there are homes without a connection to community, where houses are located in areas devoid of congenial meeting places, the enemy called boredom is ever at the gate. Much money must be spent to compensate for the sterility of the surrounding environment. Home decoration and redecoration becomes a never-ending process as people depend upon new wallpaper or furniture arrangements to add zest to their lives. Like the bored and idle rich, they look to new clothing fashions for the same purpose and buy new wardrobes well before the old ones are past service. A lively round of after-dinner conversation isn't as simple as a walk to the corner pub—one has to host the dinner.

The home entertainment industry thrives in the dearth of the informal public life among the American middle class. Demand for all manner of electronic gadgetry to substitute vicarious watching and listening for more direct involvement is high. Little expense is spared in the installation of sound and video systems, VCRs, cable connections, or that current version of heaven on earth for the socially exiled—the satellite dish. So great is the demand for electronic entertainment that it cannot be met with quality programming. Those who create for this insatiable demand must rely on formula and imitation.

Everyone old enough to drive finds it necessary to make frequent escapes from the private compound located amid hundreds of other private compounds. To do so, each needs a car, and that car is a means of conveyance as privatized and antisocial as the neighborhoods themselves. Fords and "Chevys" now cost from ten to fifteen thousand dollars, and the additional expenses of maintaining, insuring, and fueling them constitute major expenditures for most families. Worse, each drives his or her own car. About the only need that suburbanites can satisfy by means of an easy walk is that which impels them toward their bathroom.

In the absence of an informal public life, industry must also compensate for the missing opportunity for social relaxation. When the settings for casual socializing are not provided in the neighborhoods, people compensate in the workplace. Coffee breaks are more than mere rest periods; they are depended upon more for sociable human contact than physical relaxation. These and other "time-outs" are extended. Lunch hours often afford a sufficient amount of reveling to render the remainder of the working day ineffectual. The distinction between work-related communications and "shooting the breeze" becomes blurred. Once-clear parameters separating work from play become confused. The individual finds that neither work nor play are as satisfying as they should be.

30

The problem of place in America manifests itself in a sorely deficient informal public life. The structure of shared experience beyond that offered by family, job, and passive consumerism is small and dwindling. The essential group experience is being replaced by the exaggerated self-consciousness of individuals. American life-styles, for all the material acquisition and the seeking after comforts and pleasures, are plagued by boredom, loneliness, alienation, and a high price tag. America can point to many areas where she has made progress, but in the area of informal public life she has lost ground and continues to lose it.

Unlike many frontiers, that of the informal public life does not remain benign as it awaits development. It does not become easier to tame as technology evolves, as governmental bureaus and agencies multiply, or as population grows. It does not yield to the mere passage of time and a policy of letting the chips fall where they may as development proceeds in other realms of urban life. To the contrary, neglect of the informal public life can make a jungle of what had been a garden while, at the same time, diminishing the ability of people to cultivate it.

In the sustained absence of a healthy and vigorous informal public life, the citizenry may quite literally forget how to create one. A facilitating public etiquette consisting of rituals necessary to the meeting, greeting, and enjoyment of strangers is not much in evidence in the United States. It is replaced by a set of strategies designed to avoid contact with people in public, by devices intended to preserve the individual's circle of privacy against any stranger who might violate it. Urban sophistication is deteriorating into such matters as knowing who is safe on whose "turf," learning to minimize expression and bodily contact when in public, and other survival skills required in a world devoid of the amenities. Lyn Lofland notes that the 1962 edition of Amy Vanderbilt's *New Complete Book of Etiquette* "contains not a single reference to proper behavior in the world of strangers."[25] The cosmopolitan promise of our cities is diminished. Its ecumenic spirit fades with our ever-increasing retreat into privacy.

Toward a Solution: The Third Place

Though none can prescribe the total solution to the problem of place in America, it is possible to describe some important elements that any solution will have to include. Certain basic requirements of an informal public life do not change, nor does a healthy society advance beyond them. To the extent that a thriving informal public life belongs to a society's past, so do the best of its days, and prospects for the future should be cause for considerable concern.

Towns and cities that afford their populations an engaging public life are easy to identify. What urban sociologists refer to as their interstitial spaces are filled with people. The streets and sidewalks, parks and squares, parkways and boulevards are being used by people sitting, standing, and walking. Prominent public space is not reserved for that well-dressed, middle-class crowd that is welcomed at today's shopping malls. The elderly and poor, the ragged and infirm, are interspersed among those looking and doing well. The full spectrum of local humanity is represented. Most of the streets are as much the domain of the pedestrian as of the motorist. The typical street can still accommodate a full-sized perambulator and still encourages a new mother's outing with her baby. Places to sit are abundant. Children play in the streets. The general scene is much as the set director for a movie would arrange it to show life in a wholesome and thriving town or city neighborhood.

Beyond the impression that a human scale has been preserved in the architecture, however, or that the cars haven't defeated the pedestrians in the battle for the streets, or that the pace of life suggests gentler and less complicated times, the picture doesn't reveal the *dynamics* needed to produce an engaging informal public life. The secret of a society at peace with itself is not revealed in the panoramic view but in examination of the average citizen's situation.

The examples set by societies that have solved the problem of place and those set by the small towns and vital neighborhoods of our past suggest that daily life, in order to be relaxed and fulfilling, must find its balance in three realms of experience. One is domestic, a second is gainful or productive, and the third is inclusively sociable, offering both the basis of community and the celebration of it. Each of these realms of human experience is built on associations and relationships appropriate to it; each has its own physically separate and distinct places; each must have its measure of autonomy from the others.

What the panoramic view of the vital city fails to reveal is that the third realm of experience is as distinct a place as home or office. The informal public life only seems amorphous and scattered; in reality, it is highly focused. It emerges and is sustained in *core settings*. Where the problem of place has been solved, a generous proliferation of core settings of informal public life is sufficient to the needs of the people.

Pierre Salinger was asked how he liked living in France and how he would compare it with life in the United States. His response was that he likes France where, he said, everyone is more relaxed. In America, there's a lot of pressure. The French, of course, have solved the problem of place. The Frenchman's daily life sits firmly on a tripod consisting of home, place of work, and another setting where friends are engaged during the midday and evening *aperitif* hours, if not earlier and later. In the United States, the middle classes particularly are attempting a balancing act on a bipod consisting of home and work. That alienation, boredom, and stress are endemic among us is not surprising. For most of us, a third of life is either deficient or absent altogether, and the other two-thirds cannot be successfully integrated into a whole.

Before the core settings of an informal public life can be restored to the urban landscape and reestablished in daily life, it will be necessary to articulate their nature and benefit. It will not suffice to describe them in a

40

mystical or romanticized way such as might warm the hearts of those already convinced. Rather, the core settings of the informal public life must be analyzed and discussed in terms comprehensible to these rational and individualistic outlooks dominant in American thought. We must dissect, talk in terms of specific payoffs, and reduce special experiences to common labels. We must, urgently, begin to defend these Great Good Places against the unbelieving and the antagonistic and do so in terms clear to all.

The object of our focus—the core settings of the informal public life—begs for a simpler label. Common parlance offers few possibilities and none that combine brevity with objectivity and an appeal to common sense. There is the term *hangout,* but its connotation is negative and the word conjures up images of the joint or dive. Though we refer to the meeting places of the lowly as hangouts, we rarely apply the term to yacht clubs or oak-paneled bars, the "hangouts" of the "better people." We have nothing as respectable as the French *rendez-vous* to refer to a public meeting place or a setting in which friends get together away from the confines of home and work. The American language reflects the American reality— in vocabulary as in fact the core settings of an informal public life are underdeveloped.

For want of a suitable existing term, we introduce our own: the third place will hereafter be used to signify what we have called "the core settings of informal public life." The third place is a generic designation for a great variety of public places that host the regular, voluntary, informal, and happily anticipated gatherings of individuals beyond the realms of home and work. The term will serve well. It is neutral, brief, and facile. It underscores the significance of the tripod and the relative importance of its three legs. Thus, the first place is the home—the most important place of all. It is the first regular and predictable environment of the growing child and the one that will have greater effect upon his or her development. It will harbor individuals long before the workplace is interested in them and well after the world of work casts them aside. The second place is the work setting, which reduces the individual to a single, productive role. It fosters competition and motivates people to rise above their fellow creatures. But it also provides the means to a living, improves the material quality of life, and structures endless hours of time for a majority who could not structure it on their own.

Before industrialization, the first and second places were one. Industrialization separated the place of work from the place of residence, removing productive work from the home and making it remote in distance, morality, and spirit from family life. What we now call the third place existed long before this separation, and so our term is a concession to the sweeping effects of the Industrial Revolution and its division of life into private and public spheres.

The ranking of the three places corresponds with individual dependence upon them. We need a home even though we may not work, and most of us need to work more than we need to gather with our friends and neighbors. The ranking holds, also, with respect to the demands upon the individual's time. Typically, the individual spends more time at home than at work and more at work than in a third place. In importance, in claims on time and loyalty, in space allocated, and in social recognition, the ranking is appropriate.

In some countries, the third place is more closely ranked with the others. In Ireland, France, or Greece, the core settings of informal public life rank a *strong* third in the lives of the people. In the United States, third places rank a weak third with perhaps the majority lacking a third place and denying that it has any real importance.

The prominence of third places varies with cultural setting and historical era. In preliterate societies, the third place was actually foremost, being the grandest structure in the village and commanding the central location. They were the men's houses, the earliest ancestors of those grand, elegant, and pretentious clubs eventually to appear along London's Pall Mall. In both Greek and Roman society, prevailing values dictated that the *agora* and the *forum* should be great, central institutions; that homes should be simple and unpretentious; that the architecture of cities should assert the worth of the public and civic individual over the private and domestic one. Few means to lure and invite citizens into public gatherings were overlooked. The forums, colosseums, theaters, and amphitheaters were grand structures, and admission to them was free.

Third places have never since been as prominent. Attempts at elegance and grand scale continued to be made but with far less impact. Many cultures evolved public baths on a grand scale. Victorian gin palaces were elegant (especially when contrasted to the squalor that surrounded them). The winter gardens and palm gardens built in some of our northern cities in the previous century included many large and imposing structures. In modern times, however, third places survive without much prominence or elegance.

Where third places remain vital in the lives of people today, it is far more because they are prolific than prominent. The geographic expansion of the cities and their growing diversity of quarters, or distinct neighborhoods, necessitated the shift. The proliferation of smaller establishments kept them at the human scale and available to all in the face of increasing urbanization.

In the newer American communities, however, third places are neither prominent nor prolific. They are largely prohibited. Upon an urban landscape increasingly hostile to and devoid of informal gathering places, one may encounter people rather pathetically trying to find some spot in which to relax and enjoy each other's company.

Sometimes three or four pickups are parked under the shade near a convenience store as their owners drink beers that may be purchased but not consumed inside. If the habit ever really catches on, laws will be passed to stop it. Along the strips, youths sometimes gather in or near their cars

50

in the parking lots of hamburger franchises. It's the best they can manage, for they aren't allowed to loiter inside. One may encounter a group of women in a laundromat, socializing while doing the laundry chores. One encounters parents who have assumed the expense of adding a room to the house or converting the garage to a recreation room so that, within neighborhoods that offer them nothing, their children might have a decent place to spend time with their friends. Sometimes too, youth will develop a special attachment to a patch of woods not yet bulldozed away in the relentless spread of the suburbs. In such a place they enjoy relief from the confining overfamiliarity of their tract houses and the monotonous streets.

American planners and developers have shown a great disdain for those earlier arrangements in which there was life beyond home and work. They have condemned the neighborhood tavern and disallowed a suburban version. They have failed to provide modern counterparts of once-familiar gathering places. The gristmill or grain elevator, soda fountains, malt shops, candy stores, and cigar stores—places that did not reduce a human being to a mere customer, have not been replaced. Meantime, the planners and developers continue to add to the rows of regimented loneliness in neighborhoods so sterile as to cry out for something as modest as a central mail drop or a little coffee counter at which those in the area might discover one another.

Americans are now confronted with that condition about which the crusty old arch-conservative Edmund Burke warned us when he said that the bonds of community are broken at great peril for they are not easily replaced. Indeed, we face the enormous task of making "the mess that is urban America" suitably hospitable to the requirements of gregarious, social animals.[26] Before motivation or wisdom is adequate to the task, however, we shall need to understand exactly what it is that an informal public life can contribute to both national and individual life. Therein lies the purpose of this book.

Successful exposition demands that some statement of a problem precede a discussion of its solution. Hence, I've begun on sour and unpleasant notes and will find it necessary to sound them again. I would have preferred it otherwise. It is the solution that intrigues and delights. It is my hope that the discussion of life in the third place will have a similar effect upon the reader, just as I hope that the reader will allow the bias that now and then prompts me to substitute Great Good Place for third place. I am confident that those readers who have a third place will not object.

Notes

1. Richard N. Goodwin, "The American Condition," *The New Yorker* (28 January 1974), 38.
2. Kenneth Harris, *Travelling Tongues* (London: John Murray, 1949), 80.
3. Victor Gruen, *Centers for Urban Environment* (New York: Van Nostrand Reinhold Co., 1973), 217.

4. Philip E. Slater, "Must Marriage Cheat Today's Young Women?" *Redbook Magazine* (February 1971).

5. Suzanne Gordon, *Lonely in America* (New York: Simon & Schuster, 1976).

6. *Ibid.,* 105.

7. Richard Sennett, "The Brutality of Modern Families," in *Marriages and Families,* ed. Helena Z. Lopata. (New York: D. Van Nostrand Company, 1973), 81.

8. David Riesman, "The Suburban Dislocation," *The Annals of the American Academy of Political and Social Science* (November 1957), 142.

9. Dolores Hayden, *Redesigning the American Dream* (New York: W. W. Norton & Company, 1984), Chapter 2.

10. See Sennett (*op. cit.*) and Ariès, Philippe. "The Family and the City." *Daedalus,* Spring, 1977. Pp. 227–237 for succinct statements of the two views.

11. Sennett, *op. cit.,* 84.

12. Philippe Ariès, "The Family and the City," *Daedalus* (Spring 1977), 227.

13. Goodwin, *op. cit.,* 38.

14. P. F. Kluge, "Closing Time," *Wall Street Journal* (27 May 1982).

15. Frank L. Ferguson, *Efficient Drug Store Management* (New York: Fairchild Publications, 1969), 202.

16. Urie Bronfenbrenner, "The American Family: An Ecological Perspective," in *The American Family: Current Perspectives* (Cambridge, Mass.: Harvard University Press, Audiovisual Division, 1979), (audio cassette).

17. Claudia Wallis, "Stress: Can We Cope?" *Time* (6 June 1983).

18. *Ibid.*

19. *Ibid.*

20. *Ibid.*

21. Richard Goodwin, "The American Condition," *New Yorker* (4 February 1970) 75.

22. Thomas M. Kando, *Leisure and Popular Culture in Transition,* 2d ed. (St. Louis: The C. V. Mosby Company, 1980).

23. *Ibid.,* 101.

24. Generally, the Mediterranean cultures.

25. Lyn H. Lofland, *A World of Strangers* (Prospect Heights, Ill.: Waveland Press, Inc., 1973), 117.

26. Sometimes the phrase employed is "the mess that is man-made America." Planners appear to use it as much as anyone else.

Reading and Responding

1. This is a carefully organized and sequenced piece. Outline it, paying attention to Oldenburg's use of subheadings and topic sentences at the beginning of paragraphs.

2. Is Oldenburg easy or hard to read? He's the most textbookish writer in this section (not necessarily in a negative sense): Do you consider this quality a problem or a strength? Compare him to Wolfe: Did you have an easier or harder time understanding Oldenburg's main points?

3. Do a short page of freewriting explaining anything in the reading that complicated or confused something you've taken for granted. That is, have you ever thought about these topics that Oldenburg discusses? Does Oldenburg's essay help you see something you didn't see before? Does it make you uneasy?

Working Together

1. Write a quick page that (a) summarizes what Oldenburg means by a "third place" and (b) gives an example from your own experience of some "third place" you often go to, on campus or back home.

   - Sitting in a group of three to five people, pass the pages around, round-robin style: pass to the right, read that piece, pass to the right again, read another piece—until you get your own piece back.
   - With all of these ideas in mind, discuss what Oldenburg is saying. Are there third places in your lives?

2. Find the section where Oldenburg contrasts American and European experience; list three or four features of what Oldenburg identifies as European. Think about your own college campus; how does it fit (or not fit) those European features?

Rethinking and Rewriting

1. Write an essay explaining Oldenburg's idea of the third place and describing that kind of place in your own experience. Assume that your readers haven't read "The Problem of Place in America," and make sure that your essay tells them what they need to know.

2. Go to a third place, take notes on everything you see and hear for an hour, and write a portrait of that place, a profile. At some point, include Oldenburg's definition.

3. At the heart of Oldenburg's critique is an analysis of how the car has completely changed the structure of our cities and towns and the rhythms of our lives. Keep a log for a week recording how often you drive your car, where you drive your car, how far, and so on. Take notes, too, on where you live, the size of your garage, how close you are to other houses, whether you drive to malls, how many of the places you drive to are designed expressly for cars, and so on. (If you're living on campus now, you might compare the arrangement and design of the

buildings and the use of cars there with the design of your city or neighborhood back home.) Write an essay that describes what life would be like without your car. What wouldn't you be able to do? How would you go about your daily routines? Try to imagine your hometown or neighborhood without cars. What would it look like? How would the town or neighborhood have to be redesigned?

ON GOING HOME

THE ONE THOUSAND SEASONS

Donald Hall

> *Donald Hall left teaching in 1975 and retired to the family farm in Vermont, becoming a full-time writer. Over a period of forty years, he has written thirteen volumes of poetry and has become one of America's best known poets and essayists. This essay describes one aspect of Hall's life in New Hampshire.*

New York has people, the Northwest rain, Iowa soybeans, and Texas money. New Hampshire has weather and seasons. Convention speaks merely of four seasons; here, we number at least a thousand, and on one good day our spendthrift climate runs through seven or eight. Robert Frost lived his first eleven years in monoseasonal California; maybe that's why he became the laureate of climatic mutability. In "Two Tramps in Mud Time," he wrote about an April day. For a warm moment you think it's May; then with sudden wind and cloud, "you're two months back in the middle of March."

October may be more so. When we wake, we stoke the Glenwood and scrape ice off the pickup's windshield; at noon we take lunch sitting on the porch in T-shirts; the spot of rain at teatime is cold enough to send us checking the salt supply in the grainshed, but sunset blooms a soft rose in the west, promising Indian summer, a promise we remember with chagrin when we wake at midnight to the first snowfall.

However we number them, spring is the least of our seasons. It begins with the glorious disaster of winter's melt, periodic in March, interrupted by blizzards, continuing through April as rivers roll down hillsides where no rivers were, gullying tunnels under snowdrifts, hollowing gray scrap bulwarks as rag-and-tatter as snow in Manhattan. When snow goes, mud takes over. For a week or two we struggle in mud as we never struggled in snow. Transmissions bust, the pond road is travel-at-your-own-risk, the bridge is out, and Fred keeps revving up the tractor to haul flatlanders out of the ditch, the way Fred's grandfather Fred did with his oxen.

When mud goes dry, leaving stiff ridges and warps for bumping over, we do not sigh in relief, for if we sigh we inhale blackflies. We wish the mud back; it does not raise welts. Now snowdrops fly their small flags in our gardens, now daffodils rise in tentative glory—always, every year, the bravest rewarded with cupfuls of snow, in *Return of the Son of Winter,* rerun on every channel—but we do not wander happily on the daffodil hillside. We feel our joy behind windows, even storm windows, looking past the last garbage snow to the sun's blossoming hill—unless we are careless of skin or rapturous of bite and scratch. And when the blackflies go, perhaps the mosquitoes have eaten them.

But even the least of seasons is beautiful. As we drive to the store, or   *5* as we garden protected by thick socks and a beekeeper's mask, we move under the frail green of beginning leaves. There is nothing so tender as new green, smoke of red and yellow buds along with pale green smoke, loosening at the branch ends of trees released from the cold hold of winter. Whole hillsides overnight smolder up this tenderness, leaves unfolding daily and darkening week by week toward the vigorous black-green of summer's oak and maple. Now we walk, our hands slapping the air as if we bargained for a thousand rugs in a thousand Turkish markets, and inspect the winter's waste by pond and mountainside: what popples the beaver took, what birches we lost to February's icestorm.

If spring is least it is also shortest. There are those who claim it occupies only the month of May. (Some few insist that spring occurs on May 17, ten A.M. to two-thirty P.M.) But unless we confront a literalist of the calendar, there can be no controversy over the date of summer's beginning. The rest of us plant our gardens, except for the peas we scatter on snow, after the full moon closest to Memorial Day—but the summer people seed themselves on Memorial Day itself. All summer as corn inches up or doesn't, as the zucchini population of New Hampshire multiplies like Nashua, as green tomatoes wax and decide with heroic stubbornness to remain forever green, the growth of summer people outdoes every other crop. Through drought and deluge, unseasonable cold or Bostonian mug and swelter, they pop from the cracked earth of June by the hundred thousand; they spread in July up, out, and over the rural dirt of New England; they take into themselves abundancies of sun and water; they thrive, fatten, elongate, swell, ripen—only, on Labor Day, afflicted suddenly by minus three hundred degrees of school-frost, work-frost, and duty-frost, instantly to wither, blacken, die, and vanish.

On their sudden, seasonal, and predictable disappearance—we hear of them miraculously altered, no longer tanned in the flesh but brown-suited in worsted as in Worcester, and felt-hatted in the suburbs of the ordinary life—we sigh without inhaling a single insect, enjoy the huge dark end-of-summer leaves, tidy our spent gardens, and hunker down for the best of times. The red branch on the green tree starts it off, one eruption marching to a different drummer. Then whole bogs blaze with swamp maples, dear deep reds followed by the great vulgar chorus of bellowing, billowing yellows, reds, russets, and rusts. Birch, maple, rare elm, oak, beech, ash, each in its own time and with its own pitch and tone swells the outlandish chorus. It is the London Philharmonic tripling up with orchestras from Bogotá and Kuala Lumpur, Spike Jones conducting, and each shade and position contributes another violin, oboe, or triangle to the gorgeous cacophony of autumn.

Always the persistent evergreen supplies the continuo. As autumn endures and the leaves fall, the silvery sheen of empty trunks and branches becomes an increasing theme. Everywhere we walk we gaze at yellow leaves against unpainted barns, towering enormous flame-fountains beside white houses, varicolored Kearsarge altering each day, and through the day, by variety of light. Best of all, we love the hills of middle distance, with color patches distinct when we focus on them; when we refocus on the whole hill, its colors contract to a single insane tweed of pinks, oranges, reds, russets, and silvers.

After the sober and noble palette of late October and November, analytic cubism with its rectangles of granite and released stone walls, New England's seasonal journey retracts to the oneness of winter, from outrageous multiplicity to white uniformity. Usually it begins at night, the black sky flaking full with whiteness, covering brown hayfield and granite hill, boulder, road, and barn with the soft silence of its frigidity. We gather inside around the noisy Glenwood; we gather ourselves inside ourselves for the three months of our annual descent, internal Persephones of the personal underworld. On the full moon's winter night pewtery light reflects upward from snow to flicker against tin ceilings, ghost light, and we howl like coy-dogs in the moon's light.

Of the one thousand seasons, winter by actual count provides four *10* hundred and twenty-seven. Sixty-eight percent of winter's seasons cause pain. This pain's bright side is our complaining and bragging: Winter is ours, although winter people wearing skiing uniforms brighten white slopes. This long winter gives us our identity. Mixed and intense, beauty and pain together, interrupted only by January's thaw with its anticipatory melt—Miami invading from the South—winter is the name of our place. We must admit, spring is annoying, summer is not ours, autumn is best— and winter is New England's truest weather.

Reading and Responding

1. Think about a place you know well. Based on that knowledge, write your own first paragraph imitating the opening paragraph of "The One Thousand Seasons." Name the place and what it has, and mention the months of March, April, and May. (Don't worry about including a reference to a local writer; if you can include such a reference, do so.)
2. Write five sentences about what is beautiful in a place you know well. Focus three of the sentences on the countryside, the landscape itself; let the other two sentences be about the people (speak of them as "we") and what these people (presumably, you included) do.

Working Together

1. As a group, write a paragraph (of at least five sentences) about what the current season is like in the place where you live now. Model your paragraph on one of those in "The One Thousand Seasons."

2. As a group, decide on five individual sentences that you would nominate as "candidates" for the best sentence in this essay. Identify your five candidates and be ready to give two reasons supporting each candidate.
3. Some readers might argue that "The One Thousand Seasons" is really just lightweight writing—fun, and not meant to be taken seriously. What do you think? What phrases and expressions help you understand the intentions in this writing? Discuss these ideas as a group.

Rethinking and Rewriting

1. Write a letter to a friend who is not familiar with the character of the place you live in now. Following "The One Thousand Seasons" as a model (at least in part), describe the place in your letter so that someone who doesn't know it can at least begin to envision it. End your letter as Hall ends his essay, by discussing the region's "truest weather."
2. Think of a quarter or a semester or a month as being a series of seasons. Write a short essay that describes what goes on during this period of time. Use seasonal metaphors to help readers understand how you see the cycle of time. Start with any season and end with any season; just stay faithful to the character of the experiences as you understand them.

THE BEAUTIFUL PLACES

Kathleen Norris

Kathleen Norris has lived in Lemmon, South Dakota, for more than twenty years. She wrote two books of poetry and then made a name for herself as an essayist with the publication of Dakota: A Spiritual Geography *(1994), from which the following essay is taken. Since then, she has written two books that reflect more directly on spiritual themes:* The Cloister Walk *(1996) and* Amazing Grace: A Vocabulary of Faith *(1998). The essay that follows asks three questions: What is beauty? How do we find it? Where do we find it?*

The Scarecrow sighed. "Of course I cannot understand it,"
he said. "If your heads were stuffed with straw like
mine, you would probably all live in the beautiful places,
and then Kansas would have no people at all. It is
fortunate for Kansas that you have brains."

—L. FRANK BAUM, *The Wizard of Oz*

The high plains, the beginning of the desert West, often act as a crucible for those who inhabit them. Like Jacob's angel, the region requires that you wrestle with it before it bestows a blessing. This can mean driving through a snowstorm on icy roads, wondering whether you'll have to pull over and spend the night in your car, only to emerge under tag ends of clouds into a clear sky blazing with stars. Suddenly you know what you're seeing: the earth has turned to face the center of the galaxy, and many more stars are visible than the ones we usually see on our wing of the spiral.

Or a vivid double rainbow marches to the east, following the wild summer storm that nearly blew you off the road. The storm sky is gun-metal gray, but to the west the sky is peach streaked with crimson. The land and sky of the West often fill what Thoreau termed our "need to witness our limits transgressed." Nature, in Dakota, can indeed be an experience of the holy.

More Americans than ever, well over 70 percent, now live in urban areas and tend to see Plains land as empty. What they really mean is devoid of human presence. Most visitors to Dakota travel on interstate highways that will take them as quickly as possible through the region, past our larger cities to such attractions as the Badlands and the Black Hills. Looking at the expanse of land in between, they may wonder why a person would choose to live in such a barren place, let alone love it. But mostly they are bored: they turn up the car stereo, count the miles to civilization, and look away.

Dakota is a painful reminder of human limits, just as cities and shopping malls are attempts to deny them. This book is an invitation to a land of little rain and few trees, dry summer winds and harsh winters, a land rich in grass and sky and surprises. On a crowded planet, this is a place inhabited by few, and by the circumstance of inheritance, I am one of them. Nearly twenty years ago I returned to the holy ground of my childhood summers; I moved from New York City to the house my mother had grown up in, in an isolated town on the border between North and South Dakota.

More than any other place I lived as a child or young adult—Virginia, Illinois, Hawaii, Vermont, New York—this is my spiritual geography, the place where I've wrestled my story out of the circumstances of landscape and inheritance. The word "geography" derives from the Greek words for earth and writing, and writing about Dakota has been my means of understanding that inheritance and reclaiming what is holy in it. Of course Dakota has always been such a matrix for its Native American inhabitants. But their tradition is not mine, and in returning to the Great Plains, where two generations of my family lived before me, I had to build on my own traditions, those of the Christian West.

When a friend referred to the western Dakotas as the Cappadocia of North America, I was handed an essential connection between the spirituality of the landscape I inhabit and that of the fourth-century monastics who set up shop in Cappadocia and the deserts of Egypt. Like those monks, I made a countercultural choice to live in what the rest of the world considers a barren waste. Like them, I had to stay in this place, like a scarecrow in a field, and hope for the brains to see its beauty. My idea of what makes a place beautiful had to change, and it has. The city no longer appeals to me for the cultural experiences and possessions I might acquire there, but because its population is less homogeneous than Plains society. Its holiness is to be found in being open to humanity in all its diversity. And the western Plains now seem bountiful in their emptiness, offering solitude and room to grow.

I want to make it clear that my move did not take me "back to the land" in the conventional sense. I did not strike out on my own to make a go of it with "an acre and a cow," as a Hungarian friend naively imagined. As the homesteaders of the early twentieth century soon found out, it is not possible to survive on even 160 acres in western Dakota. My move was one that took me deep into the meaning of inheritance, as I had to try to fit myself into a complex network of long-established relationships.

My husband and I live in the small house in Lemmon, South Dakota, that my grandparents built in 1923. We moved there after they died because my mother, brother, and sisters, who live in Honolulu, did not want to hold an estate auction, the usual procedure when the beneficiaries of an inheritance on the Plains live far away. I offered to move there and manage the farm interests (land and a cattle herd) that my grandparents left us.

David Dwyer, my husband, also a poet, is a New York City native who spent his childhood summers in the Adirondacks, and he had enough sense of adventure to agree to this. We expected to be in Dakota for just a few years.

It's hard to say why we stayed. A growing love of the prairie landscape and the quiet of a small town, inertia, and because as freelance writers, we found we had the survival skills suitable for a frontier. We put together a crazy quilt of jobs: I worked in the public library and as an artist-in-residence in schools in both Dakotas; I also did freelance writing and bookkeeping. David tended bar, wrote computer programs for a number of businesses in the region, and did freelance translation of French literature for several publishers. In 1979 we plunged into the cable television business with some friends, one of whom is an electronics expert. David learned how to climb poles and put up the hardware, and I kept the books. It was a good investment; after selling the company we found that we had bought ourselves a good three years to write. In addition, I still do bookkeeping for my family's farm business: the land is leased to people I've known all my life, people who have rented our land for two generations and also farm their own land and maintain their own cattle herds, an arrangement that is common in western Dakota.

In coming to terms with my inheritance, and pursuing my vocation   10
as a writer, I have learned, as both farmers and writers have discovered before me, that it is not easy to remain on the Plains. Only one of North Dakota's best-known writers—Richard Critchfield, Louise Erdrich, Lois Hudson, and Larry Woiwode—currently lives in the state. And writing the truth about the Dakota experience can be a thankless task. I recently discovered that Lois Hudson's magnificent novel of the Dakota Dust Bowl, *The Bones of Plenty,* a book arguably better than *The Grapes of Wrath,* was unknown to teachers and librarians in a town not thirty miles from where the novel is set. The shame of it is that Hudson's book could have helped these people better understand their current situation, the economic crisis forcing many families off the land. Excerpts from *The Grapes of Wrath* were in a textbook used in the school, but students could keep them at a safe distance, part of that remote entity called "American literature" that has little relation to their lives.

The Plains are full of what a friend here calls "good telling stories," and while our sense of being forgotten by the rest of the world makes it all the more important that we preserve them and pass them on, instead we often neglect them. Perversely, we do not even claim those stories which have attracted national attention. Both John Neihardt and Frederick Manfred have written about Hugh Glass, a hunter and trapper mauled by a grizzly bear in 1823 at the confluence of the Little Moreau and Grand rivers just south of Lemmon. Left for dead by his companions, he crawled and limped some two hundred miles southeast, to the trading post at Fort Kiowa on the Missouri River. Yet when Manfred wanted to give a reading in Lemmon a few years ago, the publicist was dismissed by a high school principal who said, "Who's he? Why would our students be interested?" Manfred's audience of eighty—large for Lemmon—consisted mainly of the people who remembered him from visits he'd made in the early 1950s while researching his novel *Lord Grizzly.*

Thus are the young disenfranchised while their elders drown in details, "story" reduced to the social column of the weekly newspaper that reports on family reunions, card parties, even shopping excursions to a neighboring town. But real story is as hardy as grass, and it survives in Dakota in oral form. Good storytelling is one thing rural whites and Indians have in common. But Native Americans have learned through harsh necessity that people who survive encroachment by another culture need story to survive. And a storytelling tradition is something Plains people share with both ancient and contemporary monks: we learn our ways of being and reinforce our values by telling tales about each other.

One of my favorite monastic stories concerns two fourth-century monks who "spent fifty years mocking their temptations by saying 'After this winter, we will leave here.' When the summer came, they said, 'After this summer, we will go away from here.' They passed all their lives in this way." These ancient monks sound remarkably like the farmers I know in Dakota who live in what they laconically refer to as "next-year country."

We hold on to hopes for next year every year in western Dakota: hoping that droughts will end; hoping that our crops won't be hailed out in the few rainstorms that come; hoping that it won't be too windy on the day we harvest, blowing away five bushels an acre; hoping (usually against hope) that if we get a fair crop, we'll be able to get a fair price for it. Sometimes survival is the only blessing that the terrifying angel of the Plains bestows. Still, there are those born and raised here who can't imagine living anywhere else. There are also those who are drawn here— teachers willing to take the lowest salaries in the nation; clergy with theological degrees from Princeton, Cambridge, and Zurich who want to serve small rural churches—who find that they cannot remain for long. Their professional mobility sets them apart and becomes a liability in an isolated Plains community where outsiders are treated with an uneasy mix of hospitality and rejection.

"Extremes," John R. Milton suggests in his history of South Dakota, 15 is "perhaps the key word for Dakota. . . . What happens to extremes is that they come together, and the result is a kind of tension." I make no attempt in this book to resolve the tensions and contradictions I find in the Dakotas between hospitality and insularity, change and inertia, stability and instability, possibility and limitation, between hope and despair, between open hearts and closed minds.

I suspect that these are the ordinary contradictions of human life, and that they are so visible in Dakota because we are so few people living in a stark landscape. We are at the point of transition between East and West in America, geographically and psychically isolated from either coast, and unlike either the Midwest or the desert West. South Dakota has been dubbed both the Sunshine State and the Blizzard State, and both designations have a basis in fact. Without a strong identity we become a mythic void; "the Great Desolation," as novelist Ole Rolvaag wrote early in this century, or "The American Outback," as *Newsweek* designated us a few years ago.

Geographical and cultural identity is confused even within the Dakotas. The eastern regions of both states have more in common with each other than with the area west of the Missouri, colloquially called the "West River." Although I commonly use the term "Dakota" to refer to both Dakotas, most of my experience is centered in this western region, and it seems to me that especially in western Dakota we live in tension between myth and truth. Are we cowboys or farmers? Are we fiercely independent frontier types or community builders? One myth that haunts us is that the small town is a stable place. The land around us was divided neatly in 160-acre rectangular sections, following the Homestead Act of 1863 (creating many section-line roads with 90-degree turns). But our human geography has never been as orderly. The western Dakota communities settled by whites are, and always have been, remarkably unstable. The Dakotas have always been a place to be *from:* some 80 percent of homesteaders left within the first twenty years of settlement, and our boom-and-bust agricultural and oil industry economy has kept people moving in and out (mostly out) ever since. Many small-town schools and pulpits operate with revolving doors, adding to the instability.

When I look at the losses we've sustained in western Dakota since 1980 (about one fifth of the population in Perkins County, where I live, and a full third in neighboring Corson County) and at the human cost in terms of anger, distrust, and grief, it is the prairie descendants of the ancient desert monastics, the monks and nuns of Benedictine communities in the Dakotas, who inspire me to hope. One of the vows a Benedictine makes is *stability:* commitment to a particular community, a particular place. If this vow is countercultural by contemporary American standards, it is countercultural in the way that life on the Plains often calls us to be. Benedictines represent continuity in the boom-and-bust cycles of the Plains; they incarnate, and can articulate, the reasons people want to stay.

Terrence Kardong, a monk at an abbey in Dakota founded roughly a thousand years after their European motherhouse, has termed the Great Plains "a school for humility," humility being one goal of Benedictine life. He writes, "in this eccentric environment . . . certainly one is made aware that things are not entirely in control." In fact, he says, the Plains offer constant reminders that "we are quite powerless over circumstance." His abbey, like many Great Plains communities with an agricultural base, had a direct experience of powerlessness, going bankrupt in the 1920s. Then, and at several other times in the community's history, the monks were urged to move to a more urban environment.

Kardong writes, "We may be crazy, but we are not necessarily stu-   *20* pid. . . . We built these buildings ourselves. We've cultivated these fields since the turn of the century. We watched from our dining room window the mirage of the Killdeer Mountains rise and fall on the horizon. We collected a library full of local history books and they belong here, not in Princeton. Fifty of our brothers lie down the hill in our cemetery. We have become as indigenous as the cottonwood trees. . . . If you take us somewhere else, we lose our character, our history—maybe our soul."

A monk does not speak lightly of the soul, and Kardong finds in the Plains the stimulus to develop an inner geography. "A monk isn't supposed to need all kinds of flashy surroundings. We're supposed to have a beautiful inner landscape. Watching a storm pass from horizon to horizon fills your soul with reverence. It makes your soul expand to fill the sky."

Monks are accustomed to taking the long view, another countercultural stance in our fast-paced, anything-for-a-buck society which has corrupted even the culture of farming into "agribusiness." Kardong and many other writers of the desert West, including myself, are really speaking of values when they find beauty in this land no one wants. He writes: "We who are permanently camped here see things you don't see at 55 m.p.h. . . . We see white-faced calves basking in the spring grass like the lilies of the field. We see a chinook wind in January make rivulets run. We see dust-devils and lots of little things. We are grateful."

The so-called emptiness of the Plains is full of such miraculous "little things." The way native grasses spring back from a drought, greening before your eyes; the way a snowy owl sits on a fencepost, or a golden eagle hunts, wings outstretched over grassland that seems to go on forever. Pelicans rise noisily from a lake; an antelope stands stock-still, its tattooed neck like a message in unbreakable code; columbines, their long stems beaten down by hail, bloom in the mud, their whimsical and delicate flowers intact. One might see a herd of white-tailed deer jumping a fence; fox cubs wrestling at the door of their lair; cock pheasants stepping out of a medieval tapestry into windrowed hay; cattle bunched in the southeast corner of a pasture, anticipating a storm in the approaching thunderheads. And above all, one notices the quiet, the near-absence of human noise.

My spiritual geography is a study in contrasts. The three places with which I have the deepest affinity are Hawaii, where I spent my adolescent years; New York City, where I worked after college; and western South Dakota. Like many Americans of their generation, my parents left their small-town roots in the 1930s and moved often. Except for the family home in Honolulu—its yard rich with fruits and flowers (pomegranate, tangerine, lime, mango, plumeria, hibiscus, lehua, ginger, and bird-of-paradise)—and my maternal grandparents' house in a remote village in western Dakota—its modest and hard-won garden offering columbine, daisies and mint—all my childhood places are gone.

When my husband and I moved nearly twenty years ago from New York to that house in South Dakota, only one wise friend in Manhattan understood the inner logic of the journey. Others, appalled, looked up Lemmon, South Dakota (named for George Lemmon, a cattleman and wheeler-dealer of the early 1900s, and home of the Petrified Wood Park—the world's largest—a gloriously eccentric example of American folk art) in their atlases and shook their heads. How could I leave the artists' and writers' community in which I worked, the diverse and stimulating environment of a great city, for such barrenness? Had I lost my mind? But I was young, still in my twenties, an apprentice poet certain of the rightness of returning to the place where I suspected I would find my stories. As it turns out, the Plains have been essential not only for my growth as a writer, they have formed me spiritually. I would even say they have made me a human being.

St. Hilary, a fourth-century bishop (and patron saint against snake bites) once wrote, "Everything that seems empty is full of the angels of God." The magnificent sky above the Plains sometimes seems to sing this truth; angels seem possible in the wind-filled expanse. A few years ago a small boy named Andy who had recently moved to the Plains from Pennsylvania told me he knew an angel named Andy Le Beau. He spelled out the name for me and I asked him if the angel had visited him here. "Don't you know?" he said in the incredulous tone children adopt when adults seem stupefyingly ignorant. "Don't you know?" he said, his voice rising, "*This* is where angels drown."

Andy no more knew that he was on a prehistoric sea bed than he knew what *le beau* means in French, but some ancient wisdom in him had sensed great danger here; a terrifying but beautiful landscape in which we are at the mercy of the unexpected, and even angels proceed at their own risk.

Reading and Responding

1. This essay begins with an epigraph from *The Wizard of Oz,* a key to Norris's thesis. Paraphrase the epigraph in a sentence or two. Then, as you read, mark two or three key passages where Norris makes the same point in her own words.
2. Norris identifies her town in South Dakota as her "spiritual geography, the place where I've wrestled my story out of the circumstances of landscape and inheritance." In a paragraph or so, explain what you think she means by this, and continue by discussing to what extent you can identify this same kind of centrally important place in the story of your own life.

Working Together

1. List the key reasons Norris finds the Dakota landscape beautiful—important, useful, good.
2. Why for Norris is this particular landscape spiritually useful? How in her view is God revealed in this landscape? To put this another way, how does this landscape make it possible for us to experience God's

presence in the world? What's the connection between the Dakota landscape and the Benedictine spirituality Norris also celebrates?

3. As a group, discuss the places that you value most highly. Are they beautiful in the ways that Norris uses that word? What three attributes (at least three, more if you wish) make places important centers of personal and cultural identity? Compose a group paragraph (at least five sentences) discussing these issues.

Rethinking and Rewriting

1. Describe a landscape, a city, a building—some place that most people pass by without thinking about, a place people actually dislike, or a place people find uninteresting. Praise this place. Argue that it's a good place. Argue that it's a good place *because* most people don't notice it or care about it.

2. Do research on the Benedictine monastic tradition. Write a paper explaining the major tenets of this way of life.

THE SOW IN THE RIVER

Mary Clearman Blew

> *Author of two collections of stories as well as a memoir, Mary Clearman Blew was born and raised in central Montana and teaches now at Lewis-Clark State College in Lewiston, Idaho. In this, the opening piece from* All but the Waltz: A Memoir of Five Generations in the Life of a Montana Family *(1992), Blew returns to a landscape rich with childhood memories, comparing those memories to the actual ground as she finds it now.* Balsamroot: A Memoir *(1995) continues these reflections.*

In the sagebrush to the north of the mountains in central Montana, where the Judith River deepens its channel and threads a slow, treacherous current between the cutbanks, a cottonwood log house still stands. It is in sight of the highway, about a mile downriver on a gravel road. From where I have turned off and stopped my car on the sunlit shoulder of the highway, I can see the house, a distant and solitary dark interruption of the sagebrush. I can even see the lone box elder tree, a dusty green shade over what used to be the yard.

I know from experience that if I were to keep driving over the cattle guard and follow the gravel road through the sage and alkali to the log house, I would find the windows gone and the door sagging and the floor rotting away. But from here the house looks hardly changed from the summer of my earliest memories, the summer before I was three, when I lived in that log house on the lower Judith with my mother and father and grandmother and my grandmother's boyfriend, Bill.

My memories seem to me as treacherous as the river. Is it possible, sitting here on this dry shoulder of a secondary highway in the middle of Montana where the brittle weeds of August scratch at the sides of the car, watching the narrow blue Judith take its time to thread and wind through the bluffs on its way to a distant northern blur, to believe in anything but today? The past eases away with the current. I cannot watch a single drop of water out of sight. How can I trust memory, which slips and wobbles and grinds its erratic furrows like a bald-tired truck fighting for traction on a wet gumbo road?

Light flickers. A kerosene lamp in the middle of the table has driven the shadows back into the corners of the kitchen. Faces and hands emerge in a circle. Bill has brought apples from the box in the dark closet. The coil of peel follows his pocketknife. I bite into the piece of quartered apple he hands me. I hear its snap, taste the juice. The shadows hold threats: mice and the shape of nameless things. But in the circle around the lamp, in the certainty of apples, I am safe.

The last of the kerosene tilts and glitters around the wick. I cower   *5*
behind Grammy on the stairs, but she boldly walks into the shadows,
which reel and retreat from her and her lamp. In her bedroom the window
reflects large pale her and timorous me. She undresses herself, undresses
me; she piles my pants and stockings on the chair with her dress and corset.
After she uses it, her pot is warm for me. Her bed is cold, then warm. I
burrow against her back and smell the smoke from the wick she has
pinched out. Bill blows his nose from his bedroom on the other side of
the landing. Beyond the eaves the shapeless creatures of sound, owls and
coyotes, have taken the night. But I am here, safe in the center.

I am in the center again on the day we look for Bill's pigs. I am
sitting between him and Grammy in the cab of the old Ford truck while
the rain sheets on the windshield. Bill found the pigpen gate open when
he went to feed the pigs this morning, their pen empty, and now they are
nowhere to be found. He has driven and driven through the sagebrush and
around the gulches, peering out through the endless gray rain as the truck
spins and growls on the gumbo in low gear. But no pigs. He and Grammy
do not speak. The cab is cold, but I am bundled well between them with
my feet on the clammy assortment of tools and nails and chains on the
floorboards and my nose just dashboard level, and I am at home with the
smell of wet wool and metal and the feel of a broken spring in the seat.

But now Bill tramps on the brakes, and he and Grammy and I gaze
through the streaming windshield at the river. The Judith has risen up its
cutbanks, and its angry gray current races the rain. I have never seen such
a Judith, such a tumult of water. But what transfixes me and Grammy and
Bill behind our teeming glass is not the ruthless condition of the river—
no, for on a bare ait at midcurrent, completely surrounded and only inches
above that muddy roiling water, huddle the pigs.

The flat top of the ait is so small that the old sow takes up most of it
by herself. The river divides and rushes around her, rising, practically at
her hooves. Surrounding her, trying to crawl under her, snorting in apprehension at the water, are her little pigs. Watching spellbound from the cab
of the truck, I can feel their small terrified rumps burrowing against her
sides, drawing warmth from her center even as more dirt crumbles under
their hooves. My surge of understanding arcs across the current, and my
flesh shrivels in the icy sheets of rain. Like the pigs I cringe at the roar of
the river, although behind the insulated walls of the cab I can hear and feel
nothing. I am in my center and they are in theirs. The current separates us
irrevocably, and suddenly I understand that my center is as precarious as
theirs, that the chill metal cab of the old truck is almost as fragile as their
ring of crumbling sod.

And then the scene darkens and I see no more.

For years I would watch for the ait. When I was five my family   *10*
moved, but I learned to snatch a glimpse whenever we drove past our old

turnoff on the road from Lewistown to Denton. The ait was in plain view, just a hundred yards downriver from the highway, as it is today. *Ait* was a fancy word I learned afterward. It was a fifteen-foot-high steep-sided, flat-topped pinnacle of dirt left standing in the bed of the river after years of wind and water erosion. And I never caught sight of it without the same small thrill of memory: that's where the pigs were.

One day I said it out loud. I was grown by then. "That's where the pigs were."

My father was driving. We would have crossed the Judith River bridge, and I would have turned my head to keep sight of the ait and the lazy blue threads of water around the sandbars.

My father said, "What pigs?"

"The old sow and her pigs," I said, surprised. "The time the river flooded. I remember how the water rose right up to their feet."

My father said, "The Judith never got that high, and there never was   *15* any pigs up there."

"Yes there were! I remember!" I could see the little pigs as clearly as I could see my father, and I could remember exactly how my own skin had shriveled as they cringed back from the water and butted the sow for cold comfort.

My father shook his head. "How did you think pigs would get up there?" he asked.

Of course they couldn't.

His logic settled on me like an awakening in ordinary daylight. Of course a sow could not lead nine or ten suckling pigs up those sheer fifteen-foot crumbling dirt sides, even for fear of their lives. And why, after all, would pigs even try to scramble to the top of such a precarious perch when they could escape a cloudburst by following any one of the cattle trails or deer trails that webbed the cutbanks on both sides of the river?

Had there been a cloudburst at all? Had there been pigs?   *20*

No, my father repeated. The Judith had never flooded anywhere near that high in our time. Bill Hafer had always raised a few pigs when we lived down there on the river, but he kept them penned up. No.

Today I lean on the open window of my car and yawn and listen to the sounds of late summer. The snapping of grasshoppers. Another car approaching on the highway, roaring past my shoulder of the road, then fading away until I can hear the faint scratches of some small hidden creature in the weeds. I am bone-deep in landscape. In this dome of sky and river and undeflected sunlight, in this illusion of timelessness, I can almost feel my body, blood, and breath in the broken line of the bluffs and the pervasive scent of ripening sweet clover and dust, almost feel the sagging fence line of ancient cedar posts stapled across my vitals.

The only shade in sight is across the river where box elders lean over a low white frame house with a big modern house trailer parked behind it. Downstream, far away, a man works along a ditch. I think he might be the husband of a second cousin of mine who still lives on her old family place. My cousins wouldn't know me if they stopped and asked me what I was doing here.

Across the highway, a trace of a road leads through a barbed-wire gate and sharply up the bluff. It is the old cutoff to Danvers, a town that has dried up and blown away. I have heard that the cutoff has washed out, further up the river, but down here it still holds a little bleached gravel. Almost as though my father might turn off in his battered truck at fifteen miles an hour, careful of his bald wartime tires, while I lie on the seat with my head on his thigh and take my nap. Almost as though at the end of that road will be the two grain elevators pointing sharply out of the hazy olives and ochers of the grass into the rolling cumulus, and two or three graveled streets with traffic moving past the pool hall and post office and dug-out store where, when I wake from my nap and scramble down from the high seat of the truck, Old Man Longin will be waiting behind his single glass display case with my precious wartime candy bar.

Yes, that little girl was me, I guess. A three-year-old standing on the unswept board floor, looking up at rows of canned goods on shelves that were nailed against the logs in the 1880s, when Montana was still a territory. The dust smelled the same to her as it does to me now.

Across the river, that low white frame house where my cousin still lives is the old Sample place. Ninety years ago a man named Sample fell in love with a woman named Carrie. Further up the bottom—you can't see it from here because of the cottonwoods—stands Carrie's deserted house in what used to be a fenced yard. Forty years ago Carrie's house was full of three generations of her family, and the yard was full of cousins at play. Sixty years ago the young man who would be my father rode on horseback down that long hill to Carrie's house, and Sample said to Carrie, *Did your brother Albert ever have a son? From the way the kid sits his horse, he must be your brother's son.*

Or so the story goes. Sample was murdered. Carrie died in her sleep. My father died of exposure.

The Judith winds toward its mouth. Its current seems hardly to move. Seeing it in August, so blue and unhurried, it is difficult to believe how many drownings or near drownings the Judith has counted over the years. To a stranger it surely must look insignificant, hardly worth calling a river.

In 1805 the explorers Lewis and Clark, pausing in their quest for the Pacific, saw the mountains and the prairies of central Montana and the wild game beyond reckoning. They also noted this river, which they named after a girl. Lewis and Clark were the first white recorders of this place. In recording it, they altered it. However indifferent to the historical record, those who see this river and hear its name, *Judith,* see it in a slightly different way because Lewis and Clark saw it and wrote about it.

In naming the river, Lewis and Clark claimed it for a system of   *30*
governance that required a wrenching of the fundamental connections
between landscape and its inhabitants. This particular drab sagebrush
pocket of the West was never, perhaps, holy ground. None of the landmarks here is invested with the significance of the sacred buttes to the
north. For the Indian tribes that hunted here, central Montana must have
been commonplace, a familiar stretch of their lives, a place to ride and
breathe and be alive.

But even this drab pocket is now a part of the history of the West,
which, through a hundred and fifty years of white settlement and economic development, of rapid depletion of water and coal and timber and
topsoil, of dependence upon military escalation and federal subsidies, has
been a history of the transformation of landscape from a place to be alive
in into a place to own. This is a transformation that breaks connections,
that holds little in common. My deepest associations with this sunlit river
are private. Without a connection between outer and inner landscape, I
cannot tell my father what I saw. "There never was a sow in the river," he
said, embarrassed at my notion. And yet I know there was a sow in the
river.

All who come and go bring along their own context, leave their
mark, however faint. If the driver glanced out the window of that car that
just roared past, what did he see? Tidy irrigated alfalfa fields, a small green
respite from the dryland miles? That foreshortened man who works along
the ditch, does he straighten his back from his labors and see his debts
spread out in irrigation pipes and electric pumps?

It occurs to me that I dreamed the sow in the river at a time when I
was too young to sort out dreams from daylight reality or to question why
they should be sorted out and dismissed. As I think about it, the episode
does contain some of the characteristics of a dream. That futile, endless,
convoluted search in the rain, for example. The absence of sound in the
cab of the truck, and the paralysis of the onlookers on the brink of that
churning current. For now that I know she never existed outside my
imagination, I think I do recognize that sow on her slippery pinnacle.

Memory lights upon a dream as readily as an external event, upon a
set of rusty irrigation pipes and a historian's carefully detailed context
through which she recalls the collective memory of the past. As memory
saves, discards, retrieves, fails to retrieve, its logic may well be analogous to
the river's inexorable search for the lowest ground. The trivial and the
profound roll like leaves to the surface. Every ripple is suspect.

Today the Judith River spreads out in the full sunlight of August,   *35*
oblivious of me and my precious associations, indifferent to the emotional
context I have framed it with. My memory seems less a record of landscape
and event than a superimposition upon what otherwise would continue to
flow, leaf out, or crumble according to its lot. What I remember is far less

trustworthy than the story I tell about it. The possibility for connection lies in story.

Whether or not I dreamed her, the sow in the river is my story. She is what I have saved, up there on her pinnacle where the river roils.

Reading and Responding

In this essay, Blew is driving to a place that holds significance for her; as the essay opens, she pulls off the road so she can think. If you were driving to some place that holds significance for you, where would you be going? Where would you pull off the road to think? What would you think about? Write freely about these questions for a page or so.

Working Together

1. Summarize the story of the sow in the river with her offspring (the second section of this essay). Who's watching this little drama, and what do you know about her? What does she see, and how is she affected by what she sees? Concentrate only on this second section of the essay.
2. Look only at the third section of this essay. What just happened? What did the narrator learn from her father? As a group, write two or three sentences that explain what just happened. Write from Blew's point of view.
3. In the last section of this essay Blew explains the contradiction at its center, and she says "The possibility for connection lies in story." What does she mean? Write a group paragraph that explains it. If, as a group, you're too puzzled by the statement, write a list of questions that express what puzzles you in the essay.

Rethinking and Rewriting

1. At the end of this essay Blew keeps her story about the sow in the river; that is, she doesn't shrug it off as a mistake—something childish and foolish that she imagined. Write an essay that explains why she keeps the story even though she knows from her father that it never really happened.
2. Write your own essay based on "The Sow in the River," using your own personal experience. Divide your essay into at least three sections. Begin with your main character en route to some important place (as Blew begins her essay).
3. Using your own experience and Blew's essay, argue that our personal histories are inevitably caught up with the landscapes that we know best, the landscapes in which we had our most important childhood experiences.

SACRED AND ANCESTRAL GROUND

N. Scott Momaday

> *Part Kiowa and part Cherokee, N. Scott Momaday has written two novels, including* House Made of Dawn *(1968), winner of the Pulitzer Prize; several collections of poetry; and numerous essays and nonfiction books, including his best-known book,* The Way to Rainy Mountain *(1969), a collage of Kiowa legends and autobiographical stories. His collection of essays,* The Man Made of Words, *was published in 1997. Momaday teaches at the University of Arizona. In the following essay, Momaday returns to an important place in the history of his ancestors.*

There is great good in returning to a landscape that has had extraordinary meaning in one's life. It happens that we return to such places in our minds irresistibly. There are certain villages and towns, mountains and plains that, having seen them, walked in them, lived in them, even for a day, we keep forever in the mind's eye. They become indispensable to our well-being; they define us, and we say: I am who I am because I have been there, or there. There is good, too, in actual, physical return.

Some years ago I made a pilgrimage into the heart of North America. I began the journey proper in western Montana. From there I traveled across the high plains of Wyoming into the Black Hills, then southward to the southern plains, to a cemetery at Rainy Mountain, in Oklahoma. It was a journey made by my Kiowa ancestors long before. In the course of their migration they became a people of the Great Plains, and theirs was the last culture to evolve in North America. They had been for untold generations a mountain tribe of hunters. Their ancient nomadism, which had determined their way of life even before they set foot on this continent, perhaps 30,000 years ago, was raised to its highest level of expression when they entered upon the Great Plains and acquired horses. Their migration brought them to a Golden Age. At the beginning of their journey they were a people of hard circumstances, often hungry and cold, fighting always for sheer survival. At its end, and for a hundred years, they were the lords of the land, a daring race of centaurs and buffalo hunters whose love of freedom and space was profound.

Recently I returned to the old migration route of the Kiowas. I had in me a need to behold again some of the principal landmarks of that long, prehistoric quest, to descend again from the mountain to the plain.

With my close friend Charles, a professor of American literature at a South Dakota university, I headed north to the Montana-Wyoming border. I wanted to intersect the Kiowa migration route at the Bighorn Medicine Wheel, high in the Bighorn Mountains. We ascended to 8,000 feet gradually, on a well-maintained but winding highway. Then we climbed sharply, bearing upon the timberline. Although the plain below had been comfortable, even warm at midday, the mountain air was cold, and much of the ground was covered with snow. We turned off the pavement, on a dirt road that led three miles to the Medicine Wheel. The road was forbidding, it was narrow and winding, and the grades were steep and slippery; here and there the shoulders fell away into deep ravines. But at the same time something wonderful happened: we crossed the line between civilization and wilderness. Suddenly the earth persisted in its original being. Directly in front of us a huge white-tailed buck crossed our path, ambling without haste into a thicket of pines. As we drove over his tracks we saw four does above on the opposite bank, looking down at us, their great black eyes bright and benign, curious. There seemed no wariness, nothing of fear or alienation. Their presence was a good omen, we thought; somehow in their attitude they bade us welcome to their sphere of wilderness.

There was a fork in the road, and we took the wrong branch. At a   5 steep, hairpin curve we got out of the car and climbed to the top of a peak. An icy wind whipped at us; we were among the bald summits of the Bighorns. Great flumes of sunlit snow erupted on the ridges and dissolved in spangles on the sky. Across a deep saddle we caught sight of the Medicine Wheel. It was perhaps two miles away.

When we returned to the car we saw another vehicle approaching. It was a very old Volkswagen bus, in much need of repair, cosmetic repair, at least. Out stepped a thin, bearded young man in thick glasses. He wore a wool cap, a down parka, jeans and well-worn hiking boots. "I am looking for Medicine Wheel," he said, having nodded to us. He spoke softly, with a pronounced accent. His name was Jürg, and he was from Switzerland; he had been traveling for some months in Canada and the United States. Chuck and I shook his hand and told him to follow us, and we drove down into the saddle. From there we climbed on foot to the Medicine Wheel.

The Medicine Wheel is a ring of stones, some 80 feet in diameter. Stone spokes radiate from the center to the circumference. Cairns are placed at certain points on the circumference, one in the center and one just outside the ring to the southwest. We do not know as a matter of fact who made this wheel or to what purpose. It has been proposed that it was an astronomical observatory, a solar calendar and the ground design of a Kiowa sun dance lodge. What we know without doubt is that it is a sacred expression, an equation of man's relation to the cosmos.

There was a great calm upon that place. The hard, snowbearing wind that had burned our eyes and skin only minutes before had died away altogether. The sun was warm and bright, and there was a profound silence. On the wire fence that had been erected to enclose and protect the wheel were fixed offerings, small prayer bundles. Chuck and Jürg and I walked about slowly, standing for long moments here and there, looking into the wheel or out across the great distances. We did not say much; there was little to be said. But we were deeply moved by the spirit of that place. The silence was such that it must be observed. To the north we could see down to the timberline, to the snowfields and draws that marked the black planes of forest among the peaks of the Bighorns. To the south and west the mountains fell abruptly to the plains. We could see thousands of feet down and a hundred miles across the dim expanse.

When we were about to leave, I took from my pocket an eagle-bone whistle that my father had given me, and I blew it in the four directions. The sound was very high and shrill, and it did not break the essential silence. As we were walking down we saw far below, crossing our path, a coyote sauntering across the snow into a wall of trees. It was just there, a wild being to catch sight of, and then it was gone. The wilderness which had admitted us with benediction, with benediction let us go.

When we came within a stone's throw of the highway, Chuck and I 10 said goodbye to Jürg, but not before Jürg had got out his camp stove and boiled water for tea. There in the dusk we enjoyed a small ceremonial feast of tea and crackers. The three of us had become friends. Only later did I begin to understand the extraordinary character of that friendship. It was the friendship of those who come together in recognition of the sacred. If we never meet again, I thought, we shall not forget this day.

On the plains the fences and roads and windmills and houses seemed almost negligible, all but overwhelmed by the earth and sky. It is a landscape of great clarity; its vastness is that of the ocean. It is the near revelation of infinity. Antelope were everywhere in the grassy folds, grazing side by side with horses and cattle. Hawks sailed above, and crows scattered before us. The place names were American—Tensleep, Buffalo, Dull Knife, Crazy Woman, Spotted Horse.

The Black Hills are an isolated and ancient group of mountains in South Dakota and Wyoming. They lie very close to both the geographic center of the United States (including Alaska and Hawaii) and the geographic center of the North American continent. They form an island, an elliptical area of nearly 6,000 square miles, in the vast sea of grasses that is the northern Great Plains. The Black Hills form a calendar of geologic time that is truly remarkable. The foundation rocks of these mountains are older than much of the sedimentary layer of which the Americas are primarily composed. An analysis of this foundation, made in 1975, indicates an age of between two billion and three billion years.

A documented record of exploration in this region is found in the Lewis and Clark journals, 1804–6. The first white party known definitely to have entered the Black Hills proper was led by Jedediah Smith in 1823. The diary of this expedition, kept by one James Clyman, is notable. Clyman reports a confrontation between Jedediah Smith and a grizzly bear, in which Smith lost one of his ears. There is also reported the discovery of a petrified ("putrified," as Clyman has it) forest, where petrified birds sing petrified songs.

Toward the end of the century, after rumors of gold had made the Black Hills a name known throughout the country, Gen. (then Lieut. Col.)

George Armstrong Custer led an expedition from Fort Abraham Lincoln into the Black Hills in July and August, 1874. The Custer expedition traveled 600 miles in 60 days. Custer reported proof of gold, but he had an eye to other things as well:

> Every step of our march that day was amid flowers of the most exquisite colors and perfume. So luxuriant in growth were they that men plucked them without dismounting from the saddle. . . . It was a strange sight to glance back at the advancing columns of cavalry and behold the men with beautiful bouquets in their hands, while the headgear of the horses was decorated with wreaths of flowers fit to crown a queen of May. Deeming it a most fitting appellation, I named this Floral Valley.

In the evening of that same day, sitting at mess in a meadow, the   *15* officers competed to see how many different flowers could be picked by each man, without leaving his seat. Seven varieties were gathered so. Some 50 different flowers were blooming then in Floral Valley.

The Lakota, or Teton Sioux, called these mountains Paha Sapa, "Hills That Are Black." Other tribes, besides the Kiowa and the Sioux, thought of the Black Hills as sacred ground, a place crucial in their past. The Arapaho lived here. So did the Cheyenne. Bear Butte, near Sturgis, S.D., on the northeast edge of the Black Hills, is the Cheyenne's sacred mountain. It remains, like the Medicine Wheel, a place of the greatest spiritual intensity. So great was thought to be the power inherent in the Black Hills that the Indians did not camp there. It was a place of rendezvous, a hunting ground, but above all inviolate, a place of thunder and lightning, a dwelling place of the gods.

On the edge of the Black Hills nearest the Bighorn Mountains is Devils Tower, the first of our National Monuments. The Lakotas called it Mateo Tepee, "Grizzly Bear Lodge." The Kiowas called it Tsoai, "Rock Tree." Devils Tower is a great monolith that rises high above the timber of the Black Hills. In conformation it closely resembles the stump of a tree. It is a cluster of rock columns (phonolite porphyry) 1,000 feet across at the base and 275 feet across the top. It rises 865 feet above the high ground on which it stands and 1,280 feet above the Belle Fourche River, in the valley below.

It has to be seen to be believed. "There are things in nature that engender an awful quiet in the heart of man; Devils Tower is one of them." I wrote these words almost 20 years ago. They remain true to my experience. Each time I behold this Tsoai, I am more than ever in awe of it.

Two hundred years ago, more or less, the Kiowas came upon this place. They were moved to tell a story about it:

Eight children were there at play, seven sisters and their brother.   *20* Suddenly the boy was struck dumb; he trembled and began to run upon his hands and feet. His fingers became claws and his body was covered with fur. Directly there was a bear where the boy had been. The sisters were terrified; they ran, and the bear ran after them. They came to the stump of a great tree, and the tree spoke to them. It bade them climb upon it, and as they did so it began to rise into the air. The bear came to kill them, but they were just beyond its reach. It reared against the tree and scored the bark all around with its claws. The seven sisters were borne into the sky, and they became the stars of the Big Dipper.

This story, which I have known from the time I could first understand language, exemplifies the sacred for me. The storyteller, that anonymous, illiterate man who told the story for the first time, succeeded in raising the human condition to the level of universal significance. Not only did he account for the existence of the rock tree, but in the process he related his human race to the stars.

When Chuck and I had journeyed over this ground together, when we were about to go our separate ways, I reminded him of our friend Jürg, knowing well enough that I needn't have: Jürg was on our minds. He had touched us deeply with his trust, not unlike that of the wild animals we had seen. I can't account for it. Jürg had touched us deeply with his generosity of spirit, his concern to see beneath the surface of things, his attitude of free, direct, disinterested kindness.

"Did he tell us what he does?" I asked. "Does he have a profession?"

"I don't think he said," Chuck replied. "I think he's a pilgrim."

"Yes."   25

"Yes."

Reading and Responding

1. Copy out the first paragraph of this essay in your own writing. Then write a paragraph of your own that responds to it, discussing what it makes you think about.
2. Copy out any paragraph in this essay—except the first—in your own writing. Then write a paragraph of your own, talking about why you chose to copy the paragraph you did.

Working Together

1. Read to each other your responses to the first paragraph of Momaday's essay. On the basis of your individual responses, write a group paragraph explaining your group's response.
2. As a group, review the various places where Momaday uses the word *sacred*. As you look at these places, make a list of characteristics that go with *sacred*.
3. Reread the Kiowa story that accounts for the Big Dipper. Suppose that some students in class don't understand why the story is important. (For example, they think it just sounds childish.) As a group, figure out how

you'd explain to these classmates what makes the story work and why it's powerful. (*Hint:* Pay attention to the paragraph following the story.)

Rethinking and Rewriting

1. Write a three- to five-page letter that you would send to Momaday. In your letter, explain where you might go or the journey you might take to imitate the return that Momaday speaks of. If you have no such journey or place to talk about, then explain your situation as simply and clearly as you can. Once you finish the letter, add a postscript to your instructor. In the postscript, briefly tell your instructor what it was like to write this letter.
2. Research a native people who once lived where your campus is now (or who lived nearby or near your hometown). What is known about these people, and what happened to them? If you can find a story from their culture, include it in your paper. (Remember to consider not just print sources but also living ones.)
3. Tell a story from your own familial or cultural background. Introduce the story with only a few sentences, tell the story itself, and then add whatever commentary or explanation is needed to make the story and its importance clear to readers outside your family or your culture.

ON GOING HOME

Joan Didion

> *Although she is the author of several novels, Joan Didion is best known for her brilliantly imagistic essays about her own experience and the crises of American culture. Her essays have been collected in several books, including* Slouching Towards Bethlehem *(1968) and* The White Album *(1979). Her latest work is* Miami *(1998), a portrait of the Florida city. "On Going Home" was first published in 1967.*

I am home for my daughter's first birthday. By "home" I do not mean the house in Los Angeles where my husband and I and the baby live, but the place where my family is, in the Central Valley of California. It is a vital although troublesome distinction. My husband likes my family but is uneasy in their house, because once there I fall into their ways, which are difficult, oblique, deliberately inarticulate, not my husband's ways. We live in dusty houses ("D-U-S-T," he once wrote with his finger on surfaces all over the house, but no one noticed it) filled with mementos quite without value to him (what could the Canton dessert plates mean to him? how could he have known about the assay scales, why should he care if he did know?), and we appear to talk exclusively about people we know who have been committed to mental hospitals, about people we know who have been booked on drunk-driving charges, and about property, particularly about property, land, price per acre and C-2 zoning and assessments and freeway access. My brother does not understand my husband's inability to perceive the advantage in the rather common real-estate transaction known as "sale-leaseback," and my husband in turn does not understand why so many of the people he hears about in my father's house have recently been committed to mental hospitals or booked on drunk-driving charges. Nor does he understand that when we talk about sale-leasebacks and right-of-way condemnations we are talking in code about the things we like best, the yellow fields and the cottonwoods and the rivers rising and falling and the mountain roads closing when the heavy snow comes in. We miss each other's points, have another drink and regard the fire. My brother refers to my husband, in his presence, as "Joan's husband." Marriage is the classic betrayal.

Or perhaps it is not any more. Sometimes I think that those of us who are now in our thirties were born into the last generation to carry the burden of "home," to find in family life the source of all tension and drama. I had by all objective accounts a "normal" and a "happy" family situation, and yet I was almost thirty years old before I could talk to my family on the telephone without crying after I had hung up. We did not fight. Nothing was wrong. And yet some nameless anxiety colored the emotional charges between me and the place that I came from. The question of whether or not you could go home again was a very real part of the sentimental and largely literary baggage with which we left home in the fifties; I suspect that it is irrelevant to the children born of the fragmentation after World War II. A few weeks ago in a San Francisco bar I saw a pretty young girl on crystal take off her clothes and dance for the cash prize in an "amateur-topless" contest. There was no particular sense of moment about this, none of the effect of romantic degradation, of "dark journey," for which my generation strived so assiduously. What sense could that girl possibly make of, say, *Long Day's Journey into Night?* Who is beside the point?

That I am trapped in this particular irrelevancy is never more apparent to me than when I am home. Paralyzed by the neurotic lassitude engendered by meeting one's past at every turn, around every corner, inside every cupboard, I go aimlessly from room to room. I decide to meet it head-on and clean out a drawer, and I spread the contents on the bed. A bathing suit I wore the summer I was seventeen. A letter of rejection from *The Nation,* an aerial photograph of the site for a shopping center my father did not build in 1954. Three teacups hand-painted with cabbage roses and signed "E.M.," my grandmother's initials. There is no final solution for letters of rejection from *The Nation* and teacups handpainted in 1900. Nor is there any answer to snapshots of one's grandfather as a young man on skis, surveying around Donner Pass in the year 1910. I smooth out the snapshot and look into his face, and do and do not see my own. I close the drawer, and have another cup of coffee with my mother. We get along very well, veterans of a guerrilla war we never understood.

Days pass. I see no one. I come to dread my husband's evening call, not only because he is full of news of what by now seems to me our remote life in Los Angeles, people he has seen, letters which require attention, but because he asks what I have been doing, suggests uneasily that I get out, drive to San Francisco or Berkeley. Instead I drive across the river to a family graveyard. It has been vandalized since my last visit and the monuments are broken, overturned in the dry grass. Because I once saw a rattlesnake in the grass I stay in the car and listen to a country-and-Western station. Later I drive with my father to a ranch he has in the foothills. The man who runs his cattle on it asks us to the roundup, a week from Sunday, and although I know that I will be in Los Angeles I say, in the oblique way my family talks, that I will come. Once home I mention the broken monuments in the graveyard. My mother shrugs.

I go to visit my great-aunts. A few of them think now that I am my   5 cousin, or their daughter who died young. We recall an anecdote about a relative last seen in 1948, and they ask if I still like living in New York City. I have lived in Los Angeles for three years, but I say that I do. The baby is offered a horehound drop, and I am slipped a dollar bill "to buy a treat." Questions trail off, answers are abandoned, the baby plays with the dust motes in a shaft of afternoon sun.

It is time for the baby's birthday party: a white cake, strawberry-marshmallow ice cream, a bottle of champagne saved from another party. In the evening, after she has gone to sleep, I kneel beside the crib and touch her face, where it is pressed against the slats, with mine. She is an open and trusting child, unprepared for and unaccustomed to the ambushes of family life, and perhaps it is just as well that I can offer her little of that life. I would like to give her more. I would like to promise her that she will grow up with a sense of her cousins and of rivers and of her great-grandmother's teacups, would like to pledge her a picnic on a river with fried chicken and her hair uncombed, would like to give her *home* for her birthday, but we live differently now and I can promise her nothing like that. I give her a xylophone and a sundress from Madeira, and promise to tell her a funny story.

Reading and Responding

1. When someone asks you where you're from, how do you answer? Do you feel like you're really from some particular place, or is your routine answer just a way to make conversation? Explain.
2. Use metaphors to describe the voice or tone of the essay: What clothes does the writing wear? What is the weather in this essay? What kind of music is this writing most like?
3. Use metaphors to describe, in particular, the rhythm of Didion's sentences: fast or slow, hard or soft, like a clarinet or like a drum, and so on.
4. Find a sentence in this essay that seems to match something in your experience or your thinking; then find a sentence that seems quite different from your experience or your thinking. Copy each sentence, and write a paragraph that explains your choices.

Working Together

1. Outline this piece by using the TRIAC scheme. What do you notice? What slot does it fill most often? What slot does it fill least? What does this tell you about the experience of reading Didion's essay? What does it demand?
2. Take a piece of paper and draw a line down the middle from top to bottom. On the left side, write "Los Angeles—husband and I and baby." On the right side, write "Central Valley—where my family is." Now as a group, start listing the characteristics of these two places as you see them described.
3. Within your group, discuss whether you have a sense of home. If you don't have a sense of home, can you figure out why you don't? If you do have a sense of home, how do you account for that? Write a group paragraph that describes the responses in your group.

Rethinking and Rewriting

1. Write an essay of your own called "On Going Home."
2. Write an essay about how your experience differs from Didion's. Show how you're not similar. Or write an essay that shows how your experience actually echoes Didion's; show how your experience and Didion's agree in substantial ways. Whichever direction you take, make sure that your essay talks about your experience in clear, detailed ways and that it discusses your experience in comparison to Didion's.
3. At the end of her essay Didion wishes she could give her daughter a sense of home. So the essay ends by expressing sadness and regret. Write an essay of your own that aims to cheer up Joan Didion. Tell her why feeling less attachment to home might actually be a good thing.
4. Re-create a day (or part of a day) at home. Or re-create a time when you actually felt at home. Pack your essay with descriptions of that place and time.

Chapter 2 Essay Topics

1. Use two of the readings in this chapter as a starting point to help you explain your own concept of home. After reading your essay, your readers should understand home as you see it and as you feel toward it both as a place (or places) and as an idea. Don't feel that you must write a "feel-good" view of home. Simply try to tell the truth as you know it and have experienced it. Make this a personal essay that describes your home's location(s) and its people. But also show how your own experience compares to or relates to that presented in the two essays you choose. Quote at least once from each of the two essays.
2. Interview someone you know well—a family member or close friend—to learn as much as you can about that person's view of home. Compare that person's experiences and views with those presented in at least two of the essays in this chapter. Concentrate on painting as clear a picture of home as your interviewee will let you see. Quote often, if that will help your readers understand the person's experience. End this essay by discussing what you learned as an interviewer. What surprised you about this activity? What made you think more about home? What reinforced what you already thought?
3. Write an essay of return, of going home after being away for a while. Give your readers a sense of what that return was like—of what seemed different and what seemed the same. Compare your experience to that presented in at least two of the essays in this chapter so that your readers will more fully understand you. Quote from each of these essays at least once. Pay attention to two sources: (a) the physical changes you can see in places and in people, and (b) the changes in character, values, and experience you see in yourself. Make sure readers understand these changes at least as well as you do.

4. Write an essay celebrating an environment constructed by humans—the suburb, town, or large city you grew up in; the campus of your university; a highway; a car; and so on. Do your celebrating through description of physical elements and include several brief quotations from at least two of the readings in this chapter. Or write an essay condemning a specific environment constructed by humans, taking the same descriptive approach.

5. Draw on both your own experience and your reading experience of at least three of the essays in this chapter and use this knowledge to discuss the role of the car in society. How does the car help determine our lives and our experiences? How does it help determine the landscapes we live in and work in? Draw a conclusion that's new to you—something that you see now or understand now more clearly, precisely because you've done these readings and worked on this essay.

3

Where Wilderness Begins

    From the time we can crawl, we have the urge to explore whatever surrounds us, to investigate what we have not yet seen with our own eyes or heard with our own ears. Very soon, these explorations take us outside the physical structures of home. And, although most of us live amid pavement, freeways, parking lots, neon lights, and noise, even in cities we crave parks with lawns and trees, ponds. We seek the solitude and quiet that lets us hear ourselves think. We seek to reawaken our essential connection with other living things that share the air, the water, the ground.

    The readings in this chapter all show individuals acting on the impulse to seek the experience of landscape still relatively unaffected by human beings. We go toward wilderness—to be our own company for a while, to listen to fewer voices, and we do. We go toward wilderness to see it, and we do.

WALKING ON

WALKING

Henry David Thoreau

> *Henry David Thoreau's* Walden, or Life in the Woods *(1854) is one*
> *of the most important books in American literature. Its account of an attempt*
> *to live a simpler, spare life in the woods haunts all of the nature writing done*
> *since. The following excerpt from* Walking, *written shortly before Thoreau's*
> *death in 1862, contains the famous statement that "in Wildness is the*
> *preservation of the World."*

The West of which I speak is but another name for the Wild; and
what I have been preparing to say is, that in Wildness is the preservation
of the World. Every tree sends its fibres forth in search of the Wild. The
cities import it at any price. Men plough and sail for it. From the forest
and wilderness come the tonics and barks which brace mankind. Our
ancestors were savages. The story of Romulus and Remus being suckled
by a wolf is not a meaningless fable. The founders of every State which has
risen to eminence have drawn their nourishment and vigor from a similar
wild source. It was because the children of the Empire were not suckled
by the wolf that they were conquered and displaced by the children of the
Northern forests who were.

I believe in the forest, and in the meadow, and in the night in which
the corn grows. We require an infusion of hemlock-spruce or arborvitæ in
our tea. There is a difference between eating and drinking for strength and
from mere gluttony. The Hottentots eagerly devour the marrow of the
koodoo and other antelopes raw, as a matter of course. Some of our
Northern Indians eat raw the marrow of the Arctic reindeer, as well as
various other parts, including the summits of the antlers, as long as they
are soft. And herein, perchance, they have stolen a march on the cooks of
Paris. They get what usually goes to feed the fire. This is probably better
than stall-fed beef and slaughter-house pork to make a man of. Give me a
wildness whose glance no civilization can endure,—as if we lived on the
marrow of koodoos devoured raw.

There are some intervals which border the strain of the wood-thrush,
to which I would migrate,—wild lands where no settler has squatted; to
which, methinks, I am already acclimated.

The African hunter Cummings tells us that the skin of the eland, as
well as that of most other antelopes just killed, emits the most delicious
perfume of trees and grass. I would have every man so much like a wild
antelope, so much a part and parcel of Nature, that his very person should
thus sweetly advertise our senses of his presence, and remind us of those
parts of Nature which he most haunts. I feel no disposition to be satirical,

when the trapper's coat emits the odor of musquash even; it is a sweeter scent to me than that which commonly exhales from the merchant's or the scholar's garments. When I go into their wardrobes and handle their vestments, I am reminded of no grassy plains and flowery meads which they have frequented, but of dusty merchants' exchanges and libraries rather.

A tanned skin is something more than respectable, and perhaps olive is a fitter color than white for a man,—a denizen of the woods. "The pale white man!" I do not wonder that the African pitied him. Darwin the naturalist says, "A white man bathing by the side of a Tahitian was like a plant bleached by the gardener's art, compared with a fine, dark green one, growing vigorously in the open fields."

Ben Jonson exclaims,—

"How near to good is what is fair!"

So I would say,—

How near to good is what is *wild!*

[handwritten annotation: → is wilderness to superious to civilization?]

Life consists with wildness. The most alive is the wildest. Not yet subdued to man, its presence refreshes him. One who pressed forward incessantly and never rested from his labors, who grew fast and made infinite demands on life, would always find himself in a new country or wilderness, and surrounded by the raw material of life. He would be climbing over the prostrate stems of primitive forest-trees.

Hope and the future for me are not in lawns and cultivated fields, not in towns and cities, but in the impervious and quaking swamps. When, formerly, I have analyzed my partiality for some farm which I had contemplated purchasing, I have frequently found that I was attracted solely by a few square rods of impermeable and unfathomable bog,—a natural sink in one corner of it. That was the jewel which dazzled me. I derive more of my subsistence from the swamps which surround my native town than from the cultivated gardens in the village. There are no richer parterres to my eyes than the dense beds of dwarf andromeda (*Cassandra calyculata*) which cover these tender places on the earth's surface. Botany cannot go farther than tell me the names of the shrubs which grow there,—the high-blueberry, panicled andromeda, lamb-kill, azalea, and rhodora,—all standing in the quaking sphagnum. I often think that I should like to have my house front on this mass of dull red bushes, omitting other flower plots and borders, transplanted spruce and trim box, even gravelled walks,—to have this fertile spot under my windows, not a few imported barrow-fulls of soil only to cover the sand which was thrown out in digging the cellar. Why not put my house, my parlor, behind this plot, instead of behind that meagre assemblage of curiosities, that poor apology for a Nature and Art, which I call my front-yard? It is an effort to clear up and make a decent appearance when the carpenter and mason have departed, though done as much for the passer-by as the dweller within. The most tasteful front-yard fence was never an agreeable object of study to me; the most elaborate ornaments, acorn-tops, or what not, soon wearied and disgusted me. Bring your sills up to the very edge of the swamp, then, (though it may not be the best place for a dry cellar,) so that there be no access on that side to citizens. Front-yards are not made to walk in, but, at most, through, and you could go in the back way.

Yes, though you may think me perverse, if it were proposed to me to dwell in the neighborhood of the most beautiful garden that ever human art contrived, or else of a Dismal swamp, I should certainly decide for the swamp. How vain, then, have been all your labors, citizens, for me!

My spirits infallibly rise in proportion to the outward dreariness. Give me the ocean, the desert or the wilderness! In the desert, pure air and solitude compensate for want of moisture and fertility. The traveller Burton says of it,—"Your *morale* improves; you become frank and cordial, hospitable and single-minded. . . . In the desert, spirituous liquors excite only disgust. There is a keen enjoyment in a mere animal existence." They who have been travelling long on the steppes of Tartary say,—"On reëntering cultivated lands, the agitation, perplexity, and turmoil of civilization oppressed and suffocated us; the air seemed to fail us, and we felt every moment as if about to die of asphyxia." When I would recreate myself, I seek the darkest wood, the thickest and most interminable, and, to the citizen, most dismal swamp. I enter a swamp as a sacred place,—a *sanctum sanctorum*. There is the strength, the marrow of Nature. The wild-wood covers the virgin mould,—and the same soil is good for men and for trees. A man's health requires as many acres of meadow to his prospect as his farm does loads of muck. There are the strong meats on which he feeds. A town is saved, not more by the righteous men in it than by the woods and swamps that surround it. A township where one primitive forest waves above, while another primitive forest rots below,—such a town is fitted to raise not only corn and potatoes, but poets and philosophers for the coming ages. In such a soil grew Homer and Confucius and the rest, and out of such a wilderness comes the Reformer eating locusts and wild honey.

To preserve wild animals implies generally the creation of a forest for them to dwell in or resort to. So it is with man. A hundred years ago they sold bark in our streets peeled from our own woods. In the very aspect of those primitive and rugged trees, there was, methinks, a tanning principle which hardened and consolidated the fibres of men's thoughts. Ah! already I shudder for these comparatively degenerate days of my native village, when you cannot collect a load of bark of good thickness,—and we no longer produce tar and turpentine.

10

Reading and Responding

1. When you feel frustrated or downhearted, what do you do to take your mind off your troubles? Are you a walker? Write a few paragraphs or so

that tell what you do to recover what Thoreau calls "hope and the future."

2. Write a brief piece (about half a page) that disagrees with Thoreau and instead praises human company and human society.

Working Together

1. As a group, design a poster illustrating the idea that "in Wildness is the preservation of the World."
2. Design a thirty-second commercial illustrating the idea noted in item 1.

Rethinking and Rewriting

1. Write an essay in which you imagine what the world would be like if everybody believed that Thoreau were right: In wildness *is* the preservation of the world. If we really believed that, what would we do?
2. Write an essay arguing that "in *tameness* is the preservation of the world." Be serious.
3. Using this selection as your primary source (and using at least one quotation from it), write a two- or three-page "Introduction to Thoreau" that tells new readers whatever you think they need to know in order to read and appreciate what Thoreau has to say.

WINTER CREEK

Kathleen Dean Moore

Kathleen Dean Moore is professor of philosophy at Oregon State University. After writing extensively as an academic philosopher, Moore recently turned to the form of the personal essay, with Riverwalking: Reflections on Moving Water *(1995), from which this essay is taken. Her latest collection,* Holdfast, *was published in 1999. In "Winter Creek," as in all of the pieces of* Riverwalking, *Moore reflects on the values of informal, spontaneous education.*

I wish to speak a word for the art of poking around. Although the art can be practiced in libraries and antique stores and peoples' psyches, the kind of poking around I am interested in advocating must be done outdoors. It is a matter of going into the land to pay close attention, to pry at things with the toe of a boot, to turn over rocks at the edge of a stream and lift boards to look for snakes or the nests of silky deer mice, to kneel close to search out the tiny bones mixed with fur in an animal's scat, to poke a cattail down a gopher hole.

People who poke around have seeds in their socks and rocks in their pockets. They measure things with the span of their hands. They look into the sun when they see a shadow pass across a field. They spit in rivers to make fish rise. When no one is looking, they may even rub their lips where beavers have chewed, just to get a sense of it. Often they stand still for a long time, listening, and then they follow the sound, sneaky as a heron, until they are close enough to see a chickadee knocking on wood like a tiny woodpecker. But if the route to the chickadee is crossed by the tracks of a black-tailed deer, they will turn to follow the deer into the firs, unless the deer tracks cross a creek, in which case it is important to meander with the water through the fold between the hills.

Poking around is more capricious than studying, but more intense than strolling. It's less systematic than watching, but more closely focused. Unlike hiking, it has no destination. Above all, poking around is not as serious as walking, the noble art so eloquently advocated by Henry David Thoreau. This is because poking around doesn't take much sustained thought, whereas Thoreau insisted that you must think while you walk, "like a camel, which is said to be the only beast which ruminates while walking."

When you walk into a field of reedy horsetails, you could deduce that there is groundwater under your feet and remark on the fact that you are in the presence of a plant as old as the dinosaurs. If you wanted to, you could imagine huge lizards chewing the stalks and blatting like french horns to claim ownership of the marsh, and you could formulate a theory of mass extinctions and apply it to humankind. But if you're only poking around, you might prefer just to cut a section of the hollow stem and blow across it, trying to make it hoot like the mouth of a beer bottle. You could study the flatness of a skipping stone and imagine layers of mud drying in the sun, but if you're just poking around, you'll probably spin the stone into the air instead, trying to make it drop into the stream at such a perfect, vertical angle that it disappears with a small sound like wood on wood, raising a blister on the water.

Of course, there are no rules about this, and some people prefer to keep their minds engaged while they're poking around. If so, the most fitting kinds of mental activity I have found are wondering and hoping. Knocking snow into the creek, I wonder why it turns clear before it melts. I wonder where the gopher went after he raised up a lumpy mound of earth in the pasture last night. Stopping to eat my sandwich in the depression where a deer has slept, I really hope there aren't ticks. I sit on a damp log in the ash swale and wish that the varied thrush would whistle again before my pants soak through. Most of all, I hope that the late winter sun will drop below the oaks and warm my back.

The people who are best at poking around are by no means the people who work the hardest at it, and what they find is often what they least expect. Children are often good at poking around, and among children, Erin and Jonathan are premier, if I may say so. One day Erin lay on her back in the weeds by Winter Creek, blowing across a blade of grass held tight as a reed between her thumbs—idly squealing the day away— when a red-tailed hawk banked into a tight curve overhead and dropped low in the sky, screaming a territorial call that sounded just like air across a blade of grass. Another time, Jonathan played with a pair of pliers in the dark, trying to work loose the wire that held the latch shut on a lantern, not even noticing that the pliers squeaked each time they opened or closed. When he finally looked up, he found himself looking into the face of a tiny screech owl perched in a pine above his head, its eyes intent on the pliers.

When I was growing up, an entire day of poking around was a treat reserved especially for birthdays. My birthday came in the Ohio summer, and my treat was to have the whole family pile into a rented rowboat and poke around Hinckley Lake all afternoon. I can picture us still: Because it is my birthday, I am rowing, dragging strings of elodea off both oars. My father leans over the bow, looking for snails and tiny floating ferns among the duckweed. In the stern sits my mother, rejoicing beyond reason at watery smells; beside her, my little sister on her back, watching the buzzards, and my older sister with a pocketknife, sawing and sawing at the stem of a water lily. The day is aimless, usually complicated by afternoon winds, always unproductive. But each small, individually wrapped observation is a gift.

All this may make it seem that poking around is the perfect avocation for the dissolute, but, on the contrary, it's an art that takes a certain stubborn resolve. You have to drive out ideas that will dampen your spirits or dim your vision: a desk on Monday morning, the dentist's bill. You have to be alert or you will find yourself sucked away by a work ethic as strong as a vacuum: You will stop to pull a single blackberry vine, which will make you look for another and another, until you are dogging from one vine to the next and then heading back to the shed for a shovel. You have to have a strong character, or guilt will overcome you when you realize you forgot to thaw dinner, and you will get back in your car and go to the grocery store and that will be that.

Like most pleasurable activities, poking around has its solemn enemies. Thus parents call their children *slowpokes* and tell them to quit poking around or they will be left behind. Grown-ups who poke around are dismissed as *childlike,* although how that can be an insult is beyond my comprehension. Thoreau says that in the Middle Ages a saunterer was considered a *saint de terre* as he wandered the countryside gathering alms to fund a crusade to the Holy Land, but he didn't go on to say that if someone was exploring the countryside just for the joy of the exploration, he was insulted as a *poke-easy,* a lazy one. Feudal dog handlers took pains to train their dogs not to poke around. If a dog left the scent trail, even to follow the red herrings that the trainers dragged in sacks across the road, the dog was beaten with sticks. The same sort of thing sometimes happens these days to science students, who aren't allowed out in the field until they have reduced the scope of their questions, whittled away at them until the questions are narrow and pointed.

Yet poking around is a guaranteed way to learn. Ideas, after all, start *10* with sense impressions; and all learning comes from making connections among observations and ideas. Insight is born of analogy. Everything interesting is complicated. Since truth is in the details, seekers of the truth should look for it there.

Besides, poking around is recreation, re-creation, in the most literal sense. John Locke said that what gives each person his or her personal identity is that person's private store of recollections. If so, then people should be careful curators of the assortment of memories that they collect over the years. Every time you notice something, every time something strikes you as important enough to store away in your mind, you create another piece of who you are. If someone asks, "Who are you?" it is not enough to say I am Kathy, or I am a professor, or I am Dora's daughter or Frank's wife. The complete answer will acknowledge that a person is partly her memories: I am a person who remembers a flock of white pelicans over Thompson Reservoir, pelicans banking in unison into the sunlight, banking into the shadow, flashing on and off like a scoreboard.

But I don't want to make too much of the instrumental value of poking around. The whole point is that poking around is good in itself, like music, or moonrise. So I poke around at the frozen edges of Winter Creek in the late afternoon when the sun comes in low over the oak knoll and throws a long, rippling shadow from each dried cattail across the creek and up the farther bank. As Thoreau observed in *Walking,* the sun shall "perchance shine into our minds and hearts, and light up our whole lives with a great awakening light, as warm and serene and golden as on a bankside in autumn."

Reading and Responding

1. Can you recall a time when you explored a new landscape? Perhaps it was as recently as last week, or maybe when you were a young child. What such memories have in common is a sense of newness, a sense of anticipation and curiosity. Freewrite about a time when you did such exploring. If you have many such memories, choose among your earliest ones.
2. Write about a time when you (to use Moore's phrasing) "poked around" and discovered evidence of something that provoked questions or curiosity: you were looking at something or hearing something, but you didn't have a name for it or an explanation for how it came to be or why it came to be precisely that way. Include clear details, even if you can't explain how they add up or what they mean.
3. Reread "Winter Creek" and note five things that surprise you. Write a paragraph about what these things have in common. Why do they surprise you? What do they say about the sort of mind you encounter in "Winter Creek"?

Working Together

1. Discuss together the virtues of poking around as a method of education. What are the advantages of this activity, as Moore sees them? How do you and your group regard this activity? What counts for you as education?
2. Not all poking around occurs in landscapes like that portrayed in "Winter Creek." As a group, identify four other places where you've poked around without definite aim and just for the chance to look or experience. Then, as a group, discuss why you like or don't like this kind of activity. Is it valuable, or is it just a waste of time?

Rethinking and Rewriting

1. Reread the second-to-last paragraph in "Winter Creek." Then write three paragraphs, starting each one with the phrase "I am a person who . . . ." In each case, finish the sentence and fill the paragraph with a different memory of poking around. Review and rewrite the paragraphs, taking the time and care to work them toward their best expression.
2. Write a resolution (500 words or less) that announces your intention to poke around somewhere (or, if you wish, several "somewheres"). Discuss the particular form of poking around you might decide to employ. Mention the location(s) you have in mind, and clarify why this resolution you're making is important or valuable to you.

SPLENDID SWAMP

Allen de Hart

> *Allen de Hart has hiked all over the country and all over the world. He has written many popular trail books, including* North Carolina Hiking Trails *(1996), and has published articles in newspapers and magazines. Here he celebrates the beauties of a swamp.*

The brooding 396,000-acre Okefenokee Swamp in southeastern Georgia has always confounded humans. The Timucuan Indians looked at its spongy islands formed from peat-bog and dubbed the place a "land of trembling earth." Nineteenth-century developers did their best to channel its waters, but eventually gave up. (Loggers of its primeval cypress were, alas, more successful.) Showing admirable respect for the untamable, in 1937 Franklin Roosevelt protected all but 42,000 acres of the watery wild as a national wildlife refuge; today, 354,000 of its eerie acres are designated as wilderness.

This sanctuary is known for its freshwater lakes tinted mahogany by the rapid decay of vegetation, colorful orchids and carnivorous pitcher plants, and wet prairies rich in fragrant lilies, maiden cane, and golden club. It's a prime place to "view the unsurpassed spectacle of nature in her various moods," in the words of local poet Mayme A. Harris. (Others smitten by the Okefenokee's languor include cartoonist Walt Kelly, whose possum Pogo dispensed wisdom from its dark reaches, and Georgia Public Television's Okefenokee Joe, a human and more modern but equally entertaining swamp citizen.)

But of all the Okefenokee's characters, the once-endangered, now abundant American alligator is king. The swamp is home to some 75 species of reptiles, including five poisonous snakes. Less menacing creatures a visitor may encounter include black-tail deer, raccoon, river otter, round-tailed muskrat, fox, and the endangered black bear. The swamp's skies fill with more than 200 species of resident or migratory birds, among them sandhill cranes, pileated woodpeckers, egrets, ibises, and yellow-crested and great blue herons.

The best way to explore the Okefenokee is by canoe: 107 miles of water trails wind through the refuge. Paddlers can set out for up to five days, camping each night on raised wooden platforms. Travelers wary of tippy canoes or nocturnal visits from bandit-eyed raccoons can explore from one of several visitor centers, which offer interpretive exhibits, nature trails, and guided boat tours. Whether you walk or paddle, you'll come away awed by the Okefenokee's mystery, proud to count yourself a "swamper."

Reading and Responding

1. Use this short piece as an opportunity to observe how paragraphs get put together. Choose one of de Hart's paragraphs and explain in a paragraph of your own how the de Hart paragraph works as a single unit, all of the sentences doing their work. State the paragraph's organizing purpose, and show how each sentence contributes to that purpose.
2. Try to figure out how de Hart wrote this short essay without using the word *I*. How would you describe the tone or the voice of this writing? Is it stuffy, academic, boring, enthusiastic? Copy a sentence that seems to represent the voice or tone of this writing.

Working Together

1. For each paragraph of "Splendid Swamp," finish this sentence: "This paragraph discusses _____." Once you have a clear grasp of how each paragraph contributes to the whole essay, then as a group write your own essay following the same four-paragraph organizational pattern. Instead of discussing the Okefenokee Swamp, however, discuss some local building, either on campus or nearby. Be serious or satirical or whimsical, but make sure you follow the same pattern of paragraphs you see in "Splendid Swamp."
2. Work individually for about ten minutes, and identify a few places that you know well enough to write about (as de Hart has for the Okefenokee Swamp). Choose one place among these options. Make a list of the major things you know about that place. Then, working with a partner, explain this place and your knowledge of it. As a listener, your job is to ask your partner at least two questions about whatever interests you about the place he or she chose to describe.

Rethinking and Rewriting

1. Write an introduction to your school that follows the same basic pattern that de Hart uses in "Splendid Swamp." Try to adopt the same tone, too—neither stuffy nor slangy. Use your college catalog or Web site as at least one source and quote from it at least once.
2. Write an introduction to a place (wild or not) that you know well because you've been there. If necessary, conduct additional research to supplement your knowledge. Follow "Splendid Swamp" as a general model.

WHERE THE WILDERNESS BEGINS

Ofelia Zepeda

Associate professor of linguistics at the University of Arizona, Ofelia Ze-peda has published a collection of poetry, Ocean Powers: Poems from the Desert *(1995), and a grammar of the language of Arizona's Papago Indians. This essay explores the borders between cultures as well as between the urban and the wild.*

Perhaps, when it really was not necessary, since there was no one else around when the Creator formed the shape of the first human and was about to place him on the ground, he ran his hand across the spot where the human was going to be put. Perhaps the place cleared was only the size of the human's feet, or perhaps the space was the size of the state of Texas; surely he must have signified a space.

As children we have done the same. I remember playing on the cool earth floor on a hot summer day, and even though the dirt surface that was our yard and play area had been designated by our mother, we defined it further. Her signal to the space was to sprinkle it with water and sweep it every morning in order to keep the surface firm and dust free. The dirt floor was hard as cement. Once we sat down on it, whether we were playing jacks, dolls, or cars, we further ran our hands over a certain spot on this floor, clearing it and designating it as where we would play. We cleared a small space for the rag dolls to sleep. We cleared further spaces that featured roads or served as places for houses and other childhood toys. We redefined space that was already ours.

Living in the desert, we have all done the same. We have marked the space within the space that is already ours. This space, I say, is already ours, ours in the sense that this is our habitat: we are the ones who were put here to live. And even though we live here, we continue to remark it, create boundaries. We fence in, and out. We know where the "wild" desert ends and the "other space" begins. Now because we know where the desert ends, we also know *what* is in that desert. Sometimes we know these things firsthand, sometimes not. As O'odham, we know the desert is the place of wilderness. It is the place of dreams for those who must dream those kinds of dreams, and it is the place of songs for those who must sing those kinds of songs. But it is also the place where nightmares hide, nightmares so fierce that one can believe one has seen a guardian angel. For the O'odham, the desert is certainly a place of power. Because we know this essence of the desert, although sometimes we do not fully understand it, we are able to live in it.

In talking about living in the desert, I will hold some of the perspective of the Tohono O'odham, the Desert People, a tribe indigenous to the southern Arizona desert. I will pull from what I know personally, some of it certainly gained along the way from family. Other things that I say are bits of other O'odham people's stories.

As a child I grew up knowing two communities, communities that complemented each other very well. Much of my childhood was spent in the place I was born, Stanfield, Arizona. Stanfield was a cotton-farming community up until the early '70s. This community was a desert region, but with a new façade, a façade of greenery pushed up from the ground artificially. Despite its appearance, this place still had limited rainfall with the regular urgency of summer monsoons. The temperatures were extreme, the air dry and clear. The winters were the same as in any desert, mildly cold and tolerable.

The other place was a village just inside the Mexican border, which was my mother's traditional home. When I was a child, our family spent time there, too. This place was also an agricultural region of sorts. It was noted for its numerous natural springs and, at that time, its large surface ponds. We planted fields mostly of corn, melon, squash, and beans. There were also orchards of pomegranates and figs. This village was an oasis, and so special it was considered by some as a sacred place. From these two homelands in the desert, I grew up familiar with it and knowing how to live in it. Even though both places were clearly defined by their water and agricultural boundaries, in both places one did not need to look too far to see where the "wild desert" began.

It began at the end of the cotton fields or just over a low hill. It was beyond these places, the ends of fields and over desert hills, that we as children knew not to venture too far. I remember adults telling us, "Something is going to get you" should we venture toward those desert regions. These threats were not false threats of the bogeyman; no, they were real. It was the case then, as it is now, that members of society who do not fit elsewhere oftentimes find themselves on the edges of communities, in the desert, existing as well as they can. It was these people that adults warned us against. Another thing to fear is something that we cannot see but believe exists. "Something is going to get you" sometimes referred, not to anything physical, but to something psychological or spiritual. O'odham believe that one can be met by a being, a spirit, at almost any time. These meetings can happen in the most mundane places, but they can also occur in more mystical wilderness areas like the desert. And unless one actually ventures out for such a meeting because one is supposed to, it is best to keep one's chances low by avoiding the mystical places, the wilderness spaces, whenever possible.

There is a story about a male relative who after a night of partying and drinking ended up having to walk home the next day. His walk put him in the midst of dry, wild desert for a considerable stretch. The story goes that he suffered dehydration, not to mention mild sunstroke coupled with hangover, and in this state he had a meeting with a spirit animal. The animal he claims to have met was the bear who gave him his songs. My mother tells this story with some humor. She asks, where would a bear come from? It does not live in that desert. Nonetheless, this relative had the songs. Unfortunately, he did not live very long, and as far as anyone knows never had a single opportunity to take advantage of his curing power on anyone suffering sickness caused by the bear—perhaps it was just as well.

There are many accounts of O'odham men who have been called to go out in the desert for such meetings. These meetings are for gaining knowledge about a variety of traditional ways, including curing rituals, songs, and finding solutions to various major concerns, either for themselves or for the group. As children we were kept vaguely informed about such goings-on. On occasion if we asked too many questions, we were simply given the explanation that so and so went hunting and that was the reason for being gone for several days at a time. Even in our cottonfield town, we knew of men who went out into the desert because they were supposed to. I remember watching them walk down the road alongside the cottonfield, come to the end of the field, turn away, and disappear into the desert. The desert does hold all sorts of power, much of it not accessible to everyone, most of it harmless.

There are other stories from out of the desert that have nearly become folklore among many O'odham. One such story tells of something that exists in certain parts of the desert. This thing they speak of is not a physical being, and it has been ascertained by those knowledgeable that it is not a spiritual being either. And the features of this thing? Well, it has none, none yet described by anyone, since no one has really seen it. Those who have experienced this phenomenon claim it is an air, a feeling, and when one gets too close to such a place one experiences the basest, most visceral fear an evolved human is capable of. People tell how a horse will not go near an area that manifests this thing; they sense a fear unlike any other, according to those who know horses. This is a phenomenon that some people like to tell about with much relish and exaggerated detail. Some dismiss it as the bogeyman syndrome, while others are convinced this thing is truly a manifestation of Satan himself. Whether any of this is true is still in question.

Those who do not believe might perhaps think differently when they hear Mrs. Antone's story. What she saw caused her to be so overcome by such fear that the only thing that saved her from being scared out of her wits was a beautiful vision of what she believed to be a guardian angel. This experience led her to relocate to a bigger cleared space in the desert, become a born-again Christian, and join the Assembly of God Church.

She tells her story:

"I had just gotten married. I married a Mexican man. We were both young. This was around 1940, back when there was no electricity in the desert. Anyway, he took me to his home. It was just a little shack out in the middle of the desert. There were no other houses near us. We were alone except for a few of his cows. It was nighttime when we got to his place, and it was really dark, no moon. We had only been there a short

10

time when he suddenly said he had to leave. I didn't want him to leave because I didn't want to stay there alone. He told me, 'Take this and you will be all right.' He handed me his .22 and left. I didn't know what to do. I started to go about the little house and straighten up, trying to keep my mind off being alone. Suddenly, I heard something outside. At first it was like a breeze blowing through, maybe a little dust devil. But when I quickly looked outside, none of the tree limbs were moving. As I stood in the middle of that little house, I felt this thing move the walls of the house just slightly, and as suddenly as it had begun, it stopped. And then I had a sensation something was inside the house with me. It was like cold, wet air. It seemed to permeate my being. I don't know how to explain it. I know it seemed to possess me because it seemed it was holding me not the same way a man or a woman would hold another with the arms, but it held me on the inside of my body, by my backbone. I couldn't move, I couldn't feel my skin, I couldn't breathe even though I was alive. Have you ever seen someone take their last breath before they die and their blood stops running through their body? I think I felt my blood stop running. I felt dry, not wet and alive the way a human is supposed to. I stood there and just held my .22 rifle to my chest. My mind, I don't know what my mind was doing. It was either not working or it was working too fast to be of any use. Thoughts were running all around, too many, too quickly, like a bag full of marbles spilled on a concrete floor. I searched quickly, my mind. The only thing I recall was something that told me to pray. That is all. So I did. I prayed and prayed and prayed for what seemed like an eternity. That was all my mind could do. Finally, *It* released me. I felt my fingers warm up with the rush of blood. I could move. The first thing I did was look out this little hole in the door into the blackness, and I saw something floating. It was white. It floated above the house and upward until I couldn't see it anymore. It was like one of those beautiful angels I used to see in the books. Then I understood what it was—my guardian angel. It was my guardian angel that had come and saved me from that thing. I just know this is what happened."

When Mrs. Antone told me her story, she was living in a small Arizona town, which of course was in the desert but had been altered by underground water, irrigated fields, and copper mining.

I began by stating that O'odham, to a certain extent, know how to ₁₅ live in the desert because, to a certain extent, they know what is in that desert. Some of it is good, and some not. Some of it is real, and some perhaps manufactured by active imaginations. Irregardless, contemporary O'odham have available to them various insurance options they can "purchase" in order to protect the space they have set up as their homes within the desert. One option is a cleared yard and a fence, which primarily acts as a deterrent to medium-sized wild animals. The cleared yard is often a meeting ground for uninvited animals, where their host has the option of redirecting the animal back to its original trail. The fence and yard, though, are no match for the more spirit-formed intruder. The option in this case for many O'odham is to invite the local medicine man over to "clean" the house and space. This cleaning protects the building and space from nonphysical intrusions. And for many O'odham who may also happen to be Catholic, a double dose of spiritual protection can come in the form of the local padre who can, following the medicine man, "bless" the space and the house. Finally, some families may have a fiesta at their home. Part of the fiesta might include ritual dancing by the neighboring Yoeme—either Matachine dancing or, even better, Deer Dancing. This dancing offers protection insurance because wherever the Matachines dance, the ground becomes sacred; the same is true for the Deer Dancer, but with the Deer Dancer is the additional bonus of the holy water from the gourd drum. Once the celebration is completed, the water from the drum is sprinkled all about and the place is holy—to some, sacred. I have a friend who does not allow cars in the parking space next to his house because that is where the dancers danced. Even he has to park his truck out on the street.

So there we are. To live in the desert is to know the desert as well as possible, and if that is not the case, then there certainly are ways to protect oneself.

Reading and Responding

1. Write about a time and place where, as a child, you carved out a space and declared it yours. Maybe you spread an old blanket on the ground and declared it your "house." Maybe you colonized some space under stairs or took over a corner of the kitchen or threw a sheet over a card table and then crawled underneath. Write a couple of paragraphs about this experience. What did you do to make the place yours? What did you do inside its boundaries? Why do you think you were doing it? What stayed outside the boundaries you declared?

2. Zepeda says she grew up inside two communities and that in both of them the boundaries were clear enough—"one did not need to look too far to see where the 'wild desert' began." What was the "wild desert" in your own childhood? What place, nearby yet somehow wild, was scary or unknown—and off limits to you? Describe this forbidden or wild place and what resided there (or what you thought resided there). If you remember a story about that place, sketch that story.

Working Together

1. Think of places in your own experience, places where the wild or the dangerous began (thus, places you were probably told to avoid). How did people convey those dangers to you? Did they exaggerate? Were these places linked with the violent, the macabre, or the mysterious? Working together, make two lists—one of descriptions for what was home or relatively safe and known, and one for what was wild or

relatively unsafe and unknown. Then make a third list, describing any charms, rituals, or careful processes that if followed could protect one from the harms of the wild.

2. As a group, decide on one story that a member of your group could tell that would effectively illustrate the strangeness, the unpredictable terrors and forces of some place "where wilderness begins."

3. As a group, discuss how we can make "wilderness" a non-human and scary place that we tend to want to civilize or make less wild. Under what circumstances would this be a good thing—this "humanizing" or civilizing of wilderness? Under what circumstances would this be a harmful thing? In each case, what would be made safe, preserved, or enhanced?

Rethinking and Rewriting

Write an essay that re-creates your sense of some wilderness place. Begin by deciding how you want to define *wilderness:* a place left natural and uninhabited by people? a place where the wildness of life threatens or replaces a sense of civilization and order? a place of spirit and mystery, perhaps evil, outside normal human boundaries? Give your readers a physical, sensory understanding of this place. Also give readers a sense of the emotional complexity of this place and how it feels to skirt its edges or venture into it. End by discussing how this sense of a boundary between the wilderness and the known helps define your sense of community and your sense of yourself as either one who tests the boundaries and goes into the wilderness or one who avoids those boundaries and the unknown.

DAYBREAK

Bill McKibben

Author of several hundred pieces for the New Yorker *magazine, Bill McKibben is best known for* The End of Nature *(1989), a lament about the physical and spiritual effects of global warming. In this excerpt from* The Age of Missing Information *(1993), an excerpt that was adapted by the author for this anthology, McKibben explores how television has changed the way we perceive the world around us. His latest book to date is* Maybe One: A Personal and Environmental Argument for Single-Child Families *(1998).*

A little mist hangs above the pond, which is still save for a single mallard paddling slowly back and forth. From time to time it dives—sticks its rump in the air. From time to time it climbs out on a rock and airs its wings in the breeze, which is visible now and again on the surface of the pond. I watched for about an hour, and mostly the duck just swam back and forth, back and forth, back and forth.

Ducks are not necessarily placid. At certain times of the year male mallards flick water at females, or engage in what the bird books call a "grunt-whistle," while females perform "nod-swimming." At other seasons they may pull feathers from their bodies to insulate their eggs. And ducks are peculiarly susceptible to "imprinting." If, between thirteen and sixteen hours after they hatch, they are exposed to a moving object—a man or a dog or an Infiniti Q-45—they will thereafter follow it.

But on this particular morning this particular duck was doing nothing much, just swimming slowly back and forth.

We believe that we live in the "age of information," that there has been an information "explosion," an information "revolution." While in a certain narrow sense this is the case, in many important ways just the opposite is true. We also live at a moment of deep ignorance, when vital knowledge that humans have always possessed about who we are and where we live seems beyond our reach. An Unenlightenment. An age of missing information.

This account of that age takes the form of an experiment—a contrast between two days. One day, May 3, 1990, lasted well more than a thousand hours—I collected on videotape nearly every minute of television that came across the enormous Fairfax cable system from one morning to the next, and then I watched it all. The other day, later that summer, lasted the conventional twenty-four hours. A mile from my house, camped on a mountaintop by a small pond, I awoke, took a day hike up a neighboring peak, returned to the pond for a swim, made supper, and watched the stars till I fell asleep. This book is about the results of that experiment—about the information that each day imparted.

These are, of course, straw days. No one spends twenty-four hours a day watching television (though an impressive percentage of the population gives it their best shot). And almost no one spends much time alone outdoors—the hermit tradition, never strong in America, has all but died away. (Thoreau came up twice on television during May 3. Once, he was an answer on *Tic Tac Dough* in the category "Bearded Men," and later that evening, in the back of a limousine, a man toasted his fiancée with champagne and said, "You know how we've always talked about finding our Walden Pond, our own little utopia? Well, here it is. This is Falconcrest.") I'm not interested in deciding which of these ways of spending time is "better." Both are caricatures, and neither strikes me as a model for a full and happy life. But caricatures have their uses—they draw attention to what is important about the familiar. Our society is moving steadily from natural sources of information toward electronic ones, from the mountain and the field toward the television; this great transition is very nearly complete. And so we need to understand the two extremes. One is the target of our drift. The other an anchor that might tug us gently back, a source of information that once spoke clearly to us and now hardly even whispers.

About the mountain first. Crow Mountain is no Himalaya, no Alp. Even in the company of its fellow Adirondacks it keeps a low profile. It is not one of the fifty highest peaks in New York State, nor is it particularly difficult to climb—I was at the top with a two-hour hike from my back door. A day on Crow, then, offers little in the way of drama or danger or overcoming odds. Still, this mountain has its charms, including half a mile of bare ridge, with marvelous views in all directions, and an uncommonly large pond, perhaps ten acres in size, nestled just below the peak. It is an uncrowded summit—the day described here came at the end of a week I spent alone on Crow, a week in which I encountered no other human beings. And yet it is not isolated. From the ridge I could see down to the valley where my wife and I live—could see the volunteer firehouse and the few homes and grown-in pastures that form our community. Though my house was hidden behind a ridge of hemlock, I could see where Mill Creek twists through the yard. So Crow is wilderness softened by familiarity.

If climbing the mountain was easy, assembling a video record of May 3, 1990, was not. No machine exists that can tape nearly a hundred channels simultaneously; instead, you need a hundred people with video-cassette recorders who will simultaneously do you a favor. With their help I compiled what I think is a unique snapshot of American culture—a sort of video Domesday that for twenty-four hours captures the images and voices that normally vanish like birdcalls on the breeze. For even in the age of the VCR, the invisible-ink effect of television is amazing. One day last year, for instance, a reporter for *The New York Times* needed to find out how the local ABC affiliate had covered a story the previous night. He failed, reporting only that a spokesman "could not release what was said on Sunday night's newscast without the permission of William Applegate, the news director, and Mr. Applegate did not respond to repeated requests left with his secretary for a transcript." In other words, the most powerful newspaper in the world could not get its hands on a newscast watched by millions only hours before. So I was pleased with my archive of tape, even if there were hours blanked out here and there, and MTV was nothing but snow so I had to retape it and a few others a couple of days later, and several hours of CBS were in black and white.

I chose Fairfax solely because of the astounding size of the system, which in 1990 was roughly 40 percent larger than its nearest competitor. There were five Christian channels, four shopping channels, two country music video channels, even a channel that broadcasts all the arrival and departure information off the Dulles and National airport screens. Its *Cable Guide* lists nearly a thousand movies each month; in May 1990 they ranged from *About Last Night* ("1986, Romantic Comedy, A young man and woman find themselves confused, frustrated, enthralled") to *Zombie* ("1964, Horror, Friends vacationing on a remote island find it inhabited by disfigured ghouls"), with everything in between from *Slumber Party Massacre II* to *The Son of Hercules Versus Medusa* to *It Happened One Night* to *Bonzo Goes to College* to *Sagebrush Law* to *Shaft* (and *Shaft in Africa*) to *Watchers* ("1988, Science Fiction, A dog, the subject of experiments in fostering superintelligence, escapes from a CIA compound"). For those who want *more,* a six-channel pay-per-view setup offers first-run films—on May 3: *Lethal Weapon 2; Honey, I Shrunk the Kids; Welcome Home; Field of Dreams; Alienator* ("She's programmed to kill anything in her path"); and *Enraptured.* Two comedy channels, nine public-access and government channels, a national sports channel and a local one, two weather channels, even a unique "four-in-one" channel that splits your screen into quarters and lets you watch the three networks and PBS simultaneously. Before the nineties are out, technology could permit six hundred channels per set, but even with a hundred stations you can watch virtually every national TV program aired in America on Fairfax Cable. On a single day you can hear about virtually every topic on earth.

Fairfax turned out to be ideal in another way, too—it is hard to   *10* imagine a place more devoid of quirky regional tradition. The county has grown quickly in recent years, till large stretches of it have the relentlessly standardized look of neutral America, the placeless Edge City of interchange plazas and malls with crowded chain restaurants and housing developments (Foxfield, Brookfield, Century Oak) named for the things they replaced. Only in its wealth is it extreme. The town of Falls Church ranks first in the nation in per capita income; nearly 80 percent of the county's households earn more than $35,000 and 75 percent of their children, who score seventy points above the national average on the SAT, will go on to college. On the other hand, a lot of the local programming comes from the District of Columbia, which is like a photographic negative of Fairfax.

Once my friends in Fairfax had mailed me the cardboard boxes full of tape, I began spending eight or ten hours a day in front of the VCR—I watched it all, more or less. A few programs repeat endlessly, with half-hour "infomercials" for DiDi 7 spot remover and Liquid Lustre car wax leading the list at more than a dozen appearances apiece. Having decided that once or twice was enough to mine their meanings, I would fast-forward through them, though I always slowed down to enjoy the part where the car-wax guy sets fire to the hood of his car. Otherwise, however, I dutifully spent many months of forty-hour weeks staring at, say, *Outdoors Wisconsin,* the kind of show that appears on minor cable channels across the nation because there's nowhere near enough programming produced to fill all the available time. On *Outdoors Wisconsin* ("summer to fall, winter to spring, Green Bay to where the St. Croix sings") they were "sucker-grabbing" in a creek near Fond du Lac. Sucker-grabbing involves wading up behind suckers, which are a variety of fish, and grabbing them. "They're really good if you grind 'em and mix 'em with a little egg and soda cracker," the host contended.

Which leads pretty directly into the question "Why bother?" *Outdoors Wisconsin* clearly has little direct effect on anyone but the suckers. But TV is cumulative, and over a lifetime ten minutes here and there of watching fishing or car racing or *Divorce Court* has added up to a lot of hours and had a certain effect on all of us. When people write about television, especially the critics who have to do it regularly, they usually have no choice but to concentrate on the new and the interesting as if they were reviewing plays or films. But TV is different—the new is relatively unimportant. The most popular program in 1990, *Cheers,* was in its ninth season; several weeks it was topped in the ratings by twenty-two-year-old *60 Minutes,* or challenged by *Murder, She Wrote,* which turned a hardy seven. Programs that first aired twenty or thirty years ago are still on the air, shown more often than ever in ceaseless rerun. You could argue that *The Brady Bunch,* not *Twin Peaks,* is the really important show to understand—simply by dint of repetition and familiarity it has won its way into the culture. (In March of 1991, the Associated Press reported that a Florida police officer had pleaded guilty to battery charges. He had lined up four-teen juveniles he had caught skateboarding, and then gone down the line whacking them with a nightstick as he sang the theme from *The Brady Bunch.* "He was singing that *Brady Bunch* tune, and each time he'd say like two words, he would hit one person in the butt," one of the boys told investigators.) People don't watch TV the way critics have to watch it. They don't watch it the way I watched it either—I have no way of re-creating the discussions the next day at work, say, or the easy familiarity with a show that you've seen every Thursday for a decade. But I did watch everything. The commercials, the filler, the reruns, the videos—all of it counts. *My Three Sons* still alters people's orbits, at least a little, just as *Cosby* will still be a force in 2010.

I grew up in the sixties and seventies, watching a great deal of television. Not the "quality TV" of television's Golden Era in the 1950s—not *Playhouse 90* or *The Honeymooners.* I was watching TV TV. Friday night meant ABC—*The Brady Bunch, The Partridge Family,* and *Room 222* in that order. TV was like a third parent—a source of ideas and information and impressions. And not such a bad parent—always with time to spare, always eager to please, often funny. TV filled dull hours and it made me a cosmopolite at an early age. I have great affection for it—I can remember waiting anxiously for *Room 222* to come on, remember that the high school it showed (Bernie with the red Afro! Karen Valentine!) seemed impossibly, enticingly sophisticated. People who didn't grow up with television tend not to understand its real power—they already had a real world to compare with the pictures on the screen. People my age didn't—we were steeped in television, flavored for life. A few years ago my wife and I moved to a mountain-rimmed valley—there's no cable, and even with a big antenna you get mostly snow. Since necessity is the mother of acquiescence, TV proved a fairly easy habit to kick. But of course I hadn't escaped it entirely—it lingered in my temperament, attitudes, outlook. And only with some distance, some time away, was I starting to get a sense of just how much. As I embarked on this project, then, I was not some Martian suddenly confronted with television; I was a traveler returning to a cozy home, able to see that home with new eyes. Going back to television was like spending the holidays with your parents once you've grown up—in three days you comprehend more on a conscious level about your mother than you did in twenty years of living with her.

Television is the chief way that most of us partake of the larger world, of the information age, and so, though none of us owe our personalities and habits entirely to the tube and the world it shows, none of us completely escape its influence either. Why do we do the things we do? Because of the events of our childhood, and because of class and race and gender, and because of our political and economic system and because of "human nature"—but also because of what we've been told about the world, because of the information we've received.

Television researchers tend to ignore the content, taking their cue [15] from Marshall McLuhan, who argued that the "content of a medium is like the juicy piece of meat carried by the burglar to distract the watchdog of the mind." One study after another, not to mention the experience of most of us, indicates that McLuhan was largely right—that we do in fact often watch television because of our mood or out of habit, instead of tuning in to see something in particular. Even so, we're not staring at test patterns. We also often eat because we're bored or depressed, but the effects are different if we scarf carrot sticks or Doritos.

Two thirds of Americans tell researchers they get "most of their information" about the world from television, and the other statistics are so familiar we hardly notice them—more American homes have TVs than plumbing and they're on an average of seven hours a day; children spend more time watching TV than doing anything else save sleeping; on weekday evenings in the winter half the American population is sitting in front of television; as many as 12 percent of adults (that is, one in eight) feel they are physically addicted to the set, watching an average of fifty-six hours a week; and so on. The industry works hard to make this absorption seem glamorous: the Fairfax system runs an around-the-clock Cable Welcome Channel for instance, which tells viewers how to operate their systems ("If you can't get a picture on your TV, make sure it is plugged in"), but mainly congratulates them endlessly on "being part of a complete communications system that puts the whole world at your fingertips, from the far reaches of outer space to the heart of Fairfax." Outer space! Satellites! Fiber optics! Data! The final installment of an A&E series called *The Romantic Spirit* gushes, "Computers and satellites and silicon chips signal that we are in sight of a post–Romantic Age, of a fresh start." Communications are now "almost instantaneous," a documentary on the computer age explains. "Communications are the currency we trade in, the currency of the information age."

But what is this vaunted information currency? If you're a commodity broker or a bond trader, it's a blizzard of constantly changing green numbers on a flashing screen. If you're a vice president for marketing, it's a cataract of data about how much people earn in a certain zip code and what kind of car they drive. For most of us, though, this romantic, mind-boggling Niagara of communications washes up in our living rooms in the form of, say, Cory Everson's hunky husband, Jeff. Cory has an exercise program on ESPN called *Body Shaping,* and she lets Jeff handle the show's Nutrition Corner. If you're in the supermarket, Jeff advises, and you open up a carton and see that one of the eggs is broken, "don't buy that carton."

To be fair, there's a lot of other information you didn't already know, some of which is vaguely fascinating. On the Discovery Channel, for instance, Dr. Frank Field explains that in Switzerland white bread is taxed and the money is given to whole-wheat bakers so their loaves can be competitively priced. According to Casey Kasem on *Oprah,* Neil Sedaka went to the same high school as Neil Diamond and Barbra Streisand, and while he was there he wrote a song about a girl called Carole Klein who went on to become Carole King and of course have several number-one records, not only for herself but for the Shirelles. Sea otters wrap themselves in kelp before going to sleep, and three thousand matings are required to produce one lion cub that will live past its second year, and hyenas usually bear twins. And according to Showtime, the Voyager space probe carries a recording offering our planet's greetings to the entire universe in the voice of—Kurt Waldheim.

Some of the information on TV could win you fabulous prizes. "In American literature, what Mark Twain character had a girlfriend named Becky Thatcher?" As English teachers across the nation held their collective breath, a team on *Super Sloppy Double Dare* who had earlier recalled the name of the Flintstones' pet dinosaur failed to remember Tom Sawyer, and so had to turn themselves into "human tacos" by pouring vats of guacamole on their heads.

On other occasions, the information is more speculative: John Osborne, in a special edition of *Prophecy Countdown* called "Angels—God's Special Space Shuttles," calculated that angels travel eleven million miles a minute versus 283 for a NASA rocket. [20]

And once in a while the information is just a shade less than honest, as when the Travel Channel claimed that "three things make Nuremberg famous—its Christmas market, the Nuremberg gingerbread, and the Nuremberg sausage."

Most of the time, though, the information that TV has to offer is not spelled out in such tidy little factlets. It is at least a little hidden in the fabric of movies and newscasts and commercials and reruns. Not so hidden that you need to hire a team of deconstruction contractors to analyze it all—just hidden enough that the messages are passed over, absorbed through the eyes without triggering the entire brain. People used to claim you could see "sex" written on Ritz crackers in their advertisements. Despite careful examination I never could, and that's not what I'm talking about. What I'm talking about is what happens when you see an ad, over and over, for small Ritz crackers pre-smeared and pre-stuck together with peanut butter and sold under the slogan "No assembly required." What habits of mind and body does this, in concert with a hundred other similar messages, help produce? And how do those habits differ from the habits, the attitudes people got from the natural world?

Occasionally, in between old World War II documentaries on A&E, a promotion for the network showed a man named Jack Perkins who said proudly that his channel showed "the entire scope of television, which is of course the entire scope of life." This is more or less the claim of all those who herald the new age now upon us—that our flow of data replaces nearly all that came before, including nature. Mark Fowler, the Reagan-era director of the Federal Communications Commission, appeared on C-SPAN to make this point explicitly. He talked about the range of environmental problems we face, including the depletion of the ozone, the destruction of the rain forests, and the spread of acid rain. "Pretty dreary stuff," he said, "except that as the ecological system has deteriorated, I think the man-made information ecology—the ebb and flow of words, voice, data—has vastly improved, so that we now live in a world more tightly bound, more in touch one part with another, than at any moment in its history."

Set aside the question of whether it's a worthwhile trade-off to be able to fax your aunt in Australia so that you can tell her it's bloody hot out and all the fish are dying—simply realize that an awful lot of people have come to see this "information ecology" as a sort of substitute for the other, older, natural ecology. "Ours is an economy increasingly dependent not on our natural resources or geographic location," President Bush told the members of the class of 1991 as they left the California Institute of Technology. "Ours is an age of microchips and MTV." And most of us vaguely agree with the president, I think—the world seems to be evolving into an "information economy" where the occupants of every country will busy themselves selling each other computer chips and watching the whole process on Esperanto CNN.

Against such a tide of opinion it sounds a little romantic to say: If   25
you sat by a pond beside a hemlock tree under the sun and stars for a day, you might acquire some information that would serve you well. I don't fret about TV because it's decadent or shortens your attention span or leads to murder. It worries me because it alters perception. TV, and the culture it anchors, masks and drowns out the subtle and vital information contact with the real world once provided. There are lessons—small lessons, enormous lessons, lessons that may be crucial to the planet's persistence as a green and diverse place and also to the happiness of its inhabitants—that nature teaches and TV can't. Subversive ideas about how much you need, or what comfort is, or beauty, or time, that you can learn from the one great logoless channel and not the hundred noisy ones or even the pay-per-view.

For instance, as the sun comes up I'm sitting by the edge of the pond on Crow, drinking tea and wondering idly if the weather will hold all day so I can hike to the cliffs on nearby Blackberry Mountain. Ransacking my brain for weather lore, I recall that red skies at night are a sailor's delight, a ring around the moon heralds snow, and woolly caterpillars are woolliest before a hard winter, none of which is much help. I find myself wishing that I could gauge the wind direction and its speed, add the feel of the air and the type of clouds overhead, and make a reasonable guess, as most Americans once could, of what the day would bring. Of course this is no longer an essential skill—on the Fairfax cable system alone you can watch not only the twenty-four-hour national Weather Channel but also a local radar weather channel that shows storms moving inexorably, pixel by pixel, in your direction. You'd be crazy to devote any time to learning to forecast from the clouds and the wind—you wouldn't be as accurate as the giggly guy in the loud sports coat, and who would teach you anyhow? Jeffersonian farmers would doubtless have welcomed accurate predictions. Still, let this stand as one small example of information people once had and no longer possess.

Or another small example: an oft-repeated ad on May 3 was for a product called Jimmy Dean Microwave Mini Burgers, prefabricated hamburgers in a microwavable container. Silly as it sounds, think of the information you would have needed a century ago if you lived in a place like the Adirondacks and wanted to make yourself a hamburger. You'd have needed to be able to raise cattle, which implies knowing how to clear land, how to rotate pastures, how to build a barn—probably you'd have needed to know how to get your neighbors to *help* you raise a barn. You'd have needed to know how to kill an animal, and what to do with it once it was hanging there dead. You might have bought your grain at the store or you might have used cornmeal, but certainly you needed to know how to bake bread. Baking and cooking would have required wood, which meant you had to know which trees to cut down, and when, and how to build an even fire. And so on.

If we're ever to recapture these fundamental kinds of information, it's necessary to start by remembering just how divorced from the physical world many of us have become. In a refreshingly honest piece of reporting, food writer Dena Kleiman recently told readers of *The New York Times* about a trip she'd taken to the lake district of southern Chile. "I had always fantasized about eating my own catch—staring down at a plate of fresh fish and knowing it would never have got there without me. The whole idea was appealing: braving the elements, testing my skill, indulging in one of the oldest battles of time—man versus nature." So she jumped at the chance to go fishing in Chile, although not before consulting with a passel of experts. George J. Armelagos, an anthropologist at the University of Florida, told her that "it was not until about ten thousand years ago that humans first turned from hunting and fishing to farming and herding in what was the start of the Neolithic Age." After that "nothing was ever the same," explained Mr. Armelagos, who is also the author of *Consuming Passions: An Anthology of Eating*. Ultimately, added California anthropology professor Eugene Anderson, "it is capitalism that has distanced us from all stages and phases of the food preparation process." Having heard this, Kleiman was ready. The management of the hotel sent her off in a boat with a guide, and the chef promised he would sauté her catch with a touch of garlic. "Time passes slowly in a fishing boat," she reported. "The routine, in fact, is tedious. Cast out. Reel in." To fill the time, "I tried to envision what kind of weapon I would devise, what kind of skill might be required, what kind of mind-set I would need to develop if I were lost in the wilderness and confronted with starvation." While mulling over this problem, she caught a fish, the guide motored her in, and she handed it to the chef and dressed for dinner. But presented with her catch, she reports, "I was stunned to find myself suddenly feeling nauseated," unable to eat for the memory of the vibrant living creature of some hours before. Despite the assurances of one Robert Cialdini, a social psychologist at the University of Arizona, that "it is natural for us to generate food for ourselves," she went without her supper.

Her squeamishness is not the point—that may be her only natural reaction, and in any event it's not deep enough to stop her eating the flesh of animals she didn't catch herself. It's how profoundly disconnected an obviously intelligent and educated person can be from the natural world. She is perhaps a slight caricature in this regard—only a true Manhattanite would actually consult a professor for the news that it is okay for us to "generate" our own food—but she offers a pretty accurate drawing of our society as a whole. Even most of us who do hike and fish do so sporadically, and out of such a single-minded desire for recreation that we don't absorb a lot of meaning from the experience. What you do every day, after all, is what forms your mind, and precious few of us can or would spend most days outdoors. "Despite all the lip service we give to craving nature and wanting to spend more time away from cities, I suppose that in the end we are grateful to live in a society where foraging requires only a walk to the local market," Kleiman writes. And that is fine—we don't need a nation of hunter-gatherers. But it does, as she demonstrates, come at a real cost in your comprehension of the world—it robs her of the ability, in this instance, to squarely address her own participation in the drama of life and death.

Even for the few modern farmers who do appear on television, the industrial scale of the business has changed it so dramatically that much of this information is diluted, drowned out in the roar of the tractor piloting its noisy course across a vast sea of crops. The Lifetime network ran a short feature on a farm family in northern California. They ran such a large dairy operation (950 head) that the mother said she spent most of her day on the computer doing records while Dad was out minding the help. The kids took care of the house pets, and helped in other small ways, but they weren't really a part of farm life any more than a banker's children make loans. The message she tried to teach them, Mom said, was that "hard work pays off in nice things—toys, cars." Which is probably better than our culture's usual message—Buy a lottery ticket so you won't have to work hard—but it doesn't yield much in the way of wisdom about death or limits or the cycles of the seasons. Even home gardeners, presumably planting for love of working the soil, are hectored around the clock to purchase products like Miracle-Gro—hectored by "world championship gardeners," which is to say not the people who grow the tastiest vegetables or produce them most thriftily, or with the most care for their soils. No, these are the people who through constant application of chemicals have managed to produce the *largest* vegetables, great pulpy squashes and melons.

The narrow valley at the foot of Crow Mountain was once a farm— we know how grand it looked because a poet, Jeanne Robert Foster, lived in the mountain's shadow as a girl. But the farmer who had built it watched as his children left for other, shinier pursuits. An old man, he looked on in despair as his fields began the slow return to forest:

> I must find a man who still loves the soil
> Walk by his side unseen, pour in his mind
> What I loved when I lived until he builds
> Sows, reaps, and covers these hill pastures here
> With sheep and cattle, mows the meadowland
> Grafts the old orchard again, makes it bear again
> Knowing that we are lost if the land does not yield.

As I stand on the ridge this morning, looking at the sumac and the birch covering the pasture, it is clear he never found his man. And clear that most of us will need some way other than a life of growing crops to get at this fundamental information.

There are other paths to this kind of deeper understanding of the world, but they too are overgrown and hard to find; a day of watching television makes it obvious that farming is not the only skill we've lost. Often, in fact, the television culture celebrates incompetence. One American Express ad depicts a couple who have chartered a sailboat in the tropics but are having a difficult time operating it. Suddenly they see a cruise schooner round the point, and to the triumphant Big Chill strains of "Rescue Me" they ditch their scow and jump aboard the luxury yacht, where there's a crew to attend to stuff like *sails* and *wind* and *lines* and *rocks* so they can concentrate on drinking. Money supplants skill; its possession allows us to become happily stupid. Presumably the crew members on the yacht make enough money pursuing *their* specialty that they don't need to know about anything else themselves either. Certainly most TV characters don't possess many skills; except for tending bar and solving murders, virtually no one in a drama or comedy actually works.

Occasionally, though, television offers a few glimpses of people who have developed very deep mastery, become real craftsmen. There are baseball games (on this evening the Braves were losing to the Pirates) where you get to watch men employ an enormous accretion of specialized knowledge—"There's a good hitter's pitch coming here," "He's shading him to right." On public TV, a man demonstrated the art of Chinese calligraphy. And off in the back alleys of cable there are a great many cooking shows run by chefs who can chop, whisk, separate, fold, knead, and roll, all in a blur.

These kinds of skills come from long, repetitive, and disciplined apprenticeships. Societies have always, at least since the beginning of agriculture, needed and valued certain specialized abilities; while the great majority of people were learning from their parents to produce food and otherwise care for themselves, a few were spending years with a master of some craft or art. Where the one education was broad, the other was deep—deeper, say, than law school. *So deep* that it may have produced some of the same kinds of fundamental knowledge that farming produces, because the master taught not just cooking or painting but universal things. As the poet and longtime Buddhist novice Gary Snyder wrote recently, "The youngsters left home to go and sleep in the back of the potting shed and would be given the single task of mixing clay for three years. . . . It was understood that the teacher would test one's patience and fortitude endlessly. One could not think of turning back, but just take it, go deep, and have no other interests." In the TV era, we're more comfortable with, say, Robert Warren, who has a cable art show and today is teaching all of America how to paint "Majestic Mountain Meadow." No three seasons of watching Robert mix paints! Or perhaps the amazing piano course sold by former Detroit Lion Alex Karras and endorsed by Davy Jones—"Now the Monkees can play their own instruments." Or maybe you'd like the Paint by Numbers Last Supper Painting Kit from the QVC shopping channel. "Duplicate Leonardo da Vinci's beautiful painting—you get 42 shades, so many that you're going to get very close to da Vinci. . . . You'll be able to learn just what goes into making an intricate painting like this. Give yourself the pride of accomplishment."

Still, there are echoes. The notion of apprenticeship as an almost religious vocation survives best, oddly, in martial arts movies like *Bloodsport* on Showtime. Representative of its type, it featured a young Caucasian who had studied for many years under a Japanese master. His command of body and soul was complete—he had reached the point where he fought not for external reward (for the teacher gave none, not even a smile) or for his liking for blood (he hated it—his master left Japan after his family was killed at Hiroshima). Instead he fought for an essentially spiritual satisfaction—because it made him feel close to some universal force. We thrill to this in part because it's a ridiculous excuse to let people kick each other's teeth in. But there's also something deeply attractive about that depth of training, that self-abnegation. We secretly believe that people who have gone through it *may* understand more about who they are. *Bloodsport* was followed on Showtime by Championship Boxing (Michael "The Silk" Olaajide losing a decision to Thomas "Hitman" Hearns). In an even more degraded way, boxing is about the same kind of issues. The great dramas in the sport only occasionally take place in the ring—usually they're outside it, where we watch to see if young men "stick to their training" or at the first flush of victory begin buying Italian cars and fancy women and letting their hangers-on coax them into staying up late at night. That is, will they trade their secrets and their discipline for the glitter of the world? Almost invariably flash wins out, in part because by old master-apprentice standards the training is not very rigorous (and because most other sorts of apprentices don't make $20 million a year). Still, we always find ourselves hoping.

Handcrafting pottery and samurai fighting and growing corn may be outmoded skills, but perhaps all the discipline and wisdom they offer can be acquired through more modern devotions, in which case my day on the mountain would be unnecessary. That is one of the arguments Robert Pirsig makes in *Zen and the Art of Motorcycle Maintenance* when he says "the Buddha, the Godhead, resides quite as comfortably in the circuits of a digital computer or the gears of a cycle transmission as he does at the top of a mountain or in the petals of a flower." ("I am master of my fate, captain of my soul," intones an ad for BMW motorcycles.) The Buddha, for all I know, *is* as comfortable in the gearbox, but he's increasingly inaccessible. Albert Borgmann, in a book called *Technology and the Character of Contemporary Life,* argues convincingly that Pirsig's approach becomes less and less helpful as technology progresses. When Pirsig wrote his book, a motorcycle was essentially a mechanical device; with each passing year it becomes more and more a microelectronic one, and you can't sit by the road and find God by looking at a bunch of incomprehensibly microscopic silicon chips. (You also can't repair your motorcycle anymore.) TV itself began as a toy for hobbyists, a gee-whiz gadget to build in the basement. Now it is too complex even for individual corporations—great manufacturing combines are getting together to develop High Definition TV. The great push is always *away* from individual skill and engagement—a horse took all sorts of information and insight to handle, and a Model T a little, and a Honda Accord virtually none.

It's a comfortable notion that as we progress we simply add to our store of understanding about the world—that we know more about the world by kindergarten than our grandparents knew when they died, and that our grandchildren will in turn be infinitely wiser than we are. In truth, though, we usually learn a new way of doing things at the expense of the old way. In this case we've traded away most of our physical sense of the world, and with it a whole category of information, of understanding. We have a new understanding, reflected most ubiquitously by television, which in many ways is sophisticated and powerful. And democratic—TV's obvious virtues, that it is cheap and always accessible—should not be overlooked. But there's much that it leaves out, that it can't include.

For only a few people anymore will this other information come from farming, and I don't anticipate a sudden, statistically significant boom in pot-throwing apprenticeships. So I'll concentrate on contrasting television's message with the ideas about the world and our place in it that come from a day in the natural world. In a way, I suppose, I'm hunting for a shortcut, which is the curse of the age. But it's a useful shortcut, since though few of us will farm, most people can still manage regular excursions into the natural world. It's not elitist—it's subversively easy.

To pull in this broadest of broadcasts you do not need pristine wilderness—there's very little, perhaps nothing, left that's entirely "natural." A city park or a suburban woodlot or a rural hedgerow or a backyard garden will do—anyplace that will let you take a conscious step away from the entirely man-made world. In all these places you can read what John Muir called "the inexhaustible pages of nature . . . written over and over uncountable times, written in characters of every size and color, sentences composed of sentences, every part of a character a sentence."

That this broadcast has gone on since the start of time—that some of its messages still live in our genes and instincts—does not mean, however, that it will go on forever. Parts of Muir's grammar are wiped off the slate each day—species lost, ecosystems altered. You have to listen harder to the natural world so you can separate out the primal song from the songs of our civilization and from our static. A team of Canadian scientists recently finished a study of several lakes in a remote part of northern Ontario, an area where the temperature had increased 3.5 degrees in the last two decades—the kind of warming that other scientists tell us the whole planet

40

can expect in the next two generations. The Canadian researchers reported all sorts of highly complex alterations of the environment. Warmer air had meant more evaporation, for instance. Hence, stream flows dropped and the lakes became clearer and therefore warmer. As a result, many cold-water species, including trout, faced extinction. But beyond their practical impact, the changes were simply one more sign that Muir's alphabet was turning into indecipherable hieroglyphics—one more sign that the great simplification had begun.

Much of this simplification may be irreversible. If so, we had best listen closely, since we will not get another chance. And what chance we *do* have of preserving this natural world also depends on listening—on absorbing the information of the mountain and garden and park as thoroughly as we soak up the information on the screen. And on letting it play as large a role in shaping the way we live. It depends, that is, on turning the present moment into a true age of information.

Reading and Responding

1. Freewrite about a camping trip, hike, or other outdoor activity you've done. Talk specifically about what you did, what you saw, how you felt—just try to remember it on paper.
2. Brainstorm about the sources of the information you tap on any normal day. Make a list of as many of these sources as you can (at least ten). Then divide them as McKibben does—either "natural" or "electronic." If something doesn't fit either category, call it "other."
3. Fold a paper in half from left to right so that you have a crease running down the middle. To the left of the crease, write words or phrases that describe reading; to the right of the crease, write words or phrases describing watching television. Once you have at least half a dozen items on each side of the crease, look at what you've written, and write two or three sentences about what you see.
4. Freewrite about the role that television plays in your life right now. What do you tend to watch, when is it on, and why do you watch it?

Working Together

1. Bring your comparison of TV watching and reading to class and share as a class or in groups. Brainstorm on the board or on paper together about how the two activities differ.
2. In light of item 1, work together to make a list of practical tips for anyone outside the class who sits down to read this piece by McKibben. Address someone who hasn't read very much, if at all, who's grown up only with television and not with books. What, exactly, should this person do when he or she starts this assignment? (For example, should he or she turn off the TV first?) Then what?

3. Talk as a group about the outdoor activities that you do, and make a list of them. As you think about these outdoor activities, also think about what they teach you about the natural world. For example, if you go hiking in the mountains, you may learn how to pay attention to the shifting weather (and so avoid getting drenched); or walking the dog in the afternoon, you may learn that your neighbor's cherry trees have bloomed and the camas grass has sprouted in the field. Make a list of these "lessons," too. Finally, how important are these "lessons" to your everyday life? As a group, write a couple of sentences that answer that question.

4. Talk as a group about the things you make for yourself (or used to make for yourself) rather than buy. Make a list of these things. Then list the reasons you can think of to make things for yourself. Finally, as a group, write a few sentences either agreeing or disagreeing with this statement: assuming we had the money, we'd rather buy everything we need or want, even if we knew how to make it ourselves.

Rethinking and Rewriting

1. Watch television for an hour. Record everything you see; and try to record *how* you're seeing it: what your body is doing, what your eyes are doing in particular, what's going on in your mind as you watch, whether you get up to get a snack, and so on. Then go outside—to your backyard, to a park, out of town to a mountain or a stream, or to some place on campus where you can sit and simply watch things for an hour. Record everything you see. Write both of these lists into an essay, imitating the structure of McKibben's "Daybreak." At some point, include a summary of McKibben's main point in your own words. Does your own small version of McKibben's experiment support his ideas or help you understand them better?

2. Identify three of your favorite things to eat. In an essay, look at each of them in turn, paying attention to how this food is made and where it comes from. Do some research if necessary. End your essay by asking yourself how natural your favorite foods (or dishes) are. Could you trace how they're made, could you identify their ingredients, and could you find out where those ingredients were grown or raised? Finally, on the basis of these three examples, would you say that you look at food as something that comes from nature or something that comes from a box, can, or freezer case?

3. Read Neil Postman's book about television, *Amusing Ourselves to Death: Public Discourse in the Age of Television*. Summarize his main argument in the first few chapters and then compare it with McKibben's. McKibben and Postman agree about how television changes the way we process information, the way we see the world. Explain. What does Postman add to McKibben's charge?

4. Write an essay that describes the experience of making something and then using it. Talk about the process and about the frustrations and pleasures that are part of that process.
5. Do a Web search to identify at least two books and two magazine or journal pieces that discuss television and its effects on viewers. Locate and use these resources to help you write an essay that explains and supports your own conclusions about the "problem of television."

NOVEMBER SOJOURN

Karen Warren

> *Karen Warren has edited numerous books, including* The Theory of
> Experiential Education *(1996). She is an instructor for the Outdoors
> Program and Recreational Athletics of Hampshire College in Amherst, Mas-
> sachusetts, where she teaches not only experiential education but also environ-
> mental justice and feminist pedagogy. All of these interests are evident in the
> following essay.*

At the Marcy Dam trail junction I casually sipped from my water
bottle as I eavesdropped on the conversation between the Adirondack
ranger and two hikers. I had watched with curiosity as the ranger approached the two men dressed in flannel, jeans and lightweight hiking
boots on that wintry November day. My years of leading outdoor trips had
raised a red flag when I saw how they were prepared for a demanding
cold-weather hike. "Cotton kills," I had told countless students over the
years. I was glad to see that the ranger was going to do his job.

"Where you headed?" Roy, the backcountry ranger, asked the two
hikers.

"Thought we'd do Marcy," one replied. Mount Marcy, at 5,344 feet,
is the centerpiece of the High Peaks region of the Adirondacks and, while
not a technical climb, demands a keen eye to changing weather conditions
during this time of the year. *Great,* I thought to myself, *no daypacks, no
water, no margin for error.*

"Good day for it," said Roy, falling into that coffee-shop repartee
reserved for locals. "The weather is supposed to hold."

"Yup, heard it from the waitress down at the Noonmark," the taller   5
one continued. As they amiably chatted I wondered if I'd be involved in a
rescue sometime during the weekend.

What brings me out in the late November chill each year? Sometimes
it's an urge to cheat the icy rain of western Massachusetts by finding the
sacred grail of new teleskiing snow in northern Vermont or the White
Mountains. Other years it's end-of-semester burnout; too many day trips,
too many student evaluations to write, too many phone calls to return.
After facilitating countless consensus decisions at trailheads, put-ins and
campfires, I'm so used to advocating for participants' needs that I'm numb
to my own. A consensus of one forces me to decide what I want.

Most times I want to pause to take stock of my life from a perspective
that only comes when I'm alone in the woods. One year, spurred on by
my partner, I went out with the very specific reason of figuring out if I
wanted a child in my life. Here was the adventuring woman, who five

years earlier had disdained the permanency of a credit card and a car loan, now trying to decide about a child. I choked so hard it took another year and another November sojourn before I had the courage to broach the subject again.

Something entices me to make the pilgrimage each year. The sweet memory of graceful teleturns I left in the spring snow comes to me as I sit in meetings. The image of austere peaks with their cutting wind and vast whiteness sticks in my imagination weeks before as I read papers or organize the skis in the equipment room. Or the lure of losing myself by bushwhacking in my own backyard, the Berkshires, finds me with the first November gray. Rarely do I plan beforehand where I'll go. Intuition tells me what outdoor gear to toss into my truck on the morning of departure, including a huge stuff sack of topos to cover all the possibilities my whim might consider.

That November, snowshoes and skis littered the truck bed uselessly. I had come to the Adirondacks to ski but the fine dusting of white on the ground was even too thin for my "rock" skis. A new plan was needed; I perched on the tailgate and studied the map.

Some people's dreams of outdoor adventure begin with stories of intriguing places, others with breathtaking color photos of wilderness scenes. Me, I'm a map dreamer. I can fantasize adventure in the dense, brown, spaghetti contour lines of any topographical sheet. Pulse quickening, my eyes dart to the most remote peaks on the quad, searching for the ridge-line route up.

Mount Marcy commanded the center of the map. While I told myself I wasn't into peak-bagging, Marcy is the highest of the range and solitary summit stands have always held a certain romance. It was an easy decision.

These were some of the thoughts I had that morning in the Adirondacks as I screwed the top on my Nalgene bottle and watched Roy finish his banter with the two ill-prepared hikers. His parting words were a caution. "There's probably some ice up there on top," yet overall his tone had been more conversational than admonishing. I was a little surprised he wasn't more assertive about the potential dangers they faced. Maybe he didn't see that as his job.

Roy turned his attention to me. He eyed me suspiciously, giving me the once-over before uttering a word. He reminded me of a field mouse sniffing furtively around my pack to determine its contents.

"Where you headed?" It seemed this was Roy's primary conversation starter.

"I thought I'd hike up to Indian Falls and camp," I said, never quite knowing how much information to give when I'm out alone. Since he was a backcountry ranger I figured he might be useful as an emergency back-up so I divulged more than usual.

"What's in your pack?" he quizzed me curtly.

Oh no, I thought. *Here it comes; that condescending tone reserved for women outdoors that I have heard too many times in my twenty years of instructing in the field.* It takes different forms, but the theme's the same each time. Once it was the Canyonlands ranger who, when I asked him to tell me the way into Virginia Park, spread my map out before my male student co-leader and traced the route for him. Oftentimes it's an outfitter on the phone whose tone says I first have to convince him I'm qualified to lead the river trip before he'll even talk shuttle prices.

"Camping gear," I said matter-of-factly, yet steeling myself for the next question, now uncomfortable about the intrusion. Didn't he see my layers of nylon and polypropylene, my broken-in Sorrels, my worn back-pack? My gear didn't look as if I'd just taken the tags off. Didn't I look as if I belonged in the woods? Was his scrutiny because I was a woman or an outsider or alone? Or all three?

"How long are you out? Are you planning to hike up Marcy? You can't do Marcy without crampons, instep crampons at a minimum. Do you have instep crampons?"

"No," I replied, feeling myself beginning to lose my voice amid the   20
barrage of questions. I resisted the urge to tell him not to worry, that I was perfectly capable of taking care of myself out there. I resisted because to prove my competence meant he had the right to question it. I resisted because at that moment I began to wonder if I was capable. All the doubts that I've heard and assimilated came welling to the surface.

"You can't do Marcy without instep crampons," Roy repeated.

"I'm not sure I'm climbing Marcy," I said. "I'll have to see how it goes."

"I was up there yesterday; the last two hundred yards are a sheet of ice. You'll need instep crampons to keep from slipping off." Did he think I hadn't heard him?

"OK," I said. Then, trying to divert him from instep crampons, I asked, "Are there any other shelters in the High Peaks area?" and gestured to a three-sided log lean-to by the lake. I wondered because I was consid-ering bringing students to the Adirondacks later that winter, and shelters make a good base camp for beginning winter campers.

Big mistake.   25

"They've taken the shelters out of the Indian Falls area. Too much overuse." He paused. "Do you have a tent?"

"No. I mean, I'm not carrying one." Tired of the inquisition, I wasn't about to tell him I preferred a nylon tarp for its light weight and the closeness to the snow it gave me.

"Well, these are the only shelters on your route."

"That's good to know. Probably should be going," I said, shouldering my backpack. "Nice to meet you," I lied.

"Same here. Be careful out there," Roy said as I walked away. Careful   30
of what? Sexist rangers?

It would take me halfway to Indian Falls before I stopped processing my interaction with Roy. As I trudged up the trail, I probed my anger at his assumptions, making sure it was still raw to the touch. When anger no longer worked, I tried denial. I kept letting Roy off the hook—he was just doing his job, he was of the old school and couldn't be expected to treat women the way contemporaries treat me. Finally I settled on doubt. Perhaps I should have been more communicative about my ability. Maybe I did need crampons; so why was I going any farther without them? What I experienced was the age-old polarity for women: the vacillation between doubting and believing.

The antics of a chickadee darting in and out of the balsam fir boughs finally brought me back to the present. I began to notice that the snow had deepened, that it was a full-fledged winter at this higher altitude. I moved from the noise inside me to the immense silence outside. The crystal, cascading stream, the snow-clotted firs, the solitude reminded me why I love to winter camp.

Winter is my best time of reflection; the season demands introspection. Clear silent air, clear spirit voice. There is some magic in the silent winter that untangles my feelings and thoughts and brings me to my center. Perhaps it is a transcendence where I move from myself to the broader, comprehensive cycles of the earth. When exposed to those cycles I witness a truth, an inspiration that helps me understand my own life. I have little to compare it to. In yoga, the meditative breath allows me to nourish my spine, the center of my body; in Quaker meeting, the shared silence gathers my energy of introspection and translates it through a community voice. Each has elements but neither compares. In the winter woods, my kinesthetic body joins my aesthetic spirit to create an apex of communion with self and the natural community.

Winter aloneness sparks my exuberance. I dance with Orion and my seven sisters, two-step with Cassiopeia across the darkened treeline. I leap and pirouette with twinkling power-points of stars composed in winter shapes. I search for the best of myself when I'm out alone in the winter.

When I'm with others on trips we fall into an easy camaraderie based on a necessary interdependence. The wilderness allows a magnanimousness about the foibles of others that just doesn't happen in the superficial world of appointment calendars and speedy good-byes while walking away backwards. It is precisely that relationship I have experienced with others that I try to find for myself when I do a solo trip. I search to like myself in the way I love those with whom I share a cup of tea around the campfire, a Class III run in a loaded canoe or a glimpse of mountain goat babies on the open ridge.

I arrived at Indian Falls at dusk. I set up camp and cooked dinner, nestling down comfortably into my aloneness. I used my ensolite to scoop out a sleeping depression in the snow and pitched my tarp over it. I hollowed out a candleholder in the walls of my snow nest; later marveling at the intense light given off by one candle. Periodic thoughts of my morning encounter were contained by my delight at being out again in winter's sparse environment.

The deliberateness of winter camping astounds me—so organized and recipe-like. At night I am the Julia Child of the tarp as I carefully measure out each ingredient that will insure my warmth. I prepare the sleeping bag, rolling out a thick slab of down, letting it rise until double in bulk. I correct the positioning of my ensolite so I can't slip off during the night. Blending dry socks with down booties, then folding in an extra wool shirt around my feet, I stuff my legs into the bag next to the water bottle I want to keep from freezing. On nights when I'm a culinary master, I spice the water bottle with hot water to blanch my feet as I fall asleep. Zip to my waist. Rotating my upper layers so the sweat-soaked one is not next to my skin, I whisk my pile shirt around my waist to keep my midsection and kidneys at a low rolling boil. Coat the foot of my sleeping bag with my parka. Wedge my boots under my body so they won't freeze but not too much that they make a sleep-discouraging lump under my knees. Please, no icky lumps. Zip to my chin. Reserve gorp close by to stoke my metabolism to a simmer at two a.m. Mixing equal parts pulled drawstring and tightened hat, I add a weather-stripping garnish to the hole with my scarf or neck gaiter. Preheating my body with isometric exercises, I sift into sleep anticipating a night of *The Joy of Cooking* warmth.

Over breakfast the next morning I decided I had to attempt Marcy. Like a compass needle to magnetic north, the mountain pulled me. I had to know if Roy was right. Yet I would only go as far as I felt safe. Nothing heroic.

As I slowly slogged up the approach to Marcy I thought about what I teach my outdoor leadership class about risk management. Accidents in the outdoors rarely happen without some accumulation of risks or mistakes. Card-stacking, I call it. A card is piled up for each risk factor that predicates an accident. A card for improper equipment, one for fatigue, another for dehydration, maybe another for being out alone and so on. By itself, each factor doesn't cause an accident but when piled high, the stack eventually collapses. The risks become a calamity. The trick, I advise the students, is to continually unstack the pile so it can't topple.

The trick for me on solo adventures is to remember my own advice. *40*
I couldn't let my encounter with Roy impede my judgement, neither trying for the summit to prove him wrong nor turning back because of the doubt he cast on my experience. In the card game of risk management I'm convinced that if ego is the joker, then intuition is my ace in the hole. I would go with what I know to be right for me.

As I neared treeline I wondered what Roy had been so cautious about. The way up had been steep but it had been easy enough to kick steps into the snow. Then I poked my body out of the trees, popping abruptly above treeline. I was taken aback by the power of the wind. It howled fiercely, polishing the mountain top to an icy glare. The sides of the mountain dropped off steeply. A wrong step could create a fatal fall. Falling into the great abyss, I often tell my students.

I could make out the summit cairn. I was tempted to go for the top, wanting to finish, to prove it could be done. I had trudged for too many hours to be this close and not complete the climb. I figured there were probably places behind the rocks littering the cone where the wind hadn't buffed a slippery surface. I might be able to connect these protected pockets to make my way to the top. But with nothing to hold on to, I would risk the wind blowing me across the slickness, out of control. I mentally ran through a few more possibilities but they all added up to an equation of wind and ice and steepness. The cards were stacked too high.

Marcy's grand view was not to be for me this time. I scanned the summit once more and turned back. As I descended I wondered if I could tell people when I returned home that I had climbed Mount Marcy. A peak-bagger would scoff, while a Taoist might say that simply being with the mountain was what was important. For me, it was a question without an answer.

When I first saw the shining, bare cap of Marcy gleaming like a full moon in the winter light I knew Roy had been only partially right. He was correct about the icy top, but not about the crampons. I had found it wasn't instep crampons I needed. More important was to be out there alone, believing in myself, trusting my intuition, finding my center. Strapping on instep crampons could make me no safer or surer than I was at that moment.

Reading and Responding

1. List the assumptions that seem to explain the ranger's actions in the first half of this essay. What did he assume about the two hikers "dressed in flannel, jeans and lightweight hiking boots"? What did he assume about the essay's narrator? Without judging these assumptions, just list as many of them as you reasonably can think of. Only after you've made this list, decide to what extent you are personally willing to "let Roy off the hook."

2. Why does the narrator decide to take this trip to Mount Marcy? What are her personal reasons? List anything significant you know about her based on what the essay itself tells us, either directly or indirectly. Once you've made a list, assume it applies to you. Where would you personally decide to go if you wanted to get away and think?

Working Together

1. Warren's essay contrasts human interchange, human society, and solitude, self-definition. In his questions and assumptions, Roy represents some common judgments about women, men, and the outdoors. Make

a list of these judgments as the narrator sees them; that is, make a list of the things that Roy seems to think of, worry about, and communicate. Then list your group's judgments of the narrator, both in terms of what she thinks and what she does. Include in your second list all of your group's judgments, even if some items on the list contradict or disagree with other items.

2. Think of this essay as representing two almost contradictory views of nature: On the one hand nature is clearly dangerous to people; yet, on the other hand it offers a setting in which one can believe in oneself, trust one's intuition, and find one's center. Does one view seem more true than the other? As a group, write a paragraph that explains everyone's thoughts on this topic.

Rethinking and Rewriting

1. Write an account of a time that you spent solo, without company. Tell your story. Help your readers understand how you now view this experience. Use "November Sojourn" as a model to help you establish this mix of narration and commentary.

2. Write a letter to someone you feel needs to spend some time away, alone. Explain why you think this person could benefit from some solitude. Include in the letter your recommendation for where this person might go to rest and reaffirm what's important. Describe the place and, if possible, your own experience in that place. Mention in your letter that the excursion you're recommending occurred to you after reading "November Sojourn" by Karen Warren. Use her experience and your own as some of the reasoning that you hope will persuade your reader.

GONE BACK INTO THE EARTH

THE BIRD AND THE MACHINE

Loren Eiseley

A distinguished anthropologist, Loren Eiseley also wrote evocative essays about his experience of the natural world. In his first book of essays, The Immense Journey *(1957), he meditates on the evolution of life from Pre-cambrian times to the formation of the human mind. His other prose meditations include* The Firmament of Time *(1960),* The Unexpected Universe *(1969), and* Night Country *(1971). In "The Bird and the Machine," as in all of his essays, Eiseley celebrates the mystery of living things.*

I suppose their little bones have years ago been lost among the stones and winds of those high glacial pastures. I suppose their feathers blew eventually into the piles of tumbleweed beneath the straggling cattle fences and rotted there in the mountain snows, along with dead steers and all the other things that drift to an end in the corners of the wire. I do not quite know why I should be thinking of birds over the *New York Times* at breakfast, particularly the birds of my youth half a continent away. It is a funny thing what the brain will do with memories and how it will treasure them and finally bring them into odd juxtapositions with other things, as though it wanted to make a design, or get some meaning out of them, whether you want it or not, or even see it.

It used to seem marvelous to me, but I read now that there are machines that can do these things in a small way, machines that can crawl about like animals, and that it may not be long now until they do more things—maybe even make themselves—I saw that piece in the *Times* just now. And then they will, maybe—well, who knows—but you read about it more and more with no one making any protest, and already they can add better than we and reach up and hear things through the dark and finger the guns over the night sky.

This is the new world that I read about at breakfast. This is the world that confronts me in my biological books and journals, until there are times when I sit quietly in my chair and try to hear the little purr of the cogs in my head and the tubes flaring and dying as the messages go through them and the circuits snap shut or open. This is the great age, make no mistake about it; the robot has been born somewhat appropriately along with the atom bomb, and the brain they say now is just another type of more complicated feedback system. The engineers have its basic principles worked out; it's mechanical, you know; nothing to get superstitious about; and man can always improve on nature once he gets the idea. Well, he's got it all right and that's why, I guess, that I sit here in my chair, with the article crunched in my hand, remembering those two birds and that blue mountain sunlight. There is another magazine article on my desk that reads "Machines Are Getting Smarter Every Day." I don't deny it, but I'll still stick with the birds. It's life I believe in, not machines.

Maybe you don't believe there is any difference. A skeleton is all joints and pulleys, I'll admit. And when man was in his simpler stages of machine building in the eighteenth century, he quickly saw the resemblances. "What," wrote Hobbes, "is the heart but a spring, and the nerves but so many strings, and the joints but so many wheels, giving motion to the whole body?" Tinkering about in their shops it was inevitable in the end that men would see the world as a huge machine "subdivided into an infinite number of lesser machines."

The idea took on with a vengeance. Little automatons toured the country—dolls controlled by clockwork. Clocks described as little worlds were taken on tours by their designers. They were made up of moving figures, shifting scenes, and other remarkable devices. The life of the cell was unknown. Man, whether he was conceived as possessing a soul or not, moved and jerked about like these tiny puppets. A human being thought of himself in terms of his own tools and implements. He had been fashioned like the puppets he produced and was only a more clever model made by a greater designer.

Then in the nineteenth century, the cell was discovered, and the single machine in its turn was found to be the product of millions of infinitesimal machines—the cells. Now, finally, the cell itself dissolved away into an abstract chemical machine, and that into some intangible, inexpressible flow of energy. The secret seems to lurk all about, the wheels get smaller and smaller, and they turn more rapidly, but when you try to seize it the life is gone—and so, by popular definition, some would say that life was never there in the first place. The wheels and the cogs are the secret and we can make them better in time—machines that will run faster and more accurately than real mice to real cheese.

I have no doubt it can be done, though a mouse harvesting seeds on an autumn thistle is to me a fine sight and more complicated, I think, in his multiform activity than a machine "mouse" running a maze. Also, I like to think of the possible shape of the future brooding in mice, just as it brooded once in a rather mousy insectivore who became a man. It leaves a nice fine indeterminate sense of wonder that even an electronic brain hasn't got, because you know perfectly well that if the electronic brain changes, it will be because of something man has done to it. But what man will do to himself he doesn't really know. A certain scale of time and a ghostly intangible thing called change are ticking in him. Powers and potentialities like the oak in the seed, or a red and awful ruin. Either way, it's impressive; and the mouse has it, too. Or those birds, I'll never forget those birds—yet before I measured their significance, I learned the lesson of time first of all. I was young then and left alone in a great desert—part of an expedition that had scattered its men over several hundred miles in order to carry on research more effectively. I learned there that time is a series of planes existing superficially in the same universe. The tempo is a human illusion, a subjective clock ticking in our own kind of protoplasm.

As the long months passed, I began to live on the slower planes and to observe more readily what passed for life there. I sauntered, I passed more and more slowly up and down the canyons in the dry baking heat of midsummer. I slumbered for long hours in the shade of huge brown boulders that had gathered in tilted companies out on the flats. I had forgotten the world of men and the world had forgotten me. Now and then I found a skull in the canyons, and these justified my remaining there. I took a serene cold interest in these discoveries. I had come, like many a naturalist before me, to view life with a wary and subdued attention. I had grown to take pleasure in the divested bone.

I sat once on a high ridge that fell away before me into a waste of sand dunes. I sat through hours of a long afternoon. Finally, as I glanced beside my boot an indistinct configuration caught my eye. It was a coiled rattlesnake, a big one. How long he had sat with me I do not know. I had not frightened him. We were both clocked in the sleepwalking tempo of the earlier world, baking in the same high air and sunshine. Perhaps he had been there when I came. He slept on as I left, his coils, so ill-discerned by me, dissolving once more among the stones and gravel from which I had barely made him out.

Another time I got on a higher ridge, among some tough little wind-warped pines half covered over with sand in a basinlike depression that caught everything carried by the air up to those heights. There were a few thin bones of birds, some cracked shells of indeterminable age, and the knotty fingers of pine roots bulged out of shape from their long and agonizing grasp upon the crevices of the rock. I lay under the pines in the sparse shade and went to sleep once more.   *10*

It grew cold finally, for autumn was in the air by then, and the few things that lived thereabouts were sinking down into an even chillier scale of time. In the moments between sleeping and waking I saw the roots about me and slowly, slowly, a foot in what seemed many centuries, I moved my sleep-stiffened hands over the scaling bark and lifted my numbed face after the vanishing sun. I was a great awkward thing of knots and aching limbs, trapped up there in some long, patient endurance that involved the necessity of putting living fingers into rocks and by slow, aching expansion bursting those rocks asunder. I suppose, so thin and slow was the time of my pulse by then, that I might have stayed on to drift still deeper into the lower cadences of the frost, or the crystalline life that glistens pebbles, or shines in a snowflake, or dreams in the meteoric iron between the worlds.

It was a dim descent, but time was present in it. Somewhere far down in that scale the notion struck me that one might come the other way. Not many months thereafter I joined some colleagues heading higher into a remote windy tableland where huge bones were reputed to protrude like boulders from the turf. I had drowsed with reptiles and moved with the century-long pulse of trees; now, lethargically, I was climbing back up some invisible ladder of quickening hours. There had been talk of birds in connection with my duties. Birds are intense, fast-living creatures—reptiles, I suppose one might say, that have escaped out of the heavy sleep of time, transformed fairy creatures dancing over sunlit meadows. It is a youthful fancy, no doubt, but because of something that happened up there among the escarpments of that range, it remains with me a lifelong impression. I can never bear to see a bird imprisoned.

We came into that valley through the trailing mists of a spring night. It was a place that looked as though it might never have known the foot of man, but our scouts had been ahead of us and we knew all about the abandoned cabin of stone that lay far up on one hillside. It had been built in the land rush of the last century and then lost to the cattlemen again as the marginal soils failed to take to the plow.

There were spots like this all over that country. Lost graves marked by unlettered stones and old corroding rim-fire cartridge cases lying where somebody had made a stand among the boulders that rimmed the valley. They are all that remain of the range wars; the men are under the stones now. I could see our cavalcade winding in and out through the mist below us: torches, the reflection of the truck lights on our collecting tins, and the far-off bumping of a loose dinosaur thigh bone in the bottom of a trailer. I stood on a rock a moment looking down and thinking what it cost in money and equipment to capture the past.

We had, in addition, instructions to lay hands on the present. The word had come through to get them alive—birds, reptiles, anything. A zoo somewhere abroad needed restocking. It was one of those reciprocal matters in which science involves itself. Maybe our museum needed a stray ostrich egg and this was the payoff. Anyhow, my job was to help capture some birds and that was why I was there before the trucks. 15

The cabin had not been occupied for years. We intended to clean it out and live in it, but there were holes in the roof and the birds had come in and were roosting in the rafters. You could depend on it in a place like this where everything blew away, and even a bird needed some place out of the weather and away from coyotes. A cabin going back to nature in a wild place draws them till they come in, listening at the eaves, I imagine, pecking softly among the shingles till they find a hole, and then suddenly the place is theirs and man is forgotten.

Sometimes of late years I find myself thinking the most beautiful sight in the world might be the birds taking over New York after the last man has run away to the hills. I will never live to see it, of course, but I know just how it will sound because I've lived up high and I know the sort of watch birds keep on us. I've listened to sparrows tapping tentatively on the outside of air conditioners when they thought no one was listening, and I know how other birds test the vibrations that come up to them through the television aerials.

"Is he gone?" they ask, and the vibrations come up from below, "Not yet, not yet."

Well, to come back, I got the door open softly and I had the spotlight all ready to turn on and blind whatever birds there were so they couldn't see to get out through the roof. I had a short piece of ladder to put against the far wall where there was a shelf on which I expected to make the biggest haul. I had all the information I needed, just like any skilled assassin. I pushed the door open, the hinges squeaking only a little. A bird or two stirred—I could hear them—but nothing flew and there was a faint starlight through the holes in the roof.

I padded across the floor, got the ladder up and the light ready, and slithered up the ladder till my head and arms were over the shelf. Everything was dark as pitch except for the starlight at the little place back of the shelf near the eaves. With the light to blind them, they'd never make it. I had them. I reached my arm carefully over in order to be ready to seize whatever was there and I put the flash on the edge of the shelf where it would stand by itself when I turned it on. That way I'd be able to use both hands.

Everything worked perfectly except for one detail—I didn't know what kind of birds were there. I never thought about it at all, and it wouldn't have mattered if I had. My orders were to get something interesting. I snapped on the flash and sure enough there was a great beating and feathers flying, but instead of my having them, they, or rather he, had me. He had my hand, that is, and for a small hawk not much bigger than my fist he was doing all right. I heard him give one short metallic cry when the light went on and my hand descended on the bird beside him; after that he was busy with his claws and his beak was sunk in my thumb. In the struggle I knocked the lamp over on the shelf, and his mate got her sight back and whisked neatly through the hole in the roof and off among the stars outside. It all happened in fifteen seconds and you might think I would have fallen down the ladder, but no, I had a professional assassin's reputation to keep up, and the bird, of course, made the mistake of thinking the hand was the enemy and not the eyes behind it. He chewed my thumb up pretty effectively and lacerated my hand with his claws, but in the end I got him, having two hands to work with.

He was a sparrow hawk and a fine young male in the prime of life. I was sorry not to catch the pair of them, but as I dripped blood and folded his wings carefully, holding him by the back so that he couldn't strike again, I had to admit the two of them might have been more than I could have handled under the circumstances. The little fellow had saved his mate by diverting me, and that was that. He was born to it and made no outcry now, resting in my hand hopelessly but peering toward me in the shadows behind the lamp with a fierce, almost indifferent glance. He neither gave

20

nor expected mercy and something out of the high air passed from him to me, stirring a faint embarrassment.

I quit looking into that eye and managed to get my huge carcass with its fist full of prey back down the ladder. I put the bird in a box too small to allow him to injure himself by struggle and walked out to welcome the arriving trucks. It had been a long day, and camp still to make in the darkness. In the morning that bird would be just another episode. He would go back with the bones in the truck to a small cage in a city where he would spend the rest of his life. And a good thing, too. I sucked my aching thumb and spat out some blood. An assassin has to get used to these things. I had a professional reputation to keep up.

In the morning, with the change that comes on suddenly in that high country, the mist that had hovered below us in the valley was gone. The sky was a deep blue, and one could see for miles over the high outcrop-pings of stone. I was up early and brought the box in which the little hawk was imprisoned out onto the grass where I was building a cage. A wind as cool as a mountain spring ran over the grass and stirred my hair. It was a fine day to be alive. I looked up and all around and at the hole in the cabin roof out of which the other little hawk had fled. There was no sign of her anywhere that I could see.

"Probably in the next county by now," I thought cynically, but before *25* beginning work I decided I'd have a look at my last night's capture.

Secretively, I looked again all around the camp and up and down and opened the box. I got him right out in my hand with his wings folded properly and I was careful not to startle him. He lay limp in my grasp and I could feel his heart pound under the feathers but he only looked beyond me and up.

I saw him look that last look away beyond me into a sky so full of light that I could not follow his gaze. The little breeze flowed over me again, and nearby a mountain aspen shook all its tiny leaves. I suppose I must have had an idea then of what I was going to do, but I never let it come up into consciousness. I just reached over and laid the hawk on the grass.

He lay there a long minute without hope, unmoving, his eyes still fixed on that blue vault above him. It must have been that he was already so far away in heart that he never felt the release from my hand. He never even stood. He just lay with his breast against the grass.

In the next second after that long minute he was gone. Like a flicker of light, he had vanished with my eyes full on him but without actually seeing even a premonitory wing beat. He was gone straight into that towering emptiness of light and crystal that my eyes could scarcely bear to penetrate. For another long moment there was silence. I could not see him. The light was too intense. Then from far up somewhere a cry came ringing down.

I was young then and had seen little of the world, but when I heard *30* that cry my heart turned over. It was not the cry of the hawk I had captured; for, by shifting my position against the sun, I was now seeing farther up. Straight out of the sun's eye, where she must have been soaring restlessly above us for untold hours, hurtled his mate. And from far up, ringing from peak to peak of the summits over us, came a cry of such unutterable and ecstatic joy that it sounds down across the years and tingles among the cups of my quiet breakfast table.

I saw them both now. He was rising fast to meet her. They met in a great soaring gyre that turned to a whirling circle and a dance of wings. Once more, just once, their two voices, joined in a harsh wild medley of question and response, struck and echoed against the pinnacles of the valley. Then they were gone forever somewhere into those upper regions beyond the eyes of men.

I am older now, and sleep less, and have seen most of what there is to see and am not very much impressed any more, I suppose, by anything. "What Next in the Attributes of Machines?" my morning headline runs. "It Might Be the Power to Reproduce Themselves."

I lay the paper down and across my mind a phrase floats insinuatingly: "It does not seem that there is anything in the construction, constituents, or behavior of the human being which it is essentially impossible for science to duplicate and synthesize. On the other hand . . . ."

All over the city the cogs in the hard, bright mechanisms have begun to turn. Figures move through computers, names are spelled out, a thoughtful machine selects the fingerprints of a wanted criminal from an array of thousands. In the laboratory an electronic mouse runs swiftly through a maze toward the cheese it can neither taste nor enjoy. On the second run it does better than a living mouse.

"On the other hand . . . ." Ah, my mind takes up, on the other   35
hand the machine does not bleed, ache, hang for hours in the empty sky in a torment of hope to learn the fate of another machine, nor does it cry out with joy nor dance in the air with the fierce passion of a bird. Far off, over a distance greater than space, that remote cry from the heart of heaven makes a faint buzzing among my breakfast dishes and passes on and away.

Reading and Responding

1. Reading slowly and patiently, annotate this essay. Mark passages that you don't understand, ask questions in the margin, note each major transition, and record where you agree or disagree with the author. Pay attention to what time it is when you start and what time it is when you finish. Then write a paragraph that explains how long it took you to read this essay and how annotating it helped (or hurt) your understanding.
2. Write about some instance you know of in which a machine has replaced a human being. Explain your response to this substitution.

Working Together

1. In groups of four or five, read each other's annotations of this essay: read, pass to the right; read, pass to the right—until you get your own book back. Then discuss. Which passages did you and your group members mark? What challenges and demands does Eiseley present for the reader? What are the best strategies for meeting these challenges?

2. This essay falls into four sections, separated with blank space. Number each section, label or give it a subheading, outline the structure on the board, and insert transitional phrases or sentences between the sections: "and this makes me think of . . ." or "here's an example of what I was talking about" or "and that brings me back to what I was thinking of earlier."

Rethinking and Rewriting

1. Write an essay that compares any animal you know well to any machine you know well: a gerbil and a word processor, a cat and a mountain bike, a dog and a pickup truck. Think of all the comparisons you can, however odd or apparently trivial. Somewhere in your essay, quote Eiseley's main point, and agree or disagree.

2. Write an essay on any subject, imitating Eiseley's structure: the same number of sections separated with blank space, with each section performing a similar role in relation to the whole (as in Eiseley's essay).

GONE BACK INTO THE EARTH

Barry Lopez

Essayist and nature writer Barry Lopez lives and writes along the Mc-
Kenzie River in Oregon. His book Of Wolves and Men *(1978) won the*
John Burroughs Medal, and his book Arctic Dreams *(1986) won the Na-*
tional Book Award. The following piece from Crossing Open Ground
(1988) illustrates the intense environmentalism and stylistic power that have
made Lopez one of the most important environmental writers in America.
His latest collection is About This Life: Journeys on the Threshold of
Memory *(1998).*

I am up to my waist in a basin of cool, acid-clear water, at the head
of a box canyon some 600 feet above the Colorado River. I place my
outstretched hands flat against a terminal wall of dark limestone which rises
more than a hundred feet above me, and down which a sheet of water
falls—the thin creek in whose pooled waters I now stand. The water splits
at my fingertips into wild threads; higher up, a warm canyon wind lifts
water off the limestone in a fine spray; these droplets intercept and shatter
sunlight. Down, down another four waterfalls and fern-shrouded pools
below, the water spills into an eddy of the Colorado River, in the shadow
of a huge boulder. Our boat is tied there.

This lush crease in the surface of the earth is a cleft in the precipitous
desert walls of Arizona's Grand Canyon. Its smooth outcrops of purple-
tinged travertine stone, its heavy air rolled in the languid perfume of columbine, struck by the sharp notes of a water ouzel, the trill of a disturbed
black phoebe—all this has a name: Elves Chasm.

A few feet to my right, a preacher from Maryland is staring straight
up at a blue sky, straining to see what flowers those are that nod at the top
of the falls. To my left a freelance automobile mechanic from Colorado sits
with an impish smile by helleborine orchids. Behind, another man, a
builder and sometime record producer from New York, who comes as
often as he can to camp and hike in the Southwest, stands immobile at the
pool's edge.

Sprawled shirtless on a rock is our boatman. He has led twelve or
fifteen of us on the climb up from the river. The Colorado entrances him.
He has a well-honed sense of the ridiculous, brought on, one believes, by
so much time in the extreme remove of this canyon.

In our descent we meet others in our group who stopped climbing   5
at one of the lower pools. At the second to the last waterfall, a young
woman with short hair and dazzling blue eyes walks with me back into
the canyon's narrowing V. We wade into a still pool, swim a few strokes to
its head, climb over a boulder, swim across a second pool and then stand

together, giddy, in the press of limestone, beneath the deafening cascade—filled with euphoria.

One at a time we bolt and glide, fishlike, back across the pool, grounding in fine white gravel. We wade the second pool and continue our descent, stopping to marvel at the strategy of a barrel cactus and at the pale shading of color in the ledges to which we cling. We share few words. We know hardly anything of each other. We share the country.

The group of us who have made this morning climb are in the middle of a ten-day trip down the Colorado River. Each day we are upended, if not by some element of the landscape itself then by what the landscape does, visibly, to each of us. It has snapped us like fresh-laundered sheets.

After lunch, we reboard three large rubber rafts and enter the Colorado's quick, high flow. The river has not been this high or fast since Glen Canyon Dam—135 miles above Elves Chasm, 17 miles above our starting point at Lee's Ferry—was closed in 1963. Jumping out ahead of us, with its single oarsman and three passengers, is our fourth craft, a twelve-foot rubber boat, like a water strider with a steel frame. In Sockdolager Rapid the day before, one of its welds burst and the steel pieces were bent apart. (Sockdolager: a nineteenth-century colloquialism for knockout punch.)

Such groups as ours, the members all but unknown to each other on the first day, almost always grow close, solicitous of each other, during their time together. They develop a humor that informs similar journeys everywhere, a humor founded in tomfoolery, in punning, in a continuous parody of the life-in-civilization all have so recently (and gleefully) left. Such humor depends on context, on an accretion of small, shared events; it seems silly to those who are not there. It is not, of course. Any more than that moment of fumbling awe one feels on seeing the Brahma schist at the dead bottom of the canyon's Inner Gorge. Your fingertips graze the 1.9-billion-year-old stone as the boat drifts slowly past.

With the loss of self-consciousness, the landscape opens. *10*

There are forty-one of us, counting a crew of six. An actor from Florida, now living in Los Angeles. A medical student and his wife. A supervisor from Virginia's Department of Motor Vehicles. A health-store owner from Chicago. An editor from New York and his young son.

That kind of diversity seems normal in groups that seek such vacations—to trek in the Himalaya, to dive in the Sea of Cortez, to go birding in the Arctic. We are together for two reasons: to run the Colorado River, and to participate with jazz musician Paul Winter, who initiated the trip, in a music workshop.

Winter is an innovator and a listener. He had thought for years about coming to the Grand Canyon, about creating music here in response to this particular landscape—collared lizards and prickly pear cactus, Anasazi Indian ruins and stifling heat. But most especially he wanted music evoked by the river and the walls that flew up from its banks—Coconino sandstone on top of Hermit shale on top of the Supai formations, stone exposed to sunlight, a bloom of photons that lifted colors—saffron and ochre, apricot, madder orange, pearl and gray green, copper reds, umber and terra-cotta browns—and left them floating in the air.

Winter was searching for a reintegration of music, landscape and people. For resonance. Three or four times during the trip he would find it for sustained periods: drifting on a quiet stretch of water below Bass Rapids with oboist Nancy Rumbel and cellist David Darling; in a natural amphitheater high in the Muav limestone of Matkatameba Canyon; on the night of a full June moon with euphonium player Larry Roark in Blacktail Canyon.

Winter's energy and passion, and the strains of solo and ensemble   *15* music, were sewn into the trip like prevailing winds, like the canyon wren's clear, whistled, descending notes, his glissando—seemingly present, close by or at a distance, whenever someone stopped to listen.

But we came and went, too, like the swallows and swifts that flicked over the water ahead of the boats, intent on private thoughts.

On the second day of the trip we stopped at Redwall Cavern, an undercut recess that spans a beach of fine sand, perhaps 500 feet wide by 150 feet deep. Winter intends to record here, but the sand absorbs too much sound. Unfazed, the others toss a Frisbee, practice Tai-chi, jog, meditate, play recorders, and read novels.

No other animal but the human would bring to bear so many activities, from so many different cultures and levels of society, with so much energy, so suddenly in a new place. And no other animal, the individuals so entirely unknown to each other, would chance together something so unknown as this river journey. In this frenetic activity and difference seems a suggestion of human evolution and genuine adventure. We are not the first down this river, but in the slooshing of human hands at the water's edge, the swanlike notes of an oboe, the occasional hugs among those most afraid of the rapids, there *is* exploration.

Each day we see or hear something that astounds us. The thousand-year-old remains of an Anasazi footbridge, hanging in twilight shadow high in the canyon wall above Harding Rapid. Deer Creek Falls, where we stand knee-deep in turquoise water encircled by a rainbow. Havasu Canyon, wild with grapevines, cottonwoods and velvet ash, speckled dace and mule deer, wild grasses and crimson monkey flowers. Each evening we enjoy a vespers: cicadas and crickets, mourning doves, vermilion flycatchers. And the wind, for which chimes are hung in a salt cedar. These notes leap above the splash and rattle, the grinding of water and the roar of rapids.

The narrow, damp, hidden worlds of the side canyons, with their   *20* scattered shards of Indian pottery and ghost imprints of 400-million-year-old nautiloids, open onto the larger world of the Colorado River itself; but nothing conveys to us how far into the earth's surface we have come.

Occasionally we glimpse the South Rim, four or five thousand feet above. From the rims the canyon seems oceanic; at the surface of the river the feeling is intimate. To someone up there with binoculars we seem utterly remote down here. It is this known dimension of distance and time and the perplexing question posed by the canyon itself—What is consequential? (in one's life, in the life of human beings, in the life of a planet)—that reverberate constantly, and make the human inclination to judge (another person, another kind of thought) seem so eerie.

Two kinds of time pass here: sitting at the edge of a sun-warmed pool watching blue dragonflies and black tadpoles. And the rapids: down the glassy-smooth tongue into a yawing trench, climb a ten-foot wall of standing water and fall into boiling, ferocious hydraulics, sucking whirlpools, drowned voices, stopped hearts. Rapids can fold and shatter boats and take lives if the boatman enters at the wrong point or at the wrong angle.

Some rapids, like one called Hermit, seem more dangerous than they are and give us great roller-coaster rides. Others—Hance, Crystal, Upset—seem less spectacular, but are technically difficult. At Crystal, our boat screeches and twists against its frame. Its nose crumples like cardboard in the trough; our boatman makes the critical move to the right with split-second timing and we are over a standing wave and into the haystacks of white water, safely into the tail waves. The boatman's eyes cease to blaze.

The first few rapids—Badger Creek and Soap Creek—do not overwhelm us. When we hit the Inner Gorge—Granite Falls, Unkar Rapid, Horn Creek Rapid—some grip the boat, rigid and silent. (On the ninth day, when we are about to run perhaps the most formidable rapid, Lava Falls, the one among us who has had the greatest fear is calm, almost serene. In the last days, it is hard to overestimate what the river and the music and the unvoiced concern for each other have washed out.)

There are threats to this separate world of the Inner Gorge. Down inside it one struggles to maintain a sense of what they are, how they impinge.

In 1963, Glen Canyon Dam cut off the canyon's natural flow of water. Spring runoffs of more than two hundred thousand cubic feet per second ceased to roar through the gorge, clearing the main channel of rock and stones washed down from the side canyons. Fed now from the bottom of Lake Powell backed up behind the dam, the river is no longer a warm, silt-laden habitat for Colorado squawfish, razorback sucker and several kinds of chub, but a cold, clear habitat for trout. With no annual scouring and a subsequent deposition of fresh sand, the beaches show the evidence of continuous human use: they are eroding. The postflood eddies where squawfish bred have disappeared. Tamarisk (salt cedar) and camel thorn, both exotic plants formerly washed out with the spring floods, have gained an apparently permanent foothold. At the old high-water mark,

25

catclaw acacia, mesquite and Apache plume are no longer watered and are dying out.

On the rim, far removed above, such evidence of human tampering seems, and perhaps is, pernicious. From the river, another change is more wrenching. It floods the system with a kind of panic that in other animals induces nausea and the sudden evacuation of the bowels: it is the descent of helicopters. Their sudden arrival in the canyon evokes not jeers but staring. The violence is brutal, an intrusion as criminal and as random as rape. When the helicopter departs, its rotor-wind walloping against the stone walls, I want to wash the sound off my skin.

The canyon finally absorbs the intrusion. I focus quietly each day on the stone, the breathing of time locked up here, back to the Proterozoic, before there were seashells. Look up to wisps of high cirrus overhead, the hint of a mare's tail sky. Close my eyes: tappet of water against the boat, sound of an Anasazi's six-hole flute. And I watch the bank for beaver tracks, for any movement.

The canyon seems like a grandfather.

One evening, Winter and perhaps half the group carry instruments and recording gear back into Blacktail Canyon to a spot sound engineer Mickey Houlihan says is good for recording.

Winter likes to quote from Thoreau: "The woods would be very silent if no birds sang except those that sing best." The remark seems not only to underscore the ephemeral nature of human evolution but the necessity in evaluating any phenomenon—a canyon, a life, a song—of providing for change.   *30*

After several improvisations dominated by a cappella voice and percussion, Winter asks Larry Roark to try something on the euphonium; he and Rumbel and Darling will then come up around him. Roark is silent. Moonlight glows on the canyon's lips. There is the sound of gurgling water. After a word of encouragement, feeling shrouded in anonymous darkness like the rest of us, Larry puts his mouth to the horn.

For a while he is alone. God knows what visions of waterfalls or wrens, of boats in the rapids, of Bach or Mozart, are in his head, in his fingers, to send forth notes. The whine of the soprano sax finds him. And the flutter of the oboe. And the rumbling of the choral cello. The exchange lasts perhaps twenty minutes. Furious and sweet, anxious, rolling, delicate and raw. The last six or eight hanging notes are Larry's. Then there is a long silence. Winter finally says, "My God."

I feel, sitting in the wet dark in bathing suit and sneakers and T-shirt, that my fingers have brushed one of life's deep, coursing threads. Like so much else in the canyon, it is left alone. Speak, even notice it, and it would disappear.

⎾I had come to the canyon with expectations⏌ I had wanted to see snowy egrets flying against the black schist at dusk; I saw blue-winged teal against the deep green waters at dawn. I had wanted to hear thunder rolling in the thousand-foot depths; I heard Winter's soprano sax resonating in Matkatameba Canyon, with the guttural caws of four ravens which circled above him. I had wanted to watch rattlesnakes; I saw in an abandoned copper mine, in the beam of my flashlight, a wall of copper sulphate that looked like a wall of turquoise. I rose each morning at dawn and washed in the cold river. I went to sleep each night listening to the cicadas, the pencil-ticking sound of some other insect, the soughing of river waves in tamarisk roots, and watching bats plunge and turn, looking like leaves blown around against the sky. What any of us had come to see or do fell away. We found ourselves at each turn with what we had not imagined.

The last evening it rained. We had left the canyon and been carried   35
far out onto Lake Mead by the river's current. But we stood staring backward, at the point where the canyon had so obviously and abruptly ended.

A thought that stayed with me was that I had entered a private place in the earth. I had seen exposed nearly its oldest part. I had lost my sense of urgency, rekindled a sense of what people were, clambering to gain access to high waterfalls where we washed our hair together; and a sense of our endless struggle as a species to understand time and to estimate the consequences of our acts.

It rained the last evening. But before it did, Nancy Rumbel moved to the highest point on Scorpion Island in Lake Mead and played her oboe before a storm we could see hanging over Nevada. Sterling Smyth, who would return to programming computers in twenty-four hours, created a twelve-string imitation of the canyon wren, a long guitar solo. David Darling, revealed suddenly stark, again and then again, against a white-lightning sky, bowed furious homage to the now overhanging cumulonimbus.

In the morning we touched the far shore of Lake Mead, boarded a bus and headed for the Las Vegas airport. We were still wrapped in the journey, as though it were a Navajo blanket. We departed on various planes and arrived home in various cities and towns and at some point the world entered again and the hardest thing, the translation of what we had touched, began.

I sat in the airport in San Francisco, waiting for a connecting flight to Oregon, dwelling on one image. At the mouth of Nankoweap Canyon, the river makes a broad turn, and it is possible to see high in the orange rock what seem to be four small windows. They are entrances to granaries, built by the Anasazi who dwelled in the canyon a thousand years ago. This was provision against famine, to ensure the people would survive.

I do not know, really, how we will survive without places like the   40
Inner Gorge of the Grand Canyon to visit. Once in a lifetime, even, is enough. To feel the stripping down, an ebb of the press of conventional time, a radical change of proportion, an unspoken respect for others that elicits keen emotional pleasure, a quick, intimate pounding of the heart.

Some parts of the trip will emerge one day on an album. Others will be found in a gesture of friendship to some stranger in an airport, in a letter of outrage to a planner of dams, in a note of gratitude to nameless faces in the Park Service, in wondering at the relatives of the ubiquitous wren, in the belief, passed on in whatever fashion—a photograph, a chord, a sketch—that nature can heal.

The living of life, any life, involves great and private pain, much of which we share with no one. In such places as the Inner Gorge the pain trails away from us. It is not so quiet there or so removed that you can hear yourself think, that you would even wish to; that comes later. You can hear your heart beat. That comes first.

Reading and Responding

1. Freewrite (at least half a page) about the pressures and stresses in your life now. Does reading Lopez's essay have any effect on how you feel? Write a few more sentences explaining this.
2. Does it surprise you to find that part of the reason for this trip is to play music? Are you surprised to find that jazz musician Paul Winter organized the trip? What do you think of that? Would you normally associate jazz with a rafting trip? Write about half a page in response to these questions.
3. Write something you would share with no one. Then decide whether to keep it somewhere or shred it or burn it or throw it away.

Working Together

1. Assume that "Gone Back into the Earth" is an example of strong, effective narrative and descriptive writing. Reread the first seven paragraphs; as a group, decide on three reasons why this writing is in fact strong and effective narrative, descriptive writing. List your reasons and a part of Lopez's essay that illustrates each reason. (*Hint:* Look for the writing that grabs you.)
2. As a group, talk about whether you think jazz has any place on a rafting trip. Come to a consensus if you can, and write a short paragraph that explains your group's conclusion. If you can't agree, write a paragraph about why you can't agree.

Rethinking and Rewriting

1. Write about a time when you've "gone back" to some wild or natural place. Put yourself and your readers right back into that landscape and that time. In your opening paragraph, consciously try to imitate Lopez's opening paragraph. And try to end as Lopez does, too, by reflecting on the trip and what it might mean—or does mean—to you.

2. On the basis of only this one Lopez essay, write about why you would or would not be interested in reading more by this author. What does (or does not) appeal to you in this writing? Make your thoughts and opinions clear, and include at least two quotes from "Gone Back into the Earth" to further clarify your opinions.

TEXAS ON MY MIND (AND MEXICO ON MY RIGHT)

Rebecca Solnit

> *A frequent contributor to* Sierra, *Rebecca Solnit is the author of several books, including* Savage Dreams: A Journey into the Hidden Wars of the American West *(1994). Like the Saenz piece, "Exile: El Paso, Texas," in chapter 2, this essay explores many different kinds of borders— between countries, between poverty and prosperity, and between culture and landscape.*

The birds of the lower canyons of the Rio Grande were wonderful. The mammalian life, on the other hand, was dismaying, consisting almost entirely of longhorn cattle grinding the riverbank into dust and men with guns. Nothing I knew about the upper stretches of the river had prepared me for this.

The Rio Grande is to New Mexico what the Nile is to Egypt, a thirst-quenching route along which both cities and agriculture cluster in an arid land. It pours straight south from the southern Rockies, fed by the clear, rushing streams of northern New Mexico to become the broad, sluggish river that divides nothing more dramatic than, say, Albuquerque from the new developments of western Albuquerque. But as it crosses the border into Texas, two dramatic things happen. One is that the huge river has run nearly dry. Its water irrigates thousands of acres in Colorado (which siphons off nearly half the river), then continues on to quench the corn and squash fields of the Indian pueblos of northern New Mexico and the pecan orchards, alfalfa, and chile fields to the south. The other is that the Rio Grande becomes, for the rest of its course to the Gulf of Mexico, the long, meandering, southeast-slanting Texas/Mexico border. Being a border is an odd task for a river, because a river in its natural condition brings things together rather than dividing them. This is why bioregionalists often propose watersheds as the most coherent ecological—and political—boundaries. This river has a penchant for creating international incidents by changing course, notably in El Paso in the 1960s, when high flows transferred part of Mexico to the United States. Now, says El Paso poet Benjamin Saenz, "The Rio Grande is not allowed to be a river because it's a border." A concrete straitjacket encases what water makes its way to this border town, to keep it from redrawing the border again. Below El Paso, 40 percent of the river is channelized, keeping mapmakers and politicians content. Even so, the border itself is no longer synonymous with the river. After many excursions by the Rio Grande, this border was finally drawn where the deepest part of the river was during the 1967–74 survey, whether water flows there now or not.

But the Rio Grande doesn't end in El Paso. A few hundred miles downstream, in one of the more remote places in the Lower 48, the river and the landscape become wild again. (For those on the Mexican side it is named not the Rio Grande—or big river—but the Rio Bravo, or ferocious river). It's big country, with vast plains rolling toward mountains blue with distance, small scattered towns drying up, and a creosote-bush-and-cactus harshness that will probably keep its population down forever. In the right light, it is one of the most magnificent places on Earth, with pronghorns and hawks punctuating the wide sweep of grassland and abandoned farmhouses whose bladeless windmills sink silently back into the earth. The river creates a doubly anomalous landscape, both by carving a deep canyon into it and by giving sustenance to plant and bird species not found on the spare Texas plains. The lower canyons, down which our group of 17 rafted for ten days, are even more remote than Big Bend National Park just upstream, because far fewer roads lead to this wild-and-scenic stretch of river. Only 700 people raft it every year, a tiny number compared to, say, the Grand Canyon, with its 20,000 raft trips annually.

But is it wild? On its journey to the sea the Rio Grande is everywhere diverted and frequently dammed; what water stays in the riverbed contains every possible additive. A report in *National Parks* magazine declared, "The river suffers from just about every type of pollution imaginable, including radioactive sediments [from Los Alamos National Laboratory, far upstream], industrial toxins, mine wastes, agricultural runoff, erosion caused by mining and logging, and improperly treated sewage that causes outbreaks of disease among the human population living along the border." The river annually dries up altogether at four points and runs perilously low elsewhere. According to Steve Harris of Rio Grande Restoration, "Its bones are picked clean." Harris, an activist and river guide who grew up on the Texas Rio Grande, now lives far upstream, near Taos. His group advocates for water flow, an issue often neglected by those working for the other important goals of water quality and human health. Even after outlining the dire problems on this river, Harris told me that "the river's not too far gone—and we have a vision of what it could be." Restoring the river will require maintaining what natural water flows remain and working to reclaim water rights that have been lost.

The water that we floated down for ten days was largely Mexican. The river that has been sucked nearly dry in the United States is resuscitated by the Rio Conchos, a tributary flowing north through Chihuahua, and by a plethora of small springs flowing clear into the murky river. At this point what remains of the crystalline snowmelt that tumbled down from New Mexico's mountains has become a slow-moving opaque soup with the occasional clot of foam floating atop it, a river less of whitewater than of gray. Thinking too much about the water we floated on and waded, swam, and bathed in was a queasy proposition, though there was little enough of it: a more immediate hazard on this stretch of the river is running aground, which we did regularly the first few days. Wild-and-

5

scenic status will keep nearly 100 miles of the river here from being dammed or developed, but it doesn't do a thing for water flow, overgrazing, or upstream contamination. "So what does it mean that this stretch is designated wild and scenic?" I asked Harris, who seemed to know everything about the river. "Not much," he answered.

For nearly 80 miles we were sunk in the canyon of the river, surrounded by mesas and cliffs sometimes rising more than 1,000 feet from the riverbed. This steep landscape held the narrow strip of riparian life, Chihuahuan-desert-style. It was, as one of my companions said, the prickliest landscape, and she developed an affection for the thornless barometer bush—so named because its small silvery leaves respond to the least change in moisture. All around it grew cactus—prickly pear, barrel, Christmas, strawberry hedgehog, and urchin cactus—along with thorny mesquite, acacia, ocotillo, century plants, and the lecheguilla, like bouquets of curving daggers jutting from the rocks, sharper than the yuccas that also fill the niches of these hanging gardens between the rocks. Even for me, after a decade of exploring the Mojave and Great Basin deserts, this Chihuahuan landscape was hard to adjust to. Deserts are like quiet people; it takes a long time to find out who they are and how to appreciate them, to see the rich life springing up between the stones, emerging at twilight, to learn the peculiar quality of light and space that makes each distinctively majestic.

Along the river we lacked what I usually love best about deserts: the invitation and challenge of limitless space. The canyons narrowed our vision and movement and cut off our light long before the sun set—though this same landscape fostered the wealth of plant and bird life that greeted us. (This stretch of the river is a major flyway for migratory birds; letting the river run dry poses an international threat to subtropical songbirds, ducks, and cranes.) Three or four times we clambered up to a mesa to see the arid world spreading for dozens or maybe even hundreds of miles in every direction without a visible trace of civilization, and then descended again into an arena as narrow as a Manhattan avenue. And only in the last days did I start to see the beauty in the sweep of gray stone walls studded with the mud nests of roughwing swallows, in the ovoid architecture of the ubiquitous prickly pears, in the sinuous river itself looking pea-green rather than brown from high above.

For the rest of the people afloat, it was an even stranger place. All of them were from the lush landscape of British Columbia and northwest Washington State, and they found the aridity and thorniness perplexing, even as they basked like lizards in the relentless sun. To many of them, seasonal waterways were freakish; rivers were not supposed to go dry in summer, and they spoke in awe of the fact that the Rio "puddles" in summer—though here, it is true, the puddling takes place because of diversion as well as nature. The dust, too, wasn't strictly natural, but the result of hooves trampling down fragile soils and tearing up ground cover. We saw cows far more often than any other sign of civilization; longhorns chew up the banks and occasionally wash up dead, further compromising the river. The banks that were inaccessible to cattle were often covered with lush grass, but the rest were little oceans of acrid, gritty dust that would blow into every crack in a tent and across every open dish, and onto our exposed skin.

Despite the northerners' astonishment at the aridity, the place—or at least the opportunity to enjoy themselves in this place—seemed to delight them, but then they were on vacation and determined to enjoy themselves. The other environmentalists had left their troubles and concerns 1,500 miles north, in the pure blue rivers and tall forests of British Columbia. I, on the other hand, was on assignment and not so far from my home, and my concerns were all around this fierce river, with its border violence and its upstream crimes of contamination. Though I was in the same place as the other 16 people, I often felt I was in a different world. Their reference point for borders was what is often advertised as the "world's longest un-defended border," the amicable U.S./Canadian border, but the one we were floating down is the contentious, dangerous place where California's and some of the nation's most explosive political debates are centered and where border crossers and bystanders succumb regularly to crime and thirst and border patrols. So I spent my time looking into the sinister shadows of this boisterous trip under a burning sun. In the middle of the group were the young male river guides bonding noisily, and clustered around them women admiring and encouraging this, to say the least, rather old-fashioned arrangement. The guides dominated the social interactions the way, say, bears dominate a food chain, yet around the edges was more tranquil society. I managed to embark and stay, with a few other less-hectic souls, upon what we dubbed The Raft of Civilization, captained by Vancouverite Greg Roth, an expert birder and a surprising authority on cactus, given his home in the wet Northwest.

When the Mexican army arrived at Hot Springs Rapids with their *10* automatic rifles, two of the guides and several passengers were in the hot spring drinking wine and hooting out lurid speculations about guide anat-omy. The commander and his three stolid soldiers were first seen by some-one dozing in a tent who did little more than hope it was a bad dream; the second went to tell the trip leader in the spring; and I must have been the third. My primitive Spanish regressed further under the circumstances, but I figured that being female, fully dressed, and impressed with the gravity of the situation made me the best person around to take on the job of soothing diplomatic liaison anyway. (Besides, the one Spanish-speaker in the group was off hunting red-eared slider turtles. "*El busca las tortugas,*" I said, or something to that effect, and my interrogator laughed.) We were camped on the Mexican side of the river, on one of the few spots, it turns out, where a road leads all the way to its banks, 12 miles down a long canyon from the nearest ranch, used periodically by people coming to bathe in the springs.

I never found out why the Mexican army had arrived—whether we were interrupting their bathing schedule, or whether it had something to do with the old man we'd seen the day before, who with his heavily laden burro might have been a drug smuggler. It seemed unlikely to be a routine patrol, in this remote place bordered by cliffs. I did ascertain that the commander, who was in a good if unrelenting mood, preferred *la costa*— "*Acapulco y Puerto Vallarta*" to *el desierto,* and wouldn't mind being transferred soon. I was just trying to put in a good word for the desert—though I myself live on *la costa,* as he had seen when he inspected my papers, when the trip leader came along and found out that the commander didn't want to stay for a drink. Nothing, apparently, was wrong, and from then on, *no problemo* became a byword on the trip.

And with this visit, the notion that we were on the border became hard and real again. A border is not a natural landscape feature but a political abstraction drawn on maps and then imposed on the land—or not. In places like Tijuana/San Diego and Juárez/El Paso, the idea of the border is made real with a physical structure of fences and walls and concrete channels and inspection stations and patrols dividing the land. In remoter places, the border might be nothing more than a barbed-wire fence to keep livestock from going international. And here there was no marking of the border save the river, and a river is not a border, particularly when it's only a few feet deep. Once when our rafts ran aground on this border, a curious bull came over from Texas to investigate and then wandered on into Mexico; another time three of the guides sitting around the Texas campfire drank a bottle of some high-voltage concoction called Hot Damn and, around midnight, waded across to Mexico naked. The one who sat down on the prickly pear issued the pronouncement that "Mexico is uncomfortable," another phrase that became part of our daily lexicon. It was a strange Canadian take on the river-wading emigrations that gave us the unfortunate term *wetback.* (I managed to introduce *frostback,* which I'd garnered from a *Prairie Home Companion* episode parodying U.S. paranoia about Mexicans with a skit about Canadians sneaking into Minnesota, and for a little while we tried calling the whole expedition RAFTA.)

We took to navigating by saying Texas or Mexico rather than right or left, since the raft and its passengers might be facing any direction, and poor rowers like me cut a transnational course through the erratic currents of this winding river. There is no border here, ecologically speaking. The phoebes that dart among the cane and willow have no citizenship, the turkey vultures that gather by the hundreds in the evening sky carry no visas. The prickly pears that grow on the right bank are indistinguishable from those on the left, and the canyon wrens trill out their wonderful song of descending notes from both shores. You'd have to go much farther south to see the Chihuahuan desert gradually give way to the more mountainous and then more tropical regions of central Mexico, or go north hundreds of miles to reach the lusher Texas plains. These are not abrupt lines of change, but subtle gradations through which everything moves. Here, the border is conceptual—like the Iron Curtain, not literal, like the Berlin Wall—yet being on it was momentous after so many years of fierce public argument about who belongs on what side of it, after so much militarization of it in the more populous places, after so many deaths of those who tried to cross it or appeared to be on the wrong side. (After passing a herd of goats, I told my raft-mates the story of Esequiel Hernández, the teenage goatherd who was shot in the back by U.S. Marines in Redford, Texas, not far from where we floated.) The border that loomed so large in political debate took on another face as a muddy river in the fastnesses few visit.

This border river mingles the water of three U.S. states with that of Mexico and local springs on its 1,800-mile journey to the Gulf of Mexico. Killer bees are advancing north through this area, as indifferent to borders as any other nonhuman species, or so the fisherman told us, as he stood trolling for catfish on the left bank. He made a most unfortunate sample Texan, in his unclear-on-the-concept wardrobe of knee-high white socks and camouflage shorts, with a pistol on either hip. (To shoot outsize catfish? we wondered.) And on our last day we were met by a better-looking Texan, a Latino agent of the Immigration and Naturalization Service wearing jeans and a Tejano-music T-shirt (and a gun and INS badge that the northerners didn't notice, since at least some of them persisted in thinking he was a park ranger). He had apparently come down in his camouflaged pickup truck to discuss the whereabouts of a stray bull with a ragged Mexican vaquero who was mounted on a shaggy horse. He explained that when the river gets shallow, livestock emigrate across both banks.

Air, like water and wildlife and livestock, does not respect national boundaries. One of the major environmental issues of the region is air quality. Though in early spring the air looked good, in the summer visibility in Big Bend National Park often drops from 150 miles to around 10. An obvious aesthetic problem, the opaque air signifies something much more serious. Some of it contains sulfur dioxide from two huge coal-burning Mexican power plants near the border, and Texas has blithely blamed Mexico for the problem. But according to a National Park Service map of emissions sources, almost an equal amount comes from many smaller Texas locations. Local Sierra Club activists and other Texas environmental groups are still trying to get state and federal agencies to identify the sources and alleviate the air pollution. Meanwhile locals are developing respiratory problems. Frances Sage, chair of the Sierra Club's Big Bend Group says, "We're so isolated we felt immune to all those problems. People out here didn't think those kinds of city things could happen in a place so remote."

The same could be said of the Sierra Blanca nuclear-waste dump, which may open this year to receive low-level waste from Maine, Vermont,

15

and elsewhere. Several hundred miles from where we floated but a mere 16 miles from the border river, the dump—sited atop both an aquifer and an earthquake fault—would add to the radioactive threats to the Rio Grande. Like most nuclear-waste dumps, this one was chosen more for political expediency than for scientific reasons. Less than a hundred miles east of El Paso, the tiny town of Sierra Blanca wasn't expected to be able to stand up to the state of Texas on this issue, says Sierra Blanca Legal Defense Fund Director Erin Rogers. Yet it has, backed by the strong opposition of both Mexican and U.S. environmental groups (including the Sierra Club) and the Mexican government, whose congress recently passed a unanimous resolution against the dump. "We don't let the border divide us," says Rogers, pointing out that the dump would also violate the La Paz agreement signed in 1983 by Ronald Reagan and then–President Miguel de la Madrid Hurtado, which stipulated that neither country would unilaterally locate polluting sites within 100 kilometers of the border. Most recently Senator Paul Wellstone (D-Minn.) threatened to filibuster the bill authorizing funds for the dump, on the grounds of environmental racism. And desert discrimination, one might add: so many present and proposed nuclear-waste dumps—in Carlsbad, New Mexico; Yucca Mountain and Beatty, Nevada; and Ward Valley, California—are situated in the desert because deserts are imagined as inert, but geological forces and the movement of water in all these places make them as volatile as any place on Earth.

The Rio Grande is a perfect example of nature's interconnectedness. It brings the snowmelt of high western mountains through this deep desert to the subtropical Gulf of Mexico, where hundreds of species of birds stop on their migrations. But the river also suggests that no place is far enough away nowadays, that everyplace is downwind and downstream. It's a place where the old-style degradation of overgrazing meets up with the industrial age's air and water pollution, water diversion, and nuclear contamination. But even amid the murky water and the murky future and the men with guns, the lower canyons of the Rio Grande have their moments. Watching the oars cut into the reflections of canyons in calm water; watching sunlight reflected off the water spread the river's ripples across the gray canyon walls; watching a great blue heron stand camouflaged, a dull gray bird, then fly ahead of us with open wings the exhilarating blue of a desert storm cloud, the Rio Grande is still beautiful, and still surviving.

Reading and Responding

1. As you reread Solnit's account of the Rio Grande (or Rio Bravo), make a simple list of the topics or issues that the trip (and the essay) raise; make note of the place in the essay where each issue is first mentioned. Then write a couple of sentences that comment on this river as you see it now.

2. Write three or four sentences about your experience with desert landscape or about your image or notion of what deserts are like. Then write three or four sentences about how this Chihuahuan landscape compares with your experience or your images. In Solnit's account, what confirms what you already knew or thought about the desert and what surprises you or teaches you something new?

3. Why does it matter that this river is also an international border? What kinds of conflict does the border create between groups of people and between what is political and what is ecological? Write a paragraph (at least five sentences) that tries to explain these conflicts briefly but accurately.

Working Together

1. On your own, write one word that you think most accurately describes the Rio Grande as you understand it now. Then (still individually) decide on one word that describes your gut response to reading this essay; be honest and accurate. Finally (still working individually), write two sentences that explain your gut response and the word you chose to describe it. In your group, take turns explaining what you've written. Then write a group paragraph that explains the range of responses that group members had to reading this essay.

2. Work together to make a list of the various competing demands that you see being made on the Rio Grande. For each one, identify the demand and the group or entity that's making that demand.

3. Consider the issues—political, ecological, economic, and personal— that Solnit's account of the Rio Grande raises. Then compare the Rio Grande to a local river you know. To what extent is the local river affected by these same issues? Are there any issues unique to the local river? Write a paragraph that compares and contrasts the human impact of the Rio Grande and your local river, without doing additional research.

Rethinking and Rewriting

1. Use Solnit's essay on the Rio Grande as a starting point for research on a river that you know. Start by identifying two serious, important questions you have about the river (for example, what's known about the activities in the watershed that drains into this river?). Then focus your research on answering these questions. Write a paper of approximately five pages that explains what you've learned and what you'd still like to know.

2. Using Solnit's information on the Rio Grande as your sole source, write an essay that explains what you think the role of governments ought to be when it comes to managing the various activities that affect the river. In your opinion, what actions by the various governmental units in-

volved with the Rio Grande would be most beneficial? Make sure your essay identifies both the actions you'd advocate and your reasons for seeing these actions as praiseworthy. As you discuss your reasons, make it clear who or what you think would benefit most and who or what would suffer most based on your recommendations.

THE GREAT AMERICAN DESERT

Edward Abbey

> *The late Edward Abbey was famous for his passionate love of the South-west desert and his cranky impatience with those who failed to love and respect it, too. After writing several novels, Abbey wrote* Desert Solitaire *(1968), a "personal history" of his experience as a park ranger in the canyon country of Utah and Arizona. His subsequent work includes several collections of essays and a best-selling novel about eco-sabotage,* The Monkey Wrench Gang *(1975). A book of selections from his journals was published as* Confessions of a Barbarian *in 1996. The essay that follows is from* Desert Solitaire.

In my case it was love at first sight. This desert, all deserts, any desert. No matter where my head and feet may go, my heart and my entrails stay behind, here on the clean, true, comfortable rock, under the black sun of God's forsaken country. When I take on my next incarnation, my bones will remain bleaching nicely in a stone gulch under the rim of some faraway plateau, way out there in the back of beyond. An unrequited and excessive love, inhuman no doubt but painful anyhow, especially when I see my desert under attack. "The one death I cannot bear," said the Sonoran-Arizonan poet Richard Shelton. The kind of love that makes a man selfish, possessive, irritable. If you're thinking of a visit, my natural reaction is like a rattlesnake's—to warn you off. What I want to say goes something like this.

Survival Hint #1: Stay out of there. Don't go. Stay home and read a good book, this one for example. The Great American Desert is an awful place. People get hurt, get sick, get lost out there. Even if you survive, which is not certain, you will have a miserable time. The desert is for movies and God-intoxicated mystics, not for family recreation.

Let me enumerate the hazards. First the Walapai tiger, also known as conenose kissing bug. *Triatoma protracta* is a true bug, black as sin, and it flies through the night quiet as an assassin. It does not attack directly like a mosquito or deerfly, but alights at a discreet distance, undetected, and creeps upon you, its hairy little feet making not the slightest noise. The kissing bug is fond of warmth and like Dracula requires mammalian blood for sustenance. When it reaches you the bug crawls onto your skin so gently, so softly that unless your senses are hyperacute you feel nothing. Selecting a tender point, the bug slips its conical proboscis into your flesh, injecting a poisonous anesthetic. If you are asleep you will feel nothing. If you happen to be awake you may notice the faintest of pinpricks, hardly more than a brief ticklish sensation, which you will probably disregard. But the bug is already at work. Having numbed the nerves near the point of entry the bug proceeds (with a sigh of satisfaction, no doubt) to withdraw blood. When its belly is filled, it pulls out, backs off, and waddles away, so drunk and gorged it cannot fly.

At about this time the victim awakes, scratching at a furious itch. If you recognize the symptoms at once, you can sometimes find the bug in your vicinity and destroy it. But revenge will be your only satisfaction. Your night is ruined. If you are of average sensitivity to a kissing bug's poison, your entire body breaks out in hives, skin aflame from head to toe. Some people become seriously ill, in many cases requiring hospitalization. Others recover fully after five or six hours except for a hard and itchy swelling, which may endure for a week.

After the kissing bug, you should beware of rattlesnakes; we have half 5 a dozen species, all offensive and dangerous, plus centipedes, millipedes, tarantulas, black widows, brown recluses, Gila monsters, the deadly poisonous coral snakes, and giant hairy desert scorpions. Plus an immense variety and near-infinite number of ants, midges, gnats, bloodsucking flies, and blood-guzzling mosquitoes. (You might think the desert would be spared at least mosquitoes? Not so. Peer in any water hole by day: swarming with mosquito larvae. Venture out on a summer's eve: The air vibrates with their mournful keening.) Finally, where the desert meets the sea, as on the coasts of Sonora and Baja California, we have the usual assortment of obnoxious marine life: sandflies, ghost crabs, stingrays, electric jellyfish, spiny sea urchins, man-eating sharks, and other creatures so distasteful one prefers not even to name them.

It has been said, and truly, that everything in the desert either stings, stabs, stinks, or sticks. You will find the flora here as venomous, hooked, barbed, thorny, prickly, needled, saw-toothed, hairy, stickered, mean, bitter, sharp, wiry, and fierce as the animals. Something about the desert inclines all living things to harshness and acerbity. The soft evolve out. Except for sleek and oily growths like the poison ivy—oh yes, indeed— that flourish in sinister profusion on the dank walls above the quicksand down in those corridors of gloom and labyrinthine monotony that men call canyons.

We come now to the third major hazard, which is sunshine. Too much of a good thing can be fatal. Sunstroke, heatstroke, and dehydration are common misfortunes in the bright American Southwest. If you can avoid the insects, reptiles, and arachnids, the cactus and the ivy, the smog of the southwestern cities, and the lung fungus of the desert valleys (carried by dust in the air), you cannot escape the desert sun. Too much exposure to it eventually causes, quite literally, not merely sunburn but skin cancer.

Much sun, little rain also means an arid climate. Compared with the high humidity of more hospitable regions, the dry heat of the desert seems at first not terribly uncomfortable—sometimes even pleasant. But that sensation of comfort is false, a deception, and therefore all the more dangerous, for it induces overexertion and an insufficient consumption of water, even when water is available. This leads to various internal complications, some immediate—sunstroke, for example—and some not apparent until much later. Mild but prolonged dehydration, continued over a span of months or years, leads to the crystallization of mineral solutions in the urinary tract, that is, to what urologists call urinary calculi or kidney stones. A disability common in all the world's arid regions. Kidney stones, in case you haven't met one, come in many shapes and sizes, from pellets smooth as BB shot to highly irregular calcifications resembling asteroids, Vietcong shrapnel, and crown-of-thorns starfish. Some of these objects may be "passed" naturally; others can be removed only by means of the Davis stone basket or by surgery. Me—I was lucky; I passed mine with only a groan, my forehead pressed against the wall of a pissoir in the rear of a Tucson bar that I cannot recommend.

You may be getting the impression by now that the desert is not the most suitable of environments for human habitation. Correct. Of all the Earth's climatic zones, excepting only the Antarctic, the deserts are the least inhabited, the least "developed," for reasons that should now be clear.

You may wish to ask, Yes, okay, but among North American deserts   10
which is the *worst*? A good question—and I am happy to attempt to answer.

Geographers generally divide the North American desert—what was once termed "the Great American Desert"—into four distinct regions or subdeserts. These are the Sonoran Desert, which comprises southern Arizona, Baja California, and the state of Sonora in Mexico; the Chihuahuan Desert, which includes west Texas, southern New Mexico, and the states of Chihuahua and Coahuila in Mexico; the Mojave Desert, which includes southeastern California and small portions of Nevada, Utah, and Arizona; and the Great Basin Desert, which includes most of Utah and Nevada, northern Arizona, northwestern New Mexico, and much of Idaho and eastern Oregon.

Privately, I prefer my own categories. Up north in Utah somewhere is the canyon country—places like Zeke's Hole, Death Hollow, Pucker Pass, Buckskin Gulch, Nausea Crick, Wolf Hole, Mollie's Nipple, Dirty Devil River, Horse Canyon, Horseshoe Canyon, Lost Horse Canyon, Horsethief Canyon, and Horseshit Canyon, to name only the more classic places. Down in Arizona and Sonora there's the cactus country; if you have nothing better to do, you might take a look at High Tanks, Salome Creek, Tortilla Flat, Esperero ("Hoper") Canyon, Holy Joe Peak, Depression Canyon, Painted Cave, Hell Hole Canyon, Hell's Half Acre, Iceberg Canyon, Tiburon (Shark) Island, Pinacate Peak, Infernal Valley, Sykes Crater, Montezuma's Head, Gu Oidak, Kuakatch, Pisinimo, and Baboquivari Mountain, for example.

Then there's The Canyon. *The* Canyon. The Grand. That's one world. And North Rim—that's another. And Death Valley, still another, where I lived one winter near Furnace Creek and climbed the Funeral Mountains, tasted Badwater, looked into the Devil's Hole, hollered up Echo Canyon, searched for and never did find Seldom Seen Slim. Looked for *satori* near Vana, Nevada, and found a ghost town named Bonnie Claire.

Never made it to Winnemucca. Drove through the Smoke Creek Desert and down through Big Pine and Lone Pine and home across the Panamints to Death Valley again—home sweet home that winter.

And which of these deserts is the worst? I find it hard to judge. They're all bad—not half bad but all bad. In the Sonoran Desert, Phoenix will get you if the sun, snakes, bugs, and arthropods don't. In the Mojave Desert, it's Las Vegas, more sickening by far than the Glauber's salt in the Death Valley sinkholes. Go to Chihuahua and you're liable to get busted in El Paso and sandbagged in Ciudad Juárez—where all old whores go to die. Up north in the Great Basin Desert, on the Plateau Province, in the canyon country, your heart will break, seeing the strip mines open up and the power plants rise where only cowboys and Indians and J. Wesley Powell ever roamed before.

Nevertheless, all is not lost; much remains, and I welcome the pros-   15
pect of an army of lug-soled hiker's boots on the desert trails. To save what wilderness is left in the American Southwest—and in the American Southwest only the wilderness is worth saving—we are going to need all the recruits we can get. All the hands, heads, bodies, time, money, effort we can find. Presumably—and the Sierra Club, the Wilderness Society, the Friends of the Earth, the Audubon Society, the Defenders of Wildlife operate on this theory—those who learn to love what is spare, rough, wild, undeveloped, and unbroken will be willing to fight for it, will help resist the strip miners, highway builders, land developers, weapons testers, power producers, tree chainers, clear cutters, oil drillers, dam beavers, subdividers—the list goes on and on—before that zinc-hearted, termite-brained, squint-eyed, nearsighted, greedy crew succeeds in completely californicating what still survives of the Great American Desert.

So much for the Good Cause. Now what about desert hiking itself, you may ask. I'm glad you asked that question. I firmly believe that one should never—I repeated *never*—go out into that formidable wasteland of cactus, heat, serpents, rock, scrub, and thorn without careful planning, thorough and cautious preparation, and complete—never mind the expense!—*complete* equipment. My motto is: Be Prepared.

That is my belief and that is my motto. My practice, however, is a little different. I tend to go off in a more or less random direction myself, half-baked, half-assed, half-cocked, and half-ripped. Why? Well, because I have an indolent and melancholy nature and don't care to be bothered getting all those *things* together—all that bloody *gear*—maps, compass, binoculars, poncho, pup tent, shoes, first-aid kit, rope, flashlight, inspirational poetry, water, food—and because anyhow I approach nature with a certain surly ill-will, daring Her to make trouble. Later when I'm deep into Natural Bridges Natural Moneymint or Zion National Parkinglot or say General Shithead National Forest Land of Many Abuses why then, of course, when it's a bit late, then I may wish I had packed that something extra: matches perhaps, to mention one useful item, or maybe a spoon to eat my gruel with.

If I hike with another person it's usually the same; most of my friends have indolent and melancholy natures too. A cursed lot, all of them. I think of my comrade John De Puy, for example, sloping along for mile after mile like a goddamned camel—indefatigable—with those J. C. Penney hightops on his feet and that plastic pack on his back he got with five books of Green Stamps and nothing inside it but a sketchbook, some homemade jerky, and a few cans of green chiles. Or Douglas Peacock, ex–Green Beret, just the opposite. Built like a buffalo, he loads a ninety-pound canvas pannier on his back at trailhead, loaded with guns, ammunition, bayonet, pitons and carabiners, cameras, field books, a 150-foot rope, geologist's sledge, rock samples, assay kit, field glasses, two gallons of water in steel canteens, jungle boots, a case of C-rations, rope hammock, pharmaceuticals in a pig-iron box, raincoat, overcoat, two-man mountain tent, Dutch oven, hibachi, shovel, ax, inflatable boat, and near the top of the load and distributed through side and back pockets, easily accessible, a case of beer. Not because he enjoys or needs all that weight—he may never get to the bottom of that cargo on a ten-day outing—but simply because Douglas uses his packbag for general storage both at home and on the trail and prefers not to have to rearrange everything from time to time merely for the purposes of a hike. Thus my friends De Puy and Peacock; you may wish to avoid such extremes.

A few tips on desert etiquette:

1. Carry a cooking stove, if you must cook. Do not burn desert wood, which is rare and beautiful and required ages for its creation (an ironwood tree lives for over 1,000 years and juniper almost as long).
2. If you must, out of need, build a fire, then for God's sake allow it to burn itself out before you leave—do not bury it, as Boy Scouts and Campfire Girls do, under a heap of mud or sand. Scatter the ashes; replace any rocks you may have used in constructing a fireplace; do all you can to obliterate the evidence that you camped here. (The Search & Rescue Team may be looking for you.)
3. Do not bury garbage—the wildlife will only dig it up again. Burn what will burn and pack out the rest. The same goes for toilet paper: Don't bury it, *burn it.*
4. Do not bathe in desert pools, natural tanks, *tinajas,* potholes. Drink what water you need, take what you need, and leave the rest for the next hiker and more important for the bees, birds, and animals—bighorn sheep, coyotes, lions, foxes, badgers, deer, wild pigs, wild horses—whose *lives* depend on that water.
5. Always remove and destroy survey stakes, flagging, advertising signboards, mining claim markers, animal traps, poisoned bait, seismic exploration geophones, and other such artifacts of industrialism. The men who put those things there are up to no good and it is our duty to confound them. Keep America Beautiful. Grow a Beard. Take a Bath. Burn a Billboard.

Anyway—why go into the desert? Really, why do it? That sun, roar-   20
ing at you all day long. The fetid, tepid, vapid little water holes slowly
evaporating under a scum of grease, full of cannibal beetles, spotted toads,
horsehair worms, liver flukes, and down at the bottom, inevitably, the pale
cadaver of a ten-inch centipede. Those pink rattlesnakes down in The
Canyon, those diamondback monsters thick as a truck driver's wrist that
lurk in shady places along the trail, those unpleasant solpugids and unnecessary Jerusalem crickets that scurry on dirty claws across your face at
night. Why? The rain that comes down like lead shot and wrecks the trail,
those sudden rockfalls of obscure origin that crash like thunder ten feet
behind you in the heart of a dead-still afternoon. The ubiquitous buzzard,
so patient—but only so patient. The sullen and hostile Indians, all on
welfare. The ragweed, the tumbleweed, the Jimson weed, the snakeweed.
The scorpion in your shoe at dawn. The dreary wind that blows all spring,
the psychedelic Joshua trees waving their arms at you on moonlight nights.
Sand in the soup du jour. Halazone tablets in your canteen. The barren
hills that always go up, which is bad, or down, which is worse. Those
canyons like catacombs with quicksand lapping at your crotch. Hollow,
mummified horses with forelegs casually crossed, dead for ten years, leaning against the corner of a barbed-wire fence. Packhorses at night, iron-
shod, clattering over the slickrock through your camp. The last tin of
tuna, two flat tires, not enough water and a forty-mile trek to Tule Well.
An osprey on a cardón cactus, snatching the head off a living fish—always
the best part first. The hawk sailing by at 200 feet, a squirming snake in
its talons. Salt in the drinking water. Salt, selenium, arsenic, radon, and
radium in the water, in the gravel, in your bones. Water so hard it
bends light, drills holes in rock and chokes up your radiator. Why go
there? Those places with the hardcase names: Starvation Creek, Poverty
Knoll, Hungry Valley, Bitter Springs, Last Chance Canyon, Dungeon
Canyon, Whipsaw Flat, Dead Horse Point, Scorpion Flat, Dead Man
Draw, Stinking Spring, Camino del Diablo, Jornado del Muerto . . . Death
Valley.

Well then, why indeed go walking into the desert, that grim ground,
that bleak and lonesome land where, as Genghis Khan said of India, "the
heat is bad and the water makes men sick"?

Why the desert, when you could be strolling along the golden
beaches of California? Camping by a stream of pure Rocky Mountain
spring water in colorful Colorado? Loafing through a laurel slick in the
misty hills of North Carolina? Or getting your head mashed in the greasy
alley behind the Elysium Bar and Grill in Hoboken, New Jersey? Why the
desert, given a world of such splendor and variety?

A friend and I took a walk around the base of a mountain up beyond
Coconino County, Arizona. This was a mountain we'd been planning to
circumambulate for years. Finally we put on our walking shoes and did it.
About halfway around this mountain, on the third or fourth day, we paused
for a while—two days—by the side of a stream, which the Navajos call

Nasja because of the amber color of the water. (Caused perhaps by juniper roots—the water seems safe enough to drink.) On our second day there I walked down the stream, alone, to look at the canyon beyond. I entered the canyon and followed it for half the afternoon, for three or four miles, maybe, until it became a gorge so deep, narrow and dark, full of water and the inevitable quagmires of quicksand, that I turned around and looked for a way out. A route other than the way I'd come, which was crooked and uncomfortable and buried—I wanted to see what was up on top of this world. I found a sort of chimney flue on the east wall, which looked plausible, and sweated and cursed my way up through that until I reached a point where I could walk upright, like a human being. Another 300 feet of scrambling brought me to the rim of the canyon. No one, I felt certain, had ever before departed Nasja Canyon by that route.

But someone had. Near the summit I found an arrow sign, three feet long, formed of stones and pointing off into the north toward those same old purple vistas, so grand, immense, and mysterious, of more canyons, more mesas and plateaus, more mountains, more cloud-dappled sun-spangled leagues of desert sand and desert rock, under the same old wide and aching sky.

The arrow pointed into the north. But what was it pointing *at*? I 25 looked at the sign closely and saw that those dark, desert-varnished stones had been in place for a long, long time; they rested in compacted dust. They must have been there for a century at least. I followed the direction indicated and came promptly to the rim of another canyon and a drop-off straight down of a good 500 feet. Not that way, surely. Across this canyon was nothing of any unusual interest that I could see—only the familiar sun-blasted sandstone, a few scrubby clumps of blackbrush and prickly pear, a few acres of nothing where only a lizard could graze, surrounded by a few square miles of more nothingness interesting chiefly to horned toads. I returned to the arrow and checked again, this time with field glasses, looking away for as far as my aided eyes could see toward the north, for ten, twenty, forty miles into the distance. I studied the scene with care, looking for an ancient Indian ruin, a significant cairn, perhaps an abandoned mine, a hidden treasure of some inconceivable wealth, the mother of all mother lodes. . . .

But there was nothing out there. Nothing at all. Nothing but the desert. Nothing but the silent world.

That's why.

Reading and Responding

Pay attention to the various sideways glimpses you get of Abbey, the narrator of this piece. How would you describe him? (Find two places where you think Abbey shows through clearly.)

Working Together

1. Discuss the ending of this essay. Abbey doesn't so much explain his reasons as make his essay itself an arrow that points at something (or several somethings). Guess at what the arrow (this essay, that is) points at. As a group, come up with three possibilities. (*Hint:* Looking at his tips on desert etiquette might help.)
2. Each of you identify some animal mentioned in this essay. Do a little bit of research about this animal. For your next class, be ready to read a short paragraph that summarizes what you've learned about this animal. End your paragraph by talking about whether Abbey's information was accurate. Finally, as a group, decide whether Abbey's essay is a reliable source of information on what one can find in the desert.
3. As a group, decide what Abbey values and doesn't value. Make a list for each category.

Rethinking and Rewriting

1. On the basis of only your reading of "The Great American Desert," write an essay that identifies what Abbey values and doesn't value. Structure your essay so it starts by discussing what he doesn't value and ends by focusing on what you think he values most.
2. On the basis of only this essay, write a one-page introduction to Edward Abbey for those who haven't ever read anything he's written.
3. Regardless of your own beliefs, assume that you're going to write an essay that argues with Abbey. What would you argue with him about? How would you make such an argument? Who would be likely to agree with your argument?

Chapter 3 Essay Topics

1. Write an essay that describes in detail a trip you took (on foot or by water—by canoe, raft, kayak, or other boat) into relatively wild, natural country. Tell the story of where you went, what you did, saw, heard, and experienced; but also include some commentary on what the trip meant to you, how it confirmed or changed anything, and/or how writing about it now helps you further understand something about the human place on this planet (and yours in particular). Make reference to at least two essays from this chapter. Use the references either as similarities or contrasts.
2. Write an essay of your own experience of a place that you now see as somehow threatened. Discuss the place as you know it and the threat as you understand it. Use your experience to help readers understand what you would wish for this place and why your recommendation deserves serious consideration. Draw on at least two outside sources to

help readers understand. (These outside sources may be readings from this chapter, but they could also be newspaper articles, interviews, or any other useful, credible sources.)

3. Write an essay that explains why and how you have almost no direct experience with the sort of landscapes discussed in this chapter. Help your readers understand how strange or odd it is for you to read these selections, how foreign or distant they seem, and give readers a sense of your view of nature (however fragmentary or limited). End by discussing a field trip or excursion that you would like to take if you had the chance.

4. Write an essay about the kind of knowledge that you most trust. Where does such knowledge come from? Refer to at least one essay in this chapter to help readers understand what you mean. Include at least one description of a significant process or event that has resulted in this sort of secure understanding.

4

Animal Lives

When we turn off the computer screen and walk out the door, we notice suddenly that there are other creatures in the world: squirrels in the oak trees, robins in the grass, yellow labs leaping for Frisbees. They're not us. They're different. They fly or walk on all fours, they move and see and smell in ways that we don't. Most of all, they don't talk—at least not in a form that we can understand. So there is always this silence between us, this mystery, even when the lab is back in the kitchen, snoring on the rug.

The essays in this section move from accounts of the animals we live with— the pets that share our lives, the animals we visit at zoos, and so on—to butterflies and bears and the others still living in what is left of the wild. Indeed, the difference between human and wild-animal habitats is breaking down, as luxury homes crowd nature and the deer come wandering across our gardens.

SLEEPING WITH ANIMALS

DOGS, AND THE TUG OF LIFE

Edward Hoagland

> *After writing several novels, Edward Hoagland shifted to writing personal essays, producing numerous essay collections and travel books, including* The Courage of Turtles *(1971) and* Walking the Dead Diamond River *(1973). His latest book,* Tigers and Ice: Reflections on Nature and Life *(1999), looks back on his experience of losing and then recovering his sight. The following essay concerns the significance of dogs in our lives, both as social symbols and as reminders of a wildness we have left behind.*

It used to be that you could tell just about how poor a family was by how many dogs they had. If they had one, they were probably doing all right. It was only American to keep a dog to represent the family's interests in the intrigues of the back alley; not to have a dog at all would be like not acknowledging one's poor relations. Two dogs meant that the couple were dog lovers, with growing children, but still might be members of the middle class. But if a citizen kept three, you could begin to suspect he didn't own much else. Four or five irrefutably marked the household as poor folk, whose yard was also full of broken cars cannibalized for parts. The father worked not much, fancied himself a hunter; the mother's teeth were black. And an old bachelor living in a shack might possibly have even more, but you knew that if one of them, chasing a moth, didn't upset his oil lamp some night and burn him up, he'd fetch up in the poorhouse soon, with the dogs shot. Nobody got poor feeding a bunch of dogs, needless to say, because the more dogs a man had, the less he fed them. Foraging as a pack, they led an existence of their own, but served as evidence that life was awfully lonesome for him and getting out of hand. If a dog really becomes a man's best friend his situation is desperate.

That dogs, low-comedy confederates of small children and ragged bachelors, should have turned into an emblem of having made it to the middle class—like the hibachi, like golf clubs and a second car—seems at the very least incongruous. Puppies which in the country you would have to carry in a box to the church fair to give away are bringing seventy-five dollars apiece in some of the pet stores, although in fact dogs are in such oversupply that one hundred and fifty thousand are running wild in New York City alone.

There is another line of tradition about dogs, however. Show dogs, toy dogs, foxhounds for formal hunts, Doberman guard dogs, bulldogs as ugly as a queen's dwarf. An aristocratic Spanish lady once informed me that when she visits her Andalusian estate each fall the mastiffs rush out and fawn about her but would tear to pieces any of the servants who have accompanied her from Madrid. In Mississippi it was illegal for a slave owner to permit his slaves to have a dog, just as it was to teach them how to read. A "negro dog" was a hound trained by a bounty hunter to ignore the possums, raccoons, hogs and deer in the woods that other dogs were supposed to chase, and trail and tree a runaway. The planters themselves, for whom hunting was a principal recreation, whooped it up when a man unexpectedly became their quarry. They caught each other's slaves and would often sit back and let the dogs do the punishing. Bennet H. Barrow of West Feliciana Parish in Louisiana, a rather moderate and representative plantation owner, recounted in his diary of the 1840s, among several similar incidents, this for November 11, 1845: In "5 minutes had him up & a going, And never in my life did I ever see as excited beings as R & myself, ran ½ miles & caught him dogs soon tore him naked, took him Home Before the other negro(es) at dark & made the dogs give him another over hauling." Only recently in Louisiana I heard what happened to two Negroes who happened to be fishing in a bayou off the Blind River, where four white men with a shotgun felt like fishing alone. One was forced to pretend to be a scampering coon and shinny up a telephone pole and hang there till he fell, while the other impersonated a baying, bounding hound.

Such memories are not easy to shed, particularly since childhood, the time when people can best acquire a comradeship with animals, is also when they are likely to pick up their parents' fears. A friend of mine hunts quail by jeep in Texas with a millionaire who brings along forty bird dogs, which he deploys in eight platoons that spell each other off. Another friend, though, will grow apprehensive at a dinner party if the host lets a dog loose in the room. The toothy, mysterious creature lies dreaming on the carpet, its paws pulsing, its eyelids open, the nictitating membranes twitching; how can he be certain it won't suddenly jump up and attack his legs under the table? Among Eastern European Jews, possession of a dog was associated with the hard-drinking *goyishe*[1] peasantry, traditional antagonists, or else with the gentry, and many carried this dislike to the New World. An immigrant fleeing a potato famine or the hunger of Calabria[2] might be no more equipped with the familiar British-German partiality to dogs—a failing which a few rugged decades in a great city's slums would not necessarily mend. The city had urbanized plenty of native farmers' sons as well, and so it came about that what to rural America had been the humblest, most natural amenity—friendship with a dog—has been transmogrified into a piece of the jigsaw of moving to the suburbs: there to cook outdoors, another bit of absurdity to the old countryman, whose toilet was outdoors but who was pleased to be able to cook and eat his meals inside the house.

---

1. *goyishe:* Non-Jewish.
2. *Calabria:* Region in southern Italy.

There are an estimated forty million dogs in the United States (nearly   5
two for every cat). Thirty-seven thousand of them are being destroyed in
humane institutions every day, a figure which indicates that many more
are in trouble. Dogs are hierarchal beasts, with several million years of
submission to the structure of a wolf pack in their breeding. This explains
why the Spanish lady's mastiffs can distinguish immediately between the
mistress and her retainers, and why it is about as likely that one of the
other guests at the dinner party will attack my friend's legs under the table
as that the host's dog will, once it has accepted his presence in the room as
proper. Dogs need leadership, however; they seek it, and when it's not
forthcoming quickly fall into difficulties in a world where they can no
longer provide their own.

"Dog" is "God" spelled backwards—one might say, way backwards.
There's "a dog's life," "dog days," "dog-sick," "dog-tired," "dog-cheap,"
"dog-eared," "doghouse," and "dogs" meaning villains or feet. Whereas a
wolf's stamina was measured in part by how long he could go without
water, a dog's is becoming a matter of how long he can *hold* his water. He
retrieves a rubber ball instead of coursing deer, chases a broom instead of
hunting marmots. His is the lowest form of citizenship: that tug of life at
the end of the leash is like the tug at the end of a fishing pole, and then
one doesn't have to kill it. On stubby, amputated-looking feet he leads his
life, which if we glance at it attentively is a kind of cutout of our own, all
the more so for being riskier and shorter. Bam! A member of the family is
dead on the highway, as we expected he would be, and we just cart him
to the dump and look for a new pup.

Simply the notion that he lives on four legs instead of two has come
to seem astonishing—like a goat or cow wearing horns on its head. And
of course to keep a dog is a way of attempting to bring nature back. The
primitive hunter's intimacy, telepathy, with the animals he sought, surprising them at their meals and in their beds, then stripping them of their
warm coats to expose a frame so like our own, is all but lost. Sport hunters,
especially the older ones, retain a little of it still; and naturalists who have
made up their minds not to kill wild animals nevertheless appear to empathize primarily with the predators at first, as a look at the tigers, bears,
wolves, mountain lions on the project list of an organization such as the
World Wildlife Fund will show. This is as it should be, these creatures
having suffered from our brotherly envy before. But in order to really enjoy
a dog, one doesn't merely try to train him to be semihuman. The point of
it is to open oneself to the possibility of becoming partly a dog (after all,
there are plenty of sub- or semihuman beings around whom we don't wish
to adopt). One wants to rediscover the commonality of animal and man—
to see an animal eat and sleep that hasn't forgotten how to enjoy doing
such things—and the directness of its loyalty.

The trouble with the current emphasis on preserving "endangered
species" is that, however beneficial to wildlife the campaign works out to
be, it makes all animals seem like museum pieces, worth saving for senti-

mental considerations and as figures of speech (to "shoot a sitting duck"), but as a practical matter already dead and gone. On the contrary, some animals are flourishing. In 1910 half a million deer lived in the United States, in 1960 seven million, in 1970 sixteen million. What has happened is that now that we don't eat them we have lost that close interest.

Wolf behavior prepared dogs remarkably for life with human beings. So complete and complicated was the potential that it was only a logical next step for them to quit their packs in favor of the heady, hopeless task of trying to keep pace with our own community development. The contortions of fawning and obeisance which render group adjustment possible among such otherwise forceful fighters—sometimes humping the inferior members into the shape of hyenas—are what squeezes them past our tantrums, too. Though battling within the pack is mostly accomplished with body checks that do no damage, a subordinate wolf bitch is likely to remain so in awe of the leader that she will cringe and sit on her tail in response to his amorous advances, until his female co-equal has had a chance to notice and dash over and redirect his attention. Altogether, he is kept so busy asserting his dominance that this top-ranked female may not be bred by him, finally, but by the male which occupies the second rung. Being breadwinners, dominant wolves feed first and best, just as we do, so that to eat our scraps and leavings strikes a dog as normal procedure. Nevertheless, a wolf puppy up to eight months old is favored at a kill, and when smaller can extract a meal from any pack member—uncles and aunts as well as parents—by nosing the lips of the adult until it regurgitates a share of what it's had. The care of the litter is so much a communal endeavor that the benign sort of role we expect dogs to play within our own families toward children not biologically theirs comes naturally to them.

For dogs and wolves the tail serves as a semaphore of mood and social   *10* code, but dogs carry their tails higher than wolves do, as a rule, which is appropriate, since the excess spirits that used to go into lengthy hunts now have no other outlet than backyard negotiating. In addition to an epistolary anal gland, whose message-carrying function has not yet been defined, the anus itself, or stool when sniffed, conveys how well the animal has been eating—in effect, its income bracket—although most dog foods are sorrily monotonous compared to the hundreds of tastes a wolf encounters, perhaps dozens within the carcass of a single moose. We can speculate on a dog's powers of taste because its olfactory area is proportionately fourteen times larger than a man's, its sense of smell at least a hundred times as keen.

The way in which a dog presents his anus and genitals for inspection indicates the hierarchal position that he aspires to, and other dogs who sniff his genitals are apprised of his sexual condition. From his urine they can undoubtedly distinguish age, build, state of sexual activity and general health, even hours after he's passed by. Male dogs dislike running out of urine, as though an element of potency were involved, and try to save a little; they prefer not to use a scent post again until another dog has urinated there, the first delight and duty of the ritual being to stake out a territory, so that when they are walked hurriedly in the city it is a disappointment to them. The search is also sexual, because bitches in heat post notices about. In the woods a dog will mark his drinking places, and watermark a rabbit's trail after chasing it, as if to notify the next predator that happens by exactly who it was that put such a whiff of fear into the rabbit's scent. Similarly, he squirts the tracks of bobcats and of skunks with an aloof air unlike his brisk and cheery manner of branding another dog's or fox's trail, and if he is in a position to do so, will defecate excitedly on a bear run, leaving behind his best effort, which no doubt he hopes will strike the bear as a bombshell.

The chief complaint people lodge against dogs is their extraordinary stress upon lifting the leg and moving the bowels. Scatology did take up some of the slack for them when they left behind the entertainments of the forest. The forms of territoriality replaced the substance. But apart from that, a special zest for life is characteristic of dogs and wolves—in hunting, eating, relieving themselves, in punctiliously maintaining a home territory, a pecking order and a love life, and educating the resulting pups. They grin and grimace and scrawl graffiti with their piss. A lot of inherent strategy goes into these activities: the way wolves spell each other off, both when hunting and in their governess duties around the den, and often "consult" as a pack with noses together and tails wagging before flying in to make a kill. (Tigers, leopards, house cats base their social relations instead upon what ethologists call "mutual avoidance.") The nose is a dog's main instrument of discovery, corresponding to our eyes, and so it is that he is seldom offended by organic smells, such as putrefaction, and sniffs intently for the details of illness, gum bleeding and diet in his master and his fellows, and for the story told by scats, not closing off the avenue for any reason—just as we rarely shut our eyes against new information, even the tragic or unpleasant kind.

Though dogs don't see as sharply as they smell, trainers usually rely on hand signals to instruct them, and most firsthand communication in a wolf pack also seems to be visual—by the expressions of the face, by body english and the cant of the tail. A dominant wolf squares his mouth, stares at and "rides up" on an inferior, standing with his front legs on its back, or will pretend to stalk it, creeping along, taking its muzzle in his mouth, and performing nearly all of the other discriminatory pranks and practices familiar to anybody who has a dog. In fact, what's funny is to watch a homely mutt as tiny as a shoebox spin through the rigmarole which a whole series of observers in the wilderness have gone to great pains to document for wolves.

Dogs proffer their rear ends to each other in an intimidating fashion, but when they examine the region of the head it is a friendlier gesture, a snuffling between pals. One of them may come across a telltale bone fragment caught in the other's fur, together with a bit of mud to give away the location of bigger bones. On the same impulse, wolves and free-running dogs will sniff a wanderer's toes to find out where he has been roaming. They fondle and propitiate with their mouths also, and lovers groom each other's fur with tongues and teeth adept as hands. A bitch wolf's period in heat includes a week of preliminary behavior and maybe two weeks of receptivity—among animals, exceptionally long. Each actual copulative tie lasts twenty minutes or a half an hour, which again may help to instill affection. Wolves sometimes begin choosing a mate as early as the age of one, almost a year before they are ready to breed. Dogs mature sexually a good deal earlier, and arrive in heat twice a year instead of once—at any season instead of only in midwinter, like a wolf, whose pups' arrival must be scheduled unfailingly for spring. Dogs have not retained much responsibility for raising their young, and the summertime is just as perilous as winter for them because, apart from the whimsy of their owners, who put so many of them to sleep, their nemesis is the automobile. Like scatology, sex helps fill the gulf of what is gone.

The scientist David Mech has pointed out how like the posture of a   15 wolf with a nosehold on a moose (as other wolves attack its hams) are the antics of a puppy playing tug-of-war at the end of a towel. Anybody watching a dog's exuberance as it samples bites of long grass beside a brook, or pounds into a meadow bristling with the odors of woodchucks, snow-shoe rabbits, grouse, a doe and buck, field mice up on the seedheads of the weeds, kangaroo mice jumping, chipmunks whistling, weasels and shrews on the hunt, a plunging fox, a porcupine couched in a tree, perhaps can begin to imagine the variety of excitements under the sky that his ancestors relinquished in order to move indoors with us. He'll lie down with a lamb to please us, but as he sniffs its haunches, surely he must remember atavistically that this is where he'd start to munch.

There is poignancy in the predicament of a great many animals: as in the simple observation which students of the California condor have made that this huge, most endangered bird prefers the carrion meat of its old standby, the deer, to all the dead cows, sheep, horses and other substitutes it sees from above, sprawled about. Animals are stylized characters in a kind of old saga—stylized because even the most acute of them have little lee-way as they play out their parts. (*Rabbits,* for example, I find terribly affecting, imprisoned in their hop.) And as we drift away from any cognizance of them, we sacrifice some of the intricacy and grandeur of life. Having already lost so much, we are hardly aware of what remains, but to a primitive snatched forward from an earlier existence it might seem as if we had surrendered a richness comparable to all the tapestries of childhood. Since this is a matter of the imagination as well as of animal demographics, no Noah projects, no bionomic discoveries on the few sanctuaries that have been established are going to reverse the swing. The very specialists in the forefront of finding out how animals behave, when one meets them, appear to be no more intrigued than any ordinary Indian was.

But we continue to need—as aborigines did, as children do—a parade of morality tales which are more concise than those that politics, for instance, later provides. So we've had Aesop's and medieval and modern fables about the grasshopper and the ant, the tiger and Little Black Sambo, the wolf and the three pigs, Br'er Rabbit and Br'er Bear, Goldilocks and her three bears, Pooh Bear, Babar and the rhinos, Walt Disney's animals, and assorted humbler scary bats, fat hippos, funny frogs, and eager beavers. Children have a passion for clean, universal definitions, and so it is that animals have gone with children's literature as Latin has with religion. Through them they first encountered death, birth, their own maternal feelings, the gap between beauty and cleverness, or speed and good intentions. The animal kingdom boasted the powerful lion, the mothering goose, the watchful owl, the tardy tortoise, Chicken Little, real-life dogs that treasure bones, and mink that grow posh pelts from eating crawfish and mussels.

In the cartoons of two or three decades ago, Mouse doesn't get along with Cat because Cat must catch Mouse or miss his supper. Dog, on the other hand, detests Cat for no such rational reason, only the capricious fact that dogs don't dote on cats. Animal stories are bounded, yet enhanced, by each creature's familiar lineaments, just as a parable about a prince and peasant, a duchess and a milkmaid, a blacksmith and a fisherman, would be. Typecasting, like the roll of a metered ode, adds resonance and dignity, summoning up all of the walruses and hedgehogs that went before: the shrewd image of Br'er Rabbit to assist his suburban relative Bugs Bunny behind the scenes. But now, in order to present a tale about the contest between two thieving crows and a scarecrow, the storyteller would need to start by explaining that once upon a time crows used to eat a farmer's corn if he didn't defend it with a mock man pinned together from old clothes. Crows are having a hard go of it and may soon receive game-bird protection.

One way childhood is changing, therefore, is that the nonhuman figures—"Wild Things" or puppet monsters—constructed by the best of the new artificers, like Maurice Sendak or the *Sesame Street* writers, are distinctly humanoid, ballooned out of faces, torsos met on the subway. The televised character Big Bird does not resemble a bird the way Bugs Bunny remained a rabbit—though already he was less so than Br'er or Peter Rabbit. Big Bird's personality, her confusion, haven't the faintest connection to an ostrich's. Lest she be confused with an ostrich, her voice has been slotted unmistakably toward the prosaic. Dr. Seuss did transitional composites of worldwide fauna, but these new shapes—a beanbag like the *Sesame Street* Grouch or Cookie Monster or Herry Monster, and the floral creations in books—have been conceived practically from scratch by the artist ("in the night kitchen," to use a Sendak phrase), and not transferred from the existing caricatures of nature. In their conversational conflicts they offer him a fresh start, which may be a valuable commodity, whereas if he were dealing with an alligator, it would, while giving him an old-fashioned boost in the traditional manner, at the same time box him in. A chap called

Alligator, with that fat snout and tail, cannot squirm free of the solidity of actual alligators. Either it must stay a heavyweight or else play on the sternness of reality by swinging over to impersonate a cream puff and a Ferdinand.

Though animal programs on television are popular, what with the   20 wave of nostalgia and "ecology" in the country, we can generally say about the animal kingdom, "The King is dead, long live the King." Certainly the talent has moved elsewhere. Those bulbous Wild Things and slant-mouthed beanbag puppets derived from the denizens of Broadway—an argumentative night news vendor, a lady on a traffic island—have grasped their own destinies, as characters on the make are likely to. It was inevitable they would. There may be a shakedown to remove the elements that would be too bookish for children's literature in other hands, and another shakedown because these first innovators have been more city-oriented than suburban. New authors will shift the character sources away from Broadway and the subway and the ghetto, but the basic switch has already been accomplished—from the ancient juxtaposition of people, animals, and dreams blending the two, to people and monsters that grow solely out of people by way of dreams.

Which leaves us in the suburbs, with dogs as a last link. Cats are too independent to care, but dogs are in an unenviable position, they hang so much upon our good opinion. We are coming to *have* no opinion; we don't pay enough attention to form an opinion. Though they admire us, are thrilled by us, heroize us, we regard them as a hobby or a status symbol, like a tennis racquet, and substitute leash laws for leadership—expect them not simply to learn English but to grow hands, because their beastly paws seem stranger to us every year. If they try to fondle us with their handy-jack mouths, we read it as a bite; and like used cars, they are disposed of when the family relocates, changes its "bag," or in the scurry of divorce. The first reason people kept a dog was to acquire an ally on the hunt, a friend at night. Then it was to maintain an avenue to animality, as our own nearness began to recede. But as we lose our awareness of all animals, dogs are becoming a bridge to nowhere. We can only pity their fate.

Reading and Responding

1. As you reread this essay, mark in the margins two or three passages that surprise you—things you've never thought of before, or ideas that disturb you or make you uneasy. Then return to these passages and free-write about what you've marked and why in each case you've marked it. Explore whatever makes you uneasy.
2. If you've owned a dog, quickly list three different stories you could tell about that dog. Then choose one story and flesh it out so you have about a page of notes or freewriting.

Working Together

1. Make a list of three or four strange, odd, or different ideas from the Hoagland essay and discuss each one. Do you agree or disagree? How are the ideas related? Are they subpoints of a larger point? How would you draw their relationship—spokes of a wheel, islands in a stream, scattered pieces of something? Discuss these ideas in your group.
2. What is Hoagland's central idea in this piece? What reasons, observations, or arguments pushed him to write? As a group, compose a paragraph that expresses your answer(s).
3. Imagine going out to lunch with Hoagland. Describe what he looks like, what he's wearing. What kind of restaurant would you go to? What would he order? What would you talk about?

Rethinking and Rewriting

1. Describe the behavior of your own dog, if you have one. Tell a story of a dog you've loved. Variation: Tell a story about a cat you've loved.
2. Write an essay about the reasons you've kept a pet. Describe the pet, but focus mostly on whatever role the pet actually played (or still plays) in your life. Finally, does your experience lead you to agree with Hoagland that we've almost entirely lost our links to the animal world?
3. Describe the life and behavior of several people you know by describing their dogs (or other pets): How does a person's pet reveal his or her own character and values?
4. Write a paper that reports recent research on the behavior of dogs. To help you focus, assume that you're writing an article for would-be dog owners who aren't sure how the various breeds differ.

NO RMS, JUNGLE VU

Melissa Greene

> *Melissa Greene is a freelance writer and author of several books including, most recently,* The Temple Bombing *(1996), an account of the events surrounding the racially motivated bombing of Atlanta's oldest synagogue in 1954. The following essay about the design of zoos was first published in 1987 in* Atlantic Monthly.

"The Egyptians have been civilized for four thousand years . . . my own ancestors probably a lot less," Jon Charles Coe says. "We evolved over millions of years in the wild, where survival depended on our awareness of the landscape, the weather, and the animals. We haven't been domesticated long enough to have lost those senses. In my opinion, it is the business of the zoo to slice right through that sophisticated veneer, to recall us to our origins. I judge the effectiveness of a zoo exhibit in the pulse rate of the zoo-goer. We can design a zoo that will make the hair stand up on the back of your neck."

A revolution is under way in zoo design, which was estimated to be a $20 million business last year. Jon Coe and Grant Jones are the vanguard. Coe, forty-six, is a stocky man with a long, curly beard. He is an associate professor of landscape architecture at the University of Pennsylvania and a senior partner in the zoo-design firm of Coe Lee Robinson Roesch, in Philadelphia. Grant Jones, a senior partner in the architectural firm Jones & Jones, in Seattle, is at forty-eight a trendsetter in the design of riverfront areas, botanical gardens, and historical parks, as well as zoos. Coe and Jones were classmates at the Harvard School of Design, and Coe worked for Jones & Jones until 1981.

Ten years ago in Seattle they created the Woodland Park gorilla exhibit in collaboration with Dennis Paulson, a biologist, and with David Hancocks, an architect and the director of the Woodland Park Zoo. The exhibit is still praised by experts as the best ever done. It has become an international standard for the replication of wilderness in a zoo exhibit and for the art of including and engaging the zoo-goer. Dian Fossey, the field scientist who lived for fifteen years near the wild mountain gorillas of Rwanda before her murder there, in December of 1985, flew to Seattle as a consultant to the designers of Woodland Park. When the exhibit was completed, Johnpaul Jones, Grant Jones's partner (the two are not related), sent photographs to her. She wrote back that she had shown the photos to her colleagues at the field station and they had believed them to be photos of wild gorillas in Rwanda. "Your firm, under the guidance of [Mr.] Hancocks, has made a tremendously important advancement toward the captivity conditions of gorillas," Fossey wrote. "Had such existed in the past, there would undoubtedly be more gorillas living in captivity."

"Woodland Park has remained a model for the zoo world," says Terry Maple, the new director of Zoo Atlanta, a professor of comparative psychology (a field that examines the common origins of animal and human behavior) at the Georgia Institute of Technology, and the author of numerous texts and articles on primate behavior. "Woodland Park changed the way we looked at the zoo environment. Before Woodland Park, if the gorillas weren't in cages, they were on beautiful mown lawns, surrounded by moats. In good zoos they had playground equipment. In Woodland Park the staff had to teach the public not to complain that the gorilla exhibit looked unkempt."

"As far as gorilla habitats go," Maple says, "Cincinnati's is pretty good; San Diego's is pretty good; Columbus's has a huge cage, so aesthetically it loses a great deal, but socially it's terrific; San Francisco's is a more technical solution, naturalistic but surrounded by walls. Woodland Park's is the best in the world." 5

In Woodland Park the zoo-goer must step off the broad paved central boulevard onto a narrow path engulfed by vegetation to get to the gorillas. Coe planted a big-leaf magnolia horizontally, into the bank of a man-made hill, so that it would grow over the path. ("People forget that a landscape architect not only can do this," he said on a recent tour of the exhibit, indicating a pretty circle of peonies, "but can also do *this*"—he pointed to a shaggy, weed-covered little hill. "I *designed* that hill.")

The path leads to a wooden lean-to with a glass wall on one side that looks into a rich, weedy, humid clearing. Half a dozen heavy-set, agile gorillas part the tall grasses, stroll leaning on their knuckles, and sit nonchalantly among clumps of comfrey, gnawing celery stalks. The blue-black sheen of their faces and fur on a field of green is electrifying. The social organization of the gorillas is expressed by their interaction around a couple of boulders in the foreground of the exhibit. All the gorillas enjoy climbing on the boulders, but the young ones yield to their elders and the adult females yield to the adult males, two silverback gorillas. The silverbacks drum their chests with their fists rapidly and perfunctorily while briefly rising on two feet—not at all like Tarzan. The fists make a rapid thudding noise, which seems to mean, "Here I come." Each silverback climbs to his rostrum, folds his arms, and glares at the other. As in nature, their relationship is by turns civil but not friendly, and contentious but not bullying.

The zoo-goers in the lean-to, observing all this, feel fortunate that the troop of gorillas chooses to stay in view, when it apparently has acres and acres in which to romp. Moss-covered boulders overlap other boulders in the distance, a stream fringed with ferns wanders among them, birds roost in the forty-foot-high treetops, and caves and nests beyond the bend in the stream are available to the gorillas as a place of retreat. "Flight distance" is the zoological term for the distance an animal needs to retreat from an approaching creature in order to feel safe—the size of the cushion of empty space it wishes to maintain around itself. (Several years ago Jon

Coe accepted an assignment to design a nursing home, a conventional job that was unusual for him. He designed the home with flight distance. Sitting rooms and visiting areas were spacious near the front door but grew smaller as one progressed down the hall toward the residents' rooms. A resident overwhelmed by too much bustle in the outer areas could retreat down the hall to quieter and quieter environments.)

In fact the gorillas in Woodland Park do not have so much space to explore. The exhibit is 13,570 square feet (about a third of an acre), which is generous but not limitless. The arrangement of overlapping boulders and trees in the distance is meant to trick the eye. There are no fences or walls against which to calculate depth, and the visitor's peripheral vision is deliberately limited by the dimensions of the lean-to. Wider vision might allow a visitor to calculate his position within Woodland Park, or might give him an inappropriate glimpse—as happens in almost every other zoo in the world—of a snowshoe rabbit or an Amazon porcupine or a North American zoo-goer, over the heads of the West African gorillas. Coe measured and calculated the sight lines to ensure that the view was an uncorrupted one into the heart of the rain forest.

The boulders themselves contain a trick. Coe designed them to con- 10 tain heating coils, so that in the miserable, misty Seattle winter they give off a warm aura, like an electric blanket. The boulders serve two purposes: they help the tropical gorillas put up with the Seattle winter, and they attract the gorillas to within several feet of the lean-to and the zoo-goers. It is no coincidence that much of the drama of the gorillas' everyday life is enacted three feet away from the lean-to. The patch of land in front of the lean-to is shady and cool in summer. The gorillas freely choose where to spend their day, but the odds have been weighted heavily in favor of their spending it in front of the lean-to.

"Their old exhibit was a six-hundred-square-foot tile bathroom," says Grant Jones, a tall, handsome, blue-eyed man. "The gorillas displayed a lot of very neurotic behavior. They were aggressive, sad, angry, lethargic. They had no flight distance. The people were behind the glass day and night, the people pounded on the glass, the gorillas were stressed out, totally, all the time. Their only way to deal with it was to sleep or to show intense anger. They'd pick up their own feces and smear it across the glass. They were not interacting with one another.

"My assumption was that when they left their cage to enter their new outdoor park, that behavior would persist. On the first day, although they were frightened when they came into the new park, they were tranquil. They'd never felt the wind; they'd never seen a bird fly over; they'd never seen water flowing except for the drain in the bottom of their cubicle. Instantly they became quiet and curious. The male was afraid to enter into the environment and stood at the door for hours. His mate came and took him by the hand and led him. They only went about halfway. They stopped at a small stream. They sat and picked up some leaves and dipped them in the water and took a bite of the leaves. They leaned back and saw clouds moving over. It was spellbinding. I assumed they would never recover from the trauma of how they'd been kept. It turned out to be a matter of two or three days."

"Picture the typical zoo exhibit," Jon Coe says. "You stroll along a sidewalk under evenly spaced spreading maples, beside colorful bedding plants. On your right is a polar-bear exhibit. There is a well-pruned hedge of boxwood with a graphic panel in it. The panel describes interesting features of the species, including the fact that polar bears often are seen swimming far out to sea. In the exhibit a bear is splashing in a bathtub. Very little is required of the viewers and very little is gained by them. The visitor is bored for two reasons: first because the setting is too obvious, and second because of a feeling of security despite the close presence of a wild animal.

"When planning this exhibit, we learned that in the wild, gorillas like to forage at the edge of a forest, in clearings created by tribal people who fell the trees, burn off the undergrowth, farm for a couple of years, then move on. After they move on, the forest moves back in and the gorillas forage there. We set about to re-create that scene. We got lots of charred stumps, and we took a huge dead tree from a power-line clearing a few miles from here. The story is plant succession, and how the gorillas exploit the early plants growing back over the abandoned farmland."

Coe relies on stagecraft and drama to break down the zoo-goer's 15 sense of security. When walking through a client zoo for the first time, long before he has prepared a master plan, he offers a few suggestions: Get rid of the tire swings in the chimp exhibit. Get rid of the signs saying NIMBA THE ELEPHANT and JOJO THE CHEETAH. Stop the publicized feeding of the animals, the baby elephant's birthday party, and any other element contributing to either an anthropomorphized view ("Do the elephants call each *other* Nimba and Bomba?") or a view of wild beasts as tame pets.

"How can we improve our ability to get and hold the attention of the zoo-goer?" he asks. "We must create a situation that transcends the range of stimulation people are used to and enhances the visitor's perception of the animal. A zoo animal that *appears* to be unrestrained and dangerous should receive our full attention, possibly accompanied by an adrenal rush, until its potential for doing us harm is determined."

For ten years Coe and others have been experimenting with the relative positions of zoo-goers and zoo animals. Coe now designs exhibits in which the animal terrain surrounds and is actually higher than the zoo paths, so that zoo-goers must look up to see the animals. The barriers between animals and people are camouflaged so effectively that zoo-goers may be uncertain whether an animal has access to them or not. In JungleWorld, the Bronx Zoo's recently opened $9.5 million indoor tropical forest nearly an acre in size, conceived by William Conway, the director of the zoo, a python lives inside a tree trunk that apparently has fallen across the zoo-goers' walkway. "We made the interior of the log brighter and tilted the glass away from the outside light to avoid all reflections," says Charles Beier, an associate curator. "It's an old jeweler's trick. When people glance overhead, there appears to be no barrier between them and the snake." The screams of horror provoked by the python are quite a different matter from the casual conversations that people engage in while strolling past rows of terrariums with snakes inside.

"We are trying to get people to be prepared to look for animals in the forest, not have everything brightly lighted and on a platform in front of them," says John Gwynne, the deputy director for design of the New York Zoological Society, which operates the Bronx Zoo. "We have lots of dead trees and dead grass in here. It's actually very hard to train a gardener not to cut off the dead branches. We're trying to create a wilderness, not a garden—something that can catch people by surprise."

The profession of zoo design is a relatively new one. In the past, when a zoo director said that a new lion house was required, the city council solicited bids and hired a popular local architect—the one who did the suburban hospital and the new high school—and paid him to fly around the country and get acquainted with lion houses. He visited four or five and learned design tips from each: how wide to space the bars, for example, and how thick to pour the cement. Then he flew home and drew a lion house.

"As recently as fifteen years ago there was no Jones & Jones or Jon Coe," says William Conway, of the Bronx Zoo. "There were very few architects around then who had any concept of what animals were all about or who would go—as Jon Coe has gone—to Africa to see and sketch and try to understand, so that he knew what the biologist was talking about. The problem of the zoologist in the zoo was that, in the past, he was very often dealing with an architect who wanted to make a monument."

"The downfall of most zoos has been that they've hired architects," says Ace Torre, a designer in New Orleans, who holds degrees in architecture and landscape architecture. "Some of the more unfortunate zoos hired six different architects. Each one made his own statement. As a result, the zoo is a patchwork of architectural tributes."

In 1975 the City of Seattle asked Grant Jones, whose firm had restored the splendid Victorian copper-roofed pergolas and the elegant walkways and the granite statuary of the city's Pioneer Square Historic District, to design the Woodland Park Zoo gorilla house. The City of Seattle—specifically, David Hancocks, the zoo director—had made a novel choice. Jones was an anomaly in the world of architecture in that he prided himself on having never designed anything taller than three stories. Most of his buildings were made of wood, and they tended to be situated in national parks. Instead of making a grand tour of gorilla houses, Jones consulted field scientists and gorilla experts who had seen how gorillas lived in the wild.

"When they asked me to design a gorilla exhibit," Jones says, "I naturally rephrased the problem in my own mind as designing a landscape with gorillas in it. In what sort of landscape would I want to behold gorillas? I would want to include mystery and discovery. I'd like to see the gorillas from a distance first, and then up close. I'd like to be able to intrude on them and see what's going on without their knowing I'm there. I'd want to give them flight distance, a place to back off and feel secure. And I would want an experience that would take me back to a primordial depth myself. How did I spend my day some millions of years ago, living in proximity to this animal?"

"We asked Dian Fossey to visit Seattle," David Hancocks says, "and she became the most crucial member of the design team. We had so many people telling us we were being very foolish. A zoo director on the East Coast called to say he'd put a potted palm in a cage where a gorilla had lived for fifteen years. The gorilla pulled it out by the roots, ate it, and got sick."

"Driving in from the airport, we asked Fossey what the rain forest looked like," Jon Coe says. "She kept turning this way and that way in her seat, saying, 'It looks like that! It looks just like that!' Of course, Seattle is in a belt of temperate rain forest. Fossey was in an alpine tropical rain forest. The plants are not identical, but they are very similar. We realized that we could stand back and let the native plants take over the exhibit and the overall effect would be very much the same.

"And there were trees, forty-foot-tall trees, in the area slated for the gorillas. What to do about the trees? No zoo in the world had let gorillas have unlimited access to trees. We thought of the gorilla as a terrestrial animal. The wisdom at the time said that the trees had to come down. We brought George Schaller, probably the world's preeminent field scientist, to Seattle, and asked him about the trees. His response was, 'I don't know if they're going to fall out of them or not, but somebody has to do this.'"

"They didn't fall out of the trees," Jones says, "but Kiki [one of the silverbacks] escaped. We'd brought in some rock-climbers to try to get out of the exhibit when it was finished, and we'd made a few modifications based on their suggestions. Jon figured out an elaborate jumping matrix: if a gorilla can jump this far on the horizontal, how far can he go on a downward slope, et cetera. The problem is, you can't program in motivation. At some point the motivation may be so great that you'll find yourself saying, 'Whoops, the tiger can jump thirteen feet, not twelve. Guess we should have made it wider.'

"We had planted some hawthorn trees about four to five inches in diameter, ten feet high, and had hoped they were large enough that the gorillas would accept them. They accepted everything else, but these trees were standing too much alone, too conspicuous. Kiki pulled all the branches off of one, then ripped it out of the ground. It stood by itself; the roots were like a tripod. He played with that thing for a number of days.

25

"The keepers were aware of how we must never let them have a big long stick because they might put it across the moat, walk across it, and get out. They saw that tree but it was clearly not long enough to bridge the moat. We all discussed it, and decided it wasn't a problem. During that same period Kiki began disappearing for three hours at a time, and we didn't know where he was. It's a large environment, and he could have been off behind some shrubbery. One of the keepers told us later that he'd seen Kiki sitting on the edge of the big dry moat at the back of the habitat. One day Kiki climbed down into the moat.

"I imagine he took his tree with him to the far corner, leaned it up   *30*
against the wall, and considered it. At some point he must have made a firm decision. He got a toehold on the roots, pressed his body to the wall, lifted himself up in one lunge, and hung from the top of the moat. Then he pulled himself up and landed in the rhododendrons. He was out, he was in the park."

"He was sitting in the bushes and some visitors saw him," Coe says. "They raced to the director's office and reported it to Hancocks." His response was calm, according to Coe. Anxious visitors often reported that there were gorillas loose in the trees. "The gorilla's not out," said Hancocks. "The exhibit, you see, is called landscape immersion. It's intended to give you the *impression* that the gorillas are free."

The visitors thanked Hancocks and left. He overheard one remark to the other, "Still, it just doesn't seem right having him sit there on the sidewalk like that."

"Sidewalk?" Hancocks said.

"We called the police," says Hancocks, "not to control the gorilla but to stop people from coming into the zoo. Jim Foster, the vet, fed fruit to Kiki and calmed him down while we tried to figure out what to do. We put a ladder across the moat and Jim climbed on it to show Kiki how to cross. Kiki actually tried it, but the ladder wobbled and fell, and he retreated. It was getting dark. We finally had to tranquilize him and carry him back."

"It's been seven years since," Jones says, "and Kiki never has tried   *35*
again, although he clearly knows how to do it. He doesn't want to leave. In fact I am frequently called in by zoos that are having problems with escape. They always want to know, Should we make the moats wider? The bars closer together? Should we chain the animal? Yet escape is almost never a design problem. It is a question of motivation. It is a social problem."

"One of the roles a silverback has in life," Coe says, "is to patrol his territory. Kiki wasn't escaping *from* something. He was exploring outward from the center of his territory to define its edges."

"If Kiki had escaped from a conventional ape house, the city would have panicked," Hancocks says. "But in the year or two the exhibit had been open, Seattle had lost the hairy-monster-of-the-ape-house image, and saw gorillas as quiet and gentle."

Shortly after, one of the local papers carried a cartoon of Kiki roller-skating arm-in-arm with two buxom beauties through the adjacent Green-lake Park, and another had a cartoon of him pole-vaulting over the moat.

The current revolution in zoo design—the landscape revolution—is driven by three kinds of change that have occurred during this century. First are great leaps in animal ecology, veterinary medicine, landscape design, and exhibit technology, making possible unprecedented realism in zoo exhibits. Second, and perhaps most important, is the progressive disappearance of wilderness—the very subject of zoos—from the earth. Third is knowledge derived from market research and from environmental psychology, making possible a sophisticated focus on the zoo-goer.

Zoo-related sciences like animal ecology and veterinary medicine for   40 exotic animals barely existed fifty years ago and tremendous advances have been made in the last fifteen years. Zoo veterinarians now inoculate animals against diseases they once died of. Until recently, keeping the animals alive required most of a zoo's resources. A cage modeled after a scientific laboratory or an operating room—tile-lined and antiseptic, with a drain in the floor—was the best guarantee of continued physical health. In the late 1960s and early 1970s zoo veterinarians and comparative psychologists began to realize that stress was as great a danger as disease to the captive wild animals. Directors thus sought less stressful forms of confinement than the frequently-hosed-down sterile cell.

Field scientists also published findings about the complex social relations among wild animals. Zoos began to understand that captive animals who refused to mate often were reacting to the improper social configurations in which they were confined. Gorillas, for example, live in large groups in the wild. Zoos had put them in pairs, and then only at breeding time—"believing them monogamous, as we'd like to think we are," Coe says. Interaction between the male and the female gorilla was stilted, hostile, abnormal. Successful breeding among captive gorillas didn't begin until they were housed in large family groups. Golden lion tamarins, in contrast, refused to mate when they were caged in groups. Only very recently did researchers affiliated with the National Zoo discover that these beautiful little monkeys *are* monogamous.

Science first affected the design of zoos in 1735, when Linnaeus published his *Systema Naturae* and people fell in love with classification. The resultant primate house, carnivore house, and reptile house allowed the public to grasp the contemporary scientific understanding of the animal world. "At the turn of the century a zoo was a place where you went to learn what kinds of animals there were," Conway says. "The fact that they were in little cages didn't matter. You could see this was an Arabian oryx, a scimitar-horned oryx, a beisa oryx, and so on. It wasn't at that time so important to have an idea of what they do, or the way they live, or how they evolved." The taxonomic approach informed the design of science museums, aquariums, botanical gardens, and arboretums.

Today zoo directors and designers can draw on whole libraries of information about animal behavior and habitat. Exhibit designers can create entire forests of epoxy and fiber-glass trees, reinforced concrete boulders, waterfalls, and artificial vines, with mist provided by cloud machines. A zoo director can oversee the creation of astoundingly realistic habitats for the animals.

But zoo directors and designers cannot simply create magnificent animal habitats and call them a zoo. That would be something else—a wildlife preserve, a national park. A zoo director has to think about bathrooms: zoos are for people, not animals. A zoo director has to think about bond issues and the fact that the city council, which also finances garbage collection, trims a little more from his budget each year. He has to be aware that the zoo is competing with a vast entertainment industry for the leisure hours and dollars of the public.

"If you're not smiling at Disney World, you're fired the next day," says Robert Yokel, the director of the Miami Metrozoo. He is a laid-back, blue-jeaned, suntanned man with wild, scant hair. "Happy, happy, happy, that's the whole concept. They are the premier operators. They taught the rest of the industry how a park should be run: keep it clean, make it convenient, make the ability to spend dollars very easy. They do everything top drawer. They drew over thirteen million people last year. It's an escape. It's a fantasy." Obviously, the director of the Miami zoo, more than most, has to worry about Disney World. He is surrounded, as well, by Monkey Jungle, the Miami Seaquarium, Busch Gardens, Parrot Jungle, Orchid Jungle, Flamingo Gardens, Lion Country Safari, and the beach. If Florida legalizes gambling, he may never see anyone again. But Yokel is not alone in the zoo world in appreciating what commercial entertainment parks offer the public.

The public today has more leisure time and disposable income than ever before, more children than at any time since the 1950s, and more sophistication about animals—thanks to television, movies, and libraries—than at any time in history. Although a Greek in the age of Homer might not have been able to identify an anteater or a koala, many two-year-olds today can. However, there are other claims on people's time. Although, according to statistics, zoo-going is an entrenched habit with Americans, it is no longer likely that a station wagon packed with kids and heading down the highway on Sunday afternoon will turn in at the zoo. The family has been to Disney World, to Six Flags; they've been to theme parks where the hot-dog vendors wear period costumes and the concession stands look like log cabins; they've visited amusement parks where the whole environment, from the colorful banners to the trash cans, all sparkling clean and brightly painted, shrieks of fun. The local zoo, with its broad tree-lined avenues, pacing leopards, and sleeping bears, seems oddly antiquated and sobering by comparison. So zoo directors must ask, Are our visitors having a good time? Will they come back soon? Would they rather be at Disney World? What will really excite them?

Zoos used to be simpler. Once upon a time—in pharaonic Egypt, in Imperial Rome, in the Austro-Hungarian Empire, in the traveling menageries and bear shows of Western Europe and Russia in the 1800s, even in the United States at the turn of the century—it was sufficient for the zoo to pluck an animal from the teeming wild populations in Asia and Africa and display it, as an exotic specimen, to an amazed populace. (And if the animal sickened in captivity, there was nothing to do but wait for it to die and send for another one. Not only had veterinary medicine not evolved adequately but there was no pressure by concerned wildlife groups for zoos to maintain and reproduce their own stock. The animals were out there.)

Already occupied with the welfare of their animals and the amusement of their zoo-goers, zoo directors today must be responsible to the larger reality that the wilderness is disappearing and the animals with it. Today the cement-block enclosure or quarter-acre plot allotted by a zoo may be the last protected ground on earth for an animal whose habitat is disappearing under farmland, villages, or cities. The word *ark* is used with increasing frequency by zoo professionals. In this country, zoos house members of half a dozen species already extinct in the wild, and of hundreds more on the verge of extinction. Zoo-goers are confronted by skull logos denoting vanishing animals. The new designers like Coe and Jones, and directors like Conway, Maple, Graham, Dolan, George Rabb, at Chicago Brookfield, and Michael Robinson, at the National Zoo, belong as no designers or directors ever before belonged to the international community of zoologists and conservationists who have as their goal the preservation of the wild.

"This is a desperate time," William Conway says. The New York Zoological Society, under his leadership, also operates one of the largest and oldest wildlife-conservation organizations in the world, Wildlife Conservation International, which sponsors sixty-two programs in thirty-two countries. Conway is a slender, distinguished, avuncular gentleman with a pencil-line moustache. For him it seems quite a personal matter, a subject of intense private distress, that the earth is losing its wildlife and he doesn't know how many species are going, or what they are, or where they are, or how to save them.

"We are certainly at the rate of losing a species a day now, probably more," he says. "Who knows how many species there are on earth? Suppose, for the sake of argument, there are ten million species of animals out there. If we have one million in the year 2087 we will be doing very well. The human population is increasing at the rate of a hundred and fifty a minute. The tropical moist forest is decreasing at the rate of fifty acres a minute. And there is not a hope in the world of slowing this destruction and this population increase for quite some time. Most of the animals we hold dear, the big, charismatic megavertebrates, almost all of them will be endangered within the next twenty years. The people who are going to do that have already been born.

"And the destruction is being effected by some poor guy and his wife and their five children who are hacking out a few acres of ground to try to eat. That's where most of the fifty acres a minute are going: forty-eight that way and two to the bulldozers. In Rwanda there is a mountain-gorilla preserve that supports two hundred and forty gorillas. It recently was calculated that the park could sustain two thousand human families, people with no other place to live, no land. Now, how can you justify saving the land for two hundred and forty gorillas when you could have two thousand human families? That's one side of the story. Here's the other: if you were to do that, to put those two thousand families in there, the mountain gorilla would disappear completely, and that would take care of Rwanda's population-expansion needs for slightly less than three months. It's a very discouraging picture."

Michael Robinson, the director of the National Zoo, is a rotund and rosy-cheeked Englishman. "I have spent twenty years in the tropics, and it is difficult to talk about them in a detached, scientific manner," he says. "They are the richest ecosystem on earth. They have been here for millions of years. Perhaps eighty percent of all the animals in the world live there and have evolved relationships of breathtaking complexity. The northern hardwood forests have perhaps forty species of trees per hectare. The rain forest has closer to a hundred and fifty to two hundred species per hectare. Once the rain forest is cut down, it takes about a hundred years for the trees to grow back. We estimate that it would take at least six hundred years before the forest has returned to its original state, with all the plants and animals there."

"The American Association of Zoological Parks and Aquariums Species Survival Plan has only thirty-seven endangered species," Conway says. "We should have at least a thousand. How are we going to do it? My God, there are only one thousand seven hundred and eighty-five spaces for big cats in the United States. One thousand seven hundred and eighty-five. How many races of tigers are out there? Five or six. Several races of lions. Several races of leopards, to say nothing of snow leopards, jaguars, fishing cats, cheetahs, and so on. And you have to maintain a minimum population of two to three hundred animals each to have a population that is genetically and demographically sound. What in bloody hell are we going to do?"

Zoos in America are doing two things to try to save the wild animals. The front-line strategy is conservation biology and captive propagation, employing all the recent discoveries in human fertility, such as *in vitro* fertilization, embryo transplantation, and surrogate motherhood. Zoos around the world have hooked into a computerized database called ISIS, so that if a rare Indian rhino goes into heat in Los Angeles—or, for that matter, in the wilds of India—a healthy male rhino to donate sperm can be located.

The second-line strategy is to attempt to save the wilderness itself through educating the public. Zoo directors and designers point out that

55

there are 115 million American zoo-goers each year, and that if even 10 percent of them were to join conservation organizations, to boycott goods produced from the bones, horns, organs, and hides of endangered species, to vote to assist poor nations that are attempting to preserve their forests (perhaps by allowing debt payments to be eased in proportion to the numbers of wild acres preserved), their strength would be felt. The point of the landscape-immersion exhibits is to give the public a taste of what is out there, what is being lost.

It is dawning on zoo professionals that they are, in part, responsible for the American public's unfamiliarity with ecology and lack of awareness that half a dozen species a week are being driven into extinction, and that the precious tropical rain forest may vanish within our lifetime. "By itself, the sight of caged animals does not engender respect for animals," the environmental psychologist Robert Sommer wrote in 1972 in a pioneering essay titled "What Did We Learn at the Zoo?" "Despite excellent intentions, even the best zoos may be creating animal stereotypes that are not only incorrect but that actually work against the interests of wildlife preservation." Terry Maple says, "Zoos used to teach that animals are weird and they live alone."

In the past the only zoo people who paid much attention to zoo-goers were the volunteers assigned to drum up new members. The question they usually asked about zoo-goers was, Can we attract ten thousand of them in August? rather than, How have we influenced their attitudes about wildlife? With the decline of the wild and the dedication of zoos to educating the public, zoo professionals have grown curious about zoo-goers. What do they think? What are they saying as they nudge each other and point? Why do they shoot gum balls at the hippos? What exactly *are* they learning at the zoo? In search of answers to such questions, behavioral scientists are strolling through zoos around the country. They clock the number of seconds zoo-goers look at an exhibit. They count how many zoo-goers read the educational placards. They record the casual utterances of passers-by. And they note the age and gender of the zoo-goers who carve their initials on the railings. (They excite the envy of their co-equals in the science-museum world. "Researchers [at zoos] can linger for inordinate amounts of time at exhibits under the guise of waiting for an animal to do something," Beverly Serrell wrote in *Museum News* in 1980. "Standing next to a skeleton doesn't afford such a convenient cover.")

A fairly sharply focused portrait of the average North American zoo-goer has emerged. For example, data collected by the Smithsonian Institution at the National Zoo in 1979 revealed that zoo-goers arrive at the gates in any one of eighty-four "visitor constellations." One of the most common constellations is one parent accompanied by one or more children. On weekdays mothers predominate. On weekends fathers are sighted. In another study Professor Edward G. Ludwig, of State University College

at Fredonia, New York, observed that the adult unaccompanied by children seemed to have "an aura of embarrassment." A survey published in
1976 found that zoo-goers tend to have more education and larger annual
incomes than the population at large, and a 1979 survey found that zoo-
goers are ignorant of basic ecological principles much more than are back-
packers, birdwatchers, and members of wildlife organizations.

In a group of four zoo-goers, it's likely that only one or two will read
an informational sign. Nearly all conversation will be confined to the
friends and family members with whom the zoo-goer arrives. The most
common form of conversation at the zoo is a declarative sentence following "Watch!" or "Look!" The second most common form is a question.
Robert Yokel, in Miami, believes that the two questions asked most frequently by zoo-goers are "Where is the bathroom?" and "Where is the
snack bar?" Zoo-goers typically look at exhibits for about ninety seconds.
Some never stop walking. Ludwig found that most people will stop for
animals that beg, animals that are feeding, baby animals, animals that make
sounds, or animals that are mimicking human behavior. People express
irritation or annoyance with animals that sleep, eliminate, or regurgitate.

Zoo visitors do not like to lose their way within a zoo, and they get   60
disgruntled when they find themselves backtracking. "We do not enjoy
walking in circles and we invariably do," said one of the 300 respondents
to the Smithsonian study. "Then we get irritated with ourselves."

Jim Peterson, a senior partner in the natural-history exhibit design
firm of Bios, in Seattle, has identified the "first-fish syndrome." Within
twenty feet of the entrance to an aquarium, visitors need to see a fish or
they become unhappy. They will rush past the finest backlighted high-tech
hands-on exhibitry to find that first fish. Similarly, Peterson has noted that
visitors in zoos can tolerate only fifty feet between animals. Any greater
distance inspires them to plow through foliage and create their own viewing blind.

Most "noncompliant behavior" such as unauthorized feeding of animals or attempting to climb over barriers, comes from juveniles and teens
in mixed-gender groupings and children accompanied by both parents. A
1984 study by Valerie D. Thompson suggested that two parents tend to be
involved with each other, freeing the children to perform antisocial acts;
and that among teenagers there is "a close tie between noncompliant behavior and attempting to impress a member of the opposite sex."

Ted Finlay, a graduate student working with Terry Maple at Zoo
Atlanta, wrote a master's thesis titled "The Influence of Zoo Environments
on Perceptions of Animals," one of the first studies to focus on zoo design.
Finlay majored in psychology and animal behavior with a minor in architecture, with the intention of becoming a zoo psychologist. For the research for his dissertation he prepared a slide show of animals in three
environments: free, caged, and in various types of naturalistic zoo exhibits.
Two hundred and sixty-seven volunteers viewed the slides and rated their

feelings about the animals. The free animals were characterized as "free," "wild," and "active." Caged animals were seen as "restricted," "tame," and "passive." Animals in naturalistic settings were rated like the free animals if no barrier was visible. If the barrier *was* visible, they were rated like caged animals—that is to say, less favorably.

The zoo-goer who emerges from the research literature—benighted and happy-go-lucky, chomping his hot dog, holding his nose in the elephant house and scratching under his arms in the monkey house to make his children laugh—is a walking anachronism. He is the creation of an outmoded institution—the conventional zoo—in which the primate house, carnivore house, and reptile house, all lined with tile, glow with an unreal greenish light as if the halls were subterranean, and in which giraffes, zebras, and llamas stand politely, and as if on tiptoe, on the neatly mown lawns of the moated exhibits.

Once it was education enough for the public to file past the captive gorilla in its cage and simply absorb the details of its peculiar or frightening countenance. "One ape in a cage, shaking its steel bars," Terry Maple says, "was a freak show, a horror show, King Kong! You'd go there to be scared, to scream, to squeeze your girlfriend." Despite gilded, or dingy, surroundings, a tusked creature in eighteenth-century Versailles, or downtown Pittsburgh, had the aura of a savage, strange, flowered wilderness.

"Pee-you!" is the primal, universal response of schoolchildren herded into an elephant house. Adults more discreetly crinkle their noses, turn their heads, and laugh. The unspoken impressions are that elephants are filthy, tread in their own feces, attract flies, require hosing down, eat mush, and no wonder they are housed in cinder-block garages. These are not the sort of impressions that might inspire a zoo-goer to resist—much less protest—the marketing of souvenirs made of ivory.

Moated exhibits display animals in garden-like settings, with bedding plants along cement walkways. A koala seated alone in the branch of a single artificial tree above a bright-green lawn looks as if he'd be at home in a Southern California back yard, next to the patio. The visitors looking at such exhibits appreciate the animals in them more and pronounce them "beautiful" or "interesting," but the subliminal message here is that animals are like gentle pets and thrive nicely in captivity. The visitors are hard pressed to explain what the big deal is about the rain forest or why zoologists talk about it, their voices cracking, the way twelfth-century Crusaders must have discussed the Holy Land.

One evening, just at dusk, Coe hurried alone through the Woodland Park Zoo. He'd worked late on some sketches, and the zoo had closed. He would have to let himself out. The lions in the Serengeti Plains exhibit galloped back and forth through their yellow grass, whipping their tails. They ran and ran and pulled up short at the brink of their hidden moat, panting, their nostrils flaring. Coe just happened to be passing by. One of the dun-colored male lions approached and crouched at the very edge of the moat, and growled. Jon Coe froze.

Now, Coe had designed the exhibit. He knew that he was looking up at the lion because he'd elevated its territory to instill fear and respect in the zoo-goer. He knew that he seemed to be walking beside the wild, dark African plains because he'd considered issues like sight lines and cross-viewing. He knew that a concealed moat lay between him and the lion, and that the width of the moat was the standard width used by zoos all over the world. But he also knew that you can't program in motivation. The lion looked at him and crouched; he could hear it snorting. Then it growled again—king of the darkness on the grassy plain. The hair stood up on the back of Coe's neck.

Reading and Responding

1. What do zoos have in common with malls or cities? Do a ten-minute freewrite that addresses this question.
2. Visit your closest zoo and take your notebook with you. Make notes about what you see, and try to make sure that each note about what you see (or hear, or smell) also includes some mention of how this makes you feel.

Working Together

1. Assuming that you've all visited your local zoo and made notes, pool your observations. Make a list of ten of those observations, and then write a few sentences that draw some conclusions on the basis of those observations. As you think about these conclusions, ask yourself this question: is your zoo a good zoo? Be prepared to explain your reasoning.
2. Assume that, as a group, you are speaking for zoo architect Jon Coe. Write a paragraph that expresses your central philosophy regarding zoo design. Use your own words, not Coe's.
3. Reread the description of the Woodland Park gorilla exhibit, and ask yourselves why Greene devotes so many words to this part of her essay. Does she give too much detail, too little, or just about the right amount? Are you bored by it? As a group, write a paragraph about what you think this essay shows you about the use of detail.

Rethinking and Rewriting

1. Greene ends this piece by making connections between zoos and environmental awareness. Explain what she's talking about to someone who hasn't read this piece and doesn't see any immediate relationship between seeing an elephant in a zoo and deciding whether to purchase

something made of ivory. What does zoo design and the experience of zoo-goers have to do with the environment anyhow?

2. Write an essay that explains your views of the function and purpose of zoos now. Based on your views, what do you want to advocate about how zoos should or should not operate? If at all possible, anchor your discussion by including your own personal experience as a zoo-goer.

THE TUCSON ZOO

Lewis Thomas

A medical doctor and scientist, the late Lewis Thomas began writing a column for the New England Journal of Medicine *in 1971. The first of these graceful, informal essays about the physical world were collected and published as* The Lives of the Cell, *winner of the 1974 National Book Award. Several other collections followed, including* The Medusa and the Snail *(1979), from which this essay about a brief experience of animals is taken.*

Science gets most of its information by the process of reductionism, exploring the details, then the details of the details, until all the smallest bits of the structure, or the smallest parts of the mechanism, are laid out for counting and scrutiny. Only when this is done can the investigation be extended to encompass the whole organism or the entire system. So we say.

Sometimes it seems that we take a loss, working this way. Much of today's public anxiety about science is the apprehension that we may forever be overlooking the whole by an endless, obsessive preoccupation with the parts. I had a brief, personal experience of this misgiving one afternoon in Tucson, where I had time on my hands and visited the zoo, just outside the city. The designers there have cut a deep pathway between two small artificial ponds, walled by clear glass, so when you stand in the center of the path you can look into the depths of each pool, and at the same time you can regard the surface. In one pool, on the right side of the path, is a family of otters; on the other side, a family of beavers. Within just a few feet from your face, on either side, beavers and otters are at play, underwater and on the surface, swimming toward your face and then away, more filled with life than any creatures I have ever seen before, in all my days. Except for the glass, you could reach across and touch them.

I was transfixed. As I now recall it, there was only one sensation in my head: pure elation mixed with amazement at such perfection. Swept off my feet, I floated from one side to the other, swiveling my brain, staring astounded at the beavers, then at the otters. I could hear shouts across my corpus callosum, from one hemisphere to the other. I remember thinking, with what was left in charge of my consciousness, that I wanted no part of the science of beavers and otters; I wanted never to know how they performed their marvels; I wished for no news about the physiology of their breathing, the coordination of their muscles, their vision, their endocrine systems, their digestive tracts. I hoped never to have to think of them as collections of cells. All I asked for was the full hairy complexity, then in front of my eyes, of whole, intact beavers and otters in motion.

It lasted, I regret to say, for only a few minutes, and then I was back in the late twentieth century, reductionist as ever, wondering about the details by force of habit, but not, this time, the details of otters and beavers. Instead, me. Something worth remembering had happened in my mind, I was certain of that; I would have put it somewhere in the brain stem; maybe this was my limbic system at work. I became a behavioral scientist, an experimental psychologist, an ethologist, and in the instant I lost all the wonder and the sense of being overwhelmed. I was flattened.

But I came away from the zoo with something, a piece of news about   5
myself: I am coded, somehow, for otters and beavers. I exhibit instinctive behavior in their presence, when they are displayed close at hand behind glass, simultaneously below water and at the surface. I have receptors for this display. Beavers and otters possess a "release" for me, in the terminology of ethology, and the releasing was my experience. What was released? Behavior. What behavior? Standing, swiveling flabbergasted, feeling exultation and a rush of friendship. I could not, as the result of the transaction, tell you anything more about beavers and otters than you already know. I learned nothing new about them. Only about me, and I suspect also about you, maybe about human beings at large: we are endowed with genes which code out our reaction to beavers and otters, maybe our reaction to each other as well. We are stamped with stereotyped, unalterable patterns of response, ready to be released. And the behavior released in us, by such confrontations, is, essentially, a surprised affection. It is compulsory behavior and we can avoid it only by straining with the full power of our conscious minds, making up conscious excuses all the way. Left to ourselves, mechanistic and autonomic, we hanker for friends.

Everyone says, stay away from ants. They have no lessons for us; they are crazy little instruments, inhuman, incapable of controlling themselves, lacking manners, lacking souls. When they are massed together, all touching, exchanging bits of information held in their jaws like memoranda, they become a single animal. Look out for that. It is a debasement, a loss of individuality, a violation of human nature, an unnatural act.

Sometimes people argue this point of view seriously and with deep thought. Be individuals, solitary and selfish, is the message. Altruism, a jargon word for what used to be called love, is worse than weakness, it is sin, a violation of nature. Be separate. Do not be a social animal. But this is a hard argument to make convincingly when you have to depend on language to make it. You have to print up leaflets or publish books and get them bought and sent around, you have to turn up on television and catch the attention of millions of other human beings all at once, and then you have to say to all of them, all at once, all collected and paying attention: be solitary; do not depend on each other. You can't do this and keep a straight face.

Maybe altruism is our most primitive attribute, out of reach, beyond our control. Or perhaps it is immediately at hand, waiting to be released, disguised now, in our kind of civilization, as affection or friendship or attachment. I don't see why it should be unreasonable for all human beings to have strands of DNA coiled up in chromosomes, coding out instincts for usefulness and helpfulness. Usefulness may turn out to be the hardest test of fitness for survival, more important than aggression, more effective, in the long run, than grabbiness. If this is the sort of information biological science holds for the future, applying to us as well as to ants, then I am all for science.

One thing I'd like to know most of all: when those ants have made the Hill, and are all there, touching and exchanging, and the whole mass begins to behave like a single huge creature, and *thinks,* what on earth is that thought? And while you're at it, I'd like to know a second thing: when it happens, does any single ant know about it? Does his hair stand on end?

Reading and Responding

1. Reread the first paragraph of this essay. Based only on this paragraph, what would you expect to get from the rest of the essay? Write a sentence or two to explain.
2. Now reread the second paragraph and write a sentence or two discussing how this paragraph works with the first one. At the end of the second paragraph, are you more interested or less interested in reading further? Write a sentence or two to explain.
3. Reread the essay and mark at least two places where the transitions are rocky or hard to follow. Try to explain why.

Working Together

1. Do a one-page freewriting describing an intense, arresting, completely absorbing time in your recent experience when you felt fully awake and fully engaged, a time when things seemed especially clear or interesting or important to you. (*Hint:* Think in terms of moments of intense action or intense attention.) Describe this moment as clearly as you can. Talk about your freewrites in groups or in pairs. Explain why the moment was important to you. What made it stand out?
2. How does your freewriting and discussion help you understand what Thomas is doing in this essay?

Rethinking and Rewriting

Take your in-class freewriting and your thoughts from the discussion and work them into a revised personal essay. It should have the following structure: several paragraphs that provide a clear and direct description of the experience itself, followed by several paragraphs that convey just what you were thinking about during the experience (as if thinking aloud about what it meant).

AM I BLUE?

"Ain't these tears in these eyes tellin' you?" [1]

Alice Walker

> *African-American novelist, poet, and essayist Alice Walker is probably best known for* The Color Purple *(1983), her novel about the southern black experience, which won the National Book Award and the Pulitzer Prize before being made into a movie. Her essays have been collected into several books, including* Living by the Word *(1988), from which "Am I Blue?" is taken. Her most recent collection of personal essays is* Anything Can Be Saved by Love: A Writer's Activism *(1998).*

For about three years my companion and I rented a small house in the country that stood on the edge of a large meadow that appeared to run from the end of our deck straight into the mountains. The mountains, however, were quite far away, and between us and them there was, in fact, a town. It was one of the many pleasant aspects of the house that you never really were aware of this.

It was a house of many windows, low, wide, nearly floor to ceiling in the living room, which faced the meadow, and it was from one of these that I first saw our closest neighbor, a large white horse, cropping grass, flipping its mane, and ambling about—not over the entire meadow, which stretched well out of sight of the house, but over the five or so fenced-in acres that were next to the twenty-odd that we had rented. I soon learned that the horse, whose name was Blue, belonged to a man who lived in another town, but was boarded by our neighbors next door. Occasionally, one of the children, usually a stocky teen-ager, but sometimes a much younger girl or boy, could be seen riding Blue. They would appear in the meadow, climb up on his back, ride furiously for ten or fifteen minutes, then get off, slap Blue on the flanks, and not be seen again for a month or more.

There were many apple trees in our yard, and one by the fence that Blue could almost reach. We were soon in the habit of feeding him apples, which he relished, especially because by the middle of summer the meadow grasses—so green and succulent since January—had dried out from lack of rain, and Blue stumbled about munching the dried stalks half-heartedly. Sometimes he would stand very still just by the apple tree, and when one of us came out he would whinny, snort loudly, or stamp the ground. This meant, of course: I want an apple.

---

1. © 1929 Warner Bros., Inc. (renewed). By Grant Clarke and Harry Akst. All rights reserved. Used by permission.

It was quite wonderful to pick a few apples, or collect those that had fallen to the ground overnight, and patiently hold them, one by one, up to his large, toothy mouth. I remained as thrilled as a child by his flexible dark lips, huge, cubelike teeth that crunched the apples, core and all, with such finality, and his high, broad-breasted *enormity;* beside which, I felt small indeed. When I was a child, I used to ride horses, and was especially friendly with one named Nan until the day I was riding and my brother deliberately spooked her and I was thrown, head first, against the trunk of a tree. When I came to, I was in bed and my mother was bending worriedly over me; we silently agreed that perhaps horseback riding was not the safest sport for me. Since then I have walked, and prefer walking to horseback riding—but I had forgotten the depth of feeling one could see in horses' eyes.

I was therefore unprepared for the expression in Blue's. Blue was lonely. Blue was horribly lonely and bored. I was not shocked that this should be the case; five acres to tramp by yourself, endlessly, even in the most beautiful of meadows—and his was—cannot provide many interesting events, and once rainy season turned to dry that was about it. No, I was shocked that I had forgotten that human animals and nonhuman animals can communicate quite well; if we are brought up around animals as children we take this for granted. By the time we are adults we no longer remember. However, the animals have not changed. They are in fact *completed* creations (at least they seem to be, so much more than we) who are not likely *to* change; it is their nature to express themselves. What else are they going to express? And they do. And, generally speaking, they are ignored.

After giving Blue the apples, I would wander back to the house, aware that he was observing me. Were more apples not forthcoming then? Was that to be his sole entertainment for the day? My partner's small son had decided he wanted to learn how to piece a quilt; we worked in silence on our respective squares as I thought . . .

Well, about slavery: about white children, who were raised by black people, who knew their first all-accepting love from black women, and then, when they were twelve or so, were told they must "forget" the deep levels of communication between themselves and "mammy" that they knew. Later they would be able to relate quite calmly, "My old mammy was sold to another good family." "My old mammy was _____." Fill in the blank. Many more years later a white woman would say: "I can't understand these Negroes, these blacks. What do they want? They're so different from us."

And about the Indians, considered to be "like animals" by the "settlers" (a very benign euphemism for what they actually were), who did not understand their description as a compliment.

And about the thousands of American men who marry Japanese, Korean, Filipina, and other non-English-speaking women and of how happy they report they are, "*blissfully,*" until their brides learn to speak

English, at which point the marriages tend to fall apart. What then did the men see, when they looked into the eyes of the women they married, before they could speak English? Apparently only their own reflections.

I thought of society's impatience with the young. "Why are they *10* playing the music so loud?" Perhaps the children have listened to much of the music of oppressed people their parents danced to before they were born, with its passionate but soft cries for acceptance and love, and they have wondered why their parents failed to hear.

I do not know how long Blue had inhabited his five beautiful, boring acres before we moved into our house; a year after we had arrived—and had also traveled to other valleys, other cities, other worlds—he was still there.

But then, in our second year at the house, something happened in Blue's life. One morning, looking out the window at the fog that lay like a ribbon over the meadow, I saw another horse, a brown one, at the other end of Blue's field. Blue appeared to be afraid of it, and for several days made no attempt to go near. We went away for a week. When we returned, Blue had decided to make friends and the two horses ambled or galloped along together, and Blue did not come nearly as often to the fence underneath the apple tree.

When he did, bringing his new friend with him, there was a different look in his eyes. A look of independence, of self-possession, of inalienable *horse*ness. His friend eventually became pregnant. For months and months there was, it seemed to me, a mutual feeling between me and the horses of justice, of peace. I fed apples to them both. The look in Blue's eyes was one of unabashed "this is *it*ness."

It did not, however, last forever. One day, after a visit to the city, I went out to give Blue some apples. He stood waiting, or so I thought, though not beneath the tree. When I shook the tree and jumped back from the shower of apples, he made no move. I carried some over to him. He managed to half-crunch one. The rest he let fall to the ground. I dreaded looking into his eyes—because I had of course noticed that Brown, his partner, had gone—but I did look. If I had been born into slavery, and my partner had been sold or killed, my eyes would have looked like that. The children next door explained that Blue's partner had been "put with him" (the same expression that old people used, I had noticed, when speaking of an ancestor during slavery who had been impregnated by her owner) so that they could mate and she conceive. Since that was accomplished, she had been taken back by her owner, who lived somewhere else.

Will she be back? I asked. *15*

They didn't know.

Blue was like a crazed person. Blue *was*, to me, a crazed person. He galloped furiously, as if he were being ridden, around and around his five beautiful acres. He whinnied until he couldn't. He tore at the ground with his hooves. He butted himself against his single shade tree. He looked always and always toward the road down which his partner had gone. And then, occasionally, when he came up for apples, or I took apples to him, he looked at me. It was a look so piercing, so full of grief, a look so *human,* I almost laughed (I felt too sad to cry) to think there are people who do not know that animals suffer. People like me who have forgotten, and daily forget, all that animals try to tell us. "Everything you do to us will happen to you; we are your teachers, as you are ours. We are one lesson" is essentially it, I think. There are those who never once have even considered animals' rights: those who have been taught that animals actually want to be used and abused by us, as small children "love" to be frightened, or women "love" to be mutilated and raped. . . . They are the great-grand-children of those who honestly thought, because someone taught them this: "Women can't think," and "niggers can't faint." But most disturbing of all, in Blue's large brown eyes was a new look, more painful than the look of despair: the look of disgust with human beings, with life; the look of hatred. And it was odd what the look of hatred did. It gave him, for the first time, the look of a beast. And what that meant was that he had put up a barrier within to protect himself from further violence; all the apples in the world wouldn't change that fact.

And so Blue remained, a beautiful part of our landscape, very peaceful to look at from the window, white against the grass. Once a friend came to visit and said, looking out on the soothing view: "And it *would* have to be a *white* horse; the very image of freedom." And I thought, yes, the animals are forced to become for us merely "images" of what they once so beautifully expressed. And we are used to drinking milk from containers showing "contented" cows, whose real lives we want to hear nothing about, eating eggs and drumsticks from "happy" hens, and munching hamburgers advertised by bulls of integrity who seem to command their fate.

As we talked of freedom and justice one day for all, we sat down to steaks. I am eating misery, I thought, as I took the first bite. And spit it out.

1986

Reading and Responding

1. Mark the place in this essay where you think you know what it's about, what the main theme is. Briefly paraphrase this passage.
2. Write quickly and freely about a horse or other animal that you know or have known well enough to describe its personality.

Working Together

1. Do a short freewrite explaining what you think Blue represents for Walker. Then, as a group, discuss your responses. Trace each interpretation back to a particular place in the text. Finally, identify two points

you feel sure that Walker wants readers to understand. Write two or three sentences to explain each point.

2. Imagine that you're Walker and that you're getting ready to write this essay. Explain what's going through your mind. What moved you to begin writing? What main point are you planning to make? What writing strategy are you thinking about?

Rethinking and Rewriting

1. Write an essay that centers on a particular animal but that uses that animal as a way of reflecting on larger issues as well. Use the animal as a point of departure, a representative example, a symbol.

2. Write an essay arguing for vegetarianism. Use Walker's essay as a source, do other research to support your arguments, or, like Walker, draw on personal experience.

HOW SMART ARE SHEEP?

Barbara Drake

> *Poet Barbara Drake recently published a book of her personal essays,* Peace at Heart *(1998), which reflect on her ten years of living on a farm in Oregon's Yamhill Valley. She is also a professor of English at Linfield College in McMinnville, Oregon. In this dryly funny essay, Drake explains that sheep are not nearly as unintelligent as they appear.*

One indication of the intelligence of sheep is that they do not really like people. They can't help it, and it must be in their own best interest because evolution seems to have wired it into their brains. I don't mean that sheep are openly hostile—certainly, pet sheep can even seem friendly—but overall, a sheep's orientation is away from the human race.

I've been reading about it. Tests on sheep show that different parts of their brains act up when they see different figures—specifically, other sheep they know, sheep of their own breed, sheep with big horns, dogs, and people. The activity the sheep's brain exhibits when it sees a dog and a human being shows that it thinks human beings and dogs are more alike than sheep and dogs or sheep and people. Of course, from a distance, if a human being gets down on all fours, there is a little uncertainty and the sheep's brain may start sending "possible other sheep" signals until the sheep gets close enough to realize its mistake. Then a sheep might think you're a dog, until you stand up. By and large, from a sheep's viewpoint, dogs and people fall into the category of trouble.

One researcher, noticing this similarity of response to dogs and people, concluded that sheep have emotions. If you're around them much, it becomes obvious that sheep have emotions, so this is no surprise, but it's interesting to see how research proves it. According to the researcher, if a sheep were merely responding to appearance, a dog, with its long muzzle, might elicit a response that would associate the dog with a sheep. But instead, the brain waves elicited by a dog are close to those elicited by human beings, and thus we know that the sheep is experiencing an emotional response to both of us, dog and person, and that response is not thrilled.

Of course, if we are carrying a big grain bucket, the brain waves are something different. But in any case, it surely can be called an emotion—that is, a particular brain response that readies the sensate animal for some sort of action, fight or flight or pig out. My sheep always look pretty happy when the human-brings-feed image impresses itself on the optic nerve and thence to the brain.

I have run into people who don't believe that animals feel emotions 5 ("have feelings" is the way they usually put it). This is probably just a way of rationalizing what we human beings do or have done to animals, the meaning of emotion being coded into the word "feelings." If a creature has no feelings, it can feel no pain. But sheep do have emotions and feelings, however they may vary from our own.

It's true, sheep do not run to the fence in friendly curiosity when they see a person. To a sheep, a human being is almost always something to have as little to do with as possible, unless that human being is bearing alfalfa, COB, or Fatena, or preparing to open the gate into a new browsing area. Bummer lambs raised with a bottle are a dramatic exception, but they are confused by their upbringing. A bummer (a bottle-fed lamb that has been orphaned, or whose mother is unable to raise it for some reason) will see you coming or hear your voice across the pasture and come running, baaing its head off with that charming, ringing, baby baa. They'll crawl through the smallest hole in a fence, run to you, and begin butting the back of your ankles, looking for an udder and waiting for your milk to come down. It's hard not to feel loved by a sheep when this happens.

But as you wean them they become less attached, maybe even resentful after a while—another emotion. I've seen weaned bummers use a kind of body language that can only be called sulking. They plant themselves in front of you, but when you don't produce a bottle they turn and pretend to be looking at something invisible on the ground. And if they continue their fence-hopping and escape tactics, and you end up chasing them back into the pasture, after a while they get downright suspicious and will stay away from you. In the sheep's brain, sometimes you're just the thing that's standing between them and the all-you-can-eat salad bar in the kitchen garden. You're Trouble. Just the sight of you (not to mention your dog) sets off wary brain waves in the sheep.

Of course sheep have other brain waves too. Horns on sheep are signs of status, of a possibly challenging big honcho sheep, or of a sexually mature, hot-to-trot ram. Scientists have tested sheep by showing them pictures of sheep with horns, and have found that the bigger the horns, the more excitable the brain waves become. These were simple line drawings—horn porn for girl sheep. The scientists performed this test only on horned breeds. I haven't been able to find out whether hornless breeds also get turned on by big horns, but they do react positively to familiar sheep. As one study put it, "Sheep know who their friends are." That's why they get negative vibes when they look at people and dogs.

One curious thing about the way a sheep's brain reacts to different faces is that a sheep doesn't recognize its friends upside down. Though a sheep will react with familiar brain waves even to a crude drawing of a sheep right side up, if you turn that picture upside down the sheep's reaction is something like, "Whaa . . . ?"

Supposedly, arboreal primates recognize other arboreal primates right side up *and* upside down. That's because they hang from trees, sometimes upside down. But you almost never will see a live sheep upside down, and never of its own free will. Sheep don't even roll over on their backs for the

10

fun of it, as horses do. They don't roll over to scratch their backs like dogs or cats, or loll around on their backs at the beach like people on vacation. At the most, a lying-down sheep will stretch out its neck on the ground or lounge to one side, but sheep are very upright creatures.

In fact, a sheep on its back is liable to be in trouble. Our old sheep Toffee was rather fat, and once in a while, especially in rainy weather when she hadn't been sheared all winter and her wool was heavy and wet, she might lie down on a hillside and then accidentally roll over on her back. She then was unable to roll down a quarter-turn more to her other side and get back on her feet, and she certainly couldn't roll uphill, so she would lie there till we found her and rolled her over so she could get up. As she lay there, on the slope of the hill, you can imagine, being upside down, she'd see us coming and think, "Who *are* those creatures?"

With tricks like these, sheep often have been equated with stupidity, mainly because of their herding instincts, which can be so strong as to get them into trouble, such as a whole flock jumping off a cliff because the sheep in the lead goes over first. (We've never heard of human beings doing anything like that, have we?) But really, most of the time a sheep knows what a sheep needs to know.

One researcher tried to measure sheep intelligence by conducting a test that required the sheep to remove a black cloth from a box to get at feed—a test that horses and cows already had passed after varying numbers of attempts. The sheep confronted with this enigma stamped its feet, as sheep do when confronted with danger, urinated, as they do when nervous and stymied, and generally didn't get the idea until after fifty-five tries, putting them, according to this tester, below horses and cattle in intelligence.

But another test showed that sheep could learn to recognize and avoid noxious plants after only one bad experience, and that was something they had to figure out after eating a large variety of plants during the same browsing period, and with feedback (that is, a bad reaction to the noxious plant) coming as long as several hours after the plant was consumed. This is an example of single-trial learning when it comes to something a sheep needs to know. Other tests showed similar results, such as when lambs who saw their mothers eating an unfamiliar feed immediately learned to eat that feed too. Lambs normally would take a while to discover that something unfamiliar was good to eat. In further testing, researchers found that the sheep still relied on this learned information years later, even if they hadn't encountered that feed in the meantime. This indicated that lambs learn what to eat by watching what their mothers eat, and they learn it quickly.

I will not make claims that sheep are especially intelligent in human terms, but obviously they do know what they need to know to be sheep. Our older ewes are the ones who have learned which gates they can jiggle to sometimes escape the pasture when they want to. Amity, Aurora, and Bela all have learned how to lie down and crawl under a woven wire fence if there is the slightest slack in the wire, much to our inconvenience. Now it seems clear that their lambs also are learning this behavior, while other younger mothers and their lambs can't figure it out.

The sheep also know when to go in at night and how to sort themselves out. At sundown, our rams go to a pen on one side of the barn and the ewes go to the other. We just close the gates. We had a small ram born late last year that we kept to put a little more size on him. We let the lambs, male or female, go in to the ewes' side. This small ram continued to go in with the ewes and to hang on to his lamb status all through the winter. When this year's lambing started, and the ewes' side was getting crowded, we decided he needed to go into the rams' side at night. It took three nights of chasing him in there from the ewes' side. After that, he consistently went to the rams' side on his own.

Susan M. Oullette, writing about sheep in seventeenth-century America, says that although sheep in Ipswich, Massachusetts, were individually owned, during the day they were taken out to the village commons by a sheepherder hired by the community. This collectively managed flock of sheep, known as the "Great Herd," was brought home at night, with the various groups of sheep turning off to their owners' places. The essay doesn't say whether the sheep turned off on their own, knowing they were home, or whether the shepherd cut them out of the flock as appropriate. My guess is that the sheep, like our ewes and rams, would have known where their own home barn was.

Sheep know what they need to know.

This past year we had personal experience with an eight-month-old ram trying to find his way home. I like to think it's also an indicator that sheep are smarter than some people think. We sold the ram lamb to some people who live about twelve miles from here, on the other side of a wooded ridge and up their own hill. To get to their house, you have to drive north about six miles, then turn off and double back, driving down a twisting road through a narrow valley between two big ridges. Then you turn off and drive up a narrow road that passes through some other people's woods, and finally out into a clearing where their ranch is.

The week after we sold the lamb, a neighbor on the opposite side of the highway called to ask if we'd lost a lamb. She'd found one that looked like ours—a black Romney. I said, no, all my lambs were accounted for. After I got off the phone I began to wonder whether the recent buyers of the lamb had made it home with their acquisition. I called. The buyer said, ruefully, the lamb was missing. They'd brought him home and unloaded him into a pen by himself because the ewes were in another field down the road. Seeing no other sheep and panicked by the trip in the horse trailer, the lamb jumped the fence and took off. Sheep don't like to be alone, especially if they've been raised with a lot of other sheep, as ours have. If there is one instinct above all others in sheep, it's the herding instinct. The lamb would have been perfectly happy to stay where he was, had they unloaded him in with the ewes right away. They had, after all,

20

purchased him to be the sole sultan of his own harem. But so far as he could tell, after they put him in the strange truck and drove him all that way, they'd put him in isolation. It scared the heck out of him. A healthy, well-grown lamb can jump a lot higher than most people think if his adrenaline is up. This guy cleared the fence like Superlamb and took off.

When I told her about the stray lamb that had turned up in our neighborhood, she got excited and said they'd go look at him right away. Of course it turned out to be the lost lamb who had been wandering for four days and finally turned up on the sheep farm across the highway, about six miles through thickly wooded countryside and over the mountain from where he'd leaped the fence. He'd clearly been headed in the right direction.

Whether it was all by chance or not, we'll never know. Wild sheep, and sheep raised on vast ranches or downs, need to find their way. Do even small-farm domestic sheep have a strong directional sense? How would it operate considering the ram lamb had been taken to his new home via winding country roads, not at all the shortest path cross-country? How had he managed to strike off through the woods and end up that close to where he had been born? Did he know what he was doing, or was it just an accident? It wasn't exactly *Lassie Come Home,* but it was interesting.

This time when the new owners returned the lamb to their farm, they made sure there were a couple of ewes waiting for him in the pen. He took one look and was immediately happy to settle down. Sheep, after all, know what they need to know.

Reading and Responding

1. As you reread the essay, underline five separate sentences that stand out for whatever reason. Copy them in the form of a list. Underline what you think is the thesis sentence for the essay and copy it. If the sentence is already on the list, simply mark an asterisk by it.
2. Write a paragraph (at least five sentences) about a time when you wondered what a particular animal was thinking, or whether a particular animal was capable of thought.

Working Together

1. Compare your separate lists from item 1 above. How many of the same sentences did your group include, and what does this redundancy suggest about the style and structure of Drake's essay?
2. Compile your separate lists of sentences into a single list. Based only on this composite list, write a one-page summary of the idea of the essay.
3. Based only on this composite list, describe the style and voice of Drake's essay. Is it informal or formal, intimate or distant? What clothes (metaphorically) is the writing wearing? And so on.

4. Compile a list of the facts that Drake must have researched. For each one, write the question that the research answered. Then make a list of the times that members in your group have done research (not just academic research, but any instance in which you've talked with "experts" or consulted print or electronic sources) just because you wanted to.

Rethinking and Rewriting

1. Fill in the blank in this title with another animal: "How Smart Are _____?" Then write an essay about that animal, basing your essay on personal experience and on research and reading.
2. Fill in the blank with an object or machine or institution and write an essay on that subject: "How Smart Are _____?" (For example, "How Smart Are Computers?" "How Smart Are State Governments?")
3. Write an essay with this title: "How Smart Are People?" In at least two places, compare people and sheep by quoting from Drake's essay.

SLEEPING WITH ANIMALS

Maxine Kumin

> *An accomplished novelist and poet, Maxine Kumin is perhaps best known for her book* Up Country, *which draws many of its themes and locales from rural New England and which won the 1973 Pulitzer Prize for poetry. Reprinted from* Nurture *(1989), "Sleeping with Animals" turns what could easily be considered an obligation into both meditation and celebration. Kumin's* Selected Poems, 1960–1990 *was published in 1997.*

Nightly I choose to keep this covenant
with a wheezing broodmare who, ten days past due,
grunts in her sleep in the vocables
of the vastly pregnant. She lies down
on sawdust of white pine, its turp smell blending   5
with the rich scent of ammonia and manure.
I in my mummy bag just outside her stall
observe the silence, louder than the catch
in her breathing, observe gradations of
the ancient noneditorial dark; against   10
the open doorway looking south, observe
the paddock posts become a chain gang, each
one shackled leg and wrist; the pasture wall
a graveyard of bones that ground fog lifts and swirls.

Sleeping with animals,   15
loving my animals too much,
letting them run like a perfectly detached
statement by Mozart through all the other lines
of my life, a handsome family of serene
horses glistening in their thoughtlessness,   20
fear ghosts me still for my two skeletons:
one stillborn foal eight years ago.
One, hours old, dead of a broken spine.
Five others swam like divers into air,
dropped on clean straw, were whinnied to, tongued dry,   25
and staggered, stagey drunkards, to their feet,
nipped and nudged by their mothers to the teat.

Restless, dozy, between occasional coughs
the mare takes note of me and nickers. Heaves
herself up, explores the corners of   30
her feed tub. Sleeps a little, leg joints locked.
I shine my light across the bar to watch
the immense contours of her flanks rise and fall.

Each double-inhale is threaded to the life
that still holds back in its safe sac.   35
What we say to each other in the cold black
of April, conveyed in a wordless yet perfect
language of touch and tremor, connects
us most surely to the wet cave we all
once burst from gasping, naked or furred,   40
into our separate species.

Everywhere on this planet, birth.
Everywhere, curled in the amnion,
an unborn wonder.
Together we wait for this still-clenched burden.   45

Reading and Responding

1. Reread the poem and make two lists, one list detailing whatever you
   know about the person speaking in this poem and the other list relating
   to whatever you know about the horse. Read slowly and add to your
   lists as you go.
2. The speaker chooses to keep the horse company. List some of the
   reasons for this choice, highlighting the words that indicate the speaker's
   motivation.

Working Together

1. Kumin has divided this poem into four sections. As a group, look at
   each of these sections, and summarize each one in a sentence or two.
   Then from your brief summaries, make a list of questions that each
   section works to answer. For example, here's one of the questions that
   the first section works to answer: What's the horse's condition?
2. As a group, discuss the reasons that the person in this poem is spending
   the night in the barn. What connects the person and the pregnant
   mare? Decide on the three most important links or connections, and
   write a sentence for each.

Rethinking and Rewriting

1. If possible, tell the story of a birth that you watched or participated in
   and try to do justice to how it affected you.
2. Assume that someone has made a quick reading of "Sleeping with
   Animals" and just doesn't seem to understand it. Lead this reader patiently through the poem, explaining both what's going on and what
   the speaker is thinking about.
3. Using this poem as your starting point, discuss why you'd be inclined
   (or not) to read other work by Kumin. Be honest, and make your
   explanation a careful and thoughtful one.

A FRAGILE KINGDOM

A FRAGILE KINGDOM

Sue Halpern

Editor-at-large of DoubleTake *magazine, Sue Halpern has also written* Migrations to Solitude *(1992), an exploration of privacy and how our laws and ways of living reinforce or erode it. In this essay, Halpern follows and surveys the migration of monarch butterflies.*

Late last October visitors to Monarch Watch, the university Internet site that tracks monarch butterfly activity, were greeted by a message from José Sanchez, a reporter in Monterrey, Mexico. Sanchez was excited, nearly ecstatic: The butterflies were pouring into Monterrey in unprecedented numbers. So many, in fact, he said, that radio and television broadcasters were interrupting programs, urging people to drive slowly to reduce butterfly casualties.

The butterflies, which had spent late summer in the northeastern United States and Canada, were on the last leg of their annual 2,000-mile southern migration. It would be weeks before they arrived at their ultimate destination, 1 of about 15 small overwintering sites spread over just 50 acres, high in the Transverse Neovolcanic Belt of Mexico, about three hours west of Mexico City. There they would find the habitat necessary to survive the winter: thick stands of oyamel fir trees, with sufficient moisture and protection from the wind, and sources of nectar nearby. For five months the monarchs would mass in those forests, hovering in the sun, clustering on tree trunks and branches, tens of millions of them. By midwinter a visitor wandering through would be overwhelmed, as much by the chatter of 30 million wings as by the sight of butterflies so numerous they appeared to consume the trees. With the air growing warmer, the butterflies would lift off, great clouds of them moving across the sky like smoke. They would set down in fields of flowers, nectaring, mating, laying eggs, and establishing a new generation to carry on the migration, first to the north, as far as Ontario, and then, in the fall, to the south again.

How monarchs are able to find their way back to the same oyamel forests year after year is one of the great unsolved mysteries of animal biology. They are not guided by memory, since no single butterfly ever makes the entire round-trip; three or four generations separate those that came from the Neovolcanic Belt from those that go there. A monarch butterfly born in August in my New York State backyard, for instance, will probably fly all the way to Mexico and spend the winter there; it then begins the journey north in March, laying eggs on milkweed along the Gulf Coast from Texas to Florida before dying. The butterflies born of those eggs will continue northward, breeding and laying more eggs along

the way. So will their offspring. By August another monarch, four generations or so removed from the monarch that left my land for Mexico the
previous summer, will emerge from its chrysalis in my backyard and do
the same thing. It will head south, aiming for a place it has never been, an
acre or two of forest on the steep slopes of the Neovolcanics.

How it knows where to go is just as remarkable as that it gets there
at all. Researchers now believe that the monarch uses the sun as a compass,
as well as being oriented by polar magnetism and visual cues such as mountains; they are not sure if these phenomena work together, or how. What
is clear is that the monarch has a sophisticated navigation system that from
late August onward enables butterflies stretching from the eastern slopes of
the Rockies in Alberta to the Atlantic coast of Nova Scotia and the eastern
United States to begin heading south and west. Over thousands of miles
they fly as high as the clouds, often out of binocular vision. Up there they
look as evanescent, and as unlikely, as they are.

Orange and black, with a scallop of white dots on the back of their   5
wings, monarchs are the one butterfly almost all of us can identify. Yet the
monarch we see in North America is actually a tropical butterfly, native to
Central and South America and at home in Cuba, the Canary Islands, the
South Pacific. That it exists, and thrives, north of the tropics is one of the
great tricks of the natural world, an adaptation that is thought to date at
least to the Pleistocene Era, about a million years ago, when climate
changes allowed the monarchs' host plant, the milkweed, to range farther
north. Milkweed is the sole food source for the monarch caterpillar; its
leaves supply the poison that makes the butterfly, once it emerges from its
chrysalis, distasteful to most birds and other predators. Still, although milkweed is now found throughout the United States and southern Canada,
the monarch remains unable to tolerate the severe cold of a northern
winter. So the migration is an accommodation, a way for the butterflies to
make use of all that good milkweed without suffering the consequences of
weather. Breed (and feed) in the north, winter in the south—it is as familiar a pattern in the natural world as in some of our own lives.

Familiar, common, prolific—all of these describe the North American monarch population. Which is why two years ago, in January 1996,
when U.S. zoologist Lincoln Brower and Mexican poet Homero Aridjis
published an article in *The New York Times* suggesting that the monarch
was at risk, heads turned. Statistically, it seemed impossible—there were
just too many of them. The article, written shortly after a snowstorm in
the mountains that appeared to devastate a Mexican butterfly colony,
warned that changes in the land due to logging and agriculture could
change the microclimate of the overwintering sites to such an extent that
there would be a massive die-off. An intact forest, the two men argued,
serves as an umbrella and a blanket, protecting butterflies from freezing
rains. Logging creates gaps that allow rain and snow to fall through the
forest canopy and onto the butterfly clusters. As the weather clears, the

life-sustaining heat radiated from the butterflies' bodies leaks out through these holes in the blanket of trees, and the monarchs freeze to death. And so, they cautioned, though the species would survive because it is established in so many other places, the eastern migratory phenomenon itself might end.

That article marked a watershed. On one side were the scientists and preservationists like Brower and Aridjis, who saw how the logging and agricultural practices of the Mexican farmers who lived and worked where the monarchs overwintered were adversely affecting the butterfly habitat. On the other were the campesinos themselves, who needed to clear those forests to grow oats and corn to feed their families and to pasture their animals, and who also needed wood for cooking and heating and building. Though to some extent each side appreciated the argument of the other—the scientists recognized the need of the peasant community to use the forest, and the peasants valued the beauty and constancy of the returning monarchs—the division was nonetheless both poignant and acute, and the intervening years have only made it more so.

The oyamel forests are clearly in decline, and the human community is desperately poor, and even what appear to be positive signs, like the abundance of monarchs returning to the overwintering sites last fall, can be interpreted as further evidence of trouble. Brower, for one, contends that the monarchs left their overwintering sites earlier than usual in 1997 because land-clearing right up to the edge of the preserves had eliminated their nectar and water sources. With their usual staging ground for the spring migration disrupted, he says, the butterflies simply took off. Because of their early departure, they were able to produce more generations in the north prior to the return trip—hence the high numbers. If the weather in the north had not been unusually warm last spring, though, Brower contends, mortality could have been overwhelming. So, overstated as the article in the *Times* might have been—it estimated that 30 million butterflies had died when, once a proper assessment could be made, the number was put at 10 million or fewer—it did expose the fact that the *milagro*—the miracle—of migration could disappear with the trees.

It is mid-November 1997. Lincoln Brower, 66, professor emeritus at the University of Florida, the man considered to be the world's leading expert on the monarch butterfly, and his Mexican ally Homero Aridjis, are astride horses, waiting to begin an ascent of Cerro Altamirano, a mountain that looms 10,000 feet above Contupec, the village where Aridjis grew up. As a boy, Aridjis says, he and his friends would hike up the mountain to a field called Llano de la Mula—the Flat of the Donkey—to picnic and watch the butterflies, which were so thick they bowed the trees.

The region is currently suffering a drought, and so the trail up the   10
mountain is dry. If dirt can be ephemeral, this dirt is, though it gets into our lungs and our hair and our clothes. The road is eroding underfoot, one step at a time, and for those of us hiking along with Brower and

Aridjis it is important to stay clear of the small avalanches triggered by the horses. As we climb we scan the air, the trees, the ground for evidence: butterfly wings, dead butterflies, butterfly clusters, individuals sailing overhead. We see none. The oak forest gives way to oyamel as we gain altitude, and still nothing. If we want to know what the butterfly world may be coming to, the world that Brower and Aridjis in their most pessimistic moments warn about, this may be it. But that is not why we are here. Brower and Aridjis want to see butterflies, lots of them, and so we continue the upward journey to the place where Aridjis remembers their being.

It wasn't just the butterflies, Homero Aridjis says later, when we rest at Llano de la Mula, a slightly canted alpine meadow ringed by tall oyamel trees. This place used to be full of coyotes, skunks, and rabbits. Today the only thing we find are ladybugs, thousands of them—but no monarchs, and no sign of monarchs. There is evidence, still, of the fires that devastated this forest 15 years ago, fires started by people attempting to clear land for agriculture that happened to get out of control. Since then the local monarch population has been smaller and less reliable, a direct result of the fires, perhaps, as well as of logging. "I feel very frustrated," Aridjis says, mounting his horse for the ride down. "Every time I come there are fewer and fewer trees."

Cerro Altamirano, the place of Aridjis's youth, is one of five butterfly roosting sites set aside by Mexican presidential decree in 1986. All are in the Neovolcanic Belt, in the states of Michoacán and México. Although the land is privately owned, by local peasant collectives called ejidos, the decree is very specific: It designates both a core zone and a buffer zone in all the preserves, and it describes what the residents—the ejiditarios—are and are not allowed to do in each. The core zone is off-limits to logging and farming; the buffer zone is not. For the ejiditarios this means that a certain amount of their land has been effectively appropriated by the government and is no longer theirs to do with as they want. This has not precluded all logging, but it has, to a large extent, driven much of it underground and created a market for illegal trees. The ejiditarios are poor—they live, for the most part, in small, unheated houses and exist outside the cash economy—and taking the forest out of circulation has, for many, compounded their hardship. "In 1986, when the government created the five monarch butterfly reserves, we thought we'd get some benefits," recalls Silverio Tapia, president of the Ejido Jesus Nazareno near the Sierra Chincua sanctuary, "but that never happened. Finally, in 1990, because our families were starving, some of us decided to log in the area without a permit. The government noticed and treated us like criminals. We went to jail because we took out some trees to feed our families."

Trees are being taken out of the buffer zones, where it is legal, and out of the core zones, where it is not, and in both cases they are sometimes the very trees where the butterflies are roosting. (Evolved as they are, the monarchs have not yet figured out which trees are in the preserves and which are not.) Even when the trees are not home to butterflies, the effects of logging and of clearing nearby forests for pastureland are often deleterious to them. "We made a mistake," says Lincoln Brower, who worked on the plan that resulted in the presidential decrees. "We followed the U.S. Forest Service policy for buffer zones in designing these preserves, which allows for logging. We should have concentrated on the oyamel-forest ecosystem and not on the monarch butterfly."

Because the planners did not protect the entire forest, there is, for the butterflies, the problem of the changing microclimate, as well as of crowding and of diversity—problems that become obvious when you are standing in the middle of a thin stand of oyamel and thousands upon millions of monarchs are clustered on the same few trees. If those trees go, you wonder, what then? For the 75,000 or so people living off this land, the question is much the same. Given their numbers and the heavy demands they put upon the forest, how can it sustain them?

The trip down the mountain, no less treacherous than the trip up, provides one object lesson and then another. The first is observed by Brower, who points to a large oyamel tree in the core zone with a deep gash in its trunk. The gash is the size and shape of an ax head. Once he points it out, other gashes in other trees become visible—it's nearly epidemic. "These flesh wounds will invite disease," Brower explains, "and eventually the trees will die." When they do, they will be hauled out legally, for although it is illegal to take down living trees in this forest because it is a protected butterfly preserve, there is no such injunction against removing dead or diseased timber.

The second lesson is heard before it is seen. Somewhere in the distance a chainsaw whines, stops, and whines again. Wood cracks, and a tree crashes through the understory. Later we see the tree, cut into thirds and tied to the flanks of five donkeys led by two men and a boy. "How much will you get for these?" we ask the men. "Fifteen pesos per donkey," they say. Two dollars.

The extraction of wood, one piece at a time, suggests the kind of life lived by the ejiditarios in the overwintering regions. For the most part, people survive by getting what they need for free from the forest. People harvest corn, not to bring to market but to feed their families. They cut down trees for firewood, to clear the land to grow corn, and to get what little cash they can. "That is why," says Julia Carabias Lillo, the dynamic Mexican minister of the environment, "the focus can't just be about the protection of the forest. We must preserve and develop it so living conditions are adequate."

She is talking to a rapt audience of about 300 Canadians, Americans, and Mexicans who are gathered in November 1997 to talk about doing just that. All are attending the North American Conference on the Monarch

Butterfly, in Morelia, not far from the butterfly preserves—bureaucrats and loggers and environmentalists and lepidopterists and ejiditarios. Even U.S. Interior Secretary Bruce Babbitt is in attendance.

"I am here to meet the leaders of the ejidos, because they are the ones who live the reality," Babbitt tells the audience in flawless Spanish. "We have to find new models so you and your communities can live in harmony with the butterflies." Babbitt's main suggestion: Strengthen ecotourism.

It is an attractive notion, ecotourism, especially the way Babbitt en- *20* visions it: small guesthouses run by local folk who will also be able to promote and sell indigenous crafts; visitors coming year-round, even when the butterflies are not in residence. But like many such notions, this one is flawed, and not only because there is no infrastructure in the region to support it. It is flawed because it fails to take into account the butterflies and their habitat, and the impact that increased numbers of visitors would have on them. Already in the past three years more than 100,000 people— most of them Mexicans—have passed through El Campanario, the one butterfly preserve that has capitalized on the desire to experience what it is like to stand among millions of monarchs. But the dust their feet has kicked up, as well as the concomitant erosion, trash, and water pollution, has begun to worry people like Mexican biologist Benigno Salazar. "We need to determine the carrying capacity of the area," he says, making it clear that tourism is not a panacea, that it, too, will have to be regulated and limited, just like logging.

But even limits can be subverted. Just how easily was demonstrated to me one afternoon in El Campanario as I hiked the trail with three other Americans and a Mexican guide. The butterflies had just recently started to return to the area. Though there were thousands of butterflies in the air, the most dramatic clusters were about 50 feet off the trail, in the woods. Between us and those trees was a barbed wire fence—a serious, three-string fence meant to keep people like us at bay. But when one member of the group, an American naturalist, asked the guide for the fourth time if it would be possible to get closer to the butterflies—making it clear that he would make it worth the guide's while—the guide looked left and right, then quickly lifted the fence, signaling us to slip under. Later we had to hike out surreptitiously and found ourselves in the middle of a newly reforested part of the preserve, trying with moderate success to avoid trampling the seedlings. Our guide pocketed $8 for lifting the fence. What incentive did he have not to?

It is day four of the five-day North American Conference on the Monarch Butterfly. One of the campesinos has complained out loud that "putting us up in a good hotel, frankly, tires us." Nevertheless, that man and his colleagues keep on talking, pressing the Mexican government to rescind the 1986 presidential decree. Over the past week, scientists, bu-reaucrats, and farmers have made proposals, most of them having to do with compensating the local residents for preserving the forests—renting the trees, buying them outright, levying carbon taxes. Threats have been made. (If you do not give us what we want, we will take what you want.) Projects have been discussed—establishing oyamel nurseries and forestry schools, building research libraries. The ejiditarios have accused the biologists of caring only for the butterflies and not for them. The lepidopterists have wondered how their discipline became a branch of social science. The economists have declared that environmental consciousness must come after rural development. The preservationists have worried that development will destroy the environment before any consciousness can develop. Aridjis, who in many ways is responsible for the presidential decree that established the preserves and is considered to be the enemy of the campesinos because of it, is not in attendance. Brower is, shuttling between physical scientists and social scientists, Mexicans and North Americans, one part politician, two parts zoologist, trying, as always, to make sure the monarchs will have a place to return to next year, and the next.

Twenty years ago Brower and a colleague, field biologist Bill Calvert, brought the Mexican wintering sites to public attention. More than a decade ago they worked on a plan to preserve them that helped lead to the presidential decree. That plan is not working, Brower acknowledges, and a new one is needed. If, before, he had been content to focus solely on the butterflies, now Brower is acutely aware of the first principle of ecology, the interdependence of species. But he seems gratified, almost surprised, to be told that his work on the monarch may actually help the people on the ground.

The man who reminds him is Dimas Salazar, a fruit farmer from Zitácuaro, whose white cowboy hat, silver teeth, and weathered skin announce, as clearly as Brower's patched cardigan and baggy corduroys, who he is. Salazar, one of 60 campesino delegates to the conference, gets up and asks for the microphone. To the scientists he says, looking across the room at Brower, "Since you can speak the language of the monarch butterfly, please thank them for us. These little animals give us the opportunity to express ourselves as peasants."

Brower, who no doubt can speak that language, knows just what   *25* Salazar means; he has been expressing himself through the butterflies for the better part of 50 years. Though Salazar wants the decree revoked and Brower wants it rewritten, it is obvious that the two have things to say to each other. And so the real work of preservation—of habitat, of culture— will commence right here, when Dimas Salazar, the peasant, and Lincoln Brower, the professor, sit down to talk about the land, and the butterflies, and how it might be possible to save what they love.

Reading and Responding

1. This essay explores, among other things, the tension between the needs of the monarch butterfly and the needs of the people who share the

butterfly habitat to stay alive themselves. As you reread the essay, mark passages that describe both sides of this complicated issue and particular words and phrases that Halpern uses in her description. Do you detect a bias on her part? Does she treat both sides of this issue fairly?

2. Make a list of the people and organizations that have a stake in or an interest in monarch butterflies and what happens to them. Then write at least two sentences reacting to the list you've made.

Working Together

1. Suppose that someone has read "A Fragile Kingdom" and has accused Halpern of being just another "butterfly-hugging, big-city environmentalist" without any concept of the economic problems and social complexities of these issues. In your group, gather evidence that this view of Halpern is based on a misreading of the essay. Make a list of places in the essay that you would cite as evidence.

2. As a group, summarize what Halpern says about the issue of ecotourism in Mexico and why this solution to the problem is flawed. Do you agree or disagree and why?

3. Identify and discuss the point of Halpern's essay. What, in the end, does she want us to do or think about the butterfly problem in particular and environmental issues in general? Is she arguing a position? If not, what is she doing and what is the value of the essay?

Rethinking and Rewriting

1. Write an essay that reflects on one of the "great unsolved mysteries" of your life, your academic major, or some subject that interests you. Alternate in the essay, as Halpern puts it, between what people are "not sure" of and "what is clear."

2. Write an essay about another environmental problem in which the economic interests of people are in tension with the environment and the needs of animal or plant species. Imitate Halpern's style and structure.

3. Write about a familiar migratory bird or animal that you have observed. Start by explaining your knowledge or experience, then proceed to identify and try to answer at least two questions you have about where this creature goes, how it lives, and whether it is at all threatened by habitat loss.

A LIFE IN OUR HANDS

Keith Ervin

The articles of Keith Ervin, a freelance writer living in Seattle, appear in Sierra, Seattle Weekly, *and other magazines. The following essay is the first chapter of his 1989 book,* Fragile Majesty: The Battle for North America's Last Great Forest, *the result of more than four years of intensive research.*

Its nose twitching, the small mouse makes its way along the narrow branch. The animal's quivering body speaks of caution, yet it remains oblivious to its impending doom.

The owl is perched on a higher branch, his sharp eyes riveted on the prey. Silently, motionlessly, the bird calculates the best method of attack. Suddenly, he swoops down and, with scarcely a pause in his wingbeats, snatches the rodent in his talons. A few thrusts of his powerful wings and the deadly hunter is safely roosting in another tree, savoring his meal.

Watching the northern spotted owl are three other sets of eyes, the eyes of men. Two biologists and I have walked to this patch of woods on the northern edge of Washington State's Olympic Peninsula, in pursuit of the most controversial bird in America. For the spotted owl has become both a powerful symbol and the chief focus in the battle now raging to save North America's last great forest: the "old growth" of the Pacific Northwest.

On our way into the forest, before we heard the owl's first *Hoo-hoo! . . . Hooooooo!,* one of my companions, Stan Sovern, spotted a logging tower in a clearcut on the ridgetop. When Sovern climbed the ridge earlier in the year to band a female owl, the clearcut wasn't there. Sovern and Eric Forsman are after the male today. Their search will be punctuated by the occasional whine of a chain saw and the toot of a whistle on the logging site.

The owl, ready for another mouse, flies to a perch closer to the men. Forsman, the lanky young biologist directing this research sponsored by the U.S. Forest Service, walks slowly toward the bird, carrying a fishing rod with a nooselike loop at the tip. The bird calmly sits on the branch as Forsman slowly raises the pole, slips the loop around its neck, then gently lowers the now-struggling owl to the ground. Sovern takes the owl in his hands and holds the bird's wings tightly as Forsman clips colored metal bands to both legs. The bands will help scientists in their studies of the spotted owl population on the peninsula.

Forsman and Sovern carefully examine each feather on both wings to determine the progress of molting. Then they gently stuff the bird into a bag and weigh him. The men freeze, then sigh, in response to the earthshaking crash of an old-growth tree. The ancient forest is falling.

The biologists release the bird and "mouse" him once again. His second meal in his mouth, the bird watches us from a branch far beyond the reach of Forsman's fishing pole. Finally, tired of these games with humans, the owl flies off.

Walking down the hill, we notice what we had missed in our haste on the way up. A series of yellow markers are stapled to tree trunks. "BOUNDARY CLEAR-CUT," they read. The signs are familiar to those who roam the national forests of the Pacific Northwest. Part of the owl's home was torn down today. The trees in which we saw him roosting will fall soon.

The spotted owl researchers don't mix much with townsfolk here in logging country. Except when they're in the field, they stick close to the Forest Service work station where they sleep in a mobile home and raise mice for trapping owls. Likewise, the Washington Wildlife Department biologists surveying spotted owls on state land don't often leave their cabin to spend time in the nearby town of Forks.

Already, the findings of Forsman and other researchers have inflamed local passions. Logging is by far the biggest industry on the Olympic Peninsula. The nearby town of Forks bills itself, plausibly, as the logging capital of the world. Spotted owl researchers are about as popular here as freedom riders were in the Deep South. The café in Forks sells T-shirts and logging suspenders that read, "SPOTTED OWL HUNTER." A popular float in Forks' Fourth of July parade featured a logger chasing a spotted owl with a chain saw. Local managers of the Washington Department of Natural Resources—stewards of the state forestlands—drew laughs when they handed out bogus spotted owl hunting regulations.

The northern spotted owl, *Strix occidentalis caurina,* is a subspecies that has become symbolic of the battle over the last of this continent's virgin forests. The bird is unusual, though perhaps not unique, in its specialization. It doesn't just require forest for its survival. To live and breed at viable levels, it needs a special kind of forest. Only a conifer forest will do. Only a forest in the temperate zone of the Pacific Coast between northern California and southern British Columbia. Only a forest essentially undisturbed by humans. Preferably a forest in which the oldest trees took root anywhere from 200 to 1,000 years ago. And large enough that a breeding pair can forage over hundreds or even thousands of acres.

The spotted owl has become a symbol of the fragile ecosystem unique to the old-growth forests of the Pacific Northwest. It has become a symbol, too, of the threat that loggers and their families feel in the face of a growing movement to save the ancient forests. "They're putting people out of work for a danged bird," fumes one logger. "That's just sheer stupidity." Leaders of the forest-products industry have taken to calling the spotted owl "the billion-dollar bird."

Though attention has focused on the owl as an emblem for the forests, it's only one part of a greater issue. An entire ecosystem, one of the grandest on the planet, is at stake. This ecosystem is home to a yet-uncatalogued range of plant and animal life. The majestic woods are mostly gone. Less than one-fifth of the old growth that once covered the landscape of western Oregon and western Washington still stands. No one has tallied the full dimensions of this loss because no one has made a comprehensive inventory of the remaining old growth, much less figured out how much has already been cut down.

What remains is going fast. In the national forests alone, 48,000 acres of virgin forests are being cleared to feed the sawmills and pulp mills of Oregon and Washington each year. The U.S. Bureau of Land Management (BLM) is selling off another 22,000 acres. Within fifteen years—barely a summer's afternoon in the time frame of the forest—the last of the old growth on state and private lands will be gone.

Then there will be only what's left in the national parks, national   15 forests, and, in Oregon, on land administered by the BLM. To the timber industry, that's a lot of land. Over a million acres of older forests on federal land is being preserved in the Douglas fir region west of the Cascade Range crest for a number of reasons: wilderness and recreation values, habitat for the spotted owl and other species, or site-specific engineering problems such as steep and unstable soils or regeneration difficulties. A million acres that could be providing jobs and profits. A million acres that timber industry lobbyists claim the spotted owl doesn't even need.

Compared to what once was, a million acres of protected forest is a pittance. When European settlement began, an estimated 850 million acres of what are now the lower forty-eight states were covered by virgin forests. The trees were cut or burned down, first to make way for the settlers, then to produce lumber. The forests of the Pacific Coast and the Rockies are all that's left to give us an inkling of what this land may have been like three centuries ago. Even in the Northwest—where settlement began in earnest only 150 years ago—the lowland forests where trees grew to almost unimaginable size in rich alluvial soils have long disappeared.

What's left is being fragmented by patchwork clearcuts into isolated stands that are losing their ability to support spotted owls and other creatures of the ancient forests. The remaining old growth, mostly at higher elevations and on steep hillsides, sometimes is described as "the dregs."

Ah, but what dregs! In biomass alone, the Pacific forests are rivaled by no other forests on earth. The rain forests of the tropics are small things by comparison. Below the Northwest's mantle of tall trees is a unique world of plant and animal life. The Olympic rain forest's rich mantle of mosses, lichens, club mosses, and liverworts is thicker and heavier than that of any other temperate forest in the world. The Northwest forests have been called, justifiably, "the world center of mushroom diversity." Beyond the spotted owl, animals as diverse as bald eagle, red tree vole, and rough-skinned newt find their best habitat in ancient forests. Only now, when this ecosystem is in danger, have scientists come to appreciate the magnificence of these forests.

No one has done more than Jerry Franklin to demonstrate the biological opulence and uniqueness of the Pacific Northwest's old-growth forests. The Forest Service's Pacific Northwest Research Station in Corvallis, Oregon, calls Franklin its chief plant ecologist. The University of Washington's College of Forest Resources calls him professor of ecosystem analysis. Some people simply call him the guru of old growth.

Franklin grew up playing in the second-growth forests near his Camas, Washington, home. Even more special to him than those woods were the old-growth groves of the Gifford Pinchot National Forest, where his family spent vacations camping. Forests were in the family line. Franklin's parents even gave Jerry the fitting middle name of Forest. The mystique of the forest never wore out. Even today, the scientist speaks of the "aura" of old growth and of the "inspiration" he draws from the ancient forests.

The son of a worker in Crown Zellerbach's Camas paper mill, Franklin is no wild-eyed environmental radical. His soft voice and avuncular, down-home manner have only boosted his credibility in the highly politicized atmosphere surrounding the debate over management of the last old-growth forests.

Franklin has been studying the forests of Washington and Oregon since the late 1950s, when he was a forestry graduate student at Oregon State University. It wasn't until 1970, though, that serious research into the old-growth ecosystem was first undertaken. As deputy director of the Coniferous Forest Biome research project, Franklin played a crucial role in obtaining funding from the National Science Foundation and lining up researchers from Oregon State and the University of Washington.

"I think the bottom line is we learned the old-growth forest was distinctive in a number of its characteristics from younger forests," Franklin recalls, leaning back from the desk in his university office. "It's not just a younger forest grown up to a larger size. It performs some functions very well, and it has a different kind of structure than a younger forest does and because of that provides habitat for a different set of animals. It was interesting because the Forest Service had stopped doing research on old growth in about 1960 because they felt we had learned everything we needed to know about it—which was basically how to cut it down and regenerate a young forest."

Initially, the researchers weren't investigating old growth per se, rather the coniferous forests of the Douglas fir region. The focus slowly shifted toward ancient forests as it became apparent that the most distinctive features of the Northwest woods were precisely those that took centuries to develop. It was the spectacular biomass and vegetative richness of old growth that stood out in study after study. The biomass accumulated by the big trees in old growth, it turned out, produced a unique set of flora and fauna. By 1981, scientists knew enough about old growth to describe it in a landmark report authored by Franklin and seven associates, *Ecological Characteristics of Old-Growth Douglas-Fir Forests.*

As Franklin explains, big trees are the engine that drives the old-   *25*
growth ecosystem: "The trees are large, old, the crown structures are very
complex, the dead wood component—standing dead trees and logs—is
very conspicuous and that's in part because many of the species are quite
decay-resistant so that these large woody structures disappear only slowly.
And because of the canopies, they modify the environment within the
forest incredibly so that the moisture and temperature conditions are totally
different than they are outside or even in young forests. And that's one
reason why many organisms find it to be a very favorable environment. It's
extremely stable, the extremes are highly muted."

In the microclimate of the old-growth forest, animals and plants find
warmth and shelter from the snow in winter. They find coolness and
moisture in summer. From fog and clouds, the crowns of tall trees wring
moisture—in some drainages accounting for one-fourth of total precipitation in some watersheds. The wind is still on the forest floor, rarely
blowing harder than two miles an hour. The irregular canopy of old
growth lets in enough light to support a far richer understory than is found
in young forests.

The old-growth ecosystem begins with big trees, both live and dead.
Another ecologist, Elliott Norse of The Wilderness Society, says of the
forest giants, "These trees are as exceptional in the plant world as whales
are in the animal world. Ancient conifers are the whales of the forests."
The Pacific Northwest forest range, from northern California to southeast
Alaska, produces the biggest conifers in the world. Only the huge eucalyptus-
dominated forests of Australia and New Zealand come close to the biomass
of the Northwest old growth. On average, the Douglas fir and noble fir
forests of Oregon and Washington contain three times the biomass of
tropical rain forests. This "huge photosynthetic factory," as Jerry Franklin
sometimes calls old growth, accumulates biological mass more efficiently
than any ecosystem on earth. Trees simply grow crazy in the Northwest.

Temperate forests typically are deciduous or mixed deciduous-conifer
stands. The Pacific Coast, with its distinctive weather patterns, breaks the
mold. Conifers overshadow deciduous trees a thousand to one by timber
volume. Although there is ample precipitation for trees, rain and snow fall
primarily during the winter months. Drought is an annual summer event.
Seattle typically receives three inches of rain between June and August.
Less than half that amount falls on Medford, Oregon. Deciduous trees can
carry on photosynthesis only during the warm months when their leaves
are out. If rainfall is inadequate during that critical time, deciduous trees
just can't make it. Conifers, able to produce carbohydrates year-round,
have a tremendous competitive advantage on the West Coast.

Conifers aren't just unusually plentiful here, they grow like nowhere
else. Ten genera of conifers grow in the Northwest; the largest and longest-
living species of each is found on the coast. "They have a genetic makeup
that simply enables them to persist and grow for very long periods of time,"

Franklin observes. "Whereas a loblolly pine in the Southeast is pretty much pooping out by the time it gets to be fifty or sixty years old, a Douglas fir is only beginning to get started at that age."

Taken individually, none of the attributes of old growth reported in *Ecological Characteristics* was terribly surprising. Of course an ancient forest is dominated by big trees. Of course standing dead trees are abundant, as are large logs on the ground and in streams. Anyone who looked could see that mushrooms, mosses, lichens, and liverworts grew in profusion. The report galvanized the scientific community, and began to ripple through the national forests' interest groups, because it showed for the first time how the whole system worked and how it differed from other forests.

Franklin and his colleagues pointed out that the deep, irregular crown of an old-growth Douglas fir provides "ideal habitat" for such specialized creatures as the red tree vole, northern flying squirrel, and northern spotted owl. The old-growth canopy provides a home for an estimated 1,500 species of invertebrates. Large logs offer animal habitat and seedbeds for young trees. Nitrogen, often in short supply in forest soils, is built up by lichens in the forest canopy and by bacteria that proliferate in rotting logs. Large logs also provide a home for mammals that spread underground fungi. The food chain, or "energy cycle," of small old-growth streams begins with woody debris rather than green plants. Few plant or animal species are found *only* in old growth, but many find their best habitat there, and some may require a reservoir of old growth for their survival.

Between 175 and 250 years typically are required for old-growth characteristics to develop under natural conditions. Old growth "begins to come into its prime" after 350 years, says biologist Andy Carey. The term "old growth" has been used by foresters for many decades. Yet it wasn't until the mid-1980s that scientists even tried to develop an ecological definition of the term. Before that, foresters and researchers used whatever definition they found most convenient. Those wildly varying definitions generally were based on a single criterion such as tree size or age. Some foresters used the term old growth for anything that had not been cut. In 1986, the Forest Service's Old-Growth Definition Task Group, chaired by Jerry Franklin, proposed a definition that could be applied to a stand by a forester with a tape measure. The definition was both ecological and quantifiable. There had to be a certain mix of species, a certain number of live trees of various sizes per acre, along with a specified number of snags and logs of defined size.

The ecological definition set objective standards by which anyone can determine whether a forest is to be considered old growth. The standards were somewhat arbitrary; there's no magic point at which a forest is suddenly transformed from a "mature" forest into "old growth." Jerry Franklin speaks of "degrees of old-growthedness" and a "continual gradient of old-growth characteristics . . . . It becomes a little more sophisticated than a simple yes-or-no answer, 'It is or it ain't.'"

The forest in which Eric Forsman and Stan Sovern captured the spotted owl wouldn't meet the ecological definition of old growth. It had the mix of species and the deep, multilayered canopy characteristic of old growth, but it lacked the requisite number of centuries-old trees to meet the definition. A forest in the process of becoming old growth, it supports a wider range of wildlife than an even-aged tree farm but probably fewer species than true old growth. By 1989, Franklin was urging scientists to supplement the old-growth definition with more flexible measures of a forest's ecological structure.

The either-or definition is the closest thing that exists to a scientific   *35* consensus on the minimum standards for old growth. Yet even after the definition was published, national forests continued to release draft management plans that bore no relation to the definition. By continuing to use nonecological definitions, the Forest Service was able to say that millions more acres of old growth remained on its land than the ecological approach indicated.

The scientists who wrote *Ecological Characteristics* warned that the ancient forests were rapidly disappearing. It was true that the Forest Service would be selling old-growth timber for the next forty years and that some of the virgin forest was protected in national parks, wilderness areas, and research natural areas. "Nevertheless," the scientific group reported, "these reserves occupy less than 5 percent of the original landscape, and the end of the unreserved old-growth forests is in sight."

If an old-growth forest were a stage, the principal players would be the big trees. Like the protagonists of a Shakespearean drama, these nobles shape the world in which a host of lesser trees and plants live. Those others play supporting roles. Just as great men and women do much to shape society, so these trees give an ancient forest its structure.

From southern British Columbia to northernmost California, the dominant tree is Douglas fir. During its lifetime of a thousand years or more, this magnificent tree may exceed ten feet in diameter and occasionally pushes to 300 feet in height. The deeply furrowed, reddish-brown bark of old-growth specimens make this monarch instantly recognizable. Its cones are equally distinctive, bearing a sort of forked tongue like that of the serpent that tempted Eve. As a sapling, Douglas fir makes a perfectly proportioned Christmas tree. The crown of the mature tree, whether growing in the forest or in the full sunlight, takes on an irregular and highly individual shape. A single stem or "leader" points straight up from the top of the tree; the fingerlike tip of each major branch aims outward and upward.

Ironically, Douglas fir isn't a fir at all. Its Latin name, *Pseudotsuga menziesii,* identifies it as a false hemlock. Early botanists (including David Douglas himself) mislabeled it variously as pine, hemlock, fir, and spruce. Only in the late nineteenth century, after discovering a related Asian species, did scientists conclude the tree represented a new genus, and the name *Pseudotsuga* stuck.

Nowhere in what foresters call the "Douglas fir region" is the tree a 40 climax species. As a forest grows and matures, its vegetation changes until it reaches its climax, or final stage. Old growth, like the Douglas fir that so often dominates it, is a transitional stage. Intolerant of shade, Douglas fir can't grow in its own shadow; it must give way to more tolerant species. Fir manages to maintain its overall dominance because of its longevity, because thick bark sees it through most fires unscathed, and because it aggressively establishes itself in openings created by fire or other natural events.

Immense forests of giant Douglas fir standing butt to butt are no longer abundant as they were during the days when John Muir visited Puget Sound. Still, his observations on the tree he called Douglas spruce tell us much about a land that could give rise to a profusion of these giants:

> For so large a tree it is astonishing how many find nourishment and space to grow on any given area. The magnificent shafts push their spires into the sky close together with as regular a growth as that of a well-tilled field of grain. And no ground has been better tilled for the growth of trees than that on which these forests are growing. For it has been thoroughly ploughed and rolled by the mighty glaciers from the mountains, and sifted and mellowed and outspread in beds hundreds of feet in depth by the broad streams that issued from their fronts at the time of their recession, after they had long covered the land.

Like Douglas fir, western red cedar (*Thuja plicata*) is something other than what its name implies. An arborvitae rather than a true cedar, this majestic tree belongs to the cypress family. The tree's decay–resistant heart-wood is as prized by shake splitters and fence builders today as it was by the Coast Salish natives a millennium ago. Unlike Douglas fir, shade-tolerant red cedar can maintain its forest dominance over the centuries. As long–lived and as massive at the base as fir—but not as tall—western red cedar is distinguished by its scaly leaves, its shaggy fir, and its flared, amoeba-shaped butt. Alaska yellow cedar, a smaller cousin of red cedar, may live up to 3,500 years.

Western hemlock (*Tsuga heterophylla*) had little commercial value un-til the pulp industry moved into the Northwest. Now used for lumber as well as paper and cellophane products, old-growth hemlock is especially popular in Japan. The pliable tip of hemlock, whether young or old, bends earthward as if in prayer. It's a lovely understory tree; its short needles spread flatly from the stem, forming a fanlike network of lace. This lace-work of hemlock is a classic feature of a fir-hemlock forest.

Because this tree doesn't attain the mighty dimensions of Douglas fir or cedar, it's easy to dismiss it. But hemlock is a survivor. If a forest makes it through enough centuries without fire or other environmental catastrophe, this shade-tolerant tree will replace Douglas fir as the dominant tree. Hemlock is the most widespread climax species, ranging from the spruce forests of Alaska to the redwood country of California.

Sitka spruce (*Picea sitchensis*) thrives primarily in the coastal fog belt   45 from southern Alaska to the southern tip of Oregon. Sitka spruce is an extremely fast-growing tree under the proper conditions. One thirteen-foot-thick Olympic rain forest specimen reportedly added a foot to its diameter in less than thirty-five years. Like hemlock, spruce prefers to begin life in the nurturing climate of a nurse log. Once used to build aircraft and now valued as a superior wood for piano sounding boards, Sitka spruce is Alaska's most important timber species.

The mighty coast redwood (*Sequoia sempervirens*) hugs the immediate coastal region from the edge of spruce country in southernmost Oregon south to the San Francisco Bay area. The redwood is the world's tallest tree, exceeded in mass only by the incomprehensibly large giant sequoia (*Sequoiadendron giganteum*) of the Sierra Nevada. Redwood appears to be a climax species—although some scientists question whether it, like cedar, eventually gives way to hemlock through the process of forest succession. Like red cedar, redwood is remarkably resistant to rot. Virgin redwood stands have been reduced to a fraction of their original extent, and heavy logging continues.

Big trees are the key ingredient in building the forest structure that has come to be called old growth. Yet big trees do not, by themselves, add up to an ecosystem. In fact, the trees of old growth are a varied lot. Just about the only thing this ecosystem lacks is uniformity. Its living trees differ by species, by age, by size, by shape and depth of their foliage, and by soundness of their bark and wood. Centuries are required for development of the distinctive multilayered canopy that comes with a mix of young and old trees. With time, older trees die, leaving their large remains for bacteria, fungi, insects, birds, and mammals to forage in and build homes.

Seen from a steep hillside above the forest floor or from a low-flying airplane, the irregular canopy of an ancient forest is striking. In contrast to the uniform, unbroken canopy of a second-growth forest, the old-growth canopy appears random and disordered. The dominant trees vary in height, thickness, and foliage. The tops of some trees are broken; others have lost their foliage and died, still others have fallen. The gaps left by these fallen or humbled comrades allow light to filter through to the understory. The crown of an old-growth tree has been described as resembling a bottle brush—"albeit one with many missing bristles."

Early settlers and loggers, working on level ground, had little opportunity to view the remarkable forest canopy from treetop level. But today, with most of the remaining old growth limited to narrow mountain valleys, the steep mountainsides offer wondrous panoramas. At some point almost every trail through ancient forest ascends to a high point from which it's possible to look through the canopy. The tops of the trees—many of them broken off, some alive, others dead, a few charred by lightning—

may seem close enough to touch. To view the canopy from this perspective is as to feel as though one is actually in the canopy. The varying heights of the trees, their irregular spacing, the crowns of every shape and density, the quality of light, all create a more-real-than-real, super-three-dimensional effect.

Draped over the trees of old growth are mosses, lichens, club mosses, and liverworts. These "epiphytes," from the Greek prefix *epi* (upon) and suffix *phyte* (plant), grow nonparasitically atop other plants. Drawing their nutrients directly from rainfall and from particles in the air, epiphytes contribute significantly to the fertility of the forest. More than 130 epiphytic mosses have been identified in the Olympic rain forest alone. Lichens—symbiotic combinations of fungi and algae—may display tiny, delicate-looking branches or they may have a crude crustlike appearance. The most abundant epiphytic lichen is the large, leafy *Lobaria oregana*. As pieces of this and the closely related lungwort (*Lobaria pulmonaria*) break off and fall to the forest floor, they are eaten by browsing animals or they decompose to add valuable nitrogen to the soil. The waxy lungwort is named for its resemblance to the inside of the human lung. These nitrogen-fixing lichens are rare in young forests.

Until recently, it was believed that mosses and lichens had no directly beneficial or harmful effect on their host trees. It turns out, however, that some trees are more than passive hosts for the epiphytes. Nalini M. Nadkarni, a University of Washington graduate student in forest ecology, made a remarkable discovery when she used mountain climbing equipment to propel herself into the canopy of the Olympic rain forest. Weighing the epiphytes, she found three tons of dry plant mass per acre, four times the amount typical of other forests. Peeling back the vegetative mats, Nadkarni found a network of roots running along the branches and trunk of bigleaf maple. These maple roots, ranging from tiny white tips to chunky three-inch-diameter roots, were present only under moss and lichens. "Greatly excited," she wrote in *Natural History,* "I realized that here was a shortcut in the rain forest's nutrient cycling system. Host trees were capable of tapping the arboreal cupboards in their own crowns."

Nadkarni found that other deciduous trees in the Olympic rain forest—vine maple, red alder, and black cottonwood—also took water and nutrients from the organic matter created by epiphytes. Traveling to the cloud forests of Costa Rica and Papua New Guinea, she saw the same phenomenon of trees taking advantage of the nutrient treasure provided by mosses, liverworts, and lichens.

The old-growth canopy, developed to make the most of the sun's energy, has been likened to the ocean's surface. Zoologist Marston Bates put it this way in his classic book, *The Forest and the Sea:* "Most life is near the top, because that is where the sunlight strikes and everything below depends on this surface. Life in both the forest and the sea is distributed in horizontal layers." The crowns of trees are like the pelagic, or surface, layer of the ocean because that is where photosynthesis is concentrated. On the

50

forest floor, as on the benthos, or bottom, of the sea, life depends on "second-hand materials that drift down from above—on fallen leaves, on fallen fruits, on roots and logs. Only a few special kinds of green plants were able to grow in the rather dim light that reached the forest floor."

Because scientists have not had 200 years to watch old-growth forests develop, they must deduce how the process works. The 1984 report of a Society of American Foresters (SAF) task force on old growth recognized these uncertainties. "Can old growth be managed?" the task force asked. The group answered its own question this way:

> Through silviculture, foresters can grow big trees and grow them faster than nature unassisted. Yet there is no evidence that old-growth conditions can be reproduced silviculturally. In fact, the question is essentially moot, as it would take 200 years or more to find an answer. Old-growth management, for the foreseeable future, will be predicated on preservation of existing old-growth stands.

Preservation may not be the most exact word for protecting a living   *55*
system from destruction. If one fact emerges clearly from the new research on the forest ecosystem, it is that change is its very essence. The forest is forever in the process of *becoming*. Conifers are constantly struggling through the brush layer of a new clearing. Live trees keep being turned into fodder for the fungi that help to grow new trees. Like Sisyphus forever trying to reach the top of the hill, the forest continually struggles toward climax, the final and most stable stage of vegetative succession. Some natural or human-caused event inevitably sets the forest back to an earlier stage of succession, so old growth is constantly being created.

An old-growth forest "preserved" by humans inevitably will change. Old trees will fall and young trees will grow. Openings will be created and then filled with new life. The forest may reach climax. Or it may be completely toppled by windstorm or fire. Over a century, a 600-year-old stand may become a 700-year-old stand or a 100-year-old stand. But along with change, the forest maintains continuity and achieves a kind of stability. The young science of ecology teaches that complexity creates stability. The old-growth forests of the Northwest offer a wonderful laboratory—certainly the best on this continent—for studying the hidden ways in which seemingly independent creatures of the woods support one another.

The SAF task force wasn't saying that *all* old growth should be preserved. The point was that in our hubris we shouldn't assume that we can duplicate a natural process we barely understand. Not surprisingly, one of the eleven members of the task force was Jerry Franklin.

The implications of the new forest research reach far beyond the arcane interests of the scientists. The productivity of tree farms, for example, may depend more on maintaining healthy wildlife populations than on eliminating "pests." Consider the class of fungi known as mycorrhizae. The growth of conifers, like that of many other photosynthetic plants, requires the assistance of these fungi whose name means "fungus root." Unable to make direct use of the sun's energy, a fungus attaches itself to tree roots and helps itself to the sugars produced by the host plant. In return, the fungus absorbs water and nutrients, passing them along to the host tree. Antibiotics in the fungus protect the tree from root-rot pathogens, while the mycorrhizal sheath around the roots creates a physical barrier against some parasites. Tons of mycorrhizae are present in a single acre of old-growth forest, feeding the trees and storing nutrients that otherwise would be washed out of the soil and lost to the forest. The contribution that mycorrhizal fungi make to tree growth and forest fertility can scarcely be overstressed.

The story of the mycorrhiza-tree relationship doesn't end there. What at first seems a *pas de deux* is in fact a *ménage à trois*. For without the small mammals of the forest, the symbiosis would break down. Hypogeous, or underground, fungi depend on mammals for much of the dispersal of their spores. Truffles, the underground fruiting bodies of these fungi, are an important food source for a number of small animals in the old-growth forest. An animal finds a truffle by smell, digs it up, and eats it. All of the truffle is digested—except the spores, which are excreted in the animal's feces. Wherever the animal goes, the fungus goes.

Truffles were the key to a mystery that had long baffled biologists.   60
Biologists knew that bobcats and coyotes preyed on the northern flying squirrel. How do they catch an animal that presumably spent its time in the forest canopy? Analysis of the squirrels' stomach contents provided the answer. During the winter, lichens in tree crowns were the primary food source for flying squirrels. But between spring and fall, when the snow pack melted, the nocturnal animals came down to the ground to dig truffles. That's when their predators caught them. Laboratory studies of truffle-eating squirrels show that they pass nitrogen-fixing bacteria through their bodies along with fungal spores. Hypogeous fungi provide a home and small mammals a transport system for bacteria that add fertility to the forest floor.

The small California red-backed vole, whose tunnels are ubiquitous in the soil around rotting logs, shows a similar preference for truffles. The vole's environment, the Coast Range of southern Oregon and northern California, is ideal; this is one of very few places in the world where hypogeous fungi fruit year-round. If the fungus supply briefly runs short, the vole temporarily switches to lichens. Its favorite food may be *Rhizopogon vinicolor,* a mycorrhizal fungus that fruits mostly in rotten wood. *Rhizopogon* attaches itself to the roots of trees that grow in nurse logs. Forest researchers Chris Maser and James M. Trappe sum up the vole-fungus-tree relationship:

> Thus, there is a tight cycle of interdependence: the vole needs the truffle for food; the truffle depends on the vole for dispersal of spores and on a mycorrhizal tree host for energy; the tree requires mycorrhizal fungi for uptake of nutrients and provides the rotten

wood needed by the vole for cover. Moreover, since both voles and *Rhizopogon vinicolor* specialize in rotten wood as habitat, the vole disperses the *Rhizopogon* spores to the kind of substrate in which the fungus thrives.

Are the small truffle-eaters the forester's friend or foe? Townsend's chipmunk and the deer mouse, long cursed as pests that eat conifer seeds, also are eager consumers of truffles. In that second role, they assist the growth of young Douglas fir by bringing mycorrhizal fungi to their roots. Maser, raising one of the critical questions for forestry in the twenty-first century, argues that losses of wildlife and changes in soil chemistry may lead to declines in commercial forest productivity. Already, he believes, there are signs that this has happened in parts of Europe. Other scientists such as Roy R. Silen worry that the genetic diversity of the trees may be narrowed perilously far by clearcutting the virgin forests and replanting "genetically improved" trees.

In the long run, if not the short run, what's good for nature as a whole is good for the human species. The future of the timber industry depends on the hardiness and genetic diversity of the tree kingdom. Mature and old-growth forests are the reservoirs of that diversity. This era of impending climatic change would seem to be the least appropriate time to deliberately narrow the forests' genetic diversity.

More broadly viewed, the genetic variation within a particular species is only one part of the richness of life forms known as biological diversity. The other two elements of biological diversity are a variety of species and a variety of ecosystems. All three elements of genetic diversity are placed at risk as North America's last virgin forests are replaced by the even-aged monoculture of tree farms. What's happening to the forests of the Pacific Northwest mirrors a worldwide phenomenon. Global deforestation may cause the extinction of one-fourth of the earth's five million species over the next several decades. The use of plants from the tropical rain forests as sources of pharmaceuticals has been widely discussed. Only recently has the bark of the Pacific yew been identified as a potent weapon against cancerous tumors in mice. The National Cancer Institute in 1987 contracted for the harvest of 60,000 pounds of the yew's papery red bark to determine whether the taxol derivative is safe for use in humans. The yew, found in old-growth forests, is not grown on tree farms.

Jerry Franklin believes management practices on commercial forestlands may be an even more important factor in maintaining biological diversity than is the amount of old growth that's preserved. No matter how successful environmentalists are in their efforts to save the ancient forests, he points out, commercially managed forests will cover a much greater area. If timber practices on those lands aren't changed, "we're going to effectively lose the war for biologic diversity." His recipe, and that of a growing number of his colleagues, is to keep more old-growth characteristics in the managed forests.

65

"We've got to quit leaving them in a billiard-table condition," says Franklin. "We have to leave more material behind, leave trees, snags, patches of reproduction, down logs—leaving a lot more heterogeneity in the cutover areas than we've been doing until this point. What we've got to do is leave our Germanic heritage behind us and cherish a little bit of disorder and chaos in our cutover areas."

During the short time that scientists have paid serious attention to the old-growth ecosystem, they have learned that the spotted owl is just one of dozens of vertebrates that are most at home in the ancient forests. They've learned about the tree vole, whose family may live in a single tree for generations; the northern flying squirrel, which feeds on lichens in the winter and truffles in the summer; the goshawk, whose short wings are adapted for flight among the trees; the pileated woodpecker, which excavates its home in large Douglas fir snags; the Olympic salamander, which lays its eggs in the rotting wood of large logs; the marbled murrelet, a seabird that returns each night to its nest in the ancient forest; and the national symbol, the bald eagle, which prefers to build its nest in older woods.

This growing recognition of the uniqueness of the old-growth ecosystem comes at an awkward time. It's awkward for the forest-products industry because the decline of private and state timber inventories leaves the industry more dependent than ever on federal sales of virgin timber. It's awkward for those concerned about the ecosystem because the amount of low-elevation old growth is dwindling fast. We've entered an era of scarcity, and public-policy decisions will be painful. For more than a century, the timber industry has been the leading employer in the Pacific Northwest. Although aerospace-industry employment has inched ahead in Washington and tourism is growing rapidly, the importance of timber can hardly be overstated. More than one-third of Oregon's manufacturing-sector jobs still are in lumber and wood products. . . .

The more I have learned about the debate over the old growth, the more I have been struck by the complexity of the issues. We've gained some insight into the ancient forest ecosystem, but we can't quite put our finger on the glue that holds it together. We haven't taken seriously the need of Native Americans for pristine forests to practice their traditional religion. The timber industry contends that its tree farms could support a healthy population of spotted owls, but it still practices the kind of even-aged silviculture that drives owls out.

While independent sawmills are going out of business for lack of logs, two-fifths of Washington's timber harvest is sold abroad unmilled. The forest-products industry clamors for unabated timber sales but, for the most part, remains silent about the understocked second-growth forests and the conversion of the best timberlands to suburban tracts. The continuing loss of jobs in the forest-products industry has far more to do with the automation of sawmills, log exports, and conversion of private timberland than with measures designed to protect the old-growth forests.

70

We haven't figured out whether the regional economy benefits more from logging an old-growth forest or from promoting the recreational potential of the forest. Nor has anyone quantified the damage done to the Northwest's important salmon-fishing industry by logging and road building. Our growing knowledge about nutrient cycling in old-growth forests has raised disturbing questions about the sustainability of tree farming as currently practiced. Increasingly, it looks as though the future of the timber industry requires that old-growth characteristics be incorporated into tree farms.

The slash burning that typically follows clearcutting throws carbon into the atmosphere, exacerbating the greenhouse effect. Logging of the ancient forests is more than a regional problem. Virgin forests are falling around the world, from Vancouver Island to Indonesia and from the Amazon to Africa. Like the rain forests of the tropics, the temperate forests of Oregon and Washington are being stripped to keep a troubled industry afloat and to satisfy the voracious appetite of Japanese and American consumers for lovely, fine-grained wood.

The fate of the ancient forests has become the premier issue of public land management in the western United States. The basic question confronting the body politic is how much old growth should be cut for the timber industry's benefit and how much preserved. The courts have been asked to resolve the issue, but they appear to be only a detour on the way to Congress. This process may not yield the best results—and certainly won't if the issues remain as poorly understood as they are at present. A recent scene before a congressional subcommittee shouldn't surprise us. An environmentalist had been talking for some time about the importance of old-growth forests when a puzzled congressman interrupted to ask, "Okra? What's this okra you're talking about?"

What ought to concern us even more than the lack of knowledge of a decision-maker from the Southeast is the absence of constructive dialogue among those closest to the situation. Precious little problem-solving has taken place. One Seattle newspaper editor is reported to have thundered, "I hope I never read the word old growth again!" The Forest Service proposes, with none of Solomon's subtlety or wisdom, to carve the remaining old growth in two, giving half to the environmentalists and half to industry. As a solution it won't stick, because neither side is buying into it. When the courts and Congress get through deciding matters, the outcome may not do much to help an endangered ecosystem *or* industry. But an imposed settlement is exactly what's going to happen unless representatives of environmental groups and the timber industry decide there's more to be gained than lost by negotiation. A satisfactory settlement must be more creative than just carving lines through the old growth.

In desperate times, people turn to desperate measures. Environmental 75 radicals have taken to sabotaging logging equipment and "inoculating" old-growth trees with spikes that pose a deadly hazard to mill workers. Not all loggers are kidding when they talk about hunting spotted owls.

Those who earn their livelihood from the forests feel they are under attack by outsiders who understand neither their way of life nor the forests themselves. It's as if Midwestern farmers, struggling to pay their debts, had to fight a powerful political movement bent on turning their farms back into a natural prairie. If environmentalists aren't a cynical elite, then, by golly, they must be naive sentimentalists duped by the Bambi syndrome.

The alleged sentimentality of environmentalists was confronted head-on by Robert Vincent, a wildlife consultant more concerned over the prospect of board feet of timber lost to industry than over the loss of spotted owl habitat. At a conference on old growth, Vincent noted that the richness and diversity of these forests is built on the death and decay of trees. He first likened old growth to a cemetery, then to "a self-centered miser" who buries his fortune in Crisco cans. On the other hand, he continued,

> . . . there are some people who really enjoy old things. The un-changing, the stagnant, the dying. In fact, we almost seem to live in an era of ancestral worship of things. Where do people go to make a visit? Certainly not to Houston or Denver, but to Rome, Venice, Paris, and Brussels where they can see old cathedrals and stagnated cities that haven't been touched for years. In fact, the longer a city stagnates or the longer a ruin stands, the more beautiful it becomes. It's kind of ridiculous, isn't it? . . . I suppose that if we could preserve an automobile junkyard for 1,000 years, it might be considered a thing of beauty.

Ridiculous though it may seem to some, there is something in most of us that looks in awestruck wonder at a forest that has been growing stronger and wilder for a millennium. And, as those in the European tourism business know, people are willing to pay for that feeling of awe. There's money in them thar woods, whether they're chopped down or left standing. Our feelings of wonder at the ancient creations of man and nature go beyond dollars and cents, of course. As we stand at the last corner of our continent gazing at the fast-disappearing old growth, our values are being put to the test.

The determination of people in logging country to preserve their livelihoods is a legitimate desire, one that must be confronted forthrightly. So, too, is the "sentimental" view that the virgin forests are a gift of God, not to be destroyed lightly.

Eric Forsman and Stan Sovern have more work to do. As soon as the spotted owl is banded, they clamber back to the truck and head out on the logging roads toward Forks. They're going to join another member of the research team, Timm Kaminski, who is trying to locate another bird and outfit her with a radio transmitter. If the effort is successful, the scientists will be able to track her movements through the winter and into the next

80

year. The data they collect will add valuable information about the kinds of forest in which these owls nest and forage.

We follow a dirt road over state and private land that has been almost entirely cut over. Finally, we see the distinctive tree line of a natural forest. Most of these woods, Forsman explains, are "Twenty-one Blow." The hurricane that whipped through the west side of the Olympic Peninsula on January 21, 1921, tore down thousands, perhaps millions of old-growth trees. On one part of the peninsula, the 100-mile-an-hour winds left a thirty-foot-deep pile of trees; on another, an entire herd of 200 elk was wiped out by falling timber.

We pull off the road next to Kaminski's pickup. Forsman shouts to Kaminski, but there's no answer. So he shoulders a radio receiver and tunes into the channel on which the male owl's transmitter is broadcasting. By walking in on the male, he hopes to find Kaminski and the female he's after. The woods are remarkably open. Despite the young hemlocks growing beneath their mature elders, there are no impenetrable thickets here. Moss covers the ground, rotting logs support a profusion of new life, and the rotting base of a gigantic dead tree stands as a reminder of the forest that stood here before the Twenty-one Blow. This is not, strictly speaking, old growth. Like the first forest we visited, it's what Forsman calls a "mature" or "mixed stand." In common with old growth, this stand has a deep, multilayered canopy, a mottled pattern of soft sunlight, and an abundance of dead wood both standing and fallen. What it lacks are the very large trees that only centuries can produce. To see true old growth, we would have to cross the creek to a cedar grove with trees seven feet in diameter and larger. It's there, on a privately owned parcel surrounded by state land, that the birds nest.

Forsman picks up strong signals on his radio. Soon he spots Kaminski and sees the female roosting overhead. Sovern and I keep a respectful distance to avoid spooking the bird. Sovern goes through his pack and prepares his gear. The juvenile, which we can't see from our location, is begging its parents for food: *Whhhhhhhhhip! . . . Whhhhhhhhiip!* It sounds something like a preschooler trying to whistle. Forsman and Kaminski trap the female while Sovern continues to prepare the equipment needed to strap the radio to her back. The adult male, pumping his broad wings, flies above our heads toward his mate. The male and the juvenile watch from branches as Forsman makes the capture. The whole family is here.

Sovern and I walk over. Sovern takes hold of the bird. A feisty one, she snaps at Forsman as he painstakingly fits the tiny transmitter on her back and adjusts the thin straps that hold it on. With each snap of her powerful beak she makes a loud cracking sound, like the pop of two wood blocks being slammed together. Once, she manages to get Forsman's finger. The scientists cover her large brown eyes.

Not far away, the juvenile keeps begging for his dinner. The male protests his mate's treatment: *Hooo . . . hooo . . . hooo . . . hooo!*

The spotted owl is not, to some people's minds, the most intelligent of birds. Certainly it is not the most cautious. One spotted owl, oblivious to the human threat, wound up in Seattle's Woodland Park Zoo after being struck by a logging truck. The female in Sovern's hands has been moused so many times she has become quite tame. Cautious though she may be about crossing a clearcut, where she could become a great horned owl's prey, she fails to appreciate the peril that humans pose. While she lies helplessly, her family can only watch and voice their useless protest.

Perhaps it's best that they don't understand their precarious future. The birds on the branches are no safer than the bird on the ground. Their fate, like that of the forest itself, is in our hands.

Reading and Responding

1. Annotate the essay, noting major shifts in topic or subject. Write a 1 in the margin at the beginning and label it "spotted owl". Then write a new number in the margin each time you come to another topic or shift in the discussion. Then look for the important factual material—facts that make a difference to your understanding or facts that seem crucial to anyone's understanding. Mark them with a wiggly line in the margin.
2. Look for sections, sentences, or even phrases that help you understand Ervin's definition of the word *forest*. Annotate the large sections, and copy the important phrases.

Working Together

1. Review this essay as a group, and look for the introduction of each new major idea. Make a rough, one-page outline of this entire selection.
2. Pool your annotations and reading notes to make one page of notes, phrases, quotations, and paraphrasings that add up to what Ervin means by the word *forest*.
3. Assume that you are members of the "townsfolk here in logging country." How do you define the word *forest*?
4. Looking especially at what Jerry Franklin has to say, work as a group to arrive at a brief definition of *old growth*. Is this definition the same as the one for *forest*, or do these definitions differ?
5. As a group, discuss whether Ervin's piece argues in favor of "preservation." How does talking about preservation make sense and how does it not, according to Ervin?
6. As a group, discuss the primary approach that Ervin takes in this piece. Think in terms of the departments on your campus. Is Ervin's approach the English department approach? the computer science department approach?

Rethinking and Rewriting

1. In two or three pages, summarize Ervin's argument against "the even-aged monoculture of tree farms." Don't inject your own feelings; just try to accurately present what Ervin argues. Then write a page that discusses how easy or difficult it was for you to write this summary.

2. Identify two or three fundamental facts that anchor Ervin's discussion, and then do some additional research to check those facts and to see whether the thinking has changed since this article was written. End by drawing appropriate conclusions based on your research.

3. Research some aspect of forest ecology—the spotted owl or truffles or the class of fungi called mycorrhizae, for example. Try to deepen your understanding of the topic. Approach it from the viewpoint of a biologist or someone interested in biology. Assume that you're writing to your classmates and that they're eager to learn more about how a forest works.

4. Assume that Ervin were going to visit your campus. What local issues would interest him? What new facts would he need to understand in order to really appreciate the complexities of these local issues? (If you can limit this to just one issue, so much the better.) Communicate this information in the form of a letter (no more than three pages single-spaced or six pages double-spaced) that you'd send three weeks before Ervin's visit.

5. Argue that what Ervin is concerned about is really just a local issue that ought to be decided only by local input. Or argue that what Ervin is concerned about is really a national issue that ought to be decided on a national basis.

6. Ervin's piece mentions salmon fishing only briefly. Research salmon and salmon fishing and see if they are connected to forest practices. Write a paper that explains what you discover.

7. Use Ervin's description of the complex interrelationships in an old-growth forest as a metaphor for life, the writing process, relationships, family, school, whatever. How is life (or something else) like an old-growth forest?

HELPING A GREAT BEAR HANG ON

Douglas Chadwick

Douglas Chadwick is a wildlife biologist in Montana who writes regularly for National Geographic *and other magazines. He is the author of* The Fate of the Elephant *(1994) and editor of* The Company We Keep: America's Endangered Species *(1996). In this article he reports the effects that the 1973 Endangered Species Act have had on the grizzly bear.*

One quarter of a century ago, I was working as a field biologist in the Swan Mountains of western Montana when I came across two grizzlies courting. It was a growly affair with chases and cuffs at first, but the bears went on to linger side by side, rubbing heads and shoulders. Taking care not to disturb them, I watched the pair for hours—long, bright hours, for somehow these animals made time slow down and life seem richer as they moved among melting snowfields and meadows cleared by avalanches. But when I reflected that the point of the animals' togetherness was reproduction, the experience took on a bittersweet quality.

The chances were dwindling that the species—including descendants of the bears I saw that day—would survive in the United States outside of Alaska. I could see firsthand that bear habitat was under siege from road building and logging. Not only that, grizzly hunting was still legal and very much part of the culture of the West; Montana continued selling an unlimited number of bear-hunting licenses every year. The last grizzlies in the Selway-Bitterroot region of western Montana and central Idaho—one of the few populations to survive beyond the early decades of this century—had only recently vanished.

The same year I watched that mating pair, 1973, the nation's lawmakers enacted the Endangered Species Act (ESA), a revolutionary attempt to legally define our obligations to other life-forms. Two years later, grizzlies were federally listed as threatened in the contiguous 48 states. As a result, today the bears are holding on fairly well in the American West, most notably in two chunks of habitat—the Yellowstone National Park area and northern Montana. The U.S. Fish and Wildlife Service is even considering reintroducing grizzlies to the Selway-Bitterroot region.

Shock waves: Behind those few facts is a remarkable tale. For few animals have showcased the strengths and weaknesses of the landmark act that saved them quite like the strong, intelligent competitor with humans for food and space that we call *Ursus arctos horribilis.* And few people foresaw the degree to which grizzly conservation would send shock waves through the West—or how much saving the big mammals would protect an ecosystem's worth of other wildlife.

Ursus arctos, the brown bear, is native across the Northern Hemisphere, from Japan to Italy. North America is home to two subspecies.

5

Middendorffi includes only the big bears of Alaska's Kodiak Island, often referred to as Kodiaks. The rest are *horribilis,* commonly called grizzlies, though not all have the characteristic grizzled, or silvertipped, coat. Some are pure blond and others black, while the coastal ecotype tends to be solid brown.

Before European settlers arrived and began to exterminate grizzlies, 50,000 to 100,000 of the bears may have existed south of Canada. In this century, state game departments took responsibility for managing the bears. Before grizzlies were federally listed, that usually meant destroying problem animals—those that raided livestock and leftover food or simply seemed too close for comfort—while encouraging sport shooting of others. The general thinking was that as long as the death toll stayed high, plenty of bears must still be out in the woods.

The reality was altogether different. Development kept eliminating critical habitat. Bear neighborhoods were overrun by people, garbage and domestic animals. In the backcountry, road building for logging in national forests and other activities was making formerly remote populations accessible to hunters and poachers.

Desperate straits: By the 1970s, grizzlies in the West numbered fewer than 1,000, clinging to barely 2 percent of their former range. The population in Yellowstone numbered just 200 to 300 by some estimates; only about 30 were breeding females. Grizzlies reproduce more slowly than any other U.S. land mammal, giving birth for the first time at age five or six and typically waiting three years between successful litters. Cut off from other populations, Yellowstone's bears looked about to go the way of the silvertips Lewis and Clark first met on the Great Plains, or California's estimated 10,000 golden bears or the grizz of the Selway-Bitterroot region.

We know grizz can accelerate to 35 miles per hour in a couple of heartbeats and roll aside boulders with the flick of a paw. Yet perhaps their most amazing feat has been getting bureaucrats from agencies that once seldom communicated to consider the ecosystem they share. With individual home ranges as large as 600 square miles, the bears use an array of habitats from peaks to plains, ignoring the boundary lines so important to humans. "The grizzly is a landscape-level animal that requires us to go beyond the usual state and federal jurisdictions," says U.S. Fish and Wildlife biologist Chris Servheen, recovery coordinator for the species.

For the Yellowstone bears and their managers, that meant defining an area now called the Greater Yellowstone Ecosystem. Several times the size of the 2.2-million-acre park at its core, it also includes portions of state lands in Montana, Idaho, and Wyoming; five different national forests; and various wildlife refuges, Bureau of Land Management districts, private lands and municipalities.

From property owners to casual visitors, everyone in Yellowstone grizzly country has had to learn how to control food wastes. Since the bears are also lured into trouble by domestic sheep, the number allowed to graze on prime bear habitat in Idaho's Targhee National Forest was

10

reduced from 20,000 to zero through the 1980s. During the same period, sections of Yellowstone were closed to visitors so the bears would have some places free of any disturbance.

Farther north lies Glacier National Park; the Bob Marshall/Great Bear/Scapegoat wilderness complex; and adjoining public, private and tribal lands—all of which managers now treat as the Northern Continental Divide Ecosystem.

Since the 1975 listing, biologists have been estimating the grizzly population here as numbering between 300 and 600. Bears are tough to census in the rugged forests, but intensive studies in one segment clearly found that the bears avoid roads and that their numbers decline where the road density exceeds one mile per square mile of habitat. To avoid putting the grizzlies further at risk, which would violate the ESA, the Flathead National Forest has had to scale back timber harvests and gate off many existing logging roads.

The act has affected private land owners as well. The dense forests of the Flathead region's Swan Valley provide wildlife corridors between the core of the Northern Continental Divide Ecosystem and the outlying Mission Mountains, where 10 to 20 grizzlies still hold on.

To safeguard those links, the U.S. Fish and Wildlife Service forged a   15
unique grizzly conservation compact in 1995. This voluntary agreement limits harmful development on 33,000 privately owned acres. On another 83,000 acres held by a timber corporation, it also calls for closing or even obliterating roads, scheduling logging so that it disturbs no more than a fraction of the area at any one time and leaving streamside zones intact. Nationwide, more than 7 million acres of private property are now committed to management for the benefit of endangered species. Most are part of so-called Habitat Conservation Plans. These cooperative efforts allow landowners to proceed with development projects if they also agree to protect habitat for imperiled wildlife.

Good news for other species: Habitat protection for grizz has been good news for the other wildlife that shares the same space. It's no accident that many of the contiguous 48 states' last harlequin ducks, bull trout, westslope cutthroat trout, lynx, pine martens, wolverines, mountain caribou and great gray owls are found in the remaining strongholds of grizzlies. Nor is it surprising that the recent return of the gray wolf to the West has taken place largely in grizzly country.

And those relatively large creatures are only the most obvious ones to benefit. Look more closely and you'll also find wildlife on a smaller scale profiting from the protection of grizzly habitat. The water howellia, a little-known member of the bluebell family, is just one example. Much of the plant's Northwest seasonal pond habitat has been reduced by logging, grazing and the draining of wetlands. "Grizzly range overlaps with 40 percent of Montana's vascular plants of special concern," points out resource specialist Bonnie Heidel of the Montana Natural Heritage Program. "That's 148 species, from rare orchids to little-known sedges." Since 147 of them lack any special protection, their main safeguard is the fact that grizz walk among them. That was the case for the water howellia until it joined the federal list of threatened species in 1994.

Ecologists recognize the great bear as a keystone species that markedly influences the environment and the balance of other creatures within it. Formidable predators, grizzlies can kill a substantial number of hooved animals, especially young ones during the birth season. As expert scavengers, the bears hasten the release of nutrients from the carcasses they locate. In vegetarian mode, they spread seeds—as many as 7,000 in each dung pile when a grizzly is feasting on berries. As diggers of roots and underground prey such as hibernating ground squirrels and marmots, the bears excavate acres of terrain with their four-inch-long claws, opening the ground for new plants to colonize. Grizzlies have been identified as the principal movers of soil among the fauna in parts of Montana's Glacier National Park.

Numbers up: Once protected, the habitat has in turn been good for the bears. "Numbers appear to be on the rise, at least in the Greater Yellowstone Ecosystem," says recovery coordinator Servheen. "Our counts indicate an absolute minimum of 262 grizzlies there and possibly as many as 500. We intend to start delisting that population within a year."

Many bear advocates, however, feel that giving Yellowstone's bears   *20* the stamp of good health may be premature. An overriding concern is that about 90 percent of the grizzly deaths recorded since 1975 have come at the hands of humans—nearly all on private acreage—and the number of people living around Yellowstone is projected to double within the next 30 years.

As for grizzlies of the Northern Continental Divide Ecosystem, no one can say without more information just how well they are doing. The outlook is not promising for the three other remnant groups in the contiguous states. Just a handful have been counted lately in northwestern Montana's Cabinet-Yaak region, depite the reintroduction of several bears to augment the group. The Selkirk Mountains of northern Idaho and northeastern Washington host no more than 30 to 50 grizz. Another half-dozen or so inhabit the North Cascade Range of western Washington.

Sometime in the next year, the U.S. Fish and Wildlife Service will decide whether or not to reintroduce grizzlies to the Selway-Bitterroot ecosystem, where wolves were brought in from Canada during 1995 and 1996. While some area residents don't want anything to do with *horribilis,* the danger they pose or federal officials, others say the only opinions that should count are those of biologists who are supposed to determine what is best for the bears.

The middle ground in this ongoing debate has been defined by an unusual coalition led by the National Wildlife Federation, Defenders of Wildlife and representatives of the timber industry. Their Citizen Management Alternative calls for reestablishing grizzlies with less strict protection than usual along with an unprecedented level of local involvement in management. Under a special provision of the ESA intended to make the act more flexible when controversial species are returned to a range, the Selway-Bitterroot bears would be designated an "experimental, nonessential" population.

The primary recovery zone would consist of 4.1 million pristine acres already set aside as the Selway-Bitterroot Wilderness and adjoining Frank Church River of No Return Wilderness. Around this area would be an immense, 15.3 million-acre tract of national forest and private lands termed the "experimental population area." There, grizzlies would not have the same priority as in areas declared critical habitat under a traditional recovery plan. Instead, a citizen management committee would try to balance the bears' needs with those of logging and ranching operations and other human enterprises in ways that are compatible with a growing grizzly population.

Attorney Tom France of NWF's Northern Rockies Project Office in Missoula, Montana, labels this alternative "the radical center." He reasons, "Out here, folks are less afraid of bears than of government regulations and their effects on the local economy. This is a remarkable opportunity for community involvement in an endangered-species recovery."

Critics of the plan think the compromise sounds like gambling with grizzly recovery rather than ensuring it, since some of the richest habitat lies outside the main recovery zone. France and others insist the crucial point is to get the bears on the ground. Having grizzlies in the Selway-Bitterroot region could increase the species' numbers in the West by as much as 30 percent over the next half-century. And the location midway between Yellowstone and grizzly country to the north would multiply the chances of bears moving from one existing population to the next, increasing genetic interchange.

Canada connection: After all these changes, what are the great bear's chances in the West? "Without links to Canada, I would say about zero over the next century," says Troy Merrill of the Hornocker Wildlife Institute, a research foundation associated with the University of Idaho. Americans may imagine their neighbor to be a sprawling north country standing by to reseed the United States with wildlife if we lose ours, but southern Alberta and British Columbia are filling up with people and development as rapidly as the U.S. side of the border.

Once again, *Ursus arctos horribilis* is asking us to look beyond the usual boundaries. U.S. bear managers are beginning to regularly meet with their counterparts in Canada. Some conservation biologists feel that the only Rocky Mountain ecosystem truly viable over the long term would be a continuous stretch of untamed terrain running from Yellowstone to the Yukon Territory. There is even a new organization called Y2Y promoting this vision, using grizz range as a blueprint for what should be saved.

If you're lucky enough to go there yourself and to see a big, silver-tipped bear at home, it will probably take a while for your pulse to calm down. Once it finally does, you might pause to reflect on two mammal species with the power to determine how large, varied and full of promise the natural world of tomorrow will be. One is you. The other is the grizzly, in every sense a living definition of wildness.

Reading and Responding

1. In three or four sentences, summarize what Chadwick means when he says that the plight of grizzly bears "showcases the strengths and weaknesses of the landmark act that saved them."
2. Draw a line down the center of a piece of paper and make two lists: strengths of the Endangered Species Act and weaknesses of the Endangered Species Act.

Working Together

1. Discuss whether Chadwick seems like a credible reporter of facts and events. Do you believe what he says? How does Chadwick earn, or fail to earn, your trust? Make a list of the strategies that are evident—his style of description, how he uses facts, and so on—that you think affect his credibility.
2. Suppose that someone you know has just read Chadwick's essay and responds, "Who cares about grizzly bears? We don't need them anyway. They're too dangerous." Argue that this person has missed the point of the essay.
3. Write a group paragraph (at least five sentences) that summarizes and explains the range of responses you have to the Endangered Species Act.

Rethinking and Rewriting

1. Write an essay with the following format (exactly how you work this out is up to you). "The general thinking was . . . ," then complete the sentence on whatever subject you choose. Continue as necessary. Then complete the sentence, "The reality was altogether different," and provide an explanation.
2. Write an essay in which you take the middle ground in some ongoing debate, describing what arguments and issues exist on either side, how they overlap, and how there might be a way to honor both sides.

FIVE A.M. IN THE PINEWOODS

Mary Oliver

Mary Oliver's poems consistently explore the relationship between imagination and landscape. Her book American Primitive *won the Pulitzer Prize in 1984, and* New and Selected Poems *was awarded the National Book Award in 1992. The poem here tells a small story that gathers large implications by the time it ends. It originally appeared in* House of Light *(1990).*

I'd seen
their hoofprints in the deep
needles and knew
they ended the long night

under the pines, walking   5
like two mute
and beautiful women toward
the deeper woods, so I

got up in the dark and
went there. They came   10
slowly down the hill
and looked at me sitting under

the blue trees, shyly
they stepped
closer and stared   15
from under their thick lashes and even

nibbled some damp
tassels of weeds. This
is not a poem about a dream,
though it could be.   20

This is a poem about the world
that is ours, or could be.
Finally
one of them—I swear it!—

would have come to my arms.   25
But the other
stamped sharp hoof in the
pine needles like

the tap of sanity,
and they went off together through   30
the trees. When I woke
I was alone,

I was thinking:
so this is how you swim inward,
so this is how you flow outward,   *35*
so this is how you pray.

Reading and Responding

1. Read the whole poem. Write three things you're clear about; write one thing that puzzles you or that you don't quite get. (You should end up with four sentences.)
2. Write about a time when you've gotten close to a deer or other similarly impressive wild animal; tell the story in a page or so, and focus mostly on that time when you were closest to the animal.

Working Together

1. As a group, figure out why the poem goes from roughly eighteen lines of storytelling to roughly five lines of commentary. Why not just tell the story? What place does the commentary have? (*Hint:* Is the story about the deer, about the speaker, or both?)
2. This speaker gets up early to go see some deer. Why get up early to do this? What do the lines "This is a poem about the world / that is ours, or could be" mean? Do the lines help explain why the speaker goes to the pinewoods at 5 A.M.? Discuss this question as a group, and come up with some answers that make sense and do the poem justice.
3. Toward the end of this poem, one deer stamps a hoof. Explain why.

Rethinking and Rewriting

1. Write an essay that contrasts the first hour of a normal morning for you with the experience given in this poem. In the middle of your essay, discuss a time that you've been outside, somewhere in the country perhaps, just as it's getting light. End by discussing what you understand makes the experience in this poem so valuable to the speaker.
2. Assume you were going to send a copy of this poem to someone. Who would you send it to? Write that person a one-page letter that you would send with the poem.
3. Write your instructor a letter explaining why you like—or don't like—poetry. Use this poem as an example. Don't be mean or nasty or wildly enthusiastic. Just try to explain your feelings carefully and honestly.

Chapter 4 Essay Topics

1. Write an essay that reflects on a pet—a beloved dog or cat or horse—in light of any two essays in this chapter. Your thesis is that these essays

have changed or complicated or disturbed your relationship to this animal.

2. Using at least two of the essays in this chapter for supporting evidence, argue that the difference between the domestic and the wild is no longer very clear—that the grizzly bear is just as much a pet as a dog or cat; that all the world has become a zoo.

3. Visit a local zoo and reflect on your experience in light of the essays by Melissa Greene, Lewis Thomas, and at least two others in this chapter.

4. Write an essay that tells a surprising or puzzling personal experience you've had with wild animals on their own territory. Relate the experience in clear detail and identify some particular questions about this animal's behavior. Then see if your research can provide answers. End your essay by reflecting on how little or how much you now think you understand this experience and this animal species.

5. Imagine your life without *any* experience with animals—none at all. What would you have missed? What would you not understand (or understand less well)? Write an essay that explains your responses in detail.

6. Consider some local ecological conflict that pits the rights of an animal species against the rights of people and write about it. Don't take the usual slant here; don't talk politics or economics. Instead, use this local conflict as a way to focus on how the animal views its world (on the one hand) and how we view it (on the other). Don't try to resolve the conflict. Don't even try to take sides. Just use this situation as an example that shows how we view the world and how our views differ from those of other animals.

5

Limits: Challenges and Progress

Right up to the present moment, U.S. history has involved the exploitation of natural resources to the point of crisis. No one imagined that a forest could be logged completely away until it was done, over and over, as settlers moved farther west. No one believed that bodies of water could be fished out, that rivers could be diverted out of existence, that the air itself could be made so dirty it became unhealthy to breathe. But we believe it now.

At the beginning of the twenty-first century, we know for sure that as human beings dominate more and more ecosystems, the results will be increasingly serious and locally catastrophic. We know that we cannot hope to prosper unless the planet prospers, its ecologies healthy. We know this and yet are slow to change, uncertain of the processes and unsure of the local results. We wonder how our own actions can matter. The readings in this chapter point to some of the challenges—and unfortunate results—of a model based on heedless human population growth, as well as to some continuing efforts suggesting that we are capable of initiating and working toward change.

FADING COLORS

FADING COLORS: ARE WE LOSING THE SUGAR MAPLE TO ACID RAIN?

John Dillon

On a rain-soaked New Hampshire hillside, Scott Bailey is deep in dirt. Huge, gray-barked sugar maples stand starkly beautiful in the mist, but Bailey, a research geologist with the U.S. Forest Service, doesn't notice. He is focused on the minerals below the forest floor. Crouched in a three-foot-deep pit, he scrapes away some decomposing leaves to show me the tree roots threading through the damp earth. He points out where the soil separates into layers of dark organic matter above and lighter, mineral-rich zones below. The roots that penetrate this mix of leaf litter and glacial remains feed an 80-year-old sugar maple, one of a species that has evolved over millennia to withstand the Northeast's killer ice storms, leaf-munching insects, and spring cold snaps. But sugar maples, like the other trees of the northern forest, may not have had time to adapt to the dramatic changes in atmospheric chemistry caused by 50 years of industrial pollution and car exhaust. They may not have had time to adapt to acid rain.

In the early 1980s researchers first observed that spruce trees in the mountains of New England and New York were losing their needles and dying. They traced the problem to acid rain and snow, which form when sulfur dioxide or nitrogen oxides from factories, coal-fired power plants, and automobiles combine with moisture in the air. Now Bailey and other scientists want to know if the same air pollutants are affecting sugar maples.

The center for acid rain research in North America is the 7,800-acre Hubbard Brook Experimental Forest, located in Woodstock, New Hampshire, and run by the U.S. Forest Service. As Bailey and I slog through the forest, a steady rain drenches us. It has a pH of 4.6, well below the neutral level of 7. In all, the weeklong storm will dump more than four inches of acid rain on the New England landscape.

It wasn't supposed to be this way. Eight years ago, when Congress amended the Clean Air Act to curb the pollutants that cause acid rain, the atmosphere was expected to get cleaner. Yet the rain falling here in New Hampshire is still almost as acidic as it was when the controls were implemented. And as researchers have discovered, it is continuing to wreak profound changes upon forest ecosystems.

The sugar maple, which constitutes about 20 percent of the northern hardwood forest, is a prize tree. Its hard, clear wood is valued for floors and furniture; its sweet sap is boiled for amber syrup that is lavished on waffles and pancakes; and it offers a stunning show of crimson, orange, and

5

yellow foliage in the fall. But when maple trees are dying, their colorful display starts early.

Unusual levels of sugar maple mortality first began to worry foresters in the early 1980s. Because of this dieback, and because of its iconic status in the Northeast, the sugar maple quickly became the focus of research. In New England, sugar maple deaths peaked in the mid-1980s, with 14,000 acres of "significant mortality" reported in 1986 in Vermont. In Quebec, the height of forest decline came in the late 1980s. Researchers surveyed 9,600 square miles of forest and found 40 percent of the trees in decline. In recent years the sugar maples of Pennsylvania have suffered the most. In 1994 researchers found high levels of mortality on 90,000 acres of the 730,000-acre Allegheny National Forest. In the hardest-hit areas, 28 percent of the sugar maples were dead and another 31 percent were at risk (half their leaves and branches had died). In all these cases, a prime suspect was acid rain.

Scientists examining 35 years of soil-chemistry data at Hubbard Brook have found a disturbing trend: Acid rain has sapped the soil of calcium and magnesium, vital nutrients used by sugar maples—and other trees as well—to build cell walls. At Hubbard Brook the pool of available calcium in the soil has shrunk by more than 50 percent over the past four decades. The losses make the soil still more vulnerable to acid rain, since soils that contain calcium are able to buffer, or neutralize, acid. "It's like Tums," says Gene Likens, who began the acid rain research at Hubbard Brook in 1962 and who popularized the term *acid rain* back in the 1970s. "When you have an acid stomach, you take Tums. But acid rain has leached the Tums out of the soil. The system is much more sensitive to acid rain than it was before." Now he and his colleagues are trying to determine if the dramatic change in soil nutrients is stunting the forest: Its growth rate has slowed almost to zero since 1987.

Acid rain also makes trees more vulnerable to aluminum, which is toxic to them and which interferes with their calcium uptake. Aluminum is a common element in forest soils, but it is usually locked up in chemical compounds. When the compounds are soaked by acid rain, however, the chemical bonds are loosened and the aluminum can be absorbed by tree roots.

Bailey and his Forest Service colleagues are now studying the link between calcium, magnesium, and sugar maple mortality. They have found that the maples in Pennsylvania suffered a combination of stresses. The trees were rooted in soil already low in calcium and magnesium, and then they were hit by defoliating insects. Trees growing in more nutrient-rich soils and those with a lower demand for calcium, such as oaks and cherries, remained healthy.

"It seems to be a combination of nutritional stress and defoliation   *10* stress," Bailey says. "One or the other alone, you don't see the dieback." He notes that many soils in New England are as low in calcium as those in

Pennsylvania. The maple whose roots we examined at Hubbard Brook, for example, was growing in calcium-poor soil. Yet New England has not seen a major insect outbreak since the early 1980s.

Canada, Norway, and Sweden—and to a lesser extent, the United States—have been experimenting with adding lime (calcium carbonate) to forests and lakes to neutralize the effects of acid rain. But Likens says, "It doesn't get at the root of the problem: emissions from the burning of coal and oil." He worries that recent air-pollution controls have not done enough to stop the damage from acid rain. The Clean Air Act Amendments of 1990 gave factories and power plants 10 years to cut sulfur dioxide emissions to roughly half their 1980 level. Sulfur levels in the atmosphere are beginning to drop. But the law didn't tackle the other cause of acid rain: nitrogen oxides, which are released by automobiles as well as by power plants. The reason for the omission had more to do with politics than with science, according to Curtis Moore, a Washington, D.C., lawyer who helped draft the 1990 legislation while working for the U.S. Senate. During the debate, industry lobbyists beat back additional nitrogen oxide controls. Says Moore, "The large coal and utility interests have successfully avoided reductions for thirty years now."

Likens believes the lesson from the forest is clear: Emissions of nitrogen oxides must be cut. In May the governors of six New England states and the premiers of five eastern-Canadian provinces called on their two countries to reduce nitrogen oxides by 20 to 30 percent by 2007. Likens agrees that more must be done. "There is a problem here that was viewed as being solved," he says, "and it has not been."

Reading and Responding

1. Draw a chart or diagram that shows on a single page the interplay of causes and effects that define the problem of acid rain on sugar maples.
2. Who benefits from the processes that produce acid rain in the first place? Write a brief paragraph in answer to this question. If you're confused or unsure, explain why.

Working Together

1. Consider the following questions: What's wrong with acid rain falling in Vermont, Quebec, Pennsylvania, and other parts of the Northeast? Why does it matter that acid rain falls in these places and that it results in stressed or dying forests? Identify as many reasonable responses as you can generate in your group (make a list of responses). Then, in your group, identify the two or three responses that attract real support. If group members disagree, don't try to resolve the issue; instead, try merely to identify areas of greatest controversy and/or agreement.
2. Dillon's essay suggests that the "large coal and utility interests" are at least partially at fault because their electricity-generating plants produce

the air pollutants that combine with rain water to produce acid rain. Assume, for the moment at least, that this is true. Discuss who buys the output from such plants. Who, therefore, is really at fault for producing acid rain? Add to this discussion the issue of energy conservation measures that reduce electrical consumption. Now, write three statements about acid rain that everyone in your group agrees to be true.

Rethinking and Rewriting

1. Do some research to find out where the power that turns on your lights or runs your computer actually originates. Where and how is it produced? What effects does this production have on the environment? Based on this knowledge, write a letter to the generation that will follow the one in elementary school now. Assume that your local newspaper will still exist and that it will run your letter (in roughly the year 2050) as part of a "look at energy consumption and attitudes at the start of a new century." Therefore, address your letter to readers of this newspaper.

2. Research typical weather patterns in your home town (or your current locale) so that you can answer this question: which industries or other factors affect the air you breathe? Where does that same air typically go? Explain in four or five pages how your thinking about air pollution (its causes and its solutions) has changed (or why it has not changed) as a result of reading this essay and conducting research.

HETCH HETCHY VALLEY

John Muir

> *A naturalist and explorer and founder of the Sierra Club, John Muir hiked through much of the American West in the mid- to late nineteenth century, recording what he saw and arguing for the preservation of wilderness in such books as* The Mountains of California *(1894) and* Our National Parks *(1901). What follows is a good example of his efforts at persuasion, a passionate (though unsuccessful) attempt to save California's Hetch Hetchy Valley from the effects of dam building.*

Yosemite is so wonderful that we are apt to regard it as an exceptional creation, the only valley of its kind in the world; but Nature is not so poor as to have only one of anything. Several other yosemites have been discovered in the Sierra that occupy the same relative positions on the Range and were formed by the same forces in the same kind of granite. One of these, the Hetch Hetchy Valley, is in the Yosemite National Park about twenty miles from Yosemite and is easily accessible to all sorts of travelers by a road and trail that leaves the Big Oak Flat road at Bronson Meadows a few miles below Crane Flat, and to mountaineers by way of Yosemite Creek basin and the head of the middle fork of the Tuolumne.

It is said to have been discovered by Joseph Screech, a hunter, in 1850, a year before the discovery of the great Yosemite. After my first visit to it in the autumn of 1871, I have always called it the "Tuolumne Yosemite," for it is a wonderfully exact counterpart of the Merced Yosemite, not only in its sublime rocks and waterfalls but in the gardens, groves and meadows of its flowery park-like floor. The floor of Yosemite is about 4000 feet above the sea; the Hetch Hetchy floor about 3700 feet. And as the Merced River flows through Yosemite, so does the Tuolumne through Hetch Hetchy. The walls of both are of gray granite, rise abruptly from the floor, are sculptured in the same style and in both every rock is a glacier monument.

Standing boldly out from the south wall is a strikingly picturesque rock called by the Indians, Kolana, the outermost of a group 2300 feet high, corresponding with the Cathedral Rocks of Yosemite both in relative position and form. On the opposite side of the Valley, facing Kolana, there is a counterpart of the El Capitan that rises sheer and plain to a height of 1800 feet, and over its massive brow flows a stream which makes the most graceful fall I have ever seen. From the edge of the cliff to the top of an earthquake talus it is perfectly free in the air for a thousand feet before it is broken into cascades among talus boulders. It is in all its glory in June, when the snow is melting fast, but fades and vanishes toward the end of summer. The only fall I know with which it may fairly be compared is the Yosemite Bridal Veil; but it excels even that favorite fall both in height and airy-fairy beauty and behavior. Lowlanders are apt to suppose that mountain streams in their wild career over cliffs lose control of themselves and tumble in a noisy chaos of mist and spray. On the contrary, on no part of their travels are they more harmonious and self-controlled. Imagine yourself in Hetch Hetchy on a sunny day in June, standing waist-deep in grass and flowers (as I have often stood), while the great pines sway dreamily with scarcely perceptible motion. Looking northward across the Valley you see a plain, gray granite cliff rising abruptly out of the gardens and groves to a height of 1800 feet, and in front of it Tueeulala's silvery scarf burning with irised sun-fire. In the first white outburst at the head there is abundance of visible energy, but it is speedily hushed and concealed in divine repose, and its tranquil progress to the base of the cliff is like that of a downy feather in a still room. Now observe the fineness and marvelous distinctness of the various sun-illumined fabrics into which the water is woven; they sift and float from form to form down the face of that grand gray rock in so leisurely and unconfused a manner that you can examine their texture, and patterns and tones of color as you would a piece of embroidery held in the hand. Toward the top of the fall you see groups of booming, comet-like masses, their solid, white heads separate, their tails like combed silk interlacing among delicate gray and purple shadows, ever forming and dissolving, worn out by friction in their rush through the air. Most of these vanish a few hundred feet below the summit, changing to varied forms of cloud-like drapery. Near the bottom the width of the fall has increased from about twenty-five feet to a hundred feet. Here it is composed of yet finer tissues, and is still without a trace of disorder—air, water and sunlight woven into stuff that spirits might wear.

So fine a fall might well seem sufficient to glorify any valley; but here, as in Yosemite, Nature seems in nowise moderate, for a short distance to the eastward of Tueeulala booms and thunders the great Hetch Hetchy Fall, Wapama, so near that you have both of them in full view from the same standpoint. It is the counterpart of the Yosemite Fall, but has a much greater volume of water, is about 1700 feet in height, and appears to be nearly vertical, though considerably inclined, and is dashed into huge outbounding bosses of foam on projecting shelves and knobs. No two falls could be more unlike—Tueeulala out in the open sunshine descending like thistledown; Wapama in a jagged, shadowy gorge roaring and thundering, pounding its way like an earthquake avalanche.

Besides this glorious pair there is a broad, massive fall on the main river a short distance above the head of the Valley. Its position is something like that of the Vernal in Yosemite, and its roar as it plunges into a surging trout-pool may be heard a long way, though it is only about twenty feet high. On Rancheria Creek, a large stream, corresponding in position with the Yosemite Tenaya Creek, there is a chain of cascades joined here and there with swift flashing plumes like the one between the Vernal and Nevada Falls, making magnificent shows as they go their glacier-sculptured way, sliding, leaping, hurrahing, covered with crisp clashing spray made glorious with sifting sunshine. And besides all these a few small streams come over the walls at wide intervals, leaping from ledge to ledge with bird-like song and watering many a hidden cliff-garden and fernery, but they are too unshowy to be noticed in so grand a place.

The correspondence between the Hetch Hetchy walls in their trends, sculpture, physical structure, and general arrangement of the main rock-masses and those of the Yosemite Valley has excited the wondering admiration of every observer. We have seen that the El Capitan and Cathedral rocks occupy the same relative positions in both valleys; so also do their Yosemite points and North Domes. Again, that part of the Yosemite north wall immediately to the east of the Yosemite Fall has two horizontal benches, about 500 and 1500 feet above the floor, timbered with golden-cup oak. Two benches similarly situated and timbered occur on the same relative portion of the Hetch Hetchy north wall, to the east of Wapama Fall, and on no other. The Yosemite is bounded at the head by the great Half Dome. Hetch Hetchy is bounded in the same way, though its head rock is incomparably less wonderful and sublime in form.

The floor of the Valley is about three and a half miles long, and from a fourth to half a mile wide. The lower portion is mostly a level meadow about a mile long, with the trees restricted to the sides and the river banks, and partially separated from the main, upper, forested portion by a low bar of glacier-polished granite across which the river breaks in rapids.

The principal trees are the yellow and sugar pines, digger pine, incense cedar, Douglas spruce, silver fir, the California and golden-cup oaks, balsam cottonwood, Nuttall's flowering dogwood, alder, maple, laurel, tumion, etc. The most abundant and influential are the great yellow or silver pines like those of Yosemite, the tallest over two hundred feet in height, and the oaks assembled in magnificent groves with massive rugged trunks four to six feet in diameter, and broad, shady, wide-spreading heads. The shrubs forming conspicuous flowery clumps and tangles are manzanita, azalea, spiræa, brier-rose, several species of ceanothus, caly-canthus, philadelphus, wild cherry, etc.; with abundance of showy and fragrant herbaceous plants growing about them or out in the open in beds by themselves—lilies, Mariposa tulips, brodiaeas, orchids, iris, spraguea, draperia, collomia, collinsia, castilleja, nemophila, larkspur, columbine, goldenrods, sunflowers, mints of many species, honeysuckle, etc. Many fine ferns dwell here also, especially the beautiful and interesting rock-ferns—pellaea, and cheilanthes of several species—fringing and rosetting dry rock-piles and ledges; woodwardia and asplenium on damp spots with fronds six or seven feet high; the delicate maidenhair in mossy nooks by the falls, and the sturdy, broad-shouldered pteris covering nearly all the dry ground beneath the oaks and pines.

It appears, therefore, that Hetch Hetchy Valley, far from being a plain, common, rock-bound meadow, as many who have not seen it seem to suppose, is a grand landscape garden, one of Nature's rarest and most precious mountain temples. As in Yosemite, the sublime rocks of its walls seem to glow with life, whether leaning back in repose or standing erect in thoughtful attitudes, giving welcome to storms and calms alike, their brows in the sky, their feet set in the groves and gay flowery meadows, while birds, bees, and butterflies help the river and waterfalls to stir all the air into music—things frail and fleeting and types of permanence meeting here and blending, just as they do in Yosemite, to draw her lovers into close and confiding communion with her.

Sad to say, this most precious and sublime feature of the Yosemite National Park, one of the greatest of all our natural resources for the uplifting joy and peace and health of the people, is in danger of being dammed and made into a reservoir to help supply San Francisco with water and light, thus flooding it from wall to wall and burying its gardens and groves one or two hundred feet deep. This grossly destructive commercial scheme has long been planned and urged (though water as pure and abundant can be got from outside of the people's park, in a dozen different places), because of the comparative cheapness of the dam and of the territory which it is sought to divert from the great uses to which it was dedicated in the Act of 1890 establishing the Yosemite National Park.

The making of gardens and parks goes on with civilization all over the world, and they increase both in size and number as their value is recognized. Everybody needs beauty as well as bread, places to play in and pray in, where Nature may heal and cheer and give strength to body and soul alike. This natural beauty-hunger is made manifest in the little window-sill gardens of the poor, though perhaps only a geranium slip in a broken cup, as well as in the carefully tended rose and lily gardens of the rich, the thousands of spacious city parks and botanical gardens, and in our magnificent National Parks—the Yellowstone, Yosemite, Sequoia, etc.—Nature's sublime wonderlands, the admiration and joy of the world. Nevertheless, like anything else worth while, from the very beginning, however well guarded, they have always been subject to attack by despoiling gainseekers and mischief-makers of every degree from Satan to Senators, eagerly trying to make everything immediately and selfishly commercial, with schemes disguised in smug-smiling philanthropy, industriously, sham-piously crying, "Conservation, conservation, panutilization," that man and beast may be fed and the dear Nation made great. Thus long ago a few enterprising merchants utilized the Jerusalem temple as a place of business instead of a place of prayer, changing money, buying and selling cattle and sheep and doves; and earlier still, the first forest reservation, including only one tree, was likewise despoiled. Ever since the establishment of the Yosemite National Park, strife has been going on around its borders and I suppose this will go on as part of the universal battle between right and wrong, however much its boundaries may be shorn, or its wild beauty destroyed.

The first application to the Government by the San Francisco Supervisors for the commercial use of Lake Eleanor and the Hetch Hetchy Valley was made in 1903, and on December 22nd of that year it was denied by the Secretary of the Interior, Mr. Hitchcock, who truthfully said:

Presumably the Yosemite National Park was created such by law because of the natural objects of varying degrees of scenic importance located within its boundaries, inclusive alike of its beautiful small lakes, like Eleanor, and its majestic wonders, like Hetch Hetchy and Yosemite Valley. It is the aggregation of such natural scenic features that makes the Yosemite Park a wonderland which the Congress of the United States sought by law to reserve for all coming time as nearly as practicable in the condition fashioned by the hand of the Creator—a worthy object of national pride and a source of healthful pleasure and rest for the thousands of people who may annually sojourn there during the heated months.

In 1907 when Mr. Garfield became Secretary of the Interior the application was renewed and granted; but under his successor, Mr. Fisher, the matter has been referred to a Commission, which as this volume goes to press still has it under consideration.

The most delightful and wonderful camp-grounds in the Park are its three great valleys—Yosemite, Hetch Hetchy, and Upper Tuolumne; and they are also the most important places with reference to their positions relative to the other great features—the Merced and Tuolumne Cañons, and the High Sierra peaks and glaciers, etc., at the head of the rivers. The main part of the Tuolumne Valley is a spacious flowery lawn four or five miles long, surrounded by magnificent snowy mountains, slightly separated from other beautiful meadows, which together make a series about twelve miles in length, the highest reaching to the feet of Mount Dana, Mount Gibbs, Mount Lyell and Mount McClure. It is about 8500 feet above the sea, and forms the grand central High Sierra camp-ground from which excursions are made to the noble mountains, domes, glaciers, etc.; across the Range to the Mono Lake and volcanoes and down the Tuolumne Cañon to Hetch Hetchy. Should Hetch Hetchy be submerged for a reservoir, as proposed, not only would it be utterly destroyed, but the sublime cañon way to the heart of the High Sierra would be hopelessly blocked and the great camping-ground, as the watershed of a city drinking system, virtually would be closed to the public. So far as I have learned, few of all the thousands who have seen the Park and seek rest and peace in it are in favor of this outrageous scheme.

One of my later visits to the Valley was made in the autumn of 1907 *15* with the late William Keith, the artist. The leaf-colors were then ripe, and the great god-like rocks in repose seemed to glow with life. The artist, under their spell, wandered day after day along the river and through the groves and gardens, studying the wonderful scenery; and, after making about forty sketches, declared with enthusiasm that although its walls were less sublime in height, in picturesque beauty and charm Hetch Hetchy surpassed even Yosemite.

That any one would try to destroy such a place seems incredible; but sad experience shows that there are people good enough and bad enough for anything. The proponents of the dam scheme bring forward a lot of bad arguments to prove that the only righteous thing to do with the people's parks is to destroy them bit by bit as they are able. Their arguments are curiously like those of the devil, devised for the destruction of the first garden—so much of the very best Eden fruit going to waste; so much of the best Tuolumne water and Tuolumne scenery going to waste. Few of their statements are even partly true, and all are misleading.

Thus, Hetch Hetchy, they say, is a "low-lying meadow." On the contrary, it is a high-lying natural landscape garden, as the photographic illustrations show.

"It is a common minor feature, like thousands of others." On the contrary it is a very uncommon feature; after Yosemite, the rarest and in many ways the most important in the National Park.

"Damming and submerging it 175 feet deep would enhance its beauty by forming a crystal-clear lake." Landscape gardens, places of recreation and worship, are never made beautiful by destroying and burying them. The beautiful sham lake, forsooth, would be only an eyesore, a dismal blot on the landscape, like many others to be seen in the Sierra. For, instead of keeping it at the same level all the year, allowing Nature centuries of time to make new shores, it would, of course, be full only a month or two in the spring, when the snow is melting fast; then it would be gradually drained, exposing the slimy sides of the basin and shallower parts of the bottom, with the gathered drift and waste, death and decay of the upper basins, caught here instead of being swept on to decent natural burial along the banks of the river or in the sea. Thus the Hetch Hetchy dam-lake would be only a rough imitation of a natural lake for a few of the spring months, an open sepulcher for the others.

"Hetch Hetchy water is the purest of all to be found in the Sierra, 20 unpolluted, and forever unpollutable." On the contrary, excepting that of the Merced below Yosemite, it is less pure than that of most of the other Sierra streams, because of the sewerage of camp-grounds draining into it, especially of the Big Tuolumne Meadows camp-ground, occupied by hundreds of tourists and mountaineers, with their animals, for months every summer, soon to be followed by thousands from all the world.

These temple destroyers, devotees of ravaging commercialism, seem to have a perfect contempt for Nature, and, instead of lifting their eyes to the God of the mountains, lift them to the Almighty Dollar.

Dam Hetch Hetchy! As well dam for water-tanks the people's cathedrals and churches, for no holier temple has ever been consecrated by the heart of man.

Reading and Responding

1. Identify John Muir's main argument, and number the various points he makes to support that argument.

2. Highlight words and phrases that seem particularly charged, powerful, loaded, or intense.

Working Together

1. Outline Muir's argument on the board, and consider his main ways of supporting that argument.
2. Discuss Muir's other strategies of persuasion, particularly word choice and imagery.
3. Freewrite for about half a page, imitating Muir's voice and tone. Argue for a local cause—say, that the old cedars in the quad on campus shouldn't be cut down or that a new shopping center shouldn't be built. Ham it up. Exaggerate.

Rethinking and Rewriting

1. Do a profile of John Muir, drawing on library research, and put this particular essay in the context of his life and career.
2. Research the fate of the Hetch Hetchy Valley. What is it like today?
3. Write an essay that imitates Muir's style. Make a similar argument for some comparable local site threatened by development.

A STATEMENT OF
SAN FRANCISCO'S SIDE

Marsden Manson

> *Marsden Manson served as San Francisco's city engineer from 1907 to 1912. What follows is his reply to John Muir's "Hetch Hetchy Valley," a claim that the city's need for water justifies the building of the dam.*
>
> *Note that the Sierra Club's California-Nevada Conservation Committee recently established the Hetch Hetchy Restoration Task Force to coordinate its effort to remove the dam and restore the valley. For more on dam removal, see Marc Reisner's "Coming Undammed" later in this chapter.*

To the Members of the Sierra Club:

There has been sent out a ballot for an election on the Hetch–Hetchy question, to be held on Saturday, January 29, 1910. This ballot presents two questions apparently worded to draw out a vote for or against the use of the Hetch–Hetchy Valley as a reservoir. Both of these propositions are speciously arranged, and neither presents the question in its true light.

> *Proposition 1:* "I desire that the Hetch–Hetchy Valley shall remain intact and unaltered as a part of the Yosemite National Park and oppose its use as a reservoir for a water supply for San Francisco, unless an impartial federal commission shall determine that it is absolutely necessary for such use."

The facts regarding this proposition are that San Francisco made an application under the law of February 15, 1901, for the use of this reservoir space for the storage of water for domestic purposes. Such use is pointed out by the U.S. Geological Survey in the 21st Annual Report, Part IV, pages 450–453. This survey was conducted during the years 1897–99, specifically making an estimate of the volumes of water possible to store in this reservoir and of the character of the dam and work necessary for its utilization as such. Congress, acting upon the results of this work, formally made it possible to file upon this and other reservoirs in Yosemite National Park, and other parks and reservations; and *under this formal dedication to public uses of the reservoir spaces within the Yosemite National Park, and other parks and reservations* named in the law of February, 1901, made it possible for individuals, corporations and municipalities to utilize the natural resources originating in these parks, which resources had been previously prohibited by the provisions of the law of October 1, 1890, defining the limits and setting aside the Yosemite Reservation.

Lying within the floor of this reservoir are comparatively level lands, some 800 to 900 acres, of which *San Francisco owns in fee simple 720 acres under patent issued prior to the Act of October 1, 1890.* The area of the water surface when raised to about 150 feet above the level of the lower end of the Valley is about 1200 acres, which embraces quite a considerable area of gravelly and rocky soil at the upper end of the valley and the sloping sides thereof up to the level above named. The application made by San Francisco in 1901 for this permit was denied by the then Secretary of the Interior, and again denied upon a rehearing, the denial being based upon the ground that he was not authorized to make such grant. He used as the basis of his action the prior law of October, 1890, and refused to recognize the modifying effects of the subsequent law of February 15, 1901. Upon the reference of this question to the Attorney-General of the United States, the Acting Attorney-General, Judge Purdy, decided that full authority rested in the Secretary of the Interior under the law of February 15, 1901, and the then Secretary, Mr. Garfield, ultimately made the grant for the use of the remaining lands in the Hetch-Hetchy Reservoir site on May 11, 1908.

The question submitted under Proposition 1 on the ballot is therefore misleading in the extreme, and is not one that under any plea of either law or equity that can be referred to a so-called "impartial federal commission." It is misleading again in the fact that this commission is to determine that the use as a reservoir "is absolutely necessary."

By reference to the grant of May, 1908, under Stipulation No. 3, it will be observed that Lake Eleanor must first be developed to its full capacity before the development of Hetch-Hetchy shall be begun, which shall be undertaken only when the City and County of San Francisco, and adjacent cities, may require such further development. It is manifest, therefore, that the calling into effect of an "impartial federal commission" to determine what has already been determined is not making a just and equitable presentation to the members of the Sierra Club of the question at issue.

> *Proposition 2:* "I favor the use of Hetch-Hetchy Valley as a reservoir for a future water supply for San Francisco and I favor a present dedication by Congress of the right to such use without further investigation."

From the preceding discussion and statement of the facts, it will be seen that San Francisco already holds the right, under the laws of Congress as interpreted by the Attorney-General of the United States and administered by its executive officers, to use that portion of the floor of this valley which remains in the park for a reservoir after having developed Lake Eleanor to its full capacity and upon finding *that the additional supply is necessary.* So far as the laws of Congress can make this dedication, and so far as a conservative and just administrative officer of the government can guard public interests, this dedication has already been made by Congress, accepted by the people of the city under the terms imposed by the executive branch of the government, and no dedication of Congress whatever is needed, nor is asked for.

It is manifest from the above simple recital of the facts with reference to the laws and the actions taken thereunder, that neither of the propositions submitted on the ballot for the election of January 29, 1910, are fairly and equitably stated. This is made still more manifest by the re-issuance by Mr. John Muir, under date of November, 1909, of a pamphlet of some twenty odd pages of garbled quotations and specious statements protesting against the "unnecessary destruction of Hetch-Hetchy Valley." In this it is made to appear on page 3 that the Sierra Club of California formally joins in the protest against the "alleged unnecessary destruction of Hetch-Hetchy Valley." It is claimed by the undersigned that no destruction of the Valley is contemplated even in the remote future, when the use of this valley as a water supply for the homes of the cities about the bay shall become imperative. A reference to the pictures upon the latter pages of this pamphlet will make this perfectly manifest. There are nine of these pictures, and they will be referred to in order of their occurrence in the pamphlet, the pages on which they are printed not being numbered.

The first picture presents a very beautiful view of a portion of the valley opposite the falls known as Wapama. The highest level of the proposed reservoir will not reach the base of these falls. Therefore but little of the base of the granite sides of the valley will be flooded. The floor to be covered is owned in fee simple by San Francisco to the extent heretofore named, or about 720 acres. All of the floor of the valley within the limits of this picture is so owned.

In picture No. 2 the same remarks are true. Neither of the falls will be affected in any way.

Picture No. 3, the same is true.

In picture No. 4 it may be observed that San Francisco again owns the greater portion or all of the floor of the valley within sight, and that the great granite mass of Kolana will be flooded at its base by the highest dam about 10 per cent of its height.

Of pictures Nos. 5 and 6, no features will be affected except the floor of the valley, which again in these pictures embraces areas owned by San Francisco. The falls shown in these two pictures will not be affected in the least.

Pictures 7 and 8 represent landscapes in that portion of the valley owned by San Francisco. The general view given in No. 9 will be covered up to a point some fifty feet below the lowest portion of the ledge on the left side of the picture.

This pamphlet is devoted principally to three arguments: First, *that the flooding of the valley floor will destroy the scenic beauty of the Hetch-Hetchy.* The most striking natural features about the valley are all above the highest level to which it is proposed a quarter of a century or more hence to raise the level of the water. The cliffs rise to a height of more than 2500 feet above the valley floor, and as the reservoir will not in any case be more than 275 to 300 feet deep the apparent decrease in the height of the walls will not be perceptible to the eye of the ordinary observer. All of these peaks and cliffs, with their varied markings and color, will remain as now, and will be reflected in the waters of the lake, as are the cliffs surrounding the other lakes in the Sierras. Both of the falls strike the slopes of the bluffs above the level of the highest reservoir surface, and will therefore be in no way altered. The lake which will be formed in the valley by the construction of the dam will be as beautiful as the other lakes which add charm to the landscapes of the Sierras. The floor of the valley owned by San Francisco in its greater portion and for the highest purposes for which it can be used, will be flooded, and this substitution of a lake for the trees and meadows is the measure of the alleged "unnecessary destruction of the Hetch-Hetchy Valley."

It is also true that for about two months in the year the floor of this valley is a "paradise for campers," but it must be remembered that the greater portion of this paradise is owned by San Francisco for the exclusive purpose of making the homes of tens of thousands of families that will never have the opportunity of visiting this "paradise for campers" a source of health and happiness, by introducing into those homes the greatest element of health, namely, the purest water from the most available source.

Secondly: *That the use of the reservoir will make it necessary to exclude the public from the 480 square miles of watershed above it.*

It is not true that the flooding of the valley will shut out visitors from the watershed tributary thereto, for this region is not reasonably accessible for only about three and a half months, during which time the same precautions now taken in Yosemite Valley itself will be ample for many decades, and probably centuries, to keep Tuolumne Meadows clean. Even when these simple precautions shall prove inadequate, no such drastic steps as are proposed in this pamphlet, namely, the shutting out of the public from the watershed, will be necessary, as may be seen by referring to the views of an eminent authority in sanitary engineering, Prof. C. D. Marx, who, on page 341 of the Transactions of the Commonwealth Club, of November 1909, reviews and gives definite proof that there will be absolutely no necessity for in any way restricting the use of the drainage area, and that the simple precautionary measures which are deemed sufficient to protect the supplies of Boston and other cities would be sufficient, and that if the supply shall be suspected of contamination modern methods will remedy this at very small cost and without the drastic measures urged by the opponents to the use of this reservoir.

The character of the watershed above the Hetch-Hetchy is such that it is absurd to suppose that it will be necessary to shut out travel from it. This travel reaches it only in the late summer and early autumn, when dangerous germs are exposed, if upon the surface, to the glaring sun of California skies, one hour of which is fatal to any known pathogenic germ; later to the severe frosts of October, and then to the snows from November to June, and finally to the oxidizing influences in the twenty miles of foaming torrents between the meadows and Hetch-Hetchy, and to the further influences of long storage in the reservoir. When even these great natural safeguards have been overcome as pointed out by Prof. Marx, very simple remedial measures can then be applied.

Thirdly: *That there are many other sources from which San Francisco can draw its water supply, thirteen of them being named.*   20

The statements that other sources of supply are open to the city as alleged on pages 4, 5 and 6 of Mr. Muir's pamphlet do not present the facts as they stand at present. None of the supplies named on these pages is comparable in availability, abundance, nor purity. Moreover, the pleadings that San Francisco be turned over to the tender mercies of the individuals and corporations owning all of the other Sierra supplies are specious and misleading in the extreme and serve only as a screen behind which the avariciousness and selfishness of corporate greed can be used against the interests of San Francisco and the Bay municipalities. All of these sources have been fully considered, and rejected, by the engineers employed by San Francisco, and this rejection concurred in by Secretary Garfield, who points out in his very able review of the matter that it is not for him, for Congress, nor other authority to determine for San Francisco what source she should select, and it ill becomes the members of the Sierra Club to put themselves in a position in which, whether intending it or not, they are the mere screen for the selfishness of corporations and those who hold "rights to water and power" which have been secured without opposition from those who so earnestly and persistently opposed San Francisco's rights. It is suggested that the city take water from one of these companies after it has been used in their power stations. It is well known that at this elevation it cannot flow by gravity to San Francisco, and will require pumping, and that to pump this to the elevations required for delivery in San Francisco will ultimately require a yearly expenditure of $1,000,000, or a capital investment of about $25,000,000, and the plea that San Francisco accept or acquire these supplies without the necessary power to pump it over the Coast Range and to the higher elevations of the city will play into the hands of the great electrical power monopoly to the extent above named. No wonder, therefore, that if the existing monopoly of these water and power companies be appealed to to furnish funds to oppose San Francisco in the acquisition of rights, which will furnish the water as well as pump it to the homes of the city, that they would be inclined to generously contribute.

Mr. John D. Galloway, an able engineer and member of the American Society of Civil Engineers, with a thorough acquaintance with the entire field, and after going into detail over the various possible sources, says, in the Transactions of the Commonwealth Club above referred to, "As a matter of fact, the development of long distance transmission of electric power started first in California, and there is not now a single large river within two hundred miles of San Francisco except the Tuolumne and the Merced which has not one or more electric power plants upon it. Without the Hetch-Hetchy supply the city will indeed be at a loss as to where to go."

The Commonwealth Club of California, an organization formed of broad-minded citizens who take up and have presented to them both sides of the great civic problems which are brought before them, took up the question of this Hetch-Hetchy supply at its meetings of September and November, 1909. At the meeting of the latter month the "Society for the Preservation of National Parks" put the following question: "If you decide that a National Park shall be the last resort, then you must require a complete and thorough showing that no other like utility is reasonably available." To which the Club replied that it was not necessarily the first or the last resort in a municipality in need of water, and "In such a case as that of Hetch-Hetchy it should be shown that no other like utility is available under reasonable conditions of engineering, extinguishment of adverse claims, cost, etc. The city of San Francisco has fulfilled this requirement to the satisfaction of eminent engineers in and out of the city's employment, and to that of Secretary Garfield. Your committee is unwilling to pass upon the statements of those who believe that the city's investigations of other sources have not been sufficiently exhaustive. But, as the Federal authorities have, after examining the data presented by the city's engineers, approved the conclusions of the San Francisco authorities, it would seem only just that those who assert that other sources are available under reasonable conditions should set forth with equal detail the facts on which they base their opinions."

It is manifest, therefore, that the statements made in this pamphlet are only apparently substantiated by the garbled quotations presented therein, and are not in reality based upon true and correct facts, but upon a partisan presentation of selected and misleading quotations to which the city's representative is forced to take this means of refuting. These garbled quotations are grossly misleading, in that they are separated out and arranged to masquerade as the unqualified opinions of those from whom they are quoted, when in many instances the opinions are the exact opposite of the impression which this pamphlet undertakes to scatter broadcast.

As showing the trend of the best minds in San Francisco, for which we think the Commonwealth Club can fairly be said to stand, it may be noted that the Club, after sending a committee to visit the Hetch-Hetchy and make its report (the report was a most elaborate and careful document), and after devoting two evenings to a discussion of the subject, at which Mr. George Edwards, of the Society for the Preservation of National Parks, and Mr. E. T. Parsons, one of the Directors of the Sierra Club, addressed the Club, by a vote of eight to one endorsed the proposition of the immediate development of the Hetch-Hetchy water supply for San Francisco.

The City and County of San Francisco must provide for a supply in the future of at least two hundred million gallons a day. Its present plans include the acquisition of the local supply, which can economically be developed to forty million gallons a day; the building of a reservoir at Lake Eleanor, which can develop a supply of sixty million gallons a day, possibly a supply of one hundred and twenty million gallons a day, which will carry the city along for a period of thirty or forty years' development. When these sources have reached their ultimate development, it is then planned to develop the Hetch-Hetchy supply. By this development it will be a generation or longer before the Hetch-Hetchy supply will be touched. The beauties of this Valley will therefore, under this arrangement, be preserved to the present generation and perhaps to the one that follows it. Should the privileges be taken away from the city, we may well doubt whether such a source of water and power as is presented by the Hetch-Hetchy proposition can be saved for an equal length of time from acquisition by private corporations, which would use them for their own instead of the public use.

We therefore urge that the efforts of San Francisco to acquire and use this source of water for the highest purpose to which water can be devoted should receive the support of the members of the Sierra Club.

The actual reservoir areas to which this grant by Secretary Garfield applies are by no means the entire areas of the reservoirs: In the first one to be developed, Lake Eleanor, all the very desirable meadow lands are privately owned, and San Francisco is acquiring these. The remainder, *less than a square mile at the highest development, is in the Park, and constitutes less than one twelve-hundredth (1/1200) part of the Park area.*

In the second one to be developed, Hetch-Hetchy, San Francisco owns 720 acres, and the *grant of reservoir rights of way again applies to less than a square mile, or to another one twelve-hundredth (1/1200) part of the Park.*

THE GRANT THEREFORE ONLY APPLIES TO LESS THAN ONE SIX-HUNDREDTH (1/600) PART OF THE PARK AREA, and to the use of this small fraction in conjunction with the greater areas owned by the city, for the highest purpose for which they can ever be used, the Sierra Club is asked to protest in the face of a use made available and possible by Congress in the law of February 15, 1901, granted in accordance with this law and accepted by San Francisco by a vote of over six to one.

You are therefore respectfully requested and urged to vote in favor of Proposition No. 2, with the mental reservation that you do not advocate a dedication by Congress of the right to such use without further investigation, for the reason that so far as Congressional action is concerned, such dedication was made by the Act of February 15, 1901, after due and careful consideration of all the facts by a Scientific Bureau of our country, and that this supply was open to San Francisco, and if denied must inevitably be put to use for some of the great necessities of the human race, and probably through the instrumentality of some selfish corporation.

Reading and Responding

1. Freewrite for half a page or so in response to these questions: What kind of argument is Manson making in this essay? On what is it based? Why do you think he makes this kind of argument?
2. Make a list of all of the things that San Francisco owns, based on this article. Then write a paragraph in response.

Working Together

1. As a group, write an outline of Manson's argument.
2. Designate one group "Manson Allies" and another group "Friends of Muir." The Manson Allies are charged with summarizing Manson's argument and adding to it. They should think of themselves as residents of San Francisco—workers, shopkeepers, manufacturers, men, women, children. Why does San Francisco need more water? Why this particular water? In contrast, the Friends of Muir should summarize Muir's argument and add to it. They should think of themselves as the current members of the Sierra Club. Each group should be prepared to speak for ten minutes to give a summary of their position. Ultimately, the whole class has this assignment: to draft a one-page land ethics statement that accurately represents the Manson Allies and a one-page statement that accurately represents the Friends of Muir. Both statements should carry this title: "What Is the Land For?"

Rethinking and Rewriting

1. Write an essay that explains why the issue of damming or not damming a river can be complicated. Use Muir's and Manson's arguments as sources. Or extend this discussion to some local decision that's similar. Explain why the decision is difficult to make.
2. Write an essay explaining how Muir's and Manson's essays represent two different ways of approaching and arguing a question. Which method of argument seems most appealing and convincing to you? Explain why.
3. Write a three- to five-page statement of your own land ethic. Use the Muir and Manson essays as sources, and add any other sources you wish.

UNDER THE SUN

Samuel W. Matthews

> *A senior assistant editor for* National Geographic, *Samuel Matthews here gathers considerable data as well as the testimony of experts to help readers understand the issue of global warming, a result of the greenhouse effect and other factors. This article, reprinted from the October 1990 issue, suggests both the ambition and the limitations of current science.*

The road up earth's most massive mountain—Mauna Loa on the Big Island of Hawaii—is a narrow, twisting strip of tar, laid by prison labor through raw, jagged lava fields. You can drive it—with great caution and constant awe—to a small cluster of white and blue huts standing more than two miles high in the clear, cool Pacific sky.

Here for 32 years the level of carbon dioxide in the earth's atmosphere has been recorded daily at the Mauna Loa Observatory by Charles David Keeling of the Scripps Institution of Oceanography and by scientists from the National Oceanic and Atmospheric Administration (NOAA). And for 32 years the level has risen, in a wavy curve of spring-fall variations . . . , from 315 parts per million (ppm) in 1958 to more than 355 in mid-1990.

That steadily climbing CO_2 level (air locked in glacial ice a century ago held only about 280 ppm—25 percent less) is an incontrovertible measure of what man and his machines have done to the atmosphere of the earth in scarcely one lifetime. Because of it, say many scientists who study the climate, our planet is bound to become warmer—has already warmed—as more and more energy from the sun is caught and held in the thin blanket of air around us.

"As Pogo put it, the enemy is us," said Elmer Robinson, director of Mauna Loa Observatory, while we drove together up the desolate slope of the volcano. "By burning more and more fossil fuel—gasoline, natural gas, coal, peat—even ordinary firewood, we are putting into the air more of the gases that act much like a globe of glass around the planet. That's what's called the greenhouse effect.

"Up here we measure not only CO_2," he went on, as he led me 5 through a laboratory jammed with humming recorders and glowing computer terminals. "We also read methane, chlorofluorocarbons, nitrous oxide, and ozone, all of which add to the warming. We see and measure dust of various sizes in the troposphere, the weather layer of the atmosphere."

Such data, recorded by NOAA here and at American Samoa in mid-Pacific, at Point Barrow in Alaska, and at the South Pole, form the hard evidence on which climatologists base widely varying and controversial visions of the future. Average temperature worldwide, by careful calculations, has gone up about half a degree Celsius—one degree Fahrenheit—since the late 1800s.

In this century, the decade of the 1980s saw the six warmest years in weather records. Yet there are some researchers and statisticians who argue this apparent warming of the planet may be only a temporary blip, that natural warming periods have occurred before, without man's intervention, and that there is as yet no sure evidence of long-term change.

All this was in my mind under the blaze of sunlight that beautiful winter day atop Mauna Loa. Through a small occulting telescope maintained there by the National Center for Atmospheric Research at Boulder, Colorado, I stared at the darkened face of the sun, ringed by its glowing, gauzy corona.

From that blazing disk high in the Hawaiian sky comes the endless power that drives and rules all life on earth: its plant growth and the food chains of all its creatures; the winds, rains, and churning weather of the planet; the ocean currents, forests, prairies, and deserts.

Our home star in the heavens burns steadily, almost without varia-   *10* tion. It is the "almost," coupled with what man's activities are doing to the atmosphere, that this story is about. It is becoming more and more apparent that the effects of the sun upon our planet are changing. Our one and only home may be in harm's way, and we can scarcely sense just what is happening—or know what to do about it.

That burning energy of our sun works the miracle on earth called photosynthesis. Powered by sunlight, plants green with chlorophyll combine carbon dioxide from the air with water from soil or sea into energy-rich carbohydrates, releasing into the atmosphere the oxygen we need to breathe.

It is the same process by which primitive bacteria of ocean shallows, more than two billion years ago, first produced enough oxygen to permit other life on earth to develop. And it is the same process—still imperfectly understood—that grows the corn of Iowa, the grass of your lawn, the rain forests of Brazil, the floating plankton that sustains life in the seas.

"Without carbon dioxide in the atmosphere, life as we know it would be impossible," Elmer Robinson had said on Mauna Loa. "We couldn't exist if it weren't for greenhouse warming."

About half of the radiant energy reaching earth from the sun, because of its short wavelengths, can pass through the atmosphere to the earth's surface. But the longer waves of heat that radiate back toward space are absorbed and reradiated by water vapor, carbon dioxide, other gases, and clouds, and the atmosphere warms.

"That's the greenhouse effect," Elmer had said. "Without it, earth   *15* would be frozen—at least 60 degrees Fahrenheit colder—and there would be no more life here than on Mars. But if it were to increase. . . . Well, some climatologists say we face temperatures three to nine degrees higher in the next century."

Back in the last glacial age, some 20,000 years ago, world temperature averaged about nine degrees colder than today. The carbon dioxide level was only 190 to 200 parts per million, ancient ice samples from Greenland and Antarctica show. As the ice melted back, the CO_2 level gradually rose to about 280 ppm by the beginning of the industrial age.

"By the middle of the coming century—in our children's lifetime," Elmer had said, "the level will reach 550 or even 600 at its current rate of rise."

The prospect of doubled CO_2—and even more rapid rise of other gases, such as methane, which together equal the warming effect of CO_2 in the atmosphere—is what has atmospheric scientists urgently refining their computer models of the climate. World population also is predicted to double by the middle of the next century, from five billion people to ten. And as all nations become more developed and use more fuel to support those people, the release of carbon dioxide and other gases to the air is bound to keep increasing—despite the care taken or which fuels are burned.

With more warmth and more CO_2, some ask, would not more crops grow, in wider areas than today? Would we not benefit from a warmer world?

Perhaps, in some areas. The more CO_2 in the air, the more produc- 20 tive some plants become. But the biggest unknown is what changes would occur in the planet's weather patterns.

Most climate models show that in some regions—northern Scandinavia, Siberia, and Canada, for example—more rain would fall and more trees and crops grow. But in today's great mid-continent breadbasket regions, warming would lead to the drying of soil in summer. Destructive droughts, such as that of 1988 in North America, would strike more often, until the Great Plains and Ukraine turn semidesert. Storms such as hurricanes and tornadoes might become more violent. Forests would decline and change under the temperature rise, and wildlife would have to migrate—if it could—or perish. The permafrost under Arctic tundra would thaw, deep peatlands would decompose, and vast new amounts of carbon dioxide and methane could be released.

And just as inevitably, as ocean waters warm and expand and the ice on Greenland and Antarctica melts back, the seas would creep higher onto the edges of the continents. Large parts of such low countries as Bangladesh—already swept by ruinous floods and typhoons—would be submerged; cities like Miami, Venice, even New York, would cower behind dikes.

"If a rise of one to three feet, as the models have predicted, seems extreme," says environmental scientist Stephen Leatherman of the University of Maryland, "keep in mind that the oceans rose more than 300 feet after the last ice age—all in only a few thousand years."

If the ice cap on the island of Greenland were to melt completely, glaciologists estimate the oceans would rise another 20 feet. Sea level in the eastern United States has already risen a foot in this century alone, and it is predicted to go up at least another foot in the century ahead. With that one-foot rise, Leatherman says, the high-water line at Ocean City,

Maryland, will move inland 100 to 200 feet; in Florida, 200 to 1,000 feet; in Louisiana, several miles.

Yet paradoxically, say other glaciologists, the huge ice domes on both   *25* Greenland and Antarctica may not be shrinking but growing. The paradox is that this too may be a sign of global warming. As the atmosphere warms, it holds more water vapor from evaporation of oceans and soil; hence more snow falls in the polar regions, hence more ice and possibly lower sea levels. But the warmer seas eventually will melt back the fringes of the polar ice, and the oceans will creep inexorably higher.

Foretelling what may happen to the world if it should warm by even one or two degrees is the toughest problem facing climatologists today. Even though there have been times in the dim geologic past when temperatures were warmer—with no ice at all on the polar regions—there are vast differences today. No one knows whether the "wild card" of human activity will disrupt or make more extreme the cycles ordained by nature.

To try to predict the effects of human intervention, scientists mathematically simulate the weather systems of the globe. Their equations, called general circulation models (GCMs), are so complex that only a few of today's supercomputers can solve them.

The equations relate such things as the balance of radiation to and from the planet, air circulation, evaporation and rainfall, ice cover, sea-surface temperature—then try to assess what might happen if the sun were to become brighter by a tiny amount or if the carbon dioxide in the atmosphere gradually doubles as expected. The computers then calculate and map the changes in the weather of future days, weeks, seasons—or centuries.

One key to their accuracy lies in how finely they divide the planet's surface, the blanket of the atmosphere, and the seas. Most now divide the globe into blocks of at least five degrees of latitude and five of longitude: 300 nautical miles on a side, roughly the size and shape of Colorado. The best models then divide the atmosphere into as many as 20 layers and add in the oceans' currents and multiple layers. The computations are so formidable that a supercomputer might take a week to run a single change of input to determine its effect.

On a high shelf of Colorado's Front Range, where deer roam in the   *30* open above the university town of Boulder, stand the sand-hued buildings of the National Center for Atmospheric Research (NCAR), one of the principal climate-modeling centers in the nation. The others are NASA's Goddard Institute for Space Studies (GISS) on upper Broadway in New York City and NOAA's Geophysical Fluid Dynamics Laboratory (GFDL) in Princeton, New Jersey.

The computer room at NCAR, its floor carpeted with bright red squares, is a futuristic assemblage of multicolored cabinets, computer terminals, and blinking panels of lights. The chief of the center, Bill Buzbee, showed me two red-and-black cylinders, each about five feet in diameter and five feet high, with segments seemingly cut out of them like huge wedges of cheese.

"Those are our Cray supercomputers," Bill said. "Not many exist in the world. If you'd like to buy one, it might cost you about 20 million bucks. And it would not be powerful enough for much of the modeling we're asked to do."

"If our global grid were reduced to two and a half degrees on a side and the number of vertical layers increased," I had heard Jerry Mahlman, director of GFDL, say, "it would multiply the demand on the computer 16-fold; at one degree square, which might be necessary to forecast weather and climate accurately for local regions on the globe, the order of complexity—and computer time—would go up at least 500 times."

I began to appreciate what these machines do. They reduce inconceivably complicated systems of the atmosphere and oceans to logical, mathematical predictions of what might happen if man or nature changes the ways things are with the world.

All the most advanced GCMs, fed a doubling of carbon dioxide, come up with similar results: The world will warm by the middle of the next century by two to five degrees Celsius—three to nine degrees Fahrenheit—with even greater warming in the subpolar latitudes. The differences between the models show up in regional effects . . . exactly where drying or more rainfall may occur, whether the Northern and Southern Hemispheres may react differently.

The modelers acknowledge they may be as much as a decade away from full confidence in their results. At GFDL they have been trying for 20 years to couple ocean circulation to the atmosphere. Syukuro Manabe, one of GFDL's most noted modelers . . . , admits that in the early days "all sorts of crazy things happened [in the computer] . . . sea ice covered the tropical oceans, for example."

Another noted climate modeler—and spokesman for potential trouble—is James Hansen, director of NASA's Goddard Institute (GISS) in New York City. . . . During the scorching hot, dry summer of 1988 he captured international attention when he testified before a Senate subcommittee.

"The world is getting warmer," he said bluntly. "We can state with 99 percent confidence that current temperatures represent a real global warming trend, rather than a chance fluctuation. We will surely have more years like this—more droughts and many more days above a hundred degrees—in the 1990s."

He repeated these predictions in subsequent scientific meetings and climate symposiums—upsetting colleagues who felt he should hedge his concerns with more qualifications and maybes. But that is not Jim Hansen's way.

Some have heard and heeded what he and others have been saying. 40
Senator Albert Gore, Jr., of Tennessee, one of the most outspoken politicians calling for action in the face of world warming, has said bluntly: "The greenhouse effect is the most important environmental problem we have ever faced. [It threatens] loss of forests, widespread drought and famine, loss of wild species . . . topsoil, stratospheric ozone. . . . Do we have the capacity, the will, to change habits of millennia in a generation?"

Stephen H. Schneider of NCAR, an intense, curly-haired prophet of the future, has been deeply involved in climate research for more than 20 years. He writes, speaks, and travels incessantly; he is one of the worried scientists to whom policy-makers listen carefully.

"I agree with Jim Hansen and others that the world has gotten warmer over the past century—faster than ever since about 1975," he told me. "I'm not so quick to say it's entirely due to the greenhouse effect—though that's certainly there. Natural climate variations may be at work too, reinforcing—or at other times masking—the greenhouse forcing. In coming decades some years and some parts of the world may be cooler, but others will be much warmer than normal.

"The 1988 drought in North America, for example, has been linked by colleagues at NCAR with the El Niño phenomenon of the tropical Pacific Ocean. A shift in the jet stream, caused by massive ocean-atmosphere interactions in the Pacific, was the likely cause of that hot, extremely dry summer.

"But whatever the local and temporary weather changes, the world can't wait for proof of warming before trying to do something about it. We're engaged in a huge experiment, using our earth as the laboratory, and the experiment is irreversible. By the time we find the greenhouse warming *has* damaged earth's ability to feed its people, it will be too late to do much about it."

What would he have us do about it now? Try to slow the release of 45
greenhouse gases—by more rigorous energy conservation and changes in fuel use (natural gas releases half as much CO_2 as coal); by reducing the burning of rain forests, which increases the level of CO_2 in the air; and by planting many more trees, wherever possible.

"Keep in mind, it's not only carbon dioxide that's at fault," Steve Schneider points out. "Methane, which is released from decomposing tundra and marshes, rice fields, termites, and the guts of cattle, is increasing in the atmosphere faster than CO_2, at something like one percent a year. And molecule for molecule it has 20 to 30 times the greenhouse effect of CO_2. Nitrogen gases, from fertilizers as well as car exhausts and factory smokestacks, chlorofluorocarbons (CFCs) and other industrial products—all the other gases we're pouring into the air—are already doubling the warming potential of CO_2 alone.

"We can hope to reduce some of them, such as the CFCs that attack stratospheric ozone," he said. "But the others go with the industrial development of the world; all we can realistically hope is to slow their release, to gain time to cope with the results.

"If we can delay a 2°C increase of global temperature from 2025 to 2050, we will have more time to develop alternate energy sources: Nuclear—possibly fusion—is one option, despite its problems. But tapping the sun directly, by solar heat plants and converting sunlight directly into electricity, is both possible and coming down in cost."

I was to see his future in California, at the Rancho Seco nuclear plant outside Sacramento, flanked by 20 acres of solar panels slowly swinging with the sun across the sky; at a pioneering solar-cell factory near Los Angeles, where a breakthrough in "thin-film" technology was closing in on conventional electric power costs; and on a treeless mountain pass above Oakland, where a seemingly endless array of propellers taps the sun's energy from the winds sweeping in off the Pacific. . . .

Computer forecasting of climate is uncertain for reasons other than   *50* the sheer complexity of the equations. There are variables and feedbacks that even the best of the models barely approach.

The oceans are the chief reservoir of heat, controlling weather over the entire globe. As currents such as the Gulf Stream carry the heat from the tropics to high latitudes, cold water from the polar regions sinks and flows toward the Equator, overturning the seas about every thousand years.

"The tropical oceans are the driving mechanism of the climate," says climatologist Eric J. Barron of Pennsylvania State University. "The oceans are the memory of the climate system," adds Kirk Bryan of GFDL at Princeton. Yet until recently even the most advanced mathematical models treated the oceans only as vast, shallow swamps.

Carbon dioxide is absorbed by seawater, some of it incorporated into the shells of tiny marine creatures that die and become carbonate sediments on the bottom. Scientists estimate that a significant part of the seven billion metric tons of carbon released into the air each year is taken up in the seas. Oddly, the colder the water, the more CO_2 it can hold. As the oceans warm under the effect of more CO_2 in the atmosphere, there is great uncertainty about how much of that new CO_2 will be absorbed. Is there a limit to how much carbon can be locked away? Have the oceans already reached their holding capacity?

World-famed geochemist Wallace S. Broecker of Columbia University's Lamont-Doherty Geological Observatory worries that rapid switches in ocean circulation might occur under relatively small changes in global climate. Ice and seafloor core samples show that there have been sudden climate changes in the past, he says, from warming conditions to marked glaciation and back in as little time as a century. It could happen again.

As the seas and air warm, more water evaporates into the atmosphere,   *55* creating more clouds and another great enigma to the mathematical modelers. Much is yet unknown about the net effects of clouds on global weather.

"Clouds are the window shades of the planet," says Steve Schneider of NCAR. "They may be even more important than the oceans or the greenhouse gases in regulating the heat received from the sun."

In daylight low thick clouds reflect sunlight back into space and have a cooling effect. At night they hold in heat radiated from the surface and thus warm the atmosphere. High thin clouds, such as cirrus, may act differently, also adding to the greenhouse effect. Storm clouds transport and release vast amounts of heat.

The incredibly complicated interactions of the atmosphere, land, and oceans lead many scientists to doubt that local and regional weather patterns can ever be accurately predicted for more than a few days into the future. Listening to atmospheric physicists discuss the new mathematical science called chaos is a form of mental mugging; they speak of random walks, strange attractors, and climatic ripples such as the "butterfly effect"— the notion put forward by MIT meteorologist Edward Lorenz that the flap of a butterfly's wings in Peru could lead to a tornado in Kansas. Yet these are today's frontiers of understanding.

The limit of that understanding leads Eric Barron of Penn State to quote Mark Twain's famous droll remark: "The researches of many commentators have already thrown much darkness on this subject, and it is probable that, if they continue, we shall soon know nothing at all about it."

Feedbacks—the relationships between the natural forces that control climate—will be the crucial key, most modelers agree: clouds affecting surface temperatures; rainfall and droughts changing soil moisture, vegetation, and evaporation; snow and ice melting from ice caps and glaciers, changing the reflectivity of the planet and raising the level of the seas.

More volcanic eruptions, throwing fine dust and gases high into the stratosphere, might operate against the greenhouse, cooling the earth temporarily. But the best computer models suggest that to bring on marked cooling, volcanic explosions far more violent than those of Mount St. Helens in 1980 or Krakatoa in 1883 would have to occur every five years for as long as a century. The resulting dirty air and acid rain would be worse for life on earth than global warming.

If a return to ice-age conditions rather than greenhouse warming sounds farfetched, it was thought a serious possibility as recently as the mid-1970s. The nine major interglacial periods of the past million years have each lasted scarcely 10,000 years before the cold returned—and it has now been longer than that since the last great continental ice sheets melted back. And even though global temperature has been rising since the start of the industrial age, from 1940 until 1970 it leveled and even declined slightly in the Northern Hemisphere.

J. Murray Mitchell, Jr., senior climate researcher of the U.S. Weather Bureau and later of NOAA's Environmental Data Service, was one of those who documented that downward drift. Now retired, he told me recently: "We thought natural forces, such as volcanic activity or perhaps variation in the sun's radiance, might be at work. But we still don't know whether it was a real change or just a quarter-century-long twitch in the climate cycle."

Does the sun blaze absolutely uniformly, sending always the same amount of light, heat, and other radiation into space? Is its total radiance constant, as has long been assumed, or does the energy received by the earth vary, even minutely? The question is crucial in today's climate studies.

From astrophysical evidence the sun is thought to have been 25 to 30 percent dimmer when the earth was young—three and a half billion years ago. Pondering how life could have developed under this "faint young sun," earth scientists postulate that a super-greenhouse effect must have been at work, with 100 to 1,000 times as much CO_2 in the atmosphere. Otherwise the surface of the planet would have been frozen solid, and photosynthesis impossible. Yet it indeed occurred, absorbing much of the carbon dioxide and producing the oxygen in the atmosphere necessary for the evolution of life.

In the time of modern science the sun's radiation has seemed absolutely steady. Astronomers have tried for more than a century to detect any change in the "solar constant." It was only in the past decade that they succeeded.

The answer lay in taking solar instruments above the unsteady window of earth's atmosphere, into the black clarity of space. That goal was reached in February 1980 with the launch of the Solar Maximum Mission (SMM) satellite, dubbed Solar Max. It went into space to read solar output just as the number of sunspots—the dark areas on the sun's face that signal changes in its magnetic activity—had reached a peak in their 11-year cycle.

By 1985 Solar Max showed a real, though very slight, decline in the sun's brightness. The drop was only about one-tenth of one percent, but to solar physicists such as Richard Willson of the Jet Propulsion Laboratory, a principal scientist of the project, it was startling. If there is an actual fluctuation of the sun's output of even that small amount, it might have a long-term, measurable effect on global weather.

In 1986 the number of sunspots reached a minimum, as predicted. Shortly after, there began a rapid increase in sunspots—greater than in any previous solar cycle of this century. Scientists expected the upturn to continue until the next peak in 1990 or '91, but an unforeseen hazard put the Solar Max project in peril.

As the sun's activity increased, it warmed the outermost fringe of earth's atmosphere slightly, causing it to expand. The added drag began to slow the satellite, and it dropped in its orbit by a few kilometers. Instead of circling the planet at least until 1991, Solar Max began tumbling in August 1989, and by early December ended its life as a fireball of blazing metal in the sky.

"Even without the Solar Max readings—long before this century, in fact—we've known that changes occur in the sun," I heard from John A. Eddy of the Office for Interdisciplinary Earth Studies in Boulder. He is one of the world's leading solar historians.

"Chinese, Korean, and Japanese court astronomers recorded spots on the sun at least 2,000 years ago. Galileo saw them in his first telescope in 1610. The fact that the spots varied on a regular cycle wasn't recognized until 1843, by a German amateur astronomer, Heinrich Schwabe. Their number and position changed, and in some years there were more of them, in other years and decades, many fewer.

"We know today," Jack Eddy went on, "that the spots not only are real but also indicate massive changes going on in the sun. As the spots cross its face—moving with the rotating body—they affect the total energy the sun sends out into space."

As outward evidence of magnetic disturbances on the sun, the spots sometimes herald solar storms or flares, which can disrupt short-wave radio communications on earth or with satellites and cause destructive surges in high-voltage power networks. In March 1989 a massive solar flare disrupted the electric-power grid of much of eastern Canada and produced spectacular shimmering lights in the ionosphere. . . . The pulsating red, green, and white curtains called the aurora borealis, or northern lights, were seen as far south as Florida and Texas.

Do sunspots affect the planet's weather and climate? There have been times in past centuries when sunspots were very scarce—or missing entirely, if lack of any record of them can be believed. One notable period was between 1645 and 1715, the so-called Maunder Minimum, named for a British solar astronomer of the 19th century. The coincidence of their absence with the particularly cold period of the Little Ice Age, which gripped Europe from the 1400s to the 1800s, has long intrigued solar scientists. 75

Eddy and other astrophysicists point to the Maunder and a sequence of earlier minimums as the clearest evidence of long-term change in the sun's total activity, perhaps in cycles longer than the principal periods of 11 and 22 years, and of a possible connection between sunspots and the earth's climate.

The evidence remains circumstantial. "But there can be little doubt," Eddy has written, "that variability is a real feature of the sun. The challenge now is to understand it."

One clue to sunspots and their effects on the earth lies in an unlikely repository—the record of weather changes locked in the growth rings of trees. At the Laboratory of Tree-Ring Research of the University of Arizona at Tucson, director Malcolm Hughes and others showed me the 8,500-year consecutive tree-ring record acquired by that pioneering laboratory in decades of work in the U.S. Southwest. Periods of faster and slower growth in tree rings since the 17th century have been linked to wet periods and droughts—and possibly to the sunspot cycle.

"There is clear variability in much of this tree-ring record, in a pulse close to 20 years," Hughes said. "Scientists such as Murray Mitchell and my colleague Charles Stockton see this pulse as a combination of the sunspot cycle and a lunar cycle of 18.6 years and relate it to cyclical droughts in the West, such as the 1930s Dust Bowl.

80 "More than that, varying amounts of a carbon isotope in the tree rings—carbon 14—may be a clue to long-term changes in solar radiation and its effect on the earth's atmosphere," Hughes told me.

"The irregularities in the carbon-14 production rate are known as the Suess wiggles, for Hans E. Suess, their discoverer. They are extremely important in calibrating and correcting the carbon-14 calendar used to date ancient events from remnants of organic materials, such as ancient wood or bones."

Other theories of sunspot-climate relationships have come and gone, but no true "smoking gun" had been found—until the mid-1980s. Then a German atmospheric physicist, Karin Labitzke of the Free University of Berlin, together with Harry van Loon of NCAR in Boulder, published a remarkable fit between reversing winds in the stratosphere, polar air temperatures, and the sunspot cycle. If their discovery is confirmed, it will indicate a direct link between sunspots and the atmosphere of earth—a possibly crucial connection. The work has been cited as among the most significant now being pursued at NCAR.

One connection may be a better understanding of the ozone hole in the so-called polar vortex over Antarctica each winter, a giant whirlpool of stratospheric winds.

In the mid-1980s the world became suddenly aware that the protective ozone shield in the atmosphere was in danger—was, in fact, greatly depleted in a huge "hole" over the frozen wastes of Antarctica. The mysterious stuff called ozone, which until then was known to the public chiefly as an acrid, lung-burning element of smog in overcrowded cities, was being destroyed in the stratosphere by chemicals made and released in the 20th century by humans.

85 Ozone is a variant form of oxygen—the most life-sustaining gas of all. Under the intense ultraviolet bombardment from the sun at the upper reaches of the earth's atmosphere, normal two-atom molecules of oxygen are split into single atoms—O rather than O_2, in chemists' terms. Some of these single oxygen atoms rejoin with O_2 molecules to form ozone—O_3. The amount in the stratosphere is very scant, less than ten parts per million (at sea level the layer would be about as thick as a pane of window glass), but that layer is enough to stop most of the sun's dangerous ultraviolet rays from reaching the earth's surface, 10 to 30 miles below.

The possibility of ozone destruction by man-made chemicals had been predicted as early as 1974 by two farsighted researchers, F. Sherwood Rowland and Mario J. Molina, at the University of California at Irvine.

Certain industrial gases dubbed CFCs—chlorofluorocarbons—are so highly stable and inert that they do not react with other substances in nature. Thus they have long been used as the coolants in refrigerators and air conditioners, as the propellants in aerosol cans, in making foam-plastic objects such as coffee cups and fast-food containers, and as solvents for cleaning electronic circuit boards and computer chips. But there could be great danger, warned Rowland and Molina, when those same long-lived gases drift to the upper layers of the atmosphere.

In that same region where ozone is created by solar bombardment, the CFCs could break apart, they postulated, freeing chlorine atoms that could attack and destroy ozone molecules by the billions. If this were to deplete the ozone layer around the whole world, it would put all mankind at risk.

The hazard was judged serious enough for the United States to ban CFCs from aerosol cans in the late 1970s. But CFCs are still produced for other uses, and millions of tons more lie waiting to be freed from scrapped refrigerators and air conditioners.

Then came the first startling report by British scientists in 1985 of an Antarctic ozone hole, and a rash of scare stories blossomed in the world's press. Emergency field studies of the stratosphere above Antarctica were mounted by U.S. science agencies, led by NASA, NOAA, and the National Science Foundation. In 1987 an ER-2 aircraft, capable of flying to 70,000 feet in the stratosphere, and a DC-8 jammed with instruments flew from Punta Arenas, Chile, near the tip of South America, out across the ice-locked Antarctic continent.

90

The hole was real; the ozone had dropped by 50 percent. . . . Its destruction was confined within the rotating swirl of winds in the polar vortex. And it was caused by a chemical reaction, not some unfathomed atmospheric phenomenon. The reaction seemed to occur in the presence of thin polar ice clouds that form in the intense cold of late winter, just before the sun returns to strike the polar latitudes.

Less than a year later, in September 1987, more than 40 nations sent delegates to Montreal, Canada. The industrialized countries agreed to reduce production of CFCs by 50 percent by 1998. A June 1990 revision called for a 100 percent ban by the year 2000, with a ten-year time lag for less developed nations.

Does another ozone hole develop over the Arctic in its winter? If the Northern Hemisphere, far more populous than the Southern, is also being depleted of its ozone umbrella, it might pose a far more serious emergency.

The same team of atmospheric scientists and computer experts, including Robert Watson of NASA and Adrian Tuck and Susan Solomon of NOAA, spent 45 cold, bleak days in January and February 1989 in the

North Sea port of Stavanger, Norway. There the same ER-2 and DC-8 flew 28 missions, from the northernmost airstrip that could safely be used, to take readings from the air of the polar Arctic.

It took a year to analyze all the data. In March 1990 the scientists *95* published their answer. The polar vortex and ice clouds existed also in the northern stratosphere, though not to the same extent as in the southern. Ozone was being depleted in the Arctic as well, by as much as 15 to 17 percent at some altitudes.

Over the heavily populated mid-latitudes of the globe, the researchers believe, winter ozone levels may have dropped in the past decade by as much as 4 to 6 percent. And even if all CFC production worldwide were to be halted—an unlikely possibility even to the signers of the Montreal Protocol—the amount already existing and waiting to be released to the atmosphere would mean a continuing ozone drop for decades to come.

The worry is that stratospheric ozone forms the earth's principal shield against dangerous ultraviolet radiation from the sun. This short wavelength light, below the range of human visibility, kills many forms of life—bacteria, for example, which is why it is used for sterilizing surgical instruments and protecting many foods. But ultraviolet also kills beneficial forms of life, and it can affect the life cycle of many plants, both on land and in the seas.

Middle and long wavelengths of UV cause not just tanning and extreme sunburn in human skin but the most prevalent forms of skin cancer. They also can cause cataracts in the eyes and injure the immune responses of skin, which protect us from many harmful, even deadly diseases.

The Environmental Protection Agency issued a risk assessment in 1987, predicting that for every one percent drop in global ozone, there would be a one to three percent increase in skin cancers. Global ozone has dropped at least 2 percent in the past ten years, EPA said, leading to possibly four million added cases of skin cancer. In the past ten years alone, dangerous skin cancers have risen by 50 percent. Because of the long latency periods after exposure, doctors believe that case numbers will escalate even faster in coming decades.

As the public and bodies politic become ever more aware of these *100* issues and hazards to our home planet, the fundamental question remains: What can be done to safeguard our future?

Much is being proposed, both in this country and in international conferences and discussions among heads of state. Some scientists worry that not enough is yet known about the atmosphere and climate systems to justify spartan proposals of sacrifice and denial. Others counter that *something* must be done before it is too late.

One ambitious effort is the International Geosphere-Biosphere Programme (IGBP). In 1992 it will begin a 10-to-20-year study of the planet, a massive, coordinated follow-up to the historic International Geophysical Year of the mid-1950s.

In this country, planning has been taken on by the National Academy of Sciences and a federal committee whose members include NASA, NOAA, the Environmental Protection Agency, the Departments of Energy, Agriculture, and Defense, the National Science Foundation, and other agencies. Each has its own projects, such as NASA's Mission to Planet Earth, a proposed 15-to-20-billion-dollar program to study the planet from space platforms to be launched beginning in 1998. The President's budget for fiscal 1991 includes an additional billion dollars for pursuing such research efforts.

NASA's chief scientist for global change, Ichtiaque Rasool, in mid-1989 cited to me some of the basic hard facts on which the world's climatologists largely agree:

- The trace gases in the atmosphere—carbon dioxide, methane, nitrous oxide, CFCs—are rising rapidly. They are already at the highest levels of the past 160,000 years.

- These gases incontrovertibly alter the earth's radiation balance through the greenhouse effect.

- Average global temperature has risen about one degree Fahrenheit in the past century, though not steadily.

But will this unusual warmth continue? Or will cooler-than-normal seasons or years return? And what is "normal"? *105*

It is the central uncertainty about natural versus man-made forces in the climate system that causes scientists and politicians alike to hedge their concerns. It is tempting to ask: If nature will correct what we do to the atmosphere, must we give up our profligate ways?

As evidence mounts, the answer seems increasingly clear: We are the wild card in nature, in our ever increasing numbers. "Humankind has become a more important agent of environmental change than nature," Frank Press, president of the U.S. National Academy of Sciences, said bluntly at an international meeting of the Group of Seven industrial nations in Paris in mid-1989.

And what we are doing to the earth's atmosphere, to the blue planet on which we live, is not merely ominous. It may already be beyond correction.

Reading and Responding

1. Copy the facts and statistics from this essay that seem most important to you. Review your list. Circle the most important item, the one that explains the most or bothers you the most.
2. Freewrite your initial reactions to this essay.

Working Together

1. Share, as a class, the statistics, numbers, and facts that seemed central to this essay. Does one item or fact stand out to everyone? Do numerous items stand out? Are those items related, one set contained in another?
2. Translate the statistics into words; that is, summarize, in your own words, the main point of this essay.
3. Describe how you felt after reading all of these statistics.

Rethinking and Rewriting

1. Summarize Matthews's piece in no more than six hundred words. Draw on the guidelines from the first chapter to help you do this.
2. Explain why you view this essay as primarily an effort at an objective report. *Or* argue that this is really a persuasive article aimed at convincing readers of something or urging them toward some action. *Or* explain why the line between objectivity and persuasion is blurred in this essay.
3. Update Matthews's discussion of global warming with your own research. Add about seven hundred fifty words to the essay. Start your first paragraph with the phrase, "Since the publication of 'Under the Sun,' . . ." Cite at least three sources.

ANIMALS

Sandra Steingraber

In the following chapter from her book Living Downstream: A Scientist's Personal Investigation of Cancer and the Environment *(1998), biologist and poet Sandra Steingraber writes as a cancer survivor and a concerned scientist about a disturbing pair of facts: the high incidence of cancer and of environmental toxins in the part of rural Illinois where she grew up.*

Bathed in a brilliant yellow-green light, they look like bats floating in a perfectly round pond. I have seen many micrographs of cancerous tissue—reproduced neatly in atlases of human tumor cell lines or on the shiny pages of medical journals—but never before have I stared at living cancer cells. Alive, they look to me like bats.

"Now compare that one to this one."

The first petri dish is removed and replaced by another, and I look again through the microscope. In this second watery landscape, they look more like fallen leaves—some drift together in large masses, others in smaller clusters.

"Okay, here's dish number three."

Now they are everywhere. A mosaic of islands and jutting peninsulas. 5 Pieces of a crazy quilt tossed into a lake. A raft of vines tangled with shards of crockery. There is no one way to describe them. Collectively or alone, cancer cells are more chaotically arranged than the shy, scurrying animals from which the disease—as well as the zodiac constellation—derives its name. Cancer, carcinogen, carcinoma, from the Greek *karkinos,* "the crab."

The three petri dishes I have been asked to compare contain estrogen-sensitive breast cancer cells derived from a human cell line called MCF-7. The first dish is the control. Its culture medium, the broth that nourishes the growing cells, contains no estrogen. The third dish is a control of the opposite sort. Its medium was innoculated with the most potent known form of human estrogen, which is called estradiol. It's also the dish with the most luxuriant growth. By definition, estrogen-sensitive breast tumors grow faster in the presence of estrogen, and MCF-7 cells are well-known exemplifiers of this principle.

It is the second dish, the one with the intermediate growth rate, that reveals the significant finding. Its culture medium has been laced with trace amounts of endosulfan, an organochlorine pesticide. These three dishes are part of a series of experiments showing that endosulfan—introduced in 1954 and now widely used on salad crops—is estrogenic. Like the hormone it mimics, endosulfan stimulates breast cancer cells to divide and multiply.

In this ability, endosulfan is much less effective than a woman's own estradiol. However, studies similar to this one have shown that endosulfan can act in concert with other xenoestrogens, that is, chemicals foreign to the body that, directly or indirectly, act like estrogens. For example, when ten different synthetic chemicals, all estrogen mimics, are added to the culture medium at one-tenth the minimal dose required for proliferation of MCF-7 cells, proliferation ensues. Like raindrops eroding a boulder, quantities of weakly estrogenic chemicals too small to exert observable effects on their own have a significant impact when combined. Furthermore, some xenoestrogens may have the ability to interact with naturally occurring estrogens and amplify their effect. If confirmed, such results imply that "safe" levels of exposure to individual estrogen-mimicking chemicals may not exist. (The actual cellular pathways followed by xenoestrogens are described in Chapter Eleven.)

The discovery that xenoestrogens can work additively was made by the cell biologists Ana Soto and Carlos Sonnenschein, whose laboratory in downtown Boston I am visiting. Since their 1991 discovery that nonylphenol stimulates the growth of MCF-7 cells, they have continued to probe the phenomenon of estrogen mimicry and its implications for breast cancer. In addition to plastic additives, Soto and Sonnenschein have identified estrogenic activity in a variety of pesticides. Some, like endosulfan, are still in use. Others, such as dieldrin and toxaphene, are now banned.

That toxaphene—fat soluble and stubbornly persistent—should prove estrogenic is particularly frightening. Identified as an animal carcinogen in 1979 and banned in 1982, toxaphene was not so long ago the most heavily used insecticide in the United States. It was the chemical weapon of choice against boll weevils in cotton fields, where it was used in extraordinary quantities. In 1950, northern Alabama cotton fields received an average of sixty-three pounds per acre. Rachel Carson herself denounced toxaphene as an indiscriminate killer of fish, and in *Silent Spring* she described in detail the die-offs of crappies, bass, and sunfish in southern streams and farm ponds. Ironically, it rose to even greater popularity after pesticides like DDT fell into disfavor.

Toxaphene's continuing effects on wildlife are what led Soto and Sonnenschein to become concerned about its possible relationship to breast cancer. When field researchers linked toxaphene to reproductive damage in seals and documented its ongoing accumulation in the muscle fat of Arctic and Baltic salmon, these two laboratory researchers decided to test its effects on breast cancer cells. Not only does toxaphene cause MCF-7 cells to proliferate, the pair discovered, but it does so at levels well within the range of concentrations now found in the flesh of some salmon.

Soto and Sonnenschein's work thus depends on a collaboration between cell biology, which peers through magnifying lenses at the smallest units of life, and wildlife biology, which monitors the world's animals. In this way, changes in the growth rate of breast cancer cells in a Boston laboratory help elucidate the reasons for reproductive failures among sea mammals living thousands of miles away—and vice versa. The evidence

10

from animals, in turn, provides reasons for rising cancer rates among humans, as well as our routes of exposure to cancer-promoting agents.

But let's go back for a moment to the microscope and look once more at the cells named MCF-7. Whose breasts did they come from, and what was her fate?

Finding answers to such questions isn't easy. Medical researchers maintain a comfortable distance between themselves and the cancer patients who provide the human tissues used in their experiments. The results of research involving MCF-7 cells are reported in numerous published articles. Even as the cells' various properties are described in depth, these papers mention almost nothing about their human origins.

Here is what I do know. All successfully established cancer cell lines, [15] including MCF-7, are immortal, meaning that they will reproduce endlessly in covered dishes so long as they are provided with the proper nutrients. Under such conditions, most human cells—even most cancer cells—tend to die out after a finite number of cell divisions. No one knows why some cancer cells can attain immortality while others cannot. Because they can be shipped all over the world, immortal cell lines allow many laboratories to conduct research on cells from the same tumor over long periods of time. Immortal cells are to cancer researchers what sourdough starter is to bread bakers.

BT-20, VHB-1, MDA-MB-241, CAL-18B, T47D: these are the names of other famous breast cancer cell lines. MCF-7 is among the oldest and is also considered the most reliable—the coin of the realm, according to one researcher. Its name reveals a few interesting clues. *MCF* stands for Michigan Cancer Foundation, the Detroit institution that makes this cell line available to laboratories around the world. The trailing seven refers to the number of attempts that were required to establish a self-perpetuating stock of cells from the body of the particular woman patient who consented to this effort. Immortality was finally achieved on the seventh try.

"Does this mean cancerous cells were withdrawn multiple times?" I ask into the phone, trying to imagine the procedure, wondering if it was painful, wondering how many attempts she was willing to submit to.

"Yes, that's right," says Joe Michaels of the Michigan Cancer Foundation.

I learn that her birth name was Frances Mallon. At the time of her diagnosis, she was a nun—Sister Catherine Frances—at the Immaculate Heart of Mary Convent in Monroe, Michigan, a small town midway between Detroit and Toledo on the west bank of Lake Erie. Strangely enough, I have been there. The Immaculate Heart of Mary, which has a long history of involvement with social issues, was the setting for a conference I attended in 1992 concerning organochlorine contamination of the Great Lakes. So, not only have I looked at the cells of her breasts, but I have walked through the corridors of her home and eaten in her dining room.

Sister Catherine Frances died of her disease in 1970. An old news-   *20*
paper clipping reports that "she was a slightly built woman of medium
height, with auburn hair, gray eyes and hands that were remarkable for
their delicate beauty." Before entering Immaculate Heart in 1945, she had
worked for twenty-five years as a stenographer at the Mueller Brass Company in Port Huron. Both her mother and sister had died of cancer before
her. Her father had died of tuberculosis. The cancer cells that ultimately
begat the MCF-7 line were extracted from fluid trapped in her chest cavity.
This is all I know.

In 1995, at a national breast cancer meeting, I am introduced to a
well-known researcher whose work I admire. Over dinner we discuss his
current experiments, and I ask which cell line he uses.
    "MCF-7. It's a very well described line."
    "Did you know that she was a nun?"
    There is a long pause. I watch him grope toward this unexpected bit
of information. He blinks several times and takes a few swallows from his
glass of ice water.
    "Then, MCF is her name, her initials?" His voice is low and gentle.   *25*
    "Actually, no . . . ."

Now, as I'm writing, I propose a rechristening of MCF-7. Let them
be called IBFM-7: the Immortal Breasts of Frances Mallon, attempt number seven. Let them be known as a sacrament: *This is my body, which is
broken for you. This do in remembrance of me.*

In science, an assay is an evaluation of a biological or chemical substance. Estrogens, for example, are defined as substances that stimulate
proliferation of uterine and vaginal cells. Thus, the traditional assay for
estrogenicity involves injecting the substance to be evaluated into female
rats or mice, letting a period of time go by, killing the animals, and then
noting whether or not their genital tracts have gained weight, in comparison to the tracts of a control group.
    These assays are complex, messy, and expensive. For these and other
reasons, screening of environmental chemicals for possible hormone-
mimicking effects is not routinely done. The question is whether human
breast cancer cells growing in petri dishes can serve as an alternative to
rodents for an assay. So far, concordance between animal assays and breast
cancer cell line assays has been high. The pesticide endosulfan, for example, not only makes breast cancer cells proliferate but also lowers testoster-
one levels in male rats and causes their testicles to shrivel. Together, these
results tell a consistent story.
    In the attempt to identify environmental carcinogens, human studies   *30*
and animal assays remain the standard yardstick. The strongest evidence for
associations between particular chemicals and particular cancers comes
from epidemiology, but accurate information about exposure is often hard

to come by in these studies. Animal assays have a few distinct advantages over epidemiological studies. Most important, confounding factors can be controlled more easily. Laboratory rats do not smoke cigarettes or move out of state or change jobs. They can be made to have identical diets, exercise habits, and reproductive practices. Their exposures to the substance in question can also be made identical. Also, rodents have much shorter life spans. Cohorts of rats and mice can readily be followed from birth to death. In human studies, twenty to thirty years are often required between exposure and onset of cancer. Furthermore, animal assays can be conducted before a substance is marketed. Epidemiological studies, in contrast, are initiated only after evidence for harm has accumulated. Epidemiology relies on body counts.

For these reasons, evidence for carcinogenicity in laboratory animals often precedes evidence from human studies. About one-third of the agents now classified as human carcinogens were first discovered in animals. Obviously, if animal assays worked perfectly—and if human exposures to known animal carcinogens were adequately prevented—this proportion would be much higher. No human being would have to die to prove that certain chemicals cause cancer.

The history of carcinogenicity testing in animals is intimately linked to the history of organized labor. In 1918, two Japanese scientists reported that coal tar, suspected of causing cancer in workers, induced skin tumors when applied to rabbits' ears. By the 1930s, researchers working with mice were able to determine which specific chemicals within coal tar—a mixture of many ingredients—were to blame.

In 1938, in a series of now-classic experiments, exposure to synthetic dyes derived from coal and belonging to a class of chemicals called aromatic amines were shown to cause bladder cancer in dogs. These results helped explain why bladder cancers had become so prevalent among dyestuffs workers. With the invention of mauve in 1854, synthetic dyes began replacing natural plant-based dyes in the coloring of cloth and leather. By the beginning of the twentieth century, bladder cancer rates among this group of workers had skyrocketed, and the dog experiments helped unravel this mystery. The International Labor Organization did not wait for the results of these animal tests, however, and in 1921 declared certain aromatic amines to be human carcinogens. Decades later, these dogs provided a lead in understanding why tire-industry workers, as well as machinists and metal workers, also began falling victim to bladder cancer: aromatic amines had been added to rubbers and cutting oils to serve as accelerants and antirust agents.

The researcher who carried out the original dog-dye studies was none other than Wilhelm Hueper, whose work formed the basis of Rachel Carson's chapter on cancer in *Silent Spring*. All of Hueper's papers—including his typewritten autobiography—are housed in the chambers of the National Library of Medicine in Bethesda, Maryland. I once spent a bright spring day poring through them. Now that animal testing has become associated with cruelty, reading about the various attempts to squelch the results of his work is a lesson in shifting cultural perceptions. While employed as an industry scientist, Hueper endured stonewalling, harassment, threats of lawsuits, defunding, firing, and gag orders. Whatever we may now think about the ethics of exposing dogs to carcinogens, animal studies such as these were highly threatening to industries whose manufacturing processes had become dependent on certain chemicals and who feared disclosure of trade secrets.

Routine screening of chemicals for carcinogenicity in laboratory animals began in earnest in the early 1970s. As of 1993, the International Agency for Research on Cancer (IARC) had assayed about a thousand chemicals—a small fraction of the total number used in commerce—and had identified 110 definite or very probable human carcinogens. IARC is quite clear on the relevance of animal experiments for human cancers: "In the absence of adequate data on humans, it is biologically plausible and prudent to regard agents and mixtures for which there is sufficient evidence of carcinogenicity in experimental animals as if they present a carcinogenic risk to humans."

Here in the United States, the Environmental Protection Agency (EPA) combines animal evidence with the results of epidemiological studies in order to classify substances into one of five categories. These evaluations generally match those of IARC. Group A includes the *known* human carcinogens. To be so ranked, evidence from epidemiological studies alone must be strong enough to make the case. Group B are the *probable* human carcinogens. Members of this group include chemicals for which there is sufficient evidence from animal studies to regard it as a human carcinogen as well as limited evidence from human studies. A Group B ranking often means the needed human studies have never been conducted. Group C, the *possible* human carcinogens, are all those chemicals for which some evidence exists for carcinogenicity from animal studies. Group D includes chemicals not classifiable because there are simply no data on which to base a decision. Group E are noncarcinogens, chemicals that show no indication of causing cancer in any species.

Known. Probable. Possible. The fact that numerous chemicals with long-standing membership in Groups A through C are still allowed to be manufactured, sold, released, dumped, imported, exported, or otherwise used comes as a surprise to many knowledgeable people. I include myself here. It is comfortable to assume such substances are automatically expelled from human society as soon as their cancer-causing potential is demonstrated. This is not the case, but the ethical implications of any other alternative seem too much to bear.

As an antidote to innocence, I recommend a document produced every two years by the National Toxicology Program of the U.S. Department of Health and Human Services: the *Biennial Report on Carcinogens* (formerly the *Annual Report on Carcinogens*). The report exists because the National Toxicology Program is charged by law with publishing "a list of all substances (i) which either are known to be carcinogens or may reasonably be anticipated to be carcinogens; and (ii) to which a significant number of persons residing in the United States are exposed." The edition that stands next to the Toxics Release Inventory on my bookshelf is 473 pages long and features nearly 200 entries.

Some of these listings describe chemicals with large production volumes, such as benzene. When lead was outlawed as an antiknock additive in gasoline, benzene replaced it. We are therefore exposed to benzene every time we fill our cars with gasoline. Benzene is classified as a known human carcinogen.

Other listings in the National Toxicology Program's carcinogen report describe old chemical chestnuts no longer manufactured but still present, such as the PCBs. About one-third of the world's total production of PCBs is believed to have escaped into the general environment. Like thousands of tiny bombs exploding in slow motion, pieces of discarded equipment containing the oily fluid—electrical transformers, television sets, old french friers—leak their contents drop by drop into soil and water. From here, PCB molecules rise into the atmosphere, circulate with the wind, and are redeposited all over the globe. They then enter the food chain. The fatty tissues of nearly all Americans are believed to contain PCB molecules. We have accumulated most of them by eating food derived from animals: eggs, meat, milk, fish, and shellfish. In rodent assays, PCBs cause liver cancer, pituitary tumors, leukemia, lymphoma, and intestinal cancers. Manufactured from 1929 until 1977, PCBs are classified as a probable human carcinogen, as noted earlier. As more PCBs escape from obsolete equipment, human exposure is expected to continue. [40]

As the report clearly explains, carcinogens are regulated differently than noncarcinogens, and special rules intended to monitor their each and every move through human society exist. The appearance of a chemical on the government's official roster of carcinogens is only the first step toward a program of intense surveillance and assessment. Nevertheless, the very existence of this list means that trading in cancer-causing chemicals is still a perfectly legal activity.

We all know this, of course. We may even read the signs on the gas pumps that warn against inhaling the shimmery vapors that rise from the end of the nozzle. But we also all know that enforcement of any rule is imperfect, that accidents happen even when rules are followed, and that many chemicals were released into our environment before these regulations went into effect. In 1995, for example, the reopening of some public schools in Cape Cod, Massachusetts, was postponed after high levels of the banned pesticide dieldrin were found in the soil surrounding one of the grade schools. While attempting to establish the extent of this problem, investigators discovered this school was also contaminated with PCBs at levels two thousand times greater than acceptable under state regulations.

Four of the district's schools are located on the Massachusetts Military Reservation, a heavily regulated place.

Perhaps most amazing is the fact that aromatic amines—the first officially designated group of workplace carcinogens—are still among us. Benzidine dyes, for example, remained in commerce for nearly forty years after Hueper's dog studies. From a 1980 review of benzidine-based dyes conducted by the National Institute for Occupational Safety and Health:

> Benzidene-based dyes are chiefly used in the leather, textile and paper industries, but they are also used by beauticians, craft workers, and the general public. The common starting material for the manufacture of these dyes, benzidine, is acknowledged by both industry and government to cause bladder cancer. This is based on considerable evidence from studies with humans as well as with animals. . . . Both brief and prolonged exposures to benzidene have been associated with the development of bladder cancer in workers.

From a 1994 report:

> Benzidine is no longer manufactured for commercial sale in the United States. All benzidine production is for captive consumption and it must be maintained in closed systems under stringent workplace controls. . . . Prior to 1977, U.S. production of benzidine amounted to many millions of pounds per year.

From a 1996 report:

> Some benzidine-based dyes (or products dyed with them) may still be imported. Benzidine has been found in waste sites and becomes part of the bottom sediment in water. It exists in the air as very small particles, which may be brought back to the earth's surface by rain or gravity.

Perhaps it's the very matter-of-fact tone of these reports that contributes to the sense of unreality. Perhaps it is the absence of words like *pain, surgery, chemotherapy, support group, recurrence, hospice care, palliative treatment,* and all the other terms that those with cancer and those who love them learn to speak. When I read these reports, I see a urologist's waiting room full of patients and a pencil-thick, telescopic tube called a cystoscope lying on its stainless steel tray in the examination room that awaits each of them. I remember the cystoscope sliding up my urethra during an inspection for bladder tumors. And I remember the nervous, red-haired woman whose cystoscopic checkup was scheduled before mine. When I walked out of outpatient surgery, she was sobbing into the pay phone. I never found out what happened to her.

Typically, about eight hundred animals are required for a carcinogenicity assay. The first step is to assign animals of two different species— 45 usually rats and mice—and both sexes to one of four groups. Groups one through three represent high-, medium-, and low-dose exposures to whatever substance is being tested. The fourth serves as the unexposed control. Each group thus contains approximately fifty animals of each sex and species. Next, the test substance is administered by inhalation, ingestion, or skin application on a regular basis throughout the animals' life spans. At the end of the experiment, researchers compare tumor patterns in exposed and unexposed animals and determine whether differences exist among the four groups.

Using animal assays to ascertain potential human carcinogens requires two leaps of faith. One is the supposition that what causes cancer in one species will cause cancer in another. This is called transpecies extrapolation, and there is good evidence that we are on firm footing when we make this leap. Almost all substances discovered to cause cancer in humans also cause cancer in at least one species of laboratory animal. And they very often cause cancer in the same organ or tissue. The inference we make is that the reverse is also true. Significantly, five of the top ten sites for chemically induced tumor formation in laboratory rodents correspond to five of the top ten sites of cancer in the U.S. human population: lung, breast, bladder, uterus, and the blood-producing cells of the bone marrow.

Consider once again the female breast, that gland that defines all mammals. While rodent breasts and human breasts would seem to have little in common—after all, mice have ten of them and we have only two—the similarities in development and anatomy are remarkable. Early in life, both female rodents and female humans possess immature breast tissue that consists of a bundle of slender tubes. These structures—the mammary ducts—open into the nipple, which is essentially a sieve. At the other end, giving each duct the shape of a canoe paddle, are the terminal buds. Under the direction of female hormones, the ducts begin to branch. Meanwhile, the paddle-shaped buds metamorphose into clusters of lobules designed to produce milk. A cushion of fat surrounds both the ducts and their lobules, and the whole apparatus comes to resemble an orchard of fruiting trees. This process unfolds in all female mammals according to the same basic blueprint.

When women get breast cancer, the tumors most often form in the interior lining of the ducts. This is also where breast cancer in rodents is usually located. Nevertheless, some differences between species do exist. In most strains of mice, breast cancer is largely estrogen independent, while in most rats, it is estrogen dependent. Human females are vulnerable to both kinds. These sorts of variations are the reason for using more than one species in cancer assays.

Agreement between species is high—75 percent of chemicals that cause cancer in rats also do so in mice—but it is not absolute. Moreover, some anatomical differences between species do create obvious complications. Mouth breathing, for example, is impossible for a mouse. All rodents must breathe through their noses. Humans, on the other hand, often inhale through their mouths, especially when in the presence of a bad smell. Animal assays that rely on exposure to airborne contaminants become tricky. Rodents will filter the chemical through a highly developed defense system—and possibly place their sinuses and pharynx at greater risk for cancer—while humans may inspire the same chemical directly into their lungs, sparing their sinuses but possibly raising the exposure level of other tissues.

The overall concept of using one species to predict cancer in another   50
is, nonetheless, receiving renewed support from molecular biology. This field of study focuses on the intricate mechanical workings inside the body's cells. The basic truism emerging from this line of inquiry is that nature does not often reinvent the wheel. Life is conservative. Certain essential processes—such as the regulation of cell division or the extraction of energy from a molecule of glucose through its stepwise disassembly— are held in common by all members of the animal kingdom, including humans. These activities are accomplished by nearly identical enzyme systems and are governed by nearly identical genes. Because chemical carcinogens very often strike directly at these minute structures and interfere with processes basic to all life, they tend to inflict the same kind of cellular sabotage across species lines. Animals and people exposed to the same environmental contaminant frequently possess identical genetic mutations. Evidently, what is bad for the goose is bad for the gander—and for the rat, the mouse, the fish, and the bank accountant.

The second leap of faith is the assumption that the animal assays are relevant to human cancers because the results of laboratory studies conducted with high exposures to potential carcinogens can be extrapolated to human situations involving low exposures. The rationale for this extrapolating is simple. High doses must be used in the laboratory because the number of animals exposed is small compared to the human population at risk. A substance with the power to cause cancer at low doses in 1 percent of the American population, for example, could potentially kill more than two million people if all of us were so exposed. One percent of fifty rats, however, is less than one individual. Therefore, exposures are raised in excess of that to which humans are subjected in order to raise the chances of detecting any possible problems.

Animal assays are a yes-or-no instrument designed simply to pinpoint potential human carcinogens. They are not intended to provide quantitative information on responses to a wide range of doses. Too often, the necessary follow-up studies that would elucidate this relationship are never conducted. Overwhelming the protocol are the tens of thousands of chemicals in commercial use still in need of basic testing.

Without these tests, we can only guess at the number of chemical carcinogens in our midst. As of 1995, the National Toxicology Program had completed animal assays on 400-odd chemicals. Based on these results, researchers have estimated that of the 75,000 chemicals now in commercial use, somewhat fewer than 5 to 10 percent of these might reasonably be considered carcinogenic in humans. Five to 10 percent means 3,750 to 7,500 different chemicals. The number of substances we have identified and regulate as carcinogens is, at present, less than 200.

In the summer between my sophomore and junior years in college, I was diagnosed with bladder cancer of a type called transitional cell carcinoma. It is something I have in common with Hueper's dogs, as well as with at least one beluga whale in the St. Lawrence River.

Proceeding northeast from Lake Ontario, the St. Lawrence River   55
slants through the Canadian province of Quebec and flares open like a trumpet as it pours itself into the North Atlantic. Nova Scotia stands to the south, Newfoundland to the north. Where the river's current meets the ocean's tide, in the neck of the Gulf of St. Lawrence, is one of the world's deepest, longest estuaries. About five hundred beluga whales, a remnant of the thousands that once lived here, inhabit this transition zone. This estuary also receives tributarial waters that have traversed some of the most industrialized landscapes of southern Canada and the northeastern United States.
Belugas are small, toothed whales. Their skin is pure white.
Transitional cell carcinoma among the belugas was first discovered during an autopsy of a carcass that had washed ashore in 1985. It was a particularly provocative finding because workers in nearby aluminum smelters, which release their wastes into the St. Lawrence, had also been found to have an elevated incidence of this type of bladder cancer.

Gross hematuria, or noticeable blood in the urine, is the usual way bladder cancer presents itself. I do not know how a whale would experience this—perhaps through sense of smell. As for myself, gross hematuria arrived as I was finishing up a morning shift at a truck-stop diner. After making my final rounds with the ketchup bottles and syrup dispensers, I stopped in the restroom. Turning to flush, I froze. My urine looked like cherry Kool-Aid. I stood there a long time.
And then I remembered the beets—sliced red beets, which the cook had prepared for the lunch special and which I had eaten in great quantity during my break. Could beets make urine turn pink? Asparagus was certainly famous for its ability to transmit pungent odors to urine. What other explanation could there be? I felt fine.
I swore off beets. Three weeks later, I returned home from a night   60
shift at a pancake house, tore off my waitress uniform, went to the bathroom, turned to flush, and . . . the toilet was full of blood. Brilliant and thick. I drove to the emergency room.

I was wrong about the beets.

Bladder cancer is one of several cancers striking the beluga population of the St. Lawrence. In 1988, a team of veterinarians found tumors in the bodies of four dead whales from a group of thirteen that had washed up over a period of ten months along a polluted stretch of the river. In addition, the immature breast ducts of one young female showed abnormal proliferation. Called ductal hyperplasia, this condition is considered a strong risk factor for breast cancer in women. (Whales are mammals and so have breasts; in belugas, they are located on either side of the vagina, with only the nipples visible and the mammary glands themselves hidden beneath a layer of blubber.)

Autopsy reports on twenty-four other stranded carcasses were published in 1994. Twenty-one tumors were found in twelve carcasses. Among these tumors, six were malignant. The researchers concluded, "Such a high prevalence of tumors would suggest an influence of contaminants through a direct carcinogenic effect and/or a decreased resistance to the development of tumors." Both possible mechanisms are currently receiving close attention.

To date, cancers identified in the beluga include bladder, stomach, intestinal, salivary gland, breast, and ovarian. The prevalence of intestinal cancer is especially high. Of seventy-three stranded whales autopsied since 1983, fifteen had cancerous tumors somewhere in their bodies, and one-third of these were intestinal tumors. No cases of cancer have been reported in belugas inhabiting the less contaminated Arctic Ocean.

The beluga whales of the St. Lawrence estuary have more wrong   65
with them than cancer. They also have trouble reproducing. Even though belugas have been protected from hunting since the 1970s, their numbers have failed to rebound. When chemical analyses of their blubber were conducted to illuminate possible causes of both problems, PCBs, DDT, chlordane, and toxaphene—at some of the highest levels ever recorded in a living organism—were all found dissolved in the whales' fat. All four chemicals are endocrine disrupters, as well as probable carcinogens. All were banned decades ago. All are chemically very persistent.

Unlike PCBs and DDT, chlordane and toxaphene do not have a history of use in the St. Lawrence basin. And yet these two chemicals are found in the waters and sediments of the estuary, presumably because they are carried into the seaway by winds blowing up from the southern United States, where both were once used heavily. The St. Lawrence basin drains a 500,000-square-mile area; any contaminant that rains down within its vast perimeter is, sooner or later, flushed into the estuary.

There is another route of exposure. Beluga whales love to eat eels, which run through the icy, deep Lawrentian channel on their autumn migration from Lake Ontario to the warm waters of the Sargasso Sea. The eels may explain why the belugas are contaminated with Mirex, an organochlorine pesticide, now banned, that was once used against fire ants. There is no Mirex in the water of the lower St. Lawrence nor in its sediments and hardly any in the bodies of other marine mammals living in the estuary. But there is Mirex in the flesh of St. Lawrence eels. And there are two sources of Mirex in the Lake Ontario basin where the eels originate: a pesticide-manufacturing plant near Niagara and a river called the Oswego, where Mirex was once accidentally spilled. The eels are the apparent courier between these contaminated sites and the beluga whales living six hundred miles away.

Eels are very strange. Like salmon, they migrate thousands of miles to spawn, crossing between fresh and salt water to do so. However, eels make their journey in reverse: they spend twelve to twenty-four years living in lakes and rivers, and then they head out to the ocean to lay their eggs. Baby eels, each the size and shape of a willow leaf, spend their first year of life trying to swim back.

Less is known about what toxins eels might bring back from their birthplace, which is also a contaminated site. Elliptical and still, the Sargasso Sea lies within the clockwise current of the Gulf Stream. The islands of Bermuda rise from its center. Eels from freshwater rivers in North America, Europe, and Africa all converge here to spawn. The Sargasso sits at the center of a whirling gyre of currents, and so accumulates seaweed and debris from all over the Atlantic—but especially from the U.S. and Caribbean coasts. Along with the ocean's other detritus, chemical pollutants—such as DDT and balls of tar—also slowly drift in and accumulate here to join what the poet Ezra Pound once called "this sea-hoard of deciduous things."

I tried to be kind to my hospital roommate. No one else was. We were both recovering from surgery, but her situation was more typical of what happened to girls in Pekin: A fast car. Drunk boys. She was the only one pulled out alive, and the story had made the front page. When the nurses refused to tell her what had happened, I read aloud to her from the newspaper account. Mostly, she slept and watched TV. I spent a lot of time staring at her.

Outside this room, our lives were on two different tracks—in my view, at least—and I was trying to figure out how I had ended up here with her. I was the clean-living winner of the local Elks Club scholarship who viewed drink, drugs, TV, and junk food as tickets to nowhere, who was only back in this town for the summer, and now college had resumed and I was still here. Some malevolent current had deposited us together in this hospital. But unlike my partner in the next bed, no one had any explanations for my situation. The newspaper said she was expected to survive. Was I?

I examined the outline of my legs under the thin blanket, the shadow my hand cast on the sheet. Between the sheet and the blanket snaked the wretched catheter tube. I felt flattened down, like an animal wounded by something cruel and meaningless. My roommate looked over at me and touched her hands to her discolored face. Her boyfriend and brother were both dead.

70

"I think I'm going to stop partying for a while."

It was the kind of moment where laughing and crying were synonymous. What happened to her was pathetic. What was happening to me was pathetic. We started laughing.

"I think I'm going to start."   75

The belugas have local problems as well as global ones. Aluminum smelters and other industries lining the river basin have contaminated their waters with benzo[a]pyrene, a potent and well-known carcinogen.

Benzo[a]pyrene is seldom manufactured on purpose. With molecules consisting of twenty carbon atoms arranged as two hexagonal rings nestled on top of three hexagonal rings, it is created during the combustion of all kinds of organic materials from wood to gasoline to tobacco. It also occurs in coal tar, which is distilled to make a couple of familiar products. One of these is creosote, used to preserve wood (think of the smell of telephone poles on a hot summer day), and another is pitch, used in roofing and in aluminum smelting. Coal tar itself is classified as a known carcinogen, but because humans are almost always exposed to its constituent ingredients in mixtures, the data from human studies are inadequate to so classify benzo[a]pyrene individually. Animal assays, however, are unequivocal. Benzo[a]pyrene is thus listed as a probable carcinogen.

Benzo[a]pyrene causes cancer in a simple, direct way. Nearly all living things have in common a group of cellular enzymes responsible for detoxifying and metabolizing possibly harmful chemical invaders. When this enzyme group encounters benzo[a]pyrene, it inserts oxygen into the foreign molecule, the first step toward breaking it down. However, in a strange twist of fate, this addition *activates* benzo[a]pyrene rather than detoxifies it. The altered molecule now has the ability to bond tightly to a strand of DNA—that is, to one of the cell's chromosomes along which lie the organism's genes. A chemical invader so attached is called a DNA adduct, and it has the power to alter the structure of the DNA strand and produce a genetic mutation. If uncorrected, this type of damage can become a crucial step leading to the formation of cancer.

The number of adducts attached to an organism's DNA is considered a useful measure of benzo[a]pyrene exposure. DNA from the brain tissue of stranded St. Lawrence belugas bore impressively high numbers of adducts. They approached values found in laboratory animals exposed to levels of benzo[a]pyrene sufficient to cause a response in cancer bioassays. In contrast, DNA adducts were not detectable in beluga whales inhabiting Canada's more pristine estuaries.

Now we have reached the moment when, discharged at last from the   80
hospital, I opened the door to my dormitory room and saw the bare mattress. I became secretive and territorial. I staked out a favorite stall in the women's bathroom. In my return every third month to the hospital for cystoscopic checkups, cytologies, and other forms of medical surveillance,

I told no one where I was going. The interval between checkups approximated one semester's worth of time, one season. These seasons went by. I waited tables and pursued perfect grades. I finished college and began graduate school. I stopped studying grasses and started studying trees. I endured chronic bladder infections. I married.

Like breast cancer, bladder cancer can recur at any time, lying quiescent for years—sometimes decades—and then reappearing inexplicably. "Once a year for life" is the National Cancer Institute's guideline regarding cystoscopic examination of the bladder in patients, beginning five years after diagnosis. Most of my doctors seemed to agree with this. There has been more dispute about the risks and benefits of annual IVPs—intravenous pyelograms—which require X-ray imaging of the entire urinary tract, including the kidneys, to check for secondary tumors that might have seeded themselves upstream. IVPs involve considerable radiation. I navigated this controversy on my own. Transitional cell carcinomas are categorized according to aggressiveness, from stage 0 to stage 4. One pathology report describes my tumor as a stage 1; the other classifies it as stage 2.

After five years, my checkups became annual, and I was no longer tethered so tightly to the medical system. This change was almost unnerving—as though it were normal to think of the interior landscape of one's body as a study site that required constant data collection.

I immediately accepted a fellowship in Costa Rica, where I became involved in a field study of ghost crabs—delicate creatures that occupy burrows along the Pacific beaches at the edge of the rainforest. At the study's conclusion, the night before we were to fly out, I had a vivid dream: I am walking by the ocean and discover a pale orange crab, big as a whale, washed up on the beach. It is dying. I lie down next to it, and slowly it wraps a great, clawed arm around me. Reaching my arm over its carapaced body, I return the embrace. I am not afraid. As if in the final frame of a movie scene, giant letters appear in the sky above us, spelling out a single word—G-R-A-C-E.

Among those of us who had spent days out in the tropical sun trying to monitor the movements of these reclusive, lightning-fast animals, the dream was hugely funny. ("Sleep with any arthropods last night, Steingraber?") Not until I returned home did I connect the dream to the end of five intense years of monitoring the possible movements of cancer. Ghost crabs.

I mean to say two things here. First, even if cancer never comes back, one's life is utterly changed. Second, in all the years I have been under medical scrutiny, no one has ever asked me about the environmental conditions where I grew up, even though bladder cancer in young women is highly unusual. I was once asked if I had ever worked with dyes or had ever been employed in the rubber industry. (No and no.) Other than these two questions, no doctor, nurse, or technician has ever shown interest in probing the possible causes of my disease—even when I have introduced the topic. From my conversations with other cancer patients, I gather that such lack of curiosity in the medical community is usual.

Steadily increasing in incidence, bladder cancer is associated with a few lifestyle habits—especially cigarette smoking—as well as with more than a few occupations. Besides dyestuffs workers and tire manufacturers, these include janitors, mechanics, miners, printers, hairdressers, painters, truck drivers, drill press operators, and machinists. In one small factory in England, all fifteen workers distilling one particular aromatic amine, na-phthylamine, developed bladder cancer. In 1984, bladder cancer was found in excess among inhabitants of Clinton County, Pennsylvania, where a forty-six-acre toxic waste site is contaminated with aromatic amines and benzene.

Other environmental patterns exist. Among U.S. males, bladder cancer is significantly higher in counties with chemical-manufacturing plants. Bladder cancer and exposure to perchloroethylene from drinking-water pipes were linked in Massachusetts, as we have seen in Chapter Four. In Taiwan, an investigation of bladder cancer deaths among children and adolescents found that almost all those afflicted lived within a few miles of three large petroleum and petrochemical plants. In a case-control study of bladder cancer in young women, risk of developing the disease was significantly associated with having undergone a thyroid procedure that involved the use of radioactive iodine.

Household dogs have a few interesting bladder cancer trends of their own. Transitional cell carcinomas of the bladder among pet dogs are significantly associated with direct exposure to insecticidal flea and tick dips, especially if dogs were obese or lived near another potential source of pesticides. A study of more than eight thousand dogs showed that bladder cancer in these animals was significantly associated with residence in industrialized counties, a pattern that mirrors the geographic distribution of bladder cancer among humans.

In 1990, at the International Forum for the Future of the Beluga, the conservationist Leone Pippard of the Canadian Ecology Advocates asked the following questions:

> Tell me, does the St. Lawrence beluga drink too much alcohol and does the St. Lawrence beluga smoke too much and does the St. Lawrence beluga have a bad diet . . . is that why the beluga whales are ill? . . . Do you think you are somehow immune and that it is only the beluga whale that is being affected?

In Washington, D.C., the National Museum of Natural History, part   *90* of the Smithsonian Institution, can be found on Constitution Avenue midway between Capitol Hill and the Washington Monument. On any given day, its exhibit halls are busy with tourists and troops of schoolchildren. Central among the objects of their interest are the animals posed in freeze-frame action inside decorated dioramas, each an exquisite hybrid of taxidermy and landscape painting. Many contain the spoils of Teddy Roosevelt–era safaris. In a reconstructed African savanna, a lion forever slinks toward his unsuspecting prey: zebras foolishly grazing with their backs to the hunter. Will they look up in time? In the glass boxes all around, other dramas are unfolding. Animal mannequins ready the attack, startle at a sound, confront an intruder, or display their antlers. In this world of showcased trophies, nature is still a place of virility.

In an upstairs wing away from all this activity is a suite of rooms where nature appears very differently. These are the offices of the Registry of Tumors in Lower Animals, a project jointly sponsored by the Smithsonian Institution and the National Cancer Institute. (Since my visit, the registry has moved to the campus of George Washington University.) Here, too, one can look through glass at preserved animals. Whole specimens float in jars; their tumors are sliced and mounted on slides. Fish with liver cancer. Salamanders with skin cancer. Clams with genital cancers. Up here, animals are not so much triumphant warriors as casualties of toxic encroachment.

In 1964, the pathologist and physician Clyde Dawe discovered white suckers with liver cancer in Deep Creek Lake, Maryland. This was the first time this disease had been found in a wild population of fish, and Dawe was worried. While isolated incidents of fish tumors had been previously described, liver cancer in large numbers of individuals outside of hatcheries had never been seen before. What might be going on with other populations of fish or with other species?

The following year, at Dawe's instigation, the registry was founded to facilitate the study of tumors in cold-blooded vertebrates (fish, amphibians, and reptiles), as well as various invertebrates (such creatures as corals, crabs, clams, snails, and oysters). Field biologists who discover animals with tumors can send them live, frozen, or preserved to the registry. So can anyone else. Indeed, a number of the registry's accessions—and there are now over sixty-four hundred, representing nearly a thousand species—are submitted by ordinary concerned citizens.

After more than three decades of data collection and experimental research, several important patterns have emerged. All indicate that cancer in at least some species of lower animals, but especially liver cancer in fish, is intimately linked to environmental contamination. In these patterns is writ an urgent message to us higher animals.

First, the preponderance of cold-blooded animals with cancer are *95* aquatic bottom feeders. And the dark beds of rivers, lakes, and marine estuaries are precisely where the highest concentrations of contaminants are found. Each year industry releases millions of tons of suspected carcinogens directly into surface water. Adding to this burden are motorboat exhaust and toxic runoff from the surrounding landscape, as well as deposition of airborne pollutants. Adhering to fine particles of sediment and pulled to the bottom by gravity, these chemicals slowly accumulate. Scavenger fish and detritus-grazing mollusks are thus highly exposed. They are also the animals most severely afflicted by tumors. The more contaminated the sediments, researchers have found, the higher the prevalence of certain tumors among those who haunt the cool, murky bottoms of rivers, lakes, bays, and estuaries. What's more, when extracts of these sediments are painted onto healthy fish, injected into their eggs, or added to clean aquarium tanks in the laboratory, these fish contract cancer in significant numbers.

Two trends among the fish echo human trends: frequency of cancer has increased substantially during the past thirty years, and the distribution of these cancers tends to be geographically clustered around areas of environmental contamination. Obviously, no one fills out a death certificate when a fish dies. We cannot, therefore, ascertain rates of cancer incidence and mortality per every 100,000 lake trout. Instead, cancers in animals such as fish are gauged by frequency of epizootics. Like an epidemic among people, an epizootic refers to large numbers of individual animals in the same area having the same disease at the same time.

According to the registry director, John Harshbarger, epizootics of liver tumors in fish are rising and coincide with the big increase in production of synthetic organic chemicals since 1940. In North America, there are now liver tumor epizootics in sixteen species of fish in at least twenty-five different fresh- and saltwater sites. Each of these sites is considered polluted. In contrast, liver cancer among members of the same species who inhabit nonpolluted waters is virtually nonexistent. Some skin cancers among North American fish also appear linked to chemical carcinogens. Other fish epizootics under investigation include testicular cancer among yellow perch in the Great Lakes and various connective tissue cancers in Great Lakes walleye, northern pike, and muskellunge.

The registry's survey of epizootic liver cancer in marine fish from around the world identified twelve affected species on three continents. In all cases, disease was correlated with the presence of chemical pollutants, as compared to a virtually zero background rate in nonpolluted waters. William Hawkins of the Gulf Coast Research Laboratory in Mississippi collaborates with registry staff in his laboratory studies of fish cancers. "We should listen to what the fish have to tell us about our environment," says Hawkins. "When fish get certain kinds of cancers, it's almost always the result of human activities."

The new field of ecotoxicology is uncovering additional patterns. Among other projects, this line of study looks for "genetic signatures" along the organism's chromosomes that identify exposure to particular toxins that have been released into particular ecological systems. It is as though fugitive chemicals carve their initials into the genetic code, leaving their marks for us to read. DNA adducts, as found in the chromosomes of St. Lawrence belugas, are one such signature. These can be quantified, in which case, the genes themselves serve as an instrument for measuring the dose of a carcinogen received by the organism. So far, this system has been worked out for only a small number of chemicals. But for those in which it has, increased exposure correlates with increased rates of cancer. This relationship seems especially strong for liver cancer in fish.

These findings have direct implications for us. The remarkable con- *100* servatism of genetic systems spans even the four hundred million years that have passed since fish diverged from the rest of the vertebrates. "The same genes that seem to go awry in rodents and humans are also going awry in trout when they are exposed to cancer-causing agents," says the biochemist George Bailey at Oregon State University. "Cancer is cancer, is what we're finding out at the molecular level." Aquarium studies in the laboratory show that the same carcinogens known to cause cancer in humans and rodents also cause cancer in fish and mollusks—and they are often metab- olized in the same way. Concordance is not perfect, however, and plenty of exceptions exist. Lobsters, for example, do not get cancer; they seem able to sequester carcinogens in their tissues in a way that prevents damage to their chromosomes.

The appearance of cancer in wild animals—especially, it seems, liver cancer among fish—may announce the presence of carcinogenic agents in the environment. Unlike laboratory animals but very much like ourselves, wild animals living in contaminated habitats are exposed to low levels of ever-changing combinations of chemicals throughout their lifetimes. And like the proverbial canaries in the coal mine, whose sudden collapse warned miners of poisonous gas, wildlife with tumors are environmental sentinels. Not all species suitably fill this role. In some animals, infectious viruses can also cause tumors. The question of which animals are the most accurate indicator species for which environmental carcinogens is receiving consid- erable attention among wildlife biologists.

Turtles seem to serve as good sentinels for the presence of hormone- disrupting chemicals in the environment. As adults, they are not any more sensitive than other vertebrates, but as embryos, turtles possess a peculiar characteristic that dramatizes the presence of such chemicals in the envi- ronment: sex determination lability. This means that slight changes in the environment during fetal development can change the animal's sex. Tem- perature can have this effect, and so can certain chemicals. When painted onto their eggs, PCBs turn red-eared sliders from male to female. More- over, this happens at very low concentrations—levels comparable to the average level of PCBs now found in the breast milk of women living in industrialized countries. Might the turtles have something to tell us about hormone-sensitive breast cancers?

Deer Island, Massachusetts, is situated in Boston Harbor. It is actually not an island, although it once was. When a hurricane filled a narrow channel with sand in 1938, Deer Island became a swelling at the end of a peninsula. The former site of a military base and a prison, Deer Island is the current site of one of the world's largest sewage treatment plants, re- cently expanded and upgraded. The access road along the tongue of land leading out to the gate lies just below the flight path for jets landing at Boston's Logan Airport. It is not a tranquil place. Nonetheless, I like to come out here every now and then. The tidy, modest homes lining this road and the flocks of children swooping around on bicycles remind me a bit of Normandale. The island itself was granted to Boston in 1634. Deer once walked out here across the ice.

If you park your car and stand facing the harbor—as though to watch planes land—you can look out over Deer Island Flats, a shallow area where winter flounder congregate. They are down on the bottom, working hard at imitating mud and sand.

Flounder would certainly win my vote for most bizarre looking fish. 105 A flounder starts out life normally enough, but then its left eye begins to migrate across its face until it crosses sides and bumps up against the right one. The top half of its face now appears to be at a ninety-degree angle to the bottom half. The flounder then lies down on its eyeless left side and remains in the sediment, unmoving as a saucer. Unlike some bottom dwellers, it relies on the ocean sediments only for camouflage, not for food. A lie-in-wait predator, the flounder periodically shoots up from its concealed position to chase down unwary marine worms and other prey.

None of this activity is visible from the surface. Nor is the fact that the winter flounder of Deer Island Flats suffer from high rates of liver cancer. The cancer epizootic among this population—and its connection to the harbor's chemical contamination—is one of the most well-described case studies on file at the Registry of Tumors in Lower Animals. Populations of winter flounder in cleaner waters away from the harbor do not have tumors.

Two elegant experiments involving contaminated sediments from a harbor in Bridgeport, Connecticut, further support an environmental explanation for the tumors in the Boston Harbor winter flounder. In the first study, researchers exposed uncontaminated adult oysters to sediments from Bridgeport's Black Rock Harbor in Long Island Sound. This procedure was done in both the laboratory and the field (by suspending caged oysters in the harbor waters). The sediments of Black Rock Harbor are known to be contaminated with a variety of toxins, from PCBs to pesticides. Both sets of oysters accumulated these contaminants in their tissues, and both sets developed tumors. Oysters exposed to uncontaminated sediments did not acquire tumors.

In the second experiment, blue mussels were exposed to Black Rock Harbor sediments. They similarly absorbed the contaminants into their bodies. They were then fed to winter flounder. The flounder developed tumors in their kidneys and pancreases, as well as precancerous lesions in their livers. No tumors developed in flounders fed on mussels that were exposed to sediments from uncontaminated sites.

I wish the flounder beds were as visible to us as the bright interior of a Smithsonian diorama. It is easy to dismiss the problems of species we seldom see—especially bottom-dwelling, cold-blooded ones. So I wish we could watch them down there—the clownish Picasso-esque faces twisted over top of the blind, white undersides that lie in direct and constant contact with the harbor's contaminated sediments.

Out of this desire, I have developed an idea for a pilgrimage that   *110* involves people with cancer traveling to various bodies of water known to be inhabited by animals with cancer. It involves an assembly on the banks and shores of these waters and a collective consideration of our intertwined lives. We could start with the question posed by Leone Pippard at the beluga conference: Do you think you are somehow immune?

I have worked out a possible itinerary, too. Beginning on the edge of Deer Island, we would travel north to Cobscook Bay in northern Maine. Here, more than 30 percent of softshell clams have tumors in their reproductive organs. In this otherwise-pristine habitat, clams and other marine animals have been exposed to the herbicides 2,4-D and 2,4,5-T both as runoff from nearby blueberry bogs and as drift from commercial forests where they were sprayed aerially. Rebecca Van Beneden, a zoologist and molecular biologist from the University of Maine, studies the patterns of tumors in clams from these estuaries and is looking for genetic changes that might reveal the sequence of molecular events leading to carcinogenesis. Her research is made urgent by the fact that rates of ovarian and breast cancers among the women living in this county are higher than the national average. "Maybe there's a correlation; maybe there's not," she says, referring to clams, women, and herbicides. "At the least, we need to pursue it."

Next, we would travel across the continent to Puget Sound where it reaches into the mouth of the Duwarmish River. The story of liver cancer in the English sole inhabiting these waters greatly resembles that of the winter flounder. Flounder and sole, both flatfish, are mirror images of each other: one lies off Boston's shore, the other off Seattle's. The molecular epidemiologist Donald Malins and his colleagues have captured sole in the lower reaches of the Duwarmish, which is contaminated with PCBs and benzo[a]pyrene, and analyzed their tissues for DNA damage. It was diverse and extensive. Indeed, these fish had hundreds of times more DNA alterations than sole captured in Washington State's more pristine rivers. Happily, in other studies, when fish from polluted streams were moved into cleaner water, their DNA began to repair itself, and their risk of developing cancer presumably declined.

Our journey would then take us to the south branch of the Elizabeth River in Virginia, which is home to a small, common fish called the mummichog. The males are handsome—dark green or steel blue with white and yellow spots and narrow silvery bars. The females are olive green. Unlike winter flounder or English sole—all famous travelers—the mummichog is a homebody and spends its life scavenging for food within the same spot. We would gather on both banks of the river branch. On one side is a wood treatment facility. Here, residues from coal-tar creosote are found in very high concentrations in the river's sediments. About one-third of the mummichogs on this side of the river have liver cancer. On the other side of the river, where sediment contamination is much lower, no mummichogs have liver cancer.

From Virginia, we would travel north to the steel mills where the Black River of Ohio empties into Lake Erie. In the early 1980s, researchers discovered that Black River catfish living near the discharge pipes of coking facilities, where coal is turned into fuel for the mills, had very high rates of liver cancer. The facilities closed in 1983. By 1987, sediment contamination had declined dramatically, liver cancer among brown bullhead catfish had declined by 74 percent, and the percentage of fish with normal livers had doubled. In the conclusion of their study, the researchers expressed amazement at "the efficacy of natural, unassisted remediation once the source of pollution is removed." This is a phrase we would want to think about while walking the length of this river.

Finally, I would bring us to the Fox River, which flows south from Wisconsin and joins the Illinois River near the river town of Ottawa, about seventy-five miles upstream from my hometown. Tumors from an assemblage of Fox River fish—walleyes, pickerel, bullheads, carp, and hog suckers—were among some of the first identified. But I would not take us to the old industrial sites thought to be responsible. Instead, I would bring us up to Buffalo Rock, a ninety-foot-tall bluff that abuts the Illinois River just a mile or two downstream from its confluence with the Fox. From here we could see the entire river valley spread out before us.

The ecology of Buffalo Rock, which is about the size of Deer Island, was ravaged in the 1930s by a strip mine that tossed highly toxic shale and pyrite onto the topsoil. All life forms, animal and plant, were killed. For decades, it remained a landscape of jagged escarpments that funneled acidic runoff into the river.

Then in 1983, the artist Michael Heizer was commissioned to help reclaim Buffalo Rock. Inspired by ancient Native American earth mounds, Heizer used bulldozers to sculpt the thirty-foot furrows into the shapes of five river animals: water strider, frog, catfish, snapping turtle, and snake. Each of these earth sculptures is hundreds of feet long. Rye grass now grows on top of them. You can climb the catfish's whiskers, walk along the strider's legs, lie down on the snake's head, touch the grass, breathe the air.

I would choose a September afternoon with a sky as blue as cornflowers. Cancer patients and ex–cancer patients would gather on the backs of these monumental animals and, in this place of damage and reclamation, talk about all that we have seen.

Reading and Responding

1. Write the following three headings on a sheet of paper: cell biology, wildlife biology, and human biology. Quickly reread the essay and make notes under each heading.

2. Since Steingraber's subject is often complex, she tends to rely on simple comparisons to help make her points. For example, she says that "cancer cells are more chaotically arranged than the shy, scurrying animals from which the disease—as well as the zodiac constellation—derives its name. Cancer, carcinogen, carcinoma, from the Greek *karkinos*, 'the crab.'" In short, she compares cancer cells to crabs. Look for other such comparisons and identify two of them that seem particularly helpful.

3. What experience—personally or from family or friends—have you had with cancer? Write a paragraph explaining how that experience affected your reading of this essay.

4. How do you feel about the use of rodents in some kinds of cancer research? Write a paragraph that expresses your opinion.

Working Together

1. As you read this essay, did you experience moments when you wanted to resist it, to stop reading it, to not know what it tells? Were there times when you wanted to read it avidly, eager to learn more? At what point did you feel the sharpest response? In your group, discuss the experience of reading Steingraber's essay. Identify the two most dominant responses among those in your group, and list at least five reasons for each response.

2. Steingraber's essay makes an implicit argument for the connectedness of rats, dogs, beluga whales, eels, fish, turtles, and human beings. If you were to draw a visual representation of these specific connections as outlined in the essay, what would you draw? As a group, make this visual representation on paper. Be ready to show it to the class and explain why you've decided to draw it this way.

3. This essay ends without solutions to the many chemicals known to cause cancer. Why haven't all these chemicals been banned from production processes and human use? What are the arguments, as you understand them now, for not banning cancer-causing chemicals? What are the arguments for banning them? Make two lists.

Rethinking and Rewriting

1. Write an essay (about four or five pages) that details your response to "Animals." Pay attention to how the essay is written and to your own response based on whatever knowledge or experience you bring to your reading. If the essay hit you hard, explain where this happened and try to account for why it happened. Tell whatever stories you need to in order to help readers understand your response. If the essay merely seemed tedious, lengthy, and boring, explain how or why it had little effect on you.

2. Assume that this essay makes an argument. What does it argue and how can you be sure? Critique specific parts of the essay to make your

analysis clear. End your discussion by making and supporting the claim that (a) the essay makes an argument and makes it quite effectively, (b) the essay makes a muddled sort of argument that isn't effective, or (c) the essay doesn't really make an argument at all.

3. First, create a one-page map, chart, or outline of the main topics or assertions in this essay, along with examples or illustrations or reasons for each main idea. Once you have created this overall view of the whole, write a brief summary of the essay (no more than seven hundred fifty words).

WE'RE SCRAPING BOTTOM

John P. Wiley, Jr.

> *John Wiley writes a regular column for* Smithsonian *magazine. In this article he discusses the effects of drag-net fishing on ocean ecology.*

I was brought up to admire commercial fishermen, and I still do. The feeling took root during childhood summers in Gloucester, Massachusetts, when that city was still a premier fishing center. I would watch the boats pass Ten Pound Island and then the Eastern Point breakwater as they headed for the open sea, for Browns Bank or Georges Bank. I would watch them returning, and then read in the *Gloucester Daily Times* how many pounds of what kind of fish each boat had brought in. One of the high points of my early childhood was riding a boat from Gloucester to Boston and back, for ice. I can still remember sitting at lunch when the single-cylinder diesel engine missed just one beat. Every man at the table was on his feet before the engine resumed its steady *chuff chuff chuff.* Everyone sat down again and picked up the conversation where they had left off.

Some of the outbound traffic I watched towed boats in which nets called purse seines were stored. Their crews would use the boats to deploy the nets in circles around schools of mackerel and then pull in a line on the bottom of the net so it closed. Others were swordfishermen, their harpoons lashed to the bowsprit. Still others carried steel-framed dredges with chain bags to gather scallops. But most were what in the Northeast were called draggers: they would drag great bags of net across the bottom, then haul them up and dump the catch on deck. The bags are held open by floats fastened along the top, weights on the bottom and angled boards at the sides. The boards are called otter boards, and the whole rig is an otter trawl, the most widely used towed bottom-fishing gear.

These fishers are, on an industrial scale, the last hunters of wild things, men and women who go to sea to catch the finfish and shellfish the rest of us love. This is not weekend sailing on the bay. It is working on the open ocean in winter as well as summer, sometimes in weather that would keep "sensible" people indoors, not to mention off the water. It is using axes to chop frozen spray from wheelhouse and mast before the boat becomes top-heavy and rolls under. Later in life I bored my long-suffering children by pointing out to them the high bows and heavy construction of commercial fishing boats compared with the pleasure boats tied up in the same harbors. It's the difference between the Western and Eastern ways of riding horses, as explained to me once by a wrangler at a dude ranch. "Out here," he said, "we ride horses to get somewhere." Fishing boats are serious.

My admiration for commercial fishermen has not diminished by the proverbial iota. (In fact, I go through cycles of buying a monthly publication called the *National Fisherman,* written for them.) But I'm finally having to face a terrible truth, one a child could have figured out but that somehow does not seem possible in the vastness of ocean from one horizon to the next. Dragging those nets across the bottom, year after year and decade after decade, wrecks the bottom. Reality has come to face me. A couple of years ago I chanced to see on television a film of an otter trawl moving across the bottom in the clear water of the Sea of Cortez. It seemed to be having the effect a line of tanks would have had. And now scientists have quantified the damage done by dragging nets across the bottom. Think of it as clear-cutting.

The December 1998 issue of *Conservation Biology* carries seven reports   5 on what fishing does to the bottom. The lower part of the net opening moves across the bottom like a road grader, skimming off the top few inches of mud or sand and most of the invertebrates that live there, the worms and amphipods and anemones that biologists know as the benthic community. The net crushes or buries some of the organisms. Others are suddenly exposed to predators as the net sweeps away their hiding places, the complex structures created by organisms such as soft corals, brachiopods, bryozoans and crinoids. Some benthic creatures live a long time (Atlantic quahog clams live for up to 200 years, and some deepwater corals live more than 500 years) and grow and reproduce slowly; recovery from a trawler pass can take years.

Humans aren't the only ones disturbing the seabed. Feeding whales and walruses leave what look like bomb craters in the sediment. We humans do operate on a grand scale, however. Les Watling, of the Darling Marine Center at the University of Maine, and Elliott A. Norse, of the Marine Conservation Biology Institute, in Redmond, Washington, calculate that mobile fishing gear covers an area equal to all the continents' shelves, 10.8 million square miles, every two to four years. The United Nations estimates that about 39,000 square miles of forest is cut every year. Thus the damage to the seabed occurs over an area 150 times as great. Until very recently, few people took much notice. Perhaps it's because "the oceans, unlike forests, still look like the oceans after we've removed their contents," suggests James T. Carlton, of Williams College-Mystic Seaport, in Connecticut. On a deeper level, he proposes that while we have a pretty fair idea of what we've done to the terrestrial landscape and its biodiversity, we know very little of our impact on the oceans—outside the obvious cases of declining fisheries. He adds that even as long as 100 years ago life in the oceans was already profoundly affected. Carlton asks: "Where is the large, beautiful hydroid *Ectopleura americana,* first and last collected on a ship's hull in 1879 in Long Island Sound? . . . Which species were carried around the world by ships for 300 years prior to 1800 that we pretend are now native everywhere they occur?"

We don't know anywhere near as much as we'd like to about the world's oceans and the state of their biodiversity, but we do know there are fisheries in decline all over the world. Many of those declines have been blamed on overfishing, but now we are learning why the stocks don't always rebound even when moratoriums are enacted. The marine equivalent of clear-cutting leaves little or nothing for remnant populations, juveniles and their prey to live on and no place to hide.

In the Northeastern United States, and in the Gulf of Mexico and the Pacific Northwest, fishermen are suffering. Boats are tied up. Ancillary businesses are going under. In Canada, where 30,000 fishermen are no longer allowed to fish, communities are dying. Governments are doing what they can. In New England the federal government is trying to open markets for previously unsalable fish, such as skates, sculpins and dogfish. But some conservationists in turn are horrified that more species are being targeted. "People who would be outraged to find blue herons or raccoons in the meat section at the supermarket are willing to accept the hunting and marketing of previously unexploited species of marine life," wrote Tatiana Brailovskaya, of the Nereus Project, in Newcastle, Maine, in *Conservation Biology.*

If you drive up from Boston and then cross the Annisquam River into Gloucester, you will pass a memorial to the more than 7,000 men lost at sea from 1623 to 1923. Once, fishing was everything. Now modern-day Gloucester, the city of Sebastian Junger's current best-seller, *The Perfect Storm,* continues its decline as a fishing port. We've come perilously close to licking the platter clean. Large parts of the fishing grounds are closed, certain species are off-limits. Some species may recover. I just hope I never see the day when the last Gloucester fishing boat has passed the breakwater coming home from the sea and there will be no more.

Reading and Responding

1. Who owns ocean life? How well does the concept of ownership fit the oceans? Write a paragraph that explores this question and begins to explain your own view.
2. Assuming you live within one hundred miles of a coastline or other major body of water, what do you know about the local fishery and its productivity now? If you don't know much, see what you can find out just by asking people you know. Record what you discover, even if it results in more questions than answers.
3. Wiley's essay is in part about his own discovery of what he terms a "terrible truth" about commercial fishing, an activity he clearly admires. Write a paragraph about a time when you discovered a similar terrible truth—a time when your intellectual grasp of something came into clear conflict with your admiration of it.

Working Together

1. Do you think that rules should be made to lessen the sort of ocean bottom damage that Wiley discusses? If not, explain why you think no

action is needed. If you do believe rules ought to be made, who do you think should make them, and who should enforce them? Working together, outline a position paper on this issue.

2. As Wiley mentions, ocean fishing in some areas is banned, which puts commercial fishermen out of work. Should governments offer these people compensation for lost income? Should governments offer them assistance in retraining and relocating them (along with their families) to find work? Why should we be willing—or not willing—to spend tax dollars for this purpose?

Rethinking and Rewriting

1. Research the topic of over-fishing and ocean habitat destruction by focusing on one location or fishing port. Wiley mentions Gloucester, Massachusetts, as well as Browns Bank and Georges Bank as three examples. If possible, choose a port or fishing location that you know or that is relatively close to you and hence easier to research locally. See what you can discover about the current prosperity of fishing fleets at that location. Find out about the fishing methods used, and predict what will happen to this fishery over the next five years.

2. Concentrating on ocean fishing methods and the health of ocean fish populations, do some limited but focused research in current journals like *Conservation Biology.* Limit yourself to six references. Summarize what you find, and construct at least one meaningful chart, graph, or illustration to help readers understand the data. End your summary by drawing a conclusion supported by the information you've discovered.

3. Drawing on one example of ocean fishing that you know (either through personal experience or through research), write a position paper that expresses your view of the role of government (at whatever level seems important) in regulating—or not regulating—ocean fishing. Assume your readers have only a vague grasp of the topic. Therefore, your task is to educate and persuade.

OUT OF THE WOODS

IS IT TOO LATE?

Anthony Weston

> *A teacher of philosophy and global studies at Elon College, Anthony Weston is author of several books about environmental issues, including* Back to Earth: Tomorrow's Environmentalism *(1994). He also edited* An Invitation to Environmental Philosophy *(1999), from which this essay is drawn.*

Desolation

The amazement of the first Europeans at America now amazes *us;* it breaks our hearts. The first explorers smelled the land before they even saw it. In 1524, Verrazano reported smelling cedars a hundred leagues from land. Others told of sailing through vast beds of floating flowers. Ducks, turkey, deer, lynx greeted them in unimaginable abundance. Whales so crowded the waters that they were navigational hazards. Cape Cod was named for its cod–clotted waters. Salmon ran thick in every Atlantic river from Labrador to the Hudson. Lobsters were so common that they were used throughout New England for potato fertilizer, pig food, fish bait, and to feed the British navy five or six times a week until seamen's riots limited the weekly lobster dinners to four.

All gone, now. Islands once packed shore to shore with walrus or seals or nesting seabirds are now empty. The spearbill, just for one of untold possible examples, is extinct, slaughtered for its eggs or for cod bait, thousands burnt alive for fuel to melt down others' fat. Passenger pigeons who once flew in hundred–mile long rivers over the prairies, so thick they blotted out the sun, perhaps the most abundant bird species ever to live on Earth, no longer exist at all. Buffalo numbered perhaps seventy million in North America prior to Europeans' arrival on the prairies; they were reduced to only a few hundred less than a century later, and even now are regularly shot if they dare to wander out of Yellowstone or their few other sanctuaries. Some subspecies, now extinct, were larger than elephants. Pilot whales, giving birth and giving suck in shallow coastal bays, were shot with cannons or driven onto the beaches and left to die, then cut up, often still alive, sometimes after two or three days of slowly collapsing under their own weight waiting for the butchers to finish their companions. In the heyday of deep-sea whaling it was no longer live whales who were navigational hazards, but *dead* ones, stripped of their blubber and cast adrift.

The destruction goes on. Vast tracts of rainforest, harboring untold species that have not even been counted, are in flames at this moment. Spotted owl, willow flycatcher, scarlet tanager, lynx, bobcat, rhinoceros, elephant: all are or will be endangered. Three dozen species have gone extinct in the United States in the last decade just waiting for Endangered Species Act designation. Fully one quarter of the twenty thousand native plants in America are threatened with extinction. Blue whales, the largest living creatures on earth, have been reduced from a half a million in Antarctic waters alone to between 600 and 3,000 worldwide. The use of whales and other cetaceans for target-practice (machine-gunning, depth charging, ramming) by the world's navies continues to be so common that NATO commanders are surprised when there are protests. Old-growth forest in Oregon and Washington, much of it public land, may be entirely clear-cut in a generation. Almost as much land in the lower forty-eight states is dedicated to roads, rights of way, and parking lots as is designated wilderness. An area the size of Indiana is occupied just by lawns. Every major city in the country now publishes daily air pollution indices (is it safe to breathe the air? as if we had a choice), with local spice added too: the drinking water in Des Moines, Iowa, for instance, is so contaminated by leachate from fertilizers that nitrate levels are featured in the news as well. The ground water on the Wisconsin prairie where I grew up now contains so much nitrate that it could kill babies. My own children, visiting their grandfather in the country, have to drink bottled water.

Only a little less familiar are slower and more indirect processes of destruction. Many species, even those apparently well-protected, are dying out slowly as their habitat is destroyed. Migratory songbirds like tanagers are threatened by loss of habitat at both ends (they winter in the rainforests) as well as by pesticides at this end. Nitrates too, no doubt (for what do *their* babies drink?). The young produced by the twenty-seven previously wild California condors, captured and transferred to breeding programs in zoos in 1987, may or may not reacclimate to the wild, and all of the causes of their original decline still remain: loss of habitat, poison (lead shot in dead animals not recovered by hunters), high-energy powerlines. Of an unknown number of subspecies of wolves in North America (Edward Goldman distinguished twenty-three in 1945), seven are extinct (like the pure white Newfoundland wolf, *Canis lupus beothucus,* named after Newfoundland's original human inhabitants, the Beothuk Indians—likewise extinct) and the rest, surviving after a fashion even under the pressure of unparalleled destruction and dislocation, seem to have interbred with each other and with dogs and coyotes to the point that only two or three subspecies remain. Bats that once flew in huge clouds from caves have been killed by the millions by one person sealing an entrance or destroying their hearing with a bomb; yet bats are the pollinators for a wide variety of crucial species. Blue whales move in groups that may be too isolated to interbreed. Even with a global population in the thousands, the species may be dying out. North Atlantic Right Whales, after not being hunted for fifty years, still number only a few hundred.

Inconceivable pain, horror and holocaust lie behind these briefly listed facts. "Holocaust" literally means "cast whole into the fire"—think of the burning rainforests. Loss to untold numbers of animals, to the future of the whole earth, and to those human peoples who have lived close to those animals and to the land. Aboriginal peoples worldwide are being uprooted or killed off, by outright murder or starvation, dislocation, disease. Often the vanishing is quiet, hidden and of no concern to the dominant civilization that moves in to fill the vacuum, or just lets the ghost towns (ghost cultures, ghost languages, ghost possibilities) crumble into dust. Inuit communities, visited once by a whaling ship, died to a person the next winter. Indian genocide through smallpox-infected blankets was deliberate U.S. government policy. Similar things go on today in the Amazon. The extermination of the buffalo was likewise a deliberate attack on the Plains Indians. Often the natives are the only humans who can give a fully situated and *live* voice to the loss of the animals. A Nisqually Indian spokesperson, speaking of salmon—*the* being who, for all the Northwest Indians, "gathers" the landscape, but now almost completely exterminated, blocked from their breeding grounds by hydroelectric dams or chopped to bits in their turbines—tells us that the Nisqually see salmon bleeding out of light bulbs. We are the blind ones, seeing only the light.

And if this were not enough, the threats on the horizon dwarf all that has gone before. Most of these are so familiar that we can invoke them merely by the briefest reference. Global warming, brought on chiefly by the burning of fossil fuels in cars and power plants, and its threat of coastal inundation, superhurricanes, and drastic and unpredictable climate changes. Ozone depletion, starting with the infamous hole over the Antarctic and potentially continuing worldwide. Already more of the sun's ultraviolet rays reach Earth's surface than a decade ago: Australia, on the edge of the Antarctic hole, has seen skin cancers treble. Everywhere too lie hidden dangers, "risk multipliers," processes that intensify other processes: global warming may speed up the decomposition of the dead organic matter, for example, that now lies on forest floors, flooding the atmosphere with vast new quantities of carbon dioxide and accelerating further warming. Then there are other and more technological nightmares: nuclear war or meltdown, massive chemical spills, the Chernobyls and Bhopals still in our future, perhaps down the street; some sort of genetically engineered organism run amok; assorted other cataclysms. No end of nightmares. I cannot bear to begin to tell my children.

No wonder we feel ourselves in a kind of endgame: that it is already "too late." Every year I find my students more and more knowledgeable about environmental issues, and every year more fatalistic. The trends seem to be connected. There is nothing to be done, they say. The jig is up.

And Yet . . .

And yet . . . the very fact that we have awakened to all of this is also, perversely enough, a sign of progress. Only a first sign, perhaps, but a sign nonetheless. The list of cataclysms, past and possible, is no longer a surprise—*and this is itself a hopeful sign*. No problem will be solved without the awareness that it *is* a problem. For the first time in centuries, we are now aware, truly and inescapably aware, that we ourselves are *at stake with the larger living world*. And the speed with which this awareness has grown on us, seen from any historical distance, is astonishing too. Thirty years ago the United States did not even have an Environmental Protection Agency. Today it is a Cabinet-level department, its enabling legislation together with the Clean Air and Clean Water Acts and the Endangered Species Act impose direct economic costs on the scale of $125 billion a year, and three-quarters of the public approves.

More profound changes lie ahead—changes that would have seemed impossible, unimaginable, a decade or two ago. Tighter pollution control, habitat protection, limits to the factory farming of animals, usable mass transit, sustainable agriculture, an enhanced Endangered Species Act, and on and on: all of this is on the agenda. No doubt there will be immense struggles over what shape they will take and how fast they will come, but that they are coming is not in serious question. This too we know; it is no surprise. Step back from the immediate struggles and a larger movement becomes more visible. Systematic recycling is growing on everyone: municipalities can no longer afford to dispose of the current volume of garbage. There are no more landfills. The next step is to rethink the manufacture of so many "disposable" items in the first place. It is far cheaper and more sensible to plan products so that recycling is easy—planners call this "*precycling*"—than to pay attention only after the things are made, after they have been designed and manufactured with no attention to anything but the manufacturer's ease and profits. Even better, eliminate disposables entirely. Make containers to last through many reuses. Or make them edible. Or fertilize the garden with them, as we already do with some newsprint. We speak here of the growth industries of the first part of the twenty-first century.

Even the power companies are getting the message. It is far cheaper   *10*
to conserve electricity—creating what Amory Lovins calls "negawatts"—than to build new generating capacity, especially when the environmental costs of electricity generation are factored in, but even if they are not. Of necessity, it is happening. No new nuclear reactors, and few large power plants of any sort, are currently under construction in America. Hardly any dams. Willy-nilly, ecological thinking has arrived.

Other changes proceed apace. Some of my friends live in a cooperatively owned and managed development, the houses clumped around the periphery with shared open, natural, and quiet space at the center. New developments all over the country are being similarly designed. Urban creeks, buried underground or channeled straight and narrow, are coming back out of their confinement. There is now an entire organization called the National Coalition to Restore Urban Waters. Restored wetlands are replacing shopping centers. Vegetarianism, on the utter fringe twenty years ago, is now familiar enough that people feel they need excuses for eating

meat. Organic foods are common enough that conventional food producers, poor things, are starting to worry that people may actually "overreact"
to the latest pesticide scare and switch. Nearly half of all U.S. supermarkets
now carry some organic produce. And organic farming is explicitly conceived as a commitment to the health of soils and ecosystems, not just to
the food consumers at the other end. It represents a new *vision* of farming
as well as of food.

So change is the order of the day, and not all the change is downhill.
Ten minutes from my urban home there is thick forest where eighty years
ago farmland was eroded and abandoned. Succession into hardwoods is
starting. Who would have dreamed it a century ago? Now we have before
us proposals to turn vast, sparsely settled and overfarmed parts of the Great
Plains into "Buffalo Commons": back into open prairie, restoring the
native plants and animals, and making space again for the native peoples
too. Already throughout New England the wilderness trails cross old stone
walls, the walls of farms two hundred years ago. *Wilderness* now. The face
of the land may be utterly transformed again in another century.

This is what I do tell my children. I want them to awaken to a world
understood ecologically: to a vision of things according to which, for
example, buying organic food is about the health of the land and of the
people who work it; hauling the recycling to the curb (or, better, doing
our own freelance "pre-cycling") is about stewardship and creativity; and
walking the woods is partly about regeneration. Time enough later for the
horrors: first the new vision, the new century in a new key. A new *millennium,* maybe, in a new key. Perhaps, slowly, the tide is turning.

Our Fatalism

It may come as a surprise that fatalism is nothing new. Actually,
people have been lamenting that "it is too late" for millennia, almost from
the very morning of the world. The great Greek philosophers were obsessed with the theme of decay and decline. Christianity reflects a pessimism so deep that the only sources of hope have to be moved outside of
the world entirely. So now ecology is supposed to offer us a post–Christian,
scientific kind of fatalism: the Earth itself is in decline, life itself is imper-
illed. A new kind of necessity, we are told, a new wheel of fate upon
which we are once again pinned, has now been discovered.

There is of course evidence for this view, just as there is evidence for   *15*
many kinds of pessimism. Yet there is a strange and striking way in which
this fatalism treats the Earth as though its possibilities are exhausted—*at the
very moment when we are finally supposed to have learned that the Earth has
infinitely more possibilities than we ever imagined!* Is it not a little odd to give
up on the Earth just as we discover how fantastically intricate and varied
and mysterious the Earth (even a single salt marsh, even a single *duck*) really
is? The truth is that *we barely know this place.* How can we know enough to
give up on it?

In the 1960s we were told, on the best of evidence, that a billion or more people would starve to death by 1990, because population had irrevocably outgrown food supplies. Since then, population growth has slowed down while food supplies have increased, and although widespread starvation and malnutrition exist, they are arguably the result of political causes, not (primarily) population explosion. The "Population Bomb" didn't go off. Yet we were already told, in the 1960s, that it was "too late." It wasn't. Do we know it is "too late" now? Are we sure? Prediction is dangerous, as E. F. Schumacher once quipped, especially about the future.

Global warming is the disaster forecast of choice in the 1990s. But is prediction any more secure here? Almost all of our theories about the Earth are guesswork, far more uncertain than we usually admit, especially as the issues become more global, more dependent on projections, computer models, and ecological theories. Even the basic data are woefully incomplete. Surface temperatures around the world do appear to be increasing. Satellite data for the lower atmosphere are more precise but show a less clear pattern, but then again measurements from space have only been taken for seventeen years, not long enough to reliably judge trends. It is also not clear that the reported increases don't have other explanations. What determines Earth's temperature is almost incomprehensibly complicated. Variations in solar activity and even small variations in the tilt of Earth's orbit are crucial. Meanwhile none of our theories explain some of the actual empirical phenomena, such as the marked lack of warming at the poles. It is not even clear that global warming, if it really does happen, will raise the oceans. The Antarctic glacial shield was formed thirty million years ago and has withstood much warmer temperatures that are predicted at present. Since a warmer globe will experience more evaporation and precipitation, there will be more snow on the polar ice caps, thickening them: some recent estimates suggest that the sea may actually *drop*.

I do *not* mean (this had better be said emphatically: I do NOT mean) that we may as well go on as we are going. When we don't understand the dynamics of a process we depend upon, the only sane policy is not to interfere with it. Heedlessly dumping billions of tons of pollutants into the air and water is like an ignorant patient on life support polluting his own intravenous solution, flipping dials on the respirator, pulling out tubes and jacks and plugging them into other outlets. You don't have to understand the process to know that messing with the system is, to say the least, unwise. What goes around quite probably will come around. In fact it is precisely *because* we don't understand the process that it *is* so unwise. Rather than requiring proof that our present course is disastrous before we change it, then, we ought to require proof that it is *not* disastrous before we embark on it. Anything else is sheer stupidity—probably based in turn upon sheer *cupidity*.

Yet a fundamental uncertainty remains, and may always remain. So what makes caution and forbearance necessary is also precisely what also opens the space, once again, for hope. If the Earth is truly mysterious, if so many of her intricacies flow onward above or below or beyond us, then, even though she is obviously pained, there is no way that we can say that it is now "too late." Or *ever* "too late."

Believing in the latest disaster scenario, the latest fatalism, ought not   20 to be the litmus test of environmentalism. We ought to honor this Earth in her *elusiveness*. This Earth eludes the pesticide makers, who find each new chemical shortly greeted by resistant insects that are even more destructive and harder to control. It eludes the nuclear industry's planners, unable to find any place, even deep within the earth, to entomb nuclear wastes, because even the rocks move. It eludes the paleontologists, who estimate that, even now, we have discovered at best 1 percent—*1 percent!*— of dinosaur species. Who knows what awaits us, buried in the rocks? It eludes the computer modellers, who still, apparently, even now, have no idea where a billion tons of carbon dioxide—a seventh or more of the total dumped into the atmosphere from human sources—goes every year, though some of them confidently go on to predict, or deny, global warming anyway. Wholly unbelievable lifeforms may yet find their way out of the rainforests, as some already have (Who knows: an AIDS virus in reverse?). Or out of the oceans, like the coelacanth, a prehistoric, dragonlike fish, believed extinct for seventy million years, rediscovered off South Africa in 1938, brought to attention by an eccentric British scientist—a story that sounds like something out of a Gary Larson cartoon, except that it is true.

Dinosaurs are not extinct either, by the way: it turns out they evolved into birds. The littlest and flightiest from the biggest and the most plodding. Whales evolved from a dog-like land mammal who came from the sea and then, a few hundred million years later, went back. And nothing could be stranger than what is already around us: fungi (closer cousins than we thought, research suggests), flamingos, insects of all sorts (watch the movie *Microcosmos* for an amazing eyeful: slugs making love, delicately and languidly; the nativity of a mosquito . . .), elephants rumbling to each other across the savannahs (it turns out they communicate by infrasound, like the rumble of cathedral organ pipes, almost too low for us to hear). What new coelacanths must still swim below the waters we think we know so well! The proverbial grass cracks all pavements. The jig is up? Not likely.

Smash the Tube

I think the current fatalism comes primarily from watching the news. At least this much is true: most of us know what we know about nature from the media. On the one hand, I suppose, this is wonderful: perhaps only with such media can consciousness shift dramatically toward an ecological vision. But there is another and darker side too. In "the news" especially, a very specific concept of nature is at play.

Nature on TV is not something we directly experience. First and obviously, of course, it is *on* television: we are experiencing it only in a "mediated" way. In a darkened room, a tube flickers; we sit, passive, reduced to our eyes. But there is another reason too. In the time-honored fashion of television "coverage," nature is treated as such a large and complex system that we can only learn about it from the experts, the talking heads, just like the national debt or genetic engineering or politics in Russia. Or else nature makes news when trouble comes, so we have also learned to picture it as trouble-prone, threatening. For us North Carolinians, it seems that "nature" on the tube is primarily the place that hurricanes come from.

Thus television's nature is pictured as, in general, *somewhere else,* which is *why* we need experts to tell us about it, and why it can leave us so uneasy, vaguely but only vaguely sensing storms gathering over the horizon. And this in turn is part of why it seems so easy and tempting to abandon hope: because we feel no connection to television's Earth in our bones, and also, therefore, are offered no sense that it is something we can directly affect. The implicit message is: there is nothing to do, it is indeed too late, all we can do is sit back and watch the unfolding disaster, between the ads for toothpastes and senators, on TV.

But the real news is that *we are all part of nature.* We humans do not   25
stand apart, and nature does not stand apart from us. We all stand in dynamic interaction. The system is open-ended and far more resourceful, as I have been arguing, than we usually suspect: and it is also *right here,* right next to us, and we too are part of it. Nature is us.

From this perspective, all of the familiar aspects of "crisis" are still on the scene, but the overall picture is nonetheless strikingly different. Of course there are deep threats to certain parts of nature, especially the wilder and more intricate systems. Of course we may be disequilibrating some delicate global feedback mechanisms that could eventually disrupt the entire biosphere. Of course we must take these threats seriously—and again, emphatically, nothing I say here is meant to diminish them. But we also must resist the reduction or confinement of "nature" to *just that*—as if everything else were confined to some other, lesser, incomplete sort of reality, *off the screen,* as it were. Another TV image, this time from the advertisements: "nature" is something pristine far away, like a vacation destination. Never mind that if many of us vacation there it will no longer be pristine. Never mind that this entire conception is a product of the airline and hotel industries' need to generate demand for their services. All the same, it has now become reality for all too many of us.

This is a spell we need to break—and all it takes, in truth, is looking up. Look at the world, *really look;* listen and smell and touch. We do not live apart. A cat hunches over this very desk as I write, bats hang under your eaves, 100 million monarch butterflies migrate, every year, up to 4,000 miles, from all over North America, to winter on the California coast, following what nature writer John Hay calls "nature's great headings," invisible to us. All of this is going on around us, right now, all the time. The same dainty-looking butterflies (a lovely children's tale calls them "flutter-bys") welcome the spring in all our gardens. There are wild worlds under our feet: the billion or so microbes in a handful of garden soil, and beneath them bacteria living in rocks up to three miles below Earth's surface: the latest theory, in fact, is that life on Earth may have originated in the interior, and that subterranean bacteria and other forms of life feeding on the planet's chemical and thermal energy (and equally possible on, or rather *in,* other planets too, by the way) actually outweigh all life on the surface. Our own bodies harbor billions of bacteria, while we ourselves may play a role like our bodies' bacteria in the larger living organism which is now supposed, by some scientists, to include all life on earth.

These are the simplest of things: bacteria, soil, rock, air. The air itself is a kind of ocean in which we all live, a world-swaddling sea that weighs, altogether, 5,000 trillion tons. In truth we live *in* the Earth, not *on* it. In some ways the atmosphere itself is the most dynamic ocean of all, never still, full of gasses and dusts and spores and fungi; and animals of all sorts, bats and gnats and eagles, flutter-bys and bees; pollen and leaves and seeds. Air courses through our own bodies constantly, 450 cubic feet a day, 10,000 or so breaths. We are constantly and unavoidably intimate with the world; not to be intimate in this way means quick suffocation, death.

There are wild things (or: Wild Things, following that great philosopher, Maurice Sendak) right in our kitchens. Cockroaches, for example, astonishing creatures, sprinting the human equivalent of 200 miles an hour on split-second notice, so preternaturally sensitive to vibration that they are used by scientists in touch research. If cockroaches were endangered, we would regard them as one of nature's greatest marvels. (Not to worry, though: they'll outlast us.) A species of leaf-eating weevil, 1 inch long, camouflages itself by carrying a forest of tiny ferns and mosses in crevasses on its back. Still tinier insects live in that forest. Worlds within worlds. A Daddy Longlegs periodically takes up residence in my car, rides back and forth with me to work. I see one of his legs sticking out from underneath the glove compartment as I drive. Computers have "bugs" worldwide, and the original "bug" was, of course, a bug: a beetle or something that shorted out the first UNIVAC. Long live bugs!

How far we might come from the TV world of crisis, from an Earth lost in abstraction and talking heads, one more thing to learn about in school! I once took a PhD seminar (it's never too late) in the philosophy of nature to a wigwam in Hauppauge, Long Island, New York. Half a mile from the Northern State Parkway, but we did not hear the cars, perhaps because we were so immensely distant from the Parkway and all it stands for in time if not in space. It was drizzling, foggy, and cold. The mists from our voices rose to join the smoke seeking the small smoke-hole. We passed a cup, alerted to the calls of geese and wild turkeys—penned, to be sure, but still calling excitedly in the fog. We sat on the ground and talked about Abenaki creation stories. We spoke slowly, for once, not covering all other sounds with our voices. And that small matter of tempo in the end may be the best mirror of the intuition the stories spoke of, that sense of being simply part of a larger living world. There was something to hear besides ourselves: the calls of the birds and the wind; our fire echoing the hiss of the rain; and our voices, when we spoke, interweaving among the animals'. *This* is what it means to feel, as Native Americans always said, that "The Earth is Alive"—and that we are part of it. And it is all there, all still there, even on Long Island. Denise Levertov writes in "In the Woods":

> Everything is threatened, but meanwhile
> everything presents itself:
> the trees, that day and night
> steadily stand there, amassing
> lifetimes and moss, the bushes
> eager with buds sharp as green
> pencil points. Bark of cedar,
> brown braids, bark of fir, deep-creviced,
> winter sunlight favoring
> here a sapling, there an ancient snag,
> ferns, lichen. And the lake
> always ready to change its skin
> to match the sky's least inflection . . .

It is not and never can be "too late" to "save" *this* Earth, the Earth of breeze and tide, fog and bugs, lichen and moss, subterranean bacteria all a-churning and the continents themselves with all their indomitable ranges sliding around on molten rock, upsetting all the balances and changing all the maps. Perhaps this is the final and most decisive reduction introduced by TV: it reduces nature to what we have lost, or are losing. And the losses are certainly many. But they are not the whole story—not at all.

Change Begins at Home

So maybe this Earth does not need *our* saving, anyway, as if once again humans must come to the rescue in the last act, using that distinctive big brain of ours to put things right. It turns out that we do not even have the biggest brain around: that honor goes to whales, some of whom have brains up to six times bigger, with whole regions, masses of cortex, that we don't begin to understand. So just maybe, if we really are living out some sort of global drama, we are not the heroes, despite all our space travel and blazing cities and everything else. Maybe we are just extras. On the "Gaia Hypothesis," the theory that the Earth is in some sense a single living organism mediated through the atmosphere, it has been alleged that the chief human contributions are the gasses produced in our intestines, and even at outgassing we are, of course, bested hands-down by the ruminant herbivores.

A more suitable and circumspect role would be to look to ourselves. Who *we* really need to "save" is *us*. I don't mean simply looking to our own survival, though that wouldn't be a bad idea either. It is our task, now, coming into some sort of ecological awareness, to learn to live in accord with that awareness, to *learn to live as co-inhabitants of this planet.* We need to learn what might best be called a certain kind of *etiquette.* And this takes work—but on the whole it is not the kind of work we have yet had in mind when we think of responding to the environmental crisis.

We must stop what destruction we can stop—of course. Recycling and all the rest—of course. But the work that is harder to recognize are the changes necessary in more personal, everyday patterns of attention. Watch the spiders. Watch the skies. Walk. Garden. Let the lawn go wild. Feed the birds. *Learn* the birds. Talk to the animals. Seek out the stories of your place, pay attention to the names. This is the "etiquette" I mean: not claiming all the space for ourselves, learning to listen, learning how to *invite* the larger world, other presences, to re-enter our lives.

Suppose that certain places were set aside as quiet zones: deliberately   *35* protected areas, where cars, lawnmowers, stereos, and their kin do not define the soundscape, therefore a life shared with the other-than-human in the simplest ways: winds, birds, silence. We might quite literally "come back to our senses." If bright outside lights were also disallowed, we could see the stars at night, see the moons wax and wane, and feel the slow pulsations of the light over the seasons. The heaviness of the night could return. The stars could return, and the night creatures now exiled by the light.

This is not a utopian proposal. Unplug a few outdoor lights, reroute some roads, and in some places of the country we have a first approximation, even when the electricity is on. Even in my *city,* it is still possible to sit out on the back porch with my daughter in my arms and rock her to sleep with the owls and the stars. And what it would take to preserve and extend such spaces, in many regions and corners, is not necessarily so great. Return more neighborhood roads to local traffic only. Preserve owl habitat, plant wildflowers. Instead of more and more tract developments consuming cornfields and woodlots, let us try some experiments in creative zoning, make space for increasingly divergent styles of living on and with the land: experiments in recycling and energy self-sufficiency, for example, or mixed communities of humans and other species. Or other possibilities not yet even imagined. Canadian ecophilosopher Alan Drengson proposes the creation of "ecosteries"—"centers, facilities, stewarded land, nature sanctuaries, where ecosophy [ecological philosophy] is learned, taught, and practiced"—on analogy to the medieval monasteries: "places where spiritual discipline and practice are the central purpose." There is no reason that we must condemn ourselves to another ten thousand suburbs all the same.

In the midst of the worst city we can still imagine little "pocket parks," strategically placed, insulated from noise. "Quiet backs" are common in the older cities of Europe—small green areas, behind houses or public buildings, densely planted, perhaps connected by small footpaths and waterways—like the walk through the cathedral close in Chichester cited by Christopher Alexander and his colleagues in their synoptic tract *A Pattern Language,* where, "less than a block from the major crossroads of the town, you can hear the bees buzzing." This is not only in the city but in the very middle of the busiest part of the city. The remergence of the more-than-human even in the city is not at all impossible, but we must *plan* for it.

Alexander and his colleagues aim to spell out the patterns, often ancient though not necessarily even fully conscious, that define the most livable and fulfilling of our cities, neighborhoods, and houses. They propose interlocking "city-country fingers" that bring the open countryside within a short walk or bicycle ride from downtown. They calculate the maxiumum distance from home that a pocket park can still attract walkers (2–3 blocks). They calculate the optimum size for such parks. They uncover the patterns that underlie the attraction even of small but "enchanted" natural places, again in the very midst of the city: "layered" (gradual, phased) access, the presence of running and still water, the presence of animals (birds, snakes, goats, rabbits, wild cats). They plead for "site repair," for building on the *worst* parts of a piece of land rather than the best, so as to repair and improve the poorer parts while preserving the most precious, beautiful, and healthy parts (and honoring the fact that these parts are often slowly evolved and complex, not something that can be recreated elsewhere even if we or the "landscape contractor" try). They argue for the necessity of what they call "positive outdoor space": places partly enclosed by buildings and natural features so as to have a shape of their own, courtyards or partial courtyards, for example, as opposed to the shapeless outdoor space so familiar around the squarish and irregularly placed buildings of our suburbs and cities, and for "half-hidden gardens": neither the entirely decorative traditional American front yard nor the wholly private back gardens of Europe, but an intermediate kind of space.

How different life could be! Notice that we are not talking about sweeping, dictatorial, disaster-driven social change, the sort of thing that the word "environmentalism" usually implies on the news and in our politics. No: here we speak of tinkering with zoning requirements, building or retro-fitting our cities and neighborhoods in small ways that take time, like the shrubs that may take a generation to grow up to create half-hidden gardens. Rethinking the house. Modern American houses all too often function as fortresses against the supposed dangers, human and non-human, of the "outside" world. It becomes hard for us to imagine anything else. Yet here too there are alternatives, in fact entire alternative traditions. Frank Lloyd Wright used the wall, freed from its support functions, as a delicate and deliberately ambiguous transition-point between outside and in. Traditional (pre–air conditioning) Southern houses half-buried the first floor for coolness and used breezeways to amplify the faintest breeze—the winds were invited in, like friends. Native American styles still dominate parts of the Southwest, like adobe, made from the very clay of the building site, periodically replastered with the same. The buildings literally grow out of the earth. Could we not make a practice of recovering native and traditional architecture, wherever we happen to live?

No doubt bees in the parks and adobe houses are not quite what one expects of modern-day environmentalism. It is easier to bemoan the lost wilderness than to teach your children the constellations in your backyard. But even Thoreau at his cabin on Walden Pond, who it gratifies us to think of as such a hermit (so that we can also say: his life is no longer possible for *us*), in fact lived within a mile of Concord and walked there nearly every day to see his family. He lived close enough to the road that he could smell the smoke of passing pipesmokers. Fellow townspeople and farmers fished in the pond; the railroad went by one edge of it. The classic meditation on the human relation to nature, written from virtually within the city limits of Concord? But how appropriate! The "rest of the world" is not somewhere else, but *right here*. Correspondingly, the way back might be a little different than we think too.

Transhuman Etiquettes

Consider finally and again very briefly our relations to our fellow creatures, other animals. Not, by the way, just "animals," as if we weren't animals too: that little piece of language is already a first and fundamental point of etiquette here. We too are animals.

We have still not managed the most elementary politeness with respect to other creatures. Ten years or so of research aimed at getting captive apes to *talk* dead-ended when it finally dawned on someone that they don't have our kind of vocal equipment. Now we try to get them to manipulate symbols, or use sign language (ASL), and the success of some animals has been stunning. Still, why should we suppose that they even *care* about using symbols? At least outside captivity, already itself a stunning refusal of even the most minimal etiquette. Chimps trained in ASL stand by the doors of their cages begging for the keys. "You stay, I go," they say. Now that funding has dried up (Eugene Linden speculates that the research went a little *too well*) they are often caged with keepers who do not know ASL at all.

For starters, surely, we need to ask how other creatures might care to live with *us* (or not), rather than taking it upon ourselves to simply define and thereby limit them too. It is not just that the symbol-using research on apes, for example, is a little ambiguous. It is better to ask: on what terms and by what means would an ape—a free ape, not a captive one—care to communicate with us at all? And apes are our very nearest relatives. What could be the "terms" of, say, a dolphin, utterly at home in the waters, who in all probability can "see" inside his/her companions by echolocation? What would language even mean for such a creature?

So it may be that we really know almost nothing about the real possibilities of dolphins, apes, and most other creatures too: perhaps very little even about our *own* possibilities! Once again, *we* are the ones who

40

really need "saving." We are the ones who need to approach *them* in a different spirit.

Jim Nollman plays jazz rhythms with killer whales, orcas. Working in   45
their media, as it were, not primarily ours, and going to them in a way
that allows them to break off the encounter whenever they wish. Talk
about elementary politeness: this is the most basic considerateness of all:
not forcing your presence or your projects on another. Millions of official
research dollars pour into academic research on captive animals—or dead
animals, the perfect subjects—while Nollman just jury-rigs a floating drum
or puts his guitar in the canoe and paddles out to visit his friends.

To announce himself, he plays chords through an underwater sound
system. Sometimes the orca come, sometimes they do not. He recounts
some of the nights when they came:

> [One night] it seemed as if the whales vocalized constantly, not at
> all coordinated with the harmonic and rhythmical structure of the
> chord progression. [But] on the second night . . . one individual
> whale stepped out to take a kind of lead voice with the guitar
> playing. The rest of the pod chose to stay in the background,
> jibber-jabbering among themselves in a quieter tone which seemed
> unrelated to the unfolding ensemble playing at center stage. At the
> same time that the whales split into singer and Greek chorus, a
> group of humans appeared at the seaside sound studio. . . . They,
> too, began to comment among themselves at key places in the
> interaction. Sometimes the human observers would comment at
> the same moment that the observing orcas seemed also to com-
> ment. Once, the correlation was so clear that I had to stop playing
> a moment, just to get my bearings. . . .
>
> The third night evolved into pure magic . . . . I began . . . by
> mimicking the standard stereotypical vocalization of the pod: a
> three-note frequency-modulated phrase that begins and ends on
> the D note. But this pattern is never frozen. Rather it varies in
> form by the addition or deletion of the speed of the glissando, by
> the fluidity of the legato. In other words, the whales' own lan-
> guage varies just exactly the same way that a jazz musician varies a
> standardized melody. And the whales seemed very aware of my
> own attempts to vary their own song by ending each of my phrases
> with a solid obbligato amen of D to C to E to D.
>
> Unfortunately, the highest note available to my electric guitar
> is a mere C-sharp, an impenetrable half-step universe below the
> orcas' tonic note. Thus, in order to reach their register, I needed
> to bend the high string—something ordinarily not that difficult—
> but, in fact, rather clumsy to achieve hunched up in the dark fog
> while fingering up at the very top of the guitar neck. The first
> time I attempted the bend, the result sounded like a very respect-
> able approximation of the orcas' own phrasing. . . . [I] repeated the

phrase a second time. Suddenly, the high E string snapped. While I sat there in the thick night air fumbling through my guitar case for a fresh string, the orcas stepped up the intensity of their vocalizations. Calling, calling for me to rejoin the music. Every so often one of them would punctuate a long sinuous phrase with the obbligato.

I tightened up on the E string, and stubbornly plucked out the orcas' obbligato, but this time in C-sharp instead of D. The centerstage orca immediately answered by repeating the phrase in C-sharp. Otherwise, it was the exact same melody. From that point on, the dialogue between us centered around the common C-sharp chromatic scale. And the conversation continued for more than another hour in very similar fashion. . . . What the orca and the guitar player settled upon was the conversational form of dialogue. Each of us waited until the other had finished vocalizing before the other one started. In order for such a form to work properly, both of us had to become acutely conscious of each other's beginnings and endings. Once and a while, one of us would step out before the other one had completed his piece, but in general, the form of the dialogue was clearly working. And as such, the resultant musical exchange never digressed to a mere call and response. . . . There was always a feeling of care and of sensitivity, of conscious musical evolution within the time frame of a single evening's music. I might play three notes and the orca might repeat the same progression back to me, but with two or three new notes added on the end. Once, I made an error in my repetition of one of the orca's phrases. The whale repeated the phrase back again—but this time at half the speed!

After an hour of this intense concentration . . . [t]here was nothing else to do, no place else to go with the dialogue but directly into the sharply etched reggae rhythm of the previous two nights. I played it, inexplicably, in the key of A. The orca immediately responded with a short arpeggio of the A chord. When I hit the D triad on the fifth downbeat, the orca vocalized a G note, also right on the fifth downbeat. It was the suspended note of the D triad. Then back to A and the orca responded in A, again on the downbeat. The agile precision of rhythm, pitch, and harmony continued through the entire twelve-bar verse.

Jamming with whales! And we think we know what is possible in this world, enough to say that all is lost?

Utilizing the language of my own musical training, it feels very comfortable to name such an encounter a jam session. . . . But perhaps I stand guilty of bald-faced anthropomorphosing [sic]. In other words, for [the orcas'] signature whistles to be called music, must not the orca hold a concept that is at least analogous to what we humans know as music? I disagree. What we invented was neither human nor orca. Rather, it was *inter-species* music. A co-created original.

Nollman is not Saving the Earth. He is not even saving orcas. He is *joining* the orcas, with grace, with skill, with etiquette. Free and wild. Enough to hope for just that.

Across all the species and across every expressive medium there may be similar possibilities. The whole world sings. There are birds singing right outside your window, right now. Sing back. In all seriousness: sing back. On a bird walk with my environmental ethics class, several years ago, one student started whistling with a mockingbird. A ten-minute dialogue ensued; the rest of the class just stood there, agape. You can talk with a bird?

Birds are interesting as one form of more-than-human intelligence that is almost always present with us outside, though seldom attended to. Climbing in the hills or walking in rolling country, you learn to watch for unusual circling or gathering over the next hill. The birds tell you things you wouldn't otherwise know: something has died, something threatens, something has happened over there. In this way we begin to recognize a kind of sensory co-presence in the land, not at all so exotic as orcas, but, as I say, virtually omnipresent. As I drive the freeway I see the hawks perched on the high-tension wires at particular spots, or circling along with the turkey vultures overhead. Even here there is a sense of an animate presence beyond the human that broadens and deepens the human world. And correspondingly *they* watch *us.* Condors, for instance, are curious birds, like most scavengers: they enjoy watching us, apparently, which is one cause of their high mortality rate.

Other words come to mind in speaking of etiquette: tact, courtesy, generosity, humility. An alligator scientist jumps in an alligator pond (with a stick): "I was pretty sure the alligators were communicating with subtle visual signals. Slight changes in body posture and body elevation in the water—things like that. But being on this boardwalk looking down on them, I wasn't able to see those slight changes very well. I thought that if I got at an alligator's eye level, it would be pretty easy for me at least to see what's relevant to an alligator." A wonderful image. *Looking down* on the animals, he couldn't begin to understand them. Joining them, he could— or could, at least, "see what's relevant to an alligator."

It turns out that alligators, as well as other "armored" animals like turtles, are extremely sensitive to touch—odd as it may seem: in fact alligator courtship is mostly a matter of, literally, "necking." Who knows: perhaps the subtle touch will turn out to be one of the best means of human-reptile "contact," and the best human communicators will not be the scientists back on the boardwalk, and not even musicians fresh from jamming with whales, but those humans who specialize in *touch:* masseuses, maybe, or chiropractors, or practitioners of the Alexander technique. Yes:

50

touching (wild) reptiles. When *that* day comes, maybe we will be vindi-
cated as a species. Maybe we will finally have come home.

Elephants, chimps, and monkeys draw and paint. Might we not find
ways to communicate with them through pictures? Or, say, through
computer-aided graphic design? Cartooning? Entire esoteric arts are based
on just watching animals *move*. Tai Chi evolved out of careful attention to
animals' ways of fighting: a snake, finally injuring and driving off a bird,
lent its flexible and softer tactics to human fighters. Even some of the
movements are named after other life forms: one stands, for example, "like
a tree" (not at all rigid!). So here the best human communicators with
certain animals might turn out to be Aikido masters or ballet dancers,
computer artists, or Hopi Indians, who already dance with rattlesnakes.

Or high divers, mail carriers, photographers, babies. Acrobats, para-
chute jumpers, meteorologists, parents, waitresses. Just plain people. Maybe
even ethologists and philosophers. Almost anything is possible. But almost
nothing is possible until we venture to try: as equals, inviting response in
the animals' own keys, meeting the animal, as Nollman says, halfway.

Dancing with Bears

We took our children to a small powwow at a museum in downtown   55
Raleigh. Native folks much less concerned about "authenticity" than most
of us white spectators, though they were also mostly there for us: we even
had to buy tickets.

So there we sit, watching the dances and feeling the drumbeats in
our very veins, for the heartbeat seems to be its tempo. Then a break, and
we are told that some of the dancers will ask some of the spectators to join
the dance. Not just anyone. One dancer has fascinated us all night; a great
burly character, festooned, madcap but still weighty, bear-like. Now over
he comes, straight to my daughter, hand extended, no words. My child,
for half of her short life fascinated with bears, fearful and intrigued at
the same time, beckoned by a bear. Off she goes. My world spins away
from me.

When he dances her back, we talk. He's North Dakotan, he tells us
his English name and his work. Then his Indian name. Dancing Bear.
Indeed, a dancing bear. My child, bear-entranced—how could he possibly
have known this?—beckoned by a bear.

It is "too late"? I have only to watch my six-year-old Bear Dancing
to know better. Here in this crystalline moment is signalled the possibility
that we—we descendants of those who came here from elsewhere, but
born here ourselves—might finally begin to inhabit this land as *natives:*
that is, to take up our nativity, the fact that we were after all born here, as
a challenge and an invitation. We may yet *become* native Americans. Not in
the sense that we will or even could somehow imitate those who we now
call Native Americans: that would be only to join the "Wannabe" tribe, as
they call it in just derision. No: we (all of us, now, including those who

the Canadians more aptly call First Nations peoples) must find our own way, together, a new way no doubt, not a way that denies the past or the manifold traditions that the emigrants brought to this land, but no longer insensitive to the land either. The writer Barry Lopez speaks of this as "*re*discovering North America." We may well be inspired by the First Nations peoples, the original native Americans, who after all did co-inhabit this continent, relatively peacefully, for ten or twenty thousand years (they would say, forever), with that profusion of life that so amazed the first Europeans, and that was then so quickly dispatched. In the end, though, it may be that the chief inspiration must come from the land itself, and its creatures, as it did and does for First Nations peoples themselves. But it is coming. I see it as I watch, through my tears, my German-Russian-English-Jewish child dancing with a bear. Coming home. How could it be too late? In the moving unbalanced balance of things, the Earth saves us just as much as we "save" the Earth.

Reading and Responding

1. Weston's essay opens with a long catalog of what's been lost. Write briefly about the effect that this section had on you.
2. Weston says "Every year I find my students more and more knowledge-able about environmental issues, and every year more fatalistic. The trends seem to be connected. There is nothing to be done, they say. The jig is up." Do you see yourself or your peers in this statement? Write a paragraph explaining your view.
3. In the section titled "Our Fatalism," Weston makes the point that we barely understand how life processes work; he says, "*we barely know this place.*" Think about one place or one life process that you'd like to know more about—a process that you'd like to see (or see again) or learn about so thoroughly that it becomes part of what you dependably know. Write about this for ten minutes without stopping.
4. Write about a time when an animal (other than a dog or cat or other pet) observed you. How did this encounter start and how did it end? How well do you think you understood the behavior of that animal as it watched you? How well do you think the animal understood you? Answer these questions in two or three paragraphs.

Working Together

1. Look at the subheadings that Weston uses to organize his thinking. As a group, write a single-paragraph summary of each section. Then con-struct a kind of flow chart for the entire essay, showing how the logic of one section leads to the next, and so on.
2. Discuss how much or how little television you watch. Have any of you ever not watched television for extended periods (say, longer than a week)? What happens to you when you watch lots of television? How

does it make you feel? What does it make you think? What happens when you don't watch *any* television for several days in a row? How does it make you feel? Write a group paragraph that encompasses all the significant views expressed in your group.

3. Weston says, "Nature is us." Consider your own body—what it does, how it functions (or, sometimes, breaks down). To what extent does it seem true that indeed you are part of nature, part of natural processes and cycles? As a group, make a list of the ways that this seems true.

Rethinking and Rewriting

1. Write an essay that shares with readers where you go or what you do to achieve some quiet, some solitude, some balance in your life and in yourself. Narrate clearly what you do and where you go and how it feels. Provide enough detail that your readers will almost get the benefits just by reading.

2. Weston's essay is full of references to other writers and thinkers. Identify one of these references that particularly interests you and track it down. Find out all you can about this person's thinking as it pertains to ecology and the human place in nature. Write an essay that explains your interests, why you've chosen this particular writer, and what you've found out. If possible, include a list of other works by that writer.

3. Using your own experience and understandings, write an essay that defines your view of a good human life. Include at least two quotes from Weston's essay as you either agree or argue with his viewpoint.

4. Recall the beginning of Weston's essay, in which he describes the destruction and loss of nature. Think about places that you knew as a child—places that were relatively natural, relatively undisturbed. How have they fared since then? If you cannot recall any such places, can you recall your parents or other older relatives or friends ever discussing some place that you now recognize only as a parking lot or an apartment complex or a shopping center? Describe in detail one of these stories, either as you have lived it or as you remember hearing it.

OUT OF THE WOODS

David Seideman

> *David Seideman's* Showdown at Opal Creek *(1993) tells the story of two friends from Mill City, Oregon, who find themselves on opposite sides of an environmental debate. The book is also a study of what happens to resource-dependent towns once the resource is depleted. In this essay, Seideman, a reporter for* Time, *returns to Mill City for an update.*

For the past decade, a battle has been raging in the Northwest over its future. Will this region ultimately be a monument to logging's excesses or a legacy of old-growth forests to be passed on to future generations? Politicians and industrialists alike have characterized the conflict as one that pits well-paying jobs against the values of preservation. But this is a false choice. As John Muir once reflected, it is possible to have both beauty and bread. And in towns across Oregon, loggers-turned-entrepreneurs and mill-hands-turned-high-tech-workers are exposing the fallacy of a myth that claimed you couldn't have work if you didn't sacrifice nature.

At first glance, what's happening in the four states that constitute the Northwest—Idaho, Montana, Oregon, and Washington—is hard to believe. For a decade elected officials, from county commissioners to members of Congress, have made political hay out of the purported conflict between jobs in the timber industry and tough environmental regulations. Few talked less softly or carried a bigger stick than then-president George Bush. Campaigning in the Northwest in 1992, he railed against the Endangered Species Act, calling it a "sword aimed at the jobs, families, and communities of entire regions like the Northwest." Bush warned that the United States under a Clinton presidency would see "no timber workers, only a bunch of owls."

If so, the rest of the country ought to consider breeding owls. Since the late 1980s, the Northwest has successfully moved from dependence on extractive industries to a modern, widely diversified economy that is based on technology, tourism, and professional services and draws heavily on a spirit of entrepreneurial self-reliance. Today the region shows an economic growth rate more than twice the national average, with the number of jobs increasing by 940,000, or 18 percent, between 1988 and 1994. In the past two years alone, Oregon's Silicon Forest—the 1990s version of California's Silicon Valley, located predominantly along Interstate 5 between Portland and Eugene—has attracted more than $11 billion in new high-tech investments, spawning 8,300 jobs.

"It's often joked that economists can't agree on a thing, but more than five dozen reached consensus," says Tom Power, chair of the University of Montana's economics department and editor of a widely endorsed report released last December debunking the myth that conservation costs jobs. "The jobs-versus-environment folks were predicting a new Appalachia. The opposite has happened." Earlier this year, Oregon's Office of Economic Analysis released a report showing that technology—with a combined workforce of 60,860—had surpassed the wood-products industry as the state's leading manufacturing employer. Indeed, a common refrain heard on the Main Streets of the state's timber town is that anyone who wants work has it.

The region's biggest draw has been its natural resource–based amenities—water and air quality, recreational opportunities, scenic beauty, and abundant fish and wildlife. High-tech companies are flocking to Oregon because of the state's cheap land and power, lack of a sales tax, good public schools, and low unemployment rate (4.8 percent, as opposed to a national average of 5.8 percent). Above all, in no place else in the nation does the mother's milk of silicon crystals—inexpensive, ultraclean water— flow as freely.

That natural asset translates into profit. For example, Siltec, the number one manufacturing employer in Salem, Oregon's capital, has declared its opposition to potentially harmful discharges into local rivers. The company uses hundreds of gallons of water a minute to wash the silicon wafers it markets internationally, taking a cheap gift from nature that would be cost-prohibitive to duplicate artificially. "You hear about this river contaminated and that river contaminated. This area is one of the last bastions of clean water one can find anywhere," says Brad Nanke, the company's environmental engineer. "The bottom line is, water quality is a competitive advantage to Siltec." For its own part, to comply with rigid local and federal standards, the company neutralizes the chemicals it releases before sending them into Salem's municipal waste-treatment system.

Last May, Sony Disc Manufacturing became the latest addition to the Silicon Forest when its 336,000-square-foot facility opened in Springfield, a classic timber town adjoining Eugene in western Oregon, where the town's largest private employer, Weyerhaeuser, maintains its regional headquarters. Timber has for generations defined the town's culture. Among the Springfield Museum's many relics are early chainsaws; one exhibit shows a five-foot-wide old-growth stump split by a springboard, a narrow platform on which two timber cutters rocked back and forth with a crude manual saw known as a misery whip to topple mighty trees.

But that culture is changing, and Sony's riverside, state-of-the-art plant, set in parklike surroundings shadowed by the foothills of the Cascade Range, reflects the change. Where mill workers once labored in unpleasant conditions—cold in winter, hot in summer, noisy, dirty, and dangerous— Sony's workforce now pads around in an environment so clinically clean that employees use footwear that has never seen the outdoors and visitors slip paper booties over their shoes.

Sony has had no trouble attracting workers, many of whom come from the timber industry and are pinning their hopes on the newer industry's ability to pay them higher wages. In Oregon's high-tech industries the average annual wage is almost $40,000, compared with $28,000 in the lumber-and-wood-products industry. Besides, wages in the older business have been falling steadily since 1978. The high risk of injury drives up employers' labor costs, prompting them to squeeze salaries.

Kim Delaney is one of 41 ex-woodworkers at Sony who have made   *10* the transition. For the past year she has helped oversee production of 4 million compact discs and CD-ROMs each month. The products run the high-tech gamut, from multivolume, interactive encyclopedias to Michael Jackson CDs.

Wood binds together Delaney's family. A runaway log ended the life of her grandfather, a lumberjack. Her mother worked in a mill for 20 years, and her husband, Patrick, repairs machinery in a mill. For 7 of her 16 years in a Willamette Valley mill, Kim Delaney worked at "pulling the dry chain," backbreaking, dangerous work in which dry veneer is sorted on a moving chain.

In addition to the grueling physical labor, Delaney—like other timber workers—suffered through the industry's boom-and-bust cycles. During her career in the mills, she found herself out of work for as long as six months at a time.

In 1991 many mill workers appeared headed for a one-way trip to "the system," their shorthand for the welfare system. The government had mandated logging restrictions to protect the northern spotted owl and its home, the old-growth forests. Stoked by politicians and the timber industry, fear ran rampant in timber towns like Springfield, fear of the place's "drying up and blowing away like Valsetz." Seven years earlier, Boise Cascade had leveled Valsetz, a company-owned mill town 80 miles southwest of Portland, to make room for a tree farm. But instead, while Valsetz has faded into ancient history, the price of the average house in Oregon timber towns like Sweet Home and Mill City has tripled, to $90,000, in the past five years. Many of the home buyers are young commuters to nearby cities, entrepreneurs, or small-business owners seeking—as a brochure on diversification put out by Sweet Home businesspeople notes—"abundant beauty."

Like Springfield, the small logging town of Detroit, Oregon, is adjusting to a new way of life. Not much more than a wide place in the road, with a handful of stores and restaurants, it seems an unlikely tourist mecca. The timber industry here began to falter in the late 1980s, a victim not only of automation and shifting jobs but also of a reluctance to manage its resources for sustainability. Now the town is reinventing itself, preparing to cash in on a tourism boom that last year pumped more than $4 billion into the state's economy—compared with $5.5 billion from the timber industry.

In Detroit, a pair of footloose entrepreneurs in jeans and T-shirts   *15* are looking to cash in. Mike Sumner, 42, and Tom Vuyovich, 44, are remodeling the 15-room All Seasons Motel, ripping out the garish carpet and antiquated 1960s furnishings. The two have been turning handsome profits off and on for 20 years, buying and rehabilitating neglected properties. These venture capitalists expect that the $280,000 motel investment they made last fall will pay comparable dividends. "The setting has potential, and the motel was underutilized," Sumner says. "We'll get our cash flow going."

They stand a good chance of doing just that. In the Northwest, nature has become a hot commodity. Research done by the U.S. Forest Service indicates that recreation yields four times the economic benefits of timber and creates 16 jobs for each one derived from cutting trees. In Montana, for example, income from recreational tourism surpassed that from logging and mining combined in the early 1990s. In the 20 counties near Yellowstone National Park, 96 percent of new jobs over a recent two-decade period were created by businesses unrelated to extractive industries or agriculture. While Republicans in Congress sought to slash the wolf-reintroduction program in Yellowstone last summer, 40,000 visitors lined up, many before dawn, to take ranger-led "wolf walks." John Duffield, a University of Montana economist, has estimated that the wolf watchers will pump $110 million into the local economy over the next 20 years.

The loggers' lament that they would all end up flipping hamburgers has proved to be something of an overstatement. According to a report commissioned by the Oregon tourism office, salaries for full-time workers in the tourism industry average $21,000—and are edging closer to the wood-products-industry wages of $28,000. For proprietors of tourist-related businesses, income is considerably higher, averaging $42,000. The report stresses that the tourism industry provides entry-level jobs, transferable skills, and managerial and professional opportunities.

Timber towns across the Northwest have determined that tourism can underpin economic diversification. Detroit boasts an eight-and-a-half-mile-long lake frequented by anglers and boaters, as well as Breitenbush Hot Springs Retreat and Conference Center, a majestic New Age community and resort high in the Cascades where guests can hike past spotted owls and 800-year-old trees wider than the average man is tall. The retreat's business is up more than 3,500 percent since it opened in 1981. Detroit's downside, from the perspective of the local tourist industry, has been the aesthetic and ecological impact of its heavy dependence on timber. During the 1980s logging boom, the Willamette National Forest's 300,000-acre Detroit District became one of the nation's most productive, yielding enough timber to build more than 100,000 houses a year.

Vuyovich, a burly man who could pass for a lumberjack himself, stands in the parking lot counting and cursing, under his breath, the log trucks still hauling their lucrative loads out of the forest. "One day I saw thirty-five trucks near Breitenbush. Some of those logs were fat puppies," he says, tabulating the potential costs to his business. "Ecotourism isn't stumps."

This spring, to facilitate logging under the controversial salvage-   20
logging rider (a law Congress passed last summer that accelerated the logging of old growth), the Forest Service closed off Sumner and Vuyovich's
favorite hiking spots. The partners realized they had to take a stand. Working with conservationists from across the state, the new converts to the
cause organized a rally in their motel's parking lot to protest further harm
to the ancient forests. In the days leading up to the event, two of the motel
owners' antilogging signs were stolen, and Vuyovich says he received five
death threats. "They said, 'I'm gonna shoot you,'" he explains. "I responded, 'Come over, we'll hug you.' I've studied Machiavellian theory."

The pro-forest rally at the All Seasons Motel attracted 250 supporters,
including mainstream political candidates. Heeding the speakers' calls to
action, more than two dozen protesters were hauled off in handcuffs when
they defied police orders to vacate a closed federal forest road. While
several business owners expressed moral support behind the scenes, Pat
Carty, who owns the local True Value hardware store, opted to hang
above his store a yellow and green banner from the rally: DETROIT,
OREGON: HEART OF AMERICA'S ANCIENT FOREST. "It says
something very factual," Carty says. "If people don't like it, that's their
problem."

Sumner and Vuyovich believe Carty's example may embolden other
local merchants. "There's still a fair amount of polarization. There hasn't
been a political counterweight to logging in the state," Sumner says. "Now
it's beginning to change. The idea is sinking in that if you cut the old-
growth trees, the whole area is going to be toast."

The timber industry compounded its image problem early this year,
when heavy rains and a sudden thaw combined to cause the worst floods
since 1964. There was plenty of blame to go around for the torrents of
mucky water, starting with a decrease in wetlands and an increase in pavement. But most fingers pointed toward the logging industry.

From logging roads and clearcuts, mudslides cascaded down slopes
long stripped of their natural dams: trees and fields of moss. Using video-
tapes and satellite photos as evidence of the damage, city officials have
petitioned the Salem city council for preservation of Opal Creek, a pristine
ancient forest encompassing one-fifth of the city's watershed. "In the case
of Opal Creek, the vote was nine to zero," says Frank Mauldin, the city's
public-works director. "Ten years ago it would have been split. The Great
Flood of '96 has shown that some of the forest practices of the last ten to
fifteen years caused the landslides. Most of them came from logging roads,
which the Forest Service, lacking the money, has not maintained that
well." In April Gordon Grant, a Forest Service hydrologist, and Julia Jones
of Oregon State University concluded that clear-cutting and road building
increase peak flows in waterways by 20 to 50 percent and that the effects
are still evident 25 years after the cutting.

The flood exacted an enormous cost—$90 million and counting—   25
from Oregon's economy, particularly in Salem. In a development bordering

on poetic justice, Boise Cascade, lacking the necessary water, closed a mill in Salem for five days. And to the city's horror, in the five months since the flood and its mudslides, the turbidity of its water remains three times greater than normal. "If you look at it in a glass jar," says Mauldin, "there's silt so fine it did not go through the filters. We're looking at installing some sort of system costing many millions of dollars."

Mark Ottenad aims to recruit new businesses that pollute neither the air nor the water. From his sleek modern office, he serves as marketing director of the Salem Economic Development Corporation. The private group was created in the mid-1980s to enhance and diversify the city's timber-heavy economy. Attired in a business suit and tie and sporting well-trimmed hair, Ottenad, 33, performs the duties of a chamber of commerce functionary, clinking glasses with the rich and mighty at power lunches and dinners.

A decade ago, Ottenad would not have dreamed of trading in his Birkenstocks for wing tips. In late 1986, while working at the Breitenbush Hot Springs Retreat, he was among the first of 25 protesters arrested for engaging in civil disobedience at the North Roaring timber sale at Devils Ridge, where the Bugaboo Timber Company was felling stands of mammoth Douglas fir and cedar—as big as 12 feet in diameter—in what then constituted the longest contiguous stretch of unprotected old-growth left in Oregon. Ottenad's record was expunged for six months' good behavior; he assiduously pursued all legal means to save the forests.

His weapons of choice back then—high-minded newsletters, slide shows, and op-ed pieces—gave way to a more effective strategy, which he plotted inside Oregon's corridors of power. "I wanted to be more involved in the economic transition," he says. "I was touchy-feely New Age. Knowing about the destruction of these places and that the animals and birds are hurting is what drives me. But that's not going to sway the decision makers. It's going to take economic arguments. As Oregon moves into the twenty-first century, the majority of new jobs—in high tech, tourism, hospitality, retirement industries, value-added wood processing, and professional services—depend on a beautiful Oregon. The destruction of our natural resources collides with the interests of new industries dependent on marketing the scenery of our state or locating here for our clean water, a product of intact ancient forests."

In Oakridge, in the foothills of the Cascades, Don Walker ponders the dip in his standard of living. A dyed-in-the-wood timberman, he spent 34 of his 54 years as a logger, felling as many as 60 mammoth trees a day in his prime. But he found himself out of a job in 1989. For two years he gathered yew bark, which contains taxol, a cancer-fighting chemical, but then the federal government restricted the practice to protect the endangered tree.

Walker next took one of the public retraining courses offered in recent years to assist the Northwest's displaced timber workers. The latest and biggest infusion of aid came as part of President Bill Clinton's $1.2 billion stimulus initiative, enacted in 1993. Graduates now work as emergency medical technicians, accountants, computer operators, and auto mechanics, as well as in other fields. About one in five of the students, however, quit and drifted off into a professional no-man's-land.

Walker appreciates the challenges of learning new skills. "They say, 'Looky here, So-and-so went out and did this, and somebody else became a nurse, and various things.' But there's only so many people out there capable of doing that," he says. "It's a heck of a lot harder to bounce back when you're over fifty than when you're twenty-five. If you try to imagine a timber faller being a typist, it's pretty difficult." But under the guidance of a patient instructor, Walker persevered and passed his business exams.

Upon graduation, he began running a small venture raising shiitake mushrooms for restaurants and gourmet stores. He soon emerged as a sort of poster boy for the retraining program, having transformed himself from tree mower to mushroom grower.

Today, however, Walker conducts a bittersweet tour of his humid, faintly aromatic hothouse, walking past row after row of empty shelves. In the past two years his production has fallen from 2,500 pounds a month to 750 pounds, probably because of a mysterious fungus infecting the mushrooms' growing blocks. Walker is contemplating boosting the cut on his Christmas tree farm to make ends meet.

Meanwhile, his wife continues working at the Pope and Talbot mill in Halsey, 75 miles away. On weekdays she lives in an apartment there, to avoid the treacherous return trip to Oakridge. "If I could ever get it to where my wife could get back home and we could be a family like we used to be, that would be fine," Walker says, standing outside in a mist-shrouded meadow. "I like being my own boss. I'm not a quitter. If there's a breath in my body, I still have faith we're gonna get the mushroom thing ironed out."

Even as economists, environmentalists, high-tech workers, entrepreneurs, and ex-loggers play a part in the Northwest's success story, politicians persist in preparing the region for the past by working to liquidate much of the remnants of ancient forest. "The political structure is changing slower than the economic one," Ottenad says.

But public servants are finally showing signs of catching up to reality. A broad coalition of urbanites, businesspeople, and conservationists has so far blocked a proposed $21 million copper mine in the Cascades that promises 80 jobs to timber communities. At first the project's backers presumed it would sail through the state legislature. To their dismay, however, residents of Salem fear that an accident or runoff from the mine, located in the city's watershed, would degrade their crystal-clear mountain drinking water.

In Washington, D.C., Senator Ron Wyden (D-OR) owes much of his razor-thin margin of victory early this year to voters who rated the environment as a primary concern. In office he has compiled an earnest, if uneven, environmental record, attempting to moderate the Northwest delegation's stance on natural resources. And Mark Hatfield (R–OR), a longtime timber champion now in his final year in the Senate, is seeking to leave a legacy more lasting than stumps. Although public-lands preservation is as popular on Capitol Hill these days as tax hikes, in April he introduced a bill that would designate the 23,000-acre Opal Creek forest a wilderness and scenic-recreation area.

Ironically, however, the Northwest's economic expansion has been so robust that it has begun to create an entirely new set of problems. The report by economist Power sounds an alarm about overwhelming the environment with "more people, congestion, and urban sprawl." Oregon's population is projected to jump 7 percent in the next five years, to more than 3.4 million. That comes on the heels of a 10 percent gain since 1991. Portland is pushing the limits of its strict zoning, encroaching upon dwindling farmland and open space. The cacophony of honking horns, a rarity just five years ago, advertises California-style traffic jams, as evidenced by a 30 percent increase in highway traffic since 1980.

And the high-tech industries themselves have triggered a backlash. In Eugene, Oregon, environmentalists waged a fierce but futile legal battle to block Hyundai Electronics from building a $1 billion computer-chip factory in a wetland. Yamhill County, Oregon, turned down Sumitomo Sitix's demand for an $8 million tax break for its proposed $1 billion chip plant in Newberg. In the logging towns above the Willamette Valley, residents watch as the inexorable invasion of flatlanders and submission of the countryside to so-called progress threaten their bucolic way of life. "They are looking at this as a recreational backyard," snaps Tom Hirons, a third-generation Oregonian and small-scale contract logger in Mill City. "I hope it doesn't get too developed. The quality of life is dropping for many of us. A lot of people come up from the city with a vision in their mind's eye of what this ought to be. A lot of times, they're surprised that it's better, quieter, more friendly. Who the hell wants new business here? The only thing we need is a good restaurant."

In light of Mill City's dire prospects a few years ago, that request   40
represents a poignant rejection of the false choice that John Muir once defined as between beauty and bread.

Reading and Responding

1. Seideman criticizes the jobs–versus–environment debate because it reduces the complexity of the issues to simple-minded extremes. Think of other settings or other issues that we might characterize as either-or situations. Make a list of four other either-or propositions like this. Once you've made this list, write a paragraph that comments on the truthfulness or lack of truthfulness you see in such either-or characterizations.

2. As you review Seideman's essay, make a list of the conditions that have led to the prosperity in the areas once dominated by logging and timber. Include any conditions (natural, economic, personal, and so on) that seem to have made a difference.

3. Make a list of the people that Seideman mentions in his discussion to illustrate his points. For each person you identify, make a short summary of what you learn. Then write a sentence explaining why Seideman included this person in the essay.

Working Together

1. Assume that Seideman's essay makes an argument. As a group, decide what is the argument and summarize it in one sentence. Then list in order the major important moves that Seideman takes to make his argument persuasive.

2. If you were forced to reduce Seideman's entire discussion to five quotations, each no more than a sentence long, which five quotations would you select? Be ready to explain the reasons for your choices.

3. Having considered Seideman's argument carefully, what makes it a strong argument and what detracts from it or weakens it? Make a list of at least five observations.

Rethinking and Rewriting

1. At the end of the essay, Seideman quotes Mill City resident Tom Hirons, who comments on the local changes: "I hope it doesn't get too developed. The quality of life is dropping for many of us." How would you define the term "quality of life" for yourself or your loved ones? To what extent does place or landscape matter in your lives? Write an essay about the ideal place you would choose to live.

2. Write a story in response to Seideman's essay. What surprised you or encouraged you, made you skeptical or convinced you? How has this essay affected your views of the jobs-versus-environment debate?

3. Write a five hundred–word analysis of Seideman's essay that explains the degree to which you see it as successful. Critique his essay both in terms of the content and the sequence of information. In your last paragraph, indicate why you are inclined to agree or disagree with Seideman.

COMING UNDAMMED

Marc Reisner

> *Marc Reisner's* Cadillac Desert: The American West and Its Dis-
> appearing Water *(1993) won the National Book Critics Award for its*
> *investigation of the water crisis and its implications for the western United*
> *States. In this recent essay, which appeared in* Audubon *magazine (Septem-*
> *ber-October 1998), Reisner discusses the possibilities of undamming some*
> *rivers to reverse some of the damage done by generations of unrealistic water*
> *management.*

Since 1925, thousands of dams have been flung across rivers in an
explosion of concrete. As their negative effects become more and more
apparent, will these walls finally begin tumbling down?

The lower Elwha River gorge in April is a glorious green grotto of
moss-covered alders and tall cedar glades. The river, slightly milky from
glacial sediment, tumbles down rocky chutes, boils through tight canyons,
and glides across beds of agatelike stones. In the distance, poking through
storm clouds, are plunging slopes dense with virgin hemlock and fir. Aq-
uamarine glaciers spill down from turreted peaks.

Intruding into this primeval scene are two decrepit dams, the Elwha
and the Glines Canyon, built early in this century to supply power to a
nearby paper mill. The upper dam, Glines Canyon, is nearly 20 stories tall
and for its height, the slimmest dam I have ever seen, a concrete fingernail
chinked into a crevasse one could almost spit across. "It's kind of challenging to take down a dam this tall," Brian Winter mused as we gazed up at
it. "They'll notch the top to spill out some of the reservoir, then do that
again and again until they get down to the base. The real challenge is
dispersing the great big plateau of silt that's accumulated toward the back
end of the reservoir. Slurrying it out to the Strait of Juan de Fuca in a pipe
would add millions of dollars to the cost of decommissioning. I think we'll
just let floods wash it all down."

Winter—muscular, ponytailed, and laconic—is a fisheries biologist
at Olympic National Park, which was carved out of Washington's Olympic
Peninsula after the dam was built. His expertise runs to the propagation of
salmon, not the demolition of dams. But here in the Pacific Northwest,
the two are intimately linked. Removing the dams on the Elwha has been
under serious discussion for at least a decade, and the reason is fish.

At the turn of the century, before the dams went in, the Elwha River   5
churned out salmon as the Chesapeake Bay did crabs. It hosted big runs of
all the Pacific salmon species—chinook, coho, pink, chum, and sockeye—
as well as steelhead, sea-run cutthroat trout, and native char. Although a
scientific census was never taken, Winter and other biologists believe that
as many as 390,000 spawners ran up the Elwha in an average year, with

some monster chinook weighing more than 100 pounds. But the dams were built without fish ladders, and they walled off so much spawning habitat that the whole fishery crashed within a few years. Minuscule remnants of some ancestral runs have managed to hang on, propagating in the five-mile reach between the Elwha Dam and the Strait of Juan de Fuca.

But memories of the Elwha's prolific fishery could not be expunged, and in the early 1980s the National Marine Fisheries Service targeted the two Elwha dams for removal, a step that would give spawning fish renewed access to 70 miles of habitat in the river and its tributaries. According to an environmental-impact statement that the National Park Service released in 1995, the historic fishery could be fully rehabilitated within 30 years. Because Pacific salmon migrate hundreds of miles up and down the coast, the benefits would be spread from Puget Sound to Alaska.

More important are the revolutionary implications of such an act. We have come to the end of a century that historians may someday be tempted to call the Age of Dams. Nearly all of the world's most massive structures are dams, and the vast majority were erected within the past 75 years. In the United States alone, thousands of dams more than 50 feet high have gone up since the 1920s, when the U.S. Army Corps of Engineers and the Bureau of Reclamation (founded in 1902 to "reclaim" the desert for farming) led the federal public works bureaucracy in building dams to meet the nation's growing demand for water, navigation routes, and electricity.

The ecological consequences of dam building vary dramatically from river to river and dam to dam. They aren't always bad. In regions with pronounced cyclical climates—California, for example—water is released from high mountain reservoirs during the drought season, helping sustain populations of salmon and trout. In primordial North America, tens of thousands of beaver dams created a vast ecological complex in which waterfowl and amphibians thrived; after fur trappers nearly annihilated the beaver, some populations crashed, but thousands of tiny reservoirs behind mill and stock dams became substitute habitat.

By and large, however, dam building has been a potently disruptive ecological force. Deep reservoirs behind the great dams erected in the Colorado River watershed—Hoover, Glen Canyon, Flaming Gorge, and half a dozen more—have transformed a warm, muddy desert river into one that is unnaturally frigid and clear. As a result, most of its native fishes are endangered or extinct. Hydroelectric projects have inundated countless miles of scenic river canyons behind dams. Especially in the western United States, irrigation dams divert clean, cold flows from mountain streams and return them depleted, warmed, and loaded with fertilizers, pesticides, and toxic salts. As vast quantities of riverborne sediment come to rest behind dams, downriver beaches and gravel beds are frequently cannibalized. In the case of great watersheds like the Mississippi's—where hundreds of big dams have been built on the Tennessee, the Missouri, and other tributaries—not just riparian but whole coastal ecosystems have been drastically transformed, almost always for the worse.

These effects, like those of nuclear waste, are often long delayed. A   10
recent publication of the U.S. Geological Survey, *Dams and Rivers,* points
out, "Viewed in one carefully chosen dimension, many dams have been
worthwhile. [But] the adverse environmental effects of a dam may extend
in circles far wider than had been appreciated in the past." Meanwhile,
although some nuclear power plants have been decommissioned and some
test reactors dismantled, very few dams have been deliberately removed,
and almost none for environmental reasons. The great hope of the burgeoning dam-removal lobby is that liberating a star-quality river like the
Elwha could shift the Age of Dams into reverse, inaugurating an era when
more dams come down than go up. In a time of environmental enlight-
enment and exhausted fisheries, as older dams decay and their reservoirs
fill with sediment, the economics of water and watersheds are beginning
to turn upside down—or, if you prefer, right side up. In instance after
instance, getting rid of dams is making persuasive financial sense.

The 105-foot Elwha Dam has an 18-foot penstock that drapes over
its face like a monstrous metal python, swallowing most of the river's flow.
The dam is rotting quietly away; the Elwha hydroelectric complex was
built between 1910 and 1926, and the elements have taken their toll. A
dribble of water gurgles over the spillway and down a constricted eight-
foot falls. It joins the vastly larger surge released from the powerhouse, and
the reincarnated river rushes exuberantly toward the Strait of Juan de Fuca.

Most people in the region want the dams taken down, although local
feeling is decidedly edgy and mixed. The Daishowa America paper mill,
an important employer, would lose 28.6 megawatts of hydroelectric-
generating capacity; on the other hand, the Pacific Northwest is awash in
surplus electricity these days. A restored fishery would create some 450
local jobs in recreation and tourism, according to the Park Service, and the
Lower Elwha S'Kallam tribe, which once thrived on the river's fish, might
be lifted out of its current poverty. The expected cost of demolition—
including purchase of the dams—is $113 million.

In its environmental-impact statement, the Park Service concluded
that the economic value of a restored Elwha River would greatly exceed
the costs. That is why the environmental, fishing, and tribal lobbies view
Elwha-dam demolition as a no-brainer. Newspapers in the region and
across the nation have editorialized for removal. Interior Secretary Bruce
Babbitt has brought the Clinton administration along and wants the honor
of reaming out the first block of concrete.

But the Elwha dams have not come down, mainly because a single
influential politician can block dam deconstruction as effectively as a dam
blocks salmon from their spawning grounds. In this case, the politician is
Senator Slade Gorton, Republican of Washington and chair of the subcommittee on Interior Department appropriations. Despite his past support for removing the two dams, he now insists that only the Elwha Dam
should be removed and the consequences "studied." He has vowed to
withhold funds for anything more.

Winter counters that leaving the Glines Canyon Dam in place would 15 keep the water too warm in summer, all but ensuring that river restoration would fail. Juvenile and even mature salmon are exquisitely sensitive to warm water; temperatures higher than 60 degrees Fahrenheit can cause outbreaks of disease and mass mortality. Leaving the upstream dam would also block the fish from more than 80 percent of their ancestral habitat and would continue to trap sediment that the downriver ecosystem needs. As the debate continues, the Elwha dams still stand.

American Rivers, a national organization that is leading the charge to rid some rivers of their dams, keeps a list of dams that have been removed, are committed for removal, or whose removal is under active consideration. The largest dam committed for removal is the 160-year-old Edwards Dam, in Maine. Like its Elwha River counterparts, the Edwards Dam is an antiquated old fish-eater; 40 miles from the Atlantic Ocean, it blocks runs of American shad, Atlantic salmon, and eight other species from much of the once-prolific Kennebec River. So last November, after a series of public hearings, the Federal Energy Regulatory Commission ordered the dam's removal. It was a triumph for environmentalists, who have for years demanded mitigation or removal of offending dams. But in 1986 Congress ordered the commission, which licenses all privately owned dams in the United States, to include wildlife and recreation in its calculations, not just power generation. Three hundred and fifty dams have been relicensed since then; only a handful have ever been denied. In the next 15 years, 550 dams across the country will come up for relicensing, including the Hells Canyon Complex, on the Snake River in Idaho.

The most interesting of American Rivers's three lists is that of dams under active consideration for removal. The most prominent is the Glen Canyon Dam, on the Colorado River in northern Arizona. Sixty stories high, it was built in 1964 to store water for the arid Southwest and to generate hydroelectricity. Its decommissioning is now being pushed by, among others, the Sierra Club and David Brower, its most illustrious board member and former president. Brower's campaign to drain Lake Powell, the reservoir behind the dam, is tinged with tragic irony, because it was the Sierra Club's virtual acquiescence, under his leadership, that allowed the dam to be built. Obsessed with stopping a proposed dam on the Green River at gorgeous Echo Park, in eastern Utah, Brower decided that a dam in Glen Canyon was a tolerable trade-off. Later, in a memorable Sierra Club picture book called *The Place No One Knew*, he flagellated himself over his capitulation and the resulting loss. But the Glen Canyon Dam has become such a vital cog in the Southwest's economic machine—illuminating Las Vegas, Nevada; insulating southern California against drought—that it is hard to imagine it sitting idle.

After Glen Canyon, the biggest edifices on the list are four 100-foot dams erected by the Army Corps of Engineers on the lower Snake River, in eastern Washington: Ice Harbor Dam, Lower Monumental Dam, Little

Goose Dam, and Lower Granite Dam. These monoliths, erected in the 1960s and 1970s, produce 4 to 7 percent of the region's electricity. They have also transformed one of the country's largest fast-flowing rivers into a barge canal. And they have made Lewiston, Idaho, 300 miles from the Pacific Ocean, a port. Barges are raised and lowered in federally financed locks, easily negotiating the 100-foot lifts between reservoirs. The barges carry bulk commodities—lumber, wheat—down the Snake River to the Columbia, and thence to oceangoing freighters at Portland and Astoria, Oregon.

One's first impression of the Snake dams, each of which is about half a mile wide, is that they will be there forever—or at least until some biblical flood washes them away. It is conceivable, however, that their fate will be decided by the Columbia salmon fishery—once the most prolific on earth, now 7 percent of what it was, and despite several billion dollars' worth of restoration efforts, headed generally downhill.

Fourteen dams block the Columbia River, and 12 more block its largest tributary, the Snake. In the early 1930s, when the federal government recruited workers to build the first of the Columbia dams, Bonneville, the salmon fishery was already in decline from decades of overharvest and habitat degradation. Extravagant abundance had become mere plenitude.   *20*

In 1842, when the first white settlers came over the Oregon Trail, 10 to 16 million salmon surged into the Columbia watershed each year to spawn. The June hogs, a giant and now extinct race of summer-run chinook that spawned only in the Columbia's main stem, were nearly human size. In the 1940s a can of salmon cost a dime, and during the Depression it was the sustenance of the workers who built the dams—so much so that they begged for contracts limiting salmon feedings to three or four times a week.

After the dams were up, plenitude devolved into poverty. The big, fast-flowing, cold river had become a warmed escalator of reservoirs feeding into turbine generators, which took a colossal toll on juvenile fish. A female salmon lays between 2,000 and 6,000 eggs, which evolve into strikingly helpless, nail-size fry and then minnowlike smolts, utterly dependent on river currents to carry them swiftly to sea. Now, heading down the lower Snake and the Columbia, they drift lazily through reservoirs, are episodically sucked into turbines or dumped over spillways, and easily become fodder for predatory fish and birds. Juvenile salmon are genetically programmed to adapt to salt water early in life; if they are still in slow-moving fresh water when the conversion takes place, they lose the urge to migrate, and many die.

After two to four years at sea, adult salmon return to their redds, or spawning gravels, to lay their eggs. But adult spawners of the Columbia runs must climb some of the world's highest fish ladders, and at every dam, 5 to 10 percent of them don't make it. The biggest dam, the 55-story Grand Coulee, in northeastern Washington, has no fish ladders. Since it lies hundreds of miles below the Columbia's headwaters, which are in Canada, Grand Coulee alone ruined almost half of the watershed's historic spawning habitat.

Daniel P. Beard, who was the reform-minded commissioner of the Bureau of Reclamation during the first Clinton administration and is now director of public policy for the National Audubon Society, calls the Columbia River fishery debacle "the most complex and difficult natural resources dilemma in the country." Directly or indirectly, public and private interests have spent $3 billion over the past decade and a half in efforts to revive the fishery. River flows have been allowed to bypass turbines. Fish have been trucked around dams. Hatcheries have been built. High-powered diversion intakes have been carefully screened, so that juvenile fish are not sucked by the millions into irrigation canals. Antiquated fish ladders have been improved and new ones added; fish-passage improvements at Bonneville Dam alone have cost tens of millions of dollars. The gains, depending on one's point of view, have been modest or utterly negligible.

Angus Duncan, who as chair of the Northwest Power Planning   25
Council from 1990 to 1995 presided over much of this program, now says, "Things would surely be worse if we hadn't done all of the above. But the situation is still awful, and in the case of some important salmon runs and tributaries, it keeps getting worse."

For things to improve significantly, Duncan and many others believe, the lower Columbia and Snake must be restored to something like the rivers they used to be. "They're so impounded, it's hard to define them as rivers anymore," Duncan says. "Above the lower Snake dams—and before they run into the Hells Canyon dams—salmon can branch off into hundreds and hundreds of miles of tributary habitat in fairly pristine shape. . . . But to bring this fishery back to even fifteen or twenty percent of what it was, you have to get serious numbers of adult fish up beyond the lower dams. . . . I never would have said this three years ago—I wouldn't have said it a *year* ago—but it's become conceivable that we're going to breach [the lower Snake] dams." The U.S. Army Corps of Engineers is working on an environmental-impact statement that examines adapting the dams to let the river through. The draft statement is due in April 1999.

But to David Doeringsfeld, the general manager of the Port of Lewiston, breaching the four dams would be akin to tearing down the Golden Gate Bridge. "The economy here is absolutely intertwined with the many benefits those dams provide," he says. "It's not just western Idaho's economy. We handle grain shipments from as far away as eastern Montana and the Dakotas. The quantity of grain and lumber we ship down to Portland would overwhelm that city if it all went to the railroad yards downtown. No one with any common sense is looking to tear down those dams."

Duncan counters that Lewiston, which is already a sizeable railroad center, could expand its rail operations and handle most or all of what the barges carry, sending it downriver on sleek tracks that parallel the Columbia on both banks. "I'm not going to say the local socioeconomic impact wouldn't be traumatic over the short haul," he reasons. "But the impact of a devastated fishery has been traumatic, too, to the whole region. Oregon's commercial salmon fleet is disappearing, and what's left of it spends most of its time in port."

Like years of smoking and drinking, decades of dam-building have caught up with us. At least 200 runs of fish have become extinct, and many others are in serious decline—not just Pacific salmon but their Atlantic cousins as well, along with steelhead, shad, striped bass, and other species that run upriver to spawn.

"You can ask why we weren't more focused on dam removal years ago," says Lori Bodi of American Rivers's Northwest office, in Seattle. "I think it's because the cumulative impacts have just gotten worse and worse, and we see them now and have begun to appreciate their costs. More endangered-species listings is another reason. Also, removing dams is beginning to look possible. It's happening. The whole idea has captured a lot of people's imaginations. When the secretary of the interior is excited about it, you've got some momentum on your side." But experience suggests that dams—unlike office buildings and elevated freeways and sports stadiums, which have come down with some regularity—are tough to get rid of, even when all sorts of people think it's a good idea.   *30*

Half an hour after Winter and I looked over the two Elwha River dams, we were standing near the river's mouth, a couple of miles west of the city of Port Angeles, Washington. Sweeping east from the river debouchment was a long, narrow strip of rocky beach—millions and millions of wave-smoothed stones. As an environmental journalist, I have observed the effects of dams on watersheds for many years, but I came up short when Winter asked me what was wrong with the beach.

"A hundred years ago," he told me, "this was still a wide and sandy beach. There was an offshore fishery, a whole aquatic ecosystem built on a sand-bottom food chain. Now the sand and silt is trapped in the reservoirs. The strait has eaten away the sand beach and exposed all these rocks, and it's chewing into the landform that protects the western side of the port of Port Angeles."

That's one reason the mayor and the city council support dam removal, even if some of their constituents don't. If sediment doesn't start coming down the river again, they'll have to come up with an expensive fix. As Winter puts it, "The effects of all the dams we built—they just go on and on."

Reading and Responding

1. Make two columns on a piece of notebook paper, one column headed "Advantages to Dams" and the other headed "Negative Effects of Dams." As you reread the essay, make the appropriate notes in each column.

2. Before you read this essay, did you know about the environmental movement to remove dams from rivers? Freewrite one or two paragraphs in response to the essay topic.

Working Together

1. As a group, reread Reisner's essay, paying special attention to any mention of economic impact, either from keeping dams or from removing them. Looking only at the economics, what case does Reisner make? What questions would you want to ask to clarify the economic picture? As a group, write a paragraph on this topic.
2. Think of dam building and dam removal as analogous to writing a paper—putting in something and then deciding to take it out. Use this analogy to explain why it can be so hard to decide to remove a dam or to revise a paper. Work together to extend this analogy as far as you reasonably can. (What, for example, is the purpose of building a dam, and what is the purpose of building a paper?) Then decide to what extent this analogy seems truthful.

Rethinking and Rewriting

1. Which dams are within a fifty-mile radius of where you live? Research one of them. Find out when it was built, who built it, why it was built, who owned it then, who owns it now, how it works, and so on. If at all possible, visit the dam. Then write an essay about it. Speculate about what would happen locally if this particular dam were removed. Would you advocate its removal, or would you argue for its continued presence? Discuss these issues in your essay.
2. Visit the Web site for American Rivers <www.amrivers.org/hydro. html> and summarize what you find. Write only a summary; reflect whatever views and information you find at the site.
3. To what extent do you personally benefit from dams? Think in terms of recreation, of where your electricity comes from, of flood control, drinking water, and so on. Conduct research to find out, and present the information in an essay. Be specific about your own location and about the particular dams that affect you and your life. Use your analysis to help readers see why the issue of dam removal is complicated.

CLEAR PROGRESS: 25 YEARS
OF THE CLEAN WATER ACT

Paul Schneider

> *Paul Schneider is the author of a book-length study of the Adirondacks mountains. He writes frequently on environmental issues for* Audubon *and other magazines. The essay that follows appeared in a 1997 issue of* Audubon.

I still remember clearly the first time I swam in the big river near my childhood home, nearly 25 years ago. There was the smell of creosote from the sun-heated ties of the railroad bridge and the dizzy sensation of peering down into the lazy, swirling fluid the color of light coffee. Two friends and I hung from a bar until we had no option but to let go and hear the rising wind and feel the hard smack of water. It was superb fun.

To our dismay, though, the amazement of our peers and the horror of our elders centered not on our evasion of oncoming trains or our courageous plunge but on the fact that we had dared to touch the water at all. This was 1973—the Clean Water Act was brand-new—and the Connecticut River, like almost every other natural body of water near my Massachusetts home, was anathema. "You will get sick," a boy who had a pool in his yard and whom I didn't like anyway told me confidently. "Maybe you'll die."

Today, summer afternoons find that same stretch of river almost congested with canoes and speedboats, waterskiers, picnickers, anglers, and swimmers. The story of the cleanup of the Connecticut is a tale that could be told about hundreds of other rivers around the country. In parts of Cleveland, the Cuyahoga, which burst into flames in June 1969, providing a major impetus to the passage of the Clean Water Act, is now lined with restaurants and pleasure-boat slips. New Yorkers go charter fishing in the once dreaded East River, where great schools of striped bass feast on hatching red worms, just as they do in secluded New England coves. The Potomac, once known primarily for its stench, is now a major source of recreation for Washingtonians, and the Georgetown waterfront is again valuable real estate. And in Rhode Island, the Providence River was once so foul that the city of that name paved it over through the entire downtown—only to take the lid off in the early 1990s and rediscover the city's heart.

The Great Lakes are also cleaner. Erie, widely perceived to be "dead" in the late '60s, is today touted as "the walleye capital of the world." Bacteria counts and algae blooms dropped more than 90 percent between 1968 and 1991; now, like the other Great Lakes, Erie is officially safe for swimmers along 96 percent of its shoreline, and lake-based tourism contributes more than $8 billion a year to the Ohio economy. Wildlife has also benefited; for instance, there now are more than 38,000 nesting pairs of double-crested cormorants in the Great Lakes region, up from only 125 in 1973. The turnaround is largely attributed to the cleanup of the lakes.

All of this improvement and more is the result of the Clean Water   5
Act, which was enacted on October 18, 1972. The mere passage of a law, of course, does not create change. Countless hours of human effort, both professional and volunteer, both regulatory and private, went into achieving the remarkable improvement in the health of our national waters. Lawsuits against both polluters and regulators were filed and fought (and continue to be). New manufacturing technologies were invented and put to use. In the case of the Great Lakes, international treaties were negotiated.

But ultimately, it was Congress's bipartisan determination to act boldly in 1972 to "restore and maintain the chemical, physical, and biological integrity of the Nation's waters" that made clean water a national priority. The new law gave the fledgling Environmental Protection Agency (EPA) some of the muscle it desperately needed to reverse two centuries of decline in our rivers and lakes. As Senator Howard Baker, the Tennessee Republican, said at the time, it was "far and away the most significant and promising piece of environmental legislation ever enacted by Congress." And for once, it's possible to say with a quarter-century of hindsight, such political hyperbole was accurate.

The Clean Water Act is an immense piece of legislation, with more than 500 sections, so summarizing it is difficult. Suffice it to say that before it was passed there were no enforceable national standards for industrial or sewage discharge into surface waters; now all such "point sources" of pollution require state- or EPA-issued permits. The act also established a national policy on the protection of wetlands, the crucial foundation to healthy surface-water ecosystems, which were filled in or drained at a rate of about half a million acres a year between 1950 and 1970.

Just as important as the regulations was that for two decades Congress was willing to spend public money to carry out the act's mandate. Between 1972 and 1989 the EPA spent roughly $54 billion and the states were required to spend another $128 billion on new or upgraded municipal sewage-treatment facilities; in more recent years another $19 billion has been invested in revolving loan funds intended to provide permanent sources of funding for municipal-waste-treatment improvements.

The result, according to the EPA, is that even though the amount of treated sewage increased 30 percent between 1970 and 1985, there was a 46 percent reduction in the amount of organic waste released into surface waters. Controls established under the Clean Water Act have prevented the dumping of about 1 billion pounds a year of toxic pollutants. According to the EPA, more than 90 percent of the pollution coming from point sources like factories and municipal waste-treatment plants has been eliminated.

These are stunning achievements, befitting an act that was passed   10
in a post-Apollo-moon-mission era of optimism about the ability of the

government to make technical promises and keep them. Yet despite all the progress, in its most recent biennial report to Congress, in 1994, the EPA found that "about forty percent of the nation's surveyed rivers, lakes, and estuaries are too polluted for basic uses." That's far short of the Clean Water Act's original promise that "wherever attainable," rivers and lakes would be safe for swimming and fishing by 1983. Similarly, Congress predicted in 1972 that the new law would result in "zero discharge" of pollutants into navigable waters by 1985; but the EPA conservatively estimates that hundreds of millions of pounds of toxic pollutants are still dumped, perfectly legally, into public sewers and surface waters each year.

Although the act was significantly strengthened twice (in 1977 and 1987), official predictions of a cleaner future for the country's rivers and lakes have lately been replaced by more modest claims that things are not as bad as they could be. The best the EPA could say when comparing the 1994 National Water Quality Inventory with the 1992 version was a declaration that "on the whole, we have managed to hold the line or prevent further degradation."

It's no real mystery why the noble effort to "restore and maintain" the nation's waters has stalled. Chief among the reasons is the Clean Water Act's continuing inability to limit urban, suburban, and agricultural runoff, what is known as nonpoint-source pollution. Every time it rains or a field is irrigated, sediment, fertilizers, and pesticides trickle into streams, rivers, and lakes. Fertilizers load the water with nitrates and phosphates, causing boom-and-bust cycles of algae growth and decay that consume the available oxygen in the water.

But despite the fact that agriculture is the leading source of water pollution in the United States, responsible for the contamination in 60 percent of the nation's degraded rivers and in half its impaired lakes, the industry is exempt from the permitting process that regulates point sources of water pollution. Farmers are also largely exempt from the wetlands provisions of the act.

Fixing this isn't simply a matter of U.S. farms "going organic," though that would certainly help. Perfectly natural cow manure loads streams with nutrients and fecal-coliform bacteria if animals are not fenced out of every little stream and brook or if feedlots are not properly engineered and managed to contain runoff. Even plain old dirt does more than turn the water brown: It blocks light needed by aquatic plants and interferes with the reproduction of many fish and invertebrates. Sediment, in fact, is the leading cause of water-quality deterioration.

And farms are far from the only source of poisoned runoff. Most people wouldn't drink the water draining off a mall parking lot or a 21-pump gas plaza, but chances are quite good it flows into a stream or river that the Clean Water Act charges the EPA and the states with someday restoring to drinking-level quality. Scenic roads along rivers contribute salt and sand. The tens of thousands of miles of dirt roads built by the U.S.

15

Forest Service and the logging companies it serves are notorious sources of sediment in otherwise pristine waters. Construction sites erode at a rate more than 1,000 times that of forestland, and all over the West, abandoned mines leach heavy metals and other pollutants into water supplies. Finally, there's air pollution, the ultimate nonpoint source and the leading cause of continuing contamination in the Great Lakes, where airborne toxins fall into the water and fish-consumption advisories are currently in effect for 97 percent of the shoreline.

For fairly straightforward reasons, foul runoff is much more difficult to control than point-source pollution: There's no gushing pipe that regulators can point to, no corporate board of directors or town sewage authority to threaten with legal action, and often no way to conclusively prove where a given pollutant originated. But even if it were possible or desirable to identify and regulate every farm, golf course, and backyard from which pollutants leach or erode into the nation's waters, progress would likely be painfully slow. The implications of controlling poisoned runoff are enormous, simply because the problem isn't what we do to the water, it's what we do to the land.

So behind the story of a generation of Americans who, armed with a powerful new law, are reclaiming their inherited wealth of rivers and lakes lies another, more complicated tale—one of money, politics, old habits, and new ways. All over America, as the following three case studies show, there is much to celebrate after a quarter-century of effort. And there is much still to do.

The French Broad River

Bill Allen remembers the bad old days on the French Broad River. The way the Swannanoa, a major tributary that enters the river in his home city of Asheville, North Carolina, used to run different colors—red, green, yellow, blue—depending on what color blankets were being produced at the mill. The way it pretty much ran black the rest of the time. No vegetation grew along the banks below the big bleaching plant in town, and some days the air around that stretch would burn your eyes. Allen remembers the time when the farm crews over at the Biltmore estate, where his father and grandfather worked and where he grew up, tried to use water from the French Broad to irrigate a crop of corn; the plants withered within a few days.

But one day sticks in Allen's mind like no other. It was in the mid-1950s, not long after the Accousta paper plant, up on the headwaters of the French Broad, had opened a new cellophane operation with much fanfare. "I can hardly describe it," Allen recalled recently. "So many fish were dying, thousands and thousands of them. We stood there by the river, and the fish were literally jumping up on the bank trying to get out of that water. And later, the entire surface of the river in Asheville was white with their bellies.

"I remember at one point my daddy saying, 'Come here, boy, I want   20
you to take a look at this.'" What his father wanted the 10-year-old Billy
Allen to see was a medium-size muskie floating upside down, gills barely
moving, tail twitching sporadically. "Take a real good look," the man said,
"because that right there is the very last jackfish in the French Broad River.
There won't be any more."

Bill Allen paused and lit another discount cigarette from the carton
he keeps on the seat beside him in his pickup. Then he said, "That old
man was right. The French Broad was basically dead from then on. What
few fish we did see were usually deformed—both eyes on one side, big
humped backs—or covered with sores. And the thing is, people in town
in those days just sort of shrugged about it. You know: 'Gee, too bad all
those fish died.'" By the 1950s Asheville, the largest city on the French
Broad, had pretty much turned its back on the factory- and car-dump-
lined river.

But industry alone didn't destroy this fast-moving river, which flows
out of the Pisgah National Forest in the Smoky Mountains, down through
dramatic whitewater gorges and lovely farm valleys, 192 miles across the
Tennessee line to Knoxville, where it joins the Holston to form the Tennessee River. Until the Clean Water Act forced the state and local governments to take action, the French Broad was also the primary sewage-
treatment facility for all the towns along its banks.

"When I first started looking at this river, back in the mid-seventies,
the common knowledge was that you wanted to avoid whole-body contact
because the bacteria counts were so high," recalled Richard Maas in his
office at the University of North Carolina at Asheville. Maas, an aquatic
chemist, was on the board of the local sewer authority from 1989 to 1993.
The city's problem then was that even though the quality of the treatment
plant had improved dramatically, with federal help, in the first decade after
the passage of the Clean Water Act, Asheville was riddled with rotten,
leaky sewage pipes. "Just a mile from here they found a line with a hole
this big," Maas said, holding his hands apart, "and they dug it up and the
entire million and a half gallons of raw sewage just disappeared into this
huge underground cavern. It was in the stream within minutes."

So Asheville embarked on a breakneck infrastructure upgrade that
has already had a remarkable impact on water quality. Local officials also
used the power of the Clean Water Act to go after toxic releasers and force
them to pretreat their wastes. Most companies, such as the blanket factory,
were responsible corporate citizens and complied, but the owner of an
electroplating firm went to jail after a six-month FBI investigation proved
he was surreptitiously pumping chromium-laden waste down a bathroom drain.

Maas is quick to note that the French Broad is far from running truly   25
clean. From the earliest days of nonnative contact with the river, when
burly drovers herded swine and turkeys up the valley to feed the slave-and-
tobacco economy on the other side of the mountains, local agricultural

practices have added hefty loads of sediment and manure to the mix. Matching federal and state funds are beginning to encourage some large farmers to build manure-settling lagoons and fence animals away from streams, but progress is slow among the many smaller farmers. Just as worrisome is the explosive population growth in the region, with its attendant subdivisions, malls, golf courses, and increased sewage. "Land use equals water quality," Maas likes to tell his students.

Nor is point-source pollution entirely gone from the watershed; the small-time metal plater went to jail, but big players such as Accousta and the Champion paper company have permits from the EPA that allow them to "release"—not dump, of course—pollutants into the river. They've spent millions of dollars on improvements and are doing a far better job than they were before the Clean Water Act, but you need only go to the giant Champion plant on a major French Broad tributary called the Pigeon River to see the problems that remain. There's a public school just upstream from the factory, and you can stand on the riverbank and see down two or three feet to good-size trout hanging in the current. Just below the plant, on the other hand, the river is a murky brown mess. Locals say that little other than catfish and suckers lives in the Pigeon below the plant, though they quickly add that that's more than lived there 15 years ago. Downstream in Knoxville, which gets its drinking water from the French Broad, concerned citizens have formed a Dead Pigeon River Society to try to get the river cleaned up.

Despite the lingering problems, those who remember the old French Broad are optimistic. The section of river that used to change colors is full of hatchery-raised trout. Below Asheville, where the French Broad drops through a steep and lovely gorge in a series of class two, three, and four rapids, the whitewater-rafting industry has become a major seasonal employer. Riverlink, an organization dedicated to the ongoing reclamation of the river, has opened a new park near the juncture with the Swannanoa, the first piece of a planned greenbelt. "It's not the same river it was at all," says Wilma Dykeman Stokely, who 43 years ago wrote a lovely history of the French Broad that is still in print and who speaks of the goals of the Clean Water Act in almost religious tones. "But we're not yet done with the job."

For Bill Allen, who wears a baseball jacket emblazoned with the logo of the French Broad Muskie Club and who pulls 20-pounders out of the river with some regularity, the progress came just in time. "Just before he died, we took my grandfather out, and a muskie followed his lure right to the boat before turning away," Allen said. "He didn't catch it, but it was enough. He was so happy just to have seen one, he just about choked up."

The Boise River

The mayor of Boise, Idaho, keeps a purple kayak in his office, right under the city flag. "I love that sport," Brent Coles said recently in his soft, measured tones. There's a mountain bike parked near the conference table, too, which the mayor occasionally rides to work. Boise is one of those rapidly growing western cities that is justifiably proud of its quality of life. "I'll tell you," Coles said with a chuckle, "the chamber of commerce doesn't send out a single flyer or brochure that doesn't have a picture of someone fly-fishing in downtown Boise."

Ask almost anyone what they like about life in Idaho's capital, and   30
they are likely to put the Boise River and the generous greenbelt that runs along its banks near the top of the list. Miles of foot- and bike paths run along the river's edge, and they are well used. In places the riverside parks are relatively manicured and suburban-feeling, with soccer fields and picnic tables; but even in Julia Davis Park, near the state capitol building, beavers have been at work among the cottonwoods. And every summer thousands of people in inner tubes float down the river through town.

At the offices of the Boise River Festival, meanwhile, the river as a symbol of civic pride and renewal has become downright big business. There are the predictable T-shirts, of course, and posters. There are also mugs, stuffed animals, and bibs carrying the Boise River logo. Coca-Cola sponsors the festival's weeklong extravaganza of concerts, parades, and general good fun. You can even apply for a Boise River credit card.

A generation ago, most people in Boise barely took note of the river, which runs just south of downtown; it was an urban-planning consultant from California who suggested in the 1960s that the city consider creating the greenbelt along the river. "When I was a kid, we'd never think of going tubing or whatever in that river," Mayor Coles recalled. "It was full of junked cars, and there were slaughterhouses that dumped straight into the river. It was just plain unattractive." Besides the animal-rendering plants and a few other industries, there was the city's own municipal waste, which was then only minimally treated.

To its credit, Boise began the process of reclaiming its river even before the passage of the Clean Water Act; the city government decided to follow the consultant's advice and direct development away from the riverfront. But the regulatory muscle of the federal law—and more important, the matching dollars for a new municipal waste-treatment facility—were crucial to raising the water quality to a level where people could take full advantage of the new waterfront parks without fearing for their health.

"Boise succeeded in capturing and preserving most, maybe all, of the nonmonetary values associated with the river ecosystem," says David Eberle, a local economist who thinks the city's river-development plans may be a model for other places. "And the payoff has been, among other things, significantly higher real estate values."

Eberle's enthusiasm is not shared by everyone in the local conserva-   35
tion community. Some point to the daily, almost visible increase in suburban sprawl as a sign of ominous nonpoint water-quality problems to come. But the cutely named subdivisions and "private neighborhoods" creeping out from town in both directions along the greenbelt may be better for

the river than the farms they replace. After flowing through the city, the river meanders west through a rich agricultural valley. There are dairy and beef operations where you can see cattle wallowing right in the tributaries. All over the valley are irrigation ditches where water from the river is diverted and allowed to flow across fields, watering the crops but also picking up the usual brew of sediment, manure, bacteria, and chemicals. By the time the Boise gets to its juncture with the Snake River, at Idaho's border with Oregon, it's officially listed as "water quality limited" in nearly every category, including nutrients, sediment, temperature, fecal-coliform bacteria, and dissolved oxygen.

In response, the state Division of Environmental Quality is developing a watershed-wide plan for decreasing the total maximum daily load of pollution in the Boise River. Officials are attempting to include all the relevant "stakeholders" in the effort, as the Clean Water Act requires. And not only for the Boise. In a recent lawsuit brought by the Idaho Conservation League, a federal court ruled that the EPA had failed to enforce the Clean Water Act in Idaho; the state must now rapidly prepare watershed plans not just for the 36 stretches of river it had hoped to clean up but for more than 900 other degraded waterways.

Such requirements are viewed by many in Idaho as an intrusion of federal power. "It is the heavy hand of government," said Mayor Coles. Never mind that the green pastures and verdant mint and potato fields of the "treasure valley" exist mainly because of the largess of the federal government. Twelve miles upstream from town, the Boise River comes out of a pipe at the base of the first of three enormous irrigation and flood-control dams built with federal money between 1915 and 1955. Wherever you look there's a straight line of color change where the subsidized irrigation stops and the old sagebrush of the high desert begins. Like many other rivers in the west, the Boise is "fully allocated," meaning that every drop that comes out of the pipe at Lucky Peak Dam is guaranteed by right to some person, corporation, or municipal entity. As good as the fishing is in the Boise, it would be much better if the trout could afford to buy a few more water rights.

The Upper Mississippi

At the upper end of the Mississippi River is a small, limpid Minnesota lake called Itaska. Drinkable, swimmable, fishable, it is as close to pristine as any major tourist destination in America can likely be. For the next 2,350 miles, almost every success and every failure of the Clean Water Act over an area encompassing 40 percent of the United States ultimately affects this river.

At the southern end of our national river, in the Gulf of Mexico, a vast dead zone—at times nearly as big as New Jersey—waxes and wanes. It has doubled in size in the past five years. Gulf hypoxia, as the phenomenon is called, is caused by the familiar cycle of algae bloom and bust in water that is artificially enriched with fertilizers, and it has the shrimp industry very concerned.

The problem downriver has its origins in the Upper Mississippi, which is usually defined as the 868-mile stretch from Lake Itaska to the confluence with the Ohio River, at Cairo, Illinois. It's a heartbreakingly beautiful stretch of river, especially in the bluff- and backwater-strewn area above Rock Island, Illinois, and the other Quad Cities. And because there are national wildlife refuges on both banks, this stretch has more the feeling of a national park than of a national tragedy in the making. But the Upper Mississippi is in such bad shape that some government biologists worry that the amazing diversity and quantity of plant and bird life for which it is internationally known may be in jeopardy.

"We're concerned that we may reach a point of no return, where the system rapidly declines and then fails to recover," said John Duyvejonck, a biologist with the U.S. Fish and Wildlife Service. He cited recent declines in submergent plant species, such as wild celery and small invertebrates such as fingernail clams, both of which are fed on extensively by migratory waterfowl, particularly canvasback ducks. He noted that the cottonwood trees, which provide food and habitat along the river's edge and on the many backwater islands, are apparently not reproducing.

But the most pressing problem on the Upper Mississippi, Duyvejonck and most other scientists agree, is not the quality of the water but the fact that the U.S. Army Corps of Engineers manages the river through a system of locks and dams, levees, and wing dams to maintain a nine-foot navigation channel and, further downstream, to control flooding. Indeed, like so many other bodies of water in the United States, the Upper Mississippi *is* notably cleaner now than it was 25 years ago. Before the Clean Water Act, a 64-mile stretch of river below the Twin Cities was for all intents and purposes dead. Thanks to massive spending at all levels of government, the effluent coming from Minneapolis–St. Paul is now highly treated, and storm runoff no longer results in raw sewage flowing into the river.

"Most of us don't ever really even think about water quality," said Barry Drazkowski as his colleague, Rory Vose, guided a pontoon boat out of the main navigation channel and into a backwater near Wynona, Minnesota. Drazkowski, a river ecologist, used to work for the U.S. Geological Survey (USGS). Now he and Vose direct the Resource Studies Center at St. Mary's University of Minnesota. They think and talk about altering the thousands of structures that the corps has built over the past century and a half, so that instead of slowly silting in and becoming a static series of shallow lakes, the Mississippi could again act like a river. They want a dynamic river system that occasionally rages high enough to create productive new habitats and scour out overmature ones, a river that periodically recedes to allow riparian trees and plants to germinate. Although no one realistically believes that major dams will be removed in the foreseeable future, Drazkowski and others are encouraging the corps to take out or change the shape of some of the smaller structures that inhibit the river's natural flow. They also believe that occasionally opening the floodgates and drawing down the pools could produce environmental benefits that far outweigh any short-term disruption of the shipping industry.

Not surprisingly, perhaps, the corps isn't concentrating its efforts on fixing what's broken but is proceeding with plans to expand the locks on the river to allow more vessels to pass north of St. Louis. Each lock is expected to cost roughly $250 million, and not surprisingly, the various agencies and interest groups on both sides of the issue are girding for a major battle. The corps is preparing the mother of all environmental-impact statements; it is spending $21 million, primarily on studying the impact of barge wakes. "We probably know more about the effects of tugboat propellers than any other facet of the Mississippi system," said Vose as an immense barge passed on its way upstream.

Although the federal government has made admirable progress in altering its flood-control strategies in the aftermath of the 1993 flood, it's still more palatable for environmentalists to engage that worthy old nemesis the Army Corps of Engineers, and its pork barrel boondoggles, than to pick on hard-pressed American farmers. But the impact of intensive agriculture on water quality in the Upper Mississippi is devastating. The USGS estimates that 1.5 million pounds of pesticides end up in the Upper Mississippi annually; as for fertilizer runoff, at its juncture with the Ohio River, the Mississippi is carrying an estimated 100 metric tons of phosphorus and nearly 80 metric tons of nitrates each day. The watershed is so overloaded with agricultural chemicals that even the torrents of 1993 did not measurably lessen the concentration of nitrates in the water.

In another small boat, on another backwater of the Upper Mississippi, this time near Keithsburg, Illinois, Mike Coffey and Jody Millar of the Fish and Wildlife Service watched a tractor work its way across a field of rich, black riverbottom soil. "He's probably spraying Atrazine, which is an herbicide, to get the field ready to plant," Coffey said. He visits this section of the Mark Twain National Wildlife Refuge regularly, to check on some swallow nests he is using as a control group for a study on the effects of pollution from a lead smelter downriver. But the tractor, with its array of white plastic drums on the back, was a fitting backdrop to something else he wanted to point out. Not far away, a spring bubbled groundwater up into a riverside wetland. It was not, Coffey said, the kind of crystal-clear springwater you might buy in a bottle but a nitrogen-rich soup of leftovers from decades of modern agriculture.

"Even if we got control of the runoff, which we're nowhere near doing, we'd have significant water-quality problems in this refuge from groundwater contamination," he said. By midsummer, because of fertilizer loading, this bottomland hardwood forest would be almost entirely choked with algae and floating duckweed.

There are various pesticides and herbicides in the mix as well, but Coffey and Millar couldn't say for sure whether these contaminants have an adverse impact on the wildlife refuge. One reason no one has studied that particular question is the difficulty of finding a wetland in the heartland that doesn't contain agricultural chemicals.

"It rains Atrazine out here," Millar pointed out, and Coffey nodded glumly and started the boat.

Twenty-five years ago, it took both houses of Congress less than a day to muster overwhelming bipartisan majorities to override Richard Nixon's veto of the Clean Water Act. The President had made the case that too many jobs were at stake, that as admirable as the goal was, the country couldn't afford the remedy. At that time we were involved, after all, not only in a Cold War but in a very hot one as well. Nixon's own party was unconvinced.

Several times in the decades that followed, notably in 1981 and 1987, bipartisan efforts to strengthen the Clean Water Act were successful and were signed into law by a Republican president. But in 1995, only the threat of a veto from President Clinton and a flood of public outrage halted a bill passed by the new Republican House majority that would have gutted the Clean Water Act.

In that groundswell, perhaps, lies evidence of both the greatest achievement of the Clean Water Act and the hope for the future of the nation's rivers and lakes. Citizens have noticed the improvement in the past quarter-century, and they are not interested in returning to a polluters' free-for-all. The Clean Water Network, a consortium of citizen groups concerned with water issues, counts more than 900 environmental, sporting, religious, labor, and other organizations among its members. All over the country, adopt-a-river programs are springing up, and although they're not enough in themselves to finish the job of restoring U.S. rivers, they are enabling citizens to take responsibility for their local waters.

But citizen action cannot entirely replace political leadership. Nor can the federal courts, which have several times intervened in cases where the Clean Water Act is strong but political will is weak. For example, municipal waste remains the number-two source of water pollution in the country, after agriculture, and it will cost an estimated $137 billion in the next 15 years just to prevent backsliding on the progress already made in that area. That's almost as much as has been spent on municipal waste treatment since the passage of the act. Despite the current budget-cutting fervor, however, there's reason to believe Congress may find the requisite spine to act in the public interest; 19 incumbents who voted for the 1995 "dirty water bill" lost their seats two years later to opponents who highlighted their environmental record.

The Clean Water Act has not yet achieved its goal of giving Americans back the wealth of clean rivers and lakes that were taken from them over the past two centuries; but then, neither has the Civil Rights Act eliminated a legacy of racism, or the laws against murder ended violent crime. What the Clean Water Act and the resulting significant strides toward eliminating water pollution have done is permanently change expectations, giving the public the idea that progress toward clean water is possible. Not inevitable, not easy, and not cheap. But possible. And right.

Reading and Responding

1. What rivers or creeks have you waded in, fished, swam, dove into, walked or jogged next to, canoed on, camped beside, photographed, or otherwise known? Make a list of rivers or creeks (by name, if possible), and make a separate list of activities. Then consider these two related questions: (a) What evidence of water health or pollution do you remember, and (b) what influences made these waters clean or polluted? Write a paragraph addressing these two questions.
2. Have you ever fertilized a lawn, changed the car oil in the driveway, washed a car on the street, or sprayed brush killer to control weeds or vines? Assume that some of the residues of these activities wash into local creeks or into a city storm sewer that directs whatever it collects into the nearest waterway. Which bodies of water would ultimately be affected by such runoff? Write a paragraph explaining what you know for sure about the runoff path, what you're guessing at, and what you're certain you do not know.

Working Together

1. Examine one or more of Schneider's case studies, and assume they offer a formula for turning a dirty, polluted river into a somewhat healthier waterway. What are the ingredients for success? What's the formula? Write a paragraph that includes all of these ingredients and how they work together.
2. As a group, identify and list six instances in this essay in which government action or government intervention makes a significant difference in a river's health. Then write a paragraph that reflects your group's view on the role of governments in terms of the problems of water pollution. If your paragraph needs to reflect a variety of viewpoints, then make sure it does.
3. Working together, identify the three most successful aspects of the Clean Water Act and the effects it has had. Then identify the three most difficult problems or concerns still working to complicate efforts at cleaner water. Don't try to draw any conclusions.

Rethinking and Rewriting

1. Using this overview as your only source, identify the factors, situations, or issues that the Clean Water Act has addressed with some success since it was first passed in 1972. Then look to the future: will our progress toward even cleaner water be as rapid and decisive as several of

the examples that Schneider discusses, or will further progress be slower and more difficult? Explain your views clearly, quoting as often as necessary.

2. Write an essay that presents the "medical history" of a local river, starting with 1960 and moving to the present. Draw on at least one newspaper source and at least one magazine or journal source. If possible, interview someone with a knowledge of the river. Discuss what people have done to the river banks, what they have dumped into the river, how they have used the river, what lives (or used to live) in or near the river, and so on. Identify two things that, if accomplished, would significantly enhance this river's health. Discuss how easy it would be to actually accomplish these two things.

3. Find out all you can about water use in your area. What are the sources, and how plentiful is water? What are the main uses for water in your area? How clean is the water? Where does it eventually end up? If possible, visit some part of the water system that you're researching, and incorporate your firsthand knowledge in your discussion. End your report by identifying the two most controversial or problematic aspects of local water use.

FOREST OF VOICES

Chris Anderson

Chris Anderson is professor of English at Oregon State University, Composition Coordinator, and author or coauthor of several books, including Edge Effects: Notes from an Oregon Forest *(1993), a book of his personal essays. He is also a Catholic deacon active in parish and campus ministry. In this essay from* Edge Effects, *Anderson shares what he learned about the human character of the forest outside his windows.*

The forester had been dozing in the forestry truck, waiting for the satellites to come up. He was parked off the road in the northeast corner of the forest, blocking the gate to a meadow, something like a geiger counter set on a tripod next to the truck. He said there'd be four satellites in another hour—invisible in the afternoon sky—and that by bouncing signals off each he'd be able to establish the corner for a "brass cap survey" for a GIS map of this part of the forest. He showed us the actual brass cap, the size of a cookie, cemented in the ground.

A few minutes later Bob and I walked in the prairie behind him, a remnant of the prairie that covered this land for hundreds of years, most of it taken over now by the forest. It was June, and the wind blew across onion flower, clover, wild sunflower, Hooker's pink. Then: the suggestion of wagon ruts, as if two people had been walking side by side ahead of us— as if the wind were blowing harder in two narrow rows, making faint corridors in the grass. That's the Applegate Trail, Bob said to me, pointing, the southern route of the Oregon Trail. A hundred and forty years ago the horses and oxen and wagons would come up over the hill to the south, he said, curve to the west to avoid the marshy valley floor, then spread out right there, right through where the forestry truck is sitting, on their way north. You can see evidence of the trail in that row of fruit trees and oak over to the right, too, the vegetation patterns uniform and straight seen from the air. Farther down, among ash and cottonwood, we saw even clearer ruts in the widening of a cutbank on Soap Creek.

Waiting for satellites on the Applegate Trail. It's an image that sticks with me not just because of the historical irony, that brief slipping of perspective, but because it suggests how plotted and pieced and inscribed this forest is, how overlaid with the human. Past and present, the forest is everywhere enmeshed in human mapping, human measuring.

The forest in fact is an invader, I learned, the prairie much older and in some sense original. If I had looked up from my wagon 140 years ago I would have seen nothing but waving grass and an occasional isolated oak or fir. The forest I see now is the product of human intervention, existing in this form only because of the ecological impact of the settlers who flowed up this trail and into the valley.

Seen on a map Oregon State University's McDonald–Dunn Research   5
Forest looks like a lopsided wing, the apex pointing east, a ridge line of
hills and small peaks defining the V. The hills are the beginning of the
Coast Range; the wheat and grass fields of the Willamette Valley flatten
out to the east. The lower part of the wing is McDonald Forest, 6,800
acres running southwest to northeast just five miles north of Corvallis. The
upper part is Paul Dunn Forest, 4,073 acres running southeast to northwest. It's a mixed Douglas-fir and hardwood forest now, typical of this side
of the Coast Range, the fir always in the process of crowding out the oak
and maple and madrone. Hazel and oceanspray compete with seedlings in
the underbrush. The College of Forestry began acquiring the land in the
late twenties with money given by Mary McDonald, the elderly widow of
a mining and timber baron in San Francisco, buying up logged-over or
tax-delinquent tracts piece by piece for use as a research laboratory. After
sixty years of management and experimentation the forest is still a "mosaic," medium-sized clearcuts alternating with 15-, 30-, and 50-year-old
plantations up and down the V. A few pieces of 100- to 140-year-old trees
remain, and there are small sections of old-growth on the upper northern
draws.

I didn't know any of this until recently, even after I bought the new
house on the boundary of the forest (at the top of the lower wing, near
the apex). I am a person of atmospheres and moods, not by nature interested in science and historical fact, lacking a sense of topography. The
forest was just a line of timbered hills I could see from town, a place to
hike and brood when life got too complicated. I moved to its boundary
for all the sentimental reasons people move to forests, for silence and solitude and simplicity.

But then the College of Forestry decided to log part of the hillside
behind the house and I suddenly found myself attending that first meeting
of homeowners, listening to scientists and forest managers trying to explain
some of the complexities beneath the beautiful surfaces. There must have
been over a hundred people packed into Peavy Lodge that evening, all of
us in L. L. Bean khaki and flannel, it seemed, and all of us concerned,
uneasy. The scientists and managers talked about "gap dynamics" and "biodiversity assessment" and "aesthetic viewsheds," showing us computer-
enhanced photographs of the "targeted" timber "units" before and after
"treatment." Neighborhood environmentalists stood up angrily, reading
from prepared statements arguing for the integrity of the ecosystem. Several other homeowners spoke up for the forestry staff, to scattered applause,
repeating the available clichés on jobs and the timber supply.

I had moved to the forest for silence but found myself immersed in
words. I had moved for experience but found myself struggling with competing theories. I had moved for solitude but suddenly was trying to situate
myself in a tense, divided community. Interviewing forestry faculty, tromp-
ing through the poison oak, or driving the logging roads, I learned over

the course of one summer that the forest I live near is a forest of voices, of language and ideas.

Anxiety motivated my researches at first, the hope that knowledge would bring perspective at least, if not evidence for arguments and strategies for influencing policy. I joined the Sustainable Forestry New Paradigm Working Group at Oregon State, an interdisciplinary faculty research group close to decision-making in the College of Forestry. I started asking around. From the beginning the forest intrigued me as a subject for writing, too. I knew that writing an essay was probably the best way I had of getting people to pay attention to the problem; and more and more the dilemmas and conflicts of forestry began to interest me in themselves, take on a life of their own. If nothing else I knew that writing would help me handle the crisis personally, help me order my feelings. In a sense, I guess, I wanted to harvest the forest myself, exploiting the new resource for sentences and paragraphs—acting out as a writer the same paradoxes of use I kept discovering in my reading and interviews.

The research project that has entirely redesigned the hill behind my house, for example, is entitled "Comparisons of Terrestrial Vertebrate Communities and Tree Regeneration Among Three Silvicultural Systems in the East-Central Coast Range, Oregon." Its authors are John Tappeiner, a tall, bearded silviculturalist in his mid-fifties, and Bill McComb, a thirty-something wildlife biologist, deep-voiced and intense. "Examining scales, intensities, distribution and frequencies of disturbances that once occurred in unmanaged forests," they write, "can provide a basis for designing silvicultural prescriptions that produce a landscape that in structure and composition may imitate 'natural' landscapes." Trees fall over in the wind. Trees die from disease. Small fires break out at intervals. All these create "disturbances" or "gaps" in a naturally developing forest, and this may be the key to managing forests for both timber and other "values." Plants and animals apparently survive such small-scale disturbances. A number of small clear-cuts can create similar gaps—chunks of timber taken out and used—while still leaving "a matrix of mature forest" to provide suitable habitat for certain kinds of wildlife. Large-scale clear-cutting has the opposite effect, according to Tappeiner and McComb, isolating small islands of trees in a sea of disturbance, replicating rarer catastrophic wildfires. Research suggests that many birds and mammals suffer in these big openings, and there's evidence that new trees won't keep growing back rotation after rotation.

Talking with McComb over coffee one day on campus, the murmur and clatter of the commons all around us, I was struck by how academic our conversation was, how abstract and even literary. The forest is like a poem to him, a complex text whose levels he reads. But his and Tappeiner's interpretive metaphors translate into the falling of real trees, the opening of real gaps. Their "licor measurements of percent sky" have determined the amount of twilight I see as I walk the logging roads and trails, the percentage of sunrise. Their use of a "snag recruitment simulator" has left sawed-off trunks where flickers and woodpeckers are beginning to nest. Tappeiner and McComb write the forest, not just write *about* it; their paragraph indentations are new openings in the trees.

Now there are three kinds of cuts on the hill. At the end of one logging road where I often walk is a substantial clearcut with about a dozen large snags distributed across it. That's the experimental control. To the north and west are "two-story" or "shelterwood" stands, pieces where all but a third of the tall trees have been taken off. And then folded into the rest of the forest are dozens of half-acre to acre "patchcuts," the miniclear- cuts that most interest Tappeiner and McComb, replicating blowdown and disease. What are the effects of these different cuttings on mammals and birds? How successful is reforestation in these different openings—what will grow in the partial shade, and how well?

Four-thirty one July morning I went out into the patchcuts with Carol Chambers, one of McComb's graduate students, to help chart the movements of diurnal songbirds. She's a slim, soft-spoken woman from Kentucky, a long blonde braid hanging down the back of her plaid shirt. We would go to a blue- or pink-ribboned stake, sit down in the bedstraw and candy flower, and listen. The forest was alive with bird song, a cacoph- ony of dozens of species calling out, announcing their presence, repeating themselves. Carol would point and say, quietly, "olive-sided flycatcher" or "hermit warbler" or "Swainson's thrush," recording acronyms in a note- book grid and marking approximate distances on a circular target. It was a wonderful morning, the sun coming up orange through the tree trunks, a thousand blended notes in the air. Another day we walked up and down the hills checking live traps for mice and voles. Carol would reach in with a gloved hand, take the animal—usually a deer mouse—by the tail, attach the tail to a pencil-sized scale (the mouse struggling upside down for a minute, its little legs scrambling), clip a toe for marking, and let the speci- men go. We talked about nature writing as we went from site to site, sharing our enthusiasm for Annie Dillard and Wendell Berry.

The warm August day I watched part of the logging operation a graduate student from Forest Engineering was doing time and motion studies on the head faller, clocking how long it took him to angle the trees so that they fell clear in the patchcut. Marvin is a precision faller, a friendly and unassuming middle-aged man in suspenders and hard hat. He joked good-naturedly with the research coordinator showing me around, com- plaining about all the "New Forestry bullshit" and the tricky angles it requires, but you could tell he was proud of his craftsmanship, and he was quick: falling a tree, measuring it, and "bucking" it into two or three pieces in about ten minutes.

Later that day I saw the yarding operation on another site. A high- towered yarder pulled logs to the top of a slope where the swiveling tongs of the "shovel" pinched and whipped them around to a pile. As the "chasers" undid the choker cables and sawed off random limbs, I heard over the sound of their chain saws the foreman shouting about a "serious deflection" problem with the skyline, something about not enough arc between the cable and a ground bulge, a problem sure to be worse on unit ten, next up. My impression was of hugeness and loudness and danger, the swooping and swinging of big logs, though I was told that these 140-year-old trees are nothing compared to the monstrous old-growth the really big machines can yard. The question for the forest engineers on the project is how much this smaller-scale, finesse logging really costs in comparison to conventional clear-cutting (Answer: at least 22 percent more on the first harvest).

Other researchers are involved in the project, too, studying the effects of the cutting on the human community. Becky Johnson, a resource economist, is interested in "the socioeconomic impact of harvesting techniques on residents on the urban fringe." She thinks of the forest, she told me, as a "multiple output commercial asset," and she wants to measure the "non-commodity values" that are a part of that asset, how much people would pay for what they don't currently have to pay for. Questionnaires are going out. One afternoon I participated in an aesthetic-perception survey conducted by Mark Brunson, a graduate student in Forest Resources. He took us to different sites—clearcut, patchcut, old-growth, and so on—and asked us to rate our aesthetic responses on a numerical scale, taking into account sounds, smells, spatial definition, and the possibilities for camping and hiking. We carried the survey form loose as we walked, balancing the sheets awkwardly on our thighs when we wanted to write or using a stump as backing. It was a late autumn day, even the clearcuts soft and full in the fading light.

Not surprisingly, most of us in the study rated the patchcuts as more aesthetically pleasing than clearcuts. From a distance the smaller openings are almost invisible on the more level parts of the hillside. To Mark this suggests that the human habitat can be maintained within the matrix of the mature forest, too, the "viewshed" preserved.

I think of a moment from a tour that summer of the Andrews Research Forest in the Cascades outside Eugene. About thirty of us from OSU's Sustainable Forestry New Paradigm Working Group—foresters and scientists and humanists—were walking single file down a trail through 500-year–old growth, gesturing with our hands, turning around to make points, filling the air with our voices: ". . . reading streams for their level of complexity . . . the role of lichen as nitrogen-fixers in canopy microclimates . . . hierarchical scales . . . complex communities . . . structural diversity."

I think of the plastic ribbons and markers and stakes and trail signs and spray-painted numbers on the trunks of trees everywhere in McDonald Forest, as if the endless studies and reports have begun to show through on the land itself. "Wildlife Tree," one of the latest signs reads, "Please Protect / OSU Research Forests." They're bright red plastic, screwed onto many of the newly created snags, a picture of a pileated woodpecker on the side. And this sentence was tacked to a fir when the harvest began, in the forest behind the house: "The Research Management request that all individuals recreating in the adjacent area please follow these guidelines."

Much of this language infuriates me. Calling a stream "an open-water system," as I heard a hydrologist do the other day, is just silly, and potentially dangerous. The real, concrete particulars get lost in abstractions. If you think of a forest as a multiple-output commercial asset day after day, analyzable only on a spreadsheet, you forget how it smells and what it's like to walk in it in the morning. The important realities are beyond any words. Scientists, of course, don't always use the language of science, don't always view their experience scientifically, but the long-term effects of jargon—like radiation—are sometimes hard to protect against. And sometimes the abstractions are deliberate obscurings. "Treatments" and "prescriptions," after all, are just euphemisms for cutting, for killing. We can't finally trust any of this. Yet at the same time I found myself oddly soothed by the sound of the words I kept hearing, reassured that at least there was some rational method behind what was happening in the forest. Living on the level of abstraction was therapeutic for a while, giving me some perspective and detachment. Deeper than that, hearing the words and models and paradigms over and over again moved me beyond my initial naivete. The language kept showing me that the forest is a complex place, a human place, not just something to look at or find refuge within.

Jeff Garver, the manager of McDonald Forest, is a six-foot-five former track star and Eagle Scout, bearded now and still imposing. I spent two whole days bouncing around in his Chevy Blazer getting the standard tour. He drove left-handed, grabbing for a Big Gulp with his right or talking on one of his two cellular phones, dialing with his thumb. His speech is practiced and unmodulated, its cadences a mixture of law enforcement and public relations, although now and then I'd sense a sharper-edged voice underneath. He kept handing me the keys and making me fumble with the recessed locks on the metal gates blocking the entrances to logging roads.

At the Lewisburg Saddle he looked out at the far view of hills and valley and praised the "gorgeous" plantations we could see from there, their "sharp, tight points" versus the "ratty and beat-up tops" of the narrow strip of old-growth canopy. He noted "the good bird activity" in the clearcut in front of us, and the way the far clearcut, on Forest Peak, blended into the hillside. He designed that clearcut, trying to carve its edges so that they "fit better with the mind's eye." "Straight lines are as ugly as you get. I like the nice rounded contours—like a '51 Ford." Variety, "multiple-use," is what he kept stressing. There were always margins and alternating textures in the scenes he showed me, a quilting of clearcuts and various plantations. In fifty years the same "elements" will be present in these scenes, he said, just in different combinations, as if the forest is a vast temporal playing board, the same squares exchanging position over time.

The patchcuts don't make sense to him, though he's tried to accommodate the scientists. He's doing the best he can in a difficult position, answering to a divided faculty and trying to manage seventy-two separate research projects without the benefit of a coherent long-term management plan. Given public anxiety and involvement, too, he knows he has to practice what another forester I talked with called "sensitive forestry." Still, by the end of our second day, as he seemed to relax more and more, Jeff was calling the New Forestry just "weird science," "deep fungal," the product of computer jockeys and college professors with no real experience working in the woods. He thinks we need to be practical. The brush left by the patchcuts is a fire hazard, there's too much merchantable timber left on the sites, and the trees won't grow back anyway. The goal of the forest should not be research alone but the utilization of the available resources, as in any good commercial operation. Revenue is necessary to sustain the research anyway, and it costs at least a million dollars a year just to keep McDonald-Dunn going.

What Jeff honors is the paradigm of forest management that's dominated the College of Forestry, and all forestry, for two generations. His faith is in the good "site prep" of clearcut ground—poisoning and burning—then the planting of genetically strong seedlings, then judicious thinning over time. "Cut a hundred acres. Plant a hundred acres. Thin a hundred acres. Don't cut more than you grow. You can color that with all sorts of fancy computer models, but it all comes down to this."

But that, of course, is Jeff's model. He, too, reads the forest. He, too, writes it. He sculpts it, changes it over time, putting his ideas into action. His forest is just as complex a place as Tappeiner and McComb's, requiring just as precise a jargon to understand and manipulate (there are "bearing strengths" and "blind leads," "catch points" and "deflection angles," "inslopes" and "tangencies"). What I used to see as simply an expanse of trees, a hillside of fir, is in fact a silvicultural system managed day to day through hard work and insiders' knowledge.

It is a system sustained by a budget, a regular office staff, and up to thirty part-time employees. It is an institution. There are a motor pool and a coffee fund, there are staff meetings and office parties and rows of cabinets preserving old memoranda. Five other foresters—for recreation, reforestation, research, public education, and engineering—branch under Jeff on the organizational chart. There are insiders and outsiders, a pecking order. Each morning people check in at the office, gossip over coffee, return their cups to their pegs, and fan out across the forest to plant seedlings, put up signs, wait for satellites.

The Andrews Forest, coadministered by Oregon State and the Forest Service, is more impressive than McDonald-Dunn. It's only a little bigger

25

than McDonald-Dunn—around 16,000 acres—but it sits in the midst of the Willamette National Forest, miles into the Cascades from Eugene, and it's mostly old-growth, uninterrupted expanses of huge trees set aside for research. It has the old-growth mystique. Walking through its trails you have that sense of being hushed. You're always looking up.

McDonald-Dunn seems small and dull in comparison. It is close to the hubbub of town, an "urban fringe forest" cut up into littler pieces. I've heard it called a "hobby forest," too, significant only because it is convenient. There is very little old-growth except in protected draws where the fires couldn't reach.

And this the single most surprising fact about the forest to me. This is what Bob Zybach taught me that day in June when we startled the napping forester and walked in the ruts of the Applegate Trail: 150 years ago McDonald-Dunn wasn't a forest at all. It was an oak savannah, a prairie extending as far as the eye could see with just a scattering of two or three oak or fir per acre. That's why grass still grows on the forest floor and large stumps are rare. Long branches stick out from the odd big trees in the midst of newer growth, a sign they were once growing in the open, without competition. They're "hooter" trees, savannah oak and fir. Large-scale harvesting wasn't even possible on McDonald-Dunn until the late fifties and early sixties because too few of the trees were big enough. The whole Willamette Valley is the same, the result of "cultural fire"—the seasonal burning practices of the Kalapuya and other Indians.

Early trappers and explorers described the vast expanses of grass and wildflower, and the smoke that obscured them parts of the year when the Indians were burning. For instance, we have these notes from the 1826 journals of David Douglas, a Hudson's Bay botanist who gave his name to the fir:

> 9/27 Country undulating: soil rich, light with beautiful solitary oaks and pines interspersed through it and must have a fine effect, but being burned and not a single blade of grass except on the margins of the rivulets to be seen.

> 9/30 (heading south) . . . Most parts of the country burned; only on little patches in the valleys and on the flats near the low hills that verdure is to be seen.

Other explorers write of choking smoke and the absence of grass for livestock in the fall, the "grand panorama view of prairie," and "the excellent quality of grass abounding" in the spring and summer. All up and down the valley the Indians would burn, every season for perhaps thousands of years, altering the landscape to suit the berries and hazel nuts they fed on, harvesting the roasted tar-weed seeds and herding deer into unburned corners. Even more dramatically than contemporary foresters and managers, the Kalapuya and other tribes made and remade the land, "culturing" countless acres of it from Washington to California.

30

McDonald–Dunn Forest is the result of "fire suppression" in the 1840s and 50s when the first settlers arrived, which is to say that the Kalapuya quickly died out, victims of malaria and smallpox, and that the Douglas fir, after being restrained for so long, finally claimed the meadows.

Forests are supposed to be old, of course. They're supposed to be permanent, given. But McDonald Forest is actually quite young, even ephemeral, when seen from the perspective of biological and geological time, as Zybach explained to me that day in June, wading ahead of me through the wildflowers. Its Douglas fir are technically "invaders." What I took as solid suddenly seemed fragile, the trees like feathers, like false-fronts.

"Trees are cheap," Bob says. "They're everywhere." Too many in one spot make him nervous, since he's spent most of his life working beneath them. "Do you know how many people get killed by falling trees every year?" he asks, laughing. What he loves are the sweeping vistas, the tall grasses, the wildflowers remaining from the indigenous prairie. If he had his way he'd clear-cut and burn a big part of the forest, returning it to savannah. That would be aesthetically pleasing to him. That would be restoring the forest to its healthy, "natural" state, fire cleansing the forest of pests and undergrowth while returning nutrients to the soil. There were few significant snags or islands of fir in the forest before the settlers came. The Tappeiner and McComb patchcuts, their "New Forestry" snag distributions, are about as natural as a "garden," just another example of "college sense," the "weird shit" of overgrown "college boys."

Bob Zybach is a small, muscular man in his early forties, sandy hair falling to his shoulders, a former logger and private reforester with a passion for history and a contempt for academics and bureaucrats. He's a "taxpayer" more than a "tuition payer," he told me, even though he's been studying forestry at Oregon State since his business failed in the timber bust of the early 80s. A self-taught historian, lifelong student of Indians and pioneers, he was recently commissioned by the dean to compile a "Cultural Resources Inventory" of McDonald Forest. I asked him to show me some of the sites he'd catalogued. When I picked him up the first time he was wearing a "Save the Rain Forest" T-shirt, the second time a "Desert Storm" trucker's cap. He gets carried away when he talks, acknowledges that he can seem "abrasive." He says he's used to shouting at people over chain saws.

It was great fun bombing around the forest with Bob in the old Buick, debating for hours about what's natural and why that matters, what's really true and what's the product of academic self-interest, the money of the funding agencies. Off Homestead Road we gathered shards of blue crockery from the site of the old Tortora place, first settled in the 1870s. We found the rusted body of a stove reservoir there, too, a remnant from the time of World War I. Two sixty-year-old firs grew from a ten-by-fifteen hole left by the original foundation, the sides rounded now from age, and there were century-old pear and apple trees in the pasture. The rest of the homestead, what used to be oak savannah, is covered now by second-growth fir, a little forest stretching down to the bottom of the draw.

It was there, Bob claimed, in the mid-seventies, just down the hill, that Eric Forsman conducted his first spotted owl experiments as an Oregon State graduate student, coaxing the birds from the trees with mice. Consider that, Bob repeated: catching spotted owls—the symbol of old-growth—near the site of a homestead where old-growth has never been recorded, in a young forest rising from the last of a prairie long ago settled by pioneers.

Later we fought our way through vine maple and alder and dense forest to the site of the old Coote sawmill, dating from the 1930s. We passed a giant cottonwood and a very large maple. Then up ahead, sticking out of the creek like a giant rusted fin, was the perpendicular windshield frame of a Model T. Coming closer we could see the circular hole in the back of the cab where the rear window used to be. Near fallen trunks on the other side were scattered fire bricks from a kiln, the remains of a metal water tank, and indentations in the ground indicating a road and a wide staging area. All around us was deep forest, the wildest we had seen that day. "Some industrial site," Bob said, gesturing.

On the way home, by the side of the highway, we stopped and found several "bearing oaks" or "witness oaks" from the 1850s, their trunks blazed with an axe. Early settlers used these trees as fixed points to find their bearings for the first land surveys. One was inscribed with several small circles arranged in an arc. Not far away, in the same stand, were modern bearing trees, precise survey numbers marked on metal plates.

Because the valley floor was often flooded and marshy, the hills and ridges of what is now McDonald-Dunn Forest have always been the site of human habitation and culture. That is why the Kalapuya lived here, following the ridge lines to look out at their fires. That is why the California Trail of the 1820s followed the wide bench against the hillsides, taking Hudson's Bay pack trains north and south through the valley—why the Applegate Trail of the 1850s hugged the hills farther down, near what is now Highway 99, taking settlers to their promised farmlands. Jedediah Smith, the famous mountain man, traveled the California Trail, right behind where my house now stands. Peter Burnett, the first governor of California, the first leader of a wagon train on the Oregon Trail, and my wife's great-great-great-grand uncle, passed by Corvallis on his way south to the Gold Rush. My house was built on what was once the Donation Land Claim of a man named Fuller; we live on his upper pasture. Next to us was the claim of Thomas Reed, the first settler in this part of the valley. His house was framed in 1853 by Bushrod Wilson, a well-known local carpenter, and it became a famous wayside for travelers on the Applegate.

For thousands of years McDonald-Dunn Forest has been crisscrossed 40 and carved out and built on, layer after layer of culture sooner or later sifting down to the forest floor. Its cultural value far outweighs the value of its timber in Bob's mind, timber which exists in the first place precisely because of human intervention. For him the forest is not a mosaic but a "time machine," the past lives of its people recorded in vegetation patterns and old orchards merging now into fir, in hidden wells and pieces of tin, in arrowheads and fragments of flint—lives of ordinary people more admirable than the conspicuously consuming yuppies who now live on the forest edge. He imagines the people of the past living in harmony with the land, quiet and slow, wiser than any computer-generated model.

Walking into Bob's rented house near campus you see piles of old journals and documents on the couch and the coffee table and filling up the corners, maps rolled up everywhere or spread out on the floor and in the kitchen, old history books and transcribed tape recordings spilling out of file cabinets, the blurred mimeographs of family histories. Here are Alexander McLeod's Hudson's Bay journals describing the climate and vegetation of the valley, together with the notes of the Wilkes expedition of 1841. Here are the memoirs of Sarah Cummins:

> Sitting alone and glancing over my past life, long and eventful as it has been, I recall many of its scenes of pioneer adventure that were marvelous manifestations of the power and goodness of God in protecting us in our travels through wild regions, inhabited by savages and the haunt of wild beasts.

Here the day book of Lester Hulin:

> to day 5 of us laid in the bushes to watch for indians we heard them halloo but they kept at a proper distance we think they saw us go in the willows our caravan moved on to a lake, then about 3 ms up it and camped distance about 10 ms

> passed around a large swamp filled with ducks geese and cranes then passing a good spring we came to a lake watered our cattle and passed on over stony roads and at last camped without water good grass in sight of another lake distance about 14 ms

And Bob is in the process of compiling an oral history of the Soap Creek Valley, interviewing elderly residents who remember stories of what the forest was like at the turn of the century, and before:

> You asked about stories on the trail. I only remember one that they told. They come up just looking over a ridge and here was a bunch of stuff waving on ahead. They were ready to group up, and then discovered it was willows instead of a bunch of Indians.

> It snowed and snowed and snowed in 83. Dad used to talk about that. He talked about finally it quit snowing and they decided they wanted to hike over to some friends or family or something for a visit and he said that that old snow was piled up and kind of

slippery on the surface. And Dad was walking with a stick with a nail in the end of it. He got down on the side of a hill and he started slipping and sliding down, he said his mother was standing out there shouting "Jim, Jim, Jim, Jim Jim!"

A forest of voices, of stories.

The Thomas Reed house is still standing, near the entrance to Peavy Arboretum. It's a large yellow house now, expanded over the years. A riding mower and a Rototiller were parked in back, near the garage, the day Bob and I walked up the driveway. Through the front window I could see a microwave on refinished kitchen counters. We knocked on the door, but no one was home. Log trucks geared down Highway 99 behind us.

Driving my daughter to her piano lesson last week, to the top of Vineyard Mountain, I counted six minivans, three BMWs, three mountain bikers, and two pairs of white-shorted joggers. Upscale neighborhoods rim the forest, developments with names like McDonald Forest Estates and Timber Hill and Skyline West. Long, split-level houses are built into hillsides, hidden in oak and fir, their cedar decks offering views of the valley and the Cascades. Right now a developer is grubbing out a "real estate cut" at the base of Vineyard Mountain, removing the fir and leaving the madrone in preparation for a forty-eight unit housing development. I can hear the Caterpillars powering from here, over the whine of my computer fan. This morning's paper describes a neighborhood protest at the Benton County Planning Commission last night, over a hundred homeowners expressing their worry that still another development on the mountain will severely deplete the already marginal supply of drinking water.

Over 35,000 "recreation days" are spent in the forest each year, according to a recent Master's thesis. There are mountain bikers and equestrians and hikers on the roads and trails. The Timberhill Harriers run here every weekend. Once we stumbled into a timber carnival over at Cronemiller Lake. High-school timber clubs from across the state were competing in axe throwing and timber cruising and tree climbing. Trucks and campers were parked everywhere. A hotdog stand was set up. Another day we came across a mountain bike competition, the finish line at the lake. Mud-spattered riders came whizzing off the hill, numbers flapping on their jerseys.

Once I was walking with the kids on the 510 Road when I heard   45
jazz guitar seeping through the trees, then lounge music piano. Farther on we saw a wedding reception at Peavy Lodge, tuxedoed young men parking their cars, women hiking up their gowns to climb the steps. We could see a long sheet cake, balloons flying from folding chairs.

It all seems natural to me now. There has always been a "human/ forest interface" here, beginning at least as early as the first makeshift shelters of the Kalapuya.

Perhaps the central effect of my studying the forest this last year has been to complicate my understanding of the "natural." On the one hand some of the rhetoric of environmentalism seems naive and unconsidered to me now, even foolishly arrogant. We can't ground our arguments for what is right on some sentimental longing for the unspoiled, as if only what is nonhuman is good. That's to be ignorant of history, as well as to misunderstand our own responsibilities. Wendell Berry argues that just as culture depends on wilderness—just as we need to preserve wilderness to survive as a culture, spiritually and physically—wilderness now depends on culture. Setting aside the Andrews Forest to remain as old-growth is a cultural act. It is the drawing of a line, the creating of value. Preserving wilderness means erecting fences, fumbling with locks in metal gates.

But that argument also works another way. Often in my conversations with foresters and scientists a policy or practice would be explained to me as if it were inevitable, as if things had to be done that way, inexorably. Sometimes there was an arrogant privileging of expertise, an invoking of the tropes of objectivity and practicality, as if my concerns with aesthetics and spiritual values were merely subjective, merely personal. But the history of the forest argues something far different. It argues for change, for patterns too shifting and evolving to justify any single practice or claim of ownership. Clear-cutting isn't an ancient, inevitable method: the first settlers didn't have enough trees to cut; selective logging was practiced between the wars; Mary McDonald started giving money to the School of Forestry for the expressed purpose of encouraging reforestation, not harvesting.

We can do anything we want. As a nation we can choose, for example, to pay more for timber. Who's to say that the current price is inevitable, objectively right, that there aren't other values we might pay for other ways? On McDonald-Dunn Forest we can choose to pay a recreational use fee, as some have suggested, to take the financial pressures off the forest. We can decide, as a community, that the first goal of the forest should be education and research, not the generation of revenue—or we can choose to clear-cut and burn all 12,000 acres. Science imposes limits of fact. Trees grow at certain rates in certain soils in certain climates. Ecosystems function according to complex interchanges of energy. But even then these are facts to be interpreted, the basis of policies we need to construct. The history of the forest shows that it has always been cultured, shaped. It has been made. No policy can be justified on the grounds that it is pure.

One evening at the end of the summer I walked to my first meeting 50 of the McDonald Forest Trails Committee, over in the Forestry Club Cabin, a mile or so from the house. It was odd to be walking through the forest to a committee meeting instead of driving to town for one. It almost seemed as if time had fallen away and I was hiking to a gathering at the Reed place for the evening, to catch up on the news and tell stories with my neighbors.

The meeting was a potluck, pasta salad shining under the cabin's new fluorescent lights. The room smelled like a school cafeteria. The agenda

was up on a marker board in the front, items listed in ten-minute incre-
ments, and by the time I got there discussion of the "Multiple Use Trails
Map and Guide" was under way. Representatives of the equestrians were
politely complaining to representatives of the mountain bikers while Mary
Rellergert, the recreation forester, practiced her conflict-resolution skills.
Everyone kept using the term "user group": how do we accommodate the
overlapping concerns of these different "user groups"? how can we get the
full participation of this or that "user group"?

Two hours later I escaped back into the dark, familiar forest, to the
sound of crickets and the smell of smoke from the field burning in the
valley. It was early September, still warm, exactly a year since the loggers
began their work. The last of the sun glowed over the edge of the
shelterwood.

I could have named the different trees I brushed past, explained the
theory behind the shelterwood, pointed out where the California Trail
came in from the south, following the 510 Road. But I was glad to be
walking in the dark, with just the sound of the trees around me. I was glad
that the loggers were gone, the forest returned to its own rhythms and
silences. After a year of studying and learning and interviewing experts, it's
still the surfaces I value, still the feel of things, the smell of blackberry and
needle duff, the play of shadow. McDonald Forest may not be as spectacular as the Andrews, but living on and near it through the seasons I have
come to feel for it a special affection.

And this is what I want to argue for: for local knowledge, for personal
knowledge. After all the terms and ideas and paradigms, what I value most
is the sense of familiar ground, of a place I know well enough to find my
way home in the dark, and I want to argue for that, just for the feeling of
being here, fully, with the heart and the senses. I want to argue for the
mind at rest.

The difference is that I know now I will have to *argue* for these things.   *55*
I will have to fight for them and represent them publicly, and to do that I
will have to know something about current silvicultural practices and the
ecology of the forest. I will have to attend more potluck meetings at the
forestry cabin. To make possible for others the knowing of a forest by
heart, I will have to learn to speak the language of "user groups" and
"recreationists" and even "multiple-use managers." I will have to make my
own voice heard in the forest of voices.

Reading and Responding

1. Notice that Anderson uses blank space to separate the major sections of
   the essay. Number the sections in the margins of the text, and write a
   brief one- or two-line summary of each section, perhaps a subtitle.
   What is the point of each section? What is the main method of development in each section, the main kind of writing?

2. Notice the kinds of information that Anderson uses, the sources of his details. Mark and label them in the margins. What kind of research does he rely on the most?

Working Together

1. In a few sentences, explain the title, "Forest of Voices."
2. Anderson focuses on several individuals in this essay. Does any one of them come out looking better than the others? Is Anderson on the side of one more than the others, or does he treat them all equally? (Notice how much space he devotes to each one, the things he quotes them as saying, how he describes their physical appearance.)
3. Explain the following statement as it relates to Anderson's essay: "We can do anything we want."
4. Discuss these questions: How is Anderson's essay different from a traditional term paper? How is it similar?

Rethinking and Rewriting

1. Write an essay about learning something you didn't know before—something that surprised you or overturned some unconsidered assumption.
2. Do an in-depth profile of a particular piece of ground, area, or ecosystem: a park, a city block, a garden. Write a biography of that place.
3. Write an essay built out of a series of interviews, profiling several individuals associated with an issue or place.
4. Write a term paper as a series of scenes, dialogues, portraits, and stories, grounding your facts and research in your own experience.

Chapter 5 Essay Topics

1. Drawing from two (or more) essays in this section and from your own views, respond to this statement: Government plays an important role in regulating businesss and individuals in the effort to reduce pollution. Explain the extent to which you agree with this statement. Include at least one quotation from each essay you select. Variation: Instead of drawing on two essays, draw on one essay and on a local example that you research.
2. Write a personal essay about some way that you or someone you know personally has been affected by air or water pollution. Help your readers understand that pollution is more than a set of air quality measurements or water test results. Based on your experience, draw a conclusion about what should be done to lessen the impact of pollution.
3. Write a letter (five hundred words or less) to some student audience encouraging a specific action or set of actions that you want to urge them to perform to lessen a particular environmental problem. If

possible, address this letter to a group of students at your school. Make sure they understand the action(s) you advocate, the reasons for those actions, and the problem they will help relieve. Make at least one reference to one of the essays in this chapter.

4. Write a personal letter to someone in your family who is not born yet— perhaps your own children, or nieces, nephews, or cousins. Tell them your view of how the world looks to you now in terms of environmental health. Include at least one reference to an essay in this chapter. Explain that you're writing this as a class assignment. Describe briefly the class and how you view its focus, and then address the central questions of this assignment. Close the letter in an appropriate manner without being silly or flippant.

5. Using one of the readings in this chapter as a primary focus, consider the role that population increases have on the problem highlighted. Use your chosen reading as a source, but also extend your discussion (and your understanding) with research. End by identifying any strategies or practices (other than legislating the birthrate) that we could follow to lessen the problem.

6. Identify one of the readings in this chapter that really persuades you it's telling the truth. Discuss how it manages to be so persuasive. Identify the writing strategies—the intellectual moves—that make for successful persuasion. If you wish, mention a selection (or an outside source) that you do not trust or do not find particularly persuasive. Use this selection to help you discuss the strategies that do not work, do not persuade.

7. Use any one of these essays as a case study to illustrate how an environmental problem also becomes a political problem. Show how politics plays a part in the way the problem is discussed, and how politics affects what can or cannot be done (to solve the problem). If you can also use local examples to illustrate your point, do so.

6

Evolving Ethics

What is nature for? Who is it for? Do plants and animals and water and air have value apart from us? Or is their value related to what we can make from them: money, artifacts, recreation, culture?

Should we cut down trees or leave them alone? What should we refrain from exploiting? What do we owe to the generations that follow us? What right do we have to claim supremacy among species? What obligations might we incur by doing so?

To answer these questions is to be involved in ethics. To live in the world is to be faced with ethical choice: Who (or what) has rights? What is the right course of action?

The essays assembled in this chapter suggest the progress of thought about these questions over the past several decades, from the seminal thoughts of Aldo Leopold and Wallace Stegner to the recent arguments of feminists and Native Americans.

THE LAND ETHIC

EXILED IN AMERICA

Alison Hawthorne Deming

> *Poet, essayist, and direct descendant of novelist Nathaniel Hawthorne, Alison Deming is director of the University of Arizona Poetry Center, where she also teaches creative writing. She has published a book of poems, placed her work in numerous magazines and anthologies, and recently published a collection of essays titled* The Edges of the Civilized World: A Journey in Nature and Culture *(1998). In the following essay from her collection* Temporary Homelands *(1994), Deming explores what* wilderness *might have meant to her ancestors and what it means to her now.*

If only it were possible to see the unbroken New England forest through the eyes of my Puritan ancestors, to eat porridge and bear grease beside them in a dirt-floored hut, to know the fears that kept them awake at night. Certainly they feared the wilderness, its darkness, beasts, and savages. Perhaps they feared [that] the freedom for which they had risked their lives would let loose a dangerous wildness that dwelled captive inside them. They saw their own nature as depraved, yet they were visionaries bent on the radical improvement of humankind. I have wanted to understand these "Zionists," not only because they are family, but also because the story they began—leaving their homeland, separating themselves from nature as they knew it to graft themselves to a new continent—is a story still in process. We, their descendants, after having trashed the land for three hundred and fifty years, can hardly claim to have treated it as a home. What is the meaning of ancestry? What is the meaning of *this* ancestry? When I try to know those distant strangers I feel a gnarl inside myself where the authoritarian and the libertine tangle like scrapping dogs.

My ancestry is distinguished—the first American Hathorne (my great-great-grandfather Nathaniel changed the spelling to "Hawthorne") came from England in the 1630s and became one of the Fathers of Massachusetts, helping to establish domestic order and a code of justice in the pioneer colony. That was ten generations ago. Since then we've been judges and magistrates, seamen and merchants, authors and statesmen, artists, journalists, educators, psychologists, a founder of a religious order for the care of the incurably ill, and dozens of decent people devoted to raising and educating their children in a manner that would honor their cultured ancestry. And yet, bloody roots feed this tree. My Puritan ancestors committed brutal, shameful deeds in the name of their faith. Their passion for what they believed to be right fueled violence and injustice—deeds that would be unthinkable if we did not live in the century when no human cruelty became unthinkable.

William Hathorne reportedly sailed from England on the *Arbella,* one of eleven ships bearing seven hundred passengers, two hundred and forty cows, and sixty horses. Idlers and thieves had been weeded out in advance by agents of the Massachusetts Bay Colony. The voyagers sat on shipboard for two weeks waiting for the wind to be right for sailing. Stepping on board for the three-month trip must have been their first crucial test of faith. William arrived in Naumkeag harbor with dozens of pious and scurvy-weakened Puritans. They brought ballast of bricks and hardware, family chests packed with leather doublets, wool waistcoats, steeple-crowned felt hats, farthingales, stomachers, shoe buckles, a few favorite books, and packets of seed. Among the passengers were Governor John Winthrop, Lady Arbella Johnson (whose financial support helped to launch the New England migration), Sir Richard Saltonstall, Anne and Simon Bradstreet, William Hathorne and his younger brother John and sister Elizabeth. They had endured tempests and contrary winds, during which seamen and passengers alike fasted to earn God's forbearance. In rough seas they were confined below deck for days, the stench of sickness and waste as penetrating as the cold. They called the voyage a baptism. So stern was the Puritan sense of righteousness—excommunication for card playing— that it's difficult to imagine them, even in these circumstances, taking comfort from one another. More likely, sermons and long prayer lulled them, each hardship an opportunity to demonstrate the power of their faith.

I have searched through Puritan writings looking for expressions of vulnerability, fear, or intimacy, wanting to understand the emotional qual-ity of their lives. What afflictions did they suffer that gave them the courage to pull up stakes and head three thousand miles toward the probable ruin of a wilderness existence? The authors don't allow such disclosures, at least not in the letters, journals, sermons, and narratives I've come across. Falli-bility and suffering were given, the groundwork of faith, not pathology to be examined. They expressed even marital tenderness through the lan-guage of religious belief. In a letter to his wife written while the *Arbella* lay becalmed in port, John Winthrop wrote:

> And now (my sweet soul) I must once again take my last farewell of thee in Old England; it goeth verye near my heart to leaue thee, but I know to whom I haue committed thee euen to him, who loues the(e) much better than any husband can who hath taken account of the haires of thy head, and putts all thy teares in his bottle, who can, and (if it be for his glorye) will bringe us together againe with peace and comfort.

William Hathorne was the oldest and smartest child among seven   5 born to a yeoman family living on ancestral farmlands in Binfield, England. He was raised to work the land, to grow wheat, barley, oats, and hay and tend cattle, sheep, bees, and horses. But the family recognized William's promise at an early age and saw that he got an unusually good education for someone of his class. It served him well. His eloquence, earnestness, and political sense gave him the social mobility of gentry. His favorite book, the one he carried with him on the *Arbella,* was Philip Sidney's *Arcadia,* a pastoral romance about an idealized land. But William's most passionate interest was in religious matters. At the Binfield church, where his family worshiped, the Church of England preaching was vehemently opposed to religious dissent. Puritans, he was taught, were the most traitorous dissenters because of their severe code of discipline and their fervor to rid the Church of England of Roman Catholicism. But as a teenager, William spent time at his grandfather's farm near Dorchester and there began to hear firsthand the revolutionary ideology. Reverend John White, a Puritan and Calvinist, assailed the "popishly addicted" and condemned the corruption of priests: "In all excess of sin, Papists have been the ringleaders, in riotous companies, in drunken meetings, in seditious assemblies & practices, & in profaning the Sabbath, in quarrels & brawls in stage plays, greens, ales, & all heathenish customs."

Convinced that with clear will, plain worship, good deeds, and strict moral codes they could be one with God, the Puritans set out to live exemplary lives. They intended to bring Christianity back to its original humility and communal roots. Theirs was a community not only of faith, but of radical dissent from moral hypocrisy. For many of the dissenters, the answer to the ruin that European Christianity had become was to leave it behind and sow the seeds of "God's new Plantation" in the American wilderness.

By the time he was twenty-one, William had converted.

Reverend White's followers began to settle in Dorchester, Massachusetts, in 1628. Among the first was Richard Davenport, a zealous young disciple who had become a friend of the Hathornes in England and was engaged to Elizabeth when she was thirteen years old. A professional soldier, he had been called for duty in the Massachusetts Bay Colony several years before his friends and his betrothed were to join him. By the time William, Elizabeth, and John arrived, Richard had several years of experience with which to guide them. Dorchester was a rough-hewn town, the homes no more than huts with thatched roofs, mud or wooden chimneys, and oil-paper windows. For lamps, Reverend Francis Higginson wrote, they used slices of pine.

> Yea, our pine trees, that are most plentiful of all wood, doth allow us plenty of candles, which are very useful in a house, and they are such candles as the Indians burn, having no other, and they are nothing else but wood of the pine tree cloven into two little slices, something thin, which are so full of the moisture of turpentine and pitch, that they burn as clear as a torch.

William had the help of his young brother, John, still a teenager. In the custom of the times, John had papers of indenture to his older brother stipulating that he must work for him until he was eighteen. Prospective settlers had been encouraged to bring young children to the colony, because the children could earn more than the cost of their keep by working in the cornfields. For the Hathorne parents remaining in Binfield, the experience of watching three of their children fall in with the spiritual enemy and then sail off into a perilous self-exile must have been wrenching. Four other children remained in England to continue the farming tradition. The fate of the exiles was unknown to those who stayed at home. When the father made his will, he bequeathed one hundred pounds to William, forty to Elizabeth, and twenty to John, "if not dead."

The settlers endured poverty, epidemic, hurricane, drunken brawling, and a plague of caterpillars, which, it was believed, fell in a great thunder shower and decimated their crops. Nevertheless, the newcomers prospered on the bounty of the native forest and on livestock they raised for trade. With many skilled craftsmen and servants among them, they quickly raised frame-and-clapboard houses. By 1629 a brickworks had been established in nearby Salem (formerly Naumkeag, renamed for the Hebrew word for peace) and the more prosperous citizens built gracious brick homes in the thriving seaport.

Even the most devout wrote with great admiration and earnestness of the "Earth of New England." As Higginson stated: "I will endeavor to show you what New England is . . . and truly endeavor, by God's help, to report nothing of New England but what I have partly seen with mine own eyes, and partly heard and inquired from the mouths of very honest and religious persons. . . ." He went on to catalog the "commodities and discommodities" of the land, praising the air, water, and soil; the abundance of native turnips, parsnips, carrots, herbs, pumpkins, mulberries, plums, raspberries, currants, chestnuts, filberts, walnuts, hurtleberries; the varieties of wood—"There is no better in the world"; and the beasts— some bears, lions, several sorts of deer, "some whereof bring three or four young ones at once, which is not ordinary in England; also wolves, foxes, beavers, otters, martens, great wild cats, and a great beast called a molke, as big as an ox." Of the discommodities, Higginson cited mosquitoes, the cold winter season, and "snakes and serpents, of strange colors and huge greatness. Yea there are some serpents, called rattlesnakes, that have rattles in their tails, that will not fly from a man as others will, but will fly upon him and sting him so mortally that he will die within a quarter of an hour after, except the party stinged have about him some of the root of an herb called snake-weed to bite on, and then he shall receive no harm." And finally, among the discommodities he cited: "here wants as yet the good company of honest Christians . . . to make use of this fruitful land. Great pity is to see so much good ground for corn, and for grass as any is under the heavens, to lie altogether unoccupied, when so many honest men and their families in Old England, through populousness thereof, do make very hard shift to live one by the other."

Puritans wrote descriptions of how to make sugar from maple sap, how to find where the bees hive in the woods and how to collect their honey; they wrote field notes on berries, oaks, and fish, and sent specimens

10

to England for further study. The writing shows intelligence, an apprecia-
tion for complexity, attention to the thing itself, praise for nature's gener-
ative power, and careful detail: "seeds found in the gizzards of wild-fowl
which afterwards sprouted in the Earth." Even Cotton Mather, pastor at
the North Church in Boston, who is remembered for his pedantic, intolerant, and oppressive vigor, wrote about nature with an inquiring scientific
eye—at times also with wonder and love. In his essay "On Vegetables," he
wrote:

> How unaccountably is the *Figure* of *Plants* preserved? And how
> unaccountably their *Growth* determined? Our excellent *Ray* [John
> Ray, a pioneer in English natural history] flies to an intelligent
> *plastick Nature,* which must understand and regulate the whole
> Oeconomy. Every particular *part* of the *Plant* has its astonishing
> Uses. The *Roots* give it a Stability, and fetch the Nourishment into
> it, which lies in the Earth ready for it. The *Fibres* contain and
> convey the Sap which carries up that Nourishment. The *Plant* has
> also larger Vessels, which entertain the proper and specifick Juice
> of it; and others to carry the Air for its necessary respiration. The
> outer and inner *Bark* defend it from Annoyances, and contribute
> to its Augmentation. The *Leaves* embrace and preserve the *Flower*
> and *Fruit* as they come to their explication . . . How agreeable the
> *Shade* of *Plants,* let every Man say that *sits under his own Vine, and
> under his own Fig-tree!* How charming the Proportion and Pulchri-
> tude of the *Leaves,* the *Flowers,* the *Fruits,* he who confesses not,
> must be, as Dr. *More* says, *one sunk into a forlorn pitch of Degeneracy,
> and stupid as a Beast.*

Sooner or later, all Puritan writing returns to faith; all praise of nature
becomes an invitation to praise God. The historians—those who would
master the conflicting stories of the past and tell the definitive tale—say
that for the Puritans wilderness was not a place to encounter the sacred,
but a place of inherent evil, a moral emptiness where they could be tested
and prove themselves as worthy as saints. Contemporary historian Perry
Miller writes that "the Puritan felt that unless he could see the divine
purpose in the phenomenal world he had failed to interpret his facts correctly. For him nature was a revelation of the divine order which had pre-
existed in the mind of God before it was incarnated in matter, and its
highest value was symbolic."

I find the stories muddled and contradictory, replete with fearful
references to "the howling wilderness," reverent submission to God's will
as the primary survival skill, as well as an unmistakable sensual engagement
with nature, at times a rapturous love of natural beauty, and the scientific
intelligence (in 1721!) to inoculate the population of Boston against smallpox. The hope that I could understand the Puritans' relationship with the
American wilderness and how their beliefs shaped that relationship now

seems overreaching. Like us, the Puritans were inconsistent, conflicted and complex, driven by hopes they could not realize.

Without people, wilderness asks for no value or meaning—it simply   15
is. The values and meanings that people project onto the blank screen of the wild become the ground on which their relationship with nature is played out. If the wilderness is evil, we subdue it. If it is sacred, we go there to feed the soul. If wilderness is all we mean when we say "nature," then we suffer an alienation from the various forces that spawn, sustain, and limit us. I have always been taken by the sheer sensuality of the North American continent. Wild water sculpting flows and basins into rock, the dense profusion of all-terrain greenery that gentles the pitch of rocky land, the shocking and delicate appearance of flower genitals in the woods— May beauties, trout lilies, wild orchids, and the scrotal pouch of the lady's slipper. Even snow can turn the harshest land into a contour smooth as airbrushed skin. And the animals—lynx, fox, elk, moose, mustang, cougar, river otter, porpoise, hare—each name conjuring a specific liquid movement, the self-possessed physicality with which they kill, eat, breed, and wash. I sleep with two cats and the touch of their fur brushing against my naked skin is among the most beautiful sensations I can think of. They calm me, these animals who could be wild but choose not to be, who go outside to kill and lounge around, then come home every day for the food I provide and for my touch. They bridge me over to that animal country from which I came, a place in which the body poses no questions, only needs.

I go to the wilderness for spiritual comfort, to get away from the demands placed on me, and to feel closer to the mystery of the big biological enterprise in which I'm a small part. I don't hunt—though I'd like to give it a try—I fish only occasionally and eat the catch more for pleasure than need. In the woods I harvest only wild berries and chanterelles— both luxury items that have more to do with delight than with survival. I go to the city for my physical needs—food, clothing, books, hardware, friends, and sometimes for the sexiness of the city itself.

That I experience the wilderness as the nexus between sensuality and spirituality is a comfort to me. My ancestors, I suspect, experienced that nexus as a torment. Their entire subsistence came from the woods. They arrived thinking faith was their sanctuary, not the land. Yet everywhere they looked for spirit, they found confounding matter. They feared snakes, bears, wolves, and mythic animals that settlers swore they had seen—"lions and serpentlike monsters with two heads." Though game birds, deer, and firewood were more plentiful than in England, and herring so abundant that they learned from the Indians how to "fish the fields" (burying the catch as they tilled the soil) to fertilize their corn, subsistence remained an iffy proposition. Every early settler's experience of America had to have been one of grueling physicality where progress meant mastering the material world in order to survive. Many winter nights they must have sat out a gale, backdrafts of smoke leaking from the mud-and-stick chimney, taking cold comfort from cracked Indian corn boiled in seawater.

The English came from a populated country where patches of woods and heath were surrounded by settled farms, towns, and cities. They arrived in a place where fragile settlements were surrounded by enormous unmapped woods. The only roads were Indian footpaths leading from nowhere to nowhere. The "salvages" (from the Latin *silva*, woods) burned their villages behind them, leaving little trace of where they had made habitation. In England the Puritans called the outlaws who ranged in Windsor Forest "the Devil's children." They did not mean it as a metaphor. In America some argued that the Indians should be compensated for the lands the Massachusetts Bay Colony was granting to settlers. To the devout, the notion was outrageous. "The earth is the Lord's and the fullness thereof; to the saints is the earth given; we are the saints."

William Hathorne initially settled in Dorchester and rose quickly to a position of respect and prominence as a selectman and a member of the General Court. Among his duties were writing laws and determining damages in disputes between neighbors over livestock and crops. Life in the colony was hard work, which is just what he wanted—only through discipline could the faithful bring about God's new Plantation. William had contempt for those who idled, lied, or failed to conform. His totem biblical verses came from Genesis—the story of God punishing those who break the rules. Stocks and whipping posts were set up in town and he continued the customary English methods of punishment—branding, flogging, stocking, cutting off ears. Many Puritans acted out their faith with a heretical flare, defacing images of Catholic saints, naming their children Experience, Hopestill, Desire, and Supply. William's sister Elizabeth and her husband, Richard Davenport, named their first child Truecross, in honor of John Endecott's dramatic act of defiance at Salem. Ensign Davenport had been drilling his band of citizen soldiers on the town common when Endecott rode onto the scene, grabbed Davenport's standard and with the flash of his sword cut from the fabric the image of Saint George's cross, which he considered a symbol of popery. William was more traditional, naming his first daughter Sarah, and turning his attention increasingly to public discipline. In 1636, he moved to Salem where he became county judge and where the family was to flourish for five generations. In addition to his magisterial duties, he became heavily involved in trade, building a wharf and warehouse to store his "adventures."

By midcentury Salem had three thousand residents—mostly fishermen, farmers, shipbuilders, shopkeepers, and indentured servants. There were also thirty or forty Black slaves whom the Puritans had brought on ships and sold in the open market. After the Pequot War of 1637, dozens of Indian captives were shipped to the West Indies to be sold into slavery. A girl branded +IIO− on the belly was acquired by Richard Davenport. In the burgeoning theocracy, ministers were the most respected citizens, [20] and after them magistrates, whose duties included serving as trial judge, moral arbiter, director of police, prosecutor, and supervisor of informers sent to search for criminals. The accused had no defense counsel. They had to plead their own cases before the magistrate, whose judgments were considered infallible. Because the Massachusetts Bay Colony was a theocracy, by law only church members were allowed to vote (this amounted to about one in every five adult males). It also meant that a sin was considered a crime, and punished as such.

A man who had filched "soap to wash his shirts" and another who had pilfered "half a cheese, a cake, and some milk" were caught by informers. For punishment they had to pay restitution of twice the value of the goods, take a public whipping, and wear the letter *T* on their clothing for a month. William Hathorne once ordered a constable to cut off a convicted burglar's ear and brand the letter *B* on his forehead. If babies were born too soon after marriage, the mothers were sentenced to whipping and fines. Citizens were fined for failing to attend church on the Sabbath, for "speaking slightingly and scornfully" of the minister, or for mocking Christian practices as did a man from Salem who declared, "Next year I'll be a member of the church and have my dog christened." Adultery, rape, and sodomy could be tried as capital crimes. A man and a woman found "not guilty of adultery but of very suspicious acts leading to adultery" were sentenced to stand for an hour on the gallows with ropes around their necks and then to be tied to a cart and whipped while they were driven through the streets of Boston and Charlestown.

The importance placed on discipline and conformity is even clearer in the story of Mary Oliver, whose desire to worship according to her own conscience was considered heretical. In England she had been imprisoned for refusing to bow at the naming of Jesus during prayers. In the colony she was sent to jail for asking permission during church to take communion though she was not a church member. Only members were allowed to participate in the sacraments. When brought to General Court, she quoted scripture at length in her own defense, offered no penitence, and was sent back to jail. She won the sympathy of Governor Winthrop by admitting she had done wrong to disturb the church service and was released. Within a year she was back in jail, this time for criticizing the church and government within earshot of immigrants newly arrived in Salem. She was sentenced to be whipped and Winthrop reported that "she stood without tieing, and bore her punishment with a masculine spirit, glorying in her sufferings." For six years she continued to appeal for church membership, but with no success. In bitter defiance, she declaimed to an informer, "All the ministers in this country are blood-thirsty men. My blood is too thin for them to draw it out." She was sent back to court, sentenced to stand tied to the whipping post for three hours with a slit stick pinched over her tongue. The punishment served only to sharpen her criticism of Hathorne. "I do hope to live and tear his flesh in pieces, and all such as he." The battle heated. She was in and out of court for working on the Sabbath, living apart from her husband, defamation, petty theft—a barrage of actual and trumped-up infractions. She in turn brought charges of brutality against the constable, for which she was granted restitution of ten shillings, and did not cease to speak her mind. The twelve-year feud ended, talk brewing that she might be a witch, with her banishment to England in 1651. She died shortly thereafter.

There were other responses to the new land by those who came for the wealth in lumber and furs. And by those for whom the body of the land awoke a sensual engagement, inheritors of ancient wild revelry. They dressed in animal masks, skins, and horns, threading flowers into their hair and clothing, dancing in the forest with Indians, and drinking the fermented fruits of the harvest. Some settled in the town of Mount Wollaston and, in the medieval English custom, erected a maypole eighty feet tall with a pair of buck's horns nailed on top. Aroused by a barrel of excellent beer, they danced, weaving streamers and garlands around the pole. They changed the name of the town to Merry Mount. By William Bradford's account, the settlement "fell to great licentiousness," with Thomas Morton, an Anglican who had come to the colony in 1625 to set up fur trade, as the Lord of Misrule. Morton "composed sundry rhymes and verses, some tending to lasciviousness, and others to the detraction and scandal of some persons, which he affixed to this idle or idol maypole." This irreverence brought censure in the form of John Endecott and a company of soldiers (likely Lieutenant Davenport among them), who dispersed the rowdies, cut down the maypole, consigned the pagans to stocks and whipping posts, and deported Morton temporarily back to England.

There was Anne Hutchinson of Boston, who believed that salvation could be won by faith and had nothing to do with good works. She defied the Puritan fathers by holding weekly gatherings in her home. Sixty or more people would regularly come to hear her lecture. She was tried in General Court and sentenced to banishment for "traducing the ministers." And there was Reverend Roger Williams, for a time minister in Salem, a Puritan who believed in "the liberty of conscience"—that civil magistrates could have no power over matters of individual conscience, that there was room in the righteous heart for many faiths. He befriended the Indians, often serving as mediator when disputes flared. He was tried for heresy. William Hathorne voted for his banishment.

When discontent and protest grew among the people, the theocrats saw it as Satan's work—their Plantation in danger of being uprooted and an occasion to strengthen their resolve by enforcing morally correct behavior. Word came from overseas about the Friends, new radicals of the faith community in England, who believed in a doctrine of direct revelation and equality of all before God. They had no ministers and took their hats off to no one. Because the Friends believed in honoring the commandment "Thou shalt not kill" in the strictest sense, any war was considered unrighteous. Those who came to the colony believed that American land rightly belonged to the Indians. Such freethinkers were not welcome in

25

Massachusetts. They were flogged and holes were burned through their tongues with hot irons. They were hounded, banished, and hanged. Still they continued to arrive and to make converts of many Puritans, some of whom had been Hathorne's close friends. His own son John married a Quaker. The court tried to tighten its control by keeping out newcomers, establishing fines for hosting strangers in one's home. In an order to a constable, Hathorne wrote, "You are required, by virtue hereof, to search in all suspicious places for private meetings; and if they refuse to open the doors, you are to break open the door upon them, and return the names of those you find." But in 1660, Charles II was restored to the English throne and the Puritan theocracy in New England collapsed. After four Quakers had been hung in Boston, the monarch ruled that all cases against Friends would be tried in England.

Initially relations with the Indians had been peaceful, if only because the Puritans saw the locals as a source of food, and as potential converts— an essential aspect of their work in God's Plantation. As John Hooker had written during the Pequot War, "Only rebel ye not against the Lord, neither fear ye the people of the land; for they are bread for us: their defence is departed from them, & the Lord is with us: fear them not." Cotton Mather espoused this view more tenaciously than most, writing as late as the 1690s:

> The Natives of the Country now Possessed by the *New-Englanders,* had been forlorn and wretched *Heathen* ever since their first herding here; and tho' we know not *When* or *How* those *Indians* first became Inhabitants of this mighty Continent, yet we may guess that probably the Devil decoy'd those miserable Salvages hither, in hopes that the Gospel of the Lord Jesus Christ would never come here to destroy or disturb his *Absolute Empire* over them.

The Pequot War had ended in a thirty-eight-year peace with the Indians and many settlers believed that the native people would be made "faithful subjects of the King of God's State." And it seems many were— there were reportedly fourteen villages of Praying Indians in Massachusetts in 1674. Just what their conversion entailed is unclear. Mary Rowlandson wrote about seeing a Praying Indian who wore "a string about his neck, strung with Christians' fingers." When war with the Indians broke out again in 1675, Hathorne's reading of the text was predictable: "Jehovah in the wrath of his vengeance is scowling upon you, and not again will He show His smile until you return to the paths of godliness which your fathers trod." His solution was to make stricter laws: any man who wore a periwig would be fined. A "Day of Publick Humiliation, with fasting and prayer" was ordered throughout the colony. But the people, now second- and third-generation New Englanders, saw the war differently: "God is angry, and is chastising all of us for the blood the ministers and magistrates spilled in persecuting such as the Quakers."

One of the most remarkable books of the war period is Mary Rowlandson's narrative of being held captive among the Indians for nearly twelve weeks. It offers a day-by-day account of tribal life through a Puritan's eyes, a vivid sense of her biblical learning and devotion, records of savagery by all parties—both sides eagerly slaughtering, scalping, burning towns and crops, smashing babies' heads, taking and selling slaves—records of exhaustion and remorse, and insight into how profoundly the Puritans believed that God intended the wilderness for the elect alone. Fleeing from the English army, Rowlandson's captors came on a Friday to the Bacquaug River. The Indians quickly cut trees and fashioned rafts to cross over. There were a great number in the party—so many that Rowlandson could not count them—so the crossing took until Sunday night. Provisions were scant. While waiting for the remaining members of the tribe to join them, Rowlandson's band "boyled an old Horses leg which they had got, and so we drank the broth, as soon as they thought it was ready, and when it almost all gone, they filled it up again." It was the third week of her captivity and food she had thought to be "filthy trash" she had learned to savor. And her view of the moral nature of Indians was clear:

> And here I cannot but take notice of the strange providence of God in preserving the heathen: They were many hundreds, old and young, some sick, and some lame, many had Papooses at their backs, the greatest number at this time with us, were Squaws, and they travelled with all they had, bag and baggage, and yet they got over this River aforesaid; and on Munday they set their Wigwams on fire, and away they went: On that very day came the English Army after them to this River, and saw the smoak of their Wigwams, and yet this River put a stop to them. God did not give them courage or activity to go over after us; we were not ready for so great a mercy as victory and deliverance; if we had been, God would have found out a way for the English to have passed this River, as well as for the Indians with their Squaws and Children, and all their Luggage.

One might read into such an experience not the unworthiness of one's own people, but the apparently greater worth in God's eyes of the Indians. But such a possibility was not available to the Puritan imagination. At the end of her captivity, when reflecting upon "a few remarkable passages of providence" and on the remarkable survival skills of her captors, Rowlandson wrote:

> It was thought, if their Corn were cut down, they would starve and dy with hunger: and all their Corn that could be found, was destroyed, and they driven from that little they had in store, into the Woods in the midst of Winter; and yet how to admiration did the Lord preserve them for his holy ends, and the destruction of

many still amongst the English! strangely did the Lord provide for them; that I did not see (all the time I was among them) one Man, Woman, or Child, die of hunger.

Though many times they would eat that, that a Hog or a Dog would hardly touch; yet by that God strengthened them to be a scourge to his People.

The chief and commonest food was Groundnuts: They eat also Nuts and Acorns, Harty-choaks, Lilly roots, Ground-beans, and several other weeds and roots, that I know not.

They would pick up old bones, and cut them to pieces at the joynts, and if they were full of wormes and magots, they would scald them over the fire to make the vermine come out, and then boile them, and drink up the Liquor, and then beat the great ends of them in a Morter, and so eat them. They would eat Horses guts, and ears, and all sorts of wild Birds which they could catch: also Bear, Vennison, Beaver, Tortois, Frogs, Squirrels, Dogs, Skunks, Rattle-snakes; yea, the very Bark of Trees; besides all sorts of creatures, and provision they plundered from the English. I can but stand in admiration to see the wonderful power of God, in providing for such a vast number of our Enemies in the Wilderness, where there was nothing to be seen, but from hand to mouth. Many times in a morning, the generality of them would eat up all they had, and yet have some forther supply against they wanted. It is said, Psal. 81. 13,14. *Oh that my People had hearkened to me, and Israel had walked in my ways, I should soon have subdued their Enemies, and turned my hand against their Adversaries.* But now our perverse and evil carriages in the sight of the Lord, have so offended him, that instead of turning his hand against them, the Lord feeds and nourishes them up to be a scourge to the whole Land.

The moral tyranny with which William Hathorne earned his respect and prominence did not end with his death in 1681. His son John was educated in the Puritan school of moral discipline. He knew his enemies to be Indians, Quakers, Cavaliers warring in England against the Puritans, the pope and his idolatrous followers, and anyone who spoke against the rules. Unlike his father, who had renounced the religious tradition in which he'd been raised (converting from the Church of England to Puritanism) to live out a vision of spiritual renewal, John accepted the tradition in which he was raised. His piety was enforced at rigorous Sabbath services lasting all day. The passionate liturgy imprinted upon him a visceral terror of God's censure. A treatise by Thomas Hooker titled *The Soul's Preparation for Christ* might set the tone of John Hathorne's childhood:

First, judge the lion by his paw, judge the torments of hell by some little beginning of it; and the dregs of God's vengeance, by some little sips of it; and judge how unable thou art to bear the whole by thy inability to bear a little of it in this life, in the terror of conscience . . . Conceive thus much, if all the diseases in the world did seize on one man, and if all torments that all the tyrants of the world could devise, were cast upon him; and if all the creatures in heaven and earth did conspire the destruction of this man; and if all the devils in hell did labor to inflict punishments upon him; you would think this man to be in a miserable condition. And yet all this is but a beam of God's indignation. If the beams of God's wrath be so hot, what is the full sun of his wrath, when it shall seize upon the soul of a sinful creature in full measure?

John Hathorne believed the death penalty was suitable punishment for religious heresy. At the age of forty-three he became a Salem magistrate.

Witchcraft had troubled Europe since the fourteenth century. During the Spanish Inquisition, instituted by Ferdinand and Isabella, as many as a hundred accused witches had been burned in a single day: a carnival, with vendors hawking food, souvenirs, and rosaries. Executions peaked in the sixteenth and seventeenth centuries. Thousands, mostly women, were executed in England, Scotland, and the rest of Europe, accused of signing agreements with the Devil in exchange for supernatural powers. Even Francis Bacon, the father of empiricism, apparently believed in witchcraft. In retrospect, it seems grandly ironic that the religion based on two supernatural events—a virgin birth and resurrection of the dead—should find the mere suspicion of such powers to be its most dangerous enemy.

Although the witch-killing frenzy did not ignite in Massachusetts until 1692, the hanging forty years earlier of Ann Hibbins in Boston and Margaret Jones in Charlestown as witches had prepared the ground. Witchcraft was the worst of capital crimes—worse than murder, rape, or arson. It marked a crisis for the colony—the Devil retaking His land. The witch trials in Salem were conducted in the meetinghouse, where worship services also were held. Sentences came down accompanied by sermons. Some accounts say that John Hathorne was the most fervent and least repentant judge, others that he merely conducted the preliminary hearings. It's known that from June until October more than one hundred of the accused appeared before him. Twenty were executed—five hanged at one time. Dozens waited in jail either for trial or execution, several dying there from hunger and cold, until public outcry and a reprieve from the governor stopped the persecutions.

Prepared the ground . . . that's what they did, these accomplished ancestors who, in the name of God, inflicted two generations of eloquent, dictatorial, systematized, and self-righteous cruelty upon their neighbors. What did I hope to claim in examining these lives? What is there to honor in these elders? What obligation do I have to their story? What taint do I carry in my blood? I don't intend to claim any privilege here in my ancestry—we've all got some of this poison in our veins—heirs to slaughtering, torture, persecution, and injustice. So broadly rooted and branching is any family tree, who could claim to be free of this wretched aspect of the past? As Benjamin Sáenz has written, "American history is sordid and bloody and disgusting, and nothing will ever convince me that our national past has been heroic." This continent in its openness seemed to invite a particularly virulent form of greeting—a misapprehension on the part of our ancestors for which we who follow owe the land some tenderness.

My father used to joke that we had Indian blood—related to Pocahontas was how he told it. He usually said this when he was lost on back roads trying to find a new shortcut, a practice he preferred to highway frenzy. Americans love to play Indian—not the actual poverty and depletion of reservation living, but the dream of living wild, innocent, defiant, and free—in touch with the sacred powers of the land. Who wants to say, I've got Indian-killer blood, slave-trader blood, witch-hanger and tyrant blood? What would one do with this history? One cannot uproot it, but one can make it show itself. One can lament the suffering they caused. One can say that William and John Hathorne, out of blindness and good intentions, brought shame to our family. One can remember the words of Solomon Stoddard, born in Boston in 1643, who wrote this in *Concerning Ancestors*:

> The mistakes of one generation many times become the calamity of succeeding generations. The present generation are not only unhappy by reason of the darkness of their own minds, but the errors of those who have gone before them have been a foundation of a great deal of misery. Posterity is very prone to espouse the principles of ancestors, and from an inordinate veneration of them to apprehend a sacredness in their opinions, and don't give themselves the trouble to make an impartial examination of them—as if it were a transgression to call them into question, and bordered upon irreligion to be wavering about them . . . And if any particular persons have been led by God into the understanding of those mistakes, and have made their differing sentiments public, it has proved an occasion of much sorrow; and many people have fallen into parties, whereby a spirit of love has been quenched and great heats have risen, from whence have proceeded censures and reproaches, and sometimes separation and persecution.

What would one ask of such ancestors—so pious and articulate, so educated and dedicated to the common good, so committed to a better future for humankind? *How could you have been so blind?* And they would answer, *Because of our faith.* What would they ask of us? *Don't be faithless.* We would scoff, *What is faith?* They would reply, *The possibility of our goodness.* Wise and frightened ancestors, tell me this: *If faith blinds, makes us cold to another's suffering, must we be faithless to see?*

35

Reading and Responding

1. Put an asterisk beside the paragraph at which the point of the essay becomes clearest to you, when you understand the author's main idea. Summarize the main idea in a few brief phrases.
2. Make a list of questions you would like to ask in order to understand this essay better.
3. Copy five sentences that seem crucial to what Deming has to say. Choose them from any part of the essay.

Working Together

1. Discuss the following questions in your group: What audience does Deming have in mind (academics, a general readership, women or men, students)? What does she assume this audience knows or is willing to find out? If you want to be a part of this audience, what must you be willing to do and how would you go about doing it? (For example, what research would you have to do? How many times would you need to read this article? What might you gain from this extra effort?)
2. Deming says that she finds the stories of her Puritan ancestors "muddled and contradictory." Explain.
3. Deming says that her ancestors "experienced that nexus as a torment." What does she mean by "nexus," and why did the Puritans experience it as a "torment"?
4. Imagine a conversation between William Hathorne, Deming's Puritan ancestor, and a friend of yours who loves backpacking and going out into "nature" for spiritual solace and renewal. Your friend starts by saying that she escapes into the mountains to find God. How would Hathorne reply, and why?

Rethinking and Rewriting

1. Write an essay with the following thesis, borrowed from Deming's essay: "_____, like us, were inconsistent, conflicted and complex, driven by hopes they could not realize." Fill in the blank with some group of people in the past—Mormons, Native Americans, Jewish immigrants—and do the research to demonstrate the claim. As an alternative, cast this thesis in the present tense to discuss a present-day group of people—for example, environmentalists or Republicans—as inconsistent, conflicted, and complex. Or write an essay that demonstrates how *you* are inconsistent, conflicted, and complex.
2. Write a research paper that explores the values and ways of life of your own ancestors. Like Deming, focus on a particular individual. As you write, contrast his or her values with your own: how are you alike, and how are you different? Imitate Deming's precision—her close reading of facts—and her tentativeness and open-endedness—her refusal to come to easy conclusions, to claim to know the final answer.

VOICES FROM WHITE EARTH
Winona LaDuke

A graduate of Harvard, an environmentalist, and an activist, Winona LaDuke was named one of the women of the year by Ms magazine in 1997. She was also Ralph Nader's vice-presidential candidate for the Green Party in the 1996 general election. LaDuke is the author of Last Standing Woman *(1997), an attack on the oppression of Native Americans. In the following essay, a lecture originally titled "Learning from Native Peoples," she offers a Native American vision of land use. LaDuke is a member of the Anishinabeg community, who live on the White Earth Reservation in Mississippi.*

Thank you for inviting me to come here and talk about some of the things that are important to the Anishinabeg and to the wider community of native peoples. Today I would like to talk about *keewaydahn*, which means "going home" in the Anishinabeg language. It's something like what Wes Jackson said in his lecture earlier in today's program about the process of going home and finding home. I think that is essentially what we need to be talking about. It is a challenge that people of this society face in belonging to a settler culture. They have been raised in this land, but they do not know its ceremony, its song, or its naming. Early settlers re-used names from other places, calling their settlements "New England," "New Haven," and "New York." But at the same time there are many indigenous names that co-exist with them. I think naming, as well as knowing *why* names are, is very important in restoring your relationship with the earth and finding your place. Restoring this relationship is our challenge.

To introduce myself, I'll tell you a little bit about my work and about where I come from. I'm basically a community organizer, like a lot of you. I returned to the White Earth Reservation about ten years ago after being raised off-reservation, which is a common circumstance for our people. I then began to work on the land issue, trying to win back or buy back our reservation lands. In our community I am identified as Muckwuck or Bear clan, Mississippi band, Anishinabeg. That's my place in the universe. The headwaters of the Mississippi are on our reservation; where the river starts is where we are in the world.

Anishinabeg is our name for ourselves in our own language; it means "people." We are called Ojibways in Canada and Chippewas in the United States. Our aboriginal territory, and where we live today, is in the northern part of five American states and the southern part of four Canadian provinces. It's in the center of the continent and is called the Wild Rice Bowl or the Great Lakes region. Today we are probably the single largest native population in North America: there are at least two hundred and fifty thousand of us. We're on both sides of the border, and most people don't know who we are or know much about us. That ignorance stems in part from the way Americans are taught about native people.

There are about seven hundred different native communities in North America. Roughly one hundred are Ojibway or Anishinabeg communities, but we're different bands. In Alaska there are two hundred native communities; in California there are eighty. In Washington state there are fourteen different kinds of Indian people living on the Yakima Reservation alone. All different kinds of indigenous people live in North America—all culturally and historically diverse. The same situation is found on a larger scale when you look at the entire continent, the Western Hemisphere, and the world. I want you to rethink the geography of North America in terms of cultural geography, in terms of land occupancy.

Now, if you look at the United States, about 4 percent of the land is held by Indian people. That is the extent of today's Indian reservations. The Southwest has the largest native population, and there's a significant population on the Great Plains. In northern Minnesota there are seven big reservations, all Ojibway or Anishinabeg. But if you go to Canada, about 85 percent of the population north of the fiftieth parallel is native. So if you look at it in terms of land occupancy and geography, in about two-thirds of Canada the majority of the population is native. I'm not even including Nunevat, which is an Inuit-controlled area the size of India in what used to be called the Northwest Territories.

If you look at the whole of North America, you find that the majority of the population is native in about a third of the continent. Within this larger area, indigenous people maintain their own ways of living and their cultural practices. This is our view of the continent, and it is different from the view of most other North Americans. When *we* look at the United States and Canada, we see our reservations and reserves as islands in the continent. When Indian people talk about their travels, they often mention reservations rather than cities: "I went to Rosebud, and then I went over to North Cheyenne." This is the indigenous view of North America.

Going beyond North America, I want to talk about the Western Hemisphere and the world from an indigenous perspective. My intent is to present you with an indigenous worldview and our perception of the world. There are a number of countries in the Western Hemisphere in which native peoples are the majority of the population: in Guatemala, Ecuador, Peru, Bolivia. In some South American countries we control as much as 22 to 40 percent of the land. Overall, the Western Hemisphere is not predominantly white. Indigenous people continue their ways of living based on generations and generations of knowledge and practice on the land.

On a worldwide scale there are about five thousand nations and a hundred and seventy states. Nations are groups of indigenous peoples who share common language, culture, history, territory, and government institutions. That is how international law defines a nation. And that is who *we* are: nations of people who have existed for thousands of years. There are about a hundred and seventy—maybe more now, about a hundred and eighty-five—states that are recognized by the United Nations. For the most part, these states are the result of colonial empires or colonial demarcations. And whereas indigenous nations have existed for thousands of years, many of the states in existence at the end of the twentieth century have been around only since World War II. That is a big difference. Yet the dominant worldview of industrial society is determined by these young states, not by the five thousand ancient nations.

The estimated number of indigenous people in the world depends on how you define indigenous people. It is said that there are currently about five hundred million of us in the world today, including such peoples as the Tibetans, the Masai, the Wara Wara, and the Quechua. I define indigenous peoples as those who have continued their way of living for thousands of years according to their original instructions.

That is a quick background on indigenous people. It should help you   10
understand that my perspective, the perspective of indigenous peoples, is entirely different from that of the dominant society in this country.

Indigenous peoples believe fundamentally in natural law and a state of balance. We believe that all societies and cultural practices must exist in accordance with natural law in order to be sustainable. We also believe that cultural diversity is as essential as biological diversity to maintaining sustainable societies. Indigenous peoples have lived on earth sustainably for thousands of years, and I suggest to you that indigenous ways of living are the only sustainable ways of living. Because of that, I believe there is something to be learned from indigenous thinking and indigenous ways. I don't think many of you would argue that industrial society is sustainable. I think that in two or three hundred years this society will be extinct because a society based on conquest cannot survive when there's nothing left to conquer.

Indigenous people have taken great care to fashion their societies in accordance with natural law, which is the highest law. It is superior to the laws made by nations, states, and municipalities. It is the law to which we are all accountable. There are no Twelve Commandments of natural law, but there are some things that I believe to be true about natural law. And this is my experience from listening to a lot of our older people. What I am telling you is not really my opinion; it's based on what has happened in our community, on what I've heard people say, and on their knowledge. We have noticed that much in nature is cyclical: the movements of moons, the tides, the seasons, our bodies. Time itself, in most indigenous worldviews, is cyclical. We also have experienced and believe that it is our essential nature and our need always to keep a balance in nature. Most indigenous ceremonies, if you look to their essence, are about the restoration of balance. That is our intent: to restore, and then to retain, balance. Nature itself continually tries to balance, to equalize.

According to our way of living and our way of looking at the world, most of the world is animate. This is reflected in our language, Anishinabemowin, in which most nouns are animate. *Mandamin,* the word for corn, is animate; *mitig,* the word for tree, is animate; so is the word for rice, *manomin,* and the word for rock or stone, *asin.* Looking at the world and seeing that most things are alive, we have come to believe, based on this perception, that they have spirit. They have standing on their own. Therefore, when I harvest wild rice on our reservation up north, I always offer *asemah,* tobacco, because when you take something, you must always give thanks to its spirit for giving itself to you, for it has a choice whether to give itself to you or not. In our cultural practice, for instance, it is not because of skill that a hunter can harvest a deer or a caribou; it is because he or she has been honorable and has given *asemah.* That is how you are able to harvest, not because you are a good hunter but because the animal gives itself to you. That is our perception.

And so we are always very careful when we harvest. Anthropologists call this reciprocity, which means something anthropological, I guess. But from our perspective it means that when you take, you always give. This is about balance and equalness. We also say that when you take, you must take only what you need and leave the rest. Because if you take more than you need, that means you are greedy. You have brought about imbalance, you have been selfish. To do this in our community is a very big disgrace. It is a violation of natural law, and it leaves you with no guarantee that you will be able to continue harvesting.

We have a word in our language that describes the practice of living   *15*
in harmony with natural law: *minobimaatisiiwin.* This word describes how you live your life according to natural law, how you behave as an individual in relationship with other individuals and in relationship with the land and all the things that are animate on the land. *Minobimaatisiiwin* is our cultural practice; it is what you strive towards as an individual as well as collectively as a society.

We have tried to retain this way of living and of thinking in spite of all that has happened to us over the centuries. I believe we do retain most of these practices to a great extent in many of our societies. In our community they are overshadowed at times by industrialism, but they still exist.

I would like to contrast what I've told you about indigenous thinking with what I call "industrial thinking." I think the Lakota have the best term to describe it. It actually refers to white people, although they are not the only ones who think this way. Indigenous peoples have interesting terms for white people: they are usually not just words, they are descriptions encapsulated in a word. I will tell you about one: the Lakota word for a white person is *wasichu.* It derives from the first time the Lakota ever saw a white person. There was a white man out on the prairie in the Black Hills, and he was starving. He came into a Lakota camp in the middle of the night, and the Lakota of course were astonished to see him. They began to watch him to see what he was doing. He went over to the food, took something, and ran away. A little while later, the Lakota looked to see what he had taken: he had stolen a large amount of fat. So the Lakota word for a white person, *wasichu,* means "he who steals the fat." Now, that is a description that doesn't necessarily have to do with white people, but taking more than you need has to do with industrial society. He who steals the fat. That's what I'm talking about when I refer to the industrial worldview.

Industrial thinking is characterized by several ideas that run counter to indigenous ideas. First, instead of believing that natural law is preeminent, industrial society believes that humans are entitled to full dominion over nature. It believes that man—and it *is* usually man of course—has some God-given right to all that is around him, that he has been created superior to the rest.

Second, instead of modeling itself on the cyclical structure of nature, this society is patterned on linear thinking. I went all the way through its school system, and I remember how time, for example, is taught in this society. It's taught on a timeline, usually one that begins around 1492. It has some dates on it that were important to someone, although I could never figure out to whom. The timeline is a clear representation of this society's linear way of thinking. And certain values permeate this way of thinking, such as the concept of progress. Industrial society wants to keep making progress as it moves down the timeline, progress defined by things like technological advancement and economic growth. This value accompanies linear thinking.

Third, there is the attitude toward what is wild as opposed to what is cultivated or "tame." This society believes it must tame the wilderness. It also believes in the superiority of civilized over primitive peoples, a belief that also follows a linear model: that somehow, over time, people will become more civilized. Also related of course is the idea behind colonialism: that some people have the *right* to civilize other people. My experience is that people who are viewed as "primitive" are generally people of color, and people who are viewed as "civilized" are those of European descent. This prejudice still permeates industrial society and in fact even permeates "progressive" thinking. It holds that somehow people of European descent are smarter—they have some better knowledge of the world than the rest of us. I suggest that this is perhaps a racist worldview and that it has racist implications. That is, in fact, our experience.

Fourth, industrial society speaks a language of inanimate nouns. Even words for the land are becoming inanimate. Jerry Mander discusses this idea when he talks about the "commodification of the sacred." Industrial language has changed things from being animate, alive, and having spirit to being inanimate, mere objects and commodities of society. When things are inanimate, "man" can view them as his God-given right. He can take them, commodify them, and manipulate them in society. This behavior is also related to the linear way of thinking.

20

Fifth, the last aspect of industrial thinking I'm going to talk about (although it's always unpopular to question it in America) is the idea of capitalism itself. In this country we are taught that capitalism is a system that combines labor, capital, and resources for the purpose of accumulation. The capitalist goal is to use the least labor, capital, and resources to accumulate the most profit. The intent of capitalism is accumulation. So the capitalist's method is always to take more than is needed. Therefore, from an indigenous point of view capitalism is inherently out of harmony with natural law.

Based on this goal of accumulation, industrial society practices conspicuous consumption. Indigenous societies, on the other hand, practice what I would call "conspicuous distribution." We focus on the potlatch, the giveaway, an event that carries much more honor than accumulation does. In fact, the more you give away, the greater your honor. We make a great deal of these giveaways, and industrial society has something to learn from them.

Over the past five hundred years the indigenous experience has been one of conflict between the indigenous and the industrial worldviews. This conflict has manifested itself as holocaust. That is our experience. Indigenous people understand clearly that this society, which has caused the extinction of more species in the past hundred and fifty years than the total species extinction from the Ice Age to the mid-nineteenth century, is the same society that has caused the extinction of about two thousand different indigenous peoples in the Western Hemisphere alone. We understand intimately the relationship between extinction of species and extinction of peoples, because we experience both. And the extinction continues. Last year alone the Bureau of Indian Affairs, which has legal responsibility for people like myself—legally, I'm a ward of the federal government—declared nineteen different indigenous nations in North America extinct. The rate of extinction in the Amazon rainforest, for example, has been one indigenous people per year since 1900. And if you look at world maps showing cultural and biological distribution, you find that where there is the most cultural diversity, there is also the most biological diversity. A direct relationship exists between the two. That is why we argue that cultural diversity is as important to a sustainable global society as biological diversity.

Our greatest problem with all of this in America is that there has   25
been no recognition of the cultural extinction, no owning up to it, no atonement for what happened, and no education about it. When I ask people how many different kinds of Indians they can identify, they can name scarcely any. America's mythology is based on the denial of the native—of native humanity, even of native existence. Nobody admits that the holocaust took place. This is because the white settlers believed they had a God-given right to the continent, and anyone with this right wouldn't recognize what happened as holocaust. Yet it was a holocaust of unparalleled proportions: Bartholomew de las Casas and other contempo-

raries of Columbus estimated that fifty million indigenous people in the Western Hemisphere perished in a sixty-year period. In terms of millions of people, this was probably the largest holocaust in world history.

Now, it is not appropriate for me to say that my holocaust was worse than someone else's. But it is absolutely correct for me to demand that my holocaust be recognized. And that has not happened in America. Instead, nobody knows anything about us, not even educated people. Why? Because this system is based on a denial of our existence. We are erased from the public consciousness because if you have no victim, you have no crime. As I said, most Americans can hardly name a single Indian nation. Those who can are only able to name those that have been featured in television Westerns: Comanche, Cheyenne, Navajo, Sioux, Crow. The only image of a native that is widely recognized in this society is the one shown in Westerns, which is a caricature. It is a portrayal created in Hollywood or in cartoons or more recently to a minimal degree in "New Age" paraphernalia. In this society we do not exist as full human beings with human rights, with the same rights to self-determination, to dignity, and to land—to territorial integrity—that other people have.

The challenge that people of conscience in this country face is to undo and debunk the mythology, to come clean, become honest, understand the validity of our demands, and recognize our demands. People must see the interlocking interests between their own ability to survive and indigenous peoples' continuing cultural sustainability. Indigenous peoples have lived sustainably in this land for thousands of years. I am absolutely sure that our societies could live without yours, but I'm not so sure that your society can continue to live without ours. This is why indigenous people need to be recognized now and included in the discussion of the issues affecting this country's future.

I'd like to tell you now about indigenous peoples' efforts to protect our land and restore our communities. All across this continent there are native peoples—in small communities with populations of one hundred, five hundred, even five thousand—who are trying to regain control of their community and their territory. I could tell you many stories of these different struggles, but I'll use my own community as an example. Here is our story.

The White Earth Reservation, located at the headwaters of the Mississippi, is thirty-six by thirty-six miles square, which is about 837,000 acres. It is very good land. A treaty reserved it for our people in 1867 in return for relinquishing a much larger area of northern Minnesota. Of all our territory, we chose this land for its richness and diversity. There are forty-seven lakes on the reservation. There's maple sugar; there are hardwoods and all the different medicine plants my people use—our reservation is called "the medicine chest of the Ojibways." We have wild rice; we have deer; we have beaver; we have fish—every food we need. On the eastern part of the reservation there are stands of white pine. On the part farthest west there used to be buffalo, but this area is now farmland, situated in the Red River Valley. That is our area, the land reserved to us under treaty.

Our traditional forms of land use and ownership are similar to those of a community land trust. The land is owned collectively, and we have individual or, more often, family-based usufruct rights: each family has traditional areas where it fishes and hunts. In our language the words *Anishinabeg akiing* describe the concept of land ownership. They translate as "the land of the people," which doesn't infer that we own our land but that we belong on it. Our definition doesn't stand up well in court, unfortunately, because this country's legal system upholds the concept of private property.

Our community enforces its traditional practices by adhering to *minobimaatisiiwin*. Historically, this involved punishing people who transgressed these rules. For instance, in our community the worst punishment historically—we didn't have jails—was banishment. That still exists in our community to a certain extent. Just imagine if the worst punishment in industrial society were banishment! With us, each person wants to be part of the community.

We have also maintained our practices by means of careful management and observation. For example, we have "hunting bosses" and "rice chiefs," who make sure that resources are used sustainably in each region. Hunting bosses oversee trap-line rotation, a system by which people trap in an area for two years and then move to a different area to let the land rest. Rice chiefs coordinate wild rice harvesting. The rice on each lake is unique: each has its own taste and ripens at its own time. We also have a "tally man," who makes sure there are enough animals for each family in a given area. If a family can't sustain itself, the tally man moves them to a new place where animals are more plentiful. These practices are sustainable.

My children's grandfather, who is a trapper, lives on wild animals in the wintertime. When he intends to trap beavers, he reaches his hand into a beaver house and counts how many beavers are in there. (Beavers are not carnivorous; they won't bite.) By counting, he knows how many beavers he can take. Of course, he has to count only if he hasn't already been observing that beaver house for a long time. This is a very sustainable way to trap, one based on a kind of thorough observation that can come only with residency. Further, I suggest that this man knows more about his ecosystem than any Ph.D. scholar who studies it from the university.

As I have indicated, the White Earth Reservation is a rich place. And it is our experience that industrial society is not content to leave other peoples' riches alone. Wealth attracts colonialism: the more a native people has, the more colonizers are apt to covet that wealth and take it away—whether it is gold or, as in our case, pine stands and Red River Valley farmland. A Latin American scholar named Eduardo Galeano has written about colonialism in communities like mine. He says: "In the colonial to neo-colonial alchemy, gold changes to scrap metal and food to poison. We have become painfully aware of the mortality of wealth, which nature bestows and imperialism appropriates." For us, our wealth was the source of our poverty: industrial society could not leave us be.

Our reservation was created by treaty in 1867; in 1887 the General Allotment Act was passed on the national level, not only to teach Indians the concept of private property but also to facilitate the removal of more land from Indian Nations. The federal government divided our reservation into eighty-acre parcels of land and allotted each parcel to an individual Indian, hoping that through this change we would somehow become yeoman farmers, adopt the notion of progress, and become civilized. But the allotment system had no connection to our traditional land tenure patterns. In our society a person harvested rice in one place, trapped in another place, got medicines in a third place, and picked berries in a fourth. These locations depended on the ecosystem; they were not necessarily contiguous. But the government said to each Indian, "Here are your eighty acres; this is where you'll live." Then, after each Indian had received an allotment, the rest of the land was declared "surplus" and given to white people to homestead. On our reservation almost the entire land base was allotted except for some pinelands that were annexed by the state of Minnesota and sold to timber companies. What happened to my reservation happened to reservations all across the country.

The federal government was legally responsible for this; they turned our land into individual eighty-acre parcels, and then they looked the other way and let the state of Minnesota take some of our land and tax what was left. When the Indians couldn't pay the taxes, the state confiscated the land. How could these people pay taxes? In 1900 or 1910 they could not read or write English.

I'll tell you a story about how my great-grandma was cheated by a loan shark. She lived on Many Point Lake, where her allotment was. She had a bill at the local store, the Fairbanks grocery store, and she had run it up because she was waiting until fall when she could get some money from trapping or from a treaty annuity. So she went to a land speculator named Lucky Waller, and she said, "I need to pay this bill." She asked to borrow fifty bucks from him until treaty payment time, and he said: "Okay, you can do that. Just sign here and I'll loan you that fifty bucks." So she signed with her thumbprint and went back to her house on Many Point Lake. About three months later she came in to repay him the fifty bucks, and the loan shark said: "No, you keep that money; I bought land from you instead." He had purchased her eighty acres on Many Point Lake for fifty bucks. Today that location is a Boy Scout camp.

This story could be retold again and again in our communities. It is a story of land speculation, greed, and unconscionable contracts, and it exemplifies the process by which native peoples were dispossessed of their land. The White Earth Reservation lost two hundred and fifty thousand acres to the state of Minnesota because of unpaid taxes. And this was done to native peoples across the country: on a national average reservations lost a full two-thirds of their land this way.

By 1920, 99 percent of original White Earth Reservation lands were in non-Indian hands. By 1930 many of our people had died from tuberculosis and other diseases, and half of our remaining population lived off-reservation. Three generations of our people were forced into poverty, chased off our land, and made refugees in this society. Now a lot of our people live in Minneapolis. Of twenty thousand tribal members only four or five thousand live on reservation. That's because we're refugees, not unlike other people in this society.

Our struggle is to get our land back. That's what we've been trying   40
to do for a hundred years. By 1980, 93 percent of our reservation was still held by non-Indians. That's the circumstance we are in at the end of the twentieth century. We have exhausted all legal recourse for getting back our land. If you look at the legal system in this country, you will find that it is based on the idea that Christians have a God-given right to dispossess heathens of their land. This attitude goes back to a papal bull of the fifteenth or sixteenth century declaring that Christians have a superior right to land over heathens. The implication for native people is that we have no legal right to our land in the United States or in Canada. The only legal recourse we have in the United States is the Indian Claims Commission, which pays you for land; it doesn't return land to you. It compensates you at the 1910 market value for land that was seized. The Black Hills Settlement is one example. It's lauded as a big settlement—one that gives all this money to the Indians—but it's only a hundred and six million dollars for five states. That's the full legal recourse for Indian people.

In the case of our own reservation, we had the same problem. The Supreme Court ruled that to regain their land Indian people had to have filed a lawsuit within seven years of the original time of taking. Now, legally we are all people who are wards of the federal government. I have a federal enrollment number. Anything to do with the internal matters of Indian governments is subject to the approval of the Secretary of the Interior. So the federal government, which is legally responsible for our land, watched its mismanagement and did not file any lawsuits on our behalf. The Courts are now declaring that the statute of limitations has expired for the Indian people, who, when their land was taken, could not read or write English, had no money or access to attorneys to file suit, and were the legal wards of the state. We have therefore, the courts claim, exhausted our legal recourse and have no legal standing in the court system. That is what has happened in this country with regard to Indian land issues.

We have fought federal legislation for a decade without success. Yet we look at the situation on our reservation and realize that we must get our land back. We do not really have any other place to go. That's why we started the White Earth Land Recovery Project.

The federal, state, and county governments are the largest landholders on the reservation. It is good land still, rich in many things; however, when you do not control your land, you do not control your destiny. That's our experience. What has happened is that two-thirds of the deer taken on our reservation are taken by non-Indians, mostly by sports hunters from Minneapolis. In the Tamarac National Wildlife Refuge nine times as many deer are taken by non-Indians as by Indians, because that's where sports hunters from Minneapolis come to hunt. Ninety percent of the fish taken on our reservation is taken by white people, and most of them are taken by people from Minneapolis who come to their summer cabins and fish on our reservation. Each year in our region, about ten thousand acres are being clear cut for paper and pulp in one county alone, mostly by the Potlatch Timber Company. We are watching the destruction of our ecosystem and the theft of our resources; in not controlling our land we are unable to control what is happening to our ecosystem. So we are struggling to regain control through the White Earth Land Recovery Project.

Our project is like several others in Indian communities. We are not trying to displace people who have settled there. A third of our land is held by the federal, state, and county governments. That land should just be returned to us. It certainly would not displace anyone. And then we have to ask the question about absentee land ownership. It is an ethical question that should be asked in this country. A third of the *privately* held land on our reservation is held by absentee landholders: they do not see that land, do not know it, and do not even know where it is. We ask these people how they feel about owning land on a reservation, hoping we can persuade them to return it.

Approximately sixty years ago in India the Gramdan movement dealt with similar issues. Some million acres were placed in village trust as a result of the moral influence of Vinoba Bhave. The whole issue of absentee land ownership needs to be addressed—particularly in America, where the idea of private property is so sacred, where somehow it is ethical to hold land that you never see. As Vinoba said, "It is highly inconsistent that those who possess land should not till it themselves, and those who cultivate should possess no land to do so."

Our project also acquires land. It owns about nine hundred acres right now. We bought some land as a site for a roundhouse, a building that holds one of our ceremonial drums. We bought back our burial grounds, which were on private land, because we believe that we should hold the land our ancestors lived on. These are all small parcels of land. We also just bought a farm, a fifty-eight-acre organic raspberry farm. In a couple of years we hope to get past the "You Pick" stage into jam production. It is a very slow process, but our strategy is based on this recovery of the land and of our cultural and economic practices.

We are a poor community. People look at our reservation and comment on the 85 percent unemployment—they do not realize what we do with our time. They have no way of valuing our cultural practices. For instance, 85 percent of our people hunt, taking at least one or two deer annually, probably in violation of federal game laws; 75 percent of our people hunt for small game and geese; 50 percent of our people fish by net; 50 percent of our people sugarbush and garden on our reservation. About the same percentage harvest wild rice, not just for themselves; they harvest it to sell. About half of our people produce handcrafts. There is no way to quantify this in America. It is called the "invisible economy" or the "domestic economy." Society views us as unemployed Indians who need wage-earning jobs. That is not how we view ourselves. Our work is about strengthening and restoring our traditional economy. I have seen our people trained and retrained for off-reservation jobs that do not exist. I don't know how many Indians have gone through three or four carpenter and plumber training programs. It doesn't do any good if, after the third or fourth time, you still don't have a job.

Our strategy is to strengthen our own traditional economy (thereby strengthening our traditional culture as well) so that we can produce 50 percent or more of our own food, which we then won't need to buy elsewhere, and can eventually produce enough surplus to sell. In our case most of our surplus is in wild rice. We are rich in terms of wild rice. The Creator, Gitchi Manitu, gave us wild rice—said we should eat it and should share it; we have traded it for thousands of years. A lot of our political struggle is, I am absolutely sure, due to the fact that Gitchi Manitu did not give wild rice to Uncle Ben to grow in California. Commercial wild rice is totally different from the rice we harvest, and it decreases the value of our rice when marketed as authentic wild rice.

We've been working for several years now to increase the price of the rice we gather from fifty cents per pound to a dollar per pound, green. We are trying to market our rice ourselves. We try to capture the "value added" in our community by selling it ourselves. We went from about five thousand pounds of production on our reservation to about fifty thousand pounds last year. This is our strategy for economic recovery.

Other parts of our strategy include language immersion programs to 50 restore our language and revival of drum ceremonies to restore our cultural practices. These are part of an integrated restoration process that is focused on the full human being.

In the larger picture, in Wisconsin and Minnesota our community is working hard to exercise specific treaty rights. Under the 1847 treaty, we have reserved-use rights to a much larger area than just our reservations. These are called extra-territorial treaty rights. We didn't say we were going to live there, we just said we wanted to keep the right to use that land in our usual and accustomed ways. This has led us to a larger political strategy, for although our harvesting practices are sustainable, they require an almost pristine ecosystem in order to take as much fish and grow as much rice as we need. To achieve this condition the tribes are entering into a co-management agreement in northern Wisconsin and northern Minnesota to prevent further environmental degradation as a first step toward preserving an extra-territorial area in accordance with treaty rights.

There are many similar stories all across North America. A lot can be learned from these stories, and we can share a great deal in terms of your strategies and what you're trying to do in your own communities. I see this as a relationship among people who share common issues, common ground, and common agendas. It is absolutely crucial, however, that our struggle for territorial integrity and economic and political control of our lands not be regarded as a threat by this society. Deep-set in settler minds I know there's fear of the Indian having control. I've seen it on my own reservation: white people who live there are deathly afraid of our gaining control over half our land base, which is all we're trying to do. I'm sure they are afraid we will treat them as badly as they have treated us. I ask you to shake off your fear.

There's something valuable to be learned from our experiences, from the James Bay hydroelectric project in Quebec, for example, and from the Shoshone sisters in Nevada fighting the missile siting. Our stories are about people with a great deal of tenacity and courage, people who have been resisting for centuries. We are sure that if we do not resist, we will not survive. Our resistance will guarantee our children a future. In our society we think ahead to the seventh generation; however, we know that the ability of the seventh generation to sustain itself will be dependent on our ability to resist now.

Another important consideration is that traditional ecological knowledge is unheard knowledge in this country's institutions. Nor is it something an anthropologist can extract by mere research. Traditional ecological knowledge is passed from generation to generation; it is not an appropriate subject for a Ph.D. dissertation. We who live by this knowledge have the intellectual property rights to it, and we have the right to tell our stories ourselves. There is a lot to be learned from our knowledge, but you need us in order to learn it, whether it is the story of my children's grandfather reaching his hand into that beaver house or of the Haida up on the Northwest coast, who make totem poles and plank houses. The Haida say they can take a plank off a tree and still leave the tree standing. If Weyerhaeuser could do that, I might listen to them, but they cannot.

Traditional ecological knowledge is absolutely essential for the future.   *55* Crafting a relationship between us is absolutely essential. Native people are not quite at the table in the environmental movement—for example, in the management of the Great Plains. Environmental groups and state governors sat down and talked about how to manage the Great Plains, and nobody asked the Indians to come to the table. Nobody even noticed that there are about fifty million acres of Indian land out there in the middle of the Great Plains, land that according to history and law has never yet had a drink of water—that is, reservations have been denied water all these years because of water diversion projects. When water allocations are being discussed, someone needs to talk about how the tribes need a drink.

One proposal for the Great Plains is a Buffalo Commons, which would include one hundred and ten prairie counties that are now financially bankrupt and are continuing to lose people. The intent is to restore these lands ecologically, bringing back the buffalo, the perennial crops, and indigenous prairie grasses that Wes Jackson is experimenting with. I think we need to broaden the idea, though, because I don't think it should be just a Buffalo Commons; I think it should be an Indigenous Commons. If you look at the 1993 population in the area, you'll find that the majority are indigenous peoples who already hold at least fifty million acres of the land. We know this land of our ancestors, and we should rightly be part of a sustainable future for it.

Another thing I want to touch on is the necessity of shifting our perception. There is no such thing as sustainable development. Community is the only thing in my experience that is sustainable. We all need to be involved in building sustainable communities. We can each do that in our own way—whether it is European-American communities or Dené communities or Anishinabeg communities—returning to and restoring the way of life that is based on the land. To achieve this restoration we need to reintegrate with cultural traditions informed by the land. That is something I don't know how to tell you to do, but it is something you're going to need to do. Garrett Hardin and others are saying that the only way you can manage a commons is if you share enough cultural experiences and cultural values so that you can keep your practices in order and in check: *minobimaatisiiwin*. The reason we have remained sustainable for all these centuries is that we are cohesive communities. A common set of values is needed to live together sustainably on the land.

Finally, I believe the issues deep in this society that need to be addressed are structural. This is a society that continues to consume too much of the world's resources. You know, when you consume this much in resources, it means constant intervention in other peoples' land and countries, whether it is mine or whether it is the Crees' up in James Bay or someone else's. It is meaningless to talk about human rights unless you talk about consumption. And that's a structural change we all need to address. It is clear that in order for native communities to live, the dominant society must change, because if this society continues in the direction it is going, our reservations and our way of life will continue to bear the consequences. This society has to be changed! We have to be able to put aside its cultural baggage, which is industrial baggage. It's not sustainable. Do not be afraid of discarding it. That's the only way we're going to make peace between the settler and the native.

Miigwech. I want to thank you for your time. *Keewaydahn.* It's our way home.

—*1993*

Reading and Responding

1. As you review the essay, mark any statistics or facts that surprised you—anything you didn't know before or hadn't ever thought about.
2. Look for the terms "cultural geography" and "indigenous people," and write brief definitions of these terms in the margins, paraphrasing LaDuke.
3. Explain what LaDuke means by "reciprocity" and "sustainability."
4. Write a paragraph (at least five sentences) explaining your notion of property rights as you understand that term now.

Working Together

1. LaDuke says that indigenous people have an entirely different perspective than that of the "dominant society." As a group, list at least three differences in worldview.
2. LaDuke says that although there are no Twelve Commandments of "natural law," there are some things she believes to be true about natural law. List three, as mentioned in the essay. As a group, discuss the concept of natural law.
3. As a group, list five things that characterize what LaDuke calls "industrial thinking." What is your opinion of LaDuke's viewpoint? Discuss this in your group.
4. Later in the essay LaDuke explains the land use and ownership practices of the White Earth Reservation. List five of these practices. Then list at least three principles of property rights as you understand them. Write a response to each principle as you believe LaDuke might.

Rethinking and Rewriting

1. Write an essay that explains (and agrees with) the statement, "People must see the interlocking interests between their own ability to survive and indigenous peoples' continuing cultural sustainability." Draw on at least three other essays from this book.
2. LaDuke says "there's something valuable to be learned from our experiences." Write a letter to the editor of your local paper or a short essay arguing that one or two of the land use practices that LaDuke describes would be applicable, appropriate, and effective as a way of solving a land use problem in your own community. Include quotations from LaDuke's essay as appropriate. Make sure your readers will understand the quotations out of context.
3. In light of LaDuke's essay, write a personal essay about "finding your way home." Interpret and apply that phrase in whatever way makes the most sense to you. Include at least two quotations from LaDuke's essay to help make your own sentiments and ideas clear.

THE LAND ETHIC

Aldo Leopold

> *A naturalist and wildlife biologist, Aldo Leopold worked for the forest service for nearly twenty years and then was a faculty member at the University of Wisconsin until his death in 1941. As a naturalist, he pioneered the ecological approach to wildlife and land management. As a writer, he is known for* A Sand County Almanac *(1949), a series of meditations on the natural world and the human need for wilderness. What follows is a section from that book, Leopold's classic definition of ethics related to the use of natural resources.*

When God-like Odysseus returned from the wars in Troy, he hanged all on one rope a dozen slave-girls of his household whom he suspected of misbehavior during his absence.

This hanging involved no question of propriety. The girls were property. The disposal of property was then, as now, a matter of expediency, not of right and wrong.

Concepts of right and wrong were not lacking from Odysseus' Greece: witness the fidelity of his wife through the long years before at last his black-prowed galleys clove the wine-dark seas for home. The ethical structure of that day covered wives, but had not yet been extended to human chattels. During the three thousand years which have since elapsed, ethical criteria have been extended to many fields of conduct, with corresponding shrinkages in those judged by expediency only.

The Ethical Sequence

This extension of ethics, so far studied only by philosophers, is actually a process in ecological evolution. Its sequences may be described in ecological as well as in philosophical terms. An ethic, ecologically, is a limitation on freedom of action in the struggle for existence. An ethic, philosophically, is a differentiation of social from anti-social conduct. These are two definitions of one thing. The thing has its origin in the tendency of interdependent individuals or groups to evolve modes of co-operation. The ecologist calls these symbioses. Politics and economics are advanced symbioses in which the original free-for-all competition has been replaced, in part, by co-operative mechanisms with an ethical content.

The complexity of co-operative mechanisms has increased with population density, and with the efficiency of tools. It was simpler, for example, to define the anti-social uses of sticks and stones in the days of the mastodons than of bullets and billboards in the age of motors.

The first ethics dealt with the relation between individuals; the Mosaic Decalogue is an example. Later accretions dealt with the relation be-

5

tween the individual and society. The Golden Rule tries to integrate the individual to society; democracy to integrate social organization to the individual.

There is as yet no ethic dealing with man's relation to land and to the animals and plants which grow upon it. Land, like Odysseus' slave-girls, is still property. The land-relation is still strictly economic, entailing privileges but not obligations.

The extension of ethics to this third element in human environment is, if I read the evidence correctly, an evolutionary possibility and an ecological necessity. It is the third step in a sequence. The first two have already been taken. Individual thinkers since the days of Ezekiel and Isaiah have asserted that the despoliation of land is not only inexpedient but wrong. Society, however, has not yet affirmed their belief. I regard the present conservation movement as the embryo of such an affirmation.

An ethic may be regarded as a mode of guidance for meeting ecological situations so new or intricate, or involving such deferred reactions, that the path of social expediency is not discernible to the average individual. Animal instincts are modes of guidance for the individual in meeting such situations. Ethics are possibly a kind of community instinct in-the-making.

The Community Concept

All ethics so far evolved rest upon a single premise: that the individ-   *10*
ual is a member of a community of interdependent parts. His instincts prompt him to compete for his place in the community, but his ethics prompt him also to co-operate (perhaps in order that there may be a place to compete for).

The land ethic simply enlarges the boundaries of the community to include soils, waters, plants, and animals, or collectively: the land.

This sounds simple: do we not already sing our love for and obligation to the land of the free and the home of the brave? Yes, but just what and whom do we love? Certainly not the soil, which we are sending helter-skelter downriver. Certainly not the waters, which we assume have no function except to turn turbines, float barges, and carry off sewage. Certainly not the plants, of which we exterminate whole communities without batting an eye. Certainly not the animals, of which we have already extirpated many of the largest and most beautiful species. A land ethic of course cannot prevent the alteration, management, and use of these "resources," but it does affirm their right to continued existence, and, at least in spots, their continued existence in a natural state.

In short, a land ethic changes the role of *Homo sapiens* from conqueror of the land-community to plain member and citizen of it. It implies respect for his fellow-members, and also respect for the community as such.

In human history, we have learned (I hope) that the conqueror role is eventually self-defeating. Why? Because it is implicit in such a role that the conqueror knows, *ex cathedra,* just what makes the community clock tick, and just what and who is valuable, and what and who is worthless, in community life. It always turns out that he knows neither, and this is why his conquests eventually defeat themselves.

In the biotic community, a parallel situation exists. Abraham knew   *15*
exactly what the land was for: it was to drip milk and honey into Abraham's mouth. At the present moment, the assurance with which we regard this assumption is inverse to the degree of our education.

The ordinary citizen today assumes that science knows what makes the community clock tick; the scientist is equally sure that he does not. He knows that the biotic mechanism is so complex that its workings may never be fully understood.

That man is, in fact, only a member of a biotic team is shown by an ecological interpretation of history. Many historical events, hitherto explained solely in terms of human enterprise, were actually biotic interactions between people and land. The characteristics of the land determined the facts quite as potently as the characteristics of the men who lived on it.

Consider, for example, the settlement of the Mississippi valley. In the years following the Revolution, three groups were contending for its control: the native Indian, the French and English traders, and the American settlers. Historians wonder what would have happened if the English at Detroit had thrown a little more weight into the Indian side of those tipsy scales which decided the outcome of the colonial migration into the cane-lands of Kentucky. It is time now to ponder the fact that the cane-lands, when subjected to the particular mixture of forces represented by the cow, plow, fire, and axe of the pioneer, became bluegrass. What if the plant succession inherent in this dark and bloody ground had, under the impact of these forces, given us some worthless sedge, shrub, or weed? Would Boone and Kenton have held out? Would there have been any overflow into Ohio, Indiana, Illinois, and Missouri? Any Louisiana Purchase? Any transcontinental union of new states? Any Civil War?

Kentucky was one sentence in the drama of history. We are commonly told what the human actors in this drama tried to do, but we are seldom told that their success, or the lack of it, hung in large degree on the reaction of particular soils to the impact of the particular forces exerted by their occupancy. In the case of Kentucky, we do not even know where the bluegrass came from—whether it is a native species, or a stowaway from Europe.

Contrast the cane-lands with what hindsight tells us about the South-   *20*
west, where the pioneers were equally brave, resourceful, and persevering. The impact of occupancy here brought no bluegrass, or other plant fitted to withstand the bumps and buffetings of hard use. This region, when grazed by livestock, reverted through a series of more and more worthless grasses, shrubs, and weeds to a condition of unstable equilibrium. Each recession of plant types bred erosion; each increment to erosion bred a further recession of plants. The result today is a progressive and mutual

deterioration, not only of plants and soils, but of the animal community subsisting thereon. The early settlers did not expect this: on the ciénegas of New Mexico some even cut ditches to hasten it. So subtle has been its progress that few residents of the region are aware of it. It is quite invisible to the tourist who finds this wrecked landscape colorful and charming (as indeed it is, but it bears scant resemblance to what it was in 1848).

This same landscape was "developed" once before, but with quite different results. The Pueblo Indians settled the Southwest in pre-Columbian times, but they happened *not* to be equipped with range livestock. Their civilization expired, but not because their land expired.

In India, regions devoid of any sod-forming grass have been settled, apparently without wrecking the land, by the simple expedient of carrying the grass to the cow, rather than vice versa. (Was this the result of some deep wisdom, or was it just good luck? I do not know.)

In short, the plant succession steered the course of history; the pioneer simply demonstrated, for good or ill, what successions inhered in the land. Is history taught in this spirit? It will be, once the concept of land as a community really penetrates our intellectual life.

The Ecological Conscience

Conservation is a state of harmony between men and land. Despite nearly a century of propaganda, conservation still proceeds at a snail's pace; progress still consists largely of letterhead pieties and convention oratory. On the back forty we still slip two steps backward for each forward stride.

The usual answer to this dilemma is "more conservation education." No one will debate this, but is it certain that only the *volume* of education needs stepping up? Is something lacking in the *content* as well?   25

It is difficult to give a fair summary of its content in brief form, but, as I understand it, the content is substantially this: obey the law, vote right, join some organizations, and practice what conservation is profitable on your own land; the government will do the rest.

Is not this formula too easy to accomplish anything worth-while? It defines no right or wrong, assigns no obligation, calls for no sacrifice, implies no change in the current philosophy of values. In respect of land-use, it urges only enlightened self-interest. Just how far will such education take us? An example will perhaps yield a partial answer.

By 1930 it had become clear to all except the ecologically blind that southwestern Wisconsin's topsoil was slipping seaward. In 1933 the farmers were told that if they would adopt certain remedial practices for five years, the public would donate CCC labor to install them, plus the necessary machinery and materials. The offer was widely accepted, but the practices were widely forgotten when the five-year contract period was up. The farmers continued only those practices that yielded an immediate and visible economic gain for themselves.

This led to the idea that maybe farmers would learn more quickly if they themselves wrote the rules. Accordingly the Wisconsin Legislature in 1937 passed the Soil Conservation District Law. This said to farmers, in effect: *We, the public, will furnish you free technical service and loan you specialized machinery, if you will write your own rules for land-use. Each county may write its own rules, and these will have the force of law.* Nearly all the counties promptly organized to accept the proffered help, but after a decade of operation, *no county has yet written a single rule.* There has been visible progress in such practices as strip-cropping, pasture renovation, and soil liming, but none in fencing woodlots against grazing, and none in excluding plow and cow from steep slopes. The farmers, in short, have selected those remedial practices which were profitable anyhow, and ignored those which were profitable to the community, but not clearly profitable to themselves.

When one asks why no rules have been written, one is told that the   30
community is not yet ready to support them; education must precede rules. But the education actually in progress makes no mention of obligations to land over and above those dictated by self-interest. The net result is that we have more education but less soil, fewer healthy woods, and as many floods as in 1937.

The puzzling aspect of such situations is that the existence of obligations over and above self-interest is taken for granted in such rural community enterprises as the betterment of roads, schools, churches, and baseball teams. Their existence is not taken for granted, nor as yet seriously discussed, in bettering the behavior of the water that falls on the land, or in the preserving of the beauty or diversity of the farm landscape. Land-use ethics are still governed wholly by economic self-interest, just as social ethics were a century ago.

To sum up: we asked the farmer to do what he conveniently could to save his soil, and he has done just that, and only that. The farmer who clears the woods off a 75 per cent slope, turns his cows into the clearing, and dumps its rainfall, rocks, and soil into the community creek, is still (if otherwise decent) a respected member of society. If he puts lime on his fields and plants his crops on contour, he is still entitled to all the privileges and emoluments of his Soil Conservation District. The District is a beautiful piece of social machinery, but it is coughing along on two cylinders because we have been too timid, and too anxious for quick success, to tell the farmer the true magnitude of his obligations. Obligations have no meaning without conscience, and the problem we face is the extension of the social conscience from people to land.

No important change in ethics was ever accomplished without an internal change in our intellectual emphasis, loyalties, affections, and convictions. The proof that conservation has not yet touched these foundations of conduct lies in the fact that philosophy and religion have not yet heard of it. In our attempt to make conservation easy, we have made it trivial.

Substitutes for a Land Ethic

When the logic of history hungers for bread and we hand out a stone, we are at pains to explain how much the stone resembles bread. I now describe some of the stones which serve in lieu of a land ethic.

One basic weakness in a conservation system based wholly on eco- 35 nomic motives is that most members of the land community have no economic value. Wildflowers and songbirds are examples. Of the 22,000 higher plants and animals native to Wisconsin, it is doubtful whether more than 5 per cent can be sold, fed, eaten, or otherwise put to economic use. Yet these creatures are members of the biotic community, and if (as I believe) its stability depends on its integrity, they are entitled to continuance.

When one of these non-economic categories is threatened, and if we happen to love it, we invent subterfuges to give it economic importance. At the beginning of the century songbirds were supposed to be disappearing. Ornithologists jumped to the rescue with some distinctly shaky evidence to the effect that insects would eat us up if birds failed to control them. The evidence had to be economic in order to be valid.

It is painful to read these circumlocutions today. We have no land ethic yet, but we have at least drawn nearer the point of admitting that birds should continue as a matter of biotic right, regardless of the presence or absence of economic advantage to us.

A parallel situation exists in respect of predatory mammals, raptorial birds, and fish-eating birds. Time was when biologists somewhat overworked the evidence that these creatures preserve the health of game by killing weaklings, or that they control rodents for the farmer, or that they prey only on "worthless" species. Here again, the evidence had to be economic in order to be valid. It is only in recent years that we hear the more honest argument that predators are members of the community, and that no special interest has the right to exterminate them for the sake of a benefit, real or fancied, to itself. Unfortunately this enlightened view is still in the talk stage. In the field the extermination of predators goes merrily on: witness the impending erasure of the timber wolf by fiat of Congress, the Conservation Bureaus, and many state legislatures.

Some species of trees have been "read out of the party" by economics-minded foresters because they grow too slowly, or have too low a sale value to pay as timber crops: white cedar, tamarack, cypress, beech, and hemlock are examples. In Europe, where forestry is ecologically more advanced, the non-commercial tree species are recognized as members of the native forest community, to be preserved as such, within reason. Moreover some (like beech) have been found to have a valuable function in building up soil fertility. The interdependence of the forest and its constituent tree species, ground flora, and fauna is taken for granted.

Lack of economic value is sometimes a character not only of species 40 or groups, but of entire biotic communities: marshes, bogs, dunes, and "deserts" are examples. Our formula in such cases is to relegate their conservation to government as refuges, monuments, or parks. The difficulty is that these communities are usually interspersed with more valuable private lands; the government cannot possibly own or control such scattered parcels. The net effect is that we have relegated some of them to ultimate extinction over large areas. If the private owner were ecologically minded, he would be proud to be the custodian of a reasonable proportion of such areas, which add diversity and beauty to his farm and to his community.

In some instances, the assumed lack of profit in these "waste" areas has proved to be wrong, but only after most of them had been done away with. The present scramble to reflood muskrat marshes is a case in point.

There is a clear tendency in American conservation to relegate to government all necessary jobs that private landowners fail to perform. Government ownership, operation, subsidy, or regulation is now widely prevalent in forestry, range management, soil and watershed management, park and wilderness conservation, fisheries management, and migratory bird management, with more to come. Most of this growth in governmental conservation is proper and logical, some of it is inevitable. That I imply no disapproval of it is implicit in the fact that I have spent most of my life working for it. Nevertheless the question arises: What is the ultimate magnitude of the enterprise? Will the tax base carry its eventual ramifications? At what point will governmental conservation, like the mastodon, become handicapped by its own dimensions? The answer, if there is any, seems to be in a land ethic, or some other force which assigns more obligation to the private landowner.

Industrial landowners and users, especially lumbermen and stockmen, are inclined to wail long and loudly about the extension of government ownership and regulation to land, but (with notable exceptions) they show little disposition to develop the only visible alternative: the voluntary practice of conservation on their own lands.

When the private landowner is asked to perform some unprofitable act for the good of the community, he today assents only with outstretched palm. If the act costs him cash this is fair and proper, but when it costs only fore-thought, open-mindedness, or time, the issue is at least debatable. The overwhelming growth of land-use subsidies in recent years must be ascribed, in large part, to the government's own agencies for conservation education: the land bureaus, the agricultural colleges, and the extension services. As far as I can detect, no ethical obligation toward land is taught in these institutions.

To sum up: a system of conservation based solely on economic self-interest is hopelessly lopsided. It tends to ignore, and thus eventually to eliminate, many elements in the land community that lack commercial value, but that are (as far as we know) essential to its healthy functioning. It assumes, falsely, I think, that the economic parts of the biotic clock will function without the uneconomic parts. It tends to relegate to government many functions eventually too large, too complex, or too widely dispersed to be performed by government.

An ethical obligation on the part of the private owner is the only visible remedy for these situations.

The Land Pyramid

An ethic to supplement and guide the economic relation to land presupposes the existence of some mental image of land as a biotic mechanism. We can be ethical only in relation to something we can see, feel, understand, love, or otherwise have faith in.

The image commonly employed in conservation education is "the balance of nature." For reasons too lengthy to detail here, this figure of speech fails to describe accurately what little we know about the land mechanism. A much truer image is the one employed in ecology: the biotic pyramid. I shall first sketch the pyramid as a symbol of land, and later develop some of its implications in terms of land-use.

Plants absorb energy from the sun. This energy flows through a circuit called the biota, which may be represented by a pyramid consisting of layers. The bottom layer is the soil. A plant layer rests on the soil, an insect layer on the plants, a bird and rodent layer on the insects, and so on up through various animal groups to the apex layer, which consists of the larger carnivores.

The species of a layer are alike not in where they came from, or in what they look like, but rather in what they eat. Each successive layer depends on those below it for food and often for other services, and each in turn furnishes food and services to those above. Proceeding upward, each successive layer decreases in numerical abundance. Thus, for every carnivore there are hundreds of his prey, thousands of their prey, millions of insects, uncountable plants. The pyramidal form of the system reflects this numerical progression from apex to base. Man shares an intermediate layer with the bears, raccoons, and squirrels which eat both meat and vegetables. *50*

The lines of dependency for food and other services are called food chains. Thus soil-oak-deer-Indian is a chain that has now been largely converted to soil-corn-cow-farmer. Each species, including ourselves, is a link in many chains. The deer eats a hundred plants other than oak, and the cow a hundred plants other than corn. Both, then, are links in a hundred chains. The pyramid is a tangle of chains so complex as to seem disorderly, yet the stability of the system proves it to be a highly organized structure. Its functioning depends on the co-operation and competition of its diverse parts.

In the beginning, the pyramid of life was low and squat; the food chains short and simple. Evolution has added layer after layer, link after link. Man is one of thousands of accretions to the height and complexity of the pyramid. Science has given us many doubts, but it has given us at least one certainty: the trend of evolution is to elaborate and diversify the biota.

Land, then, is not merely soil; it is a fountain of energy flowing through a circuit of soils, plants, and animals. Food chains are the living channels which conduct energy upward; death and decay return it to the soil. The circuit is not closed; some energy is dissipated in decay, some is added by absorption from the air, some is stored in soils, peats, and long-lived forests; but it is a sustained circuit, like a slowly augmented revolving fund of life. There is always a net loss by downhill wash, but this is normally small and offset by the decay of rocks. It is deposited in the ocean and, in the course of geological time, raised to form new lands and new pyramids.

The velocity and character of the upward flow of energy depend on the complex structure of the plant and animal community, much as the upward flow of sap in a tree depends on its complex cellular organization. Without this complexity, normal circulation would presumably not occur. Structure means the characteristic numbers, as well as the characteristic kinds and functions, of the component species. This interdependence between the complex structure of the land and its smooth functioning as an energy unit is one of its basic attributes.

When a change occurs in one part of the circuit, many other parts must adjust themselves to it. Change does not necessarily obstruct or divert the flow of energy; evolution is a long series of self-induced changes, the net result of which has been to elaborate the flow mechanism and to lengthen the circuit. Evolutionary changes, however, are usually slow and local. Man's invention of tools has enabled him to make changes of unprecedented violence, rapidity, and scope.

One change is in the composition of floras and faunas. The larger predators are lopped off the apex of the pyramid; food chains, for the first time in history, become shorter rather than longer. Domesticated species from other lands are substituted for wild ones, and wild ones are moved to new habitats. In this world-wide pooling of faunas and floras, some species get out of bounds as pests and diseases, others are extinguished. Such effects are seldom intended or foreseen; they represent unpredicted and often untraceable readjustments in the structure. Agricultural science is largely a race between the emergence of new pests and the emergence of new techniques for their control.

Another change touches the flow of energy through plants and animals and its return to the soil. Fertility is the ability of soil to receive, store, and release energy. Agriculture, by overdrafts on the soil, or by too radical a substitution of domestic for native species in the superstructure, may derange the channels of flow or deplete storage. Soils depleted of their storage, or of the organic matter which anchors it, wash away faster than they form. This is erosion.

Waters, like soil, are part of the energy circuit. Industry, by polluting waters or obstructing them with dams, may exclude the plants and animals necessary to keep energy in circulation.

55

Transportation brings about another basic change: the plants or animals grown in one region are now consumed and returned to the soil in another. Transportation taps the energy stored in rocks, and in the air, and uses it elsewhere; thus we fertilize the garden with nitrogen gleaned by the guano birds from the fishes of seas on the other side of the Equator. Thus the formerly localized and self-contained circuits are pooled on a worldwide scale.

The process of altering the pyramid for human occupation releases stored energy, and this often gives rise, during the pioneering period, to a deceptive exuberance of plant and animal life, both wild and tame. These releases of biotic capital tend to becloud or postpone the penalties of violence.   60

* * *

This thumbnail sketch of land as an energy circuit conveys three basic ideas:

1. That land is not merely soil.
2. That the native plants and animals kept the energy circuit open; others may or may not.
3. That man-made changes are of a different order than evolutionary changes, and have effects more comprehensive than is intended or foreseen.

These ideas, collectively, raise two basic issues: Can the land adjust itself to the new order? Can the desired alterations be accomplished with less violence?

Biotas seem to differ in their capacity to sustain violent conversion. Western Europe, for example, carries a far different pyramid than Caesar found there. Some large animals are lost; swampy forests have become meadows or plowland; many new plants and animals are introduced, some of which escape as pests; the remaining natives are greatly changed in distribution and abundance. Yet the soil is still there and, with the help of imported nutrients, still fertile; the waters flow normally; the new structure seems to function and to persist. There is no visible stoppage or derangement of the circuit.

Western Europe, then, has a resistant biota. Its inner processes are tough, elastic, resistant to strain. No matter how violent the alterations, the pyramid, so far, has developed some new *modus vivendi* which preserves its habitability for man, and for most of the other natives.

Japan seems to present another instance of radical conversion without disorganization.   65

Most other civilized regions, and some as yet barely touched by civilization, display various stages of disorganization, varying from initial symptoms to advanced wastage. In Asia Minor and North Africa diagnosis is confused by climatic changes, which may have been either the cause or the effect of advanced wastage. In the United States the degree of disorganization varies locally; it is worst in the Southwest, the Ozarks, and parts of the South, and least in New England and the Northwest. Better land-uses may still arrest it in the less advanced regions. In parts of Mexico, South America, South Africa, and Australia a violent and accelerating wastage is in progress, but I cannot assess the prospects.

This almost world-wide display of disorganization in the land seems to be similar to disease in an animal, except that it never culminates in complete disorganization or death. The land recovers, but at some reduced level of complexity, and with a reduced carrying capacity for people, plants, and animals. Many biotas currently regarded as "lands of opportunity" are in fact already subsisting on exploitative agriculture, i.e. they have already exceeded their sustained carrying capacity. Most of South America is overpopulated in this sense.

In arid regions we attempt to offset the process of wastage by reclamation, but it is only too evident that the prospective longevity of reclamation projects is often short. In our own West, the best of them may not last a century.

The combined evidence of history and ecology seems to support one general deduction: the less violent the man-made changes, the greater the probability of successful readjustment in the pyramid. Violence, in turn, varies with human population density; a dense population requires a more violent conversion. In this respect, North America has a better chance for permanence than Europe, if she can contrive to limit her density.

This deduction runs counter to our current philosophy, which assumes that because a small increase in density enriched human life, that an indefinite increase will enrich it indefinitely. Ecology knows of no density relationship that holds for indefinitely wide limits. All gains from density are subject to a law of diminishing returns.

70

Whatever may be the equation for men and land, it is improbable that we as yet know all its terms. Recent discoveries in mineral and vitamin nutrition reveal unsuspected dependencies in the up-circuit: incredibly minute quantities of certain substances determine the value of soils to plants, of plants to animals. What of the down-circuit? What of the vanishing species, the preservation of which we now regard as an esthetic luxury? They helped build the soil; in what unsuspected ways may they be essential to its maintenance? Professor Weaver proposes that we use prairie flowers to reflocculate the wasting soils of the dust bowl; who knows for what purpose cranes and condors, otters and grizzlies may some day be used?

Land Health and the A-B Cleavage

A land ethic, then, reflects the existence of an ecological conscience, and this in turn reflects a conviction of individual responsibility for the health of the land. Health is the capacity of the land for self-renewal. Conservation is our effort to understand and preserve this capacity.

Conservationists are notorious for their dissensions. Superficially these seem to add up to mere confusion, but a more careful scrutiny reveals a single plane of cleavage common to many specialized fields. In each field one group (A) regards the land as soil, and its function as commodity-production; another group (B) regards the land as a biota, and its function as something broader. How much broader is admittedly in a state of doubt and confusion.

In my own field, forestry, group A is quite content to grow trees like cabbages, with cellulose as the basic forest commodity. It feels no inhibition against violence; its ideology is agronomic. Group B, on the other hand, sees forestry as fundamentally different from agronomy because it employs natural species, and manages a natural environment rather than creating an artificial one. Group B prefers natural reproduction on principle. It worries on biotic as well as economic grounds about the loss of species like chestnut, and the threatened loss of the white pines. It worries about a whole series of secondary forest functions: wildlife, recreation, watersheds, wilderness areas. To my mind, Group B feels the stirrings of an ecological conscience.

In the wildlife field, a parallel cleavage exists. For Group A the basic commodities are sport and meat; the yardsticks of production are ciphers of take in pheasants and trout. Artificial propagation is acceptable as a permanent as well as a temporary recourse—if its unit costs permit. Group B, on the other hand, worries about a whole series of biotic side-issues. What is the cost in predators of producing a game crop? Should we have further recourse to exotics? How can management restore the shrinking species, like prairie grouse, already hopeless as shootable game? How can management restore the threatened rarities, like trumpeter swan and whooping crane? Can management principles be extended to wildflowers? Here again it is clear to me that we have the same A-B cleavage as in forestry.

In the larger field of agriculture I am less competent to speak, but there seem to be somewhat parallel cleavages. Scientific agriculture was actively developing before ecology was born, hence a slower penetration of ecological concepts might be expected. Moreover the farmer, by the very nature of his techniques, must modify the biota more radically than the forester or the wildlife manager. Nevertheless, there are many discontents in agriculture which seem to add up to a new vision of "biotic farming."

Perhaps the most important of these is the new evidence that poundage or tonnage is no measure of the food-value of farm crops; the products of fertile soil may be qualitatively as well as quantitatively superior. We can bolster poundage from depleted soils by pouring on imported fertility, but we are not necessarily bolstering food-value. The possible ultimate ramifications of this idea are so immense that I must leave their exposition to abler pens.

The discontent that labels itself "organic farming," while bearing some of the earmarks of a cult, is nevertheless biotic in its direction, particularly in its insistence on the importance of soil flora and fauna.

The ecological fundamentals of agriculture are just as poorly known to the public as in other fields of land-use. For example, few educated people realize that the marvelous advances in technique made during recent decades are improvements in the pump, rather than the well. Acre for acre, they have barely sufficed to offset the sinking level of fertility.

In all of these cleavages, we see repeated the same basic paradoxes: *80* man the conqueror *versus* man the biotic citizen; science the sharpener of his sword *versus* science the searchlight on his universe; land the slave and servant *versus* land the collective organism. Robinson's injunction to Tristram may well be applied, at this juncture, to *Homo sapiens* as a species in geological time:

> Whether you will or not
> You are a King, Tristram, for you are one
> Of the time-tested few that leave the world,
> When they are gone, not the same place it was.
> Mark what you leave.

The Outlook

It is inconceivable to me that an ethical relation to land can exist without love, respect, and admiration for land, and a high regard for its value. By value, I of course mean something far broader than mere economic value; I mean value in the philosophical sense.

Perhaps the most serious obstacle impeding the evolution of a land ethic is the fact that our educational and economic system is headed away from, rather than toward, an intense consciousness of land. Your true modern is separated from the land by many middlemen, and by innumerable physical gadgets. He has no vital relation to it; to him it is the space between cities on which crops grow. Turn him loose for a day on the land, and if the spot does not happen to be a golf links or a "scenic" area, he is bored stiff. If crops could be raised by hydroponics instead of farming, it would suit him very well. Synthetic substitutes for wood, leather, wool, and other natural land products suit him better than the originals. In short, land is something he has "outgrown."

Almost equally serious as an obstacle to a land ethic is the attitude of the farmer for whom the land is still an adversary, or a taskmaster that keeps him in slavery. Theoretically, the mechanization of farming ought to cut the farmer's chains, but whether it really does is debatable.

One of the requisites for an ecological comprehension of land is an understanding of ecology, and this is by no means co-extensive with "education"; in fact, much higher education seems deliberately to avoid ecological concepts. An understanding of ecology does not necessarily originate in courses bearing ecological labels; it is quite as likely to be labeled geography, botany, agronomy, history, or economics. This is as it should be, but whatever the label, ecological training is scarce.

The case for a land ethic would appear hopeless but for the minority   *85* which is in obvious revolt against these "modern" trends.

The "key-log" which must be moved to release the evolutionary process for an ethic is simply this: quit thinking about decent land-use as solely an economic problem. Examine each question in terms of what is ethically and esthetically right, as well as what is economically expedient. A thing is right when it tends to preserve the integrity, stability, and beauty of the biotic community. It is wrong when it tends otherwise.

It of course goes without saying that economic feasibility limits the tether of what can or cannot be done for land. It always has and it always will. The fallacy the economic determinists have tied around our collective neck, and which we now need to cast off, is the belief that economics determines *all* land-use. This is simply not true. An innumerable host of actions and attitudes, comprising perhaps the bulk of all land relations, is determined by the land-users' tastes and predilections, rather than by his purse. The bulk of all land relations hinges on investments of time, forethought, skill, and faith rather than on investments of cash. As a land-user thinketh, so is he.

I have purposely presented the land ethic as a product of social evolution because nothing so important as an ethic is ever "written." Only the most superficial student of history supposes that Moses "wrote" the Decalogue; it evolved in the minds of a thinking community, and Moses wrote a tentative summary of it for a "seminar." I say tentative because evolution never stops.

The evolution of a land ethic is an intellectual as well as emotional process. Conservation is paved with good intentions which prove to be futile, or even dangerous, because they are devoid of critical understanding either of the land, or of economic land-use. I think it is a truism that as the ethical frontier advances from the individual to the community, its intellectual content increases.

The mechanism of operation is the same for any ethic: social appro-   *90* bation for right actions: social disapproval for wrong actions.

By and large, our present problem is one of attitudes and implements. We are remodeling the Alhambra with a steam-shovel, and we are proud of our yardage. We shall hardly relinquish the shovel, which after all has many good points, but we are in need of gentler and more objective criteria for its successful use.

Reading and Responding

1. Find four places in Leopold's essay that make clear sense to you. Write about each one briefly.

2. Though it's simplistic to do so, read this essay only in terms of dualities: make one list of stuff that Leopold likes or approves of, and make another list of whatever he dislikes.
3. Write five questions that, if answered, would really help you understand this essay more thoroughly.

Working Together

1. Divide this essay into sections, and let each group in the class focus on a different section. In your group, work to condense your section into five (or fewer) core statements. Write them in your own words. Once the groups are ready, combine these core statements to form a whole-class summary of Leopold's "The Land Ethic."
2. As a group, write a 500- to 750-word introduction to "The Land Ethic." Tell readers whatever you think they need to hear to make their reading less difficult, easier and richer.

Rethinking and Rewriting

1. Once you're fairly sure that you understand what Leopold argues for in "The Land Ethic," write about why you agree or disagree with him.
2. Choose a page or less from the essay, a section that seems to you to present the very heart of what Leopold has to say. Write an essay that gives a close reading of just this section, quoting it often and leading readers through it slowly and carefully, so that they understand this section as fully and completely as you do.
3. Make a connection between "The Land Ethic" and any other course you've had or are taking now. Show how the material in the other course adds to your understanding or prompts you to think about Leopold's essay in a new way.

WOMEN AND THE CHALLENGE OF THE ECOLOGICAL ERA

Dana Lee Jackson

> *Dana Lee Jackson is cofounder of The Land Institute in Salina, Kansas, and is currently associate director of the Land Stewardship Project, an organization in Minnesota dedicated to sustainable agriculture. In this article, Jackson systematically presents the history and major tenets of both environmentalism and feminism.*

When E. F. Schumacher visited The Land Institute in March 1977, we were only seven months old. We were small, but our place was not beautiful. Three partially paid staff members and eight students worked and studied in a building under construction. Outside, in the mud around the building, there were piles of scavenged materials: lumber, 220 patio doors bought for a bargain price, scrap iron, and more. But Dr. Schumacher affirmed our efforts, and his ideas influenced the developing mission of this newest nonprofit devoted to sustainable alternatives.

Now we are fourteen years old with thirteen staff members and nine student interns. The Land Institute is still small by most standards but, we think, much more beautiful with our gardens, boardwalks, trees, research plots, and nearly one hundred acres of never-plowed native prairie. We have an office building in addition to the classroom we were constructing in 1977 plus barns and farm equipment. The two Carpathian walnut trees we planted in memory of Schumacher are thriving.

Many of the problems we discuss at The Land Institute would have interested Schumacher, but I doubt if my topic is one he would have chosen. While he obviously respected and quoted prominent women of his day, like the rest of the society he considered that the main role for women was predetermined by their sex. They were to care for their children at home. In the important essay on Buddhist economics in *Small Is Beautiful,* he described the three functions of work: to give a man a chance to utilize and develop his faculties, to enable him to overcome his ego-centeredness by joining with others in a common task, and to bring forth the goods and services needed for a becoming existence. When he said "a man," he meant a man. Women were not part of this description. "Women on the whole," he said, "do not need an outside job." The legitimate need for women to have fulfilling work in addition to parenting responsibilities was not part of his range of considerations.

Attitudes about women's roles were already undergoing change in 1977 when Schumacher visited us, but I think he would be surprised at how actively women participate in mainstream society now. In general, society approves when they "utilize and develop their faculties" and engage in meaningful work, and it does not expect them to provide all the support services (cooking, cleaning, and laundry) that free their husbands to pursue careers. And just in time. Women's perspectives, values, and skills are needed as we respond to the complex problems making up the environmental crisis that is the theme of this year's lectures. We are in an age of ecology, what we might call the ecological era.

The challenge of the first part of the ecological era has largely been   5 to recognize and understand our dependence upon nature, upon ecological systems, and to realize that humans cannot continue to ruthlessly exploit the nonhuman world to satisfy our needs and greeds.

The challenge of the second part of the ecological era—from 1990 on—is to transform our society so we can act on our ecological knowledge, change destructive patterns, and develop a sustainable society. Women must have a large part in this. I shall describe here the ecological era and, occurring in the same time frame, the feminist era. In my view, and the view of a growing number, the coming together of the ecological and feminist movements gives us a greater opportunity to change patterns that not only lead to the extinction of countless other species but also destroy what supports humans. We must change the underlying conceptual framework of Western society: a hierarchy that ranks white, heterosexual, male values, ideas, and work above that of women, people of color, and all other life forms. Certain attributes of women's culture must be employed to help us adapt to sustainable, ecological living patterns. What we might call a feminization of the culture will come about in response to the environmental crisis in the most decentralist social organizations of all, our families and partnerships. Let me begin by describing the ecological era.

The Ecological Era

In *Nature's Economy* Donald Worster writes that the Age of Ecology began "on the desert outside Almagordo, New Mexico, on July 16, 1945, with a dazzling fireball of light and a swelling mushroom cloud of radioactive gases." We had created a force capable of destroying the planet. Before Worster, in 1948 Fairfield Osborne, in his book *This Plundered Planet,* said he had come to understand towards the end of World War II that humans were involved in *another* war, one against nature. This was not the age-old literary theme of conflict with nature, in which nature was a worthy opponent. Osborne and Worster both recognized that nature was now the *victim* of our aggressive actions.

But I think we did not actually start the ecological era until this understanding became a part of the general public awareness, something that came about in the mid-1960s. By the time of the first Earth Day in 1970 the thinking, reading public in this country had become acquainted with several ecological concepts and had extended them to the human experience. We could see ecological damage that humans had created; we began to understand that what we do to nature, we do to ourselves.

Rachel Carson's *Silent Spring*, published in 1962, called attention to the flagrant misuse of persistent pesticides such as DDT, chlordane, heptachlor, and dieldrin and to their devastating effect on species other than insects. The chapter "Earth's Green Mantle" explained connections between plants and animals and described the concept of the web. This ecological concept was popularized around the time of the first Earth Day. And though, as David Ehrenfeld pointed out in *The Arrogance of Humanism,* "we greatly exaggerated the fragility of that web in developing our economic arguments for preserving natural resources," for those who had never thought much about our dependence upon nature, the concept was an eye-opener.

Next it was "carrying capacity" that became widely discussed when   *10* Paul Ehrlich's book *The Population Bomb* was published in 1968. The book stimulated people to ask questions like the following: How many people can the earth support? At what standard of living? By replacing what other life forms?

The idea of cycles in nature—nutrient cycles, life cycles, reproductive cycles—also became part of the public's awareness in the early stage of the ecological era.

The awakening of our minds to these and other ecological concepts led to an active grass-roots environmental movement in the early 1970s and the founding of alternative organizations such as the New Alchemy Institute, already established in 1969, and later The Land Institute in 1976. National environmental organizations had the support of their local letter-writing constituencies when promoting the significant national legislation of the period: the National Environmental Quality Act requiring environmental impact statements, establishment of the Environmental Protection Agency to enforce new laws regulating air and water quality, and legislation protecting wilderness. The Arab oil embargo of 1973 led to a growing awareness that natural resources were finite. We began to think about the fuel "cycles" of power plants, about net energy balances, and we experimented with conservation and renewable energy.

The ecological era continued into the 1980s in spite of Ronald Reagan and James Watt. Perhaps because of James Watt, the national environmental organizations became stronger and their leadership more professional but, sadly, not in proportion to the destructive forces that increased their membership. Three Mile Island, Bhopal, Chernobyl, Prince William Sound, Alaska—these plus other environmental catastrophes caused the public to acknowledge increasingly the inherent dangers of large-scale industrial technology. In the 1980s we wrestled with the clean-up and safe storage of toxic and radioactive wastes. We realized that both capitalism and socialism externalized the environmental costs of industrial growth and acted in ignorance of the second law of thermodynamics.

The relevance of ecology to farming became clearer in the 1980s as we studied the negative consequences of industrialized agriculture: soil loss, groundwater contamination, and the demise of family farm communities. In 1980 The Land Institute launched a research program based on nature as the teacher and the measure in agriculture. We set out to learn the wisdom of the prairie, a self-sustaining ecosystem that produced the soil that made Midwest corn and wheat fields productive. We continue our efforts to bring ecology and agriculture together as we attempt to develop prairie-like mixtures of perennial plants that produce seeds for people and livestock. We expect these domestic prairies to replace conventional crops on highly erodible soil. They will require no pesticides or herbicides and will use little or no chemical fertilizer. Tractor fuel consumption will be lower as we eliminate annual tillage for planting.

The conservation provisions in the 1985 farm bill were put there by   15
the American people—city and country folk alike—to protect soil and water. Farmers were told that they must comply with conservation requirements on highly erodible land or be ineligible for subsidies. The discussion of ecology in agriculture increased as some researchers studied predator-prey relationships to control insect pests. We began hearing about studies of the role of legumes in the nitrogen fertilizer cycle and research on decomposition of organic material and release of soil nutrients.

In 1990 we are in the second stage of the ecological era. The second Earth Day celebration on April 22, 1990, focused on global environmental problems such as acid rain, the greenhouse effect, and ozone depletion. But everyone was reminded that solutions should be carried out *locally,* in particular places. One wonders if we will ever go beyond the Earth Day T-shirt level of consciousness. In this next stage of our ecological era we must do more than pick away at the symptoms of ecological disruption. It is essential to gain control over that which is responsible for our aggression against the earth, the hierarchal framework for society that is the basis of interaction between humans and the nonhuman world.

The Feminist Era

The ecological era appeared simultaneously with the feminist era. Changes in the status of women, in women's perception of themselves, in the opportunities and challenges they face have never before been so widespread nor so widely recognized as they have been in the period from the mid-sixties until now. I speak, of course, as a white, middle-class, married woman with three grown children, someone for whom the last twenty-five years have been a period of slow awakening. My own experience and the influence of women writers and feminist activists make me see the world in an entirely different way than I once did. My daughters and the young women interns at The Land Institute continue to enlighten me. Though I share much with women of color and lesbians, I am aware that their experiences have been in different contexts, and I know they have other opinions and proposals for change that I cannot adequately express.

Though I choose to describe the feminist era as beginning in the mid-sixties, parallel to the ecological era, I know that the groundwork of feminist philosophy was laid by women in the nineteenth century and feminist activism was born of the suffragettes in the early twentieth century. How much we owe to our foremothers—Sojourner Truth, Elizabeth Cady Stanton, Charlotte Perkins Gilman, Margaret Sanger, and others—for revealing the realities of sexist oppression. And how deprived our whole culture has been by the suppression of such books as *Woman, Church and State,* written by Matilda Joslyn Gage, first published in 1893 and reprinted in 1980.

I did not learn about these women when I was in school, nor in college. I was not taught that women abolitionists who attended the international anti-slavery convention in 1840 were not allowed to sit in the convention hall with the delegates or participate in the deliberations. Many women abolitionists were among the early advocates for women's rights: they spoke against the injustice of the common-law doctrine that considered wives to be chattel of husbands, that denied women the right to own property, that would not allow women to vote or hold office. When African-Americans were given the right to vote, white men still denied women—of all races—the same right. Why did the textbooks clearly teach the immorality of African-American slavery but not the immorality of women's oppression?

Women becoming adults in the 1950s, like me, did not question   20
much. Textbook stereotypes, women's magazines, and movies all reinforced the belief that "a woman's place is in the home." This attitude kept women from competing for jobs with men who were World War II veterans, and it stimulated the consumer economy as women made a career of purchasing household goods for life in suburbia. Those who went to college and earned academic honors were not as much of a success by societal standards as those who dropped out after "catching a husband" and became adept at home decorating, dinner parties, and raising well-scrubbed children.

When I was twenty, I read Henrik Ibsen's play *A Doll's House,* first performed in 1879, and suddenly recognized the tyranny of patriarchy. I was horrified and depressed. But there was no one to talk to about my feelings, so I soon was again absorbed by the culture, became engaged, bought a copy of one of those glossy bride magazines and a cedar chest, and got married.

My mother-in-law approved of my temporary teaching job, saying that I was earning a PHT degree, Putting Hubby Through (a graduate program). She fully expected me to become a full-time homemaker again and stay home with our two preschool children when my husband finished his Ph.D. I expected this of myself. Friends in the Graduate Student Wives Club and I discussed our dissatisfactions, our buried intellectual interests, and the conflicts we felt because of our belief that it was the mother's duty to be home with the children.

The involvement of many women in the environmental movement has been an extension of the motherhood role. Women have always been involved in reform movements that they see as related to the welfare of their home and children. From promoting spittoons in the streets of frontier towns to prohibition of alcohol to working for air-pollution abatement and the safe disposal of hazardous or radioactive wastes, family well-being has been the impetus for action.

Friends and I arranged a "teach in" for homemakers at the Salina, Kansas, YWCA on Earth Day 1970, which then led to the organization of the Salina Consumers for a Better Environment. We lobbied grocery stores for less plastic packaging and more recyclable containers. We promoted tree planting. We also set up a speakers' bureau with self-educated women available to speak to clubs and service organizations about all the environmental issues of the day, everything from overpopulation to pesticides to declining fossil fuel supplies. My own interest in the issues—the personal environmental crusade I took on—kept me busy for most of the next decade as a professional citizen. The challenge of learning about many new subjects so we could give speeches and lobby lawmakers eased some of the suburban homemaker dissatisfaction Betty Friedan described in *The Feminine Mystique,* which had hit me hard when I read it in 1966. While still loyal homemakers for our husbands and children, we could also spend our days working in common cause with other women environmentalists. Undoubtedly we did some good, but from another perspective our involvement in working for the public good and our children's future sidetracked us from seeking personal fulfillment and independence.

Women became important in local chapters of mainstream environmental organizations in the 1970s. Too often they left the leadership to men and fell into the housekeeping chores: telephoning, licking stamps, baking cookies, and writing letters. This volunteer work force declined in the 1980s as more women took full-time jobs and professionals did more of the lobbying and office work. If we are to think globally and act locally, if we are to develop decentralist responses to the environmental crisis, we need to revitalize grass-roots organizations. But who will do the important volunteer work?   25

This brings us to the challenge for the next phase of the feminist era. The women's movement to this point has affected the way women work, how they relate to their families, and especially what they think about themselves and their aspirations. Contrasted to the 1950s, women *expect* to find careers in business, medicine, politics, and law. But greater equity in the workplace has not led to greater equity in the home. Studies show that women do a disproportionate share of the housework, take most of the responsibility for the children, and get less personal support from men than they give. Women develop their faculties on the job but still provide most of the physical and emotional support for the family. We have made great strides in social justice—except in our basic social unit, the home.

This inequity persists because the underlying conceptual framework for society is a hierarchy with white heterosexual men at the top. Men are considered to be more important than women and to pursue more important work. Men's patterns of thinking and making moral choices, of organizing ideas or work, of determining justice, of judging esthetics have been the *standards* for Western culture and the Judeo-Christian tradition.

These standards, carried out through industrialization, have molded the workplace in our country. Industrial values dominate: high production for profit is the bottom line, growth and more growth is the major goal, bigger or more is better. People must work at least forty hours a week—or fifty or sixty if they are aspiring corporate executives or academics—in order to hold jobs with decent pay. We cannot ignore the fact that many women are employed outside the home *not* because they have fulfilling work but because the family needs two salaries. Men—and now women—on that treadmill cannot reestablish a proper relationship with the earth, let alone an adequate relationship with their families and communities.

Women increasingly understand that working for their own release from male dominance cannot succeed unless they work to eliminate the dominance of one race over another, one age group over another. Sexism, heterosexism, ageism, racism, classism, and naturism are all the same problem. Women are not out to replace male dominance with female dominance but to correct the problem of dominance. Our goal must not be to change who dominates but to get rid of the model that justifies and promotes domination.

The environmental crises we face are the result of human domination over the natural environment. Humans have exploited the nonhuman world, treating other life forms as "the other" just as the dominant race has treated people of color as "the other" and just as men have treated women as the "other." The difference is that the consequence of our subjugating nature could be the destruction of ecosystems and the extinction of people of all races as well as many other species.   *30*

Now we must conclude that to live within the limits of natural ecosystems, to live sustainably, will require an entirely different way of relating to one another and to the earth. Rather than set up hierarchies of value, we must learn to deal with differences (gender, race, and species) by a process Riane Eisler, in *The Chalice and the Blade,* calls "linking" instead of "ranking." We must reestablish relationships with the natural world that will make us sensitive to the needs of other species.

A Synthesis of the Ecological Era and the Feminist Era

In this next phase of the ecological era and the feminist era, we must learn from nature and from women in order to transform our destructive patterns, but we cannot learn in a system that oppresses nature and women.

The first step away from this system is to cultivate and elevate in importance some of the qualities and values most generally associated with
women that can help us abandon our suicidal patterns. These are not to
be considered innate characteristics, and they are not universally found in
women, but they *are* identified more often with women than men, even
though men express them also. Until recently, men have been criticized
for exhibiting such qualities . . . that identified them with the inferior
gender. But as we face a large number of environmental threats, not the
least of which is still nuclear annihilation, we desperately need new standards of behavior. The feminization of our culture has already produced
beneficial results in many workplaces, which leads us to believe that
women's cultural patterns can benefit society on a broader scale also. These
qualities are described in slightly different ways by different people. I've
grouped them in four general categories, each of which includes a number
of related traits.

First, women are considered to be nurturers. They take care of the
physical and emotional needs of their families, but their strong nurturing
impulse extends to all living things. They tend to place individual growth
and fulfillment above abstractions. Women are attentive to the needs of
nonhuman growing things such as pets, garden flowers and vegetables, and
houseplants. Some claim that women are closer to nature, perhaps because
their monthly cycle and their capacity to give birth and produce milk make
them more tuned in to the world around them.

Second, women see themselves in relationship to others. Psychologists say that men are more likely to think of themselves as individuals who
must accomplish things independently, while women tend to exhibit co-
operative individualism. They see themselves as wives, mothers, friends,
and members of groups and communities. Women empathize with others
and are more adaptable and cooperative in group situations. They tend to
integrate rather than separate, preferring networks to hierarchies.

Third, women have an attachment to the day-to-day process of sus-   35
taining life. They are used to taking care of many details at the same time.
They will do the nitty-gritty work necessary to keep the household in
good condition, complete projects, and organize events.

Fourth, women have a preference for negotiation as a means of problem solving that springs from an antipathy to violence. They tend to make
moral choices based on causing the minimum of hurt, while men will tend
to make moral choices based on rights and justice. Carol Gilligan points
out in her book *In a Different Voice* that women do not like to make moral
decisions based on dichotomies: either this is right or that is right. They
prefer to look at the *context* of a problem and find a way out that causes
the least hurt for those involved.

Why are these qualities associated with women? I think they are the
consequences of the history of women's position. We've had to learn these
patterns as subordinates, in some cases using them as techniques for survival. They are needed to do parenting and housekeeping, tasks tradition-

ally relegated to women and passed on from mother to daughter. Society at large has benefited from the display or expression of women's qualities that help groups to work harmoniously, and society would benefit more if these qualities could replace some qualities of the dominant gender, such as aggressiveness and competitiveness and the tendency to prefer large and sweeping solutions or generalizations.

Women's culture has generally been disdained, and many women have forsaken much of it to become "honorary men" and succeed in the corporate business world. If gender differences are wiped out by women becoming men, then the earth will get a double whammy. But in a recent article in *Working Women* Thomas J. Peters, co-author of *In Search of Excellence,* says that women are feminizing corporate offices and being praised by their employers for introducing different ways of organizing work and relating to other employees.

Now we seem to be in a new trap. Because women's culture could be a dose of good medicine for society, are women responsible for solving our problems? Does this mean that women must be earthkeepers and work out the truce in the human war against nature? This sounds as if women are expected to clean up after men again. But we don't want to do that anymore. We want to share the clean-up jobs as partners and equals.

In a conversation I had with the organizer Byron Kennard in 1980, he referred to women activists as the "conscience of the community." They feel personally responsible for righting the wrongs in a community and volunteer their time for the organizing of causes. Women cannot carry this role alone, however, if they seek fulfilling work outside the home.

For progress to be made in the new stages of the ecological era and the feminist era, men and women must cooperate. It is time for the old domination structure to crumble, time for men to share the housekeeping and earthkeeping tasks, unglamorous as they may be. Instead of women sacrificing their talents and goals to enable their husbands to succeed, it is time for husbands and wives to help each other. But partnership and sharing must be extended beyond the household. Just as more working men now do share the laundry and shopping on evenings and weekends with their working wives, more men must share the tasks of community building, of earthkeeping.

We have problems even with this arrangement, however, if children are in the household and the parents' full-time work and volunteer schedules deny children loving attention. Varying the industrial model in the workplace by means of shared jobs, part-time work, and flexible working hours would enable us to express our nurturing natures more adequately.

Many fathers now do take care of their children. They are not babysitting; they are parenting. As men consider childcare a shared responsibility and are able to be with their children, a pattern unfolds that benefits men and the whole society as well as women.

To make progress in the second stage of the ecological era, humans must remake the relationship between nature and culture. The notion that women were closer to nature, thus wild, led men in the past to believe that women were not to be trusted but must be controlled and tamed. Our challenge is to learn from nature, from the wild, to study nature as the standard for agriculture and nature's economy as the basis of our human economy. As Ynestra King said, "Freedom lies in becoming natural beings in the deepest sense, rather than beings against nature."

Our Next Steps

The scope of our environmental problems is enormous: we must address our excessive faith in and dependence on technology, the overconsumption and waste of resources, overreliance on nonrenewable energy, destruction of habitats, and above all the question of how many people the earth can support. We must redefine national security and subdue costly militarism. We have so far been unsuccessful in turning around our bent for destruction through state and national legislation. (I do not mean by this that we should abandon protective laws such as the Clean Air Act.) And we will not be successful until we stop believing that an increasing domination of nature is a measure of human progress.

In his book *Envisioning a Sustainable Society: Learning Our Way Out* Lester Milbrath discusses the concept of social learning. He says that social learning, which is impossible to define in a phrase, comes about in different ways, generally recognizable only after it has happened. One way to explain it is to say that social learning occurs when society comes to understand something sufficiently for one dominant institution or practice to be replaced by another. We are in the midst of social learning about the relationship between men and women and our human relationship with nature, which has created the environmental crisis, but we have not reached the point where significant social change is imminent.

Milbrath suggests that we might open up our collective mind for social learning to take place because of a "slowly accelerating cascade of unfortunate developments." More industrial accidents like those at Bhopal and Chernobyl, increased ozone depletion, cancer threats, contaminated drinking water, population growth, and famines will finally convince us. As stories accumulate that show us the world is not working, he says, we may finally come to our senses. Then social learning will soak in, and we will have the potential for a sudden shift from the dominant social paradigm to a new paradigm.

David Ehrenfeld concludes the chapter "The Conservation Dilemma" in *The Arrogance of Humanism* with a similar position: "Nonhumanistic arguments [for conservation] will carry full and deserved weight only after prevailing cultural attitudes have changed." The change may come only by a miracle, that is (he quotes Lewis Mumford), "'not something outside the order of nature but something occurring so infrequently and bringing about such a radical change that one cannot include it in any statistical prediction.'" He reassures the reader that those who have considered the nonhumanistic arguments for conservation of nature will be ready to take advantage of the favorable circumstances. And in a broader context, those of us who have considered the advantages of a world in which patriarchy is no longer the conceptual framework and in which people understand and value our linkage with the natural world, will be ready for the paradigm shift or the miracle, and we can help it to happen. In the meantime, we should continue our work to effect social learning.

Social learning is underway in many parts of our culture. I am encouraged by what I see as an effort to integrate ecology and feminism into agriculture, religion, the arts, and community development.

Most people begin to understand their connection to the natural world when they start learning about food production. I think social learning has begun in agriculture as the environmental consequences of industrial farming have become public information. The connections between heavy use of agricultural chemicals and drinking water contamination led to revolutionary groundwater protection legislation in Iowa. The treatment of animals raised in confinement now really troubles consumers. Farmers themselves are looking for a way out of the costly input treadmill, and a transition from conventional agribusiness to sustainable farming has begun for many. In the grain/livestock agriculture of the Midwest, farmers like Dick and Sharon Thompson and their fellow members of Practical Farmers of Iowa talk about practices that will prevent soil erosion and nurture soil organisms. The Thompsons emphasize care and attention in their livestock programs, which are unlike large-scale hog confinement operations in Iowa. Each year several hundred farmers attend the Thompson field days and learn about their crop rotations and, most importantly, about their philosophy of working with nature. Similar learning goes on in sustainable agriculture organizations and on-farm experiments in Wisconsin, Minnesota, and Nebraska. The U.S. Department of Agriculture has not provided leadership; it is the decentralist organizations that are guiding us to a more ecological agriculture and making social learning happen.

The Land Institute goes further than other organizations in aiming for long-term sustainability in agriculture. We want to develop crops that can feed us when cheap fossil fuel is no longer available. This means creating a partnership with nature in which elements of the ecosystem contribute to soil fertility and to insect and disease control. Our focus on bringing ecology and agriculture together naturally embraces some of the feminine qualities I mentioned. For example, we must think about how the species of our planet will relate to one another and the places where they grow. Researchers must pay close attention to the growth habits and particular needs of each species. Our ecological model is not a pyramid with humans at the top of the food chain but a network of organisms linked together. Though the mixtures of grain crops we develop will mimic the prairie of the plains and Midwest states, we think the ecological principles we learn can apply to other ecosystems around the world.

50

The historical connections among food, religion, and women may be revitalized as churches recognize a new role in the ecological era. The newly appointed spiritual leader of the Church of England and seventy million Anglicans worldwide say that "God is Green." Although churches and synagogues in the United States mostly ignored the first Earth Day in 1970, they actively participated on April 22, 1990. From a concern about hunger and rural justice, religious leaders saw connections to soil and water stewardship. Now they regularly preach environmental messages from the pulpit and urge a higher ecological consciousness among their members. Jewish and Christian theologians are trying to renew a philosophy of nature and ethical guidelines for the human-nature relationship. Ten years ago women clergy were scarce, but now women are spiritual leaders throughout several Protestant denominations, and gender-inclusive language is found in church ritual. Books on theology by women have opened up discussions on the similarity between domination over women and domination over nature, and social learning is taking place.

The arts are also contributing to social learning and will help us change our conceptual framework for human-earth relations. The emotional response that the arts elicit affects social learning. Of course, the arts should not be forced to serve a particular moral vision or political position; artists respond to the world as they experience it, and the ecological era and feminist era have been a part of their experience. I think it is significant that more women artists are writing and exhibiting their works and that ecological themes are used more often by both women and men.

Our arts associate at The Land Institute is Terry Evans, a photographer whose book *Prairie: Images of Ground and Sky* has taught an esthetic understanding of prairie to many people. She is collaborating with nine other landscape photographers, three women and six men, in a special "Water in the West" project, which will depict many kinds of water use in western states. All the artists are concerned about problems resulting from the use of land and water. The project is unique in the way these independent artists learn from one another and work together developing the project.

Simone de Beauvoir said: "Representation of the world, like the world itself, is the work of men. They describe it from their own point of view, which they mistake for the absolute truth." Representation of the world from the perspective of women and their ethical sense of relatedness to living things and their propensity to nurture life are needed now. More than ever, we should encourage the feminization of the arts. We need an alternative to what Ynestra King calls the "androcentric master narrative."

Last is *praxis,* defined by David Orr as "the science of effective action." Action can contribute to social learning, and social learning must prepare us for action—that is, political action. William Ophuls, in *Ecology and the Politics of Scarcity,* describes politics as "the art of creating new possibilities for human progress." New possibilities and effective action seem most likely to materialize within the context of communities.

Faith in the small-scale, local approach turns into action in projects such as those begun through the Schumacher Society. The activities of community-based programs—land trusts, organic farm marketing cooperatives, and economic renewal projects such as Self-Help Association for a Regional Economy—are models of local politics as defined by Ophuls that open our minds to social learning. As communities stop trying to solve their economic problems by bringing in large polluting industries or expecting federal government assistance, they can improve their support of what is already there and develop more locally owned and locally controlled enterprises.

The most local situation of all, the smallest political unit, is the home. Here is where effective action toward social transformation begins—with partners in households helping each other develop as individuals, as individuals in relationships with others and the natural world. By caring for each other and sharing in the tasks of living, we undermine the old hierarchical framework that keeps us on the path of environmental destruction.

I conclude with three stanzas of a poem, a prayer, by Barbara Deming:

Spirit of love
That flows against our flesh
Sets it trembling
Moves across it as across grass
Erasing every boundary that we accept
And swings the doors of our lives wide—
This is a prayer I sing
Save our perishing earth!

Spirit that cracks our single selves—
Eyes fall down eyes,
Hearts escape through the bars of our ribs
To dart into other bodies—
Save this earth!
The earth is perishing.
This is a prayer I sing.

Spirit that hears each one of us,
Hears all that is—
Listens, listens, hears us out—
Inspire us now!
Our own pulse beats in every stranger's throat,
And also there within the flowered
    ground beneath our feet,
And—teach us to listen!—
We can hear it in water, in wood, and even in stone.
We are earth of this earth,

and we are bone of its bone.
This is a prayer I sing, for we have
    forgotten this and so
The earth is perishing.

                                                                    —1990

Reading and Responding

1. Is Jackson's article easy or hard to read? Freewrite for one minute to answer this question.
2. Reread the article and make a list of qualities in Jackson's writing that you think account for your response about whether the essay is easy or hard to read. For example, if you thought the article was easy to read, what strategies of form and style made it readable?

Working Together

1. As a group, construct a timeline of major dates and their corresponding events or people in "the ecological era," according to Jackson. Construct a similar timeline of dates, events, and people of "the feminist era." Now, on a separate sheet, synthesize the two timelines by summarizing Jackson's four main points under the subheading "A Synthesis of the Ecological Era and the Feminist Era." Discuss what you learned from this exercise about the environmental movement or environmental ideas. Do you find this overview of history useful? Why or why not? Which ideas attract or interest you, and which ideas do you find problematic?
2. As a group, identify three instances in the essay that provoke strong responses. Discuss your reactions and determine what it is that provokes such a strong response.

Rethinking and Rewriting

1. Write an essay that defines the phrase, "the tyranny of patriarchy." Explain its importance, according to Jackson, for an understanding of the environmental movement. Reflect on its usefulness and significance, and extend it to some particular example in your own reading and experience. Summarize the major points in Jackson's essay, but use the essay as a point of departure.
2. Jackson lists several qualities that are associated generally with women—that women are nurturers, for example. Write an essay that agrees or disagrees with one of these general qualities—or that expresses your comfort or discomfort with such generalizations—and draw on your own experience.

UNCHOPPING A TREE

W. S. Merwin

W. S. Merwin is one of the best known and most acclaimed poets in America. His collection of poems The Carrier of Ladders *won the Pulitzer Prize in 1970. In this carefully constructed essay, Merwin proceeds from a startling assumption.*

Start with the leaves, the small twigs, and the nests that have been shaken, ripped, or broken off by the fall; these must be gathered and attached once again to their respective places. It is not arduous work, unless major limbs have been smashed or mutilated. If the fall was carefully and correctly planned, the chances of anything of the kind happening will have been reduced. Again, much depends upon the size, age, shape, and species of the tree. Still, you will be lucky if you can get through this stage without having to use machinery. Even in the best of circumstances it is a labor that will make you wish often that you had won the favor of the universe of ants, the empire of mice, or at least a local tribe of squirrels, and could enlist their labors and their talents. But no, they leave you to it. They have learned, with time. This is men's work. It goes without saying that if the tree was hollow in whole or in part, and contained old nests of bird or mammal or insect, or hoards of nuts or such structures as wasps or bees build for their survival, the contents will have to be repaired where necessary, and reassembled, insofar as possible, in their original order, including the shells of nuts already opened. With spiders' webs you must simply do the best you can. We do not have the spider's weaving equipment, nor any substitute for the leaf's living bond with its point of attachment and nourishment. It is even harder to simulate the latter when the leaves have once become dry—as they are bound to do, for this is not the labor of a moment. Also it hardly needs saying that this is the time for repairing any neighboring trees or bushes or other growth that may have been damaged by the fall. The same rules apply. Where neighboring trees were of the same species it is difficult not to waste time conveying a detached leaf back to the wrong tree. Practice, practice. Put your hope in that.

Now the tackle must be put into place, or the scaffolding, depending on the surroundings and the dimensions of the tree. It is ticklish work. Almost always it involves, in itself, further damage to the area, which will have to be corrected later. But as you've heard, it can't be helped. And care now is likely to save you considerable trouble later. Be careful to grind nothing into the ground.

At last the time comes for the erecting of the trunk. By now it will scarcely be necessary to remind you of the delicacy of this huge skeleton. Every motion of the tackle, every slight upward heave of the trunk, the branches, their elaborately re-assembled panoply of leaves (now dead) will draw from you an involuntary gasp. You will watch for a leaf or a twig to be snapped off yet again. You will listen for the nuts to shift in the hollow limb and you will hear whether they are indeed falling into place or are spilling in disorder—in which case, or in the event of anything else of the kind—operations will have to cease, of course, while you correct the matter. The raising itself is no small enterprise, from the moment when the chains tighten around the old bandages until the bole hangs vertical above the stump, splinter above splinter. Now the final straightening of the splinters themselves can take place (the preliminary work is best done while the wood is still green and soft, but at times when the splinters are not badly twisted most of the straightening is left until now, when the torn ends are face to face with each other). When the splinters are perfectly complementary the appropriate fixative is applied. Again we have no duplicate of the original substance. Ours is extremely strong, but it is rigid. It is limited to surfaces, and there is no play in it. However the core is not the part of the trunk that conducted life from the roots up into the branches and back again. It was relatively inert. The fixative for this part is not the same as the one for the outer layers and the bark, and if either of these is involved in the splintered section they must receive applications of the appropriate adhesives. Apart from being incorrect and probably ineffective, the core fixative would leave a scar on the bark.

When all is ready the splintered trunk is lowered onto the splinters of the stump. This, one might say, is only the skeleton of the resurrection. Now the chips must be gathered, and the sawdust, and returned to their former positions. The fixative for the wood layers will be applied to chips and sawdust consisting only of wood. Chips and sawdust consisting of several substances will receive applications of the correct adhesives. It is as well, where possible, to shelter the materials from the elements while working. Weathering makes it harder to identify the smaller fragments. Bark sawdust in particular the earth lays claim to very quickly. You must find your own ways of coping with this problem. There is a certain beauty, you will notice at moments, in the pattern of the chips as they are fitted back into place. You will wonder to what extent it should be described as natural, to what extent man-made. It will lead you on to speculations about the parentage of beauty itself, to which you will return.

The adhesive for the chips is translucent, and not so rigid as that for the splinters. That for the bark and its subcutaneous layers is transparent and runs into the fibers on either side, partially dissolving them into each other. It does not set the sap flowing again but it does pay a kind of tribute to the preoccupations of the ancient thoroughfares. You could not roll an egg over the joints but some of the mine-shafts would still be passable, no doubt. For the first exploring insect who raises its head in the tight echoless passages. The day comes when it is all restored, even to the moss (now dead) over the wound. You will sleep badly, thinking of the removal of the scaffolding that must begin the next morning. How you will hope for sun and a still day!

The removal of the scaffolding or tackle is not so dangerous, perhaps, to the surroundings, as its installation, but it presents problems. It should be taken from the spot piece by piece as it is detached, and stored at a distance. You have come to accept it there, around the tree. The sky begins to look naked as the chains and struts one by one vacate their positions. Finally the moment arrives when the last sustaining piece is removed and the tree stands again on its own. It is as though its weight for a moment stood on your heart. You listen for a thud of settlement, a warning creak deep in the intricate joinery. You cannot believe it will hold. How like something dreamed it is, standing there all by itself. How long will it stand there now? The first breeze that touches its dead leaves all seems to flow into your mouth. You are afraid the motion of the clouds will be enough to push it over. What more can you do? What more can you do?

But there is nothing more you can do.

Others are waiting.

Everything is going to have to be put back.

Reading and Responding

Write a short, step-by-step record of what it was like to read this piece. Make your narrative at least half a page long.

Working Together

1. In a few sentences, summarize what you think Merwin's main point is. Put it as bluntly as you can.
2. Discuss why Merwin just doesn't come out and say his point? Why does he make his point in this indirect, odd way?

Rethinking and Rewriting

1. Write an essay with this title, filling in the blanks: "Un _____ ing a _____" (Unwriting a Paper, Unreading a Book, Undrinking a Bottle of Wine, Unhurting a Friend, Undriving a Car).
2. Describe any process in reverse.
3. Argue any position or make some point about something without coming out and stating your position. Do it obliquely, through some trick or shift in perspective.

IS NATURE TOO GOOD FOR US?

IS NATURE TOO GOOD FOR US?

William Tucker

> *A contributing editor to* Forbes, *journalist William Tucker has written for a variety of national magazines. He is also the author of several books about American social issues, including* Zoning, Rent Control, and Affordable Housing *(1991) and* Progress and Privilege: America in the Age of Environmentalism *(1982), from which the following excerpt is taken.*

Probably nothing has been more central to the environmental movement than the concept of wilderness. "In wildness is the preservation of the world," wrote Thoreau, and environmental writers and speakers have intoned his message repeatedly. Wilderness, in the environmental pantheon, represents a particular kind of sanctuary in which all true values—that is, all nonhuman values—are reposited. Wildernesses are often described as "temples," "churches," and "sacred ground"—refuges for the proposed "new religion" based on environmental consciousness. Carrying the religious metaphor to the extreme, one of the most famous essays of the environmental era holds the Judeo-Christian religion responsible for "ecological crisis."

The wilderness issue also has a political edge. Since 1964, longstanding preservation groups like the Wilderness Society and the Sierra Club have been pressuring conservation agencies like the National Forest Service and the Bureau of Land Management to put large tracts of their holdings into permanent "wilderness designations," countering the "multiple use" concept that was one of the cornerstones of the Conservation Era of the early 1900s.

Preservation and conservation groups have been at odds since the end of the last century, and the rift between them has been a major controversy of environmentalism. The leaders of the Conservation Movement—most notably Theodore Roosevelt, Gifford Pinchot, and John Wesley Powell—called for rational, efficient development of land and other natural resources: multiple use, or reconciling competing uses of land, and also "highest use," or forfeiting more immediate profits from land development for more lasting gains. Preservationists, on the other hand, the followers of California woodsman John Muir, have advocated protecting land in its natural state, setting aside tracts and keeping them inviolate. "Wilderness area" battles have become one of the hottest political issues of the day, especially in western states—the current "Sagebrush Revolt" comes to mind—where large quantities of potentially commercially usable land are at stake.

The term "wilderness" generally connotes mountains, trees, clear streams, rushing waterfalls, grasslands, or parched deserts, but the concept has been institutionalized and has a careful legal definition as well. The one given by the 1964 Wilderness Act, and that most environmentalists favor, is that wilderness is an area "where man is a visitor but does not remain." People do not "leave footprints there," wilderness exponents often say. Wildernesses are, most importantly, areas in which *evidence of human activity is excluded;* they need not have any particular scenic, aesthetic, or recreational value. The values, as environmentalists usually say, are "ecological"—which means, roughly translated, that natural systems are allowed to operate as free from human interference as possible.

The concept of excluding human activity is not to be taken lightly. One of the major issues in wilderness areas has been whether or not federal agencies should fight forest fires. The general decision has been that they should not, except in cases where other lands are threatened. The federal agencies also do not fight the fires with motorized vehicles, which are prohibited in wilderness areas except in extreme emergencies. Thus in recent years both the National Forest Service and the National Park Service have taken to letting forest fires burn unchecked, to the frequent alarm of tourists. The defense is that many forests require periodic leveling by fire in order to make room for new growth. There are some pine trees, for instance, whose cones will break open and scatter their seeds only when burned. This theoretical justification has won some converts, but very few in the timber companies, which bridle at watching millions of board-feet go up in smoke when their own "harvesting" of mature forests has the same effect in clearing the way for new growth and does less damage to forest soils.

The effort to set aside permanent wilderness areas on federal lands began with the National Forest Service in the 1920s. The first permanent reservation was in the Gila National Forest in New Mexico. It was set aside by a young Forest Service officer named Aldo Leopold, who was later to write *A Sand County Almanac,* which has become one of the bibles of the wilderness movement. Robert Marshall, another Forest Service officer, continued the program, and by the 1950s nearly 14 million of the National Forest System's 186 million acres had been administratively designated wilderness preserves.

Leopold and Marshall had been disillusioned by one of the first great efforts at "game management" under the National Forest Service, carried out in the Kaibab Plateau, just north of the Grand Canyon. As early as 1906 federal officials began a program of "predator control" to increase the deer population in the area. Mountain lions, wolves, coyotes, and bobcats were systematically hunted and trapped by game officials. By 1920, the program appeared to be spectacularly successful. The deer population, formerly numbering 4,000, had grown to almost 100,000. But it was realized too late that it was the range's limited food resources that would threaten the deer's existence. During two severe winters, in 1924–26, 60 percent of the herd died, and by 1939 the population had shrunk to only 10,000. Deer populations (unlike human populations) were found to have no way of putting limits on their own reproduction. The case is still cited as the classic example of the "boom and bust" disequilibrium that comes from thoughtless intervention in an ecological system.

The idea of setting aside as wilderness areas larger and larger segments of federally controlled lands began to gain more support from the old preservationists' growing realizations, during the 1950s, that they had not won the battle during the Conservation Era, and that the national forests were not parks that would be protected forever from commercial activity.

Pinchot's plan for practicing "conservation" in the western forests was to encourage a partnership between the government and large industry. In order to discourage overcutting and destructive competition, he formulated a plan that would promote conservation activities among the larger timber companies while placing large segments of the western forests under federal control. It was a classic case of "market restriction," carried out by the joint efforts of larger businesses and government. Only the larger companies, Pinchot reasoned, could generate the profits that would allow them to cut their forest holdings *slowly* so that the trees would have time to grow back. In order to ensure these profit margins, the National Forest Service would hold most of its timber lands out of the market for some time. This would hold up the price of timber and prevent a rampage through the forests by smaller companies trying to beat small profit margins by cutting everything in sight. Then, in later years, the federal lands would gradually be worked into the "sustained yield" cycles, and timber rights put up for sale. It was when the national forests finally came up for cutting in the 1950s that the old preservation groups began to react.

The battle was fought in Congress. The 1960 Multiple Use and Sus- 10 tained Yield Act tried to reaffirm the principles of the Conservation Movement. But the wilderness groups had their day in 1964 with the passing of the Wilderness Act. The law required all the federal land-management agencies—the National Forest Service, the National Park Service, and the Fish and Wildlife Service—to review all their holdings, keeping in mind that "wilderness" now constituted a valid alternative in the "multiple use" concept—even though the concept of wilderness is essentially a rejection of the idea of multiple use. The Forest Service, with 190 million acres, and the Park Service and Fish and Wildlife Service, each with about 35 million acres, were all given twenty years to start designating wilderness areas. At the time, only 14.5 million acres of National Forest System land were in wilderness designations.

The results have been mixed. The wilderness concept appears valid if it is recognized for what it is—an attempt to create what are essentially "ecological museums" in scenic and biologically significant areas of these lands. But "wilderness," in the hands of environmentalists, has become an all-purpose tool for stopping economic activity as well. This is particularly crucial now because of the many mineral and energy resources available on western lands that environmentalists are trying to push through as wilderness designations. The original legislation specified that lands were to be surveyed for valuable mineral resources before they were put into wilderness preservation. Yet with so much land being reviewed at once, these inventories have been sketchy at best. And once land is locked up as wilderness, it becomes illegal even to explore it for mineral or energy resources.

Thus the situation in western states—where the federal government still owns 68 percent of the land, counting Alaska—has in recent years become a race between mining companies trying to prospect under severely restricted conditions, and environmental groups trying to lock the doors to resource development for good. This kind of permanent preservation—the antithesis of conservation—will probably have enormous effects on our future international trade in energy and mineral resources.

At stake in both the national forests and the Bureau of Land Management holdings are what are called the "roadless areas." Environmentalists call these lands "de facto wilderness," and say that because they have not yet been explored or developed for resources they should not be explored and developed in the future. The Forest Service began its Roadless Area Resources Evaluation (RARE) in 1972, while the Bureau of Land Management began four years later in 1976, after Congress brought its 174 million acres under jurisdiction of the 1964 act. The Forest Service is studying 62 million roadless acres, while the BLM is reviewing 24 million.

In 1974 the Forest Service recommended that 15 million of the 50 million acres then under study be designated as permanent wilderness. Environmental groups, which wanted much more set aside, immediately challenged the decision in court. Naturally, they had no trouble finding flaws in a study intended to cover such a huge amount of land, and in 1977 the Carter administration decided to start over with a "RARE II" study, completed in 1979. This has also been challenged by a consortium of environmental groups that includes the Sierra Club, the Wilderness Society, the National Wildlife Federation, and the Natural Resources Defense Council. The RARE II report also recommended putting about 15 million acres in permanent wilderness, with 36 million released for development and 11 million held for further study. The Bureau of Land Management is not scheduled to complete the study of its 24 million acres until 1991.

The effects of this campaign against resource development have been 15 powerful. From 1972 to 1980, the price of a Douglas fir in Oregon increased 500 percent, largely due to the delays in timber sales from the national forests because of the battles over wilderness areas. Over the decade, timber production from the national forests declined slightly, putting far more pressure on the timber industry's own lands. The nation has now become an importer of logs, despite the vast resources on federal lands. In 1979, environmentalists succeeded in pressuring Congress into setting aside 750,000 acres in Idaho as the Sawtooth Wilderness and National

Recreational Area. A resource survey, which was not completed until *after* the congressional action, showed that the area contained an estimated billion dollars' worth of molybdenum, zinc, silver, and gold. The same tract also contained a potential source of cobalt, an important mineral for which we are now dependent on foreign sources for 97 percent of what we use.

Perhaps most fiercely contested are the energy supplies believed to be lying under the geological strata running through Colorado, Wyoming, and Montana just east of the Rockies, called the Overthrust Belt. Much of this land is still administered by the Bureau of Land Management for multiple usage. But with the prospect of energy development, environmental groups have been rushing to try to have these high-plains areas designated as wilderness areas as well (cattle grazing is still allowed in wilderness tracts). On those lands permanently withdrawn from commercial use, mineral exploration will be allowed to continue until 1983. Any mines begun by then can continue on a very restricted basis. But the exploration in "roadless areas" is severely limited, in that in most cases there can be no roads constructed (and no use of off-roads vehicles) while exploration is going on. Environmentalists have argued that wells can still be drilled and test mines explored using helicopters. But any such exploration is likely to be extraordinarily expensive and ineffective. Wilderness restrictions are now being drawn so tightly that people on the site are not allowed to leave their excrement in the area.

Impossible Paradises

What is the purpose of all this? The standard environmental argument is that we have to "preserve these last few wild places before they all disappear." Yet it is obvious that something more is at stake. What is being purveyed is a view of the world in which human activity is defined as "bad" and natural conditions are defined as "good." What is being preserved is evidently much more than "ecosystems." What is being preserved is an *image* of wilderness as a semisacred place beyond humanity's intrusion.

It is instructive to consider how environmentalists themselves define the wilderness. David Brower, former director of the Sierra Club, wrote in his introduction to Paul Ehrlich's *The Population Bomb* (1968):

> Whatever resources the wilderness still held would not sustain (man) in his old habits of growing and reaching without limits. Wilderness could, however, provide answers for questions he had not yet learned how to ask. He could predict that the day of creation was not over, that there would be wiser men, and they would thank him for leaving the source of those answers. Wilderness would remain part of his geography of hope, as Wallace Stegner put it, and could, merely because wilderness endured on the planet, prevent man's world from becoming a cage.

The wilderness, he suggested, is a source of peace and freedom. Yet setting wilderness aside for the purposes of solitude doesn't always work very well. Environmentalists have discovered this over and over again, much to their chagrin. Every time a new "untouched paradise" is discovered, the first thing everyone wants to do is visit it. By their united enthusiasm to find these "sanctuaries," people bring the "cage" of society with them. Very quickly it becomes necessary to erect bars to keep people *out*— which is exactly what most of the "wilderness" legislation has been all about.

In 1964, for example, the Sierra Club published a book on the relatively "undiscovered" paradise of Kauai, the second most westerly island in the Hawaiian chain. It wasn't long before the island had been overrun with tourists. When *Time* magazine ran a feature on Kauai in 1979, one unhappy island resident wrote in to convey this telling sentiment: "We're hoping the shortages of jet fuel will stay around and keep people away from here." The age of environmentalism has also been marked by the near overrunning of popular national parks like Yosemite (which now has a full-time jail), intense pressure on woodland recreational areas, full bookings two and three years in advance for raft trips through the Grand Canyon, and dozens of other spectacles of people crowding into isolated areas to get away from it all. Environmentalists are often critical of these inundations, but they must recognize that they have at least contributed to them.

I am not arguing against wild things, scenic beauty, pristine landscapes, and scenic preservation. What I am questioning is the argument that wilderness is a value against which every other human activity must be judged, and that human beings are somehow unworthy of the landscape. The wilderness has been equated with freedom, but there are many different ideas about what constitutes freedom. In the Middle Ages, the saying was that "city air makes a man free," meaning that the harsh social burdens of medieval feudalism vanished once a person escaped into the heady anonymity of a metropolitan community. When city planner Jane Jacobs, author of *The Death and Life of Great American Cities,* was asked by an interviewer if "overpopulation" and "crowding into large cities" weren't making social prisoners of us all, her simple reply was: "Have you ever lived in a small town?"

It may seem unfair to itemize the personal idiosyncrasies of people who feel comfortable only in wilderness, but it must be remembered that the environmental movement has been shaped by many people who literally spent years of their lives living in isolation. John Muir, the founder of the National Parks movement and the Sierra Club spent almost ten years living alone in the Sierra Mountains while learning to be a trail guide. David Brower, who headed the Sierra Club for over a decade and later broke with it to found the Friends of the Earth, also spent years as a mountaineer. Gary Snyder, the poet laureate of the environmental

20

movement, has lived much of his life in wilderness isolation and has also spent several years in a Zen monastery. All these people far outdid Thoreau in their desire to get a little perspective on the world. There is nothing reprehensible in this, and the literature and philosophy that merge from such experiences are often admirable. But it seems questionable to me that the ethic that comes out of this wilderness isolation—and the sense of ownership of natural landscapes that inevitably follows—can serve as the basis for a useful national philosophy.

That Frontier Spirit

The American frontier is generally agreed to have closed down phys-ically in 1890, the year the last Indian Territory of Oklahoma was opened for the settlement. After that, the Conservation Movement arose quickly to protect the remaining resources and wilderness from heedless stripping and development. Along with this came a significant psychological change in the national character, as the "frontier spirit" diminished and social issues attracted greater attention. The Progressive Movement, the Social Gospel among religious groups, Populism, and Conservation all arose in quick succession immediately after the "closing of the frontier." It seems fair to say that it was only after the frontier had been settled and the sense of endless possibilities that came with open spaces had been constricted in the national consciousness that the country started "growing up."

Does this mean the new environmental consciousness has arisen be-cause we are once again "running out of space"? I doubt it. Anyone taking an airplane across almost any part of the country is inevitably struck by how much greenery and open territory remain, and how little room our towns and cities really occupy. The amount of standing forest in the coun-try, for example, has not diminished appreciably over the last fifty years, and is 75 percent of what it was in 1620. In addition, as environmentalists constantly remind us, trees are "renewable resources." If they continue to be handled intelligently, the forests will always grow back. As farming has moved out to the Great Plains of the Middle West, many eastern areas that were once farmed have reverted back to trees. Though mining operations can permanently scar hillsides and plains, they are usually very limited in scope (and as often as not, it is the roads leading to these mines that environmentalists find most objectionable).

It seems to be that the wilderness ethic has actually represented an attempt psychologically to reopen the American frontier. We have been desperate to maintain belief in unlimited, uncharted vistas within our bor-ders, a preoccupation that has eclipsed the permanent shrinking of the rest of the world outside. Why else would it be so necessary to preserve such huge tracts of "roadless territory" simply because they are now roadless, regardless of their scenic, recreational, or aesthetic values? The environ-mental movement, among other things, has been a rather backward-looking effort to recapture America's lost innocence.

The central figure in this effort has been the backpacker. The back-packer is a young, unprepossessing person (inevitably white and upper middle class) who journeys into the wilderness as a passive observer. He or she brings his or her own food, treads softly, leaves no litter, and has no need to make use of any of the resources at hand. Backpackers bring all the necessary accouterments of civilization with them. All their needs have been met by the society from which they seek temporary release. The backpacker is freed from the need to support itself in order to enjoy the aesthetic and spiritual values that are made available by this temporary *removal* from the demands of nature. Many dangers—raging rivers or pre-cipitous cliffs, for instance—become sought-out adventures.

Yet once the backpacker runs out of supplies and starts using re-sources around him—cutting trees for firewood, putting up a shelter against the rain—he is violating some aspect of the federal Wilderness Act. For example, one of the issues fought in the national forests revolves around tying one's horse to a tree. Purists claim the practice should be forbidden, since it may leave a trodden ring around the tree. They say horses should be hobbled and allowed to graze instead. In recent years, the National Forest Service has come under pressure from environmental groups to enforce this restriction.

Wildernesses, then, are essentially parks for the upper middle class. They are vacation reserves for people who want to rough it—with the assurance that few other people will have the time, energy, or means to follow them into the solitude. This is dramatically highlighted in one Sierra Club book that shows a picture of a professorial sort of individual back-packing off into the woods. The ironic caption is a quote from Julius Viancour, an official of the Western Council of Lumber and Sawmill Workers: "The inaccessible wilderness and primitive areas are off limits to most laboring people. We must have access. . . ." The implication for Sierra Club readers is: "What do these beer-drinking, gun-toting, working peo-ple want to do in *our* woods?"

This class-oriented vision of wilderness as an upper-middle-class pre-serve is further illustrated by the fact that most of the opposition to wil-derness designations comes not from industry but from owners of off-road vehicles. In most northern rural areas, snowmobiles are now regarded as the greatest invention since the automobile, and people are ready to fight rather than stay cooped up all winter in their houses. It seems ludicrous to them that snowmobiles (which can't be said even to endanger the ground) should be restricted from vast tracts of land so that the occasional city visitor can have solitude while hiking past on snowshoes.

The recent Boundary Waters Canoe Area controversy in northern 30 Minnesota is an excellent example of the conflict. When the tract was first designated as wilderness in 1964, Congress included a special provision that allowed motorboats into the entire area. By the mid-1970s, outboards and inboards were roaming all over the wilderness, and environmental groups began asking that certain portions of the million-acre preserve be set aside exclusively for canoes. Local residents protested vigorously, arguing that fishing expeditions, via motorboats, contributed to their own recreation. Nevertheless, Congress eventually excluded motorboats from 670,000 acres to the north.

A more even split would seem fairer. It should certainly be possible to accommodate both forms of recreation in the area, and there is as much to be said for canoeing in solitude as there is for making rapid expeditions by powerboat. The natural landscape is not likely to suffer very much from either form of recreation. It is not absolute "ecological" values that are really at stake, but simply different tastes in recreation.

Not Entirely Nature

At bottom, then, the mystique of the wilderness has been little more than a revival of Rousseau's Romanticism about the "state of nature." The notion that "only in wilderness are human beings truly free," a credo of environmentalists, is merely a variation on Rousseau's dictum that "man is born free, and everywhere he is in chains." According to Rousseau, only society could enslave people, and only in the "state of nature" was the "noble savage"—the preoccupation of so many early explorers—a fulfilled human being.

The "noble savage" and other indigenous peoples, however, have been carefully excised from the environmentalists' vision. Where environmental efforts have encountered primitive peoples, these indigenous residents have often proved one of the biggest problems. One of the most bitter issues in Alaska is the efforts by environmentalists groups to restrict Indians in their hunting practices.

At the same time, few modern wilderness enthusiasts could imagine, for example, the experience of the nineteenth-century artist J. Ross Browne, who wrote in *Harper's New Monthly Magazine* after visiting the Arizona territories in 1864:

> Sketching in Arizona is . . . rather a ticklish pursuit. . . . I never before traveled through a country in which I was compelled to pursue the fine arts with a revolver strapped around my body, a double-barreled shot-gun lying across my knees, and half a dozen soldiers armed with Sharpe's carbines keeping guard in the distance. Even with all the safeguards . . . I am free to admit that on occasions of this kind I frequently looked behind to see how the country appeared in its rear aspect. An artist with an arrow in his back may be a very picturesque object . . . but I would rather draw him on paper than sit for the portrait myself.

Wilderness today means the land *after* the Indians have been cleared away but *before* the settlers have arrived. It represents an attempt to hold that particular moment forever frozen in time, that moment when the visionary

American settler looked out on the land and imagined it as an empty paradise, waiting to be molded to our vision.

In the absence of the noble savage, the environmentalist substitutes himself. The wilderness, while free of human dangers, becomes a kind of basic-training ground for upper-middle-class values. Hence the rise of "survival" groups, where college kids are taken out into the woods for a week or two and let loose to prove their survival instincts. No risks are spared on these expeditions. Several people have died on them, and a string of lawsuits has already been launched by parents and survivors who didn't realize how seriously these survival courses were being taken.

The ultimate aim of these efforts is to test upper-middle-class values against the natural environment. "Survival" candidates cannot hunt, kill, or use much of the natural resources available. The true test is whether their zero-degree sleeping bags and dried-food kits prove equal to the hazards of the tasks. What happens is not necessarily related to nature. One could as easily test survival skills by turning a person loose without money or means in New York City for three days.

I do not mean to imply that these efforts do not require enormous amounts of courage and daring—"survival skills." I am only suggesting that what the backpacker or survival hiker encounters is not entirely "nature," and that the effort to go "back to nature" is one that is carefully circumscribed by the most intensely civilized artifacts. Irving Babbitt, the early twentieth-century critic of Rousseau's Romanticism, is particularly vigorous in his dissent from the idea of civilized people going "back to nature." This type, he says, is actually "the least primitive of all beings":

> We have seen that the special form of unreality encouraged by the aesthetic romanticism of Rousseau is the dream of the simple life, the return to a nature that never existed, and that this dream made its special appeal to an age that was suffering from an excess of artificiality and conventionalism.

Babbitt notes shrewdly that our concept of the "state of nature" is actually one of the most sophisticated productions of civilization. Most primitive peoples, who live much closer to the soil than we do, are repelled by wilderness. The American colonists, when they first encountered the unspoiled landscape, saw nothing but a horrible desert, filled with savages.

What we really encounter when we talk about "wilderness," then, is one of the highest products of civilization. It is a reserve set up to keep people *out,* rather than a "state of nature" in which the inhabitants are "truly free." The only thing that makes people "free" in such a reservation is that they can leave so much behind when they enter. Those who try to stay too long find out how spurious this "freedom" is. After spending a year in a cabin in the north Canadian woods, Elizabeth Arthur wrote in *Island Sojourn:* "I never felt so completely tied to *objects,* resources, and the tools to shape them with."

What we are witnessing in the environmental movement's obsession with purified wilderness is what has often been called the "pastoral impulse." The image of nature as unspoiled, unspotted wilderness where we can go to learn the lessons of ecology is both a product of a complex, technological society and an escape from it. It is this undeniable paradox that forms the real problem of setting up "wildernesses." Only when we have created a society that gives us the leisure to appreciate it can we go out and experience what we imagine to be untrammeled nature. Yet if we lock up too much of our land in these reserves, we are cutting into our resources and endangering the very leisure that allows us to enjoy nature.

The answer is, of course, that we cannot simply let nature "take over" 40
and assume that because we have kept roads and people out of huge tracts of land, then we have absolved ourselves of a national guilt. The concept of stewardship means taking responsibility, not simply letting nature take its course. Where tracts can be set aside from commercialism at no great cost, they should be. Where primitive hiking and recreation areas are appealing, they should be maintained. But if we think we are somehow appeasing the gods by *not* developing resources where they exist, then we are being very shortsighted. Conservation, not preservation, is once again the best guiding principle.

The cult of wilderness leads inevitably in the direction of religion. Once again, Irving Babbitt anticipated this fully.

> When pushed to a certain point the nature cult always tends toward sham spirituality. . . . Those to whom I may seem to be treating the nature cult with undue severity should remember that I am treating it only in its pseudo-religious aspect. . . . My quarrel is only with the asthete who assumes an apocalyptic pose and gives forth as a profound philosophy what is at best only a holiday or weekend view of existence. . . .

It is often said the environmentalism could or should serve as the basis of a new religious consciousness, or a religious "reawakening." This religious trend is usually given an Oriental aura. E. F. Schumacher has a chapter on Buddhist economics in his classic *Small Is Beautiful*. Primitive animisms are also frequently cited as attitudes toward nature that are more "environmentally sound." One book on the environment states baldly that "the American Indian lived in almost perfect harmony with nature." Anthropologist Marvin Harris has even put forth the novel view that primitive man is an environmentalist, and that many cultural habits are unconscious efforts to reduce the population and conserve the environment. He says that the Hindu prohibition against eating cows and the Jewish tradition of not eating pork were both efforts to avoid the ecological destruction that would come with raising these grazing animals intensively. The implication in these arguments is usually that science and modern technology have somehow dulled our instinctive "environmental" impulses, and that Western "non-spiritual" technology puts us out of harmony with the "balance of nature."

Perhaps the most daring challenge to the environmental soundness of current religious tradition came early in the environmental movement, in a much quoted paper by Lynn White, professor of the history of science at UCLA. Writing in *Science* magazine in 1967, White traced "the historical roots of our ecological crisis" directly to the Western Judeo-Christian tradition in which "man and nature are two things, and man is master." "By destroying pagan animism," he wrote, "Christianity made it possible to exploit nature in a mood of indifference to the feelings of natural objects." He continued:

> Especially in its Western form, Christianity is the most anthropocentric religion the world has seen. . . . Christianity, in absolute contrast to ancient paganism and Asia's religions (except, perhaps, Zoroastrianism), not only established a dualism of man and nature but also insisted that it is God's will that man exploit nature for his proper ends. . . . In antiquity every tree, every spring, every stream, every hill had its own *genius loci,* its guardian spirit. . . . Before one cut a tree, mined a mountain, or dammed a brook, it was important to placate the spirit in charge of that particular situation, and keep it placated.

But the question here is not whether the Judeo-Christian tradition is worth saving in and of itself. It would be more than disappointing if we canceled the accomplishments of Judeo-Christian thought only to find that our treatment of nature had not changed a bit.

There can be no question that White is onto a favorite environmental theme here. What he calls the "Judeo-Christian tradition" is what other writers often term "Western civilization." It is easy to go through environmental books and find long outbursts about the evils that "civilization and progress" have brought us. The long list of Western achievements and advances, the scientific men of genius, are brought to task for creating our "environmental crisis." Sometimes the condemnation is of our brains, pure and simple. Here, for example, is the opening statement from a book about pesticides, written by the late Robert van den Bosch, an outstanding environmental advocate:

> Our problem is that we are too smart for our own good, and for that matter, the good of the biosphere. The basic problem is that our brain enables us to evaluate, plan, and execute. Thus, while all other creatures are programmed by nature and subject to her whims, we have our own gray computer to motivate, for good or evil, our chemical engine. . . . Among living species, we are the only one possessed of arrogance, deliberate stupidity, greed, hate, jealousy, treachery, and the impulse to revenge, all of which may erupt spontaneously or be turned on at will.

At this rate, it can be seen that we don't even need religion to lead us astray. We are doomed from the start because we are not creatures of *instinct,* programmed from the start "by nature."

This type of primitivism has been a very strong, stable undercurrent in the environmental movement. It runs from the kind of fatalistic gibberish quoted above to the Romanticism that names primitive tribes "instinctive environmentalists," from the pessimistic predictions that human beings cannot learn to control their own numbers to the notion that only by remaining innocent children of nature, untouched by progress, can the rural populations of the world hope to feed themselves. At bottom, as many commentators have pointed out, environmentalism is reminiscent of the German Romanticism of the nineteenth century, which sought to shed Christian (and Roman) traditions and revive the Teutonic gods because they were "more in touch with nature."

But are progress, reason, Western civilization, science, and the cerebral cortex really at the root of the "environmental crisis?" Perhaps the best answer comes from an environmentalist himself, Dr. René Dubos, a world-renowned microbiologist, author of several prize-winning books on conservation and a founding member of the Natural Resources Defense Council. Dr. Dubos takes exception to the notion that Western Christianity has produced a uniquely exploitative attitude toward nature:

> Erosion of the land, destruction of animal and plant species, excessive exploitation of natural resources, and ecological disasters are not peculiar to the Judeo-Christian tradition and to scientific technology. At all times, and all over the world, man's thoughtless interventions into nature have had a variety of disastrous consequences or at least have changed profoundly the complexity of nature.

Dr. Dubos has catalogued the non-Western or non-Christian cultures that have done environmental damage. Plato observed, for instance, that the hills in Greece had been heedlessly stripped of wood, and erosion had been the result; the ancient Egyptians and Assyrians exterminated large numbers of wild animal species; Indian hunters presumably caused the extinction of many large paleolithic species in North America; Buddhist monks building temples in Asia contributed largely to deforestation. Dubos notes:

> All over the globe and at all times . . . men have pillaged nature and disturbed the ecological equilibrium . . . nor did they have a real choice of alternatives. If men are more destructive now . . . it is because they have at their command more powerful means of destruction, not because they have been influenced by the Bible. In fact, the Judeo-Christian peoples were probably the first to develop on a large scale a pervasive concern for land management and an ethic of nature.

The concern that Dr. Dubos cites is the same one we have rescued out of the perception of environmentalism as a movement based on aristocratic conservatism. That is the legitimate doctrine of *stewardship* of the land. In order to take this responsibility, however, we must recognize the part we play in nature—that "the land is ours." It will not do simply to worship nature, to create a cult of wilderness in which humanity is an eternal intruder and where human activity can only destroy.

"True conservation," writes Dubos, "means not only protecting na-   50
ture against human misbehavior but also developing human activities which favor a creative, harmonious relationship between man and nature." This is a legitimate goal for the environmental movement.

Reading and Responding

Do any of William Tucker's arguments surprise you or seem more reasonable than you might have expected? For example, if you think of yourself as a strong environmentalist, someone who supports preservation efforts, you might find yourself agreeing with some of what Tucker says, despite yourself, or at least considering his ideas seriously. Or if you think of yourself as already agreeing with the kind of stance Tucker takes here, you might be surprised by a new, more powerful argument than you'd thought of before. In other words, what does Tucker make you consider that you haven't considered before?

Working Together

Divide the class into three groups: a Tucker Group, a Leopold Group, and a Mediator Group. The Mediator Group is in charge of the proceedings.

- Take some local controversy about preservation—land to be set aside as a park or a green belt, for example, or an old building people want to save—or take some national preservation controversy currently in the news, something that everyone in the class knows about. Imagine that the Mediator Group has called a meeting of both sides to negotiate a compromise action on this issue. The Tucker Group summarizes the author's main arguments and applies them to this particular issue, arguing for a specific action. The Mediators write these arguments on one side of the board, simply recording what is said.

- The Leopold Group then counters each argument, point by point, with ideas and reasoning drawn from John Muir, Aldo Leopold, and other conservationists, and uses these arguments to propose a different action. Mediators write these arguments on the board.

- The Mediators then take charge of the meeting, working to find common ground in these two positions, areas of overlap, possible agreement as a way of brokering a compromise solution. The group might list on the board, for example, any way, however broad or apparently trivial, that the two sides fundamentally agree.

• As a class, draw up a document that represents the compromise. All concerned parties should sign it.

Rethinking and Rewriting

1. Write an essay that describes and reflects on the negotiation process that took place in class. The paper can focus on the issues—summarizing the two sides and then explaining the compromise—or it can focus on the process of negotiation, the issues of rhetoric, argument, and relationship.
2. Use Tucker's arguments to argue against the preservation of a specific local landmark or piece of ground.
3. Write a letter to Tucker politely questioning his positions and proposing alternatives. Disagree with him. Try to persuade him that he's wrong.
4. Write a personal essay in response to Tucker's argument. Describe a relevant experience, something that might illustrate his ideas, counter them, or at least complicate them. You don't need to come to a conclusion. Tell the story in as much detail as you can and conclude with questions and concerns.

SAVE THE WHALES,
SCREW THE SHRIMP

Joy Williams

Recipient of fellowships from both the National Endowment for the Arts and the Guggenheim Foundation, Joy Williams is best known as a fiction writer. In this essay, which originally appeared in Esquire, *Williams gives readers a monologue with an attitude.*

I don't want to talk about *me,* of course, but it seems as though far too much attention has been lavished on *you* lately—that your greed and vanities and quest for self-fulfillment have been catered to far too much. You just want and want and want. You haven't had a mandala dream since the eighties began. To have a mandala dream you'd have to instinctively know that it was an attempt at self-healing on the part of Nature, and you don't believe in Nature anymore. It's too isolated from you. You've abstracted it. It's so messy and damaged and sad. Your eyes glaze as you travel life's highway past all the crushed animals and the Big Gulp cups. You don't even take pleasure in looking at nature photographs these days. Oh, they can be just as pretty, as always, but don't they make you feel increasingly . . . anxious? Filled with more trepidation than peace? So what's the point? You see the picture of the baby condor or the panda munching on a bamboo shoot, and your heart just sinks, doesn't it? A picture of a poor old sea turtle with barnacles on her back, all ancient and exhausted, depositing her five gallons of doomed eggs in the sand hardly fills you with joy, because you realize, quite rightly, that just outside the frame falls the shadow of the condo. What's cropped from the shot of ocean waves crashing on a pristine shore is the plastics plant, and just beyond the dunes lies a parking lot. Hidden from immediate view in the butterfly-bright meadow, in the dusky thicket, in the oak and holly wood, are the surveyors' stakes, for someone wants to build a mall exactly there—some gas stations and supermarkets, some pizza and video shops, a health club, maybe a bulimia treatment center. Those lovely pictures of leopards and herons and wild rivers, well, you just know they're going to be accompanied by a text that will serve only to bring you down. You don't want to think about it! It's all so uncool. And you don't want to feel guilty either. Guilt is uncool. Regret maybe you'll consider. *Maybe.* Regret is a possibility, but don't push me, you say. Nature photographs have become something of a problem, along with almost everything else. Even though they leave the bad stuff out—maybe because you *know* they're leaving all the bad stuff out—such pictures are making you increasingly aware that you're a little too late for Nature. Do you feel that? Twenty years too late, maybe only ten? Not *way* too late, just a little too late? Well, it appears that you are. And since you are, you've decided you're just not going to attend this particular party.

Pascal said that it is easier to endure death without thinking about it than to endure the thought of death without dying. This is how you manage to dance the strange dance with that grim partner, nuclear annihilation. When the U.S. Army notified Winston Churchill that the first atom bomb had been detonated in New Mexico, it chose the code phrase BABIES SATISFACTORILY BORN. So you entered the age of irony, and the strange double life you've been leading with the world ever since. Joyce Carol Oates suggests that the reason writers—*real* writers, one assumes—don't write about Nature is that it lacks a sense of humor and registers no irony. It just doesn't seem to be of the times—these slick, sleek, knowing, objective, indulgent times. And the word *Environment.* Such a bloodless word. A flat-footed word with a shrunken heart. A word increasingly disengaged from its association with the natural world. Urban planners, industrialists, economists, and developers use it. It's a lost word, really. A cold word, mechanistic, suited strangely to the coldness generally felt toward Nature. It's their word now. You don't mind giving it up. As for *Environmentalist,* that's one that can really bring on the yawns, for you've tamed and tidied it, neutered it quite nicely. An environmentalist must be calm, rational, reasonable, and willing to compromise, otherwise you won't listen to him. Still, his beliefs are *opinions* only, for this is the age of radical subjectivism. Not long ago, Barry Commoner spoke to the Environmental Protection Agency. He scolded them. They loved it. The way they protect the environment these days is apparently to find an "acceptable level of harm from a pollutant and then issue rules allowing industry to pollute to that level." Commoner suggested that this was inappropriate. An EPA employee suggested that any other approach would place limits on economic growth and implied that Commoner was advocating this. Limits on economic growth! Commoner vigorously denied this. Oh, it was a healthy exchange of ideas, healthier certainly than our air and water. We needed that little spanking, the EPA felt. It was refreshing. The agency has recently lumbered into action in its campaign to ban dinoseb. You seem to have liked your dinoseb. It's been a popular weed killer, even though it has been directly linked with birth defects. You must hate weeds a lot. Although the EPA appears successful in banning the poison, it will still have to pay the disposal costs and compensate the manufacturers for the market value of the chemicals they still have in stock.

That's ironic, you say, but farmers will suffer losses, too, oh dreadful financial losses, if herbicide and pesticide use is restricted.

Farmers grow way too much stuff anyway. They grow surplus crops with subsidized water created by turning rivers great and small into a plumbing system of dams and canals. Rivers have become *systems.* Wetlands are increasingly being referred to as *filtering systems*—things deigned *useful* because of their ability to absorb urban run–off, oil from roads, et cetera.

We know that. We've known that for years about farmers. We know   5
a lot these days. We're very well informed. If farmers aren't allowed to
make a profit by growing surplus crops, they'll have to sell their land to
developers, who'll turn all that *arable land* into office parks. Arable land
isn't Nature anyway, and besides, we like those office parks and shopping
plazas, with their monster supermarkets open twenty-four hours a day with
aisle after aisle after aisle of *products.* It's fun. Products are fun.

Farmers like their poisons, but ranchers like them even more. There
are well-funded predominantly federal and cooperative programs like the
Agriculture Department's Animal Damage Control Unit that poison,
shoot, and trap several thousand animals each year. This unit loves to kill
things. It was created to kill things—bobcats, foxes, black bears, mountain
lions, rabbits, badgers, countless birds—all to make this great land safe for
the string bean and the corn, the sheep and the cow, even though you're
not consuming as much cow these days. A burger now and then, but
burgers are hardly cows at all, you feel. They're not all *our* cows in any
case, for some burger matter is imported. There's a bit of Central American
burger matter in your bun. Which is contributing to the conversion of
tropical rain forest into cow pasture. Even so, you're getting away from
meat these days. You're eschewing cow. It's seafood you love, shrimp most
of all. And when you love something, it had better watch out, because you
have a tendency to love it to death. Shrimp, shrimp, shrimp. It's more
common on menus than chicken. In the wilds of Ohio, far, far from
watery shores, four out of the six entrées on a menu will be shrimp, for
some modest sum. Everywhere, it's all the shrimp you can eat or all you
care to eat, for sometimes you just don't feel like eating all you *can.* You are
intensively *harvesting* shrimp. Soon there won't be any left and then you
can stop. It takes that, often, to make you stop. Shrimpers shrimp, of
course. That's their *business.* They put out these big nets and in these nets,
for each pound of shrimp, they catch more than ten times that amount of
fish, turtles, and dolphins. These, quite the worse for wear, they dump
back in. There is an object called TED (Turtle Excluder Device), which
would save thousands of turtles and some dolphins from dying in the nets,
but the shrimpers are loath to use TEDs, as they say it would cut the size
of their shrimp catch.

We've heard about TED, you say.

They want you, all of you, to have all the shrimp you can eat and
more. At Kiawah Island, off the coast of South Carolina, visitors go out on
Jeep "safaris" through the part of the island that hasn't been developed yet.
("Wherever you see trees," the guide says, "really, that's a lot.") The safari
comprises six Jeeps, and these days they go out at least four times a day,
with more trips promised soon. The tourists drive their own Jeeps and the
guide talks to them by radio. Kiawah has nice beaches, and the guide talks

about turtles. When he mentions the shrimpers' role in the decline of the turtle, the shrimpers, who share the same frequency, scream at him. Shrimpers and most commercial fishermen (many of them working with drift and gill nets anywhere from six to thirty miles long) think of themselves as an *endangered species*. A recent newspaper headline said, "Shrimpers Spared Anti-Turtle Devices." Even so, with the continuing wanton deple-tion of shrimp beds, they will undoubtedly have to find some other means of employment soon. They might, for instance, become part of that vast throng laboring in the *tourist industry*.

　　Tourism has become an industry as destructive as any other. You are no longer benign in your traveling somewhere to look at the scenery. You never thought there was much gain in just looking anyway, you've always preferred to *use* the scenery in some manner. In your desire to get away from what you've got, you've caused there to be no place to get away *to*. You're just all bumpered up out there. Sewage and dumps have become prime indicators of America's lifestyle. In resort towns in New England and the Adirondacks, measuring the flow into the sewage plant serves as a business barometer. Tourism is a growth industry. You believe in growth. *Controlled* growth, of course. Controlled exponential growth is what you'd really like to see. You certainly don't want to put a moratorium or a cap on anything. That's illegal, isn't it? Retro you're not. You don't want to go back or anything. Forward. Maybe ask directions later. Growth is *desirable* as well as being *inevitable*. Growth is the one thing you seem to be power-less before, so you try to be realistic about it. Growth is—it's weird—it's like cancer or something.

　　Recently you, as tourist, have discovered your national parks and are quickly *overburdening* them. Spare land and it belongs to you! It's exotic land too, not looking like all the stuff around it that looks like everything else. You want to take advantage of this land, of course, and use it in every way you can. Thus the managers—or *stewards*, as they like to be called—have developed *wise* and *multiple-use* plans, keeping in mind exploiters' interests (for they have their needs, too) as well as the desires of the back-packers. Thus mining, timbering, and ranching activities take place in the national forests, where the Forest Service maintains a system of logging roads eight times larger than the interstate highway system. The national parks are more of a public playground and are becoming increasingly Eu-ropeanized in their look and management. Lots of concessions and motels. You deserve a clean bed and a hot meal when you go into the wilderness. At least your stewards think that you do. You keep your stewards busy. Not only must they cater to your multiple and conflicting desires, they have to manage your wildlife *resources*. They have managed wildfowl to such an extent that the reasoning has become, If it weren't for hunters, ducks would disappear. Duck stamps and licensing fees support the whole rickety duck-management system. Yes! If it weren't for the people who killed them, wild ducks wouldn't exist! Managers are managing all wild creatures,

10

not just those that fly. They track and tape and tag and band. They relocate, restock, and reintroduce. They cull and control. It's hard to keep it all straight. Protect or poison? Extirpate or just mostly eliminate? Sometimes even the stewards get mixed up.

This is the time of machines and models, hands-on management and master plans. Don't you ever wonder as you pass that billboard advertising another MASTER-PLANNED COMMUNITY just what master they are actually talking about? Not the Big Master, certainly. Something brought to you by one of the tiny masters, of which there are many. But you like these tiny masters and have even come to expect and require them. In Florida they've just started a ten-thousand-acre city in the Everglades. It's a *megaproject,* one of the largest ever in the state. Yes, they must have thought you wanted it. No, what you thought of as the Everglades, the Park, is only a little bitty part of the Everglades. Developers have been gnawing at this irreplaceable, strange land for years. It's like they just *hate* this ancient sea of grass. Maybe you could ask them about this sometime. Roy Rogers is the senior vice president of strategic planning, and the old cowboy says that every tree and bush and inch of sidewalk in the project has been planned. Nevertheless, because the whole thing will take twenty-five years to complete, the plan is going to be constantly changed. You can understand this. The important thing is that there be a blueprint. You trust a blueprint. The tiny masters know what you like. You like *a secure landscape* and *access to services.* You like grass—that is, lawns. The ultimate lawn is the golf course, which you've been told has "some ecological value." You believe this! Not that it really matters, you just like to play golf. These golf courses require a lot of watering. So much that the more inspired of the masters have taken to watering them with effluent, *treated* effluent, but yours, from all the condos and villas built around the stocked artificial lakes you fancy.

I really don't want to think about sewage, you say, but it sounds like progress.

It is true that the masters are struggling with the problems of your incessant flushing. Cuisine is also one of their concerns. Advances in sorbets—sorbet intermezzos—in their clubs and fine restaurants. They know what you want. You want A HAVEN FROM THE ORDINARY WORLD. If you're A NATURE LOVER in the West you want to live in a $200,000 home in A WILD ANIMAL HABITAT. If you're eastern and consider yourself more hip, you want to live in new towns—brand-new reconstructed-from-scratch towns—in a house of NINETEENTH-CENTURY DESIGN. But in these new towns the masters are building, getting around can be confusing. There is an abundance of curves and an infrequency of through streets. It's the new wilderness without any trees. You can get lost, even with all the "mental bread crumbs" the masters scatter about as visual landmarks—the windmill, the water views, the various groupings of landscape "material." You *are* lost, you know. But you trust a Realtor will show you the way.

There are many more Realtors than tiny masters, and many of them have to make do with less than a loaf—that is, trying to sell stuff that's already been built in an environment already "enhanced" rather than something being planned—but they're everywhere, willing to show you the path. If Dante returned to Hell today, he'd probably be escorted down by a Realtor, talking all the while about how it was just another level of Paradise.

When have you last watched a sunset? Do you remember where you were? With whom? At Loews Ventana Canyon Resort, the Grand Foyer will provide you with that opportunity through lighting which is computerized to diminish with the approaching sunset!

The tiny masters are willing to arrange Nature for you. They will compose it into a picture that you can look at your leisure, when you're not doing work or something like that. Nature becomes scenery, a prop. At some golf courses in the Southwest, the saguaro cacti are reported to be repaired with green paste when balls blast into their skin. The saguaro can attempt to heal themselves by growing over the balls, but this takes time, and the effect can be somewhat . . . baroque. It's better to get out the pastepot. Nature has become simply a visual form of entertainment, and it had better look snappy.

Listen, you say, we've been at Ventana Canyon. It's in the desert, right? It's very, very nice, a world-class resort. A totally self-contained environment with everything that a person could possibly want, on more than a thousand acres in the middle of zip. It sprawls but nestles, like. And they've maintained the integrity of as much of the desert ecosystem as possible. Give them credit for that. *Great* restaurant, too. We had baby bay scallops there. Coming into the lobby there are these two big hand-carved coyotes, mutely howling. And that's the way we like them, *mute*. God, why do those things howl like that?

Wildlife is a personal matter, you think. The attitude is up to you. You can prefer to see it dead or not dead. You might want to let it mosey about its business or blow it away. Wild things exist only if you have the graciousness to allow them to. Just outside Tucson, Arizona, there is a brand-new structure modeled after a French foreign legion outpost. It's the *International Wildlife Museum,* and it's full of dead animals. Three hundred species are there, at least a third of them—the rarest ones—killed and collected by one C. J. McElroy, who enjoyed doing it and now shares what's left with you. The museum claims to be educational because you can watch a taxidermist at work or touch a lion's tooth. You can get real close to these dead animals, closer than you can in a zoo. Some of you prefer zoos, however, which are becoming bigger, better, and bioclimatic. New-age zoo designers want the animals to *flow right out into your space.* In Dallas there will soon be a Wilds of Africa exhibit; in San Diego there's a simulated rain forest, where you can thread your way "down the side of a lush canyon, the air filled with a fine mist from 300 high-pressure nozzles"; in New Orleans you've constructed a swamp, the real swamp not far away on the verge of disappearing. Animals in these places are abstractions—wandering relics of their true selves, but that doesn't matter. Animal behavior in a zoo is nothing like natural behavior, but that doesn't really matter, either. Zoos are pretty, contained, and accessible. These new habitats can contain one hundred different species—not more than one or two of each thing, of course—on seven acres, three, one. You don't want to see *too much* of anything, certainly. An *example* will suffice. Sort of like a biological Crabtree & Evelyn basket selected with *you* in mind. You like things reduced, simplified. It's easier to take it all in, park it in your mind. You like things inside better than outside anyway. You are increasingly looking at and living in proxy environments created by substitution and simulation. *Resource economists* are a wee branch in the tree of tiny masters, and one, Martin Krieger, wrote, "Artificial prairies and wildernesses have been created, and there is no reason to believe that these artificial environments need be unsatisfactory for those who experience them. . . . We will have to realize that the way in which we experience nature is conditioned by our society—which more and more is seen to be receptive to responsible intervention."

Nature has become a world of appearances, a mere source of materials. You've been editing it for quite some time; now you're in the process of deleting it. Earth is beginning to look like not much more than a launching pad. Back near Tucson, on the opposite side of the mountain from the dead-animal habitat, you're building Biosphere II (as compared with or opposed to Biosphere I, more commonly known as Earth)—a 2½-acre terrarium, an artificial ecosystem that will include a rain forest, a desert, a thirty-five-foot ocean, and several thousand species of life (lots of microbes), including eight human beings, who will cultivate a bit of farmland. You think it would be nice to colonize other worlds after you've made it necessary to leave this one.

Hey, that's pretty good, you say, all that stuff packed into just 2½ acres. That's only about three times bigger than my entire *house.*

It's small all right, but still not small enough to be, apparently, useful.   20
For the purposes of NASA, say, it would have to be smaller, oh much smaller, and energy-efficient too. Fiddle, fiddle, fiddle. You support fiddling, as well as meddling. This is how you learn. Though it's quite apparent the environment has been grossly polluted and the natural world abused and defiled, you seem to prefer to continue pondering effects rather than preventing causes. You want proof, you insist on proof. A Dr. Lave from Carnegie-Mellon—and he's an expert, an economist, and an environmental *expert*—says that scientists will have to prove to you that you will suffer if you don't become less of a "throwaway society." *If you really want me to give up my car or my air conditioner, you'd better prove to me first that the earth would otherwise be uninhabitable,* Dr. Lave says. *Me* is *you,* I presume, whereas *you* refers to them. You as in me—that is, *me, me, me*—certainly

strike a hard bargain. Uninhabitable the world has to get before you rein in your requirements. You're a consumer after all, *the* consumer upon whom so much attention is lavished, the ultimate user of a commodity that has become, these days, everything. To try to appease your appetite for proof, for example, scientists have been leasing for experimentation forty-six pristine lakes in Canada.

They don't want to *keep* them, they just want to *borrow* them.

They've been intentionally contaminating many of the lakes with a variety of pollutants dribbled into the propeller wash of research boats. *It's one of the boldest experiments in lake ecology ever conducted.* They've turned these remote lakes into huge *real-world test tubes.* They've been doing this since 1976! And what they've found so far in these *preliminary* studies is that pollutants are really destructive. The lakes get gross. Life in them ceases. It took about eight years to make this happen in one of them, everything carefully measured and controlled all the while. Now the scientists are slowly reversing the process. But it will take hundreds of years for the lakes to recover. They think.

Remember when you used to like rain, the sound of it, the feel of it, the way it made the plants and trees all glisten. We needed that rain, you would say. It looked pretty too, you thought, particularly in the movies. Now it rains and you go, Oh-oh. A nice walloping rain these days means *overtaxing our sewage treatment plants.* It means *untreated waste discharged directly into our waterways.* It means . . .

Okay. Okay.

Acid rain! And we all know what this is. Or most of us do. People of power in government and industry still don't seem to know what it is. Whatever it is, they say, they don't want to curb it, but they're willing to study it some more. Economists call air and water pollution "externalities" anyway. Oh, acid rain. You do get so sick of hearing about it. The words have already become a white-noise kind of thing. But you think in terms of *mitigating* it maybe. As for *the greenhouse effect,* you think in terms of *countering* that. One way that's been discussed recently is the planting of new forests, not for the sake of the forests alone, oh my heavens, no. Not for the sake of majesty and mystery or of Thumper and Bambi, are you kidding me, but because, as every schoolchild knows, trees absorb carbon dioxide. They just soak it up and store it. They just love it. So this is the plan: you plant millions of acres of trees, and you can go on doing pretty much whatever you're doing—driving around, using staggering amounts of energy, keeping those power plants fired to the max. Isn't Nature remarkable? So willing to serve? You wouldn't think it had anything more to offer, but it seems it does. Of course these "forests" wouldn't exactly be forests. They would be more like trees. *Managed* trees. The Forest Service, which now manages our forests by cutting them down, might be called upon to evolve in their thinking and allow these trees to grow. They would probably be patented trees after a time. Fast-growing, uniform, genetically-created-to-be-toxin-eating *machines.* They would be *new-age* trees, because the problem with planting the old-fashioned variety to *combat* the greenhouse effect, which is caused by pollution, is that they're already dying from it. All along the crest of the Appalachians from Maine to Georgia, forests struggle to survive in a toxic soup of poisons. They can't *help* us if we've killed them, now can they?

All right, you say, wow, lighten up will you? Relax. Tell me about yourself.

Well, I say, I live in Florida . . .

Oh my God, you say. Florida! Florida is a joke! How do you expect us to take you seriously if you still live there! Florida is crazy, it's pink concrete. It's paved, it's over. And a little girl just got eaten by an alligator down there. It came out of some swamp next to a subdivision and just carried her off. That set your Endangered Species Act back fifty years, you can bet.

I . . .

Listen, we don't want to hear any more about Florida. We don't want   30
to hear about Phoenix or Hilton Head or California's Central Valley. If our wetlands—our *vanishing* wetlands—are mentioned one more time, we'll scream. And the talk about condors and grizzlies and wolves is becoming too de trop. We had just managed to get whales out of our minds when those three showed up under the ice in Alaska. They even had *names.* Bone is the dead one, right? It's almost the twenty-first century! Those last condors are *pathetic.* Can't we just get this over with?

Aristotle said that all living things are ensouled and striving to participate in eternity.

Oh, I just bet he said that, you say. That doesn't sound like Aristotle. He was a humanist. We're all humanists here. This is the age of humanism. And it has been for a long time.

You are driving with a stranger in the car, and it is the stranger behind the wheel. In the back seat are your pals for many years now—DO WHAT YOU LIKE and his swilling sidekick, WHY NOT. A deer, or some emblematic animal, something from that myriad natural world you've come from that you now treat with such indifference and scorn—steps from the dimming woods and tentatively upon the highway. The stranger does not decelerate or brake, not yet, maybe not at all. The feeling is that whatever it is *will get out of the way.* Oh, it's a fine car you've got, a fine machine, and oddly you don't mind the stranger driving it, because in a way, everything has gotten too complicated, way, way out of your control. You've given the wheel to the masters, the managers, the comptrollers. Something is wrong, *maybe,* you feel a little sick, *actually,* but the car is luxurious and fast and you're *moving,* which is the most important thing by far.

Why make a fuss when you're so comfortable? Don't make a fuss, make a baby. Go out and get something to eat, build something. Make *another* baby. Babies are cute. Babies show you have faith in the future. Although faith is perhaps too strong a word. They're everywhere these days, in all the crowds and traffic jams, there are the babies too. You don't seem to associate them with the problems of population increase. They're just babies! And you've come to believe in them again. They're a lot more tangible than the afterlife, which, of course, you haven't believed in in ages. At least not for yourself. The afterlife now belongs to plastics and poisons. Yes, plastics and poisons will have a far more extensive afterlife than you, that's known. A disposable diaper, for example, which is all plastic and wood pulp—you like them for all those babies, so easy to use and toss—will take around four centuries to degrade. Almost all plastics do, centuries and centuries. In the sea, many marine animals die from ingesting or being entangled in discarded plastic. In the dumps, plastic squats on more than 25 percent of dump space. But your heart is disposed toward plastic. Someone, no doubt the plastics industry, told you it was convenient. This same industry is now looking into recycling in an attempt to get the critics of their nefarious, multifarious products off their backs. That should make you feel better, because *recycling* has become an honorable word, no longer merely the hobby of Volvo owners. The fact is that people in plastics are born obscurants. Recycling (practically impossible) won't solve the plastic glut, only reduction of production will, and the plastics industry isn't looking into that, you can be sure. Waste is not just the stuff you throw away, of course, it's the stuff you use to excess. With the exception of *hazardous waste,* which you do worry about from time to time, it's even thought you have a declining sense of emergency about the problem. Builders are building bigger houses because you want bigger. You're trading up. Utility companies are beginning to worry about your constantly rising consumption. Utility companies! You haven't entered a new age at all but one of upscale nihilism, deluxe nihilism.

In the summer, particularly in *the industrial Northeast,* you did get a little excited. The filth cut into your fun time. Dead stuff floating around. Sludge and bloody vials. Hygienic devices—appearing not quite so hygienic out of context—all coming in on the tide. The air smelled funny, too. You tolerate a great deal, but the summer of '88 was truly creepy. It was even thought for a moment that the environment would become a political issue. But it didn't. You didn't want it to be, preferring instead to continue in your politics of subsidizing and advancing avarice. The issues were the same as always—jobs, defense, the economy, maintaining and improving the standard of living in this greedy, selfish, expansionistic, industrialized society.

You're getting a little shrill here, you say.

You're pretty well off. You expect to be better off soon. You do. What does this mean? More software, more scampi, more square footage?

You have created an ecological crisis. The earth is infinitely variable and alive, and you are killing it. It seems safer this way. But you are not safe. You want to find wholeness and happiness in a land increasingly damaged and betrayed, and you never will. More than material matters. You must change your ways.

What is this? *Sinners in the Hands of an Angry God?*

The ecological crisis cannot be resolved by politics. It cannot be solved by science or technology. It is a crisis caused by culture and character, and a deep change in personal consciousness is needed. Your fundamental attitudes toward the earth have become twisted. You have made only brutal contact with Nature, you cannot comprehend its grace. You must change. Have few desires and simple pleasures. Honor nonhuman life. Control yourself, become more authentic. Live lightly upon the earth and treat it with respect. Redefine the word *progress* and dismiss the managers and masters. Grow inwardly and with knowledge become truly wiser. Make connections. Think differently, behave differently. For this is essentially a moral issue we face and moral decisions must be made.

A *moral issue!* Okay, this discussion is now toast. A *moral* issue . . .   *40*
And who's this *we* now? Who are *you* is what I'd like to know. You're not me, anyway. I admit, someone's to blame and something should be done. But I've got to go. It's getting late. That's dusk out there. That is dusk, isn't it? It certainly doesn't look like any dawn I've ever seen. Well, take care.

Reading and Responding

1. What seems to you the single most important factor in this essay? Write a paragraph explaining this.
2. Write a paragraph that imitates Williams's voice; focus on some local or campus concern.

Working Together

1. Use metaphors to describe the voice of this essay: What's the weather, the clothing, the music? Who would play the writer in the movie? And so on.
2. In a plain, matter-of-fact, straightforward way, summarize the main point Williams is making.
3. Discuss these questions: Why doesn't Williams simply come out and make her point? Why go about it in this indirect, oblique way? What do her tone and approach accomplish?
4. Working as a class or in a group, write a portrait of the kind of person Williams is satirizing in this piece, the target of her satire. How old is this person? What does he or she wear? How much money does he or she make? Where does the person live? Do you know anybody like this? Describe the person.
5. Respond to Williams: "Wait a minute, what right have you to . . . ?"

Rethinking and Rewriting

1. Watch a sunset and describe it, using Williams's essay as justification—a defense for why this isn't a silly, stupid thing to do after all.

2. Write an essay about growing up with all of the ecological doomsaying and catastrophic science to which Williams alludes. You've heard all these warnings and predictions all your life. How has that affected your outlook on life and the things you do day to day? Has the "end of nature" made you callous and self-centered, as Williams argues? Assume that's true and that you've changed, that you want others to change. How do you move people out of this frame of mind? What can be done?

A CRITICAL ANALYSIS OF HUNTERS' ETHICS

Brian Luke

> *Animal liberationist Brian Luke is an assistant professor of philosophy at the University of Dayton in Ohio. In this academic article, published in 1997, he submits the activity of hunting to sustained philosophical critique.*

I analyze the "Sportsman's Code," arguing that several of its rules presuppose a respect for animals that renders hunting a *prima facie* wrong. I summarize the main arguments used to justify hunting and consider them in relation to the *prima facie* case against hunting entailed by the sportsman's code. Sport hunters, I argue, are in a paradoxical position—the more conscientiously they follow the code, the more strongly their behavior exemplifies a respect for animals that undermines the possibilities of justifying hunting altogether. I consider several responses, including embracing the paradox, renouncing the code, and renouncing hunting.

> My father told me more than once that there were killers and there were hunters, good and bad ways to kill animals, worst men and best men.
>
> —ROBERT FRANKLIN GISH[1]

How to Hunt

A survey of hunting literature reveals a high degree of consensus regarding what constitutes ethical sport hunting.[2] The primary rules of the "Sportsman's Code" are the following:

SC1. Safety first;
SC2. Obey the law;
SC3. Give fair chase;
SC4. Harvest the game;
SC5. Aim for quick kills;
SC6. Retrieve the wounded.[3]

---

1. Robert Franklin Gish, *Songs of My Hunter Heart: A Western Kinship* (Albuquerque: University of New Mexico Press, 1992), p. 63.
2. *Sport hunting* is defined here as hunting done for its own sake, in contrast to subsistence hunting (done as a means of survival) and market hunting (done to sell parts of the animals' bodies).
3. I have attempted to express succinctly the ideas most frequently reiterated by those Westerners concerned with developing a hunting ethic. The best single source that affirms

Attention to safety and obedience to the law (SC1 and SC2) are the bare minimum requirements expected of every shooter, while SC3 through SC6 form additional rules that one must follow to be considered a truly ethical hunter. Hunters who violate SC2 are called "poachers," while hunters who routinely disregard any or all of SC1 through SC6 are known as "slob hunters," in distinction from the conscientious followers of the code known as "true sportsmen."

What general principles are entailed by the sportsman's code? Most of the rules of the code are susceptible to a multitude of interpretations, some anthropocentric, some nonanthropocentric. Since the *prima facie* case against hunting arises from a nonanthropocentric principle of respect for animals, it is important to determine whether an anthropocentric or a nonanthropocentric reading of the sportsman's code has greater validity. Moreover, the strength of the *prima facie* case against hunting depends on the precise nature of the respect for animals (e.g., whether the respect is for nonhuman species or for nonhuman individuals). Thus, in the following discussion I attempt to be as precise as possible about what is entailed by the sportsman's code. I do so by considering the rules not as isolated formulae, but in the context of how hunters apply them and how they understand them. I conclude in this section that although some parts of the sportsman's code are straightforwardly anthropocentric, the code as a whole entails a strong principle calling for the minimization of the harm done to nonhuman individuals.

Safety is highly stressed by hunters. The purpose, of course, is to protect hunters and other humans from the dangerous weapons used by hunters. Thus, SC1 implies no ethical principles regarding the treatment of nonhuman animals. However, SC2, the injunction to obey the law, may be interpreted nonanthropocentrically if the law is understood to be protecting animals for their own sakes. Hunting regulations limit the number of animals of each kind that a licensed hunter may kill over a given time period. These regulations are promulgated mainly to protect species from overhunting. How SC2 should be interpreted thus depends on hunters' understanding of the reasons for this animal protection. Legal regulation of hunting could be taken as a furtherance of healthy ecosystemic functioning for its own sake or as a recognition of the species' own interest in survival. Nevertheless, there are plenty of human-centered reasons to protect non-

---

and discusses each of these rules is Jim Posewitz, *Beyond Fair Chase: The Ethic and Tradition of Hunting* (Helena, Mont.: Falcon Press, 1994). Ted Nugent includes versions of each of these rules in his "Sportsman's Creed," printed on page one of his book, *Blood Trails: The Truth about Bowhunting* (Jackson, Mich.: Ted Nugent, 1991). Other sources that articulate some or all of these rules include James Swan, *In Defense of Hunting* (New York: Harper-Collins, 1995); Ted Kerasote, *Bloodties: Nature, Culture, and the Hunt* (New York: Kodansha, 1993); James Whisker, *The Right to Hunt* (North River Press, 1981); Robert Franklin Gish, *Songs of My Hunter Heart*; and José Ortega y Gasset, *Meditations on Hunting* (New York: Charles Scribner's Sons, 1972).

human species, and these seem to be foremost in hunters' understanding of SC2. In explaining the need to obey hunting regulations, hunters most often refer to obligations to future human hunters. For instance:

> As a hunter, you have a responsibility to future generations to see to the conservation of the animals you hunt. . . . Hunting seasons and bag limits are established to allow the taking of some animals while sustaining wildlife populations. In this way hunters are allowed a harvest, and breeding populations are maintained.[4]

Thus, rules SC1 and SC2 are straightforwardly anthropocentric, primarily functioning to further a human interest in pursuing hunting in a safe and sustainable fashion. The rule SC3, "give fair chase," is more ambiguous. "Fair chase" refers to the restrictions on the means of hunting that sport hunters feel they must apply to remain ethical. Fair chase, as Jim Posewitz explains it, is "a balance that allows hunters to occasionally succeed while animals generally avoid being taken."[5] Although there is disagreement at times between hunters over whether a particular restriction is necessary for a chase to be fair, the techniques most universally denounced include pursuing animals whose flight is restricted by water, deep snow, or fencing, using motorized vehicles to chase or herd animals, tracking animals electronically, employing automatic weaponry, and hunting animals placed outside of their native habitat.

Fair chase is about letting "the hunted animal have his *chance,* that he be able, in principle, to avoid capture."[6] Stated this way, with the emphasis on the animal potentially escaping, it might seem that SC3 embodies some respect for the hunted animals, that the hunters are trying to be fair *to their targets* by refraining from totally overwhelming them with technology. Although hunters do at times understand fair chase this way, as a mark of respect for their prey, it is a superficial fairness insofar as it is not in the interests of any particular game animal to be hunted "sportingly," but rather not to be hunted at all. Joy Williams sarcastically refutes the idea that sport hunting is "a balanced jolly game of mutual satisfaction between the hunter and the hunted—*Bam, bam, bam, I get to shoot you and you get to be dead.*"[7]

Indeed, some hunters insist that the rule of fair chase is not followed out of consideration for the animals themselves. Ortega chides those who assume that fair chase "arises from the pure gentlemanliness of a Knight of the Round Table."[8] He argues that the total absence of restrictions on the

5

---

4. Posewitz, *Beyond Fair Chase,* pp. 13, 27. Cf. Whisker, *The Right to Hunt,* pp. 88 and xvi.
5. Posewitz, *Beyond Fair Chase,* p. 57.
6. Ortega, *Meditations on Hunting,* p. 49.
7. Joy Williams, "The Killing Game," in *Women on Hunting,* ed. Pam Houston (Hopewell, N.J.: Ecco Press, 1995), p. 252.
8. Ortega, *Meditations on Hunting,* p. 50.

means of killing wild animals would "annihilate the essential character of the hunt"⁹ because

> . . . hunting is precisely the series of efforts and skills which the hunter has to exercise to dominate with sufficient frequency the countermeasures of the animal which is the object of the hunt. If these countermeasures did not exist, if the inferiority of the animal were absolute, the opportunity to put the activities involved in hunting into effect would not have occurred.[10]

The point of fair chase is to preserve the hunting experience *for the hunter,* in particular to maintain *hunting* as the development and application of certain skills in distinction from effortless *killing* via high technology. Hunting becomes dull in the absence of fair chase restrictions: "Boredom occurs when the hunt is always a failure or always a success. Neither our superiority nor our inferiority to the hunted may be absolute."[11] From this point of view, the ultimate standard used to decide how to balance human hunting technology against the elusive abilities of the prey is the maximization of the sportsman's pleasure in the hunt, particularly whether the pursuit requires the application of hunting skills or "disciplines." This standard is applied in Nugent's discussion of whether hunting hogs on private preserves violates fair chase:

> [T]he anti-hunters like to claim it is considered "slob hunting." Not true. . . . A wild hog is a wild hog, and I've found no difference in or out of an enclosure. I get a blast out of it either way (and of course they are delicious regardless). It will demand all the disciplines that all good bowhunting takes.[12]

Thus, the primary motivation for following SC3—retaining the hunt as an enjoyable exercise of certain skills—centers on the interests of human hunters. In other words, this part of the sportsman's code, like SC1 and SC2, entails no particular respect for animals and no *prima facie* case against hunting.

"Today, using what is killed is essential to ethical hunting."[13] The rule SC4, "harvest the game," is stated as something the hunter does *after* the kill, but in practice this rule affects the sportsman's behavior prior to the kill as well, since the hunter will leave off killing specific animals when he or she anticipates finding their harvest distasteful: "I will not shoot coots or mergansers as I can't find a way to get them to taste good enough to

---

9. Ibid., p. 45.
10. Ibid., p. 49.
11. Whisker, *The Right to Hunt,* p. 6.
12. Nugent, *Blood Trails,* p. 71. Compare Leopold's statement that "the recreational value of game is inverse to the artificiality of its origin" (quoted in Posewitz, *Beyond Fair Chase,* p. 60).
13. Posewitz, *Beyond Fair Chase,* p. 90.

eat."[14] Matt Cartmill notes that only since World War II has the injunction to harvest the kill been widely applied in the West.[15] Today, however, SC4 is such an established part of the sportsman's code that even pure trophy hunters seek a way to portray themselves as satisfying it. They do so by extending the notion of "harvest" from its primary connotation of eating the flesh to include the taking of the antlers. Mounting the head is translated from a display of conquest into a "responsible use." We must "responsibly utilize the products of the game we harvest, appreciating the God-given flesh, hides, bone, *horn & antlers* with respect and dignity."[16]

In his book, *The Right to Hunt,* Whisker attempts to give a purely anthropocentric analysis of hunting practices. He thus interprets SC4 as a rule intended to safeguard other people against wasted resources. As Whisker notes, it follows from such an analysis that harvesting the kill is *not* required if there is an overabundance of game relative to people's needs: "If game is scarce, or if some are in need, and he wantonly kills and wastes he will have committed an offense against charity. If, however, game is plentiful, and if there is no known need, he may not have sinned at all."[17] It is only by thus contextualizing the application of SC4 that one can read it anthropocentrically. However, hunters today generally do not contextualize this rule; rather, they see it as applying to all hunting situations: "Under *all* circumstances, the ethical hunter cares for harvested game in a respectful manner, leaving no waste,"[18] and "my father taught me my first lesson about fishing and hunting ethics and conservation: You *always* eat what you catch and keep."[19] Hunter Robert Franklin Gish criticizes the jackrabbit hunting he tried and rejected growing up in New Mexico:

> [D]ead jackrabbits were never picked up, never treated as "game" to take home and eat. Those jackrabbits were nothing more than motion to try to stop. It was the cruelest kind of hunting. . . . Three or four guns shooting over the cab and to the side of a bouncing truck is not the kind of hunting any person who values life would confess to.[20]

There is no suggestion here that leaving the rabbit carcasses in the brush was wrong because people were in need of meat; rather, the failure to harvest is deemed cruel because it is seen as linked to a deficient perception of the value of animal life—seeing rabbits as nothing more than "motion to try to stop."

---

14. Swan, *In Defense of Hunting,* p. 155. See also Kerasote, *Bloodties,* p. 194.
15. Matt Cartmill, *A View to a Death in the Morning: Hunting and Nature through History* (Cambridge: Harvard University Press, 1993), p. 232.
16. "A Sportsman's Creed," bylaw 8. Nugent, *Blood Trails,* p. 1 (emphasis added).
17. Whisker, *The Right to Hunt,* p. 89.
18. Posewitz, *Beyond Fair Chase,* pp. 90–91 (emphasis added).
19. Swan, *In Defense of Hunting,* p. 126 (emphasis added).
20. Gish, *Songs of My Hunter Heart,* p. 63.

In his defense of hunting, Theodore Vitali starts with the premise   10
that "the life of the animal is a good. For the animal in question, it is
better to be alive than dead."[21] The intrinsic value of the hunted animal's
life entails that there must be a good reason for the kill:

> [K]illing is an evil, . . . in such acts there is a loss of something
> good, in this case, the life of the animals. And for there ever to be
> the deliberate taking away of something good, there needs to be a
> proportionate good that provides an adequate reason for this delib-
> erate loss.[22]

The use of parts of the animal's body enjoined by SC4 is an attempt to
provide such an adequate reason for the deliberately inflicted loss. Sport
hunters are not aiming for true mercy kills, for they generally shoot healthy
animals. Rule SC4 represents the hunters' recognition that they must have
a good reason for committing the *prima facie* wrong act of ending a healthy
animal's life. This recognition leads naturally to the sense that the greater
use they make of the animal's body, the more ethical they become as
hunters. Nugent writes, "It is our ultimate legal and ethical responsibility
to *maximize* the utilization of this animal at the dinner table and beyond."[23]
Likewise, Carmill writes:

> Some hunters . . . make a point of trying to eat, wear, or utilize in
> some other way every possible scrap of their quarry's body. "I
> don't waste anything," proclaims one hunter held up as a model in
> a 1985 National Rifle Association ad. "I process the meat, tan the
> buckskin, make thread and lacings from the sinew, even scrimshaw
> the bones."[24]

By making use of the dead body, the hunter hopes to redeem his act of
prematurely ending the animal's life. The sportsman's insistence on harvesting the kill presupposes a recognition of the intrinsic value of the
hunted individual's life.

The general point of the next rule, SC5, is well stated by Jim Posewitz: "When the time comes to kill an animal, your responsibility is to do it
efficiently. . . . The ethical hunter will constantly work toward the ideal of
making all shots on target and instantly fatal."[25] This principle is affirmed
by all those who promulgate hunting ethics. The ideal of always killing
instantly leads to numerous practical injunctions: ethical hunters must be
familiar with their weaponry and choose weapons appropriate for the in-

---

21. Theodore Vitali, "Sport Hunting: Moral or Immoral?" *Environmental Ethics* 12 (1990): 76.
22. Theodore Vitali, "The Ethics of Hunting: Killing as Life-Sustaining," *Reason Papers* 12 (1987): 37.
23. Nugent, *Blood Trails,* p. 101 (emphasis added). See also p. 135.
24. Cartmill, *A View to a Death in the Morning,* pp. 231–32.
25. Posewitz, *Beyond Fair Chase,* p. 35.

tended prey; they must practice sufficiently to become a reliable shot; they must be conscientious about shot selection, passing up those shots that may only wound the target or miss entirely.[26]

Anthropocentric interpretations of SC5 are possible, but they are not consistent with the hunters' expressed attitudes. For instance, one might read SC5 as encouraging the hunter to practice shooting and acquire familiarity with weapons so as not to unnecessarily lose game. If the concern were merely to maximize the hunter's take, then the advice would be to work diligently to improve one's shooting skill *and* to take uncertain shots when it is clear that no better opportunity is forthcoming. However, this approach is inconsistent with the sportsman's commitment always to *pass up* uncertain shots:

> [I]f the first shot is a miss, and a better shooting opportunity does not present itself, do not continue firing. . . . Continuing to shoot at fleeing targets or groups of birds, hoping to "get lucky," is blatantly unethical. It risks crippling animals and hitting the wrong animal.[27]

Posewitz's comment about crippling animals or hitting the wrong animal supports an interpretation of SC5 focused on consequences for animals rather than on hunters' interests. Maurice Wade quotes one hunter's evidently nonanthropocentric interpretation of SC5, but then suggests a deeper anthropocentric explanation for hunters' commitment to this rule:

> C. H. D. Clarke, himself a sport hunter, wrote the following: "A hunter who, deliberately, ignorantly, thoughtlessly, or through lack of the skill which an ethical sportsman would strive for, needlessly risks inflicting pain is unethical and imperils his moral right to hunt." That sport hunters accept this anticruelty ethic should not be surprising for, like other aspects of the hunting ethic, it contributes to the challenge of the hunt. Making a clean kill is often more difficult than making a dirty kill.[28]

As in the case of fair chase, while hunters do construct their code out of concern to maximize the pleasure of hunting, including particularly the challenge, it would be a mistake to understand SC5 completely in terms of hunters' self-interest. First, note that sportsmen advocate developing one's shooting skill by practicing at the shooting range, not by taking difficult and uncertain long shots at live animals, even though this latter practice could well be challenging and enjoyable for some hunters. Thus,

---

26. See, for example, Vitali, "The Ethics of Hunting," p. 39.
27. Posewitz, *Beyond Fair Chase,* pp. 36–37. See also Swan, *In Defense of Hunting,* p. 220.
28. Maurice Wade, "Animal Liberation, Ecocentrism and the Morality of Sport Hunting," *Journal of the Philosophy of Sport* 17 (1990): 17.

SC5 is evidently not motivated exclusively by hunters' self-interest.[29] Further support for this interpretation comes from hunters' explanations of SC5—unlike fair chase, which hunters often explain anthropocentrically, SC5 is consistently explained in terms of the importance of minimizing animal suffering. Consider the comments above by Clarke and by any number of other hunting defenders,[30] which show the sportsman's determination to minimize the suffering that he or she is responsible for inflicting on hunted animals.

Rule SC6, "retrieve the wounded," also shows this sense of personal responsibility toward individual animals. Swan summarizes it as follows: "A hunter always hopes that his shots will kill quickly and cleanly. If not, I was taught, it is your duty to find and kill the wounded animal as quickly as possible."[31] Hunters do not like the idea of game animals suffering. This aversion can be seen in their strained arguments for the benignity of shooting: "In most cases, a well-placed, sharp arrowhead causes imperceptible pain, zero hydrostatic shock, and literally puts the animal to sleep on its feet."[32] The commitment to aim for instant kills and follow up on all woundings expresses the hunter's desire to minimize the suffering that he or she causes to wild animals by hunting. As with SC5, a prudential interpretation of SC6 in terms of maximizing the hunter's take is implausible, given the hunters' insistence on retrieving the wounded under *all* circumstances.[33] There are times at which the likelihood of retrieving a wounded animal is so small that the expected gain for the hunter is not worth continuing the search. Yet, even under such circumstances, the hunter who perseveres is valorized, as in Posewitz's tale of the bowhunter who for thirty consecutive days returned to the woods to track an elk that he had fatally wounded. His friends encouraged him to "abandon his obsession" and shoot another elk that season, but "He was no longer looking for any elk; he was looking for the elk he shot . . . the hunter stayed with the hunt until he satisfied himself that it was over. He had mortally wounded an animal and did not rest until he sat with that animal. This is a profound expression of respect."[34] In this case, the tracking continued past the point at which any alleviation of suffering or even harvesting of flesh was likely, since well before the elk was found he was certainly dead and picked over

---

29. See Swan, *In Defense of Hunting*, p. 182.

30. For example, "Her slender, once-powerful leg was ripped nearly off. What had the pain been like? . . . The first doe's sacrifice impressed upon me that I never wanted to wound or wing an animal. To hunt must be to kill as swiftly as possible" (Gish, *Songs of My Hunter Heart*, p. 127); and Vitali, "The Ethics of Hunting," p. 39; Ann Causey, "On the Morality of Hunting," *Environmental Ethics* 11 (1989): 334–35; Swan, *In Defense of Hunting*, p. 181; Nugent, *Blood Trails*, p. iv.

31. Swan, *In Defense of Hunting*, p. 132.

32. Nugent, *Blood Trails*, p. 135. Cf. *Deer & Deer Hunting*, October 1991, p. 51.

33. Posewitz, *Beyond Fair Chase*, pp. 39–40; Swan, *In Defense of Hunting*, p. 188; Nugent, *Blood Trails*, p. 1; etc.

34. Posewitz, *Beyond Fair Chase*, pp. 80–83.

by scavengers. Yet the perseverance was still seen as profoundly respectful by Posewitz because the hunter was acting on a sense of personal responsibility for the animal that he shot. Viewed in this way, rules SC5 and SC6 are not abstract injunctions to minimize suffering in the aggregate; rather they represent the hunters' sense of personal responsibility for the suffering of the specific individual that they shoot.

Whether to Hunt

Of the six parts of the sportsman's code, only SC1, SC2, and SC3 can be interpreted anthropocentrically. The rest of the code presumes two nonanthropocentric principles: a recognition of the intrinsic value of individual animal lives and a sense of personal responsibility for minimizing one's imposition of animal suffering. Given a prior decision to hunt, these principles give rise to the practical injunctions detailed above—avoid wanton killing, aim for instant kills, etc. Nevertheless, these principles also put into question the acceptability of hunting itself. The intrinsic value of animal life implies that we should avoid unnecessary killing altogether, not that we may kill provided that we find a use for the corpse. The commitment to avoid causing unnecessary pain implies leaving healthy animals alone, not just shooting them more carefully, the rules hunters have developed to prescribe *how* to hunt ethically presume principles that pointedly raise the question of *whether* to hunt at all. In other words, the sportsman's code entails that hunting is *prima facie* wrong.

Hunters have developed a number of arguments in various attempts to overcome this *prima facie* case against hunting. In this section, I consider the four major defenses of hunting that are usually given, not to assess these arguments on their own terms, but rather to relate them to the sportsman's code and the nonanthropocentric principles that the code entails. The key question is: have hunters successfully rebutted their own case against hunting?

Meat Procurement. The first defense of hunting is that it is an acceptable way to obtain food: "one of the more legitimate arguments for hunting is to hunt your own food and take responsibility for it."[35] Many hunters point out that death in the slaughterhouse is by no means more humane than the death imposed by hunters. This argument is directed toward Anglo-European non-hunters (most of whom eat the flesh of slaughtered animals) and is evidently telling—most Americans support hunting for meat and oppose hunting for trophies.[36] However, in the context of the sportsman's code such *ad hominem* arguments against non-hunting meat eaters are insufficient: being committed to minimizing their infliction of

_____
35. Gish, *Songs of My Hunter Heart*, p. 100. Also Nugent, *Blood Trails*, p. 9.
36. Swan, *In Defense of Hunting*, p. 9.

suffering, hunters must determine whether there is a source of nutrition entailing less harm than either game or factory-farmed flesh—i.e., they must address the possibility of vegetarianism.

Two recent defenders of hunting, Swan and Kerasote, do so. Swan writes that he tried a vegetarian diet for a year and it made him ill,[37] while Kerasote, who also abstained from meat for a while, returned to hunting after calculating that his consumption of vegetarian food imported from outside his bioregion was indirectly costing more animal lives than if he killed and ate one elk a year.[38] Although these points are useful for rendering Swan's and Kerasote's own hunting consistent with their commitment to minimize their imposition of unnecessary harm, neither point can be used as the basis of a generalized defense of North American meat hunting. American vegetarians are typically as healthy or healthier than American meat eaters, and few Americans live in that particular combination of ecological circumstances that Kerasote needs to support a utilitarian defense of his hunting. For hunters in general, killing wild animals and eating their flesh is an unnecessary imposition of harm and is thus inconsistent with the principles entailed by the sportsman's code.

Atavism. One of the most frequently presented defenses of hunting is the atavism argument. According to this argument, "Man" has been a hunter throughout most of "his" existence,[39] acquiring predatory instincts that cannot have been totally lost in the brief period of time since the development of agriculture.[40] It is suggested that modern sport hunting is an expression of these lingering instincts,[41] and a way of linking civilized man with his prehistoric origins.[42] Various conclusions are drawn from this analysis, including the claims that hunting, being instinctive, is not subject to moral evaluation,[43] that hunting today is necessary for emotional stability, fulfillment and happiness,[44] and that the abolition of hunting, by repressing an instinctive need, has led or could lead to various seriously negative consequences such as drug abuse and intrahuman violence.[45]

There are major problems with the atavism argument. Sport hunting can be explained easily without recourse to predatory instincts,[46] and the

---

37. Ibid., p. 15.
38. Kerasote, *Bloodties,* pp. 232–33.
39. Ortega, *Meditations on Hunting,* p. 102; Whisker, *The Right to Hunt,* pp. ix, 24.
40. Swan, *In Defense of Hunting,* p. 175; Whisker, *The Right to Hunt,* pp. 18–20, 66.
41. Ortega, *Meditations on Hunting,* p. 119; Gish, *Songs of My Hunter Heart,* p. xii; Swan, *In Defense of Hunting,* pp. 12–13; Whisker, *The Right to Hunt,* pp. 18, 30–31.
42. Posewitz, *Beyond Fair Chase,* p. 110; Nugent, *Blood Trails,* p. 116.
43. Causey, "On the Morality of Hunting," p. 338.
44. Ortega, *Meditations on Hunting,* p. 27; Swan, *In Defense of Hunting,* p. 177.
45. Paul Shepard, *The Tender Carnivore and the Sacred Game* (New York: Scribner's, 1973), p. 150; Swan, *In Defense of Hunting,* pp. 126–27; Nugent, *Blood Trails,* p. 129.
46. Evelyn Pluhar, "The Joy of Killing," *Between the Species* 7 (1991): 123.

empirical evidence for the evolution of such instincts is shaky. The presumption that "Man" evolved as a hunter has been challenged by recent anthropological theory, according to which humans have been foragers, not hunters, throughout most of our existence, gathering plants, insects and perhaps a few stray small animals, so that scavenging is as likely as hunting to be the first means by which the flesh of large mammals was acquired.[47] Moreover, several writers have pointed out that the occurrence of prehistoric hunting does not necessitate the evolution of predatory instincts.[48] Finally, the presumption of an inherited hunting instinct is difficult to maintain in the face of the preponderance of non-hunters and anti-hunters today—a population that is evidently no less well-adjusted than the hunters themselves.[49]

In addition to these points, there are two other difficulties related directly to the sportsman's code that are important in assessing the atavism argument. The first is that the code indicates a significant ambivalence by hunters about their killing. Hunting is hedged by an elaborate network of restrictions, conditions, and guidelines to prevent it from lapsing into a completely unacceptable activity. Thus, when Swan suggests that "in each of us there is a leopard,"[50] or Nugent claims that he is as "much a natural predator as any Canis Lupus or Ursa Horribilus,"[51] they are evidently forgetting that wolves, bears, and leopards show none of the compunction over killing their prey that human hunters do. Even if sport hunting is an expression of some kind of predatory instinct, the sportsman's code indicates that human hunters are also disposed *against* killing and inflicting pain. Thus, humans are not *natural* predators; rather, they are *conflicted* predators. Because it is not clear that emotional adjustment, happiness, fulfillment, etc., can ever come from expressing a disposition (the predatory "instinct") in such a way that it conflicts with some other disposition (our compassion for animals) that may be just as "instinctive," this conflict undermines the atavism argument.[52]

Hunters reject the obvious resolution of this conflict—for example, such nonlethal stalking practices as wildlife photography—insisting in various ways that the intent to kill is essential to the hunt. Yet, it is precisely

20

---

47. See Cartmill, *A View to a Death in the Morning,* pp. 15–18; Andree Collard with Joyce Contrucci, *Rape of the Wild: Man's Violence against Animals and the Earth* (Bloomington: Indiana University Press, 1989), chap. 2; Mason, *An Unnatural Order,* chap. 2.
48. Marc Bekoff and Dale Jamieson, "Sport Hunting as an Instinct," *Environmental Ethics* 13 (1991): 375–78; Pluhar, "The Joy of Killing," p. 123.
49. See Causey, "On the Morality of Hunting," p. 338; Pluhar, "The Joy of Killing," p. 123; Cartmill, *A View to a Death in the Morning,* p. 229.
50. Swan, *In Defense of Hunting,* p. 13.
51. Nugent, *Blood Trails,* p. v.
52. Daniel Dombrowski argues that moral concern for nonhuman animals is as likely to be part of our evolutionary heritage as the urge to kill (Daniel Dombrowski, "Comment on Pluhar," *Between the Species* 7 (1991): 130–31).

this part of hunting, the killing, that is most difficult to interpret as instinctive, given our frequent reluctance and resistance to harming animals. For example, Pluhar writes:

> One of my colleagues, an avid hunter, once told me in exasperation that his 13-year-old son had just ruined his chance to "get" his first buck. Although the child was in perfect position to shoot the deer, he did not pull the trigger. "I couldn't do it, Dad," the boy explained: "he was looking right into my eyes!"[53]

The first kill is the most difficult.[54] Helping boys "work through this problem" is part of the process that Swan describes as a primary challenge facing hunters today—overcoming guilt.[55] After killing his first animal, Gish's anguish was so severe that he worried for weeks that his mother would die from plague transmitted to her from a flea jumping off the carcass. He writes:

> When I killed my first rabbit with my new Benjamin air rifle, . . . I was overcome with a . . . pervasive sadness. I shot the rabbit in the back and paralyzed it. And it took another shot to stop its wild cries and suffering. My father coaxed me into the responsibility of finishing it off myself, albeit with tears in my eyes.[56]

Pluhar's comment about another child seems apt here: "Such children do not appear to be genetically programmed to kill."[57]

The second difficulty for the atavism argument raised by the sportsman's code is that although the code greatly conditions the practice of modern sport hunting, it is not part of our evolutionary inheritance, but rather is a social construction developed within a particular time and place. Ortega writes:

> This is the reason men hunt. When you are fed up with the troublesome present, with being "very twentieth century," you take your gun, whistle for your dog, go out to the mountain, and, without further ado, give yourself the pleasure during a few hours or a few days of being "Paleolithic."[58]

---

53. Pluhar, "The Joy of Killing," p. 123.

54. "The film [*After the First*] tells the story of a young boy who goes on his first deer hunt with his father. When the boy looked at the beauty of the deer poised in the early morning, its antlered head raised above the bushes, he had hesitated, then shot; and as father and son looked down together at the dead deer, the father had said, 'After the first it won't be so hard.'" Helen Prejean, *Dead Man Walking* (New York: Vintage Books, 1993), p. 185.

55. Swan, *In Defense of Hunting*, p. 29.

56. Gish, *Songs of My Hunter Heart*, p. 62.

57. Pluhar, "The Joy of Killing," pp. 123–24; see also Cartmill, *A View to a Death in the Morning*, pp. 229–31.

58. Ortega, *Meditations on Hunting*, p. 116.

While North American hunters today do often fantasize that they are acting as their Paleolithic forefathers, the reality is quite different. Note that even though the sportsman's code can be summarized with just six rules, some of the rules, particularly SC1, SC2 and SC3, are actually rubrics for whole lists of specific injunctions. These injunctions are complicated and specific to time and place: they are not instinctive; they must be carefully studied; and they greatly condition the modern experience of hunting. For example, Swan describes the process of hunting for waterfowl in California: how to sign up for the lottery that determines who may shoot, where and when you must go to be assigned a blind, which types of weapons and ammunition are allowed, the complicated determination of how many of which kinds of birds one may legally shoot ("four per day, eight in possession . . . no more than three mallards, only one of which is a female, only one pintail of either sex, and no more than two redheads and/or canvasbacks"). Swan concludes: "If I haven't got all these regulations exactly correct, I apologize. I only have a Ph.D. in natural resources, and I have a little trouble reading eight-point condensed-type manuals of regulations."[59]

One might argue that prehistoric hunting was most likely also highly ritualized and rule-bound so the regulations surrounding hunting today do not prevent it from being atavistic. However, the specific forms that the rules take differ between cultures, and those who deploy the atavistic argument never address the crucial question of which rules so significantly alter the hunting experience that their adoption decisively separates modern hunting from the primal experience. For example, it is presumed that prehistoric hunters did *not* self-impose limits on their means of hunting. The supposition is that early men hunted out of necessity, and it is generally agreed that it makes no sense for the truly needy to restrict their means of killing: "It would be as absurd for a hunter in need of food to wait until dawn to kill a deer as it would be for a cougar to wait."[60] Because today's North American hunters are generally not facing starvation regardless of the outcome of their hunt, they have the luxury to apply the rules of fair chase to make the hunting experience a more exciting challenge. How do we know that the one who staves off hunger by using any means at his disposal to kill is expressing the same "instinctive" disposition as one who self-consciously restricts his means of killing in order to construct the most thrilling hunting experience?

Conservation. Another common defense of hunting is the conservation argument, according to which "there would be few wild animals if there were no hunters"[61] because hunters as a group form "one of the

---

59. Swan, *In Defense of Hunting,* pp. 259–60.
60. Vitali, "The Ethics of Hunting," pp. 38–39. Compare Swan, *In Defense of Hunting,* pp. 181–82; Gish, *Songs of My Hunter Heart,* p. 51; Kerasote, *Bloodties,* p. 77.
61. Posewitz, *Beyond Fair Chase,* p. 105.

most effective pressure groups in existence working to preserve" natural habitat.[62]

The premise regarding the relative contribution of hunters to conservation can be challenged.[63] Even granting this premise, there are still problems with the conservation argument given the nonanthropocentric principles behind the sportsman's code. Rules SC5 and SC6 entail a commitment to minimize the unnecessary harm that one inflicts on individual animals; however, if there are ways to generate funds for conservation other than through the sale of hunting licenses and the taxation of weapons and ammunition, then hunting is an unnecessary imposition of harm. Causey (who defends the atavism argument) agrees with anti-hunters such as Pluhar that conservation can *more* effectively be served by using general tax revenues than by charging hunters.[64]

The hunter who defends his sport with the conservation argument faces a particular difficulty at the culminating moment of the hunt just before he shoots. Because, at this point, his or her financial contribution to conservation has already been made, no further benefit will come from continuing the hunt to its fatal conclusion. The kill is in this sense an unnecessary harm for which the hunter is personally responsible. On the other hand, hunters might know that given the opportunity they will conclude the hunt with a killing shot, and simultaneously recognize that they would not contribute much to conservation except to further their hunting experiences. Thus, their contribution to conservation is impossible without the deaths and possible injuries of some wild animals.[65] Indeed, those who use the conservation argument generally recognize that hunters support conservation because they enjoy hunting and want to preserve game species so as to continue their sport.[66] However, this desire for enjoyment again puts the conservation argument into tension with the sportsman's code because rule SC4 entails the intrinsic value of the individuals, that their continued lives are a good for the animals themselves. By saying in effect that "we will conserve animals only if we can enjoy tracking and shooting them," hunters are precisely denying the value of animal lives independent of their utility as moving targets.[67]

---

62. Robert Loftin, "The Morality of Hunting," *Environmental Ethics* 6 (1984): 248. See also Swan, *In Defense of Hunting,* pp. 6, 147; and Whisker, *The Right to Hunt,* pp. 83–84.

63. Williams, "The Killing Game," pp. 264–65; Pluhar, "The Joy of Killing," p. 126, n 8.

64. Causey, "On the Morality of Hunting," p. 341; Pluhar, "The Joy of Killing," pp. 121–22.

65. On this basis Loftin calls animals killed by hunters "martyrs" and argues that "their deaths should be seen as a sacrificial act in the best sense" (Loftin, "The Morality of Hunting," p. 248).

66. E.g., Nugent, *Blood Trails,* pp. 14, 115; Whisker, *The Right to Hunt,* pp. 152–53.

67. Williams calls sportsman's conservation a "contradiction in terms (We protect things now so that we can kill them later)" (Williams, "The Killing Game," p. 258). Roger King points out the essentially anthropocentric attitude behind the conservation argument (Roger J. H. King, "Environmental Ethics and the Case for Hunting," *Environmental Ethics* 13 (1991): 81–82).

25

Hunters are interested not just in the *continuation* of those species that they enjoy hunting, but also in the proliferation of those game species in sufficient numbers to maximize pleasurable hunting opportunities. The proliferation of game animals sometimes requires the complete or near extermination of natural predators—a case in point being the recent killing of wolves in Alaska to generate greater numbers of elk and caribou for human hunters to pursue.[68] This eradication underscores the inconsistency between the conservation argument and hunters' own ethics. The intrinsic value of hunted animals recognized by SC4 applies equally well to wolves and other natural predators since they also seek to continue their lives. Yet, these animals are at times subjected to extermination efforts funded by the "conservation" dollars of hunters.

Wildlife Management. Hunters often attempt to overcome the *prima facie* case against hunting through the wildlife management argument. According to this argument, the absence of natural nonhuman predators necessitates the regulated use of human hunting to maintain the populations of prey species at healthy, sustainable levels.[69] Although this argument is one of the most common defenses of hunting, it applies at most to only a few hunting situations. Deer comprise about two percent of the animals that North Americans kill each year; yet, for the remaining 98 percent (doves, rabbits, squirrels, quail, pheasant, ducks and geese),[70] no one even suggests there are overpopulation problems.[71] Deer hunters cannot realistically portray themselves as "Florence Nightingales with rifles"[72]—euthanizing deer to save them from an agonizing death by starvation—because, whether hunting for meat or for trophies, deer hunters select the healthy adults for killing, just those individuals most likely to survive a hard winter.[73] As a result, human hunters cannot be said to be replacing natural predators, since natural predators are more likely to kill the young, the old, and the unhealthy.[74] Deer hunters might grant that the individuals they kill are not really being helped, but still maintain that their killing is justified because by helping decrease the herd size they save others from starvation. This idea actually reverses reality, since it is because of hunting that U.S. deer herds are often unnaturally large—in order to boost deer herd size to

68. See Pluhar, "The Joy of Killing," pp. 121–22; Causey, "On the Morality of Hunting," p. 342.
69. See Vitali, "Sport Hunting," and Nugent, *Blood Trails*, p. 8, for just two examples.
70. Swan, *In Defense of Hunting*, p. 8.
71. See Pluhar, "The Joy of Killing," p. 121; Loftin, "The Morality of Hunting," p. 244; Cartmill, *A View to a Death in the Morning*, p. 232.
72. Kerasote, *Bloodties*, p. 218.
73. See Byron Dalrymple, *Deer Hunting with Dalrymple* (New York: Arco, 1983), pp. 53–54, on the selection involved in meat hunting for deer, and Vitali, "Sport Hunting," p. 70, on the negative consequences of trophy hunting for the healthiest males.
74. Loftin, "The Morality of Hunting," p. 245; Vitali, "Sport Hunting," p. 71.

please hunters, wildlife managers (both public and private) feed deer, manipulate flora, and decimate natural predators.[75] Once the herd has become unnaturally large through such measures, wildlife managers make sure it stays that way, insuring an annual "harvestable surplus" for hunters by carefully regulating how many does are killed.[76] Even in the absence of natural predators, deer herds that are not hunted by humans tend to reach and maintain a stable population level below the carrying capacity of the habitat, and below the levels fostered by states managing wildlife for hunters.[77] Therefore, since the wildlife management system functions primarily to further the interests of hunters, it is question begging to assert the importance of hunting as a wildlife management tool in response to the *prima facie* case against hunting raised by the sportsman's code.

The Paradox of Hunters' Ethics

The sportsman's code, particularly SC4 through SC6, enjoins hunters to hunt in a way that recognizes both the moral burden of killing and the importance of minimizing one's infliction of pain. Because hunters aim to kill and at times cannot help inflicting pain, the sportsman's code raises a strong *prima facie* case against hunting altogether. According to the analysis of the preceding section, this case against hunting has not been successfully rebutted. Thus, hunters' ethics are paradoxical: hunters become more ethical by hunting in a way that is sensitive to the animal's interests in avoiding pain and in continuing to live; nevertheless, this very sensitivity and respect for animals entails that hunting is not justifiable, that even true sportsmen are not acting ethically. There are three major responses to this paradoxical situation: embracing the paradox, renouncing the code, and renouncing hunting.

Embracing the Paradox. The first response is the most common in   30
hunting literature: hunters attempt to make a virtue out of necessity by claiming that the whole world is essentially paradoxical, with good and evil inextricably tied to each other. Hunters feel that they alone are honest enough to admit the existence of this paradox of nature and that they consciously engage themselves in it. Violence is the way of the world, they claim, and virtue comes not from nonviolence but from acknowledgment of this basic truth. Hunters are emphatic in describing the inescapable violence of nature and life: "Life is a terrible conflict, a grandiose and atrocious confluence,"[78] "We are murderers and cannot live without mur-

75. Swan, *In Defense of Hunting*, p. 77; Nugent, *Blood Trails*, pp. 113–14; Kerasote, *Bloodties*, p. 214; Pluhar, "The Joy of Killing," p. 121; Wenz, "Ecology, Morality, and Hunting," pp. 193–94; King, "Environmental Ethics and the Case for Hunting," p. 68.

76. Ron Baker, *The American Hunting Myth* (New York: Vantage Press, 1985), p. 81.

77. Ibid., pp. 73–77.

78. Ortega, *Meditations on Hunting*, p. 98.

dering. The whole of nature is based on murder,"[79] "There is not a man, woman, or child alive who has not caused a blood trail. . . . Life lives off of life," etc.[80] In a world based on violence, advocacy of nonviolence is not virtuous or compassionate, it is a dangerous and immoral ignorance: "We fall, therefore, [in replacing hunting with wildlife photography] into a new immorality, into the worst of all, which is a matter of not knowing those very conditions without which things cannot be."[81] While non-hunters buy processed meat wrapped in cellophane, protected from any painful awareness of the bloodshed intrinsic to this process, hunters have advanced to a higher ethical stage, confronting the truth.[82] Thus, Swan quotes a fellow hunter (a former priest) who describes killing his first deer as "the most profound spiritual experience" that he ever felt because he was "finally being honest about killing the meat" he ate.[83] The final stage of spiritual and ethical growth is not just to acknowledge and accept the blood and horror "inherent in all life," but to embrace and enjoy it: "Hunters do not prefer death to life; rather, they simply seek to participate in the reality of life and embrace it, deriving joy from accepting life as it is."[84]

Hunters attempt to transcend compassion, claiming that acknowledgement of the "truth" of inescapable violence is the highest virtue. It is ironic that this whole position is based on half-truths and distortions. Swan concludes his book-long defense of hunting by citing Joseph Campbell's "wise" observation that "the trouble with society today is that people have forgotten the basic law of life that 'flesh eats flesh.'"[85] Yet, "flesh eats flesh" is obviously *not* the basic law of life, given that most animals are herbivorous. The comment is not even apt for human life, given that many, perhaps most, human individuals and cultures have lived healthy lives without consuming flesh. The clear, undeluded vision of the spiritually advanced hunter evidently requires a blind spot for most animals and many people. Statements such as Ortega's "Every animal is in a relationship of superiority or inferiority with regard to every other"[86] can only be based on a self-servingly selective observation of nature, one that blocks awareness of the

---

79. von Franz, quoted in Swan, *In Defense of Hunting,* p. 132.
80. Nugent, *Blood Trails,* p. i. Also: "There is almost no way for one form of life to exist *except* at the expense of another" (Thomas McIntyre, *The Way of the Hunter: The Art and the Spirit of Modern Hunting* [New York: Dutton, 1988], p. 101); and Whisker, *The Right to Hunt,* p. 98; Nugent, *Blood Trails,* pp. 13, 135; Vitali, "The Ethics of Hunting," p. 36; Causey, "On the Morality of Hunting," p. 340.
81. Ortega, *Meditations on Hunting,* p. 94. Compare: "Man's worst crime against nature is not progress, but disassociation" (Nugent, *Blood Trails,* p. 89).
82. E.g., Gish, *Songs of My Hunter Heart,* p. 15; Cartmill, *A View to a Death in the Morning,* pp. 181, 236; Nugent, *Blood Trails,* pp. iii–iv; Swan, *In Defense of Hunting,* p. 134.
83. Swan, *In Defense of Hunting,* p. 240. Cf. Nugent, *Blood Trails,* p. 4.
84. Swan, *In Defense of Hunting,* p. 175.
85. Ibid., p. 270.
86. Ortega, *Meditations on Hunting,* p. 98.

myriad ways that species have adapted through symbiotic mutual cooperation rather than through exploitation (not to mention all those species who are simply indifferent to each other).

Sometimes nature is violent and exploitative; sometimes it is peaceful and symbiotic. There are also varying degrees of violence. The sportsman's code, by distinguishing better from worse reasons for killing and by enjoining hunters to minimize their infliction of pain, recognizes that less violence is better than more. When hunters describe nature as intrinsically exploitative, they retain the use of terms with highly negative connotation—"murder," "violence," "horror," etc.—thus still implying that less violence is better than more. It makes no sense to suggest that because some bloodshed in nature is inescapable, we might as well just wade right in and *add* to it. Causey writes that "it is naive of [animal protectionists] to believe that all animal suffering at the hands of humans can be avoided."[87] Such remarks are irrelevant, however, because the exhortations of animal protectionists *and* the sportsman's code are not to eliminate our imposition of animal suffering, but to avoid imposing unnecessary suffering.

Renouncing the Code. Since the contradiction within hunting ethics is between the respect for animals embodied in parts of the code and the harms inflicted through hunting, one potential way to resolve the contradiction is to renounce the nonanthropocentric rules, keeping only the purely anthropocentric rules SC1 through SC3. In this way, hunters at least achieve a consistent practice and ethic of animal exploitation. Hunters who violate the code are sometimes portrayed by sportsmen as a small minority of "bad apples" who can be rehabilitated or thrown out through a determined effort by the ethical majority.[88] However, because it is SC4 through SC6 that create the difficult ethical problems, ignoring these rules is one way of responding to the tension within hunting ethics. Thus, slob hunting can be seen not as an unusual and inexplicable deviation, but rather as one alternative choice motivated by the nature of hunting itself.

Given this alternative, one might wonder whether the constructors of hunting ethics would do better for themselves to renounce the nonanthropocentric elements of the code altogether. There are two reasons why they have not done so. On the one hand, hunters are very sensitive to the opinions of the non-hunting majority. Posewitz has pointed out that "The future of hunting depends upon how the majority of people view hunters. These people form their opinions when they see how we hunt and how we care for, and about, wildlife."[89] Hunters want to secure hunting privileges and access to public lands, and they feel that to do so requires curbing

---

87. Causey, "On the Morality of Hunting," p. 340.
88. Swan, *In Defense of Hunting,* p. 188; Nugent, *Blood Trails,* p. 118.
89. Posewitz, *Beyond Fair Chase,* p. 14.

behaviors that most blatantly display disrespect for animals.[90] Those who construct hunting ethics in North America are particularly aware of the studies showing that most Americans oppose hunting for trophies but support hunting for meat.[91] Given their politically vulnerable minority status, hunters thus feel compelled to promulgate rules such as SC4, "harvest the kill":

> Using venison as a basic source of food gives the sport of deer hunting a sound, utilitarian foundation. We must remember that the non-hunting public does not accept deer hunting for either recreational purposes or antler collecting; the non-hunting public, however, accepts hunting when it is done to put deer meat on the table.[92]

Although putting on an ethical show to placate the majority certainly   *35* involves some bad faith, it would be a mistake to think that the nonanthropocentric elements of the sportsman's code are purely motivated by a concern about outsider opinion. The deeper reason comes from within. In their discussions of wounding animals and causing protracted deaths, hunters describe such a depth of personal anguish that their concern over minimizing the infliction of animal suffering must be taken to be sincere. Nugent, for example, writes: "I made a poor hit. . . . I get sick when that happens."[93] Jim Fergus recalls wounding a squirrel with his slingshot; subsequently killing that squirrel with a stick "was a nasty, messy business and the squirrel suffered. . . . I still, all these years later, feel terrible thinking about it."[94] Kerasote writes:

> I think of this elk tossed off his feet and lying still—one of those careful and lucky stalks ending in the magic bullet, the instantaneous death from a high neck shot, . . . Would that they were all like that instead of the times that I've knelt by their heads, and their breath has grated and their legs have kicked and shivered, their eyes filming over—another life prematurely departed between my hands. The first elk I shot died like that, and I swore that I would never hunt again. I even thought of running away and forgetting the carcass. But I sat by her, holding her head, then finally started my penance.[95]

---

90. "The eyes of the world are on us," Nugent, *Blood Trails,* p. 118; and Swan, *In Defense of Hunting,* p. 188.

91. Posewitz, *Beyond Fair Chase,* p. 111; Swan, *In Defense of Hunting,* p. 9.

92. Robert Wegner, *Deer & Deer Hunting,* bk. 3 (Harrisburg, Pa.: Stackpole Books, 1990), p. 165.

93. Nugent, *Blood Trails,* p. 58.

94. Jim Fergus, *A Hunter's Road: A Journey with Gun and Dog across the American Uplands* (New York: Henry Holt and Company, 1992), p. 2.

95. Kerasote, *Bloodties,* p. 184.

Swan discusses the moral hesitation, or "guilt," faced by today's hunters as follows:

> The modern hunter, on the other hand, is challenged not so much by fear as by overcoming guilt. Most animals killed by hunters are not taken for protection or self-defense, but for food, and perhaps for a trophy. There is a special fondness in our hearts for wild things, and a hunter must work through guilt feelings to be successful. The more one learns about wild animals, the more one develops a fondness for them.[96]

Note that the fondness for wild animals that puts the moral acceptability of hunting into question arises from the practice of hunting itself—the fondness develops from learning about wild animals. This learning is intrinsically tied to hunting since the successful hunter's anticipation of the prey's location and movements comes from long observation and, often, eventual identification with the hunted.[97] Kerasote, for example, comments on a hunting partner's ambivalence over killing elk: "He has watched too long not to be conflicted when taking . . . their playful lives."[98]

The hunter's understanding of the real value that continued life has for the hunted animal comes not from some animal rights position developed externally to the hunting community, but from the observation of and identification with game animals that are intrinsic to hunting itself. Thus dropping SC4, SC5, and SC6 from the sportsman's code would be a superficial move not really addressing the root cause of the ethical tension internal to hunting.

Renouncing Hunting. Because (1) the sportsman's code raises an unmet moral case against hunting, (2) embracing animal exploitation as a law of nature is a self-deceptive position, and (3) the sportsman's code cannot be renounced because the respect for animal well-being it expresses arises from the practice of hunting itself, it follows that sport hunting is an unethical institution. The only moral choice left is to renounce hunting as such. Hunters do not practice their sport because they have succeeded in making it ethical through the promulgation of a code distinguishing sportsmen from slobs. Rather, they hunt in spite of the fact that hunting is im-

---

96. Swan, *In Defense of Hunting*, p. 29.
97. Hunters often develop an identification with their prey. For example, "The nature hunter . . . must develop an acute sympathy with the animals he hunts. He must not only have a good deal of knowledge about them, he must have a feeling for them, which is a reflection of how he views himself. . . . The Zen archers maintain that you ultimately shoot yourself by blending your consciousness with that of your target" (Swan, *In Defense of Hunting*, pp. 33, 183).
98. Kerasote, *Bloodties*, p. 227 (ellipsis in original).

moral on their own terms. They shoot animals unnecessarily even though the practice of hunting brings them close enough to their prey to cause an awareness that it is not in the animal's interests to be shot and wounded or killed.

One study indicates that fully twenty percent of Americans who hunt in their youth give it up because they become convinced that it is wrong.[99] This twenty percent does not include the many sportsmen who continue to "hunt," but quietly curtail or halt their *shooting*—their field trips become little more than carrying a gun into the woods with their friends.[100] Kerasote believes that older hunters frequently stop killing because of the time outside with animals: "If a person spends that time really watching, listening, and getting close . . . it becomes harder to look at animals as a 'resource,' or merely meat to harvest, or a certain number of points in a record book. They become endowed with qualities that must be respected. Eventually it becomes impossible to take their lives for shallow reasons."[101] Gish's book affirms Kerasote's view that the practice of hunting itself leads men to reject killing. Gish describes how he and an old hunting buddy wounded a duck in the wing. Rather than wring the duck's neck as usual, they took him to the Rio Grande Zoo to mend. The "contradiction of shooting a duck to save it" led to Gish's realization that his hunting days were over. Gish speculates that "Perhaps because we had caused death, seen its ugly, permanent transformations, we didn't really like to hunt anymore."[102]

People who hunt frequently express regret, remorse, sadness, and   *40* shame over the killing that they do.[103] The editor of one hunting magazine notes that he doesn't "know any hunter who hasn't felt a sense of sadness after he's shot a deer."[104] Given these feelings in seasoned hunters, the reluctance to kill that frequently must be overcome in young hunters, and the internal inconsistency of hunters' ethics, the question is not so much whether people should hunt, but why they hunt at all. Gish sums up the

---

99. Dena Jolma, "Why They Quit: Thoughts from Ex-Hunters," *Animals' Agenda* (July/August 1992): 39.
100. "As they grow older, most men become less intense about hunting, and it isn't always because their reflexes have slowed and their joints stiffened. Some quit altogether. Others engage in token sorties which might or might not result in game being taken" (Nelson Bryant, in Gish, *Songs of My Hunter Heart*, pp. xii–xiii).
101. Ted Kerasote, "The Spirit of Hunting: What Native Americans Knew," *Sports Afield* 211, no. 6 (June 1994): 60.
102. Gish, *Songs of My Hunter Heart*, pp. 107–08.
103. See Gish, *Songs of My Hunter Heart*, p. xii; Kerasote, *Bloodties*, pp. 127–28; Jolma, "Thoughts from Ex-Hunters," p. 40; Cartmill, *A View to a Death in the Morning*, p. 231 (citing Mitchell, *The Hunt*, p. 46); Stuart Marks, *Southern Hunting in Black and White* (Princeton: Princeton University Press, 1991), p. 226.
104. "The Sadness of the Hunter," *New York Times*, 10 December 1995, p. E3.

problem in this way: "[T]he act of not so much hunting as shooting an animal as beautiful and vital as the antelope now bouncing lifeless in the back of the truck carried with it a strange regret that took on the general outline of the question, 'Why?'"[105]

Reading and Responding

1. As in many forms of academic writing, this article begins with an abstract or summary of what follows. Use the abstract to construct a sketchy outline of the essay. As you review the essay, check off each point on the outline.
2. Underline words like *anthropocentric* or phrases like *prima facie* or any words and phrases that you need to look up. List them on a separate sheet and write their definitions.
3. Underline all words like *thus* and *therefore*. Note how many times such transitional words are used in this article. Write a brief explanation of why you think the author uses this type of construction.

Working Together

1. Luke's essay draws explicitly on the form of philosophical analysis known as syllogism. A simple example of a syllogistic argument is:
   All people are mortal.
   I am a person.
   Therefore I am mortal.
   In other words, if the premise, the first statement, is true, and if the second statement is also true, then a certain conclusion must follow. Summarize Luke's article into one or two syllogisms. Then, as a group, discuss the argument. Do you agree or disagree? (*Hint:* the key to arguing about syllogisms is to dispute the initial premise.)
2. Describe the style or tone or voice of this essay. Use metaphors: What clothes is the writing wearing? What is the weather in the writing? How effective is this voice in persuading you of Luke's thesis?

Rethinking and Rewriting

1. Write an essay that agrees or disagrees with Luke in light of your own experience. Include a summary of Luke's position.
2. Imitate the syllogistic approach of Luke's article for an essay on any other subject, applying the title, "A Critical Analysis of _____" and filling in the blank. For example, analyze college composition classes, a political campaign, a local or national controversy, or a personal prob-

---

105. Gish, *Songs of My Hunter Heart,* p. 106.

lem. Look for contradictions and paradoxes, and, like Luke, suggest alternate ways out of the dilemma.

3. Write an introduction to Luke's essay (400–500 words) that gives readers some idea of what they're about to read and suggests how they should read it. Assume that you're writing to other students who are getting ready to read Luke's piece themselves.

WILDERNESS LETTER

Wallace Stegner

> *Wallace Stegner was one of the most influential novelists in America, best known for* Angle of Repose *(1971), winner of the Pulitzer Prize, and* The Spectator Bird *(1976), winner of the National Book Award. Throughout his life Stegner was also a committed conservationist, writing numerous essays and travel articles in the cause of preserving the landscape and ecology of the American West. "Wilderness Letter," published in the early 1980s, is a seminal argument for the spiritual value of the wild.*

Los Altos, Calif.
Dec. 3, 1960

David E. Pesonen
Wildland Research Center
Agricultural Experiment Station
243 Mulford Hall
University of California
Berkeley 4, Calif.

Dear Mr. Pesonen:

I believe that you are working on the wilderness portion of the Outdoor Recreation Resources Review Commission's report. If I may, I should like to urge some arguments for wilderness preservation that involve recreation, as it is ordinarily conceived, hardly at all. Hunting, fishing, hiking, mountain-climbing, camping, photography, and the enjoyment of natural scenery will all, surely, figure in your report. So will the wilderness as a genetic reserve, a scientific yardstick by which we may measure the world in its natural balance against the world in its man-made imbalance. What I want to speak for is not so much the wilderness uses, valuable as those are, but the wilderness *idea,* which is a resource in itself. Being an intangible and spiritual resource, it will seem mystical to the practical-minded—but then anything that cannot be moved by a bulldozer is likely to seem mystical to them.

I want to speak for the wilderness idea as something that has helped form our character and that has certainly shaped our history as a people. It has no more to do with recreation than churches have to do with recreation, or than the strenuousness and optimism and expansiveness of what historians call the "American Dream" have to do with recreation. Nevertheless, since it is only in this recreation survey that the values of wilderness are being compiled, I hope you will permit me to insert this idea between the leaves, as it were, of the recreation report.

Something will have gone out of us as a people if we ever let the remaining wilderness be destroyed; if we permit the last virgin forests to be turned into comic books and plastic cigarette cases; if we drive the few remaining members of the wild species into zoos or to extinction; if we pollute the last clear air and dirty the last clean streams and push our paved roads through the last of the silence, so that never again will Americans be free in their own country from the noise, the exhausts, the stinks of human and automotive waste. And so that never again can we have the chance to see ourselves single, separate, vertical, and individual in the world, part of the environment of trees and rocks and soil, brother to the other animals, part of the natural world and competent to belong in it. Without any remaining wilderness we are committed wholly, without chance for even momentary reflection and rest, to a headlong drive into our technological termite-life, the Brave New World of a completely man-controlled environment. We need wilderness preserved—as much of it as is still left, and as many kinds—because it was the challenge against which our character as a people was formed. The reminder and the reassurance that it is still there is good for our spiritual health even if we never once in ten years set foot in it. It is good for us when we are young, because of the incomparable sanity it can bring briefly, as vacation and rest, into our insane lives. It is important to us when we are old simply because it is there—important, that is, simply as idea.

We are a wild species, as Darwin pointed out. Nobody ever tamed or domesticated or scientifically bred us. But for at least three millennia we have been engaged in a cumulative and ambitious race to modify and gain control of our environment, and in the process we have come close to domesticating ourselves. Not many people are likely, any more, to look upon what we call "progress" as an unmixed blessing. Just as surely as it has brought us increased comfort and more material goods, it has brought us spiritual losses, and it threatens now to become the Frankenstein that will destroy us. One means of sanity is to retain a hold on the natural world, to remain, insofar as we can, good animals. Americans still have that chance, more than many peoples; for while we were demonstrating ourselves the most efficient and ruthless environment-busters in history, and slashing and burning and cutting our way through a wilderness continent, the wilderness was working on us. It remains in us as surely as Indian names remain on the land. If the abstract dream of human liberty and human dignity became, in America, something more than an abstract dream, mark it down at least partially to the fact that we were in subtle ways subdued by what we conquered.

The Connecticut Yankee, sending likely candidates from King Arthur's unjust kingdom to his Man Factory for rehabilitation, was overoptimistic, as he later admitted. These things cannot be forced, they have to grow. To make such a man, such a democrat, such a believer in human individual dignity, as Mark Twain himself, the frontier was necessary, Hannibal and the Mississippi and Virginia City, and reaching out from those the wilderness; the wilderness as opportunity and as idea, the thing that has helped to make an American different from and, until we forget it in   5 the roar of our industrial cities, more fortunate than other men. For an American, insofar as he is new and different at all, is a civilized man who has renewed himself in the wild. The American experience has been the confrontation by old peoples and cultures of a world as new as if it had just risen from the sea. That gave us our hope and our excitement, and the hope and excitement can be passed on to newer Americans, Americans who never saw any phase of the frontier. But only so long as we keep the remainder of our wild as a reserve and a promise—a sort of wilderness bank.

As a novelist, I may perhaps be forgiven for taking literature as a reflection, indirect but profoundly true, of our national consciousness. And our literature, as perhaps you are aware, is sick, embittered, losing its mind, losing its faith. Our novelists are the declared enemies of their society. There has hardly been a serious or important novel in this century that did not repudiate in part or in whole American technological culture for its commercialism, its vulgarity, and the way in which it has dirtied a clean continent and a clean dream. I do not expect that the preservation of our remaining wilderness is going to cure this condition. But the mere example that we can as a nation apply some other criteria than commercial and exploitative considerations would be heartening to many Americans, novelists or otherwise. We need to demonstrate our acceptance of the natural world, including ourselves; we need the spiritual refreshment that being natural can produce. And one of the best places for us to get that is in the wilderness where the fun houses, the bulldozers, and the pavements of our civilization are shut out.

Sherwood Anderson, in a letter to Waldo Frank in the 1920s, said it better than I can. "Is it not likely that when the country was new and men were often alone in the fields and the forest they got a sense of bigness outside themselves that has now in some way been lost. . . . Mystery whispered in the grass, played in the branches of trees overhead, was caught up and blown across the American line in clouds of dust at evening on the prairies. . . . I am old enough to remember tales that strengthen my belief in a deep semi-religious influence that was formerly at work among our people. The flavor of it hangs over the best work of Mark Twain. . . . I can remember old fellows in my home town speaking feelingly of an evening spent on the big empty plains. It had taken the shrillness out of them. They had learned the trick of quiet. . . ."

We could learn it too, even yet; even our children and grandchildren could learn it. But only if we save, for just such absolutely nonrecreational, impractical, and mystical uses as this, all the wild that still remains to us.

It seems to me significant that the distinct downturn in our literature from hope to bitterness took place almost at the precise time when the frontier officially came to an end, in 1890, and when the American way of life had begun to turn strongly urban and industrial. The more urban it has become, and the more frantic with technological change, the sicker and more embittered our literature, and I believe our people, have become.

For myself, I grew up on the empty plains of Saskatchewan and Montana and in the mountains of Utah, and I put a very high valuation on what those places gave me. And if I had not been able periodically to renew myself in the mountains and deserts of western America I would be very nearly bughouse. Even when I can't get to the back country, the thought of the colored deserts of southern Utah, or the reassurance that there are still stretches of prairie where the world can be instantaneously perceived as disk and bowl, and where the little but intensely important human being is exposed to the five directions and the thirty-six winds, is a positive consolation. The idea alone can sustain me. But as the wilderness areas are progressively exploited or "improved," as the jeeps and bulldozers of uranium prospectors scar up the deserts and the roads are cut into the alpine timberlands, and as the remnants of the unspoiled and natural world are progressively eroded, every such loss is a little death in me. In us.

I am not moved by the argument that those wilderness areas which *10*
have already been exposed to grazing or mining are already deflowered, and so might as well be "harvested." For mining I cannot say much good except that its operations are generally short-lived. The extractable wealth is taken and the shafts, the tailings, and the ruins left, and in a dry country such as the American West the wounds men make in the earth do not quickly heal. Still, they are only wounds; they aren't absolutely mortal. Better a wounded wilderness than none at all. And as for grazing, if it is strictly controlled so that it does not destroy the ground cover, damage the ecology, or compete with the wildlife it is in itself nothing that need conflict with the wilderness feeling or the validity of the wilderness experience. I have known enough range cattle to recognize them as wild animals; and the people who herd them have, in the wilderness context, the dignity of rareness; they belong on the frontier, moreover, and have a look of rightness. The invasion they make on the virgin country is a sort of invasion that is as old as Neolithic man, and they can, in moderation, even emphasize a man's feeling of belonging to the natural world. Under surveillance, they can belong; under control, they need not deface or mar. I do not believe that in wilderness areas where grazing has never been permitted, it should be permitted; but I do not believe either that an otherwise untouched wilderness should be eliminated from the preservation plan because of limited existing uses such as grazing which are in consonance with the frontier condition and image.

Let me say something on the subject of the kinds of wilderness worth preserving. Most of those areas contemplated are in the national forests and in high mountain country. For all the usual recreational purposes, the alpine and forest wildernesses are obviously the most important, both as genetic banks and as beauty spots. But for the spiritual renewal, the recognition of identity, the birth of awe, other kinds will serve every bit as well. Perhaps, because they are less friendly to life, more abstractly non-human, they will serve even better. On our Saskatchewan prairie, the nearest neighbor was four miles away, and at night we saw only two lights on all the dark rounding earth. The earth was full of animals—field mice, ground squirrels, weasels, ferrets, badgers, coyotes, burrowing owls, snakes. I knew them as my little brothers, as fellow creatures, and I have never been able to look upon animals in any other way since. The sky in that country came clear down to the ground on every side, and it was full of great weathers, and clouds, and winds, and hawks. I hope I learned something from knowing intimately the creatures of the earth; I hope I learned something from looking a long way, from looking up, from being much alone. A prairie like that, one big enough to carry the eye clear to the sinking, rounding horizon, can be as lonely and grand and simple in its forms as the sea. It is as good a place as any for the wilderness experience to happen; the vanishing prairie is as worth preserving for the wilderness idea as the alpine forests.

So are great reaches of our western deserts, scarred somewhat by prospectors but otherwise open, beautiful, waiting, close to whatever God you want to see in them. Just as a sample, let me suggest the Robbers' Roost country in Wayne County, Utah, near the Capitol Reef National Monument. In that desert climate the dozer and jeep tracks will not soon melt back into the earth, but the country has a way of making the scars insignificant. It is a lovely and terrible wilderness, such a wilderness as Christ and the prophets went out into: harshly and beautifully colored, broken and worn until its bones are exposed, its great sky without a smudge of taint from Technocracy, and in hidden corners and pockets under its cliffs the sudden poetry of springs. Save a piece of country like that intact, and it does not matter in the slightest that only a few people every year will go into it. That is precisely its value. Roads would be a desecration, crowds would ruin it. But those who haven't the strength or youth to go into it and live can simply sit and look. They can look two hundred miles, clear into Colorado: and looking down over the cliffs and canyons of the San Rafael Swell and the Robbers' Roost they can also look as deeply into themselves as anywhere I know. And if they can't even get to the places on the Aquarius Plateau where the present roads will carry them, they can simply contemplate the *idea,* take pleasure in the fact that such a timeless and uncontrolled part of earth is still there.

These are some of the things wilderness can do for us. That is the reason we need to put into effect, for its preservation, some other principle than the principles of exploitation or "usefulness" or even recreation. We simply need that wild country available to us, even if we never do more than drive to its edge and look in. For it can be a means of reassuring ourselves of our sanity as creatures, a part of the geography of hope.

Very sincerely yours,

When I wrote my "wilderness letter" to David Pesonen 20 years ago, I had probably been prompted to do so by David Brower. He was usually the cattleprod that woke me from other preoccupations and from my workaholism and directed my attention to something important. In this case what he woke me to was close to my heart. I had been lucky enough to grow up next to wilderness, or quasi-wilderness, of several kinds, and I was prepared to argue for the preservation of wilderness not simply as a scientific reserve, or a land-bank, or a playground, but as a spiritual resource, a leftover from our frontier origins that could reassure us of our identity as a nation and a people. The Wilderness Bill, already debated for years and the subject of hundreds of official pages, had not yet passed. The ORRRC report,* with its inventory of what remained of our outdoors and its promise of reorganization of the bureaus managing it, seemed a good place to put in a word.

By luck or accident or the mysterious focusing by which ideas whose time has come reach many minds at the same time, my letter struck a chord. Before it had time to appear in the ORRRC report, Secretary of the Interior Stewart Udall had picked it up and used it as the basis of a speech before a wilderness conference in San Francisco, and the Sierra Club had published it as a document of that conference. It was published in the *Washington Post* and the ORRRC report, and I included it in my collection of essays, *The Sound of Mountain Water.* Before long, some friend of mine saw it posted on the wall in a Kenya game park. From there, someone in South Africa or Rhodesia carried it home and had an artist named C. B. Cunningham surround it with drawings of African animals and birds, and turned it into a poster which the Natal Park Board, a Rhodesian kindness-to-animals organization, and perhaps other groups have distributed all over south and east Africa. A quotation from it captions a Canadian poster, with a magnificent George Calef photograph of caribou crossing river ice; and I have heard of, but not seen, a similar Australian poster issued with the same intent. The Sierra Club borrowed its last four words, "the geography of hope," as the title for Eliot Porter's book of photographs of Baja California. Altogether, this letter, the labor of an afternoon, has gone farther around the world than other writings on which I have spent years.

I take this as evidence not of special literary worth, but of an earnest, worldwide belief in the idea it expresses. There are millions of people on every continent who feel the need of what Sherwood Anderson called "a sense of bigness outside ourselves"; we all need something to take the shrillness out of us.

Returning to the letter after twenty years, I find that my opinions have not changed. They have actually been sharpened by an increased urgency. We are twenty years closer to showdown. Though the Wilderness Bill in which we all placed our hopes was passed, and though many millions of acres have been permanently protected—the magnificent Salmon

15

---

* *Outdoor Recreation for America: A Report to the President and to the Congress by the Outdoor Recreation Resources Review Commission,* U.S. Government Printing Office, January 1962.

River wilderness only a few weeks ago—preservation has not moved as fast as it should have, and the Forest Service, in particular, has shown by its reluctance and foot-dragging that it often puts resource use above preservation. Its proposed wilderness areas have consistently been minimal, and RARE II was a travesty.

Nevertheless, something saved. And something still to fight for.

And also, since the BLM Organic Act, another plus-minus development. It is now possible that out of the deserts and dry grasslands managed by the BLM there may be primitive areas set aside as wilderness, as I suggested in my letter to Pesonen and as some of us proposed to Secretary Udall as early as 1961. Unhappily, the Organic Act was contemporary with the energy crisis and the growing awareness that the undeveloped country in the Rocky Mountain states is one of the greatest energy mines on earth. That discovery, at a time of national anxiety about energy sources, has brought forward individuals, corporations, and conglomerates all eager to serve their country by strip mining the BLM wasteland, or drilling it for oil and gas. Economic temptation begets politicians willing to serve special economic interests, and they in turn bring on a new wave of states'-rights agitation, this time nicknamed the Sagebrush Rebellion. Its purpose, as in the 1940s when Bernard DeVoto headed the resistance to it (it was then called Landgrab), is to force the transfer of public lands from federal control to the control of the states, which will know how to make their resources available to those who will know what to do with them. After that they can be returned to the public for expensive rehabilitation

The Sagebrush Rebellion is the worst enemy not only of long-range management of the public lands, but of wilderness. If its counterpart in the 1940s had won, we would have no wilderness areas at all, and deteriorated national forests. If it wins in the 1980s we will have only such wilderness as is already formally set aside. Federal bureaus are imperfect human institutions, and have sins to answer for, and are not above being influenced by powerful interests. Nevertheless they represent the public interest, by and large, and not corporate interests anxious to exploit public resources at the public's expense.

In my letter to David Pesonen twenty years ago I spoke with some feeling about the deserts of southern Utah—Capitol Reef, the San Rafael Swell, the Escalante Desert, the Aquarius Plateau. That whole area has been under threat for nearly a decade, and though the Kaiparowits Complex was defeated and the Intermountain Power Project forced to relocate northward into the Sevier Desert near Lynndyl, the Union Pacific and thirteen other companies are still pushing to mine the coal in the Kaiparowits Plateau, surrounded by national parks; and a group of utilities wants to open a big strip mine at Alton, four miles from Bryce, and a 500-megawatt power plant in Warner Valley, seventeen miles from Zion, and a 2,000-megawatt plant north of Las Vegas, and two slurry pipelines to serve them. The old forest road over the Aquarius is being paved in from both ends, the equally beautiful trail over the Hightop from Salina to Fish Lake is being widened and improved. Our numbers and our energy demands inexorably press upon this country as beautiful as any on earth, country of an Old Testament harshness and serenity.

It is in danger of being made—of helping to make itself—into a sacrifice area. Its air is already less clear, its distances less sharp. Its water table, if these mines and plants and pipelines are created, will sink out of sight, its springs will dry up, its streams will shrink and go intermittent. But there will be more blazing illumination along the Las Vegas Strip, and the little Mormon towns of Wayne and Garfield and Kane Counties will acquire some interesting modern problems.

What impresses me after twenty years is how far the spoiling of that superb country has already gone, and how few are the local supporters of the federal agencies which are the only protection against it. They would do well to consider how long the best thing in their lives has been pre-served for them by federal management, and how much they will locally lose if the Sagebrush Rebellion wins. Furthermore, the land that the Sage-brush Rebellion wants transferred, the chickenhouse that it wants to put under the guard of the foxes, belongs as much to me, or to a grocer in Des Moines, or a taxi driver in Newark, as to anyone else. And I am not willing to see it wrecked just to increase corporate profits and light Las Vegas.

Reading and Responding

1. Write what you think are the three most important statements in the original letter. Leave space between them. Below each of these state-ments, write a quick response of three or four sentences. Do you un-derstand or not understand? Are you moved or not moved? Do you agree or disagree?
2. Stegner says, "Something will have gone out of us as a people if we ever let the remaining wilderness be destroyed." Explain and then re-flect on what these words mean to you, here and now, in your own situation. Be honest. Write at least five sentences.

Working Together

1. Stegner argues, "We need wilderness preserved because it was the chal-lenge against which our character as a people was formed." As a group, write a paragraph that explains what Stegner means and that tells to what extent your group agrees with him.
2. "The more urban it has become, and the more frantic with techno-logical change, the sicker and more embittered our literature, and I be-lieve our people, have become." As a group, do you agree or disagree? What personal experiences are behind your responses? Discuss these questions.

Rethinking and Rewriting

1. Write your own version of a "Wilderness Letter," revealing your own beliefs about the value of wilderness. Imitate Stegner's structure and style. Address it to a particular person, whether a government official or a local leader.
2. Stegner returned to his wilderness letter twenty years later and found that, given events, his opinions hadn't changed. Things were still bad and the argument still had to be made. Many years have passed since the follow-up piece was written. Return to the original letter and argue that if Stegner were alive today he would still believe what he believed about the future of wilderness in America—or that he would be more optimistic about that future.

Chapter 6 Essay Topics

1. Suppose you are a landowner who has paid a considerable sum to purchase fifty acres of trees. A stream runs through it. Market prices for timber are high and you could make a healthy profit logging the entire acreage. Hire one of the authors in this chapter as a consultant. From the ethical principles implied in this author's essay, write an essay explaining what you think he or she would tell you to do with your land.
2. Choose any two essays from this chapter. Assume that the authors are discussing your own backyard instead of public land. Translate each argument in terms of your own backyard. Be as literal as you can. Then end your essay by discussing what this comparison has taught you.
3. Write an "As I See It" essay for your local or campus newspaper arguing a position on some local environmental issue. Use at least one quotation from each of three writers in this chapter.
4. Write an essay discussing your view of the American habit of equating money and success. Show how your own environmental ethics affect your views on this topic, and include quotations from at least two essays in this chapter.

7

Practicing Knowledge

    In "Save the Whales, Screw the Shrimp," an essay in the previous chapter, *Joy Williams invokes the shell-shock that many people feel when confronted with all of our environmental crises. There are, we wail, just too many of them. What can possibly be done? It turns out that much can be done. We are an imaginative species, and the many kinds of action suggested in this chapter, which offers a mere sampling, offer cause for both appreciation and commitment.*

    The selections in this final chapter demonstrate that many individuals and groups are engaged in ecological action that is both wide-ranging and effective. Activists are effecting change quietly, place by place, species by species, challenge by challenge. Individually, we cannot save the planet, but we can act in our own communities. Our actions add up to reclaim a common future.

MAKING CHANGE

WOMEN, HOME, AND COMMUNITY: THE STRUGGLE IN AN URBAN ENVIRONMENT

Cynthia Hamilton

> *Cynthia Hamilton is an associate professor in the Pan African Studies Department at California State University, Los Angeles. She also has been a grassroots organizer for many years, helping to halt construction on a solid waste incinerator in Los Angeles. She describes this effort in the following essay, first published in* Reweaving the World: The Emergence of Eco-feminism *(1990), edited by Irene Diamond and Gloria Feman Orestein.*

In 1956, women in South Africa began an organized protest against the pass laws. As they stood in front of the office of the prime minister, they began a new freedom song with the refrain "now you have touched the women, you have struck a rock." This refrain provides a description of the personal commitment and intensity women bring to social change. Women's actions have been characterized as "spontaneous and dramatic," women in action portrayed as "intractable and uncompromising."[1] Society has summarily dismissed these as negative attributes. When in 1986 the City Council of Los Angeles decided that a 13-acre incinerator called LANCER (for Los Angeles City Energy Recovery Project), burning 2,000 tons a day of municipal waste, should be built in a poor residential, Black, and Hispanic community, the women there said "No." Officials had indeed dislodged a boulder of opposition. According to Charlotte Bullock, one of the protestors, "I noticed when we first started fighting the issue how the men would laugh at the women . . . they would say, 'Don't pay no attention to them, that's only one or two women . . . they won't make a difference.' But now since we've been fighting for about a year the smiles have gone."[2]

Minority communities shoulder a disproportionately high share of the by-products of industrial development: waste, abandoned factories and warehouses, leftover chemicals and debris. These communities are also asked to house the waste and pollution no longer acceptable in White communities, such as hazardous landfills or dump sites. In 1987, the Com-

---

1. See Cynthia Cockburn, "When Women Get Involved in Community Action," in Marjorie Mayo (ed.), *Women in the Community* (London: Routledge & Kegan Paul, 1977).
2. All of the quotes from Charlotte Bullock and Robin Cannon are personal communications, 1986.

mission of Racial Justice of the United Church of Christ published *Toxic Wastes and Race.* The commission concluded that race is a major factor related to the presence of hazardous wastes in residential communities throughout the United States. Three out of every five Black and Hispanic Americans live in communities with uncontrolled toxic sites; 75 percent of the residents in rural areas in the Southwest, mainly Hispanics, are drinking pesticide-contaminated water; more than 2 million tons of uranium tailings are dumped on Native American reservations each year, resulting in Navajo teenagers having seventeen times the national average of organ cancers; more than 700,000 inner city children, 50 percent of them Black, are said to be suffering from lead poisoning, resulting in learning disorders. Working-class minority women are therefore motivated to organize around very pragmatic environmental issues, rather than those associated with more middle-class organizations. According to Charlotte Bullock, "I did not come to the fight against environmental problems as an intellectual but rather as a concerned mother. . . . People say, 'But you're not a scientist, how do you know it's not safe?' I have common sense. I know if dioxin and mercury are going to come out of an incinerator stack, somebody's going to be affected."

When Concerned Citizens of South Central Los Angeles came together in 1986 to oppose the solid waste incinerator planned for the community, no one thought much about environmentalism or feminism. These were just words in a community with a 78 percent unemployment rate, an average income ($8,158) less than half that of the general Los Angeles population, and a residential density more than twice that of the whole city. In the first stages of organization, what motivated and directed individual actions was the need to protect home and children; for the group this individual orientation emerged as a community-centered battle. What was left in this deteriorating district on the periphery of the central business and commercial district had to be defended—a "garbage dump" was the final insult after years of neglect, watching downtown flourish while residents were prevented from borrowing enough to even build a new roof.

The organization was never gender restricted but it became apparent after a while that women were the majority. The particular kind of organization the group assumed, the actions engaged in, even the content of what was said, were all a product not only of the issue itself, the waste incinerator, but also a function of the particular nature of women's oppression and what happens as the process of consciousness begins.

Women often play a primary part in community action because it is   5
about things they know best. Minority women in several urban areas have found themselves part of a new radical core as the new wave of environmental action, precipitated by the irrationalities of capital-intensive growth, has catapulted them forward. These individuals are responding not to "nature" in the abstract but to the threat to their homes and to the health of their children. Robin Cannon, another activist in the fight against the Los Angeles incinerator, says, "I have asthma, my children have asthma, my

brothers and sisters have asthma, there are a lot of health problems that people living around an incinerator might be subjected to and I said, 'They can't do this to me and my family.'"

Women are more likely than men to take on these issues precisely because the home has been defined and prescribed as a woman's domain. According to British sociologist Cynthia Cockburn, "In a housing situation that is a health hazard, the woman is more likely to act than the man because she lives there all day and because she is impelled by fear for her children. Community action of this kind is a significant phase of class struggle, but it is also an element of women's liberation."[3]

This phenomenon was most apparent in the battle over the Los Angeles incinerator. Women who had no history of organizing responded as protectors of their children. Many were single parents, others were older women who had raised families. While the experts were convinced that their smug dismissal of the validity of the health concerns these women raised would send them away, their smugness only reenforced the women's determination. According to Charlotte Bullock:

> People's jobs were threatened, ministers were threatened . . . but I said, "I'm not going to be intimidated." My child's health comes first, . . . that's more important than my job.
>
> In the 1950s the city banned small incinerators in the yard and yet they want to build a big incinerator . . . the Council is going to build something in my community which might kill my child. . . . I don't need a scientist to tell me that's wrong.

None of the officials were prepared for the intensity of concern or the consistency of agitation. In fact, the consultants they hired had concluded that these women did not fit the prototype of opposition. The consultants had concluded:

> Certain types of people are likely to participate in politics, either by virtue of their issue awareness or their financial resources, or both. Members of middle or higher socioeconomic strata (a composite index of level of education, occupational prestige, and income) are more likely to organize into effective groups to express their political interests and views. All socioeconomic groupings tend to resent the nearby siting of major facilities, but the middle and upper socioeconomic strata possess better resources to effectuate their opposition. Middle and higher socioeconomic strata neighborhoods should not fall at least within the one mile and five mile radii of the proposed site.
>
>   . . . although environmental concerns cut across all subgroups, people with a college education, young or middle aged,

---

3. Cockburn, "When Women," p. 62.

and liberal in philosophy are most likely to organize opposition to the siting of a major facility. Older people, with a high school education or less, and those who adhere to a free market orientation are least likely to oppose a facility.[4]

The organizers against the incinerator in South Central Los Angeles are the antithesis of the prototype: they are high school educated or less, above middle age and young, nonprofessionals and unemployed and low-income, without previous political experience. The consultants and politicians thus found it easy to believe that opposition from this group could not be serious.

The intransigence of the City Council intensified the agitation, and the women became less willing to compromise as time passed. Each passing month gave them greater strength, knowledge, and perseverance. The council and its consultants had a more formidable enemy than they had expected, and in the end they have had to compromise. The politicians have backed away from their previous embrace of incineration as a solution to the trash crisis, and they have backed away from this particular site in a poor, Black and Hispanic, residential area. While the issues are far from resolved, it is important that the willingness to compromise has become the official position of the city as a result of the determination of "a few women."

The women in South Central Los Angeles were not alone in their battle. They were joined by women from across the city, White, middle-class, and professional women. As Robin Cannon puts it, "I didn't know we all had so many things in common . . . millions of people in the city had something in common with us—the environment." These two groups of women, together, have created something previously unknown in Los Angeles—unity of purpose across neighborhood and racial lines. According to Charlotte Bullock, "We are making a difference . . . when we come together as a whole and stick with it, we can win because we are right." 10

This unity has been accomplished by informality, respect, tolerance of spontaneity, and decentralization. All of the activities that we have been told destroy organizations have instead worked to sustain this movement. For example, for a year and a half the group functioned without a formal leadership structure. The unconscious acceptance of equality and democratic process resulted practically in rotating the chair's position at meetings. Newspeople were disoriented when they asked for the spokesperson and the group responded that everyone could speak for the neighborhood.

It may be the case that women, unlike men, are less conditioned to see the value of small advances.[5] These women were all guided by their

---

4. Cerrell Associates, *Political Difficulties Facing Waste to Energy Conversion Plant Siting* (Los Angeles: California Waste Management Board, 1984), pp. 42–43.
5. See Cockburn, "When Women," p. 63.

vision of the possible: that it *was* possible to completely stop the construction of the incinerator, that it is possible in a city like Los Angeles to have reasonable growth, that it is possible to humanize community structures and services. As Robin Cannon says, "My neighbors said, 'You can't fight City Hall . . . and besides, you work there.' I told them I would fight anyway."

None of these women was convinced by the consultants and their traditional justifications for capital-intensive growth: that it increases property values by intensifying land use, that it draws new businesses and investment to the area, that it removes blight and deterioration—and the key argument used to persuade the working class—that growth creates jobs. Again, to quote Robin Cannon, "They're not bringing real development to our community. . . . They're going to bring this incinerator to us, and then say 'We're going to *give* you fifty jobs when you get this plant.' Meanwhile they're going to shut down another factory [in Riverside] and eliminate two hundred jobs to buy more pollution rights. . . . They may close more shops."

Ironically, the consultants' advice backfired. They had suggested that emphasizing employment and a gift to the community (of $2 million for a community development fund for park improvement) would persuade the opponents. But promises of heated swimming pools, air-conditioned basketball courts and fifty jobs at the facility were more insulting than encouraging. Similarly, at a public hearing, an expert witness' assurance that health risks associated with dioxin exposure were less than those associated with "eating peanut butter" unleashed a flurry of derision.

The experts' insistence on referring to congenital deformities and   15
cancers as "acceptable risks" cut to the hearts of women who rose to speak of a child's asthma, or a parent's influenza, or the high rate of cancer, heart disease, and pneumonia in this poverty-stricken community. The callous disregard of human concerns brought the women closer together. They came to rely on each other as they were subjected to the sarcastic rebuffs of men who referred to their concerns as "irrational, uninformed, and disruptive." The contempt of the male experts was directed at professionals and the unemployed, at Whites and Blacks—all the women were castigated as irrational and uncompromising. As a result, new levels of consciousness were sparked in these women.

The reactions of the men backing the incinerator provided a very serious learning experience for the women, both professionals and nonprofessionals, who came to the movement without a critique of patriarchy. They developed their critique in practice. In confronting the need for equality, these women forced the men to a new level of recognition—that working-class women's concerns cannot be simply dismissed.

Individual transformations accompanied the group process. As the struggle against the incinerator proceeded to take on some elements of class struggle, individual consciousness matured and developed. Women began to recognize something of their own oppression as women. This led to new forms of action not only against institutions but to the transformation of social relations in the home as well. As Robin Cannon explains:

> My husband didn't take me seriously at first either. . . . He just saw a whole lot of women meeting and assumed we wouldn't get anything done. . . . I had to split my time . . . I'm the one who usually comes home from work, cooks, helps the kids with their homework, then I watch a little TV and go to bed to get ready for the next morning. Now I would rush home, cook, read my materials on LANCER . . . now the kids were on their own . . . I had my own homework. . . . My husband still wasn't taking me seriously. . . . After about 6 months everyone finally took me seriously. My husband had to learn to allocate more time for baby sitting. Now on Saturdays, if they went to the show or to the park, I couldn't attend . . . in the evening there were hearings . . . I was using my vacation time to go to hearings during the workday.

As parents, particularly single parents, time in the home was strained for these women. Children and husbands complained that meetings and public hearings had taken priority over the family and relations in the home. According to Charlotte Bullock, "My children understand, but then they don't want to understand. . . . They say, 'You're not spending time with me.'" Ironically, it was the concern for family, their love of their families, that had catapulted these women into action to begin with. But, in a pragmatic sense, the home did have to come second in order for health and safety to be preserved. These were hard learning experiences. But meetings in individual homes ultimately involved children and spouses alike—everyone worked and everyone listened. The transformation of relations continued as women spoke up at hearings and demonstrations and husbands transported children, made signs, and looked on with pride and support at public forums.

The critical perspective of women in the battle against LANCER went far beyond what the women themselves had intended. For these women, the political issues were personal and in that sense they became feminist issues. These women, in the end, were fighting for what they felt was "right" rather than what men argued might be reasonable. The coincidence of the principles of feminism and ecology that Carolyn Merchant explains in *The Death of Nature* (San Francisco: Harper & Row, 1981) found expression and developed in the consciousness of these women: the concern for Earth as a home, the recognition that all parts of a system have equal value, the acknowledgment of process, and, finally, that capitalist growth has social costs. As Robin Cannon says, "This fight has really turned me around, things are intertwined in ways I hadn't realized. . . . All these social issues as well as political and economic issues are really intertwined. Before, I was concerned only about health and then I began to get into the politics, decision making, and so many things."

In two years, what started as the outrage of a small group of mothers has transformed the political climate of a major metropolitan area. What these women have aimed for is a greater level of democracy, a greater level of involvement, not only in their organization but in the development process of the city generally. They have demanded accountability regarding land use and ownership, very subversive concerns in a capitalist society. In their organizing, the group process, collectivism, was of primary importance. It allowed the women to see their own power and potential and therefore allowed them to consolidate effective opposition. The movement underscored the role of principles. In fact, we citizens have lived so long with an unquestioning acceptance of profit and expediency that sometimes we forget that our objective is to do "what's right." Women are beginning to raise moral concerns in a very forthright manner, emphasizing that experts have left us no other choice but to follow our own moral convictions rather than accept neutrality and capitulate in the face of crisis.

The environmental crisis will escalate in this decade and women are   20
sure to play pivotal roles in the struggle to save our planet. If women are able to sustain for longer periods some of the qualities and behavioral forms they have displayed in crisis situations (such as direct participatory democracy and the critique of patriarchal bureaucracy), they may be able to reintroduce equality and democracy into progressive action. They may also reintroduce the value of being moved by principle and morality. Pragmatism has come to dominate all forms of political behavior and the results have often been disastrous. If women resist the "normal" organizational thrust to barter, bargain, and fragment ideas and issues, they may help set new standards for action in the new environmental movement.

Reading and Responding

1. To what extent are you surprised by this discussion of environmental problems in an urban setting? Write about this for half a page or so.
2. To what extent do you define yourself in terms of your race, gender, and socioeconomic class? How important are these factors to Hamilton? Write a paragraph or so to discuss these questions.

Working Together

1. Do an in-class freewrite, quickly paraphrasing the following passage and reflecting on what it means: "For these women, the political issues were personal and in that sense they became feminist issues. These women, in the end, were fighting for what they felt was 'right' rather than what men argued might be reasonable."
2. In what sense are personal issues also feminist issues? What's the difference between the right and the reasonable? How do men and women see these issues differently? Discuss these questions in your group.

3. Share your own personal experiences in which a political issue also became a personal issue—or a time when you fought for the right as opposed to the reasonable.

Rethinking and Rewriting

1. Research and report on the issue Hamilton reports, using newspaper and magazines indexes for the time of the event and looking, too, at letters to the editor, editorials, and so on. What were the other points of view? Did others see the same situation differently? What other facts can you discover about the event?
2. Write an essay about a time in your own life when political issues also became personal issues. Be clear and specific enough that readers will feel the same shift from personal to political or political to personal.
3. Write an essay with this thesis: "If taking the political personally is feminist, then I'm a feminist."

LEARNING FROM LOVE CANAL: A 20TH-ANNIVERSARY RETROSPECTIVE

Lois Marie Gibbs

Known now as the "Mother of Superfund," Lois Marie Gibbs was a mother and housewife in Niagara Falls, New York, in 1978 when she discovered that her neighborhood had been built on top of a toxic dump. Ultimately she became the leader of the grassroots effort that led to the relocation of more than 900 families. She is now the executive director of the Center for Health, Environment, and Justice, an organization that helps community-based groups throughout the country in their environmental efforts. The article that follows appeared in the spring 1998 issue of Orion Afield.

Twenty years ago the nation was jolted awake when a blue-collar community uncovered a serious public health crisis resulting from the burial of chemical wastes in their small suburban neighborhood. As the events unfolded, network television, radio, and print media covered the David and Goliath struggle in Love Canal, New York. The country watched as mothers with children in their arms and tears in their eyes cried out for help.

The words "Love Canal" are now burned in our country's history and in the memory of the public as being synonymous with chemical exposures and their adverse human health effects. The events at Love Canal brought about a new understanding among the American people of the correlation between low-level chemical exposures and birth defects, miscarriages, and incidences of cancer. The citizens of Love Canal provided an example of how a blue-collar community with few resources can win against great odds (a multi-billion-dollar international corporation and an unresponsive government), using the power of the people in our democratic system.

Now, 20 years later, science has shown that some of the same chemicals found at Love Canal are present in our food, water, and air. As important now as ever, the main lesson to be learned from the Love Canal crisis is that in order to protect public health from chemical contamination, there needs to be a massive outcry—a choir of voices—by the American people demanding change.

The Love Canal crisis began in the spring of 1978 when residents discovered that a dump site containing 20,000 tons of chemical wastes was leaking into their neighborhood. The local newspaper ran an extensive article, explaining that the dump site was once a canal that connected to the Niagara River five miles upstream of Niagara Falls. This canal, 60 feet wide and 3,000 feet long, was built by William T. Love in the 1800s in an attempt to connect the upper and lower Niagara River. Mr. Love ran out of money before completing the project, and the abandoned canal was sold at public auction, after which it was used as a municipal and chemical dump site from 1920 until 1953. Hooker Chemical Corporation, a subsidiary of Occidental Petroleum, was the principal disposer of chemical wastes at the site. Over 200 different chemicals were deposited, including pesticides such as lindane and DDT (both since banned from use in the U.S.), multiple solvents, PCBs, dioxin, and heavy metals.

In 1953, after filling the canal and covering it with dirt, Hooker sold the land to the Niagara Falls Board of Education for one dollar. Included in the deed was a "warning" about the chemical wastes buried on the property and a disclaimer absolving Hooker of any future liability. The board of education, perhaps not understanding the potential risks associated with Hooker's chemical wastes, built an elementary school near the perimeter of the canal in 1954. Home building around the canal also began in the 1950s, and by 1978, there were approximately 800 single-family homes and 240 low-income apartments, with about 400 children attending the 99th Street School next to the dump.

After reading the newspaper article about Love Canal in the spring of 1978, I became concerned about the health of my son, who was in kindergarten at the 99th Street School. Since moving into our house on 101st Street, my son, Michael, had been constantly ill. I came to believe that the school and playground were making him sick. Consequently, I asked the school board to transfer Michael to another public school, and they refused, stating that "such a transfer would set a bad precedent."

Receiving no help from the school board, city, or state representatives, I began going door to door with a petition to shut down the 99th Street School. The petition, I believed, would pressure the school board into investigating the chemical exposure risks to children and possibly even into closing the school. It became apparent, after only a few blocks of door knocking, that the entire neighborhood was sick. Men, women, and children suffered from many conditions—cancer, miscarriages, still-births, birth defects, and urinary tract diseases. The petition drive generated news coverage and helped residents come to the realization that a serious problem existed. The media attention and subsequent inquiries by residents prompted the New York State Department of Health (NYSDOH) to undertake environmental testing in homes closest to the canal.

On August 2, 1978, the NYSDOH declared a state of emergency at Love Canal, ordering closure of the 99th Street School, recommending that pregnant women and children under the age of two evacuate, and mandating that a cleanup plan be undertaken immediately. These pronouncements, based on the unsafe level of chemicals found in the air of 239 homes and the soils in yards located closest to the canal, were devastating to pregnant women and families with small children.

Other residents were panicked about the risk of disease to their three, five, and ten year olds—and themselves—pleading, "Our fetuses are our canaries and you are removing the canaries. Why are you leaving the rest of us here to die?" The health department, unable to justify their age-specific decisions scientifically, and Governor Carey, feeling tremendous pressure from the public, agreed on August 7 to evacuate all 239 families, regardless of the number or age of children in the households.

In October cleanup began on the dump site. A drainage trench was installed around the perimeter of the canal to catch waste that was permeating into the surrounding neighborhood. A clay cap was placed on top of the site to reduce water infiltration from rain or melting snow. Sewer lines and the creek to the north of the canal were also cleaned up. However, the waste that had migrated throughout the neighborhood and into the homes remained.

At that time, there were approximately 660 families living in the community who were not given the option to relocate. They continued to pressure the governor and federal authorities, including President Carter, to expand the evacuation area. A health study was conducted by volunteer scientists and community members, revealing that 56 percent of children born between 1974 and 1978 suffered birth defects. The miscarriage rate increased 300 percent among women who had moved to Love Canal. And urinary-tract disease had also increased 300 percent, with a great number of children being affected.

These results prompted the NYSDOH to issue a second evacuation order on February 8, 1979, for pregnant women and children under the age of two from all 660 families. As with the previous order, this too created great panic and fear among the remaining residents. Finally, on October 1, 1980, President Carter visited Niagara Falls to sign a bill authorizing funding to permanently relocate all families who wished to leave. All but 67 families moved out of the Love Canal neighborhood.

President Carter's decision, like Governor Carey's, was due partly to the public pressure generated during an election year. Love Canal Homeowners Association (LCHA) deliberately focused pressure on elected representatives to make the Love Canal crisis a campaign issue, protesting at political conventions and giving hundreds of interviews to the news media, always singling out candidates by name, and always asking for their positions on hazardous-waste issues—Love Canal specifically.

It is unfortunate that every action at Love Canal, from the first health study to the final evacuation, was taken for political reasons. Members of LCHA truly believe that if we hadn't assembled this large, strong citizen organization, we would still be living at Love Canal, with authorities still maintaining that there are no health problems. There are many reasons why the various levels of government did not want to evacuate the people in this community. These reasons include:

1. The expense incurred. Together, state and federal governments spent over $60 million on Love Canal, which was later repaid by Occidental Chemical through a government lawsuit.

2. The precedent that would be set by evacuating a neighborhood because of chemical exposures. At the time, there were an estimated 30–50,000 similar sites scattered across the nation.

3. The lack of peer-reviewed scientific studies. The scientific understanding of human health effects resulting from exposure to low-level chemicals had been based on adult workers exposed over a 40-hour workweek, while at Love Canal the threat was residential, involving pregnant women and children exposed to multiple chemicals 24 hours a day.

Eventually, the 239 homes closest to the canal were demolished and   *15* the southern sections of the neighborhood declared unsuitable for residential use. But in September 1988, the 200 homes in the northern section of Love Canal were declared "habitable," which should not be confused with "safe." This decision to move people back into Love Canal is an appalling idea that cannot be justified by legitimate scientific or technical data. These homes are still contaminated, as are the yards around the adjacent evacuated homes. The only separation between them and those still considered uninhabitable is a suburban street. Anyone can freely cross the street and walk through the abandoned sections of the neighborhood. In fact, children ride their bikes and play frequently among the abandoned homes. And 20,000 tons of waste still remain in the dump.

The world is a very different place now for families who lived through the Love Canal crisis. What was once taken for granted is no longer—that if you work hard, pay your taxes, vote on election days, and teach your children right from wrong, you can achieve the American Dream. Eyes were opened to the way our democracy works—and doesn't work. Former residents of this blue-collar community have come to see that corporate power and influence are what dictated the actions at Love Canal, not the health and welfare of citizens.

Each step in the events as they unfolded shocked and stunned the public. It was not conceivable to families that their government would lie or manipulate data and studies to protect corporate interests. It was difficult to grasp the reality—obvious, in retrospect—that corporations have more influence and rights than tax-paying citizens. This realization left us feeling alone, abandoned, and empty inside. Love Canal taught us that government will protect you from such poisoning only when you force it to.

If you think you're safe, think again. And, if you're ever in doubt about what a company is doing, or what government is telling you, talk with your neighbors, seek out the truth beyond the bland reassurances of the authorities, and don't be afraid to dig your heels in to protect your community. The number of children with cancer is increasing, as are the incidences of breast and prostate cancer in adults. Children suffer more today than ever before from birth defects, learning disabilities, attention-deficit disorders, and asthma. These diseases and adverse health problems are no longer located in someone else's backyard; they're in everyone's backyard, and in our food, water, and the air we breathe.

Over the past 20 years, the U.S. has come a long way in identifying buried wastes, cleaning up sites, reducing some air and water pollution, and cutting back on both industrial and household waste. We have cleaned up the rivers that once caught fire and removed the ugly barrels that sat in abandoned industrial sites or fields. We cleaned up what we can see—the obvious, the ugly—but there are deadly poisons invisible to the eye that remain in our everyday environment and food supply. The challenge for the next decade will be to eliminate the poisons we can't see, but that are evidenced in the state of our health, in the growing number of diseases in our society.

As we move forward to correct the pollution mistakes of the past, we   *20* are bound to uncover new information and new problems. Waste facilities like the one at Love Canal continue to be discovered—a national phenomenon that has created a flurry of communities organizing themselves to wage their own David and Goliath struggles. These urban and suburban neighborhoods and rural communities now make up the new grassroots movement for environmental justice. Their efforts are critical, but, like Love Canal, they are only first steps.

It will take a massive effort to move society from corporate domination, in which industry's rights to pollute and damage health and the environment supersede the public's right to live, work, and play in safety. This is a political fight. The science is already there, showing that people's health is at risk. To win, we will need to keep building the movement, networking with one another, planning, strategizing, and moving forward. Our children's futures, and those of their unborn children, are at stake.

Reading and Responding

1. What did you know about Love Canal before reading this article?
2. What do you think you should have known about Love Canal, and why?
3. How would you react to a discovery that where you live now—your apartment or house—was built over hazardous materials and that this knowledge was concealed from you? Write a paragraph explaining what you would be worried about, what you would be angry about, and what you would want done.

Working Together

1. Assuming that you never heard of Love Canal (or heard very little) before reading this article, what does your lack of knowledge say about American culture or human nature? Is your lack of knowledge typical?

What are the consequences of this lack of knowledge? Discuss these questions in your group.

2. In light of this article and the experience of Gibbs, respond to these frequently heard questions: "What good can I do? What difference can one person make?"

3. Gibbs says of the Love Canal crisis, "What was once taken for granted is no longer—that if you work hard, pay your taxes, vote on election days, and teach your children right from wrong, you can achieve the American Dream." Explain what Gibbs means. Do you agree or disagree, based on your own reading and experience? Conduct a group discussion.

4. As a group, consider what you think constitutes the property rights of the owner of a piece of ground. What do you think property owners are obligated to do or not do in terms of how they use their property? What are property owners obligated to do or not do before selling their land? Based on your discussion, write two principles for property ownership.

Rethinking and Rewriting

1. Develop your discussion from item 3 of "Working Together" into an essay. Agree or disagree with Gibbs and illustrate your point with your own experience or with library research. Answer the question, Do hard work and good citizenship necessarily pay off with the American dream?

2. Write an essay that reflects on anything—an idea, a belief, a fact—that you once took for granted but that you cannot take for granted any longer.

3. Write a research paper that illustrates Gibbs's claim that "corporations have more influence and rights than tax-paying citizens." Use another example besides the Love Canal disaster.

OUT OF YOUR CAR,
OFF YOUR HORSE

Wendell Berry

> *Wendell Berry lives on a small farm in Kentucky where he writes poems,*
> *stories, and scores of eloquent essays arguing for the balanced way of life that*
> *he himself lives. Among his many collections of essays are* The Unsettling
> of America *(1977) and* Home Economics *(1987). The following essay*
> *was first published in a 1991 issue of* Atlantic.

I. Properly speaking, global thinking is not possible. Those who have "thought globally" (and among them the most successful have been imperial governments and multinational corporations) have done so by means of simplifications too extreme and oppressive to merit the name of thought. Global thinkers have been, and will be, dangerous people. National thinkers tend to be dangerous also; we now have national thinkers in the northeastern United States who look upon Kentucky as a garbage dump.

II. Global thinking can only be statistical. Its shallowness is exposed by the least intention to do something. Unless one is willing to be destructive on a very large scale, one cannot do something except locally, in a small place. Global thinking can only do to the globe what a space satellite does to it: reduce it, make a bauble of it. Look at one of those photographs of half the earth taken from outer space, and see if you recognize your neighborhood. If you want to *see* where you are, you will have to get out of your space vehicle, out of your car, off your horse, and walk over the ground. On foot you will find that the earth is still satisfyingly large, and full of beguiling nooks and crannies.

III. If we could think locally, we would do far better than we are doing now. The right local questions and answers will be the right global ones. The Amish question "What will this do to our community?" tends toward the right answer for the world.

IV. If we want to put local life in proper relation to the globe, we must do so by imagination, charity, and forbearance, and by making local life as independent and self-sufficient as we can—not by the presumptuous abstractions of "global thought."

V. If we want to keep our thoughts and acts from destroying the globe, then we must see to it that we do not ask too much of the globe or of any part of it. To make sure that we do not ask too much, we must learn to live at home, as independently and self-sufficiently as we can. That   5 is the only way we can keep the land we are using, and its ecological limits, always in sight.

VI. The only sustainable city—and this, to me, is the indispensable ideal and goal—is a city in balance with its countryside: a city, that is, that would live off the *net* ecological income of its supporting region, paying as it goes all its ecological and human debts.

VII. The cities we now have are living off ecological principal, by economic assumptions that seem certain to destroy them. They do not live at home. They do not have their own supporting regions. They are out of balance with their supports, wherever on the globe their supports are.

VIII. The balance between city and countryside is destroyed by industrial machinery, "cheap" productivity in field and forest, and "cheap" transportation. Rome destroyed the balance with slave labor; we have destroyed it with "cheap" fossil fuel.

IX. Since the Civil War, perhaps, and certainly since the Second World War, the norms of productivity have been set by the fossil-fuel industries.

X. Geographically, the sources of the fossil fuels are rural. Techni-   10
cally, however, the production of these fuels is industrial and urban. The facts and integrities of local life, and the principle of community, are considered as little as possible, for to consider them would not be quickly profitable. Fossil fuels have always been produced at the expense of local ecosystems and of local human communities. The fossil-fuel economy is the industrial economy par excellence, and it assigns no value to local life, natural or human.

XI. When the industrial principles exemplified in fossil-fuel production are applied to field and forest, the results are identical: local life, both natural and human, is destroyed.

XII. Industrial procedures have been imposed on the countryside pretty much to the extent that country people have been seduced or forced into dependence on the money economy. By encouraging this dependence, corporations have increased their ability to rob the people of their property and their labor. The result is that a very small number of people now own all the usable property in the country, and workers are increasingly the hostages of their employers.

XIII. Our present "leaders"—the people of wealth and power—do not know what it means to take a place seriously: to think it worthy, for its own sake, of love and study and careful work. They cannot take any place seriously because they must be ready at any moment, by the terms of power and wealth in the modern world, to destroy any place.

XIV. Ecological good sense will be opposed by all the most powerful economic entities of our time, because ecological good sense requires the reduction or replacement of those entities. If ecological good sense is to prevail, it can do so only through the work and the will of the people and of the local communities.

XV. For this task our currently prevailing assumptions about knowl-edge, information, education, money, and political will are inadequate. All our institutions with which I am familiar have adopted the organizational patterns and the quantitative measures of the industrial corporations. *Both* sides of the ecological debate, perhaps as a consequence, are alarmingly abstract.

XVI. But abstraction, of course, is what is wrong. The evil of the industrial economy (capitalist or communist) is the abstractness inherent in its procedures—its inability to distinguish one place or person or creature from another. William Blake saw this two hundred years ago. Anyone can see it now in almost any of our common tools and weapons.

XVII. Abstraction is the enemy *wherever* it is found. The abstractions of sustainability can ruin the world just as surely as the abstractions of industrial economics. Local life may be as much endangered by "saving the planet" as by "conquering the world." Such a project calls for abstract purposes and central powers that cannot know, and so will destroy, the integrity of local nature and local community.

XVIII. In order to make ecological good sense for the planet, you must make ecological good sense locally. You can't act locally by thinking globally. If you want to keep your local acts from destroying the globe, you must think locally.

XIX. No one can make ecological good sense for the planet. Every-one can make ecological good sense locally, *if* the affection, the scale, the knowledge, the tools, and the skills are right.

XX. The right scale in work gives power to affection. When one works beyond the reach of one's love for the place one is working in, and for the things and creatures one is working with and among, then destruc-tion inevitably results. An adequate local culture, among other things, keeps work within the reach of love.

XXI. The question before us, then, is an extremely difficult one: How do we begin to remake, or to make, a local culture that will preserve our part of the world while we use it? We are talking here not just about a kind of knowledge that *involves* affection but also about a kind of knowledge that comes from or with affection—knowledge that is unavailable to the unaffectionate, and that is unavailable to anyone as what is called information.

XXII. What, for a start, might be the economic result of local affection? We don't know. Moreover, we are probably never going to know in any way that would satisfy the average dean or corporate executive. The ways of love tend to be secretive and, even to the lovers themselves, somewhat inscrutable.

XXIII. The real work of planet-saving will be small, humble, and humbling, and (insofar as it involves love) pleasing and rewarding. Its jobs will be too many to count, too many to report, too many to be publicly noticed or rewarded, too small to make anyone rich or famous.

XXIV. The great obstacle may be not greed but the modern hankering after glamour. A lot of our smartest, most concerned people want to come up with a big solution to a big problem. I don't think that planet-saving, if we take it seriously, can furnish employment to many such people.

XXV. When I think of the kind of worker the job requires, I think of Dorothy Day (if one can think of Dorothy Day herself, separate from the publicity that came as a result of her rarity), a person willing to go down and down into the daunting, humbling, almost hopeless local presence of the problem—to face the great problem one small life at a time.

XXVI. Some cities can never be sustainable, because they do not have a countryside around them, or near them, from which they can be sustained. New York City cannot be made sustainable, nor can Phoenix. Some cities in Kentucky or the Midwest, on the other hand, might reasonably hope to become sustainable.

XXVII. To make a sustainable city, one must begin somehow, and I think the beginning must be small and economic. A beginning could be made, for example, by increasing the amount of food bought from farmers in the local countryside by consumers in the city. As the food economy became more local, local farming would become more diverse; the farms would become smaller, more complex in structure, more productive; and some city people would be needed to work on the farms. Sooner or later, as a means of reducing expenses both ways, organic wastes from the city would go out to fertilize the farms of the supporting region; thus city people would have to assume an agricultural responsibility, and would be properly motivated to do so both by the wish to have a supply of excellent

food and by the fear of contaminating that supply. The increase of economic intimacy between a city and its sources would change minds (assuming, of course, that the minds in question would stay put long enough
to be changed). It would improve minds. The locality, by becoming partly
sustainable, would produce the thought it would need to become more
sustainable.

Reading and Responding

1. Mark the three propositions that are the clearest to you, that you like
   the best, or that seem the most powerful.
2. Mark the three propositions you don't understand, that you don't agree
   with, or that don't seem to fit for whatever reason.
3. Do a freewrite at the end of your first reading: Record anything in
   your mind at that moment—thoughts, images, questions, observations,
   experiences.

Working Together

1. Work to agree on the three propositions that seem to your group the
   best or most powerful. Then write a group paragraph that explains your
   rationale.
2. Arrange related propositions. Put them in categories and label the categories. How many categories are there? How are they connected?
3. Determine the logical relationships between these propositions, and insert transitional words and phrases between each of them. (Sample transition words and phrases include *that is, in other words, for example, on the
   other hand, to repeat*.)
4. Find a proposition that summarizes the theme for all the rest. Where is
   it positioned, and why do you think it is positioned there?
5. Which propositions (if any) could be deleted without taking away from
   the meaning? What do these propositions contribute to the whole?
6. What would you have to do to make this list of propositions into an
   essay? What would have to be added or deleted?

Rethinking and Rewriting

1. In an essay, discuss the effect on you as a reader of these separate and
   discrete units of meaning. How do they force you to read and reflect?
   What are the advantages and disadvantages of arranging ideas in this way?
2. Write a paper composed of twenty-seven propositions—on any subject.
   Arrange it exactly as Berry does this essay.
3. Write an essay that illustrates the idea that "Abstraction is the enemy
   wherever it is found." Draw from your own experience and reading,
   applying it to some particular subject or question.

4. Write an essay explaining how the notion presented in item 3 applies to the writing of papers. How is abstraction "the enemy" in writing?
5. Apply the following statement to your life right now, particularly in light of the amount of homework you have to do for school: "The right scale in work gives power to affection."
6. Use at least three readings from previous chapters in this book to illustrate the statement, "Both sides of the ecological debate are alarmingly abstract." Or use examples from recent or local newspapers, letters to the editor, and magazines.

PRINTING MONEY, MAKING CHANGE:
THE PROMISE OF LOCAL CURRENCIES

Susan Witt

> *Executive director of the E. F. Schumacher Society, Susan Witt founded the SHARE micro-credit program and administers the Community Land Trust in the southern Berkshires, a region in western Massachusetts. The article that follows appeared in the autumn 1998 issue of* Orion Afield.

On May 30, 1998, the *New York Times* Metro Section carried a front-page story about Thread City Bread, a local currency issued in Willimantic, Connecticut. Within a few days CNBC, "ABC World News Tonight," "Voice of America," Fox News in Boston, *Northeast Magazine,* as well as several regional papers, TV and radio stations had swooped into Willimantic to interview selectpersons, bankers, and shop owners about their home-made money.

Popular during the Great Depression of the 1930s when federal dollars were in short supply, local currencies are experiencing a revival in North America, but for new reasons. In the 1990s small towns and inner-city neighborhoods are discovering that local scrip helps to define regional trading areas, educate consumers about local resources, and build community. Willimantic joins the more than 65 different places in the United States and Canada where you can use colorful bills with names like Dillo Hours and Barter Bucks for anything from buying groceries to having your hair cut or your computer repaired.

It started in 1989 when Frank Tortoriello, the owner of a popular restaurant in the southern Berkshires of Massachusetts, was rejected for a bank loan to finance a move to a new location. In a small community word spreads quickly. All of us at the E. F. Schumacher Society office frequented The Deli. We recognized that Frank had a committed clientele who could afford to take a risk to keep the cherished luncheon spot in business. So, we suggested that Frank issue "Deli Dollars" as a self-financing technique. Customers could purchase these notes during a month of sale and redeem them over a one-year period once The Deli had moved to its new location.

Martha Shaw, a local artist, donated the design for the notes, which were dated and read "redeemable for meals up to a value of ten dollars." Frank sold ten-dollar notes for eight dollars and in 30 days had raised $5,000. Over the next year, Frank repaid the loan, in sandwiches and soup, rather than hard-to-come-by federal dollars. Berkshire Farm Preserve Notes, Monterey General Store Notes, and Kintaro Notes soon followed in what began to look like a movement.

Paul Glover of Ithaca, New York, heard about Berkshire notes on the radio in 1991. He liked the idea of a hand-to-hand currency that let   5 consumers support local businesses through prepurchase of products, but he wanted to broaden the concept. Instead of each business issuing its own notes, why couldn't the community as a whole issue a local scrip? To learn how this might be done, he spent a week researching the history and theory of regional scrip at the E. F. Schumacher Library. He engaged in long discussions with one of the Society's founders, Robert Swann, who has spent a lifetime promoting local currencies.

Back in Ithaca, Paul talked to those who were running small businesses out of their homes. As is typical in rural areas, many people support themselves not with one $25,000-a-year job, but with five $5,000-a-year cottage industries. They bake pies, repair lawn mowers, do landscaping, paint houses, bookkeep, tutor, and dog sit. Most of these businesses are undercapitalized and underpublicized and would benefit from more customers. Paul asked various owners if they would agree to accept a local scrip for their goods and services. With nothing to lose, people signed up.

Everyone initially enrolled was "issued" 40 dollars worth of local scrip, denominated in units of hourly labor. Each HOUR note was valued at ten federal dollars—a fair hourly wage for the region. Paul printed several denominations of HOUR notes with pictures celebrating Ithaca's natural wonders, children, and famous persons. Heat-sensitive ink, high-rag-content paper, serial numbers, and embossing helped prevent counterfeiting. *HOURTown,* a free newsprint paper listing businesses that accept Ithaca HOURS, was printed, featuring stories of successful exchanges to draw in new participants.

Behind the scenes, Paul is always at work to keep HOURS circulating. He finds out which businesses have too many HOURS in their till, then sits down with the owners to recommend ways of expanding their HOUR usage. Paul knows which carpenter among the HOUR traders does the finest carpentry work, knows if the farmer down the road has a reputation for delivering carefully washed lettuce, and knows if the guy with the rototiller will get the job done before the weekend.

Largely as a result of this persistent attention to detail, $65,000 in Ithaca HOURS are in circulation today, representing several million dollars in trade. An informal advisory board, the Municipal Reserve, keeps an eye on scrip circulation, deciding whether and how more should be issued. There are 370 area businesses—contractors, farmers, restaurants, movie theaters, masseurs, even the local credit union—that now accept partial payment in Ithaca HOURS. In fact, when bidding the contract for improvements to their new offices, Bill Meyers, the president of Alternatives Federal Credit Union, specified that the contractor take partial payment in Ithaca HOURS. The message was loud and clear: nonlocals need not apply. Meyers explained that the winning contractor became of necessity a promoter of Ithaca HOURS to subcontractors, further accelerating trade in scrip and adding new businesses to the growing list of participants.

The Ithaca HOURS Hometown Money Starter Kit has inspired *10* groups around the country, who have worked to develop currencies that are right for their particular communities. For Paul Glover and other visionaries of the movement, local scrip is much more than a device for revitalizing the local economy. It provides a direct way to respond to the alienation we experience in an expanding global economy, and to restore the possibility of regional economies based on social and ecological principles.

In a simple barter economy, production methods are highly visible. The value of the carrots we offer in trade is directly linked to memories of hoeing in the garden, of building the compost pile, and of waiting for the rain after planting. And though our understanding of the cordwood for which we are bartering is probably not as detailed, still we have seen our neighbor's progress as he split and stacked the wood from the ash tree. Barter transactions link us inextricably to a particular place and time.

Money, for all its many obvious advantages, introduces an element of abstractness into the process. This was less so in the past, when real goods were used as currency, or to back or denominate units of currency. Value was still derived from the amount of labor applied to natural resources. When a Tibetan herdsman traded a brick of tea (once used as currency in Tibet) for his lamb, he could picture tea brewing in a bucket over a fire in a yurt, and could imagine the days it took to cultivate the tea plant on its mountainside plantation and the hours spent bending to gather the tiny new tea leaves. He could compare in his mind the value of a generalized brick of tea to that of the lamb in his arms.

Most of today's national currencies are no longer commodity-based. They are pegged to each other, or tied in a vague way to the general productivity of their country of origin. At the end of the twentieth century, money has become altogether abstracted from our daily experience. We talk of earning six percent interest, but have no picture of "what our money is doing tonight"—whether it is building wheelbarrows in Brazil, growing corn on chemically fertilized land in Iowa, or making shoes in a crowded factory in Thailand.

One of the crucial tasks of the new century will be to shape our economic system so that environmental and social safeguards are built into its design. Theoretical knowledge of poor working conditions and toxic dumping will not necessarily stimulate a change in consumer habits. When we can picture manufacturing processes clearly, because they're familiar, and involve our community's human and natural resources, we'll then be compelled to demand secure conditions for workers and nonpolluting methods of production.

By intentionally narrowing our choices of consumer goods to those 15 locally made, local currencies allow us to know more fully the stories of items purchased—stories that include the human beings who made them and the minerals, rivers, plants, and animals that were used to form them. Such stories, shaped by real life experience, work in the imagination to foster responsible consumer choices and re-establish a commitment to the community. In this sense, local currencies become a tool not only for economic development but for cultural renewal.

This multilayered nature of local currencies has captivated and energized an informal network of practitioners who regularly communicate via e-mail and articles, and who convene periodically at conferences, where they share successes, problems, and new ideas. The 1996 and 1997 Decentralist Conferences sponsored by the E. F. Schumacher Society drew a strong showing of activists from around North America. Pioneers of the movement came to give workshops—people like Paul Glover, Diana McCourt, and Jane Wilson, founders of Womanshare in New York City, and Tim Mitchell and Gurunam Kaur Khalsa of Valley Trade Connection in Massachusetts. George Washington University law professor Lewis Solomon provided legal expertise (to the frequently asked question, are these currencies legal, the answer is, yes), and Australian businessman Shann Turnbull explained how local currencies can be used to finance appropriately scaled businesses in developing countries. Informal discussions lasted late into the night, as participants struggled over such practical questions as how to determine the optimum amount of scrip in circulation.

In February of 1998 in San Francisco, Jim Masters of the Center for Community Futures held a conference that introduced social service organizations to the possibilities of integrating local currencies into their programs. Jim, who has been working with government-funded social service agencies since the Johnson Administration, felt intuitively that in a time of collapsing public budgets, local currencies offer a powerful and creative tool for building sustainable communities. The conference brought representatives of social service groups from Chicago to Honolulu together with local-currency activists and experts in nonscrip programs of local exchange. Edgar Cahn spoke of how Time Dollars, which are issued by nonprofit organizations to those providing volunteer services, could be utilized to foster a climate of neighbor helping neighbor. Canadian Michael Linton explained the Local Economic Trading System (LETS), which has no hand-to-hand scrip but rather uses a centralized computer to keep track of exchanges.

The social service providers were especially attracted to the job-creating potential of HOUR systems and had lots of questions. As managers of large organizations, they know what it takes to sustain a successful program. They wondered how a local-currency system could support professional management to oversee long-term operations. All three conferences devoted a significant amount of discussion time to this question, and to the related one, how to involve more mainstream businesses in regional scrip trading. The future direction of the local-currency movement will be shaped by developments in these areas.

The small home-business owners who first enroll in HOUR programs may be the folks most in need of a revitalized local economy, but they lack the income margin to pay for the management these programs require. The coordination for most HOUR programs has been carried out by volunteers. As a result, while they are often showered with media attention, the majority of local-currency systems do not have the staff and financial capability to meet their full potential.

Some local-currency systems issue a small percentage of the total   *20* amount of scrip in circulation to make a token payment to administrators. Ithaca HOURS keeps a tight cap at five percent. But as a general policy, issuing for administrative purposes can jeopardize the soundness of the issue. Administration is more appropriately paid from fees for service. Other local-currency groups are being formed as programs of existing organizations, using administrative structures that are already in place. In Calgary, Alberta, for example, the Bow Chinook Barter Community formed out of a committee of the Arusha Centre and has received substantial organizational funding from the Calgary United Way, which views the program as a means for creating jobs. Other groups are looking to affiliate with established local economic-development organizations.

Several large social service agencies have embraced local currencies as in-house projects, since changes in federal welfare laws are forcing them to find employment for clients. Unwilling to take single mothers from their homes and place them in low-paying fast-food service jobs, the agencies use local currencies to develop opportunities for home businesses, thereby keeping neighborhoods healthy and mothers at home when their children return from school. In Philadelphia, Resources for Human Development, a nonprofit organization contracted to distribute state and federal government assistance funds, has invested significant time and resources to issue Equal Dollars. In North Carolina, Suzanne Kinder coordinates the DEPC Dollar program of the Down East Partnership for Children. Clients are paid for work at a number of nonprofit organizations in DEPC Dollars, which can be spent for donated food, clothing, toys, and other items in the DEPC store.

While these agencies have been effective, they are constrained by federal tax code to serve only their low-income clientele. If they wish to continue building support for the newly formed businesses created through their efforts, they will need to evolve their local-currency programs to include the banking community, main street businesses, and professional service providers. Ultimately it will take a coalition of nonprofit groups and for-profit businesses working together to form the kind of regionally based, democratically structured organization that can provide long-term management of a local-currency program. In such a model, administrative costs would be paid from membership fees. Broad usage of scrip would assure that wealth is recirculated within the community where it is generated, supporting a diverse group of regional producers. Several groups are already laying the groundwork for these developments.

In the southern Berkshire region of Massachusetts, we are lucky to have a healthy local banking community with a strong record of community reinvestment and partnership. Of the six banks operating in the region, five remain locally owned. It was a Berkshire banker who came forward with a proposal to involve a broad segment of the established business community in the issue of a local scrip. The program would be based on a simple ten-percent discount note. Consumers would come to their favorite bank and purchase 100 "BerkShares" for 90 federal dollars. As long as the BerkShares remain in circulation they would be traded at full dollar value, encouraging merchants to seek locally produced goods for their shops and thus opening new local markets for small home-based businesses. Bank participation would make it easier for many businesses to begin trading in local scrip. At the end of the day, merchants would simply deposit excess scrip at 90 cents on the dollar.

The increased volume of business brought about by a fully operational local scrip program would more than offset the ten-percent discount. With a significant base of participants, the system could charge businesses a yearly fee for service and so raise sufficient funds to pay for professional management. Home-based businesses might join at a different fee schedule. The system could be run by a committee of the nonprofit Chamber of Commerce with representation from various sectors of the community.

In Toronto author Joy Kogawa and merchant Susan Braun are spearheading a similar initiative that would combine the bank–issued ten-percent discount note with the HOUR model. The project has already won significant merchant support in the thriving St. Lawrence neighborhood.   25

The BerkShare and Toronto projects are just two examples of programs building on the compelling Ithaca model. In the future, local currencies could be issued solely through productive loans, which introduce into the economy new goods whose value is in excess of the loan itself. A familiar example would be a farmer who receives a loan in the spring to purchase seeds that will yield a bountiful crop of vegetables in the fall. The interest rate for such loans could be zero percent, encouraging local manufacturing, plants that generate renewable energy, and other small enterprises that are not currently economically competitive. Eventually, a nonprofit issuer could untie the local scrip from the federal dollar, establishing a local backing such as cordwood, or a basket of commodities—corn, soy beans, and wheat, for instance—as was done in Exeter, New Hampshire, in the 1970s. In such a scenario, currency would retain a constant local value related to a natural resource, making visible once again the connection between the health of the local economy and the health of the land.

Such ideas might have seemed utopian until just a few years ago, when the HOURS programs and other alternative currencies began to gather momentum. Today when local-currency activists get together, there is no mistaking the positive dynamic at work. The movement has all the energy, idealism, and mobility of young adulthood—still experimenting to find the right form, not afraid to take risks, able to alter direction as needed, and determined to change the economic system to reflect deeply held social and environmental values.

Reading and Responding

1. In one or two paragraphs, explain the concept of local currency.
2. Explain the following statement in one or two paragraphs: "Money, for all its many obvious advantages, introduces an element of abstractness into the process."
3. Write a list of at least three specific questions, based on Witt's article, to bring to class.

Working Together

1. Compare your questions from item 3 of "Reading and Responding" and answer them, as a group, as best you can.
2. As a group, compare the barter system and the local currency system. Discuss the advantages and disadvantages of each system.
3. As a group, write a paragraph to explain how a local scrip program can restore the "connection between the health of the local economy and the health of the land."
4. Sketch a poster or a one-page promotional brochure that explains the idea of local currency to people who are not familiar with the concept.

Rethinking and Rewriting

1. Write a paper that proposes a local currency for your campus or your hometown. Explain how it would work and argue for its advantages.
2. Find out more about local scrip programs and modern barter systems. Write a research report that demonstrates what you've found. You might begin by visiting <www.schumachersociety.org>.

THE CLAN OF
ONE-BREASTED WOMEN

Terry Tempest Williams

> *Terry Tempest Williams lives in Salt Lake City, Utah, where she is Naturalist-in-Residence at the Utah Museum of Natural History. As an essayist, Williams has written several books in which she ponders the spiritual beauty of the natural world. Her books include* Refuge *(1991) and, more recently,* Desert Quartet *(1995). The following essay is from* Refuge.

I belong to a Clan of One-breasted Women. My mother, my grand-mothers, and six aunts have all had mastectomies. Seven are dead. The two who survive have just completed rounds of chemotherapy and radiation.

I've had my own problems: two biopsies for breast cancer and a small tumor between my ribs diagnosed as "a border-line malignancy."

This is my family history.

Most statistics tell us breast cancer is genetic, hereditary, with rising percentages attached to fatty diets, childlessness, or becoming pregnant after thirty. What they don't say is living in Utah may be the greatest hazard of all.

We are a Mormon family with roots in Utah since 1847. The word-of-wisdom, a religious doctrine of health, kept the women in my family aligned with good foods: no coffee, no tea, tobacco, or alcohol. For the most part, these women were finished having their babies by the time they were thirty. And only one faced breast cancer prior to 1960. Traditionally, as a group of people, Mormons have a low rate of cancer.

Is our family a cultural anomaly? The truth is we didn't think about it. Those who did, usually the men, simply said, "bad genes." The women's attitude was stoic. Cancer was part of life. On February 16, 1971, the eve before my mother's surgery, I accidently picked up the telephone and overheard her ask my grandmother what she could expect.

"Diane, it is one of the most spiritual experiences you will ever encounter."

I quietly put down the receiver.

Two days later, my father took my three brothers and me to the hospital to visit her. She met us in the lobby in a wheelchair. No bandages were visible. I'll never forget her radiance, the way she held herself in a purple velour robe and how she gathered us around her.

"Children, I am fine. I want you to know I felt the arms of God around me."

We believed her. My father cried. Our mother, his wife, was thirty-eight years old.

Two years ago, after my mother's death from cancer, my father and I were having dinner together. He had just returned from St. George where his construction company was putting in natural gas lines for towns in southern Utah. He spoke of his love for the country: the sandstoned landscape, bare-boned and beautiful. He had just finished hiking the Kolob trail in Zion National Park. We got caught up in reminiscing, recalling with fondness our walk up Angle's Landing on his fiftieth birthday and the years our family had vacationed there. This was a remembered landscape where we had been raised.

Over dessert, I shared a recurring dream of mine. I told my father that for years, as long as I could remember, I saw this flash of light in the night in the desert. That this image had so permeated my being, I could not venture south without seeing it again, on the horizon, illuminating buttes and mesas.

"You did see it," he said.

"Saw what?" I asked, a bit tentative.   15

"The bomb. The cloud. We were driving home from Riverside, California. You were sitting on your mother's lap. She was pregnant. In fact, I remember the date, September 7, 1957. We had just gotten out of the Service. We were driving north, past Las Vegas. It was an hour or so before dawn, when this explosion went off. We not only heard it, but felt it. I thought the oil tanker in front of us had blown up. We pulled over and suddenly, rising from the desert floor, we saw it, clearly, this golden-stemmed cloud, the mushroom. The sky seemed to vibrate with an eerie pink glow. Within a few minutes, a light ash was raining on the car."

I stared at my father. This was new information to me.

"I thought you knew that," my father said. "It was a common occurrence in the fifties."

It was at this moment I realized the deceit I had been living under. Children growing up in the American Southwest, drinking contaminated milk from contaminated cows, even from the contaminated breasts of their mother, my mother—members, years later, of the Clan of One-breasted Women.

It is a well-known story in the Desert West, "The Day We Bombed   20 Utah," or perhaps, "The Years We Bombed Utah."[1] Above ground atomic testing in Nevada took place from January 27, 1951, through July 11, 1962. Not only were the winds blowing north, covering "low use segments of the population" with fallout and leaving sheep dead in their tracks, but the climate was right.[2] The United States of the 1950s was red, white, and blue. The Korean War was raging. McCarthyism was rampant. Ike was it and the Cold War was hot. If you were against nuclear testing, you were for a Communist regime.

---

1. Fuller, John G., *The Day We Bombed Utah* (New York: New American Library, 1984).
2. Discussion on March 14, 1988, with Carole Gallagher, photographer and author, *Nuclear Towns: The Secret War in the American Southwest,* Doubleday, 1990.

Much has been written about this "American nuclear tragedy." Public health was secondary to national security. The Atomic Energy Commissioner, Thomas Murray, said, "Gentlemen, we must not let anything interfere with this series of tests, nothing."[3]

Again and again, the American public was told by its government, in spite of burns, blisters, and nausea, "It has been found that the tests may be conducted with adequate assurance of safety under conditions prevailing at the bombing reservations."[4] Assuaging public fears was simply a matter of public relations. "Your best action," an Atomic Energy Commission booklet read, "is not to be worried about fallout." A news release typical of the times stated, "We find no basis for concluding that harm to any individual has resulted from radioactive fallout."[5]

On August 30, 1979, during Jimmy Carter's presidency, a suit was filed entitled "Irene Allen vs. the United States of America." Mrs. Allen was the first to be alphabetically listed with twenty-four test cases, representative of nearly 1200 plaintiffs seeking compensation from the United States government for cancers caused from nuclear testing in Nevada.

Irene Allen lived in Hurricane, Utah. She was the mother of five children and had been widowed twice. Her first husband with their two oldest boys had watched the tests from the roof of the local high school. He died of leukemia in 1956. Her second husband died of pancreatic cancer in 1978.

In a town meeting conducted by Utah Senator Orrin Hatch, shortly   25
before the suit was filed, Mrs. Allen said, "I am not blaming the government, I want you to know that, Senator Hatch. But I thought if my testimony could help in any way so this wouldn't happen again to any of the generations coming up after us . . . I am really happy to be here this day to bear testimony of this."[6]

God-fearing people. This is just one story in an anthology of thousands.

On May 10, 1984, Judge Bruce S. Jenkins handed down his opinion. Ten of the plaintiffs were awarded damages. It was the first time a federal court had determined that nuclear tests had been the cause of cancers. For the remaining fourteen test cases, the proof of causation was not sufficient. In spite of the split decision, it was considered a landmark ruling.[7] It was not to remain so for long.

In April, 1987, the 10th Circuit Court of Appeals overturned Judge Jenkins' ruling on the basis that the United States was protected from suit

---

3. Szasz, Ferenc M., "Downwind From the Bomb," *Nevada Historical Society Quarterly,* Fall, 1987 Vol. XXX, No. 3, p. 185.
4. Fradkin, Philip L., *Fallout* (Tucson: University of Arizona Press, 1989), 98.
5. Ibid., 109.
6. Town meeting held by Senator Orrin Hatch in St. George, Utah, April 17, 1979, transcript, 26–28.
7. Fradkin, Op. cit., 228.

by the legal doctrine of sovereign immunity, the centuries-old idea from England in the days of absolute monarchs.[8]

In January, 1988, the Supreme Court refused to review the Appeals Court decision. To our court system, it does not matter whether the United States Government was irresponsible, whether it lied to its citizens or even that citizens died from the fallout of nuclear testing. What matters is that our government is immune. "The King can do no wrong."

In Mormon culture, authority is respected, obedience is revered, and independent thinking is not. I was taught as a young girl not to "make waves" or "rock the boat."

"Just let it go—" my mother would say. "You know how you feel, that's what counts."

For many years, I did just that—listened, observed, and quietly formed my own opinions within a culture that rarely asked questions because they had all the answers. But one by one, I watched the women in my family die common, heroic deaths. We sat in waiting rooms hoping for good news, always receiving the bad. I cared for them, bathed their scarred bodies and kept their secrets. I watched beautiful women become bald as cytoxan, cisplatin and adriamycin were injected into their veins. I held their foreheads as they vomited green-black bile and I shot them with morphine when the pain became inhuman. In the end, I witnessed their last peaceful breaths, becoming a midwife to the rebirth of their souls. But the price of obedience became too high.

The fear and inability to question authority that ultimately killed rural communities in Utah during atmospheric testing of atomic weapons was the same fear I saw being held in my mother's body. Sheep. Dead sheep. The evidence is buried.

I cannot prove that my mother, Diane Dixon Tempest, or my grandmothers, Lettie Romney Dixon and Kathryn Blackett Tempest, along with my aunts contracted cancer from nuclear fallout in Utah. But I can't prove they didn't.

My father's memory was correct, the September blast we drove through in 1957 was part of Operation Plumbbob, one of the most intensive series of bomb tests to be initiated. The flash of light in the night in the desert I had always thought was a dream developed into a family nightmare. It took fourteen years, from 1957 to 1971, for cancer to show up in my mother—the same time, Howard L. Andrews, an authority on radioactive fallout at the National Institutes of Health, says radiation cancer requires to become evident.[9] The more I learn about what it means to be a "downwinder," the more questions I drown in.

_____

8. U.S. vs. Allen, 816 Federal Reporter, 2d/1417 (10th Circuit Court 1987), cert. denied, 108 S. CT. 694 (1988).
9. Fradkin, Op. cit., 116.

What I do know, however, is that as a Mormon woman of the fifth generation of "Latter-Day-Saints," I must question everything, even if it means losing my faith, even if it means becoming a member of a border tribe among my own people. Tolerating blind obedience in the name of patriotism or religion ultimately takes our lives.

When the Atomic Energy Commission described the country north of the Nevada Test Site as "virtually uninhabited desert terrain," my family members were some of the "virtual uninhabitants."

One night, I dreamed [about] women from all over the world circling a blazing fire in the desert. They spoke of change, of how they hold the moon in their bellies and wax and wane with its phases. They mocked at the presumption of even-tempered beings and made promises that they would never fear the witch inside themselves. The women danced wildly as sparks broke away from the flames and entered the night sky as stars.

And they sang a song given to them by Shoshoni grandmothers:

> *Ah ne nah, nah*
> *nin nah nah—*
> *Ah ne nah, nah*
> *nin nah nah—*
> *Nyaga mutzi*
> *oh ne nay—*
> *Nyaga mutzi*
> *oh ne nay—*[10]

The women danced and drummed and sang for weeks, preparing   40
themselves for what was to come. They would reclaim the desert for the sake of their children, for the sake of the land.

A few miles downwind from the fire circle, bombs were being tested. Rabbits felt the tremors. Their soft leather pads on paws and feet recognized the shaking sands while the roots of mesquite and sage were smoldering. Rocks were hot from the inside out and dust devils hummed unnaturally. And each time there was another nuclear test, ravens watched the desert heave. Stretch marks appeared. The land was losing its muscle.

The women couldn't bear it any longer. They were mothers. They had suffered labor pains but always under the promise of birth. The red hot pains beneath the desert promised death only as each bomb became a stillborn. A contract had been broken between human beings and the land.

---

10. This song was sung by the Western Shoshone women as they crossed the line at the Nevada Test Site on March 18, 1988, as part of their "Reclaim the Land" action. The translation they gave was: "Consider the rabbits how gently they walk on the earth. Consider the rabbits how gently they walk on the earth. We remember them. We can walk gently also. We remember them. We can walk gently also."

A new contract was being drawn by the women who understood the fate of the earth as their own.

Under the cover of darkness, ten women slipped under the barbed wire fence and entered the contaminated country. They were trespassing. They walked toward the town of Mercury in moonlight, taking their cues from coyote, kit fox, antelope squirrel, and quail. They moved quietly and deliberately through the maze of Joshua trees. When a hint of daylight appeared they rested, drinking tea and sharing their rations of food. The women closed their eyes. The time had come to protest with the heart, that to deny one's genealogy with the earth was to commit treason against one's soul.

At dawn, the women draped themselves in mylar, wrapping long streamers of silver plastic around their arms to blow in the breeze. They wore clear masks that became the faces of humanity. And when they arrived on the edge of Mercury, they carried all the butterflies of a summer day in their wombs. They paused to allow their courage to settle.

The town which forbids pregnant women and children to enter because of radiation risks to their health was asleep. The women moved through the streets as winged messengers, twirling around each other in slow motion, peeking inside homes and watching the easy sleep of men and women. They were astonished by such stillness and periodically would utter a shrill note or low cry just to verify life. 45

The residents finally awoke to what appeared as strange apparitions. Some simply stared. Others called authorities, and in time, the women were apprehended by wary soldiers dressed in desert fatigues. They were taken to a white, square building on the other edge of Mercury. When asked who they were and why they were there, the women replied, "We are mothers and we have come to reclaim the desert for our children."

The soldiers arrested them. As the ten women were blindfolded and handcuffed, they began singing:

> You can't forbid us everything
> You can't forbid us to think—
> You can't forbid our tears to flow
> And you can't stop the songs that we sing.

The women continued to sing louder and louder, until they heard the voices of their sisters moving across the mesa.

> Ah ne nah, nah
> nin nah nah—
> Ah ne nah, nah
> nin nah nah—
> Nyaga mutzi
> oh ne nay—
> Nyaga mutzi
> oh ne nay—

"Call for re-enforcement," one soldier said.

"We have," interrupted one woman. "We have—and you have no   50
idea of our numbers."

On March 18, 1988, I crossed the line at the Nevada Test Site and
was arrested with nine other Utahns for trespassing on military lands. They
are still conducting nuclear tests in the desert. Ours was an act of civil
disobedience. But as I walked toward the town of Mercury, it was more
than a gesture of peace. It was a gesture on behalf of the Clan of One-
breasted Women.

As one officer cinched the handcuffs around my wrists, another
frisked my body. She found a pen and a pad of paper tucked inside my left
boot.

"And these?" she asked sternly.

"Weapons," I replied.

Our eyes met. I smiled. She pulled the leg of my trousers back over   55
my boot.

"Step forward, please," she said as she took my arm.

We were booked under an afternoon sun and bussed to Tonapah,
Nevada. It was a two-hour ride. This was familiar country to me. The
Joshua trees standing their ground had been named by my ancestors who
believed they looked like prophets pointing west to the promised land.
These were the same trees that bloomed each spring, flowers appearing
like white flames in the Mojave. And I recalled a full moon in May when
my mother and I had walked among them, flushing out mourning doves
and owls.

The bus stopped short of town. We were released. The officials
thought it was a cruel joke to leave us stranded in the desert with no way
to get home. What they didn't realize is that we were home, soul-centered
and strong, women who recognized the sweet smell of sage as fuel for our
spirits.

Reading and Responding

1. When you hear the word *cancer,* what comes to mind? Freewrite about
   this for half a page or so.
2. When you hear the word *radiation,* what comes to mind? Freewrite
   about this for half a page or so.

Working Together

1. In order to get your group discussion rolling, start by individually writing one sentence about the experience of reading this selection; then
   read your sentences aloud. Once you've heard each person, what conclusions can you begin to draw about how your group was affected by
   this piece? Make a list of the issues or reactions that stay in your mind
   after you've finished reading.

2. As a group, discuss what surprised you in this selection. What information was entirely new or startling to you? Make a list of these things.
3. As a group, decide whether you agree with the decision of the 10th Circuit Court of Appeals to affirm that the United States government cannot be sued. Assume that you're the Supreme Court and you've agreed to review the appeals court decision. What are the major issues of the case? How would you vote?

Rethinking and Rewriting

1. Write your opinion regarding *Irene Allen vs. the United States of America*. Assume that you're a Supreme Court judge and you're either going to uphold the appeals court decision or you're going to overturn it.
2. Assume that you are Terry Tempest Williams—that her family history is your family history and that her medical history is your medical history. Write an open letter to the Supreme Court explaining why you feel so passionately that the Court should agree to reconsider the appeals court decision. Make sure that your letter makes clear all that you feel is at stake.
3. Look at how this essay ends. Then argue that the protest action that Williams took was foolish, that it accomplished nothing. Or argue that her action was significant and important. Either way, explain carefully.
4. Explain how a case can be made that many cancers are caused by human actions that alter our environment, often in ways that we do not fully grasp. Include in your discussion some mention of the way that cancer has touched your own family or friends.

THE IDEA OF A GARDEN

TRAVELING THROUGH THE DARK

William Stafford

> *William Stafford was Oregon's poet laureate and was much loved through-out the country. His many books of poems include* Traveling through the Dark, *winner of the 1962 National Book Award. In the following poem Stafford suggests that we cannot predict when we might be called on to take action, or what action we might take.*

Traveling through the dark I found a deer
dead on the edge of the Wilson River road.
It is usually best to roll them into the canyon:
that road is narrow; to swerve might make more dead.

By glow of the tail-light I stumbled back of the car   5
and stood by the heap, a doe, a recent killing;
she had stiffened already, almost cold.
I dragged her off; she was large in the belly.

My fingers touching her side brought me the reason—
her side was warm; her fawn lay there waiting,   10
alive, still, never to be born.
Beside that mountain road I hesitated.

The car aimed ahead its lowered parking lights;
under the hood purred the steady engine.
I stood in the glare of the warm exhaust turning red;   15
around our group I could hear the wilderness listen.

I thought hard for us all—my only swerving—,
then pushed her over the edge into the river.

Reading and Responding

1. Imagine this poem rewritten as prose—the line breaks taken out and the sentences arranged in one or two paragraphs. How would it read? Would any particular lines or phrases stand out as poetic?
2. Which lines stand out as especially "unpoetic"? Why? What do *poetic* and *unpoetic* mean, anyway?
3. What relationship does this poem have to the other selections in this chapter? How does it convey "practicing knowledge"? Freewrite an

answer, and don't worry if you start by saying "I don't know" or "I'm not sure."

Working Together

Here are several possible interpretations of this poem. Divide the class into groups, and have each group take an interpretation, finding details in the poem to support it.

- The poem is about the inevitable conflict between technology and the natural world, a conflict that always results in the destruction of nature.
- The poem is about the poet's guilt, his struggling with an insolvable moral problem.
- The poem is about the poet's midlife crisis.
- The poem is about the moral dilemma of abortion.
- The poem isn't about any of these other things; it's just about pushing a deer over the edge of the canyon.

Rethinking and Rewriting

1. Write an essay about a difficult, insolvable moral choice—some decision you felt you had to make at the time but that still troubles you, still feels unresolved.
2. Write an essay that speculates about Stafford's use of the phrase "my only swerving" in this poem. What is this "swerving," and how does it explain (or not explain) the action in the last line?
3. Tell the story that this poem reveals, but tell it as though it actually happened to you and you actually did it all. That is, tell the story using *I*. As you tell the story—your story—include any useful commentary about what you were thinking or feeling at the time (that night) and what you feel now.
4. Write an essay arguing that learning to read poetry is good training for the critical thinking required in all reading—and in life.

RETURNING THE NATIVES
Bringing Endangered Species Back to the Wild Involves More than Just Opening a Cage Door

Don Stap

Don Stap is the author of A Parrot without a Name: The Search for the Last Unknown Birds on Earth *(1990) and a collection of poetry,* Letter of the End of Winter *(1987). The essay that follows was published in a 1996 issue of* Audubon.

For three centuries, by way of neglect and persecution, we have driven hundreds of species of plants and animals from the regions they once inhabited, reducing many to remnant populations so small and scattered that we can represent them with pins on a map. Now, in these late years of the 20th century, we are trying to put some of them back where they belong. Reestablishing a plant or an animal in parts of its former range is a biologically complex and—in the United States at least—a bureaucratically convoluted process. A species slide toward extinction often has a glacial momentum. For those involved, the biology of fixing what's broken in an ecological system must some days have a nightmarish confusion about it, as if they are trying to reassemble a pocket watch dropped in a darkened room, with the tiny gears and springs spilled out—they know time is running out, but without the watch they can only guess how quickly.

Reintroducing a species to its historical range is the most challenging of all the multifaceted actions that have sprung from the Endangered Species Act of 1973, which mandates the use of "all methods and procedures which are necessary to bring any endangered species or threatened species to the point at which the measures provided pursuant to this Act are no longer necessary"—in other words, until the species is no longer threatened. The U.S. Fish and Wildlife Service, charged with preparing a recovery plan for each federally listed species, develops its reintroduction programs primarily for species with populations so few in number or limited in range that they might be destroyed by a single catastrophic event. In the well-publicized cases of the black-footed ferret and the California condor in the late 1980s, the provisions of the act were taken to their extreme: The few remaining individuals from a wild population deemed too small to be self-sustaining were removed from the wild, and biologists, with not much more than Noah had to work with, regenerated the population in captivity, then began reestablishing it in its native habitat. By contrast, two of the earliest and most successful projects, reintroducing the bald eagle and the peregrine falcon, had sufficient healthy populations to draw from. Both species had been eliminated from large portions of their range primarily because of the pesticide DDT; but in the 1970s, after DDT was banned, Fish and Wildlife began reestablishing both birds throughout their full range.

The peregrine falcon, bald eagle, California condor, black-footed ferret, and a few other ecocelebrities, such as the gray wolf and whooping crane, dominate the news. Headlines and television news clips of their releases create a rabbit-out-of-the-hat illusion that returning a species to the wild is simply a matter of transporting the animal to the woods and letting it go. Of the 961 plants and animals currently federally listed as endangered or threatened, only a few have been successfully reestablished in areas they disappeared from, including such less publicized cases as those of the Aleutian Canada goose and the greenback cutthroat trout. Exactly how many reintroduction projects are under way no one seems to know. Fish and Wildlife does not keep such a list, and most administrators and biologists, when asked about reintroductions, point to the same few, well-known megafauna.

In fact, out of the spotlight, biologists across the country are working on many unpublicized, unglamorous reintroduction efforts, among them bringing back the American burying beetle, northeastern beach tiger beetle, Mitchell's satyr, fat pocketbook pearly mussel, Arkansas fatmucket, Apache trout, Arctic grayling, pallid sturgeon, lakeside daisy, kearney's blue-star, running buffalo clover, Virginia round-leaf birch, Stock Island tree snail, and Wyoming toad. The problems are large and small. You can put a radio collar on a wolf but not a butterfly. How do you teach a captive-bred prairie-chicken to quench its thirst in the wild by drinking the dew off plants? How do you know if fox squirrels prefer forests of hardwoods or pines?

This last question I know something about. On a cool, windy morn- 5 ing last April on the Delmarva Peninsula, I pulled on a pair of hip boots and followed retired U.S. Fish and Wildlife Service biologist Guy Willey into a partially flooded pine woods. Willey, now a consultant to the service, had set 25 traps at dawn, baiting them with corn, and now he was check-ing them. These Maryland woods held one of the few remaining natural populations of the endangered Delmarva fox squirrel, one of 10 subspecies of the Eastern fox squirrel. Unlike the more common gray squirrels, with which they share their range, fox squirrels do not adapt well to forest fragmentation and are unlikely to venture far from the woods. One will not find a fox squirrel eating peanuts in a city park. They remain wild; thus their current crisis.

Heavy spring rains had left water in every depression, some ankle deep, some above the calf. We sloshed along, from one empty trap to the next. Willey, a congenial, talkative man and a native of the area, has had a lifetime of experience with the Delmarva fox squirrel. "Delmarvas prefer mature hardwoods, where the understory is more open," he told me. "We've found some in pines like these, but we don't really know whether or not a pine woods can sustain a population."

Brushing aside a holly branch, Willey saw movement in one of the traps ahead of us. "We got a squirrel here," and then a second later he added, "but it's the wrong kind." He bent down to the wire trap, the size of a shoe box, and opened one end. The gray squirrel bolted out and clambered wildly up a tree.

At the turn of the century the Delmarva fox squirrel could be found throughout the Delmarva Peninsula, a thick stalactite of land framed by the Chesapeake Bay to the west and the Atlantic Ocean to the east. By the 1960s more than three-quarters of the hardwoods that once covered much of the peninsula had been cut, and only a few populations of Delmarva fox squirrels remained, 80 percent of them in Maryland's Dorchester County, where Willey and I had spent the morning.

That afternoon, at a field office of the Maryland Department of Natural Resources, I spoke with Glenn Therres, an endangered-species biologist in charge of the recovery of the Delmarva fox squirrel for the state of Maryland. In 1978, in a sweeping effort to reestablish the fox squirrel throughout its historical range, the U.S. Fish and Wildlife Service approved a plan to trap Delmarvas in their few remaining populations and translocate them. Between 1978 and 1991 nearly 300 squirrels were translocated to 17 sites throughout the Delmarva Peninsula. Finding suitable habitat was the principal challenge. All but 3 of the 17 sites were on private land. "Trying to convince landowners to allow the government to place an endangered species on their property, well. . . ." Therres shook his head, leaving the sentence unfinished.

Because loss of habitat is usually the primary cause of a species' decline, it becomes the key issue in most reintroduction efforts. Michael Bean, an attorney with the Environmental Defense Fund who has 20 years of experience with endangered-species issues, spends much of his time dealing with private landowners' concerns. "The level of anxiety for private landowners runs very high when it comes to putting an endangered species back into the wild," Bean says. "Private landowners worry about what will happen if the animal ends up on their land." 10

This past summer the effort to release California condors in Arizona stalled when local communities protested. Robert Mesta, who coordinates the Fish and Wildlife Service's role in the recovery of the condor, points to the heart of the problem: "Even a species as benign as the California condor has trouble because it has the moniker *endangered species,* and what pops into people's minds when they hear the term is spotted owl or gray wolf—all the controversies."

When Therres got involved in the translocation effort in 1986, he took a practical approach to finding release sites. "We needed to work with the private landowners," he said. When Therres found a landowner who would cooperate, they settled the matter with a handshake: "People don't like to sign a piece of paper with the government, and the squirrels don't care." Therres admits this was hardly ideal. In one case a site was logged five years after a group of squirrels had been released on it.

The translocation effort was halted in 1991, but not because of sites threatened with logging. In fact, the project appeared to be successful. The problem was that no one knew with certainty what constituted a "successful" population of Delmarva fox squirrels because so many questions about natural populations remained unanswered. How many squirrels are needed for a healthy population, and how many acres do they require? The facts are limited—squirrels don't attract many researchers. Thus, each spring for the past four years, Guy Willey has trapped and tagged Delmarva fox squirrels from five undisturbed natural populations, accumulating data.

Late that afternoon I walked the trapline with Willey once again. The wind had died down, and the day had warmed up. Trap number six held a Delmarva fox squirrel, a beautiful silver-and-cream-colored animal with a large, fluffy tail—foxlike, hence the name. Willey picked up the cage and lifted it above his head to look at the squirrel's underside. "A female," he said. "She's nursed recently." Frank Hughes, another retired Fish and Wildlife employee who had accompanied us, noted this on a chart. In order to minimize the squirrel's stress, Willey worked quickly. He put the cage back on the ground, placed a funnel-shaped cloth bag over the entrance, opened the trapdoor, and then blew gently in the squirrel's face so the animal would turn around. The squirrel, noticing what appeared to be an escape route, crawled out the now open door and into the cloth bag. Hughes quickly clamped his fingers around the bag just behind the squirrel's tail, creating a straitjacket. Willey then slowly opened a zipper at the other end until the squirrel's head poked out like a toe out of a sock. Within moments, Willey had placed tags on each ear, dabbed salve on the pierced ears, suspended the squirrel-in-a-sock from a spring scale ("She's a fat one: 1.05 kilograms"), and released the Delmarva, which fled, leaping across pools of water and disappearing into the woods.

Considering the complexity of the endeavor, and the time and money involved, it's fair to ask, Why don't we simply protect the existing populations? Why try to return species to their former ranges? "Because we can," Robert Mesta says. Mesta, who has worked not only with the California condor project but also with restoring bald eagles and peregrine falcons, refers first to our moral obligation: "We have developed the methods to reintroduce species, when the need arises, and we have the responsibility to do so. If we caused the problem, it's our responsibility to do something about it." 15

Moreover, Mesta points out that reintroduction is necessary to save a species from potential extinction when it is restricted to a few localized populations. Still, one might wonder if this is an exaggerated threat. Ask University of Florida entomologist Tom Emmel whether or not the threat is real, and he'll tell you that small populations are as fragile as a butterfly in a hurricane, which was exactly the case of the Schaus swallowtail butterfly.

The Schaus swallowtail, another victim of habitat loss, once was found throughout the Florida Keys and on the southeastern tip of mainland Florida. As hardwood hammocks were destroyed to make way for residential development, the butterfly began disappearing. It was last reported on the Florida mainland in 1924 and was eliminated on one key after another, until in the 1970s it was found only on northern Key Largo and on several islands in Biscayne National Park. In 1977 it was federally listed as a threatened species; in 1984 it was reclassified as endangered, at which point its known range was one site on Key Largo and three keys in Biscayne National Park. The populations fluctuated from year to year and were often on the brink of disappearing completely. By 1992 the only healthy population that remained was on Elliott Key in Biscayne National Park. On August 24, 1992, Hurricane Andrew hit Elliott Key dead on, leveling the hardwood hammocks and covering the island with saltwater surges that killed the butterfly's pupae.

The following spring Tom Emmel led a team of eight researchers on a two-week search of Elliott Key for any signs of the Schaus swallowtail. Where they had counted 600 butterflies the year before, they found only 17 adults. In the wild, Schaus swallowtails live, on average, between three and four days. They are preyed upon by birds, spiders, bees, lizards, and mice, among other things, and are victims of disease and bad weather. Each female lays about two dozen eggs, and less than 1 percent of all eggs escape being eaten or otherwise destroyed before reaching the adult stage. Seventeen butterflies could not likely sustain a population.

Nine years earlier, in 1984, when Emmel first began looking closely at the Schaus swallowtail, he asked the Fish and Wildlife Service and the Florida game commission for permission to remove a number of butterflies from the wild to begin a captive-propagation program as a safeguard against natural disasters. Year after year Emmel asked and both agencies said no, citing the risk of further weakening the small populations. Finally, Emmel devised a method to remove eggs without taking any butterflies from the wild by temporarily holding eight females inside a mesh enclosure on Elliott Key as they laid their eggs. After eight years of requests, Emmel finally received permission and removed 100 eggs in the late spring of 1992—two months before Hurricane Andrew struck.

That summer Emmel knew how important it was that he successfully breed Schaus swallowtails from the eggs he had collected. Despite some unnerving setbacks (he lost 50 percent of the pupae in 1993 to desiccation caused by keeping them in an air-conditioned room), Emmel had 3,000 eggs by the spring of 1994. At this point, after 10 years of working to save the Schaus swallowtail, he thought he had learned what he was up against. In 1984, after he completed the first comprehensive census of Schaus swallowtails to date, Emmel reported his finding to the state. "I naively put down the exact locations of the remaining Schaus swallowtail populations," he told me. "Contractors [concerned about Endangered Species Act restrictions] got the report, and one of them went right out and bulldozed one of the sites. Somehow he missed the exact location by ten yards."

20

In March 1995, three years after Hurricane Andrew, Emmel was ready to begin reintroducing Schaus swallowtails to their former habitat. But at what stage of the life cycle does one release a butterfly? "In 1995 we tried the pupae," Emmel said, "thinking it was the most secure stage to put out: It was inconspicuous, and, we could just put it on a tree and leave it." Twenty students worked for 10 days, laboriously painting the sticks the pupae were attached to so they would match the color of each individual pupa, making them less noticeable to predators once they were set out. At the beginning of April, Emmel's research team placed 760 pupae near torchwood and wild lime trees (the Schaus swallowtail's food plants) at seven different sites. Three cold fronts hit south Florida that April. Migrating warblers dropped out of the turbulent skies onto the land and ate anywhere from 60 to 99 percent of the pupae at the sites.

So it was that in May 1996, when I met up with Emmel in south Florida, his plan was to release *adult* butterflies, 750 of them. This year, however, he had a new problem: funding. Despite an understanding that Fish and Wildlife would provide partial support of captive propagation of the Schaus swallowtail, Emmel had not received any funds since July 1995. The University of Florida had advanced him $52,000 to keep the project going, but now he was out of money. I recalled the sign in Emmel's office when I visited him in early April: "Due to financial restraints, the light at the end of the tunnel will be turned off indefinitely."

On May 13, I joined Emmel at the site of the first release, 100 acres of tropical hardwoods just south of Miami, and the following morning we headed for Elliott Key. In a short while, Emmel was running down a trail with a butterfly net in hand, a Schaus swallowtail fluttering just out of reach. He had released 20 Schaus swallowtails as soon as we reached the study site and then set out to recapture as many as possible. Each butterfly released had a number on its wing, not as efficient as a radio collar, but how else could one track a butterfly? As time-consuming as it was, by continuing to capture and release the butterflies over the next several days, Emmel could learn much about how far they ranged and other information about the basic biology of the Schaus swallowtail.

Five weeks later I was getting ready for a trip to south Texas, where northern aplomado falcons and Attwater's prairie-chickens were being reestablished in what was left of the coastal prairie that once spread across more than 6 million acres of Texas and southwestern Louisiana. The northern aplomado falcon, once fairly common in those coastal grasslands, disappeared from the United States when its native habitat gave way to farmland and urban development. The last nest was found in 1952. But in the spring of 1995, after nearly 10 years of work that included several releases in south Texas of captive-bred falcons (the offspring of birds taken from the Mexican population), a Fish and Wildlife biologist discovered a pair of banded falcons nesting near the port of Brownsville, not far from the 1952 nest.

Officials at the Peregrine Fund, who were raising the falcons in co-   25
operation with Fish and Wildlife, were jubilant. The captive-propagation
and release program was beginning to yield results. In 1995, 39 falcons
were released, the most ever in one year, and the Peregrine Fund expected
to release more than 50 birds in south Texas between June and August
1996. Four days before I was to fly to Brownsville, I called Bill Heinrich,
the fund's coordinator for the aplomado falcon, to confirm my plans to
meet with field-workers who would be putting 12 subadult falcons in
hacking towers at Laguna Atascosa National Wildlife Refuge. Heinrich's
voice was filled with alarm and despair. "We have a problem here," he said.
Fifteen of the young aplomado falcons that were to be released during the
summer had died in the last week, probably victims of an avian herpes
virus. "Nothing like this has ever happened before," Heinrich said. "We've
lost six of the twelve birds we were going to bring down next week. I
don't know if there'll be any left to bring."

When I got to Brownsville, only two of the group were still alive.
The virus apparently had originated in the falcons' food supply, quail raised
for the purpose. Fortunately, there were still 19 unhatched eggs, and the
seven falcons that had been put in a hacking tower at Laguna Atascosa
before the herpes outbreak appeared healthy.

At 7 A.M. the day after my arrival, I met the Peregrine Fund's Brian
Mutch at Laguna Atascosa. We drove to the site, a salt flat chosen for its
absence of brush or trees, where owls, the chief avian predator of aplomados, might perch. Mutch wanted the falcons to have a chance to acclimate
themselves and learn to fly before they had to elude predators. Last year,
shortly after he released a group of aplomados, a coyote had approached
the tower. Two of the falcons were so agitated, Mutch recalled, that they
fell off the tower and landed on the ground. The coyote swept in, grabbed
one of the birds, and headed off with it. Mutch jumped into a truck and
followed the coyote, which eventually dropped the dead aplomado. When
Mutch stopped to examine the bird, the coyote circled back and grabbed
the other one. Mutch gave chase again and, to his amazement, the second
falcon was still alive when the coyote dropped it.

The seven falcons to be released that morning had been placed in a
box atop the hacking tower when they were five weeks old. Now, a week
later, the falcons were at their natural fledging age. Mutch climbed up to
the box, about 15 feet off the ground, and placed a three-day supply of
quail meat around it. Although the birds had been fed daily, they had not
seen people since they were placed at the site, and Mutch didn't want to
disturb them during the first days of learning to fly, because he was afraid
they might spook and fly off before they were familiar with their surroundings. Field-workers would continue to place food at the tower for eight
weeks. The birds would make longer and longer flights away from the
tower, eventually dispersing.

Mutch slowly opened a door on the side of the box, only an inch at
first. The falcons fluttered about noisily. To quiet them, he picked up a

spray bottle filled with water and began misting the birds as he opened the door wider. For five minutes he continued spraying the falcons, blocking their attempts to bolt out the door and wetting them down thoroughly to discourage them from trying to fly out in a state of panic. I wondered who had first thought to use a spray bottle this way, one of the innumerable and invaluable tricks of the trade for handling wild creatures in unnatural conditions. It reminded me of the entomologist's solution to the problem of how to transport hundreds of live butterflies without damaging their delicate features: Place each butterfly, wings folded, into a stamp collector's glassine envelope, then place them in a picnic cooler, each envelope held upright by toothpicks stuck into a slab of Styrofoam.

When Mutch was satisfied that the birds had calmed down, he fixed the door to remain open and climbed down from the tower. An observation platform had been set up 150 yards away, where field-workers would sit watching and noting each move the falcons made. Within minutes, several falcons approached the opened door, ventured out, and looked at the Texas sky their ancestors had graced for thousands of years before there was a Texas.

It was the same sky, and it was a different sky. Unlike the Delmarva fox squirrel and Schaus swallowtail butterfly, the northern aplomado falcon was not being released in its native habitat. It appeared that the falcon, given time, could adapt to the cattle ranches and agricultural land that have replaced the coastal prairies, an unusual case of restoring the animal but not the ecosystem it originally inhabited. In most cases a species' decline is inextricably linked to habitat loss, and recovery of the species depends on protecting the remaining suitable habitat.

The Attwater's prairie-chicken, like the aplomado falcon, declined as the Texas and Louisiana coastal prairie dwindled to 200,000 acres, a 97 percent loss. However, the Attwater's prairie-chicken, a subspecies of the greater prairie-chicken, is a ground-dwelling bird that cannot survive outside the few remaining parcels of this dry, warm ecosystem dominated by clump grasses such as little bluestem, Indian grass, and switchgrass. An estimated 1 million Attwater's prairie-chickens once were found throughout the coastal grasslands. When the bird was federally listed as endangered in 1967, roughly a thousand of them were thought to remain in the wild. The decline continued. A series of drought years in the late 1980s followed by several exceptionally wet years brought prairie-chicken reproduction to a virtual standstill. The population dropped to 456 birds in the spring of 1992 before a captive-propagation program got under way. It seems clear the prairie-chicken's lack of charisma has been a liability to its recovery. Currently, the total wild prairie-chicken population has fallen to an estimated 70 birds. Terry Rossignol, manager of Attwater Prairie Chicken National Wildlife Refuge, has had to resort to getting help from Boy Scouts to build the release pens. Three of seven staff positions were vacant when I visited the refuge. The entrance sign sat on the ground, propped against the base it had broken off from, unrepaired.

30

The 8,000-acre refuge, about 60 miles west of Houston, contains 4,000 acres of untouched prairie. Last spring, Rossignol counted only five males there. Usually from January through May, beginning near sunrise, the males gather for two to three hours to attract females by stamping their feet in a ritualized "dance" and uttering a low booming sound that can carry for a mile or more. This past spring they didn't start until late February and ended in April, often leaving the booming grounds within 30 minutes. "It seemed like they didn't care anymore," Rossignol said.

In 1992, 49 Attwater's prairie-chicken eggs were taken from the wild and incubated at the Fossil Rim Wildlife Center in Glen Rose, Texas, one of four facilities now involved in the project. Forty-two eggs hatched, but by August only seven chicks had survived. "We started too late," Rochelle Plassé, curator of birds at the Houston Zoo, told me when I visited her the day after watching the falcon release. Captive breeding is a risky endeavor, a corner we paint ourselves into by letting the population of an animal dwindle and fragment to the point that raising it in captivity may be the only way to restore its numbers and genetic diversity. "The saving grace of the project to breed California condors," Plassé said, "was that we knew how to breed condors because zoos had been breeding Andean condors for years." Likewise, the aplomado falcons benefited from methods devised to raise peregrine falcons.

When Fish and Wildlife asked Plassé for help in 1992, she curtailed much of the zoo's other avian breeding to concentrate on the Attwater's prairie-chicken. Each year she has learned more about the process. With this year's group of birds, she is tracking each chick hatched, beginning with exactly where the egg was found in the nest, whether it was clean or dirty, wet or dry, and so on. "That might tell us nothing, but you never know," she said. "What if we learn something important that will give us a better success rate in the future?" For comparison, 20 chicks are being raised by Attwater's hens, 20 others by domestic hens, and the remaining 76 in specially built brooder boxes. Plassé is also experimenting with how best to prepare the chicks to find food and water on their own. Last year 13 captive-raised subadults, fitted with radio collars, were released at the refuge; a week and a half later, seven of them died suddenly. When the birds' bodies were recovered, they appeared emaciated. One guess was the young birds had wandered from the release site, where water had been set out for them, and did not know how to drink dew off the plants.

Plassé took me to a back lot of the zoo to show me the adult prairie-chickens that had bred this past spring. "This was the first problem we had to solve," Plassé said. "How do you let the males gather in a group, in which a dominant male does most of the breeding, and still control which male breeds with which female in order to ensure genetic diversity?" Plassé devised a system of enclosures that allowed all the males to see one another but enabled her to shuttle females into whichever enclosure she chose.

"And what do you feed prairie-chickens?" Plassé asked. "Crickets. But what do you feed the crickets? What nutrients do *they* need?"

What to feed crickets? Do Delmarva fox squirrels prefer hardwoods or pines? What is the home range of a Schaus swallowtail? But the questions go far beyond practical considerations. At the heart of the matter is our desire, confused and uncertain, to keep parts of the world wild. Plassé, who is keenly aware of the tensions between zoo biologists, aviculturalists, and conservationists, recalled a conversation with Fish and Wildlife officials: "They kept saying, 'You have to keep the birds *wild*'—but first you have to keep the birds alive! And what does it mean to 'keep them wild'? Do we try to breed a prairie-chicken capable of avoiding a wolf? Wolves, historically, preyed on prairie-chickens, but there are no wolves left in prairie-chicken habitat. And what is wild about the environment we're putting them back into? Today there are telephone poles for hawks to perch on and prey on prairie-chickens. That's not natural. These birds will be living differently than their ancestors, but they will be living."

That is more than we can say for the Carolina parakeet, the passenger pigeon, or the dusky seaside sparrow, which had the sad distinction of being the first bird to go extinct since the Endangered Species Act was passed in 1973. Thirteen years ago I stood outside an enclosure at Santa Fe Community College in Gainesville, Florida, where the last five dusky seaside sparrows were housed, having been removed from the wild the year before. As a species, they were what University of Pennsylvania biologist Daniel Janzen refers to as "the living dead." A plan was being developed to crossbreed the duskies with another closely related race of sparrow that would, after successive crossbreeding, produce a number of birds whose genetic makeup would be approximately 95 percent dusky. The late ornithologist Herb Kale, a former vice-president of the Florida Audubon Society, hoped that eventually the descendants of the last wild duskies could be reintroduced to their habitat, the spartina grass marshes along a section of the St. John's River and mid-Florida Atlantic coast. Kale was upset that the U.S. Fish and Wildlife Service refused to fund the crossbreeding because it would not be saving a species but creating a hybrid, which Kale called a "racist attitude."

The biological challenges of reintroduction efforts are sometimes entangled with such philosophical conundrums—what is wild?—and with the knowledge that we have not only destroyed most of our wilderness but have also compromised the basic integrity of ecosystems and the species that inhabit them.

At the time, the effort to crossbreed the dusky seemed to me misguided, and futile. Let them go in peace, I thought. Two years later I moved to Florida, and in the past 11 years have spent countless hours in the marshes where the dusky once lived. If I looked out into the spartina and saw a sparrow perched on a swaying blade of grass, would I care if the bird was 95 percent dusky or 100 percent dusky? And would the ecosystem be richer or poorer, more or less vital, than it was? 40

Reading and Responding

1. As you review the essay carefully, make notes in the margins about the travel and research needed to write the essay. What trips did Stap take? What did he do on those trips? How did he prepare for them beforehand? On a sheet of paper, list the activities and estimate the amount of time the trips took in all.
2. Does this article give you hope for the future? Why or why not?

Working Together

1. Stap quotes a biologist: "We have developed the methods to reintroduce species, when the need arises, and we have the responsibility to do so. If we caused the problem, it's our responsibility to do something about it." Write a group paragraph about this quote. Describe in general the methods that the biologist mentions. Agree or disagree with his conclusion that we have a responsibility to restore endangered species.
2. Stap concludes his article with a paragraph asking two questions. Answer them for yourselves and discuss.

Rethinking and Rewriting

1. Write an essay about some effort of your own that took place "out of the spotlight" and that required much "unpublicized, unglamorous effort."
2. Write an essay that explains how the intellectual life of a student in a university can be defined in the same way that Stap describes biologists' efforts—as slow, careful, small-scale, and steady over time. As you write, continue to compare your effort as a student with the efforts of the biologists that Stap profiles. Is intellectual life of any sort somehow "ecological"?
3. Using Stap's article as a starting point, see what you can discover about the reintroduction of a particular species. Write a report that discusses and details your actual research effort step-by-step: what you do, why you do it, what is the result, what you discover, and so on. Detail your actual process honestly and clearly. Consult both print and online materials. At the end of your discussion, summarize what you have learned about research and about the reintroduction effort you've investigated.

PIECES OF PAPER PROTECTING THE LAND
How Field Notes Saved Montana Open Space

Carolyn Duckworth

> *Carolyn Duckworth met environmental activist Will Kerling while writing a master's thesis on the power of field journals. The essay that follows, which appeared in the summer 1998 issue of* Orion Afield, *describes Kerling's efforts to protect native habitats around the city of Missoula.*

With just paper and pen, people who are passionate about a place may be as well equipped as anyone to protect it. Perhaps they will list what they see, sketch maps of animal movement, record their emotions, or ask a chain of questions about what they observe. Whether taken by a conservation biologist or a neophyte naturalist, the resulting field notes become powerful tools for conserving open space and wild places.

The people of western Montana know this is true, for the evidence is in view. There, a mountain shines gold against charcoal skies; a sensuous, fertile, reclining nude of a mountain that bears the name of a circus elephant. If you stand beside a certain hedged-in white cottage on Locust Street in Missoula, Montana, your peripheral vision fills with Mount Jumbo. A quiet man may rise from tending his herbs, walk over to the fence, and begin a conversation with you. Will Kerling notices people who notice Jumbo; the mountain has been his passion for more than 25 years. His hundreds of pages of field notes helped save this piece of urban wild for the elk, bear, deer, birds, and butterflies that live there.

Urban? You may ask. In Montana? In addition to this state's more familiar wild places, Montana does have large cities—and Missoula is one. It's a metropolitan area by the U.S. Census Bureau definition (more than 50,000 people), recognizable as a city by the grim trio of pollution, traffic jams, and crime. Missoula's fast-growing population is pushing hard against the boundaries of undeveloped land.

Mount Jumbo is one of two rounded mountains that form the eastern entrance to the city. Jumbo is already divided from its geological neighbor, Mount Sentinel, by a river and two highways. Real-estate development threatens to separate Jumbo from the Rattlesnake Wilderness and National Recreation Area. Houses have already been built on the slopes of the low, broad saddle that provides a safe migration route for the elk and mule deer that descend from the Rattlesnake to Jumbo's sunny slopes for the winter.

Will and other open-space advocates have been working for years to secure that saddle and all of Jumbo for wildlife. Their efforts have been closely monitored by the local paper, *The Missoulian,* which published several articles describing the human impact on Jumbo after Will documented that elk were altering their behavior as human presence increased. From his field notes:

> *Dec. 24, 1991:* 12+ elk grazing toward far horizon; observed them from 8:55–11:15 A.M.

> *Jan. 1, 1992:* 30+ elk at daybreak, went for timber between 9–9:30 A.M. 40–50 elk over horizon at 5:30 P.M.

> *Jan. 5:* 10 hikers on face of Jumbo at 4. Elk not out by 5:45.

> *Jan. 6:* No elk in morning. 7:10 P.M., 40–50 of them near lone large pine.

> *As of Jan. 7,* the elk are coming out progressively later after dark and going back before daylight. I feel this is definitely because of human activity, which includes dogs.

Elk incite Will to action—sometimes even before dawn. One December morning he awoke to the sound of a bull elk bugling from the slopes of Jumbo. He rolled out of bed and walked down the dark alley in his pajamas and clogs to hear this ethereal mating call more clearly. His journals are jammed with maps that show where he has seen elk, alongside descriptions of them eating, resting, running. He even documented what few biologists thought possible—elk calving on this dry, exposed hill.

Through the newspaper, and through workshops that winter, Will and other activists were able to help Missoulians understand that their recreational behavior could place stress on Jumbo's animals. They also succeeded in limiting human access to Jumbo during the critical winter months. Will's notes were key to this success; by recording his observations regularly, he had established evidence of the disturbance, evidence that the decision makers could not ignore. But it would be another three years before Will Kerling could relax with the knowledge that Mount Jumbo, indeed, would be protected from further development.

For the last 25 years, Will has used his field notes and observations to turn skeptical neighbors and politicians toward enthusiastic preservation of Missoula's open space. In addition to Jumbo, he has been engaged in efforts related to two other significant areas: The Rattlesnake Mountains and a cluster of islands in the Clark Fork River.

"The Rattlesnake was my best friend," Will explains, "so I thought I could go there and document a vision of what a unique place it is and how crucial it is that we do something special with it. I had a sense that the community in Missoula was special, that they would understand. So I went for it."

Will spent a year studying the Rattlesnake Mountains. Imagining what evidence he might need to convince the skeptics, he began carrying a camera and notebook. He photographed everything he saw and kept detailed field notes—especially about the birds. Flipping through the notebook pages, each labeled with a species' name, he would record his daily observations, including time, location, and what the bird was doing. From his notes:

> *Common raven:* Sept. 1, 1977—heard one nearby from the air back of base camp . . . voice was changing locations, another indication of being airborne. Saw it and another fly by shortly heading toward Sanders Lake area. Black adults, they were alternating flapping with soaring. Soaring on flat wings. Call was a cr-r-ruck.

He was especially careful to describe animals he was unfamiliar with or those that displayed unusual behavior—some he simply described as "mystery mammals." One of those mystery animals turned out to be a wolverine—a documentation that proved significant in the fight for the Rattlesnake.

From those notes and his stack of slides, Will developed a powerful new tool in the campaign to have the Rattlesnake designated as wilderness: a slide presentation entitled "Timeless Journey." More than 10,000 Missoulians attended Will's presentations during the next year, witnessing the presence of wolverine and mountain goats and grizzlies in a wild land so close to their home. The program was also presented to the major private landowner in the Rattlesnake Mountains, the Montana Power Company. Will's field notes and photos helped convince the company that its holdings should be included in the wilderness and recreation area being considered by Congress.

Will believed the Rattlesnake would sell itself through the images. "I've always been consistent with my field notes and my politics," he says. "I don't go in thinking it would be nice to find certain mammals or birds. I bring back what is there and I think that is good enough." It was good enough. In 1980, the Rattlesnake Wilderness and National Recreation Area was established.

"Is he the guy that I see in a big floppy hat down around the river all the time?" a friend asked. Indeed, it was Will. In 1994, he learned from a friend that a proposed bridge expansion would change the natural qualities of several small islands in the section of the Clark Fork River that flows through Missoula's downtown. Will decided to document the wildlife in preparation for a public hearing. He spent more than 500 hours visiting the islands at least five days a week, stopping for an hour each time he bicycled by on his way to or from work.

"I'm educating myself, surprising some conservationists, and anguishing some business people by what I'm discovering, because the downtown area is teeming with wildlife." Will documented 82 species of birds on the islands. Some of them—such as red-necked grebes and yellowlegs—pass through on migration. Others—mergansers, yellow warblers, blackbirds—nest on the islands.

Will didn't file away his notes or leave them tucked in notebooks. *15* "All of my notes are being shared," he said, "with the engineering firm that's studying the bridge project, the environmental subcontractor that's writing the environmental assessment, and also at informational public meetings." Will used his field notes when he testified before the city council, and the council subsequently recommended that the islands be protected as a wildlife sanctuary and an environmental education area.

His notes are especially helpful to the conservation groups working to protect land. When the local group, the Five Valleys Land Trust, wants to protect a piece of property, it usually commissions a baseline report from a scientist or naturalist who documents what species are present on the property. To prepare the report, the consultant may visit the property two or three times, and interview the landowner. Duplicating Will's detailed, long-term observations would cost thousands of dollars.

"My journals have been disorganized ever since day one," Will said with a laugh as he looked for examples of his field notes. "I'm doing so much that it's hard to focus on something that's not my main job, not a source of income—to keep it organized the way I'd like." An archivist would simultaneously be enthralled and appalled at the plastic binders and their contents—hundreds of notes in blue ball-point ink on inexpensive lined paper. Recently, Will began using a computer to organize his notes. He is also experimenting with entering his daily observations directly on the machine. "I'm caught up with getting information organized now, but I don't want to depersonalize field journaling. I try to balance using the computer with keeping field notes like I always have."

Describing how he uses his notes, Will says, "I write up what I see each day on these pieces of paper that are falling out of this tablet and at the same time I have an overview from my observations that I keep up to date—a summary of different things I think are important."

Will's "pieces of paper" have been the start of multiple records for each site. For Mount Jumbo, he maintains a bound journal describing each outing. From that account he extracts lists of the birds, mammals, butterflies, and reptiles. These lists are used by university students, scientists, and anyone else who wants to learn about wildlife on Jumbo. He has similar lists for his backyard, his neighborhood, and for the parts of the city through which he regularly rides his bike.

When Will was younger, he earned a degree in science education *20* and taught high school math and science for a year. "I have enough background to claim I'm a scientist, but I don't speak as a scientist and I've gone as far as I want that way," he says. At one time Will considered entering a master's degree program in environmental studies. He enrolled in a few classes, discussed his ideas with one of the professors, and concluded that maybe he didn't need that advanced degree after all; he could be an effective advocate without it. "Life's a trade-off," he says, "I spend a lot of time settling on what is important to me in the outdoors and how to share it with people."

His balance and focus have helped Will succeed. "Instead of scattering myself, I pick a focus and become an expert with that," he explains. "I keep dedicating myself to the field work. I grow personally and enjoy the hell out of it."

His years of patience and persistence paid off. In April 1993, *The Missoulian* devoted two color pages to Mount Jumbo, explaining its geologic history and its significance to wildlife and native plant communities. The reporter, Sherry Devlin, opened the article with a description of Will's field journal: "In an 80-sheet spiral notebook stained by the seasons he chronicles, Will Kerling records the beauty and diversity of life on Mount Jumbo." She quoted Will and cited his observations throughout the article. On the second page, she featured excerpts from his notes such as, "50-plus elk bedded in forest island near top . . . at 1:05 P.M., saw the last 21 of the elk going back into the heavy timber to the north on Jumbo."

Then, in 1995, Missoulians passed a historic open-space bond that helped protect Mount Jumbo. During the following year, Will and many other volunteers worked tirelessly to raise additional funds to purchase private land still at risk. Their goals were reached, and Will stepped back.

He continues to enjoy Mount Jumbo and other wild places through his photography, writing, and teaching. He writes a column about butterflies for *WOW,* a children's magazine, and contributes seasonal articles to *The Missoulian.* He also leads field trips through the grasses and thickets of Missoula's beloved mountain.

Will encourages people to keep field notes about the places they cherish. "I know how powerfully it works," he says, "There's a strong sense of place that comes from keeping field notes." And he knows that field notes change the history of a place. "Even if a project is not successful, people will know what they've lost."   25

Thanks in large part to Will Kerling, Mount Jumbo's natural values will endure. Its sensuous ridgeline remains home to elk, bear, deer, birds, and butterflies. It will always be there, a shining gold symbol of the power of people and pieces of paper.

Reading and Responding

1. Write one or two paragraphs to explain something that surprised you in what Duckworth says. Reread the essay and write one or two paragraphs to record your reaction. Is the text clearer than it was before? Do you find Duckworth more persuasive?

2. Position yourself somewhere on your own campus or near where you live—somewhere that will give you a view of trees, bushes, and relatively undeveloped landscape (if possible). Following Duckworth's description of field notes, list what you see. Describe what each item

looks like, estimate its size, describe its shape, and note its movements and their causes. Record your own thoughts or emotions as you observe, and make a list of any specific questions that occur to you. Fill at least half a page with your notes, and draw at least one picture of something (or part of something) that you observe.

Working Together

1. As a group, rewrite the examples of field notes included in this essay so that they are no longer interesting or useful. What exactly have you done? What writing or speech does this "translation" resemble? What does this exercise tell you about the power of Kerling's writing?
2. Suppose someone tells you that keeping field notes is just a waste of time, that nature writers are doing nothing of much use to anyone. You've read this article by Duckworth. Set this person straight.
3. Discuss a problem or issue on your campus or in your local community that might benefit from close observation over time. What's the problem, what needs to be observed, what might be the implications of observation?

Rethinking and Rewriting

Over a two-week period, keep your own field notes as you observe a place and its inhabitants. It doesn't have to be a natural place or a piece of "urban wild," though it can be. Try a park, a path along a river, a coffee shop, a fraternity house, or a street in your neighborhood. Apply the style and approach of Will Kerling, keeping regular and detailed notes.

At the end, write an essay reflecting on the experience and the implications of the data you've assembled. Accurate field notes about a fraternity house, for example, may or may not confirm the stereotype that "frat boys" are more concerned with partying than with studying.

THE IDEA OF A GARDEN

Michael Pollan

> *A former editor at* Harper's *magazine, Michael Pollan is the author of* Second Nature: A Gardener's Education *(1991), from which the following selection (one chapter of the book) is taken, and, more recently,* A Place of My Own: The Education of an Amateur Builder *(1998). The essay that follows tries to strike a delicate balance between the human and the natural.*

The biggest news to come out of my town in many years was the tornado, or tornadoes, that careened through here on July 10, 1989, a Monday. Shooting down the Housatonic River Valley from the Berkshires, it veered east over Coltsfoot Mountain and then, after smudging the sky a weird gray green, proceeded to pinball madly from hillside to hillside for about fifteen minutes before wheeling back up into the sky. This was part of the same storm that ripped open the bark of my ash tree. But the damage was much, much worse on the other side of town. Like a gigantic, skidding pencil eraser, the twister neatly erased whole patches of woods and roughly smeared many other ones, where it wiped out just the tops of the trees. Overnight, large parts of town were rendered unrecognizable.

One place where the eraser came down squarely was in the Cathedral Pines, a famous forest of old-growth white pine trees close to the center of town. A kind of local shrine, this forty-two-acre forest was one of the oldest stands of white pine in New England, the trees untouched since about 1800. To see it was to have some idea how the New World forest must have looked to the first settlers, and in 1985 the federal government designated it a "national natural landmark." To enter Cathedral Pines on a hot summer day was like stepping out of the sun into a dim cathedral, the sunlight cooled and sweetened by the trillions of pine needles as it worked its way down to soft, sprung ground that had been unacquainted with blue sky for the better part of two centuries. The storm came through at about five in the evening, and it took only a few minutes of wind before pines more than one hundred fifty feet tall and as wide around as missiles lay jackstrawed on the ground like a fistful of pencils dropped from a great height. The wind was so thunderous that people in houses at the forest's edge did not know trees had fallen until they ventured outside after the storm had passed. The following morning, the sky now clear, was the first in more than a century to bring sunlight crashing down onto this particular patch of earth.

"It is a terrible mess," the first selectman told the newspapers; "a tragedy," said another Cornwall resident, voicing the deep sense of loss shared by many in town. But in the days that followed, the selectman and the rest of us learned that our responses, though understandable, were shortsighted, unscientific, and, worst of all, anthropocentric. "It may be a calamity to us," a state environmental official told a reporter from the *Hartford Courant,* but "to biology it is not a travesty. It is just a natural occurrence." The Nature Conservancy, which owns Cathedral Pines, issued a press release explaining that "Monday's storm was just another link in the continuous chain of events that is responsible for shaping and changing this forest."

It wasn't long before the rub of these two perspectives set off a controversy heated enough to find its way into the pages of *The New York Times.* The Nature Conservancy, in keeping with its mandate to maintain its lands in a "state of nature," indicated that it would leave Cathedral Pines alone, allowing the forest to take its "natural course," whatever that might be. To town officials and neighbors of the forest this was completely unacceptable. The downed trees, besides constituting an eyesore right at the edge of town, also posed a fire hazard. A few summers of drought, and the timber might go up in a blaze that would threaten several nearby homes and possibly even the town itself. Many people in Cornwall wanted Cathedral Pines cleared and replanted, so that at least the next generation might live to see some semblance of the old forest. A few others had the poor taste to point out the waste of more than a million board-feet of valuable timber, stupendous lengths of unblemished, knot-free pine.

The newspapers depicted it as a classic environmental battle, pitting   5
the interests of man against nature, and in a way it was that. On one side were the environmental purists, who felt that *any* intervention by man in the disposition of this forest would be unnatural. "If you're going to clean it up," one purist declared in the local press, "you might as well put up condos." On the other side stood the putative interests of man, variously expressed in the vocabulary of safety (the fire hazard), economics (the wasted lumber), and aesthetics (the "terrible mess").

Everybody enjoys a good local fight, but I have to say I soon found the whole thing depressing. This was indeed a classic environmental battle, in that it seemed to exemplify just about everything that's wrong with the way we approach problems of this kind these days. Both sides began to caricature each other's positions: the selectman's "terrible mess" line earned him ridicule for his anthropocentrism in the letters page of *The New York Times;* he in turn charged a Yale scientist who argued for noninterference with "living in an ivory tower."

But as far apart as the two sides seemed to stand, they actually shared more common ground than they realized. Both started from the premise that man and nature were irreconcilably opposed, and that the victory of one necessarily entailed the loss of the other. Both sides, in other words, accepted the premises of what we might call the "wilderness ethic," which is based on the assumption that the relationship of man and nature resembles a zero-sum game. This idea, widely held and yet largely unexamined, has set the terms of most environmental battles in this country since the very first important one: the fight over the building of the Hetch Hetchy

Dam in 1907, which pitted John Muir against Gifford Pinchot, whom Muir used to call a "temple destroyer." Watching my little local debate unfold over the course of the summer, and grow progressively more shrill and sterile, I began to wonder if perhaps the wilderness ethic itself, for all that it has accomplished in this country over the past century, had now become part of the problem. I also began to wonder if it might be possible to formulate a different ethic to guide us in our dealings with nature, at least in some places some of the time, an ethic that would be based not on the idea of wilderness but on the idea of a garden.*

* * *

Foresters who have examined sections of fallen trees in Cathedral Pines think that the oldest trees in the forest date from 1780 or so, which suggests that the site was probably logged by the first generation of settlers. The Cathedral Pines are not, then, "virgin growth." The rings of felled trees also reveal a significant growth spurt in 1840, which probably indicates that loggers removed hardwood trees in that year, leaving the pines to grow without competition. In 1883, the Calhouns, an old Cornwall family whose property borders the forest, bought the land to protect the trees from the threat of logging; in 1967 they deeded it to the Nature Conservancy, stipulating that it be maintained in its natural state. Since then, and up until the tornado made its paths impassable, the forest has been a popular place for hiking and Sunday outings. Over the years, more than a few Cornwall residents have come to the forest to be married.

Cathedral Pines is not in any meaningful sense a wilderness. The natural history of the forest intersects at many points with the social history of Cornwall. It is the product of early logging practices, which clear-cut the land once and then cut it again, this time selectively, a hundred years later. Other human factors almost certainly played a part in the forest's history; we can safely assume that any fires in the area were extinguished before they reached Cathedral Pines. (Though we don't ordinarily think of it in these terms, fire suppression is one of the more significant effects that the European has had on the American landscape.) Cathedral Pines, then, is in some part a man-made landscape, and it could reasonably be argued that to exclude man at this point in its history would constitute a break with its past.

But both parties to the dispute chose to disregard the actual history of Cathedral Pines, and instead to think of the forest as a wilderness in the commonly accepted sense of that term: a pristine place untouched by white men. Since the romantics, we've prized such places as refuges from

10

---

*In developing some of the ideas for this chapter, I've drawn from a panel discussion on environmental ethics that I moderated for the April 1990 issue of *Harper's* magazine. The participants were James Lovelock, Frederick Turner, Daniel Botkin, Dave Foreman, and Robert Yaro. This chapter also owes a lot to the work of Wendell Berry, René Dubos, William Cronon, William Jordan III, and Alston Chase.

the messiness of the human estate, vantages from which we might transcend the vagaries of that world and fix on what Thoreau called "higher laws." Certainly an afternoon in Cathedral Pines fostered such feelings, and its very name reflects the pantheism that lies behind them. Long before science coined the term *ecosystem* to describe it, we've had the sense that nature undisturbed displays a miraculous order and balance, something the human world can only dream about. When man leaves it alone, nature will tend toward a healthy and abiding state of equilibrium. Wilderness, the purest expression of this natural law, stands out beyond history.

These are powerful and in many ways wonderful ideas. The notion of wilderness is a kind of taboo in our culture, in many cases acting as a check on our inclination to dominate and spoil nature. It has inspired us to set aside such spectacular places as Yellowstone and Yosemite. But wilderness is also a profoundly alienating idea, for it drives a large wedge between man and nature. Set against the foil of nature's timeless cycles, human history appears linear and unpredictable, buffeted by time and chance as it drives blindly into the future. Natural history, by comparison, obeys fixed and legible laws, ones that make the "laws" of human history seem puny, second-rate things scarcely deserving of the label. We have little idea what the future holds for the town of Cornwall, but surely nature has a plan for Cathedral Pines; leave the forest alone and that plan—which science knows by the name of "forest succession"—will unfold inexorably, in strict accordance with natural law. A new climax forest will emerge as nature works to restore her equilibrium—or at least that's the idea.

The notion that nature has a plan for Cathedral Pines is a comforting one, and certainly it supplies a powerful argument for leaving the forest alone. Naturally I was curious to know what that plan was: what does nature do with an old pine forest blown down by a tornado? I consulted a few field guides and standard works of forest ecology hoping to find out.

According to the classical theory of forest succession, set out in the nineteenth century by, among others, Henry Thoreau, a pine forest that has been abruptly destroyed will usually be succeeded by hardwoods, typically oak. This is because squirrels commonly bury acorns in pine forests and neglect to retrieve many of them. The oaks sprout and, because shade doesn't greatly hinder young oaks, the seedlings frequently manage to survive beneath the dark canopy of a mature pine forest. Pine seedlings, on the other hand, require more sunlight than a mature pine forest admits; they won't sprout in shade. So by the time the pine forest comes down, the oak saplings will have had a head start in the race to dominate the new forest. Before any new pines have had a chance to sprout, the oaks will be well on their way to cornering the sunlight and inheriting the forest.

This is what I read, anyway, and I decided to ask around to confirm that Cathedral Pines was expected to behave as predicted. I spoke to a forest ecologist and an expert on the staff of the Nature Conservancy. They told me that the classical theory of pine-forest succession probably does describe the underlying tendency at work in Cathedral Pines. But it turns out that a lot can go, if not "wrong" exactly, then at least differently. For what if there are no oaks nearby? Squirrels will travel only so far in search of a hiding place for their acorns. Instead of oaks, there may be hickory nuts stashed all over Cathedral Pines. And then there's the composition of species planted by the forest's human neighbors to consider; one of these, possibly some exotic (that is, nonnative), could conceivably race in and take over.

"It all depends," is the refrain I kept hearing as I tried to pin down   15
nature's intentions for Cathedral Pines. Forest succession, it seems, is only a theory, a metaphor of our making, and almost as often as not nature makes a fool of it. The number of factors that will go into the determination of Cathedral Pines' future is almost beyond comprehension. Consider just this small sample of the things that could happen to alter irrevocably its future course:

A lightning storm—or a cigarette butt flicked from a passing car—ignites a fire next summer. Say it's a severe fire, hot enough to damage the fertility of the soil, thereby delaying recovery of the forest for decades. Or say it rains that night, making the fire a mild one, just hot enough to kill the oak saplings and allow the relatively fire-resistant pine seedlings to flourish without competition. A new pine forest after all? Perhaps. But what if the population of deer happens to soar the following year? Their browsing would wipe out the young pines and create an opening for spruce, the taste of which deer happen not to like.

Or say there is no fire. Without one, it could take hundreds of years for the downed pine trees to rot and return their nutrients to the soil. Trees grow poorly in the exhausted soil, but the seeds of brambles, which can lie dormant in the ground for fifty years, sprout and proliferate: we end up with a hundred years of brush. Or perhaps a breeze in, say, the summer of 1997 carries in seedpods from the Norway maple standing in a nearby front yard at the precise moment when conditions for their germination are perfect. Norway maple, you'll recall, is a European species, introduced here early in the nineteenth century and widely planted as a street tree. Should this exotic species happen to prevail, Cathedral Pines becomes one very odd-looking and awkwardly named wilderness area.

But the outcome could be much worse. Let's say the rains next spring are unusually heavy, washing all the topsoil away (the forest stood on a steep hillside). Only exotic weed species can survive now, and one of these happens to be Japanese honeysuckle, a nineteenth-century import of such rampant habit that it can choke out the growth of all trees indefinitely. We end up with no forest at all.

Nobody, in other words, can say what will happen in Cathedral Pines. And the reason is not that forest ecology is a young or imperfect science, but because *nature herself doesn't know what's going to happen here.* Nature has no grand design for this place. An incomprehensibly various and complex set of circumstances—some of human origin, but many not—will determine the future of Cathedral Pines. And whatever that future turns out to be, it would not unfold in precisely the same way twice. Nature may possess certain inherent tendencies, ones that theories such as forest succession can describe, but chance events can divert her course into an almost infinite number of different channels.

It's hard to square this fact with our strong sense that some kind of *20* quasi-divine order inheres in nature's workings. But science lately has been finding that contingency plays nearly as big a role in natural history as it does in human history. Forest ecologists today will acknowledge that succession theories are little more than comforting narratives we impose on a surprisingly unpredictable process; even so-called climax forests are sometimes superseded. (In many places in the northern United States today, mature stands of oak are inexplicably being invaded by maples—skunks at the climax garden party.) Many ecologists will now freely admit that even the concept of an ecosystem is only a metaphor, a human construct imposed upon a much more variable and precarious reality. An ecosystem may be a useful concept, but no ecologist has ever succeeded in isolating one in nature. Nor is the process of evolution as logical or inexorable as we have thought. The current thinking in paleontology holds that the evolution of any given species, our own included, is not the necessary product of any natural laws, but rather the outcome of a concatenation of chance events—of "just history" in the words of Stephen Jay Gould. Add or remove any single happenstance—the asteroid fails to wipe out the dinosaurs; a little chordate worm called *Pikaia* succumbs in the Burgess extinction—and humankind never arrives.

Across several disciplines, in fact, scientists are coming to the conclusion that more "just history" is at work in nature than had previously been thought. Yet our metaphors still picture nature as logical, stable, and ahistorical—more like a watch than, say, an organism or a stock exchange, to name two metaphors that may well be more apt. Chance and contingency, it turns out, are everywhere in nature; she has no fixed goals, no unalterable pathways into the future, no inflexible rules that she herself can't bend or break at will. She is more like us (or we are more like her) than we ever imagined.

To learn this, for me at least, changes everything. I take it to be profoundly good news, though I can easily imagine how it might trouble some people. For many of us, nature is a last bastion of certainty; wilderness, as something beyond the reach of history and accident, is one of the last in our fast-dwindling supply of metaphysical absolutes, those comforting transcendental values by which we have traditionally taken our measure and set our sights. To take away predictable, divinely ordered nature is to pull up one of our last remaining anchors. We are liable to float away on the trackless sea of our own subjectivity.

But the discovery that time and chance hold sway even in nature can also be liberating. Because contingency is an invitation to participate in history. Human choice is unnatural only if nature is deterministic; human change is unnatural only if she is changeless in our absence. If the future of Cathedral Pines is up for grabs, if its history will always be the product of myriad chance events, then why shouldn't we also claim our place among all those deciding factors? For aren't we also one of nature's contingencies?

And if our cigarette butts and Norway maples and acid rain are going to shape the future of this place, then why not also our hopes and desires?

Nature will condone an almost infinite number of possible futures for Cathedral Pines. Some would be better than others. True, what we would regard as "better" is probably not what the beetles would prefer. But nature herself has no strong preference. That doesn't mean she will countenance *any* outcome; she's already ruled out many possible futures (tropical rain forest, desert, etc.) and, all things being equal, she'd probably lean toward the oak. But all things aren't equal (*her* idea) and she is evidently happy to let the free play of numerous big and little contingencies settle the matter. To exclude from these human desire would be, at least in this place at this time, arbitrary, perverse and, yes, unnatural.

* * *

Establishing that we should have a vote in the disposition of Cathedral   25
Pines is much easier than figuring out how we should cast it. The discovery of contingency in nature would seem to fling open a Pandora's box. For if there's nothing fixed or inevitable about nature's course, what's to stop us from concluding that anything goes? It's a whole lot easier to assume that nature left to her own devices knows what's best for a place, to let ourselves be guided by the wilderness ethic.

And maybe that's what we should do. Just because the wilderness ethic is based on a picture of nature that is probably more mythical than real doesn't necessarily mean we have to discard it. In the same way that the Declaration of Independence begins with the useful fiction that "all men are created equal," we could simply stipulate that Cathedral Pines *is* wilderness, and proceed on that assumption. The test of the wilderness ethic is not how truthful it is, but how useful it is in doing what we want to do—in protecting and improving the environment.

So how good a guide is the wilderness ethic in this particular case? Certainly treating Cathedral Pines as a wilderness will keep us from building condos there. When you don't trust yourself to do the right thing, it helps to have an authority as wise and experienced as nature to decide matters for you. But what if nature decides on Japanese honeysuckle— three hundred years of wall-to-wall brush? We would then have a forest not only that we don't like, but that isn't even a wilderness, since it was man who brought Japanese honeysuckle to Cornwall. At this point in history, after humans have left their stamp on virtually every corner of the Earth, doing nothing is frequently a poor recipe for wilderness. In many cases it leads to a gradually deteriorating environment (as seems to be happening in Yellowstone), or to an environment shaped in large part by the acts and mistakes of previous human inhabitants.

If it's real wilderness we want in Cathedral Pines, and not merely an imagined innocence, we will have to restore it. This is the paradox faced by the Nature Conservancy and most other advocates of wilderness: at this point in history, creating a landscape that bears no marks of human intervention will require a certain amount of human intervention. At a minimum it would entail weeding the exotic species from Cathedral Pines, and that is something the Nature Conservancy's strict adherence to the wilderness ethic will not permit.

But what if the Conservancy *was* willing to intervene just enough to erase any evidence of man's presence? It would soon run up against some difficult questions for which its ethic leaves it ill-prepared. For what is the "real" state of nature in Cathedral Pines? Is it the way the forest looked before the settlers arrived? We could restore that condition by removing all traces of European man. Yet isn't that a rather Eurocentric (if not racist) notion of wilderness? We now know that the Indians were not the ecological eunuchs we once thought. They too left their mark on the land: fires set by Indians determined the composition of the New England forests and probably created that "wilderness" we call the Great Plains. For true untouched wilderness we have to go a lot further back than 1640 or 1492. And if we want to restore the landscape to its pre-Indian condition, then we're going to need a lot of heavy ice-making equipment (not to mention a few woolly mammoths) to make it look right.

But even that would be arbitrary. In fact there is no single moment 30 in time that we can point to and say, *this* is the state of nature in Cathedral Pines. Just since the last ice age alone, that "state of nature" has undergone a thorough revolution every thousand years or so, as tree species forced south by the glaciers migrated back north (a process that is still going on), as the Indians arrived and set their fires, as the large mammals disappeared, as the climate fluctuated—as all the usual historical contingencies came on and off the stage. For several thousand years after the ice age, this part of Connecticut was a treeless tundra; is *that* the true state of nature in Cathedral Pines? The inescapable fact is that, if we want wilderness here, we will have to choose *which* wilderness we want—an idea that is inimical to the wilderness ethic. For wasn't the attraction of wilderness precisely the fact that it relieved us of having to make choices—wasn't nature going to decide, letting us off the hook of history and anthropocentrism?

No such luck, it seems. "Wilderness" is not nearly as straightforward or dependable a guide as we'd like to believe. If we do nothing, we may end up with an impoverished weed patch of our own (indirect) creation, which would hardly count as a victory for wilderness. And if we want to restore Cathedral Pines to some earlier condition, we're forced into making the kinds of inevitably anthropocentric choices and distinctions we turned to wilderness to escape. (Indeed, doing a decent job of wilderness restoration would take all the technology and scientific know-how humans can muster.) Either way, there appears to be no escape from history, not even in nature.

* * *

The reason that the wilderness ethic isn't very helpful in a place like Cathedral Pines is that it's an absolutist ethic: man or nature, it says, pick one. As soon as history or circumstance blurs that line, it gets us into trouble. There are times and places when man or nature is the right and necessary choice; back at Hetch Hetchy in 1907 that may well have been the case. But it seems to me that these days most of the environmental questions we face are more like the ambiguous ones posed by Cathedral Pines, and about these the wilderness ethic has less and less to say that is of much help.

The wilderness ethic doesn't tell us what to do when Yellowstone's ecosystem begins to deteriorate, as a result not of our interference but of our neglect. When a species threatens to overwhelm and ruin a habitat because history happened to kill off the predator that once kept its population in check, the ethic is mute. It is confounded, too, when the only hope for the survival of another species is the manipulation of its natural habitat by man. It has nothing to say in all those places where development is desirable or unavoidable except: Don't do it. When we're forced to choose between a hydroelectric power plant and a nuclear one, it refuses to help. That's because the wilderness ethic can't make distinctions between one kind of intervention in nature and another—between weeding Cathedral Pines and developing a theme park there. "You might as well put up condos" is its classic answer to any plan for human intervention in nature.

"All or nothing," says the wilderness ethic, and in fact we've ended up with a landscape in America that conforms to that injunction remarkably well. Thanks to exactly this kind of either/or thinking, Americans have done an admirable job of drawing lines around certain sacred areas (we did invent the wilderness area) and a terrible job of managing the rest of our land. The reason is not hard to find: the only environmental ethic we have has nothing useful to say about those areas outside the line. Once a landscape is no longer "virgin" it is typically written off as fallen, lost to nature, irredeemable. We hand it over to the jurisdiction of that other sacrosanct American ethic: laissez-faire economics. "You might as well put up condos." And so we do.

Indeed, the wilderness ethic and laissez-faire economics, antithetical 35 as they might at first appear, are really mirror images of one another. Each proposes a quasi-divine force—Nature, the Market—that, left to its own devices, somehow knows what's best for a place. Nature and the market are both self-regulating, guided by an invisible hand. Worshippers of either share a deep, Puritan distrust of man, taking it on faith that human tinkering with the natural or economic order can only pervert it. Neither will acknowledge that their respective divinities can also err: that nature produces the AIDS virus as well as the rose, that the same markets that produce stupendous wealth can also crash. (Actually, worshippers of the market are a bit more realistic than worshippers of nature: they long ago stopped relying on the free market to supply us with such necessities as food and shelter. Though they don't like to talk about it much, they accept the need for society to "garden" the market.)

Essentially, we have divided our country in two, between the kingdom of wilderness, which rules about 8 percent of America's land, and the kingdom of the market, which rules the rest. Perhaps we should be grateful for secure borders. But what do those of us who care about nature do when we're on the market side, which is most of the time? How do we behave? What are our goals? We can't reasonably expect to change the borders, no matter how many power lines and dams Earth First! blows up. No, the wilderness ethic won't be of much help over here. Its politics are bound to be hopelessly romantic (consisting of impractical schemes to redraw the borders) or nihilistic. Faced with hard questions about how to confront global environmental problems such as the greenhouse effect or ozone depletion (problems that respect no borders), adherents of the wilderness ethic are apt to throw up their hands in despair and declare the "end of nature."

The only thing that's really in danger of ending is a romantic, pantheistic idea of nature that we invented in the first place, one whose passing might well turn out to be a blessing in disguise. Useful as it has been in helping us protect the sacred 8 percent, it nevertheless has failed to prevent us from doing a great deal of damage to the remaining 92 percent. This old idea may have taught us how to worship nature, but it didn't tell us how to live with her. It told us more than we needed to know about virginity and rape, and almost nothing about marriage. The metaphor of divine nature can admit only two roles for man: as worshipper (the naturalist's role) or temple destroyer (the developer's). But that drama is all played out now. The temple's been destroyed—if it ever was a temple. Nature *is* dead, if by nature we mean something that stands apart from man and messy history. And now that it is, perhaps we can begin to write some new parts for ourselves, ones that will show us how to start out from here, not from some imagined state of innocence, and let us get down to the work at hand.

* * *

Thoreau and Muir and their descendants went to the wilderness and returned with the makings of America's first environmental ethic. Today it still stands, though somewhat strained and tattered. What if now, instead of to the wilderness, we were to look to the garden for the makings of a new ethic? One that would not necessarily supplant the earlier one, but might give us something useful to say in those cases when it is silent or unhelpful?

It will take better thinkers than me to flesh out what such an ethic might look like. But even my limited experience in the garden has persuaded me that the materials needed to construct it—the fresh metaphors about nature we need—may be found there. For the garden is a place with long experience of questions having to do with man *in* nature. Below are some provisional notes, based on my own experiences and the experiences of other gardeners I've met or read, on the kinds of answers the garden is apt to give.

1. An ethic based on the garden would give local answers. Unlike the wilderness idea, it would propose different solutions in different places and times. This strikes me as both a strength and a weakness. It's a weakness because a garden ethic will never speak as clearly or univocally as the wilderness ethic does. In a country as large and geographically various as this, it is probably inevitable that we will favor abstract landscape ideas—grids, lawns, monocultures, wildernesses—which can be applied across the board, even legislated nationally; such ideas have the power to simplify and unite. Yet isn't this power itself part of the problem? The health of a place generally suffers whenever we impose practices on it that are better suited to another place; a lawn in Virginia makes sense in a way that a lawn in Arizona does not.

So a garden ethic would begin with Alexander Pope's famous advice to landscape designers: "Consult the Genius of the Place in all." It's hard to imagine this slogan ever replacing Earth First!'s "No Compromise in Defense of Mother Earth" on American bumper stickers; nor should it, at least not everywhere. For Pope's dictum suggests that there are places whose "genius" will, if hearkened to, counsel "no compromise." Yet what is right for Yosemite is not necessarily right for Cathedral Pines.

2. The gardener starts out from here. By that I mean, he accepts contingency, his own and nature's. He doesn't spend a lot of time worrying about whether he has a god-given right to change nature. It's enough for him to know that, for some historical or biological reason, humankind finds itself living in places (six of the seven continents) where it must substantially alter the environment in order to survive. If we had remained on African savanna things might be different. And if I lived in zone six I could probably grow good tomatoes without the use of plastic. The gardener learns to play the hand he's been dealt.

3. A garden ethic would be frankly anthropocentric. As I began to understand when I planted my roses and my maple tree, we know nature only through the screen of our metaphors; to see her plain is probably impossible. (And not necessarily desirable, as George Eliot once suggested: "If we could hear the squirrel's heartbeat, the sound of the grass growing, we should die of that roar." Without the editing of our perceptions, nature might prove unbearable.) Melville was describing all of nature when he described the whiteness of the whale, its "dumb blankness, full of meaning." Even wilderness, in both its satanic and benevolent incarnations, is an historical, man-made idea. Every one of our various metaphors for nature—"wilderness," "ecosystem," "Gaia," "resource," "wasteland"—is already a kind of garden, an indissoluble mixture of our culture and whatever it is that's really out there. "Garden" may sound like a hopelessly anthropocentric concept, but it's probably one we can't get past.

The gardener doesn't waste much time on metaphysics—on figuring out what a "truer" perspective on nature (such as biocentrism or geocentrism) might look like. That's probably because he's noticed that most of the very long or wide perspectives we've recently been asked to adopt (including the one advanced by the Nature Conservancy in Cathedral Pines) are indifferent to our well-being and survival as a species. On this point he agrees with Wendell Berry—that "it is not natural to be disloyal to one's own kind."

4. That said, though, the gardener's conception of his self-interest   45 is broad and enlightened. Anthropocentric as he may be, he recognizes that he is dependent for his health and survival on many other forms of life, so he is careful to take their interests into account in whatever he does. He is in fact a wilderness advocate of a certain kind. It is when he respects and nurtures the wilderness of his soil and his plants that his garden seems to flourish most. Wildness, he has found, resides not only out there, but right here: in his soil, in his plants, even in himself. Over-cultivation tends to repress this quality, which experience tells him is necessary to health in all three realms. But wildness is more a quality than a place, and though humans can't manufacture it, they can nourish and husband it. That is precisely what I'm doing when I make compost and return it to the soil; it is what we could be doing in Cathedral Pines (and not necessarily by leaving the place alone). The gardener cultivates wild-ness, but he does so carefully and respectfully, in full recognition of its mystery.

5. The gardener tends not to be romantic about nature. What could be more natural than the storms and droughts and plagues that ruin his garden? Cruelty, aggression, suffering—these, too, are nature's offspring (and not, as Rousseau tried to convince us, culture's). Nature is probably a poor place to look for values. She was indifferent to humankind's arrival, and she is indifferent to our survival.

It's only in the last century or so that we seem to have forgotten this. Our romance of nature is a comparatively recent idea, the product of the industrial age's novel conceit that nature could be conquered, and probably also of the fact that few of us work with nature directly anymore. But should current weather forecasts prove to be accurate (a rapid, permanent warming trend accompanied by severe storms), our current romance will look like a brief historical anomaly, a momentary lapse of judgment. Na-ture may once again turn dangerous and capricious and unconquerable. When this happens, we will quickly lose our crush on her.

Compared to the naturalist, the gardener never fell head over heels for nature. He's seen her ruin his plans too many times for that. The gardener has learned, perforce, to live with her ambiguities—that she is neither all good nor all bad, that she gives as well as takes away. Nature's apt to pull the rug out from under us at any time, to make a grim joke of our noblest intention. Perhaps this explains why garden writing tends to be comic, rather than lyrical or elegiac in the way that nature writing usually is: the gardener can never quite forget about the rug underfoot, the possibility of the offstage hook.

6. The gardener feels he has a legitimate quarrel with nature—with her weeds and storms and plagues, her rot and death. What's more, that quarrel has produced much of value, not only in his own time here (this garden, these fruits), but over the whole course of Western history. Civilization itself, as Freud and Frazer and many others have observed, is the product of that quarrel. But at the same time, the gardener appreciates that it would probably not be in his interest, or in nature's, to push his side of this argument too hard. Many points of contention that humankind thought it had won—DDT's victory over insects, say, or medicine's conquest of infectious disease—turned out to be Pyrrhic or illusory triumphs. Better to keep the quarrel going, the good gardener reasons, than to reach for outright victory, which is dangerous in the attempt and probably impossible anyway.

7. The gardener doesn't take it for granted that man's impact on nature will always be negative. Perhaps he's observed how his own garden has made this patch of land a better place, even by nature's own standards. His gardening has greatly increased the diversity and abundance of life in this place. Besides the many exotic species of plants he's introduced, the mammal, rodent, and insect populations have burgeoned, and his soil supports a much richer community of microbes than it did before. 50

Judged strictly by these standards, nature occasionally makes mistakes. The climax forest could certainly be considered one (a place where the number and variety of living things have declined to a crisis point) and evolution teems with others. At the same time, it should be acknowledged that man occasionally creates new ecosystems much richer than the ones they replaced, and not merely on the scale of a garden: think of the tall-grass prairies of the Midwest, England's hedgerow landscape, the countryside of the Ile de France, the patchwork of fields and forests in this part of New England. Most of us would be happy to call such places "nature," but that does not do them (or us) justice; they are really a kind of garden, a second nature.

The gardener doesn't feel that by virtue of the fact that he changes nature he is somehow outside of it. He looks around and sees that human hopes and desires are by now part and parcel of the landscape. The "environment" is not, and has never been, a neutral, fixed backdrop; it is in fact alive, changing all the time in response to innumerable contingencies, one of these being the presence within it of the gardener. And that presence is neither inherently good nor bad.

8. The gardener firmly believes it is possible to make distinctions between kinds and degrees of human intervention in nature. Isn't the difference between the Ile de France and Love Canal, or a pine forest and a condo development, proof enough that the choice isn't really between "all or nothing"? The gardener doesn't doubt that it is possible to discriminate; it is through experience in the garden that he develops this faculty.

Because of his experience, the gardener is not likely to conclude from the fact that some intervention in nature is unavoidable, therefore "anything goes." This is precisely where his skill and interest lie: in determining what does and does not go in a particular place. How much is too much? What suits this land? How can we get what we want here while nature goes about getting what she wants? He has no doubt that good answers to these questions can be found.

9. The good gardener commonly borrows his methods, if not his goals, from nature herself. For though nature doesn't seem to dictate in advance what we can do in a place—we are free, in the same way evolution is, to try something completely new—in the end she will let us know what does and does not work. She is above all a pragmatist, and so is the successful gardener.

By studying nature's ways and means, the gardener can find answers to the questions, What is apt to work? What avails here? This seems to hold true at many levels of specificity. In one particular patch of my vegetable garden—a low, damp area—I failed with every crop I planted until I stopped to consider what nature grew in a similar area nearby: briars. So I planted raspberries, which are of course a cultivated kind of briar, and they have flourished. A trivial case, but it shows how attentiveness to nature can help us to attune our desires with her ways.

The imitation of nature is of course the principle underlying organic gardening. Organic gardeners have learned to mimic nature's own methods of building fertility in the soil, controlling insect populations and disease, recycling nutrients. But the practices we call "organic" are not themselves "natural," any more than the bird call of a hunter is natural. They are more like man-made analogues of natural processes. But they seem to work. And they at least suggest a way to approach other problems—from a town's decision on what to do with a blown-down pine forest, to society's choice among novel new technologies. In each case, there will be some alternatives that align our needs and desires with nature's ways more closely than others.

It does seem that we do best in nature when we imitate her—when we learn to think like running water, or a carrot, an aphid, a pine forest, or a compost pile. That's probably because nature, after almost four billion years of trial-and-error experience, has wide knowledge of what works in life. Surely we're better off learning how to draw on her experience than trying to repeat it, if only because we don't have that kind of time.

10. If nature is one necessary source of instruction for a garden ethic, culture is the other. Civilization may be part of our problem with respect to nature, but there will be no solution without it. As Wendell Berry has pointed out, it is culture, and certainly not nature, that teaches us to observe and remember, to learn from our mistakes, to share our experiences, and perhaps most important of all, to restrain ourselves. Nature does not teach its creatures to control their appetites except by the harshest of lessons—epidemics, mass death, extinctions. Nothing would be more natural than for humankind to burden the environment to the extent that it was rendered unfit for human life. Nature in that event would not be the loser,

nor would it disturb her laws in the least—operating as it has always done, natural selection would unceremoniously do us in. Should this fate be averted, it will only be because our culture—*our* laws and metaphors, our science and technology, our ongoing conversation about nature and man's place in it—pointed us in the direction of a different future. Nature will not do this for us.

The gardener in nature is that most artificial of creatures, a civilized human being: in control of his appetites, solicitous of nature, self-conscious and responsible, mindful of the past and the future, and at ease with the fundamental ambiguity of his predicament—which is that though he lives in nature, he is no longer strictly *of* nature. Further, he knows that neither his success nor his failure in this place is ordained. Nature is apparently indifferent to his fate, and this leaves him free—indeed, obliges him—to make his own way here as best he can.

60

* * *

What would an ethic based on these ideas—based on the idea of the garden—advise us to do in Cathedral Pines? I don't know enough about the ecology of the place to say with certainty, but I think I have some sense of how we might proceed under its dispensation. We would start out, of course, by consulting "the Genius of the Place." This would tell us, among other things, that Cathedral Pines is not a wilderness, and so probably should not be treated as one. It is a cultural as well as a natural landscape, and to exclude the wishes of the townspeople from our plans for the place would be false. To treat it now as wilderness is to impose an abstract and alien idea on it.

Consulting the genius of the place also means inquiring as to what nature will allow us to do here—what this "locale permits, and what [it] denies," as Virgil wrote in *The Georgics*. We know right off, for instance, that this plot of land can support a magnificent forest of white pines. Nature would not object if we decided to replant the pine forest. Indeed, this would be a perfectly reasonable, environmentally sound thing to do.

If we chose to go this route, we would be undertaking a fairly simple act of what is called "ecological restoration." This relatively new school of environmentalism has its roots in Aldo Leopold's pioneering efforts to re-create a tall-grass prairie on the grounds of the University of Wisconsin Arboretum in the 1930s. Leopold and his followers (who continue to maintain the restored prairie today) believed that it is not always enough to conserve the land—that sometimes it is desirable, and possible, for man to intervene in nature in order to improve it. Specifically, man should intervene to re-create damaged ecosystems: polluted rivers, clear-cut forests, vanished prairies, dead lakes. The restorationists also believe, and in this they remind me of the green thumb, that the best way to learn about nature's ways is by trying to imitate them. (In fact much of what we know about the role of fire in creating and sustaining prairies comes from their efforts.) But the most important contribution of the restorationists has been to set forth a positive, active role for man in nature—in their conception, as equal parts gardener and healer. It seems to me that the idea of ecological restoration is consistent with a garden ethic, and perhaps with the Hippocratic Oath as well.

From the work of the ecological restorationists, we now know that it is possible to skip and manipulate the stages of forest succession. They would probably advise us to burn the fallen timber—an act that, though not strictly speaking "natural," would serve as an effective analogue of the natural process by which a forest is regenerated. The fires we set would reinvigorate the soil (thereby enhancing *that* wilderness) and at the same time clear out the weed species, hardwood saplings, and brush. By doing all this, we will have imitated the conditions under which a white pine forest is born, and the pines might then return on their own. Or else—it makes little difference—we could plant them. At that point, our work would be done, and the pine forest could take care of itself. It would take many decades, but restoring the Cathedral Pines would strain neither our capabilities nor nature's sufferance. And in doing so, we would also be restoring the congenial relationship between man and nature that prevailed in this place before the storm and the subsequent controversy. That would be no small thing.

Nature would not preclude more novel solutions for Cathedral Pines—other kinds of forest-gardens or even parks could probably flourish on this site. But since the town has traditionally regarded Cathedral Pines as a kind of local institution, one steeped in shared memories and historical significance, I would argue that the genius of the place rules out doing anything unprecedented here. The past is our best guide in this particular case, and not only on questions of ecology.

But replanting the pine forest is not the only good option for Cathedral Pines. There is another forest we might want to restore on this site, one that is also in keeping with its history and its meaning to the town.

Before the storm, we used to come to Cathedral Pines and imagine that this was how the New World forest looked to the first settlers. We now know that the precolonial forest probably looked somewhat different—for one thing, it was not exclusively pine. But it's conceivable that we could restore Cathedral Pines to something closely resembling its actual precolonial condition. By analyzing historical accounts, the rings of fallen trees, and fossilized pollen grains buried in the soil, we could reconstruct the variety and composition of species that flourished here in 1739, the year when the colonists first settled near this place and formed the town of Cornwall. We know that nature, having done so once before, would probably permit us to have such a forest here. And, using some of the more advanced techniques of ecological restoration, it is probably within our competence to re-create a precolonial forest on this site.

We would do this not because we'd decided to be faithful to the "state of nature" at Cathedral Pines, but very simply because the precolonial forest happens to mean a great deal to us. It is a touchstone in the

65

history of this town, not to mention this nation. A walk in a restored version of the precolonial forest might recall us to our culture's first, fateful impressions of America, to our thoughts on coming upon what Fitzgerald called the "fresh green breast of the new world." In the contemplation of that scene we might be moved to reconsider what happened next—to us, to the Indians who once hunted here, to nature in this corner of America.

This is pretty much what I would have stood up and said if we'd had a town meeting to decide what to do in Cathedral Pines. Certainly a town meeting would have been a fitting way to decide the matter, nicely in keeping with the genius of *this* place, a small town in New England. I can easily imagine the speeches and the arguments. The people from the Nature Conservancy would have made their plea for leaving the place alone, for "letting nature take her course." Richard Dakin, the first selectman, and John Calhoun, the forest's nearest neighbor, would have warned about the dangers of fire. And then we might have heard some other points of view. I would have tried to make a pitch for restoration, talking about some of the ways we might "garden" the site. I can imagine Ian Ingersoll, a gifted cabinetmaker in town, speaking with feeling about the waste of such rare timbers, and the prospect of sitting down to a Thanksgiving dinner at a table in which you could see rings formed at the time of the American Revolution. Maybe somebody else would have talked about how much she missed her Sunday afternoon walks in the forest, and how very sad the place looked now. A scientist from the Yale School of Forestry might have patiently tried to explain, as indeed one Yale scientist did in the press, why "It's just as pretty to me now as it was then."

This is the same fellow who said, "If you're going to clean it up, you might as well put up condos." I can't imagine anyone actually proposing that, or any other kind of development in Cathedral Pines. But if someone did, he would probably get shouted down. Because we have too much respect for this place; and besides, our sympathies and interests are a lot more complicated than the economists or environmentalists always seem to think. Sooner than a developer, we'd be likely to hear from somebody speaking on behalf of the forest's fauna—the species who have lost out in the storm (like the owls), but also the ones for whom doing nothing would be a boon (the beetles). And so the various interests of the animals would be taken into account, too; indeed, I expect that "nature"—all *those* different (and contradictory) points of view—would be well represented at this town meeting. Perhaps it is naïve of me to think so, but I'm confident that in the course of a public, democratic conversation about the disposition of Cathedral Pines, we would eventually arrive at a solution that would have at once pleased us and not offended nature.

But unfortunately that's not what happened. The future of Cathedral Pines was decided in a closed-door meeting at the Nature Conservancy in September, after a series of negotiations with the selectmen and the owners of adjacent property. The result was a compromise that seems to have pleased no one. The fallen trees will remain untouched—except for a fifty-

foot swath clear-cut around the perimeter of the forest, a firebreak intended to appease the owners of a few nearby houses. The sole human
interest taken into account in the decision was the worry about fire.

I drove up there one day in late fall to have a look around, to see
what the truce between the Conservancy and the town had wrought.
What a sad sight it is. Unwittingly, and in spite of the good intentions on
both sides, the Conservancy and the selectmen have conspired to create a
landscape that is a perfect symbol of our perverted relation to nature. The
firebreak looks like nothing so much as a no-man's-land in a war zone, a
forbidding expanse of blistered ground impounding what little remains of
the Cathedral Pines. The landscape we've made here is grotesque. And yet
it is the logical outcome of a confrontation between, on the one side, an
abstract and mistaken concept of nature's interests and, on the other, a
pinched and demeaning notion of our own interests. We should probably
not be surprised that the result of such a confrontation is not a wilderness,
or a garden, but a DMZ.

Reading and Responding

1. Review the essay, looking for passages that define the main controversy.
   Mark these, and make a list of how Pollan describes each side of the
   controversy.
2. Based on just the title alone, what did you think this essay was about?
   Freewrite a paragraph to explain.
3. Briefly define an "environmental purist" and an "ecological restoration-
   ist," according to Pollan.

Working Together

1. Establish the basic facts of the controversy—what is it, how did it originate, what courses of action have been suggested as remedies? Once
   you're clear about these facts, write them in a group paragraph.
2. Write a group paragraph that explains why it's not easy to decide what
   to do with Cathedral Pines.
3. See whether you can collectively summarize what Pollan has to say
   about the wilderness ethic. Summarize what you understand, and write
   a list of questions about whatever's confusing.
4. As a group, put Pollan's garden ethic in your own words. Write six
   sentences about it that you can all agree on.

Rethinking and Rewriting

1. Look at the ten-point discussion of the garden ethic. Of the ten points,
   choose three as central and argue that if any one of the three were
   discarded, the garden ethic would fall apart.

2. Pollan mentions several of the writers included elsewhere in this book. Choose one of the selections by one of those writers and show how understanding that selection helps you understand Pollan. Show how this other selection lays the groundwork for Pollan or provides a useful contrast. (Use at least three quotations to help you make your points.)

3. Compare Pollan's recommended actions with the actual decisions and actions made by the Nature Conservancy. Who do you agree with, and why?

4. Apply Pollan's garden ethic to some local issue or controversy regarding land use or land preservation. Model your essay on the last section of Pollan's essay.

Chapter 7 Essay Topics

1. Suppose you have been asked to address a group of juniors at your old high school on the subject of environmental action. You know that these students are bored by the whole environmental debate and convinced that nothing they can do makes any difference anyway. Drawing on at least three essays in this chapter, write your speech. Your aim is to convince these students that action is not only possible but necessary, and that they should get involved now.

2. Suppose you have a friend or relative who expresses the notion that ecology and commerce are at odds, saying things like, "All environmentalists have their heads in the clouds," and "People have to eat; we can't have pretty forests *and* good jobs." Drawing on at least three essays in this chapter, write a letter to this friend or relative disagreeing with his or her characterization of environmentalists and the assumption about the economic implications of ecological ideas.

3. Examine the archives of your city or campus newspaper to find a recent grassroots environmental effort in your own community. After taking notes on the essential facts and progress of the effort, contact and interview the principal people involved. Write an article based on your research and modeled after any article in this chapter.

4. Survey the recycling programs, energy conservation programs, and any other efforts on your campus to conserve resources and act in ecologically responsible ways. What are these programs or organizations? Who runs them? Who provides the funding? Are the staff happy with the success of their programs? (If your campus is large or if it houses many such programs, you may wish to limit this survey.) Based on what you discover, write an article that could be published in your campus newspaper or local newspaper.

5. Work in a small group to brainstorm various ways that a particular environmental program on your campus could be publicized or promoted to increase its effectiveness. Write a group report proposing these efforts and aimed at those decision makers who could effect change. Structure your report in three parts:

a. Strengths and weaknesses of the program now
b. Proposed new actions for promotion or publicity
c. Expected results

Credits

EDWARD ABBEY, "The Great American Desert," from *The Journey Home* by Edward Abbey. Copyright © 1977 by Edward Abbey. Reprinted by permission of Dutton Signet, a division of Penguin Putnam, Inc.

CHRIS ANDERSON, "A Forest of Voices," from *Edge Effects* by Chris Anderson. Copyright © 1993 University of Iowa Press.

WENDELL BERRY, "Out of Your Car, Off Your Horse," from *Sex, Economy, Freedom & Community* by Wendell Berry. Copyright © 1992, 1993 by Wendell Berry. Reprinted by permission of Pantheon Books, a division of Random House, Inc.

MARY CLEARMAN BLEW, "The Sow in the River," from *All But the Waltz* by Mary Clearman Blew. Copyright © 1991 by Mary Clearman Blew. Used by permission of Viking Penguin, a division of Penguin Putnam, Inc.

DOUGLAS CHADWICK, "Helping A Great Bear Hang On." Copyright © 1999 by the National Wildlife Federation. Reprinted with permission for *National Wildlife* magazine's December/January 1999 issue.

ALLEN DE HART, "Splendid Swamp." Reprinted with permission of *Sierra* magazine, 85 Second Street, 2nd Floor, San Francisco, CA 94105. "Splendid Swamp," Allen de Hart, 1997, January/February. Reproduced by permission of the publisher via Copyright Clearance Center, Inc.

ALISON HAWTHORNE DEMING, "Exiled in America," from *Temporary Homelands*. Copyright © 1994 by Alison Hawthorne Deming. Published by Mercury House, San Francisco, CA and reprinted by permission.

JOAN DIDION, "On Going Home," from *Slouching Towards Bethlehem* by Joan Didion. Copyright © 1968 and copyright renewed © 1996 by Joan Didion. Reprinted by permission of Farrr, Straus & Giroux, Inc.

ANNIE DILLARD, "The Silent Neighborhood," from *An American Childhood* by Annie Dillard. Copyright © 1987 by Annie Dillard. Reprinted by permission of HarperCollins Publishers, Inc.

JOHN DILLON, "Fading Colors: Are We Losing the Sugar Maple to Acid Rain?" Copyright © 1998 John Dillon. First published in *Audubon* Magazine, September/October 1998. To subscribe to Audubon, call: 800-274-4201.

BARBARA DRAKE, "How Smart Are Sheep?" from *Peace at Heart: An Oregon Country Life* by Barbara Drake, Oregon State University Press, 1998. Copyright © 1998 by Barbara Drake. Used by permission.

CAROLYN DUCKWORTH, "Pieces of Paper Protecting the Land," *Orion Afield,* Summer 1998, pp. 28–31. Copyright © 1998 The Orion Society. Reprinted from *Orion Afield* and used by permission. 195 Main Street, Great Barrington, MA 01230, (888) 909-6568, *www.orionsociety.org/afield.html*

LOREN EISELEY, "The Bird and the Machine," from *The Immense Journey* by Loren Eiseley. Copyright © 1995 by Loren Eiseley. Reprinted by permission of Random House, Inc.

KEITH ERVIN, "A Life In Our Hands," reprinted by permission of the publisher from *Fragile Majesty: The Battle for North America's Latest Great Forest* by Keith Ervin. Copyright © 1989 The Mountaineers, Seattle.

LOIS MARIE GIBBS, "Learning from Love Canal: A 20th Anniversary Retrospective," *Orion Afield,* Spring 1998, pp. 10–14. Copyright © 1998 The Orion Society. Reprinted from

Index of Rhetorical Terms

Index of Authors and Titles

EYES:

Herb Pharm.

Rue fennel → (they

eyecup to wash out

½ cup water 20 drops

cool off until you can

put in your eyes.